Readings in American Military History

Edited by
James M. Morris

PEARSON

Prentice
Hall

Upper Saddle River, New Jersey 07458

Library of Congress Cataloging-in-Publication Data
Readings in American military history / edited by James M. Morris.
p. cm.
ISBN 0-13-182516-X
1. United States—History, Military.   I. Morris, James M. (James
Matthew)
E181 .R285 2003
355' .00973—dc21

2003001597

Senior Acquisitions Editor: Charles Cavaliere
Editorial Director: Charlyce Jones-Owen
Associate Editor: Emsal Hasan
Editorial Assistant: Adrienne Paul
Production Liaison: Joanne Hakim
Marketing Manager: Claire Bitting
Marketing Assistant: Jennifer Bryant
Manufacturing Buyer: Sherry Lewis
Cover Designer: Bruce Kenselaar
Cover Photos: Library of Congress; U.S. Naval Academy Museum; Library of
    Congress
Composition/Full-Service Project Management: Pine Tree Composition, Inc./
    Karen Berry
Printer/Binder: Courier Stoughton, Inc.

Credits and acknowledgments borrowed from other sources and reproduced, with
permission, in this textbook appear on appropriate pages within text.

Pearson Education LTD.
Pearson Education Singapore, Pte. Ltd
Pearson Education, Canada, Ltd
Pearson Education–Japan
Pearson Education Australia PTY,
    Limited

Pearson Education North Asia Ltd
Pearson Educación de Mexico, S.A.
    de C.V.
Pearson Education Malaysia, Pte. Ltd
Pearson Education, Upper Saddle River,
    New Jersey

10 9 8 7 6 5 4 3 2 1
0-13-182516-X

Contents

Preface

Events and developments in the military history of the United States have played a major role in the nation's evolution since its early days as a colonial extension of Great Britain. And ever since independence was attained in the late eighteenth century, military affairs have continued to be considerable, if not always dominant, factors in its existence as it evolved from a new and comparatively weak upstart among nations to its position in the twentieth century as the leading economic and military power in the world. From colonial wars against the French while fighting alongside the British during the Wars for Empire, to the Revolutionary War and the War of 1812, to the Mexican-American War fueled by Manifest Destiny, to the fratricidal Civil War, to World Wars I and II, to Korea, Vietnam, and the Persian Gulf, and to the opening years of the twenty-first century when terrorists launched their suicidal attacks on American citizens in New York City and the Pentagon, and through all the years in between, military responses and developments have been a major part of the nation's vibrant, colorful, and sometimes violent history.

It is an easy and patently false cliché—however fashionable in certain quarters—to say that "wars never settle anything." A more accurate assertion would be to say, "wars often settle almost everything." This was surely the case in the colonists' bid for independence from Great Britain, in the Confederates' claim to the right to secede from the Union, in the drive by Hitler to bring all of Europe under his control, in the Japanese attempt to conquer the entire western Pacific for their co-prosperity sphere, in the unsuccessful attempt by North Korea to conquer South Korea, in the North Vietnamese long and successful crusade to dominate the entire peninsula despite South Vietnam's and America's failed efforts to thwart them, and in a hundred more scenarios that can be easily recalled. Wars may not always settle everything, but they do settle some things, and for that reason wars and preparation for wars must be studied and understood by the American people if they are to continue to enjoy their many benefits as a matter of course. Americans must be aware of how threats to the nation and its allies and friends from without at times permit no other than a military solution. War should always be the last solution, but sometimes it is the only solution.

It is, therefore, fortunate that the American people have throughout their history been blessed with historians and other people of letters who have recorded and interpreted the major military events in their history, although sometimes romantically, sometimes superpatriotically, and sometimes with little depth or breadth. But whether presented as solid, verifiable truth as can best be ascertained or in a less professional manner, the people of this country have enjoyed at least a passing knowledge of the nation's military heritage. Obviously those who have been involved in warfare have had a ringside—if horrible—seat on history. Again fortunately, in the last half century much solid military scholarship, going beyond the "drums and bugles" type of military history popular during the first century and a half of the nation's existence, has emerged from among the fads of history as politics, history as social or economic conflict, history as white or male domination, and so on to reassert its rightful and crucial place in the nation's store of valuable knowledge necessary for an informed citizenry.

In this reemergence, however, despite library shelves continuing to groan every year under the weight of new military history volumes ranging from the scholarly and insightful to the trite and ephemeral, those who teach American military history in the nation's colleges and universities have been aware of the lack of a suitable collateral reader to supplement their lectures, texts, and journal and monograph assignments, a reader designed to give their students greater depth and breadth in the subject. To that end, after collecting and reviewing literally hundreds of articles and monograph chapters, I have selected 28 to be reprinted here. They range from the writings of some of America's best-known military historians (with whom all students of military history should be familiar) to lesser known but outstanding scholars, who by their research and writing are making significant contributions to the field. To the best of my ability, I have selected readings that will induce the students to attain greater depth and breadth in this important subfield of American history. Some selections fall into the category of narrative; others are analytical; some combine both approaches to the subject at hand. By presenting a variety of approaches to military history, it is my hope that students will "see the elephant," appreciate the impact of civil affairs and technology on the art of war, and be able to understand how battles and wars are won or lost.

In the introduction to each essay I have indicated where it was originally published. My thanks to the authors of the selections, to those publications that allowed me to reprint their articles for fees that were not prohibitive, and to their representatives, who were consistently cooperative and helpful in leading me through the reprint legal jungle. My thanks also to the primary reviewers of this project, Dr. William Thomas Allison of Weber State University, Dr. Robert Wooster of Texas A&M–Corpus Christi, and Dr. James C. Bradford of Texas A&M University, for their criticisms and their suggestions as to how to strengthen this reader. Thanks, too, to the staff of Captain John Smith Library of Christopher Newport University, especially to Andrea Kross, Amy Boykin, Leslie Condra, and Susan Barber, who bore with me beyond the call of duty as I implored their help in finding materials I deemed important in the shortest possible time. Finally, my thanks to my wife, Nancy, who bore with me once again when my research and writing sometimes made deep dents in my attention span regarding other important matters.

December 9, 2002
James M. Morris

I

Colonial Wars

The Siege of Louisbourg, 1745

Eric Niderost

During the Wars for Empire from 1689 to 1763, the British and French fought four wars over the question of which nation would dominate both in Europe and in North America. During the third of these wars, the War of the Austrian Succession of 1744–1748, or "King George's War" as the American colonists called it, a key victory was won by the British-American colonials when they placed under siege the French fortress at Louisbourg on Cape Breton Island, guarding the entrance to the vital St. Lawrence River. They achieved this improbable victory between March and June 1745— only to see the Crown return the prize to the French at the end of the war in exchange for Madras in India. In this essay, originally titled "Pride Taken from Victory," Eric Niderost of Chabot Community College in California reveals the details of this memorable contest of arms that, from the colonists' point of view, came to naught. From Military History, October 1989, by Eric Niderost. Copyright © 1989 by Military History. Reprinted by permission of PRIMEDIA Enthusiasts Publications (History Group).

The great French fortress of Louisbourg had never known such a celebration. The year was 1744, the month was May, and France had just struck the first North American blow against England in the newly declared War of the Austrian Succession.

As soon as he received definite news of war, Louis le Prevost, *Seigneur du* Quesnel, had dispatched an expedition against the English outpost of Canso some 50 miles down the coast. Governor Quesnel's instincts apparently had been sound, for the raiders were returning home victorious, their ships' holds bulging with booty and English prisoners.

1

Cannon salutes thundered over the harbor, vibrating windows with their earsplitting reports. The civilian population flocked to the waterfront, happy to welcome the conquering heroes and grateful for anything that might break the tedium of their bleak lives. White-coated marines and red-coated Swiss mercenaries marched about smartly, and officers collected near the waterfront to form an official welcoming committee.

After some delay, the British prisoners were landed and prodded through the fortress town, tangible proof of the success of Gallic arms. Citizens craned their necks to get a better view of the spectacle. Here, before their very eyes, were the hated *Anglais*! More specifically, these captives were British colonials, called *Bostonnais* by the French because most hailed from New England.

The long file of prisoners trudged dejectedly through the narrow cobbled streets of Louisbourg. Some wore masks of indifference or hostility, but others bore expressions of undisguised admiration. They gazed in awe at the magnificent stone fortifications, the imposing multistory buildings, the harbor crowded with ships.

This brooding pile of stone, mortar and cannon indeed had the look of a European stronghold, a far cry from the flimsy wooden stockades or block-houses the New Englanders were used to. And as they marched ever closer to their waiting cells, a few observed Louisbourg with a more practiced eye, duly noting every feature of the defenses and committing those details to memory. Once these men were released—and they would be since Louisbourg had few provisions to feed them—they would provide the British with valuable information on the fortress town.

Louisbourg was France's answer to the encroaching British Empire. Ever since 1689, England and France had been at each other's throats. The two rivals would go to war, fight for a number of years, then sign a peace that was only a thinly disguised truce. The name of the war might change, and allies would be swapped with the ease of changing partners at a court ball, but England and France were always on opposing sides.

The New World reflected the rivalries of the Old. A scattering of English colonies clung to the Atlantic seaboard, from the fringes of French Canada in the frigid north to the borders of Spanish Florida in the humid south. By the early 1700s, the British colonies boasted a combined population of some 400,000, while French Canada could barely muster 25,000 inhabitants.

In 1713, under the terms of the Treaty of Utrecht that had ended the War of the Spanish Succession, France ceded Newfoundland and Arcadia (today's Nova Scotia) to the victorious English. As a sop to Gallic pride, the English allowed the French to keep Cape Breton Island, a fist of land that juts into the Atlantic just off Nova Scotia. The French knew Cape Breton as Isle Royale, but there was nothing regal about the place. The island was literally a howling wilderness, where fierce Atlantic gales blew off the open ocean with undiminished force. Though some fertile patches existed, Cape Breton was largely barren, a place of marshes and wind-blown pines.

Nevertheless, King Louis XIV of France grasped the strategic value of the island. To begin with, Cape Breton was near the mouth of the St. Lawrence River, and the St. Lawrence was a watery highway into the very heart of French Canada. Then, too, the seas near the island boasted some of the best fisheries in the world—the seas teemed with cod and other species. With a fortress built on Cape Breton, the whole strategic picture vis-a-vis the English would change. Like a cork in a bottle, a fortress would block the seaward approaches of the St. Lawrence to the British Royal Navy. Louis-bourg—named in honor of the aging French monarch—would provide a base for French fishermen in time of peace and French privateers in time of war.

Louis XIV ordered the fortress plans to be drawn up at once, but France was war-weary and her bureaucrats notoriously corrupt and lazy. A full seven years were to pass before the first spadeful of earth was turned, and by that time Louis XIV had died and been replaced by the boy-king, Louis XV. French engineers chose *Havre a la Anglais*, the ironically named English harbor, as the site for Louisbourg. English fishermen had once frequented the area, giving the place its name, and its harbor simply was the best for miles around.

Slowly but surely, the great fortress then rose beside its magnificent harbor. The site encompassed 57 acres, and plans were based on the designs of Sebastien le Prestre, *Seigneur de* Vauban, one of the greatest military engineers of all time. On the landward side of the fortress, stone walls bristling with cannon rose 30 feet high and at least a foot thick. The walls were angled to form a scarp to a ditch, and on the far side of the ditch a covered way and counterscarp completed what was in effect a dry moat. Beyond the ditch, sloped mounds of earth formed a glacis to absorb or deflect cannonballs.

At select points along the wall, bastions thrust out from the main emplacements. The *Dauphin Bastion* anchored the landward walls to the north, the *Bastion du Roy*, or King's Bastion, guarded the center, and the *Bastion de la Reine*, or Queen's Bastion, loomed near the sea side of the fortress. It was the protruding bastions, together with the pointed glacis, that gave Louisbourg the characteristic star shape of the classic Vauban fort.

The harbor side of the fortress seemed less formidable. A low-slung wall ran along the waterfront, and *Bastion Maurepas* stood alone, save for a few supplementary batteries.

But the harbor defenses did not end there. Near the harbor mouth, a small *demi-lune* fort perched on a protruding outcrop of rock. Dubbed Island Battery, this fort had 30 24-pounder cannons peering from its embrasures. Just across the bay stood Grand Battery, its field of fire designed to complement that of its island neighbor.

In addition, Nature herself was enlisted in the French cause. Though seemingly wide, the harbor entrance was really quite narrow. Dangerous shoals lurked beneath the placid waters, and a necklace of small islands lay scattered in a wide arc. A British warship lucky enough to negotiate these natural obstacles would come under the guns of Grand and Island batteries, as well as those from Louisbourg itself. The combined crossfire of formidable 24- and 42-pounder cannons would blow any ship out of the water.

Inside its forbidding walls, Louisbourg was more like a French provincial town than a frontier outpost. Sturdy homes of wood or stone rose beside a grid of cobblestone or gravel streets. The governor of Cape Breton Island was housed in Chateau St. Louis, an imposing three-story structure that nestled behind the *Bastion du Roy*. His office and reception rooms echoed the splendors of Versailles with their gilt-frame mirrors, rich tapestries and elegant furniture. Yet, 500 garrison troops were lodged in the same building, crammed into barracks noted for their filth and lack of privacy.

On the frontier, Louisbourg had the amenities—and vices—of European civilization. Stores abounded, offering goods of many kinds. A tavern, grog shops and brothels attracted off-duty soldiers and visiting sailors. But Louisbourg's pride was the Hospital of St. John. Built at a time when medical facilities were rare in America, this 112-bed institution boasted kitchens, a bakery, brewhouse and laundry.

Far to the south, meanwhile, trouble was in the offing for the French fortress. The Massachusetts Bay Colony was larger than the state of today— its Eastern District, now Maine, was on the very borders of French Canada. When prominent merchant William Vaughan heard of the French attack on Canso, his anger knew no bounds. Vaughan and other colonial businessmen weary of French attacks found this latest provocation to be a last straw. In the doughty merchant's mind, there could be no peace until Louisbourg was captured by the colonies.

As Vaughan then laid his case before Massachusetts Governor William Shirley, the merchant argued so persuasively that Shirley was quickly won over. The Massachusetts legislature, initially reluctant, eventually voted in favor of a Louisbourg expedition.

Vaughan and Shirley proposed that the colonies take the fortress themselves, without the aid of British troops. It was a novel, bold and perhaps foolhardy idea—that a few thousand civilians-in-arms could singlehandedly capture the greatest fortress in North America. Nevertheless, the plans were approved and word of the Louisbourg expedition spread across the length and breadth of New England.

With the Puritan tradition still strong in the northern colonies, ministers mounted their pulpits to preach a holy "crusade" against the French Catholic "papists." Louisbourg was the Citadel of Satan, they thundered, the hotbed of idolatry. Their exhortations fell on receptive ears. French privateers had wreaked havoc on the high seas. On land, the French led or encouraged Indian attacks against British settlements. The whole frontier lived in terror of the tomahawk and scalping knife. Yes, now was the time to deal with the French menace once and for all.

Recruitment began in February 1745, while much of New England was still under a mantle of snow. Men came from near and far, breath misting in the cold air as they trudged to Boston. Massachusetts and what is now Maine supplied most of the men, though Connecticut and New Hampshire also sent contingents. Enthusiasm for the venture cooled in direct proportion to the distance from French Canada. In Philadelphia, a printer named Ben Franklin wrote his brother in Boston: "Fortified towns are hard nuts to crack; and your teeth are not accustomed to it."

British naval support would be of prime importance, a key to the project's ultimate success. The colonists possessed a few armed sloops, but none would be a match for a French ship-of-the-line. Most of England's powerful navy was tied up in Europe, guarding the home island from a threatened French invasion. At last, though, their lordships of the Admiralty relented and allowed Commodore Peter Warren's West Indian squadron to join the proposed Louisbourg expedition. Warren's squadron included his flagship *Superb*, 60 guns; and three other ships of 40 guns each.

William Pepperrell of Kittery was appointed supreme commander of the assembling colonial forces. Like most of his men, Pepperrell had never heard a shot fired in anger, but he was intelligent and a natural leader. A prominent lumber merchant, his bewigged features fairly radiated confidence. He was also well liked, and charisma, not discipline, was the cement that would hold his untrained army together.

Without sufficient artillery, though, the enterprise was questionable from the start. A hodgepodge of guns was hastily assembled, including eight 22-pounders, ten 18s, twelve 9s and a few mortars. Most of the available ammunition didn't fit the ordnance, but the colonials were confident. Many believed it would be a simple matter to storm the walls of Louisbourg, capture the enemy guns and turn them on the French.

By mid-March, Boston harbor was a forest of masts as vessels of every size and description gathered to take the Provincial army to Louisbourg. The army itself was at full strength—4,200 farmers, apprentices and woodsmen. Save for a few officers, most didn't have uniforms, but wore an odd assortment of civilian garb. Most of the amateur soldiers had muskets, though, and would make first-class warriors if given the proper training.

On March 24, 1745, the colonials set sail with the cheers of Boston ringing in their ears. Unfortunately, most of the soldiers were landlubbers and the winter seas were rough. Packed in smelly holds, swaying and pitching with every wave, the men became violently seasick. As one queasy warrior noted in his diary, "Our distress Encreas'd inasmuch as our sickness not only Continued, but the weather grew, Thicker and more Stormy. . . ."

After 12 tempest-tossed days, the invasion fleet finally reached Canso, scene of the successful French raid the previous summer and only 50 miles from their objective. Grateful to see dry land, the volunteers landed and quickly recovered from their ordeal. The brief sojourn stretched to three weeks when scout ships reported ice still clogged Louisbourg's harbor area. The extra time was put to good use as the few trained drillmasters on hand tried to whip the raw recruits into some kind of shape. By the end of April, the New Englanders reboarded their transports for the last leg of the journey.

On the morning of April 30, the Provincial fleet hove to off Gabarus Bay, an inlet about five miles from Louisbourg proper. Though forewarned of the attack, French observers stood in awe of the enemy armada. Ships dotted the ocean almost as far as the eye could see. Counting escort vessels, there were nearly 100 ships in this vast assemblage.

Hoping to distract the defenders, Commodore Warren cruised just outside the harbor and began lobbing broadsides at the fortress town. Island Battery took up the gauntlet, and the morning air was filled with the booming reports of their duel. Inside Louisbourg, bells rang the *tocsin* or alarm as soldiers hurried to their posts and citizens ran for cover. In spite of its formidable appearance, Louisbourg had some serious weaknesses. No more than 90 guns were in place, though the walls were pierced for 148. Parts of the fortress were poorly built; corrupt contractors had used large amounts of government money to buy cheap materials, then pocketed the difference.

Even the garrison could not be trusted. A brief mutiny had broken out a few months earlier when Swiss mercenaries demanded better conditions. The mutiny had been suppressed, but the soldiers were unreliable and might go over to the enemy if given the chance. Years of neglect, corruption and bureaucratic inertia were bearing bitter fruit.

While Warren slugged it out with Island Battery, the first wave of invaders prepared to land. Men clambered down the sides of bobbing troopships to fill whaleboats alongside. After a brief skirmish on the beach, a party of defenders withdrew to the main works, but not before torching some outlying houses to cover their retreat. Large-scale sorties were out of the question; the garrison could not be trusted.

For the next several days, troops, supplies and artillery were ferried ashore in spite of rough seas and treacherous currents. It took Herculean efforts to lash cumbersome cannons to rafts in the face of high winds and crashing surf. Mishaps were frequent; rafts were smashed to kindling on the rocky shore and some men drowned. Nevertheless, the bulk of the army's ordnance and supplies managed to reach shore.

A fairly flat stretch of ground facing the landward walls was selected as the main Provincial encampment. Canvas tents sprang up like grey-white mushrooms, each placed according to its owner's whim or fancy. Shelter was of the utmost concern; the nights were bitterly cold and the men wet from frequent work details in the surf. Survival-wise frontiersmen went to nearby forests and cut pine boughs to use as bedding. City-bred apprentices and gangly farm boys wrapped themselves in sodden blankets, crouched around smokey fires, and drained rum containers to fortify themselves against the cold. In spite of such precautions, the sick list grew with every passing day.

On May 2, a party of 400 men, led by the same William Vaughan who suggested the expedition, set off to probe the hilly country north of the fortress. As the march progressed, small groups pared off from the main body to forage among the small French farms in the interior.

After giving the guns of Louisbourg a wide berth, Vaughan's party followed a path that paralleled the inner harbor. Progress was slow, since the ground was rough, thickly wooded, and little better than an Indian hunting trail. After burning some abandoned fishing shacks, Vaughan and his men encountered a series of large wooden warehouses. Just beyond these buildings, the sinister profile of Grand Battery loomed in the distance.

The warehouses were found to contain naval stores—pitch, tar, cordage and wood. As property of the French king, they were legitimate spoils of war and would be valuable assets to the British Royal Navy. Unfortunately, landlubbing provincials had no use for naval stores—particularly if a pyrotechnic display would provide a few moment's diversion. Lighted brands were thrust into each warehouse, then the men stood back to watch the show. Flames greedily consumed the stores, turning thousands of livres' worth of supplies into ash and billowing coils of oily smoke.

Though the blazing warehouses were well within range of Grand Battery, its guns were strangely silent. Suspecting a trap, and unwilling to hazard the lives of his own men, Vaughan sent an Indian scout forward to reconnoiter the position. To sweeten what was obviously a dangerous mission, the colonel produced a pocket flask of brandy and gave the Indian a swig before sending him on his way. Moments later the native climbed the battery wall and disappeared through one of its embrasures.

The scout brought back incredible news: The battery was abandoned. Vaughan and his men—now only 13 individuals—quickly took possession of this prize, and once inside could scarcely believe their eyes. The battery was intact, though the touchholes of the cannons had been spiked. There was powder and shells in abundance, and neat pyramids of cannonballs stood by each gun. Once the spikes were removed from the 42-pounder cannon—a difficult but not impossible task—these massive weapons could be turned on the main fortress.

Vaughan had no flag, so the scarlet coat of 18-year-old William Tufts was pressed into service. The homemade garment was run up the battery flagstaff, a grand if rather limp symbol of British colonial defiance. It was

Governor Louis Dupont du Chambon who had ordered the evacuation of the Grand Battery upon recommendation of a council of war. It was argued at the time that the battery was untenable and its 200-man garrison would be put to better use in Louisbourg itself. Battery Captain Chassin de Thierry had suggested the entire outwork be leveled to the ground, but his proposals fell on deaf ears.

Now regretting his decision, Governor du Chambon dispatched four boatloads of marines—about 100 men in all—to retake the fallen battery.

Straining at their oars, the French flotilla plowed through the fingers of fog that misted and swirled about the harbor. When the boats were in musket range, Vaughan and his handful of men unleashed a telling fire on the approaching whitecoats. Guns from Louisbourg boomed in reply, but their covering fire did the marines more harm than good. Great geysers of water mushroomed near the boats as the "friendly" fire fell far short of its intended target. Caught in the middle of an ironic crossfire, the marines veered off and returned to base.

The capture of Grand Battery and its ample supplies was a welcome development, but when General Pepperrell and his senior officers scanned the ground before Louisbourg their faces were etched with concern. Much of the land was a watery bog, a viscous, muddy expanse barely able to support a carpet of moss, let alone the weight of a full-grown man. And if a man could be swallowed up in this unstable "pudding," what would happen to a cannon?

Yet firm ground *did* exist. A mound called Green Hill rose right in the middle of the swamp, a gun platform designed by the hand of nature. The obviously solid island in a swampy, liquid sea seemed to taunt the New Englanders by its very nearness. In order to reach the hill, however, guns would have to be dragged over a half-mile of bog, a seemingly impossible task.

Lieutenant Colonel Nathaniel Meserve of New Hampshire came forward with a solution: stone boats. Familiar to every New Englander, "stone boats" were wooden sledges used to gather boulders when farm fields were cleared. As axemen hurriedly felled timber, sledges 16 feet long were constructed. Though the army had few (if any) draft animals, it did have manpower in abundance. While human harnesses called "bricoles" attached to the sledges, scouts were sent into the swamp to blaze a trail through the mire. After careful probing, a relatively shallow area about three feet deep was discovered and marked.

Once a cannon was secure on a sledge, 200 men attached themselves to the guide cables and began to pull with all their might. Backs bent, shoulders hunched against the pull, they made slow but steady progress. Whenever a man took a step, he sank knee-deep—sometimes waist-deep—in the primordial slime. Movement was difficult, and often achieved at the cost of losing one's shoes and stockings to the mud. The men worked in relays; when one toiler neared exhaustion, another would take his place. In a spirit of equality rare for that era, even General Pepperrell took his turn on the ropes.

After four days of back-breaking labor, six cannon were in place on Green Hill, well protected by stone-faced earthworks. Barefooted, befouled with mud, lacerated and bleeding from the hidden rocks and roots encountered along the way, these grimy warriors had achieved the impossible. The work had been done under the cover of darkness or when a blanket of fog enveloped the swamp. From the French perspective, the Green Hill Battery seemed more like a feat of magic than a feat of arms. Their own engineers had assured them the swamp was impenetrable. Suddenly, one of the six Green Hill behemoths sprang to life and hurled a cannonball that crashed into a barracks roof behind the King's Bastion.

It was the beginning of an intense bombardment that would last for weeks. As the days passed, and more and more Provincial batteries were brought into action, Louisbourg was engulfed in a ring of fire. Unfortunately, trained gunners were few in the Provincial army, and could not be everywhere at once. All too frequently, novice artillerymen overloaded their pieces with fatal results. One Provincial diarist recorded that: "I am inform'd that we have Lost five men at our batteries this day. One was killed by the Breaking of a cannon . . . a Large Piece of it . . . Fell and Ground him to Pieces."

In spite of the accidents, a somewhat festive mood prevailed, and the gunners took long "pulls" of rum between firing each shot. As Pepperrell laconically remarked, "We are in great want of gunners that have a disposition to be sober in daytime."

Nevertheless, these farm boys and apprentices were quick learners, and their marksmanship steadily improved. Fingers of flame lanced through blossoms of smoke as gun crews worked their pieces with a will. Mortars peppered the air with bombs, dark spheres that could be seen as they arched in graceful parabolas. When they touched earth, they exploded in great gouts of fire, spewing masonry, earth, and hapless people in all directions.

In reply, the great French bastions flamed in counterbattery. Gallic bombs ("bums" as one diarist spelled it) caused havoc in Provincial siege lines, and French muskets picked off unwary gunners as they peered over their earthworks. On the whole, though, Yankee casualties from the French fire were light.

The Provincials were conducting a queer kind of war. Freed from the toil of farm and workshop, these men and boys were out to have a good time. Discipline was almost nonexistent.

It is estimated that only one-half to one-third of the army worked the cannons at any given time. Highly individualistic, supremely self-reliant,

"Pepperrell's boys" seemed more like an armed mob than an army. The main encampment was in a state of near anarchy. Men wandered about, loafed, or went fishing. Elsewhere, a country-fair spirit pervaded the camp. Soldiers ran foot races, wrestled and engaged in various games while others fought and bled a mile or two away. As cannonballs flew, idlers wasted precious powder on shooting competitions.

Yet not all was fun and games. Armed bands of hostile Indians lurking in the woods killed and scalped many who wandered too far from camp. In addition, fever and dysentery laid many low, until at one point half the army was on the sick list. Most recovered, but the cordon around Louisbourg was so thinly manned it was stretched to the breaking point.

Still, the enemy was faring far worse. As Provincial gunnery improved, not a single foot of Louisbourg was safe from bombardment. French civilians cowered in cellars while their houses crashed over their heads. Shell holes pocked the ground, the debris of shattered buildings was everywhere, and the air was heavy with the acrid stench of powder smoke. A Louisbourg official named Bigot noted sadly that "the enemy established their batteries to such effect that they soon destroyed the greater part of the town, broke the right flank of the King's Bastion and ruined the Dauphin Battery. . . ."

The outer walls held firm, since they were designed to absorb such punishment. Breaches were made, to be sure, but they were too small to make an assault practicable. To solve the impasse, Commodore Warren suggested that his Royal Navy squadron force an entrance to the harbor and add the weight of its guns to those already pounding the fortress. The idea contained one problem: Though Grand Battery had been neutralized, Island Battery still guarded the mouth of the harbor.

On the night of May 26, 400 volunteers boarded whaleboats for an attack on Island Battery. Somehow, this operation brought out the worst in the men. Ill-disciplined in the best of times, now they were a boisterous rabble, loud and querulous even when their officers stressed the need for silence.

The assault on Island Battery was an extremely hazardous mission. The New Englanders' greatest weapon would be the element of surprise; if they could manage to get up and over the battery walls without detection, the night would be theirs. Unfortunately, many volunteers felt the need for copious amounts of liquid "Dutch courage." Hard liquor passed from hand to hand before the men embarked; by the time they were in the boats many were roaring drunk.

After an "eternity" of suspense, the whaleboats touched shore on Island Battery. Luck seemed to be with them—there was no sign of life on the ramparts, and the sound of heavy surf masked their debarkation. In spite of some confusion caused by darkness, leading elements of the attacking force reached the battery and began placing scaling ladders against its wall.

All at once, things began to unravel. Without warning, one of the drunken volunteers raised three cheers. In moments, the rampart seemed to explode as French cannon were discharged pointblank into the struggling mass of Provincials. Few survivors would forget the horror of those minutes; all was darkness, save for the orange-yellow muzzle flashes of the French guns and the occasional stabs of flame from muskets. Cannon reports mingled with screams and shouts to produce a horrible din, and men scrambled over the rocks and the torn bodies of their fallen comrades as they sought shelter from the rain of death.

But the Provincials refused to give in and actually pressed their attack home. Though no man reached the top of the wall, no less than 12 scaling ladders were placed on the ramparts. The colonials also maintained a steady musket fire from whatever natural cover was available.

Some of the troops were still in whaleboats when the battle began; heavy French fire forced them to withdraw. Others were not so lucky—the harbor was filled with the bodies of soldiers and the debris of smashed boats. Those on shore were trapped. The coming of dawn put an end to the unequal contest. At least 60—and perhaps as many as 150—had been killed and wounded; the French claimed an additional 119 prisoners.

The Island Battery fiasco raised French morale and plunged the Provincial camp into gloom. In spite of appearances, however, a New England victory was near. Commodore Warren's squadron had recently captured the French warship *Vigilant*, 64 guns, after a hard-fought battle at sea. *Vigilant* was carrying supplies and reinforcements to the beleaguered garrison, and its loss would be keenly felt. Even more importantly, a strong relief effort from the Canadian mainland had been repulsed at the so-called "Gut of Canso," the narrow strait that separated Cape Breton from Nova Scotia. There, about 1,300 French and Indians had been caught in mid-crossing by alert Provincial warships that made short work of flimsy birchbark canoes.

On June 15, French drummer boys climbed the rubblestrewn ramparts and beat a steady tattoo. The drumbeats requested a parley, which was granted. Governor du Chambon had finally accepted reality. His gunpowder was low, supplies were dwindling, and most of the guns were out of action. Louisbourg looked more like ancient ruins than a modern fortress. There were now so many breaches, an assault was inevitable, and du Chambon wished to spare the citizens the horror of a possible sacking.

The final capitulation took place June 17. After a siege of seven weeks, the ragged, but triumphant, Yankees marched into Louisbourg and claimed it as their own. New England casualties had amounted to 130 dead and 200 wounded. Another 30 men—a suspiciously low figure—were carried off by disease. French casualty figures are disputed; the French claimed 50 killed and 80 wounded, but the victors maintained 300 of the garrison were killed.

Whatever the figures, the colonials had every right to be proud. Raw amateurs in the art of war, they had reduced a fortress designed by one of the greatest military engineers of all time. Yet, when the Peace of Aix-la-Chapelle was signed in 1748, British negotiators callously gave Louisbourg back to France in return for some territory in India. (A repaired and strengthened Louisbourg was retaken by British regulars in 1758.)

The Yankees, though, came away from Louisbourg a more confident, more united people. Even colonies that had not directly participated were infused with a new sense of *American* pride. When united in a common cause, the colonials found they could achieve wonders. It was a lesson well remembered during the American Revolution.

The Colonial Militia as a Social Institution: Salem, Massachusetts, 1764–1775

Ronald L. Boucher

While the importance of the militia as a local defensive force notably declined during the late seventeenth and early eighteenth centuries, the role it played in the colonial towns' social and political life remained strong. However, as the late Ronald Boucher of Clark University points out, as troubles with the mother country emerged in the 1760s and 1770s, the political opinions of militia leaders regarding the actions of the English and the readiness of the militiamen to assume the defense of their towns and counties led to a reemphasis on the militia as an integral part of colonial life. This resulted in a corresponding demand that these citizen military units be reinvigorated in defense of the colonists' rights and liberties. This essay was originally published in Military Affairs *(37/4 [Dec. 1973], 125–30) and is reprinted with permission.*

The Militia system established by English settlers in America became in time one of the most important institutions in colonial life. By the eighteenth century a pattern of development by the militia was clearly evident. In the beginning the militia was a necessity in safeguarding small and isolated communities against a hostile and threatening environment. By the end of the Great War for Empire, its military vigor and effectiveness had seriously declined, only to be revived again during the Revolutionary crisis. These changes reflect the growth and maturity of the American colonies.

When the colonies became more secure and permanent, and the militia's defense activities decreased, its importance within colonial communities became increasingly social. John Adams, for instance, noted in 1782 that four institutions—the towns, congregations, schools and militia—provided the key to understanding American history. To Adams, these institutions "produced the American Revolution," and were the foundations of the liberty, happiness and prosperity of the American people. The militia was one of the most enduring colonial institutions, theoretically including almost all white males, and was active or present in nearly every community. Since it was so thoroughly integrated into the complex pattern of colonial society, an investigation into the militia's social aspects offers new insights into colonial history, particularly the changes and conflicts as the Revolution approached. The legal structure and regulations of the militia have been thoroughly studied, but its importance as a social institution often has been neglected.

Such an inquiry demands that the militia be studied in specific geographic settings became it was basically a local institution. Community attitudes and conflicts regarding the militia and its relationship to other social organizations and processes are undoubtedly more important than its legal framework in revealing the social significance of the militia. The community of Salem, Massachusetts provides a unique opportunity to examine the colonial militia as a social institution. As a result of Salem's location on the seacoast, the military functions of its militia were very limited by the eighteenth century, but its social importance was increased. The Salem militia was also a focus of conflict and dramatic change in the Revolutionary period, and this attempt to revive the militia as an effective military force, only partly successful in Salem, illustrates the difficulties of the Revolutionary movement.

The militia was first organized in Salem in 1630, and by the mid-eighteenth century it had gradually expanded to include four companies in the First Essex Regiment. Both active and inactive militia titles were commonplace in Salem. Yet, there were so many exemptions from militia service in this seacoast town, such as fishermen and seamen, that its militia was smaller than that in many other communities. Due to Salem's importance in Essex County, however, it was able to dominate important officer positions of leadership in its militia regiment.

Many community attitudes in Salem were related to its militia. The colonists, in general, viewed a standing army as a threat to their liberties and rights. And in Salem, the most vociferous militia analyst, Timothy Pickering, contended in his first letter written as "A Military Citizen" and published in the *Essex Gazette*, that a well-organized militia rendered permanent professional armies unnecessary on American soil. When British regulars were stationed in Boston in 1768, the *Essex Gazette* stated: "The thoughts of a Standing Army are more and more alarming to this People, who hitherto supported the due Execution of constitutional Law without the Necessity of such Aid." As the Revolution approached these beliefs had important implications for the colonial militia because, as will be shown, the initial defense efforts of the colonists reemphasized the militia system of earlier days.

The public often took an active interest in Salem's militia, at times responding with pride and enthusiasm on muster days. In fact, public approval appears to have been one of the main concerns of these events held four times each year. In 1770, in the *Essex Gazette*, it was reported that "The good Order and Regularity with which they performed all parts of their Duty, very sensibly pleased a numerous crowd of Respectable Spectators, and reflected great Honor on the Assiduity and military Skills of their Officers." Training days were secular holidays when the militia "performed their Exercises to such general Acceptance as would do Honor to any Militia."

To Salem's militia leadership such occasions were also socially important. Muster days were opportunities to gather together as a group and reinforce their distinctive importance as militia leaders. After one day of training, for instance, it was reported, "the officers prepared an elegant dinner at Mr. Goodhue's Tavern . . . (and) they spent the Evening together at the same House, when they made a Collection and released a Debtor from Prison." On special occasions in Salem, such as a visit by the governor in 1774, the mustering and review of the militia was usually an integral part of civil celebrations. In the decade prior to the Revolution, social interest in militia activities often outweighed military purposes.

An anonymous letter to the *Essex Gazette*, however, indicates that not everyone in Salem was so interested in the militia. "F," a correspondent in the *Essex Gazette*, took ". . . the Freedom to mention the Fault that some of my Neighbors find with it." He thought that the militia held only slight interest for the average person (those who "have time only in the Evening to read News."). It was a vital concern only to men "impatient to be promoted." "F" implied that persons active in militia affairs were seeking their own social or individual aims, and asked the printer, referring to Pickering's letters, "If the Old Gentleman should come again (as I fear he will after the next Training) pray desire him to have Pity on your Readers, and not be so lengthy."

The militia in Salem also came in for some criticism. Timothy Pickering's interest was highly critical, and even before the prospect of armed conflict with England became likely, he agitated for militia reforms. According to Pickering, one of the main reasons why the militia was so "truly contemptible" in 1770 was because it was now mainly composed of "Children, Apprentices and Men of Low Rank." The lower classes had come to dominate the militia because "everyone who could pay a small Fine, thought it beneath them to appear on a Muster."

The militia's leadership also drew criticism. One attitude reported in the *Essex Gazette* was voiced by "A Common Soldier," who thought "the conduct of the officers of that company to which I have the misfortune to belong," was so neglectful of militia affairs that it actually discouraged many young men from taking interest or pride in their own defense. With disgust he declared that the present officers were "so lazy and incompetent" that they actually ridiculed those sincere militiamen who tried to improve themselves. This critic attributed the problem to "an amazing infatuation of many militia officers . . . that the only end of giving them commissions was that they might be addressed by the title of captain, lieutenant or ensign." The importance of titles was emphasized in town meetings, he cynically noted, where moderators were extremely careful "lest they should offend their honors by omitting these notable marks of distinction." To "A Common Soldier," the militia was being misused by those who saw it as a means of securing or maintaining social recognition.

Timothy Pickering declared that the main problem was that "Officers in the Militia have sometimes descended from Persons of Interest, Inflence and

Abilities, to others Inferior in all those Respects, and these last to a Class still lower, and so on till at length, in the Course of a few Years, the Officers have gotten into the lowest Hands." The best gentlemen have mistakenly paid "little attention to military exercises, though it behooves *them* more than any others." The better classes should be involved in the militia "greater in Proportion to the greater Interests they have to be defended and guarded." The solution according to Pickering was to attract more men of "Fortune, Weight and Figure." The social structure of the militia should conform more closely to the hierarchical social order prevailing in colonial society.

The efforts to rejuvenate Salem's militia provide insight into the colonial attitudes towards warfare. Many problems such as tardiness, absenteeism and drunkenness were identified, but the basic failing appeared to be a lack of "military discipline," i.e. the ability to perform many complicated exercises and maneuvers in large formations. In one respect, therefore, the militia leaders of Salem reflected the rigid, mechanistic views of the British. On the other hand, the military manual most strongly recommended was the "Norfolk Manual" which presented military discipline in a simplified manner, compared to other eighteenth century manuals. The difficulties of teaching military discipline under colonial conditions was often recognized, and therefore the colonials sought the most practical guidelines. At least one Salem officer, Captain Samuel Barton, Jr., made a brief attempt at improving and standardizing militia drills at the "Exercises of the 2nd Day." But the most important effort was made by Timothy Pickering who in 1775 published *An Easy Plan of Discipline for a Militia*. Pickering's approach was clearly pragmatic. Because of the limited time available for training, he sought to simplify earlier manuals even more by eliminating "the custom and prejudice (that) are the foundations of many practices among the military, and maxims . . . blindly adopted without any examination of the principles upon which they are founded." The ordinary militiaman must understand the exercises performed, and if the motions are taught because they are "convenient, useful and necessary," they will be accepted and learned more easily.

The social importance of the militia also may be investigated by examining the relationship of its leaders to other aspects of Salem society. For example, a variety of typical occupations were represented by the militia leaders. Although "merchant" was the most commonly identified occupation, the list also includes several "gentlemen," a draper, blacksmith, anchorsmith, gristmill operator, farmer and chairmaker. It must be remembered that the colonials frequently did not specialize and many of these individuals may have been engaged in several activities. Yet, it is evident that this group included a broad spectrum of Salem's economy in the 1760s and 1770s.

The wealth of the militia officers also indicates their relative position in Salem. A reasonably accurate measurement of this wealth may be found in the Salem tax records. . . . The average total tax paid by militia officers was £7.10/11, and by town officers £7.16/10. For the same years a random 7–8 percent sampling of the town's population shows the average tax paid by Salem's residents was £1.11/02. The range of taxes levied, moreover, was similarly distributed. In the average year only three of eighteen militia officers and two of thirty town officers paid less than the town mean. In general, militia and town positions of authority were filled by men of approximately equal economic means and, despite a few obvious exceptions, the wealth of both groups was far above that of the average citizen.

The rate of turnover among Salem's militia officers is another factor in analyzing its leadership. Major appointments were made in 1765–1767, and again in 1771 (commissions were given irregularly and were held for an indefinite term). Fifteen men were commissioned at the earlier dates, but only four were reappointed in 1771. The last group of militia commissions prior to the Revolution therefore included fourteen out of eighteen individuals who had not previously held military office. In 1771 there was only one town officer who had belonged to the same group during the years 1765–1767. There was a basically similar pattern of leader turnover in the militia and town even though the method of selection to each group was fundamentally different. These facts reflect, in part, the colonial attitude that obligated a man to serve his community. This idea of duty demanded that an individual serve in public office when requested or expected to do so. But many also sought to restrict such duty to as short a time as possible. This rapid rate of turnover implies that militia commissions probably were often based upon nonmilitary considerations determined at the provincial level of government rather than by local military concerns for the effectiveness of the militia.

A further indication of the social recognition given to militia officers is the frequency of plural office-holding by these men. Of the twenty-nine active militia officers between 1765 and 1774, twelve also held positions of civil importance in Salem. Conversely, 39 per cent of the town leaders held militia commissions during the same period. This integration of leadership again indicates that nonmilitary considerations were an important factor in the selection of militia officers. Contrary to the assertions of Timothy Pickering, whose opinions were influenced mainly by the problems of military effectiveness, the militia leadership obviously included the wealthier men of Salem, and while this was a rapidly changing rather than static group, these were also men who generally enjoyed more than the usual social recognition.

During the decade after 1764 political interests and factions appear to have exercised a decisive influence upon the Salem militia. Since appointments were the responsibility of the provincial government, there was frequently a conflict between it and town authorities. Two incidents involving William Browne illustrate the importance of provincial control over militia commissions. In 1768 Salem had instructed its representatives to the General Assembly, Browne and Peter Frye, to support the "rescinding petition" from Massachusetts against English duties. When Browne and Frye disobeyed these orders they were quickly removed from their posts by the town. Salem's sentiments were indicated by their replacements, Richard Derby, Jr. and John Pickering, both ardent patriots during the 1770s and annually returned to office for the next six years. However, both Browne and Frye retained their militia posts, and in 1771 were promoted to colonel and major respectively in the First Essex Regiment.

In a second episode, William Browne was arrested in 1769 in connection with the beating of James Otis by John Robinson in a Boston tavern. When Otis was strongly supported by the *Essex Gazette*, which also printed Robinson's apology for his actions, Browne discontinued his subscription to Salem's local newspaper on the grounds that it had become too radical. He was publicly criticized for this behavior. It is clear that Browne, Frye and others leaning towards Toryism were becoming politically unacceptable in Salem. However, because militia appointments were controlled by provincial authorities, this group of future Loyalists remained in their militia posts for several more years. Provincial officals indicated their attitude in 1771 when three of the only four re-appointments to the Salem militia were men who would soon decide on loyalty to England.

The label of Tory was a serious charge in Salem even several years before the Revolution. As early as 1770 Timothy Pickering became embroiled in a newspaper controversy when "Y" accused him of leading a pro-British party that sought its own self-interest rather than the public good. In three vigorous replies Pickering denied these charges, asserting that he had long since disassociated himself from his earlier Tory friends, supported colonial resistance to British infringements of American rights, and had never embraced Tory principles. He offered his constant endeavors to improve the militia as proof of his patriotism.

In most respects, the militia resembled Salem society in the eighteenth century, with one important difference—local communities had only limited control over militia commissions. In times of crisis, conflict over the militia between the colonists and the British was almost certain. The resolution of this conflict and the hurried attempts to prepare the militia for an active military role must be analyzed to understand the initial impact of the Revolution upon the militia in Salem.

One important aspect of the militia as a social institution has remained obscure. Little is known of the "common man" in the militia. As recent efforts to study the common man in American history have indicated, this is usually a difficult task. The brief glimpses offered by contemporary observers, such as Timothy Pickering, are undoubtedly biased. During peaceful years inadequate militia records were kept or preserved to investigate the socio-economic status of the average militia member, and their attitudes towards the militia have also remained largely unknown.

As the American Revolution approached, the militia became increasingly important to the colonists. An investigation of its role in this crisis is a revealing study of institutional change. The dramatic changes in the militia after 1774 stemmed partly from the sudden demand that it become militarily more effective, but the colonists also sought to make the militia conform with patriotic attitudes. This second motive for change was especially important in Salem where partisan politics influenced almost every aspect of life.

In the years prior to the Revolution Salem's attitudes towards the British changed significantly. While joining the protests over the Stamp Act in 1765, for instance, Salem maintained its loyalty to England. Ten years later the transformation had been so complete that it was declared: "The Colonies are convinced that their Libertieis [sic] depend upon their Power, and are generally attentive to military Discipline."

Many members of the militia in Salem reflected this shift in attitudes by their involvement in organized protest. Forty percent of the committee elected to draft Salem's protest concerning the Stamp Act held military titles. Militia leaders also comprised 66 per cent of the Boycott Committee in 1770 and 55 per cent of the Committee of Correspondence. In 1774 militia officers made up 63 per cent of the delegates to the Essex County Convention and provided both of Salem's representatives to the Provincial Congress in the same year. These facts become more meaningful when compared to the letter welcoming Governor Gage to Salem in 1774; only eight of forty-eight signatures belonged to militia officers, three of whom soon after apologized for this mistake. There was a significant group of at least twelve militia officers, however, who did not participate in any rebellious activities. A sharp division had therefore developed within the militia's leadership. Despite the fact that its leaders comprised a high percentage of those involved in organized patriotic activities, they still constituted slightly less than half of the militia officers in Salem. Most of these pro-patriot leaders had emerged in the years after 1765 and were part of a three-way split within the militia—patriots, Tories and undecided. Therefore, prior to its reorganization in 1774 it is doubtful that the militia could have acted as a unified body because of these political divisions.

Salem became inescapably involved in the forces leading to the decisive break with England when Governor Thomas Gage attempted to escape the unsettled, radical atmosphere of Boston by moving the General Court to Salem in 1774. Conflict within Salem was quickly apparent. After being welcomed at a ball hosted by Colonel William Browne, Gage received two contradictory letters, the *Salem Gazette* reported. One expressed the support of many citizens for Gage's recent actions, and the other criticized British policies with uncompromising harshness. Tensions were further heightened when the justices of the Essex County court assured Gage that they would preserve "law and order" in Salem, and also upon the removal of British troops from Boston to Salem.

The General Court that convened in Salem confronted Gage with a legislature as stubbornly resistant to his wishes as any he had faced in Boston. Realizing that he could not control this legislature, and fearful that they might decide to defy British authority, he issued a message of dismissal to the lower house. But it refused to bow to his orders, and proceeded to endorse the motion for a provincial congress to meet that Fall.

Gage then turned his frustrated anger upon Salem. In August 1774, the Committee of Correspondence had announced a special town meeting to select delegates to the Essex County Convention that was to be held soon. As the meeting was assembling, Gage informed the Committee that it was illegal and should be immediately dispersed. When the Committee refused to cooperate and Salem proceeded to elect its representatives, Gage issued a warrant for the Committee's arrest, delivered by Peter Frye. Two Committee members were arrested as a result, but realizing the futility of his position Gage soon dropped the charges against them. For the future of the militia, however, these events were decisive.

The Essex County Convention met at Ipswich on 6 and 7 September 1774. Its decisions concerning the militia clearly were influenced by recent events in Salem which required "immediate opposition." The Convention resolved that any officers or magistrates who cooperated with England to restrict American liberties "are and will be considered its unnatural and malignant enemies." William Browne and Peter Frye, both regimental militia officers in Salem, were singled out for special criticism. Condemnation of Frye for his part in the arrest of two members of the Committee of Correspondence was suspended awaiting his apology and pledge to reform. Browne was censured more severely for his acceptance of a position as Mandamus Councilor, and the Convention demanded that he resign his current offices and refuse other appointments.

Frye quickly deferred to the Convention and assured Salem that, "I will not accept any Commission under said Act of Parliament . . . and therefore hope to be restored to that Friendship and Regard with my Fellow-Citizens and Countrymen which I heretofore enjoyed." Despite these efforts, Frye's patriotism remained doubtful in Salem, and soon after his house and store were set afire and totally destroyed. Frye was left with little choice but to join the Loyalists and flee Massachusetts when the Revolution began.

Browne, however, steadfastly refused to alter his stance. Even after conferring with a special committee and receiving public encouragement to associate himself with the patriots, he stated, "I cannot consent to defeat His Majesty's Intentions and disappoint His Expectations by abandoning a Post to which He has Graciously pleased to appoint me . . . I will therefore give

Him no Cause to suspect my Fidelity." Browne's property was also damaged by zealous patriots and he was forced to leave Salem for the safety of Boston.

The Provincial Congress which met in Concord stressed the need for increased defense preparations and ordered county and town militia units to be reorganized. An important feature of their recommendations revived the practice of local election of officers. On 26 October, 1774, it suggested that those companies which "have not already chosen and appointed officers, that they meet forthwith and elect officers to command their respective companies."

Colonel Browne's refusal to resign his various offices had given Essex County the opportunity to take militia affairs into their own hands even before this decision by the Provincial Congress. On 4 October 1774, many of the militia officers resigned their commissions because of Browne's "exertions for carrying into execution acts of Parliament calculated to enslave and ruin his native land." The militia in effect was dissolved and could now be reorganized free of British influence. Only through such direct and radical action were the Essex County towns able to exert sufficient power to determine the political persuasion of its militia officers. A minority of the county's militia leaders were responsible for the action. Less than half of the officers resigned (twenty-three in all, nine from Salem). There is nothing to suggest that either Tories or even those who were at the time moderates or undecided participated in this decision. The reorganized militia, as might be expected, consisted mainly of the most enthusiastic supporters of independence from England.

While many Essex County towns quickly elected new officers and intensified militia training, little of this activity was evident in Salem for many months. An attempt to select officers in December 1774, was apparently unsuccessful because when Timothy Pickering was appointed Colonel of the First Essex Regiment two months later, he was compelled to instruct the militia companies of Salem "to hold themselves in readiness to march at the shortest notice under the command of such officers as they shall choose." Unlike other towns, it took a minor crisis to prod Salem into serious military preparations.

In February 1775, the British received rumors of cannon placements in the Salem area, and dispatched a small unit from Boston to investigate. The British troops confronted a hastily assembled group of militiamen at the North Bridge entrance to Salem. With little hope of accomplishing their purpose, the British avoided armed conflict. The disorganized response of the Salem militia, particularly its leadership, demonstrated its inadequate preparation. Soon afterwards the first general training session was held at which "Every person liable by law to train, and to muster upon an Alarm, belonging to the Militia of this Town, have been warned to appear in School Street . . . with Arms Ammunitions and Accoutrements." Two minutemen companies were formed, additional money was appropriated for defense and Salem "Voted that there be a constable's watch kept in the town consisting of ten persons nightly."

But events moved swiftly, and when the "British commenced hostilities upon the People of this Province," the Salem militia was still not completely prepared. On 19 April 1775, several hundred militiamen under the command of Timothy Pickering rather than their elected captains failed to intercept the British retreat from Lexington and Concord. The transformation of Salem's militia into an effective military force was not a task that was easily or quickly accomplished, but there could be no doubt regarding its attitude towards Independence.

By April 1775, the Salem militia had been significantly changed by the events of the previous decade. During most of that time the militia had lapsed as a military organization, and much of the interest in it was non-military. Beginning in mid-1774, however, renewed emphasis was placed upon the militia's original purpose—the defense of Salem. This caused the militia to assume new importance, and indicates why Adams thought it continued to be one of the most fundamental colonial institutions. The alternative to a militia defense system, a professional standing army, again was proven unnecessary, for the time being at least.

The importance of the militia, however, cannot be assessed solely in military terms. The militia reflected many of the issues and conflicts that were crucial in pre-Revolutionary colonial society. Through both its leadership and the increased importance placed upon its role in the colony, the militia was directly involved in the crises in Salem and Essex County as the Revolution approached. It was a focus of conflict that witnessed a growing polarization and struggle for control, and by 1774 had reached a point in which the opposing factions were virtually irreconcilable. These divisions, scarcely evident in the early 1760s, increased and became determining forces as the complex interplay of revolutionary events and issues quickened.

While the militia was being transformed into a more effective military organization, it remained an important social institution. In fact, social and political concerns had become more decisive, as was the case in many other aspects of colonial life in the 1770s. The developments and changes in the militia, and the conflicts in which it was involved, are an interesting study of institutional transformation in revolutionary America. But while this study suggests several important aspects of the militia as a social institution, it also serves to raise further questions. Important insights, for example, might arise from a more extensive comparison of the new militia officers after 1774 with the earlier leadership. Greater understanding of the social impact of the American Revolution upon the colonies might be gained by examining the continuing transformations of the militia during the Revolution.

The conclusion reached in 1775, when it was generally agreed to revive the earlier and basically seventeenth century militia structure is particularly important. Greater universality of service was required, the urgency of day-to-day preparedness was emphasized, and most importantly, the direct control of each community over its militia was reasserted. This reorganization of the militia demonstrates a distinctive thrust of the American Revolution that sought to return to simpler, more direct institutions—the militia included—that many Americans felt had always been successful in preserving their rights and liberties.

II

〜〜◆〜〜

Wars for Independence, 1763–1815

George Washington, General
Thomas Fleming

Contrary to negative opinion sometimes voiced by historians regarding George Washington's military leadership, Thomas Fleming, a biographer of Washington, argues in this essay that the commander of the American forces displayed a near military genius during the American Revolution. He did so by abandoning the accepted idea of a great decisive battle, "a general action," in favor of a winning strategy of keeping his army intact, retreating if necessary, and striking the enemy only when success seemed assured. This long-range strategy of avoiding all-out confrontation was complemented by rejecting the idea of conducting guerrilla warfare, by cautious tactical audacity, by relying on the militia as supplemental forces only, and by assuring the loyalty of his soldiers to the cause by asking them to make sacrifices only when success appeared attainable. From MHQ: The Quarterly Journal of Military History, Winter 1990, *by Thomas Fleming. Copyright © 1990 by* MHQ: The Quarterly Journal of Military History. *Reprinted by permission of PRIMEDIA Enthusiasts Publications (History Group).*

How good a general was George Washington? If we consult the statistics as they might have been kept if he were a boxer or a quarterback, the figures are not encouraging. In seven years of fighting the British, from 1775 to 1782, he won only three clear-cut victories—at Trenton, Princeton, and Yorktown. In seven other encounters—Long Island, Harlem Heights, White Plains, Fort Washington, Brandywine, Germantown, and Monmouth—he either was defeated or at best could claim a draw. He never won a major battle: Trenton was essentially a raid; Princeton was little more than a large skirmish; and Yorktown was a siege in which the blockading French fleet was an essential component of the victory.

Most contemporary Americans, even if unacquainted with these statistics, are inclined to see General Washington as a figurehead, an inspiring symbol whose dedication and perseverance enabled his starving men to endure the rigors of Valley Forge and Morristown winter quarters. He wore the British out by sheer persistence, with little reference to military skill, much less genius. The recent spate of books devoted to how Washington's image was invented either by himself or by skillful propagandists bolsters this idea. Almost as misleading is our post-Vietnam fascination with guerrilla warfare and comparisons of our defeat in Southeast Asia with the British failure in America. If American guerrillas defeated the British, Washington the general seems almost superfluous.

A general's ability to inspire his men is not, of course, to be discounted, and Washington unquestionably had this gift. But in the final analysis, the great captains of history are rated on their ability to conceive a winning strategy and devise tactics to execute it. Does Washington, the man the British called "a little paltry colonel of militia" in 1776, belong in this select group? The answer is complicated by Washington's character. He was, as the historian J.A. Carroll has pointed out, "not an architect in ideas; he was essentially a man of deeds." He never set down in a neat volume his military (or political) principles. The best way to grasp his superior qualities, Carroll maintains, is to examine his thoughts and actions at climactic moments of his career.

To judge his generalship this way requires a look at the strategy of the Revolutionary Army when Washington became its commander on July 3, 1775. By that time the Americans had fought two battles, Lexington-Concord and Bunker Hill, from which their politicians and soldiers drew ruinously wrong conclusions. At Lexington-Concord they saw proof that militia could spring to the defense of their homes and farms and rout British regulars on a day's notice. At Bunker Hill they thought they had found a secret weapon, the entrenching tool, that would enable them to inflict crippling casualties on the attacking British even if, at the very end of the battle, the Americans ignominiously ran away.

In fact, the minutemen who fought at Lexington and Concord were a well-trained rudimentary army that had been drilling and marching for six months. They outnumbered the British five to one and knew it—a fact that added immensely to their élan. At Bunker Hill the overconfident British commander, William Howe, ordered a frontal assault on the entrenched colonials. Why the Americans assumed he would repeat this mistake in the future remains a mystery. As early as March 17, 1776, when the Americans outflanked the British defenses in Boston by seizing Dorchester Heights and fortified them with cannon dragged from Fort Ticonderoga in New York,

Howe demonstrated he had learned his lesson by evacuating the city—something he had planned to do anyway.

A corollary to these ideas was the conviction that the war would be settled in one tremendous battle—what in the eighteenth century was called "a general action." Thus there was no need to sign men up for long enlistments—a year was considered more than enough time. There was even less need for a large regular army, which might endanger the liberties of the embryonic republic. Militia could operate as well as regulars from behind Bunker Hill–like barricades. As Israel Putnam, the commander at Bunker Hill, summed it up: "Cover Americans to their chins and they will fight until doomsday."

Still another corollary—though the term may be paying too much of a compliment to the Continental Congress's foggy military thinking—was the idea that if the Americans could push the British off the continent, the war would be won. So Washington obediently detached some of his best regiments and officers, such as Daniel Morgan and Benedict Arnold, to wrest Canada from royal control—a campaign that consumed close to half the 20,000 regulars Congress had empowered him to enlist. And the British evacuation of Boston was hailed as a stupendous victory, for which Congress issued Washington a medal.

Washington did not question these strategic assumptions—or Congress's order to abide by a majority vote of his generals in councils of war—until mid-1776, when the main theater of conflict shifted to New York. Congress told him to defend the city; he did it Bunker Hill–style. On Brooklyn Heights and at various points around Manhattan, his men expended immense amounts of energy building forts on which the British were expected to impale themselves. One, on the corner of Grand and Greene streets, was appropriately named Bunker Hill.

Meanwhile, in mid-July, William Howe proceeded to land 25,000 men unopposed on Staten Island, underscoring the idiocy of Congress's continental redoubt strategy in a war with the world's dominant sea power. Washington had only about 10,000 regulars to defend a city surrounded by rivers that permitted the enemy to land where and when they chose. The rest of his 23,000-man army was militia.

A few weeks later Howe shifted his field army to Long Island and defeated the Americans in a battle of feint and maneuver. Faking a frontal assault in order to pin Washington's men in their entrenchments, Howe swung half his army in a night march around the exposed American left wing, creating rout and panic.

A shaken Washington was able to move his surviving troops to Manhattan by night. But a few weeks later Howe outflanked the American forts on lower Manhattan, landing at Kips Bay (now Thirty-fourth Street) after a ferocious naval bombardment. The Connecticut Militia guarding the shore fled without firing a shot. Washington, watching this stampede, cried out, "Are these the men with which I am to defend America?" Again, mostly thanks to British sloth, Washington managed to extricate the bulk of his army, this time to strong positions on Harlem Heights, where a brisk skirmish with British patrols temporarily steadied their collapsing morale.

During "hours allotted to sleep," Washington began rethinking the strategy of the war in a series of letters to the president of Congress. Henceforth, he wrote, the Americans should "avoid a general action or put anything to the Risk, unless compelled by a necessity into which we ought never to be drawn." Their goal should be "to protract the war."

In cutting terms, Washington demolished congressional prejudice against a large standing army. It was imperative to recruit regulars committed to serve for the duration, and end their dependence on militia. "Men just dragged from the tender Scenes of domestick life, unaccustomed to the din of arms," had no confidence in themselves or their officers on a battlefield. They were impatient, impossible to discipline, and they infected the regulars with similar vices.

But Washington and his generals were themselves still infected with the Bunker Hill virus, which they now called "a war of posts." When Howe outflanked him again, landing troops on the Westchester shore of the Hudson who threatened to trap the Americans on Manhattan Island, Washington retreated to the hills around White Plains. Behind him he left almost 3,000 regulars in Fort Washington, overlooking the Hudson at present-day 181st Street. These men were supposed to deny the British full use of Manhattan Island and the river.

At White Plains, Howe did little more than feint an attack, then detached a hefty portion of his army to assault Fort Washington. Masterfully combining artillery with flank and frontal attacks, the British took the fort in two hours, bagging irreplaceable regulars and scores of cannon. A chagrined Washington confessed there had been "warfare in my mind" about whether to evacuate the place. He had let Major General Nathanael Greene, at this point one of the leading Bunker Hillists, talk him into leaving them there.

That bitter pill purged the last vestige of entrenchment-tool illusions from Washington's mind. Two weeks later General Greene was across the Hudson River in Fort Washington's New Jersey twin, Fort Lee, when he learned from a local farmer that four or five thousand British troops had crossed the river at Dobbs Ferry, a few miles to the north, and were marching on the fort. Greene rushed a dispatch to Washington in Hackensack, asking for instructions. Should he stay and fight it out? Instead of a written answer, he got General Washington in person on a lathered horse. His instructions were one word: Retreat. Cannon, food, ammunition—everything was abandoned.

That was the day Washington began fighting a new kind of war in America. He was just in time, because in New Jersey the British, too, had some new ideas. Having demonstrated their ability to defeat the American army almost at will, they launched a campaign to win what post-Vietnam Americans would call hearts and minds. Along their line of march, they distributed a proclamation offering rebels pardons and guaranties against "forfeitures, attainders and penalties." All they had to do was appear before a British official within sixty days and sign a statement promising to "remain in a peaceable Obedience to His Majesty." New Jersey, the British hoped, would become a model of how to defuse the Revolution. It had a large percentage of loyalists who would support a restoration of royal government and back the king's troops against "the disaffected."

At first Washington thought he had a good chance to defend New Jersey. He had brought 2,500 regulars across the Hudson with him, leaving some 7,000 men in Westchester to bar the British from the Hudson highlands and New England. New Jersey had 16,000 militiamen on its muster rolls. He asked Governor William Livingston to call them all out. He told the commander of the Westchester force, Major General Charles Lee, to cross the Hudson and join him for a stand on the Raritan River around New Brunswick.

These hopes rapidly unraveled. The British reinforced their invading army until it was 10,000 men strong, under the command of one of their most aggressive generals, Charles, Lord Cornwallis. Charles Lee, a headstrong compound of radical political opinions and careening military ambition, ignored Washington's request to join him. Meanwhile New Jersey's militia declined to turn out. Not a single regiment responded to the governor's call. Only about 1,000 individuals showed up at mustering sites, almost as useless as none at all. It was grim evidence of the power of Britain's shrewd combination of carrot and bayonet.

On November 29, Washington was in New Brunswick with an army riven by three months of retreat and defeat. Some militiamen broke into stores of rum and got drunk. Others, mostly Pennsylvanians, deserted in droves, although they had been paid to stay until January 1. Those whose contracts expired on December 1 announced they were going home then, no matter what was happening to the glorious cause.

Soon down to 3,000 men, and with the British crunching toward the bridges over the Raritan, Washington told Congress, "We shall retreat to the west side of the Delaware." Although New Jersey and the rest of the country saw this decision as mere flight, Washington was still thinking strategically. He wrote Charles Lee that he hoped the British would pursue him and attempt to pacify New Jersey by detaching garrisons across the state. He planned to "lull them into security" and, when he saw an opportunity, "beat them up."

The Revolution in New Jersey slid toward collapse. The legislature disbanded. As many as three to four hundred people a day flocked to British army posts to renew their allegiance. Brigadier General Alexander McDougall wrote from Morristown: "This state is totally deranged, without Government or officers, civil or military . . . that will act with any spirit." Another contemporary observer remarked that at this point the British could have bought New Jersey for eighteen pence a head.

Finally realizing that the fate of the infant nation was at stake in New Jersey, Charles Lee crossed the Hudson into Bergen County. He was not encouraged by what he encountered along his line of march: The mass of the people were "strangely contaminated" with loyalty to the king. He urged Congress to recruit a new army immediately by drafting every militiaman they could find. A few days later Lee was captured by a British cavalry patrol and the remnants of his force straggled across the Delaware to join Washington's handful.

Major General Israel Putnam, the architect of Bunker Hill, was also wandering through New Jersey telling everyone the war was lost. The current army was about to disband, he said, and even if Congress could raise another one, there was no hope of resisting the British "in the plain country to the southward." Without a hill to fight from, Putnam was devoid of ideas.

Washington took a different view. In a letter to General William Heath, who was guarding the Hudson highlands, the American commander in chief wrote that "the defection of the people . . . has been as much owing to the want of an Army to look the Enemy in the face, as any other cause."

In this offhand, intuitive way, Washington enunciated the central idea of the strategy that would win the American Revolution. It merits his inclusion in the select circle of great revolutionary generals who invented a new kind of war—with an additional laurel for conceiving this winning strategy while most of the others around him were losing their heads.

This central statement coincided with the rest of the new strategic ideas Washington had enunciated in the previous chaotic months of defeat and disillusion: recruiting a regular army for the duration, protracting the war, never risking a general action, retreating until the enemy exposed a part of their army to insult or destruction.

Washington swiftly demonstrated his ability to implement tactics to match his strategy. He ordered General Heath to invade northern New Jersey from the Hudson highlands, seize arms, and intimidate the many loyalists the British had encouraged to come out of hiding there. He gave Alexander McDougall three of Charles Lee's continental regiments to support a fairly good turnout of militia in Morris County. Finally, he marshaled the 2,500 shivering regulars under his command and led them across the ice-choked Delaware River on Christmas night of 1776 to kill or capture two-thirds of the 1,500-man royal garrison at Trenton.

A few days later, Washington again invaded New Jersey. Cornwallis came at him with 9,000 men. On January 2, 1777, Washington wheeled his army around the British left flank by night and chewed up three regiments at Princeton, then headed for the royal army's main base at New Brunswick. The frantic British abandoned west Jersey and marched all night to get there first. They flung themselves into defensive positions around the town—only to discover that Washington had slipped away to winter quarters in Morristown. There, he coolly issued a proclamation announcing that anyone who had switched sides could return to the cause by showing up at any American post and pledging fresh allegiance to the United States.

With an army to look the enemy in the face and British power reduced to a narrow enclave along the Raritan, New Jersey's revolutionary ardor underwent a magical revival. British commissaries and foraging parties were ambushed on the roads. Loyalism beyond the army's enclave collapsed. Brilliantly combining military force and patriotic persuasion, Washington had rescued the state—and the country.

Recruiting for a new army revived in the rest of the nation, and General Howe glumly reported to London that he now saw no hope of ending the war "but by a general action." Here was irony indeed: Washington had maneuvered the British into adopting the flawed strategy with which the Americans had begun the war.

Washington had already decided that a climactic battle was precisely what Howe was never going to get. And for the next five years he stuck to his strategy despite criticism from hotheads in Congress and in the army, who still envisioned a general action as the answer to everything. In early 1777 Congressman John Adams, who fancied himself a military expert, was still drinking toasts to "a short and violent war."

When the British tried to advance across New Jersey that summer to assault Philadelphia, they found Washington's army on the high ground in the center of the state, waiting to pounce on them—and absolutely declining to come down from the hills to give all-out battle. A disgusted Howe abandoned the stunned loyalists of east Jersey as he had deserted those in the west after Trenton and Princeton, marched his army to Perth Amboy and sailed them down the coast, then up Chesapeake Bay to attack Philadelphia in a roundabout fashion.

Howe found the hard-marching American army waiting for him in line of battle on Brandywine Creek, apparently ready to offer him the general action he wanted. But Washington positioned his men to give them the whole state of Pennsylvania into which to retreat if—as it transpired—victory eluded them. He followed the same policy a few weeks later at Germantown. Retreat, a dirty word in the American vocabulary in 1776, was no longer considered disgraceful. When the frustrated Howe settled into winter quarters in Philadelphia, former Bunker Hillist Nathanael Greene exulted that British rule in America did not extend beyond "their out-sentinels."

Meanwhile, to make sure the British did not conquer America piece-meal, Washington was extending his central strategic concept of an army to look the enemy in the face. When a British army under General John Burgoyne descended from Canada in 1777, Washington sent some of his best troops, in particular a regiment of Virginia riflemen under Daniel Morgan, to help Major General Horatio Gates's northern army. These men played a crucial part in the victory at Saratoga, inspiring thousands of militiamen to turn out to support the regulars. Although the regulars did almost all the fighting, the militia blocked Burgoyne's line of retreat and destroyed his supply lines, giving him no alternative but surrender.

Washington followed the same strategy in the South when the British shifted their main effort to that region in 1779. They swiftly pacified Georgia and ensconced a royal governor in Savannah. Washington detached one of his most dependable generals, Benjamin Lincoln, and some of his best regiments to meet the threat, but the British trumped this hand by trapping Lincoln and his army in Charleston and forcing them to surrender—a victory that more than balanced Saratoga.

Grimly, Washington detached more regulars he could not spare and assigned them to an army led by Horatio Gates, the victor at Saratoga. They inspired another good turnout of militiamen, but Gates made the mistake of putting the amateurs into line of battle alongside the regulars at Camden. A bayonet charge routed them, exposing the regulars to defeat.

This time Washington riposted with his best general, Nathanael Greene, who had learned a great deal about the art of war at Washington's side since sponsoring the disaster at Fort Washington in 1776. Although he began with barely 800 ragged regulars, Greene adapted Washington's strategy to the South, summing it up admirably in a letter to the guerrilla leader Thomas Sumter:

> The salvation of this country don't depend upon little strokes nor should the great business of establishing a permanent army be neglected to pursue them. Partisan strokes in war are like the garnish of a table, they give splendor to the Army and reputation to the officers, but they afford no national security. . . . You may strike a hundred strokes and reap little benefit from them unless you have a good army to take advantage of your success. . . . It is not a war of posts but a contest for States.

Greene soon demonstrated what he meant. He dispatched 350 regulars to South Carolina under Daniel Morgan when the state was on the verge of total surrender. These regulars rallied enough militiamen to win a stunning victory at the Cowpens and reverse the momentum of the war.

While Washington supported armies to the north and south, he never forgot New Jersey. The state remained the cockpit of the Revolution for him. In three out of five years, he made it the site of his winter quarters. In the other two years, the ones he spent at Valley Forge and at Newburgh in

Westchester, he was never more than a day's march away. The payoff came in June 1780, when swarms of New Jersey militiamen turned out to join 3,500 continentals in stopping a 7,000-man invading army. After two bloody collisions at Connecticut Farms and Springfield, the British withdrew and never invaded the state again.

One thing should now be apparent: Washington's strategy was far more complex than guerrilla warfare. Instead, it posited a regular army as an essential force to sustain a war, aided when necessary by guerrilla elements. In spite of his criticism of militia, Washington used them throughout the war. He had no other choice. He soon resigned himself to never achieving the 40,000-man army Congress voted him in the aftermath of Trenton and Princeton. For most of the war, he was lucky to have a fourth of that number under his command. He called out militia again and again to flesh out his forces, but he never depended on them the way he and his fellow generals had in 1776. In 1780 he told the president of Congress that militia were useful "only as light troops to be scattered in the woods and plague rather than do serious injury to the enemy." This kind of fighting, which he called *petite guerre*—a first cousin of the Spanish word *guerrilla*—was, as his lieutenant Greene made clear, never decisive.

In 1778 Washington met the greatest challenge to his strategy. It came from Charles Lee, who returned from British captivity with a plan to disband the regular army and commit the country to a guerrilla war. Washington rejected the idea as firmly as he turned aside proposals for summoning all the militiamen within reach and hurling them and the regulars at the British for the one big battle John Adams and other fire-eaters wanted.

Washington got the most out of his thin line of regulars because he seldom used them in a European way—and because he was generously endowed with a trait essential to a great general: audacity. It runs like a bright thread through his whole career, beginning with his dawn attack on a French patrol on Virginia's frontier in 1754, a burst of gunfire that started the Seven Years' War. Even in early 1776, during the stalemated siege of Boston, he startled his Bunker Hill–infatuated colleagues by proposing a dawn assault across the ice of Back Bay on the entrenched British—a gamble that might have ended the war on the spot. A council of war voted him down.

Trenton and Princeton were, of course, masterpieces of audacity, but not enough credit has been given to Germantown. Here, just four weeks after losing a major battle on the Brandywine, he hurled his entire army in four columns at the main British camp. Only the confusion generated by an early-morning fog prevented him from winning. In Europe, it was Germantown as much as Saratoga that convinced France the Americans were capable of winning the war and were worth the risk of an alliance.

Even after he went into winter quarters at Valley Forge, Washington's audacity continued to manifest itself. He insisted on constant skirmishing and harassment of the enemy in Philadelphia. Although driven to cries of exasperation and despair at the way Congress failed to feed and clothe the army, he found time to plan a winter attack on the British, which Nathanael Greene narrowly persuaded him was too "hassardous."

By this time Washington had stopped paying much attention to Congress's military thinking. He refused to split up his army to give various parts of the country an unfounded feeling of security. Not even the president of Congress could persuade him to station some units closer to the politicians' 1778 headquarters in York. "It would give me infinite pleasure to afford protection to every individual and to every spot of ground in the whole United States. Nothing is more my wish . . . [but] I cannot divide the army. If this is done I cannot be answerable for the consequences," Washington wrote. For the same reason he vetoed a plan to give the marquis de Lafayette a chunk of the main army and let him invade Canada in 1778.

But Washington never stopped looking for a chance to strike at an exposed British position. In July and August of 1779, when the war in the north seemed stalemated, he struck two ferocious blows. First, bayonet-wielding light infantry under Anthony Wayne killed or captured the entire garrison at Stony Point on the Hudson. A month later Washington's favorite cavalryman, Light-Horse Harry Lee, repeated the performance against the smaller British outpost at Paulus Hook in present-day Jersey City.

Surprize [sic] was one of the favorite words in Washington's military vocabulary, and he was constantly studying ways to improve his technique for achieving it. Because the enemy expected surprise attacks at dawn, he recommended midnight. "A dark night and even a rainy one if you can find the way, will contribute to your success," he told Anthony Wayne, advice Wayne put to good use at Stony Point.

But Washington tempered his audacity with caution. When Benedict Arnold wanted to organize an assault on British-held Newport in 1777, Washington told him to forget it unless he had "a moral certainty" of succeeding. More and more, as the war dragged on, he sought to avoid giving the British even the appearance of a victory. He was ever aware of the importance of maintaining popular support. This not only was important politically but was a vital part of his military strategy. Militia would not turn out for a loser.

In this context, Brandywine, which seems at first glance to contradict Washington's determination to avoid a general action, fits his strategy of maintaining an army to look the enemy in the face. He recognized that in the struggle for hearts and minds up and down a 2,000-mile-long continent, there were times when the Americans had to fight even if the odds were heavily against them. To have allowed the British to march into Philadelphia without a battle would have ruined the patriots' morale.

A similar blend of pugnacity and public relations motivated the last major battle under Washington's command—Monmouth in June 1778. The

French had entered the war, and the panicky British abandoned Philadelphia to retreat to New York. Now more than ever Washington was disin-
clined to risk everything in a general action. But he sensed the need to strike
a blow. After a day of ferocious fighting in nightmarish heat in the New Jersey Pine Barrens, satisfied that he had won the appearance of a victory, he
let the redcoats continue their retreat.

To maintain civilian morale, Washington at one point suggested Congress provide the army with "a small traveling press" to supply "speedy
and exact information of any military transactions that take place." When
the bankrupt Congress refused, Washington did the next best thing. He fur-
loughed an ex-newspaperman, Lieutenant Sheppard Kollock of the continental artillery, and set him up as editor of the New Jersey *Journal*, which at
least stabilized public opinion in the cockpit state.

On another front Washington displayed an audacity—and an imagination—few generals have matched. Throughout most of the war, he was his
own intelligence director. He proved himself a master of the game, running
as many as a half dozen spy rings in Philadelphia and New York, and constantly urged his fellow generals to follow suit. "Single men in the night will
be more likely to ascertain facts than the best glasses in the day," he wrote to
Anthony Wayne in 1779.

One of the keys to his victory at Trenton was his use of a double agent,
John Honeyman, to give him a thorough briefing on the enemy's defenses—
and to lull the local commander with stories of the American Army's collapse. At Valley Forge, Washington manufactured documents in his own
handwriting full of returns from imaginary infantry and cavalry regiments.
Double agents handed those documents over to the British in Philadelphia,
convincing them that the main army had been reinforced with 8,000 men
and was too strong to molest.

In July 1780 Sir Henry Clinton decided to launch a preemptive attack on
a French army that had just landed at Newport. A brilliant idea, it might
well have succeeded if one of Washington's best New York agents had not
rushed him news of the plan. Clinton actually had his men aboard ships
when he was distracted by the capture of some "secret" papers that showed
Washington was planning an all-out attack on New York. The jittery British
general reluctantly abandoned his *coup de main*.

The Yorktown campaign was the ultimate proof of the genius of Washington's generalship. The idea of trapping Cornwallis in the little tobacco
port came from the French commander, the comte de Rochambeau; Washington was skeptical of its chances for success. But the execution of the plan
depended totally on Washington's tactics and strategy. First he befuddled
Sir Henry Clinton with a veritable blizzard of false information about an attack on New York. Then he took the huge gamble of marching his men
south in a long, exposed line through New Jersey. Benedict Arnold, by that

time a British general, begged Clinton to attack, but Sir Henry declined another encounter with "the bold persevering militia of that populous province" and let Washington march to victory.

Perhaps the most appealing thing about Washington's strategy was its strong link to freedom. It eschewed the militaristic idea of hauling every man into the ranks at the point of a gun. It rested instead on faith in the courage of free men. It was a realistic faith: He did not expect men to commit suicide in defense of freedom, but he did believe men would take grave risks if they thought they had a reasonable chance of succeeding.

Looking back later, Washington, an innately modest man, was often inclined to attribute victory to the "interposition of Providence." But those who study the evidence, and ignore the statistics, are inclined to think Providence wore the shape of a tall Virginian who had the brains to conceive a way to win a war when it was on the brink of being lost—and the ability to provide the leadership that converted this strategy into a military victory won by free men.

The Battle of Lake Erie: A Narrative

Gerard T. Altoff

One of the most significant victories of the War of 1812 was won by an American fleet under Commodore Oliver Hazard Perry over a British fleet under Robert Heriot Barclay off Put-in-Bay on western Lake Erie on September 10, 1813. Whatever losses the American forces suffered elsewhere in "The Second War of American Independence," this victory assured American control of the upper Great Lakes and contributed to the Crown's decision to terminate hostilities against its former colonies across the Atlantic. This epic battle is described in detail by Gerard Altoff, historian and Chief Ranger, National Park Service, at the Perry's Victory and International Peace Memorial, in the following essay and illustrates how the "fog of war" can play a major role in achieving victory or incurring defeat. It was first published in a different form as Chapter 1 in William Jeffrey Welsh and David Curtis Skaggs, eds., War on the Great Lakes (Kent, OH & London: Kent State University Press, 1991), 118–48, and is reprinted, text only, by permission of The Kent State University Press.

Blood streamed in crimson rivulets along the seams of the stricken ship's gouged deck. As their lifeblood flowed from ghastly wounds, tortured seamen writhed in agony, their heart-rending screams and moans competing with the roar of cannon and musketry. The broken and maimed bodies lying on deck or stretched out in the surgery below far outnumbered the exhausted and mentally stunned sailors still on their feet. Thick clouds of dirty white gunsmoke drifted across the restless lake, its rancid, sulfurous smell pervading every corner of the ravaged vessel, stinging the eyes and wrinkling the nostrils of the ship's dazed crew. Like walking zombies they stumbled about their assigned duties, brains refusing to register the horror surrounding them.

The little 20-gun brig, battered and beaten, shuddered under the impact of each British cannonball, as if in sympathy for the wretched men bleeding on her deck. Her gunports were mostly silent, only a few of the giant 32-pounders still capable of disgorging their deadly iron spheres. Shredded strips of canvas flapped helplessly in the wind, all that remained of the ship's once majestic sails. Rigging hung limply from her spars and trailed in the water alongside, not unlike a stately willow after a hailstorm. Her tall, heavily punctured frame resembled a bull's-eye after a long day of target practice.

On the flayed quarterdeck the young commodore, hatless and wearing a common seaman's round-jacket to conceal him from British sharpshooters, gazed despairingly at the wasted wreck that only two hours earlier had been the proud flagship of his fleet. Peering up at the large blue banner floating above his head on the main truck—his battle flag bearing the determined epithet "DONT GIVE UP THE SHIP"—he perceived that its taunting words belied his desperate situation. Surrender appeared his only logical alternative.

It was an incredible predicament for an officer who exactly one month earlier had resigned his commission from the U.S. Navy. Master Commandant Oliver Hazard Perry had undoubtedly suffered a number of both real and imagined slights from his superior, Commodore Isaac Chauncey, during the summer of 1813. Not least of these affronts was Chauncey's railing vilification after Perry bypassed his commanding officer and appealed directly to Secretary of the Navy William Jones for assistance, an obvious error in judgment by Perry.

Throughout the previous spring Chauncey had supported Perry while the American fleet was under construction at Erie, Pennsylvania, and the latter was able to solve most of his shipbuilding problems through diligence and hard work. However, as the time neared to fight his fleet, Perry was forced to rely on Chauncey to provide sailors, but progress to resolve his manpower shortage was nil. All reinforcements for the Great Lakes were routed through Sacket's Harbor, New York, for distribution by Chauncey who churlishly, though perhaps understandably, elected to retain the cream of the crop for his own Lake Ontario fleet. Even after Chauncey relented, thanks to Perry's missive and Jones's intervention, and provided two contingents of sailors for the Erie fleet, Perry still fell far short of his manpower requirements. Needing a minimum of 720 able-bodied seamen to man his numerous vessels, Perry could muster only about 400 men by August 10. Of this number fully one-fourth were soldier volunteers or marines, and a large number were prostrated by a debilitating lake-induced fever, a malady with which Perry himself was intermittently afflicted.

Chauncey's apparent disregard for both Perry's military situation and personal feelings compelled Perry to submit his resignation to Secretary Jones. While deadly serious, Perry was nevertheless cognizant of his greater responsibilities, those being duty to his country and Major-General William Henry Harrison's critical situation in northwest Ohio. Several weeks would pass before a suitable replacement could reach Lake Erie. Meanwhile, Perry would strive to accomplish his assigned task, the destruction of British naval power on Lake Erie.

Realizing that further reinforcements from Sacket's Harbor would not be forthcoming, Perry decided to sail for western Lake Erie. Although hindered by his lack of seamen, Perry was determined this handicap would not inhibit him. On August 12, with barely enough men to navigate his ships, Perry aimed his bowsprits toward the setting sun. Even though at this point he commanded too few men to even fill his gun crews, Perry was confident his dilemma would somehow be rectified. He had labored too long and hard to be deprived of the opportunity to fight his fleet.

The American fleet, ten vessels strong, arrived off Sandusky Bay on August 16. Harrison, Perry, and their combined staffs held a conference on board the flagship *Lawrence* to determine strategy. Here it was decided that Perry would utilize Put-in-Bay harbor on South Bass Island as his base of operations. From that strategic location Perry could easily observe British fleet movements in the event they opted to sail, or interdict enemy supply vessels if they attempted a hasty resupply mission.

Twice in the next three weeks, sailing from his new base, Perry conducted reconnaissance cruises in the proximity of Fort Malden. Perry hoped a direct approach and bombardment of both the fort and the Amherstburg Navy Yard might prove the simplest and easiest means of destroying the British. Such was not the case. The fort was too strongly defended, the current in the Detroit River too swift, the winds too fickle, and the channel too narrow for fleet maneuvers. In any event, it was not necessary for Perry to risk his fleet in an ill-conceived attack; time was now on the American side.

With the American fleet perched in western Lake Erie the British confronted numerical superiority. More importantly, their water supply route along Lake Erie's northern shore between Fort Malden and Long Point was compromised. Perry need only return to Put-in-Bay, train his hybrid crews of soldiers and sailors, and wait for the British to sail forth and fight.

Perry's adversary, Robert Heriot Barclay, was younger than Perry by a year, yet he was an experienced Royal Navy officer who had lost an arm fighting against the French in the Napoleonic Wars. There was little doubt in Barclay's mind that a battle was forthcoming, and even less doubt that he would wage the fight at a considerable disadvantage. Despite the fact that Barclay commanded fewer ships than Perry, he nevertheless counted more cannon lining his broadsides—nine American ships with fifty-four guns versus six British vessels with sixty-three artillery pieces. But it was not the number of muzzles that really mattered. What would determine the outcome of the upcoming battle was the weight of metal those broadsides fired. The American ships were armed primarily with heavy 32-pounders, while Barclay's largest guns were 24-pounders, and he was equipped with all too few of those. Barclay's meager hopes lay in the fact that most of his guns were long-range weapons.

Perry relied on carronades for his two largest ships. Although they were endowed with numerous practical advantages over the traditional naval cannon, carronades possessed less than half the effective range of the British long guns. Essentially, the Americans traded firepower for distance. Thus, if Barclay could maintain his fleet at long range, he could pulverize the American vessels before Perry's short-range guns inflicted fatal damage.

Guns, however, were not Barclay's only worry. As destitute as Perry was of trained sailors, Barclay found himself even more shorthanded. The British commodore on Lake Ontario and Barclay's immediate superior, Sir James Lucas Yeo, proved even more parsimonious with resources than Chauncey. When Barclay arrived at Amherstburg, his largest vessel could boast only twenty experienced seamen, a situation that did not greatly improve. As a result, crews on the English ships were comprised mostly of British soldiers, Canadian militia, and merchant mariners. Barclay surely contemplated the upcoming engagement with nervous uncertainty.

Significant though these deficiencies were, it was an entirely different factor that forced Barclay's hand. With the British supply line severed by Perry's presence at Put-in-Bay, the store of rations at Fort Malden was soon depleted. By September 9, only one day's supply of flour remained, so there was really no option. The British could either regain control of Lake Erie and their interrupted supply line, or abandon Fort Malden, their Indian allies, and the fruits of their earlier hard-won victories.

Whereas Barclay could expect no additional help, Perry received welcome reinforcements upon returning to Put-in-Bay from his Fort Malden sojourn. After discovering Perry's paucity of seamen during their initial meeting two weeks earlier, Harrison issued a call for volunteers from among his regiments. Altogether approximately 130 men volunteered, soldiers from all the regular regiments in the Old Northwest plus a number of militia units. Of Perry's eventual total of 532 men on his ten vessels, over 40 percent were assimilated soldiers and marines emanating from nearly twenty different army units representing at least ten different states; an incredible amalgamation of diverse elements never before nor since assembled to fight a fleet of American warships.

The stage was set. Barclay consulted with Major-General Henry Procter, commander of combined British operations in the Old Northwest, and it was decided Barclay would fight the American fleet. Regardless of his problems and shortages, no choice remained for Barclay except a fleet action at a time and place not of his choosing. On the afternoon of September 9, 1813, the British ships hauled their hooks, floated down the Detroit River, and slipped into Lake Erie.

As a crisp dawn slowly crept across the placid waters and peaceful islands, a lookout perched at dizzying heights above the deck of the American flagship suddenly bellowed a warning. Perry, in his cabin below, rushed on deck barking commands. Scurrying about in disciplined chaos, barefoot sailors responded to their lieutenants' shouted orders and hurriedly executed a myriad of complex evolutions. As the stars and stripes lazily floated from the main gaffs, the long line of nine vessels eased out of Put-in-Bay—the schooner *Ohio* having been dispatched a few days earlier for supplies.

Perry's first concern after clearing the harbor was to position his fleet to windward of the British so as to acquire the crucial advantage of the weather gauge. A small forest of British masts stood starkly visible several miles north of Rattlesnake Island. A gentle breeze, barely strong enough to ruffle the calm waters, puffed intermittently from the southwest. To secure the weather gauge Perry would find it necessary to work his vessels well to the westward of Rattlesnake Island, but the southwesterly breeze was blowing almost directly in his face, obviating any opportunity of headreaching to windward. If the British continued to hold the wind advantage, they could maintain a sufficient distance to windward and destroy Perry's fleet with their long guns before the American commodore managed to deploy his short-range carronades. Perry's small schooners did carry heavy long guns, but only one or two each, certainly not enough to deflect the British onslaught. With the leverage of the weather gauge the British could focus on one American vessel at a time and destroy Perry's fleet piecemeal.

For almost three hours Perry's heels rapped a steady tattoo as he impatiently paced back and forth across the *Lawrence*'s quarterdeck, interrupted only occasionally by a frustrated scowl in the direction of the British ships. No matter how arrantly he willed it, Perry's ships failed to make headway into the wind. Finally, at four bells in the forenoon watch (ten o'clock A.M.), a disgusted Perry succumbed to nature's vagary and passed the order to wear ship and steer an easterly course. Conceding the salient advantage of the weather gauge to the British, Perry now intended to fight to leeward among the islands, where Barclay's superiority of long guns might conceivably eliminate American naval power on Lake Erie. Perry's action illustrates his overpowering desire to fight and prove his squadron, but it also points to a certain rashness and impetuosity in his personality.

Fortunately the consequences of Perry's headstrong decision will never be known. No sooner was this inexpedient order issued than the mutable wind suddenly backed ninety degrees and blew from the southeast. An incredible stroke of good fortune, the change of wind direction, as Barclay later recounted, proffered a prodigious advantage to the American fleet. Mother Nature had conferred upon Perry the one factor over which he had no control: a wind at his back.

The sinking feeling in Barclay's chest served only to emphasize a rapidly deteriorating state of affairs. Barclay had just lost his one great advantage but he was not about to submit. With a little ingenuity and a modicum of good fortune the battle could still be won. Although the breeze favored the Americans, it was barely strong enough to propel a ship through the water. Perry's approach would thus be exceedingly prolonged, and a slow approach would allow time for Barclay's more numerous long guns to play upon the American ships virtually unchallenged. If Barclay could dismast or disable one or both of the American brigs before Perry's deadly carronades floated into range the day could yet belong to the British.

Barclay's iota of optimism increased as he stared intently at the still distant American line. Ever so slowly the American fleet appeared to be splitting apart. The smaller converted merchant vessels bringing up the rear of Perry's line were deep-hulled vessels designed to carry cargo, not cannon. Unfortunately the combination of deep draft and impotent winds soon forced three schooners and a sloop to lag behind, isolating half of Perry's heavy long guns far astern and temporarily out of the battle. Even though these four small vessels carried only one or two long guns each, all were 32- or 24-pounders, a heavy punch indeed. Barclay's fortunes were steadily improving.

Perry elected not to wait for his wayward schooners, once again exhibiting a lack of constraint and displaying possibly faulty judgment. There was obviously no hurry since the British had no option but to fight, they were going nowhere. Perry must have realized that, yet he deliberately dashed pell-mell into range of the enemy long guns, leaving many of his own heavy long guns trailing in his wake, guns that could equally contest the British and somewhat negate the enemy advantage.

The light airs instead insured that Perry, in such a great hurry, would make only faltering progress. The two fleets converged with painful slowness. Perry opted to use this pregnant interval to display his as-yet-unseen battleflag. Sewn by a dowager acquaintance of Perry's in Erie, the banner was a blue rectangle sporting crude white letters. The message on the flag, though negative in connotation, left no doubt as to its meaning. It was the dying utterance of Perry's friend, the epitaph of the man for whom his flagship was named—James Lawrence. As the navy blue bunting fluttered to the maintruck and its words were read by upraised eyes, the phrase "DONT GIVE UP THE SHIP" inspired a chorus of throaty, boisterous cheers—tension-relieving cheers, just as Perry intended. But as the dying echoes of the spirited shouting dissipated over the open water, the trepidation again began to mount. Nothing now remained except the intolerable waiting and last minute preparations.

Reticence gripped the crewmen as they nervously pondered the coming few hours. Hearts thumped irregularly, muscles knotted in tensed shoulders, eyes squinted against the shimmering glare, dry tongues licked parched lips, sweaty palms stroked cotton trousers, stiffened fingers clenched and unclenched, restless feet shuffled against white holy-stoned decks. Only a few nervous coughs punctuated the silence.

The clean decks were sanded to help retain footing on the inevitably blood-splattered, smooth wood. Buckets of water dotted the planking, to quell both thirst and the nemesis of all sailors—fire. Ramrods clinked as soldiers and marines jammed musketballs down long-barreled smoothbores. Slow-match burned in sand-filled tubs. Gun captains minutely inspected the bulbous cannonballs, searching for imperfections that would prevent the iron spheres from flying true. Gun crews triple-checked rammers, sponges, thumbstalls, tackleblocks, and flaked gun tackle; inexperienced officers paced anxiously; marines with fixed bayonets guarded the hatches, ordered to cut down cowards attempting to skulk below. In the sick bays, surgeons in leather aprons laid out orderly rows of scalpels, probes, lancets, and bone saws, while their hated loblolly boys waited patiently, unemotionally to restrain the bloodied, mangled wounded; powder monkeys scampered to and fro with deadly fodder for the insatiable big guns; agitated and frightened men craned flushed faces above bulwarks, swearing the opposing fleets were drawing no closer. But they were!

At 11:45 A.M. the unearthly silence was broken when a brilliant flash highlighted the steep profile of Barclay's flagship and a thunderous crash echoed across the tranquil water. A ranging shot which splashed harmlessly short of the *Lawrence*. The waiting was over.

The encore was not long in coming as the British soon opened a steady fire. Ten minutes after the opening volley Perry hoisted a signal for all vessels to close the range and engage their previously designated adversaries. Obviously that was impossible for the lagging schooners, yet Perry was not overly concerned. *Lawrence* was moving slowly but steadily and *Niagara* coasted under all sail only a quarter mile astern. The brigs *Lawrence* and *Niagara* carried forty of Perry's fifty-four guns, thirty-six of which were the heavy 32-pounder carronades. As long as *Lawrence,* Perry's flagship, closed with *Detroit,* Barclay's flagship, and *Niagara* converged with *Queen Charlotte,* Barclay's second largest ship, then Perry would maintain better than a three-to-two advantage in weight of broadsides. If only he could absorb the punishment until the range shortened, Perry knew Barclay was finished.

For thirty minutes British metal crashed into the *Lawrence* and American soldiers and sailors died horribly or were smashed screaming to her deck. Retribution was impossible; the range was too great. The Americans could only grit their teeth, brave the storm of shot, and pray for a stronger breeze.

Finally, at 12:15 P.M., the *Lawrence* eased into range. Perry luffed and his ponderous 32-pounders belched iron death at the British. His ship had been hurt, but not mortally, and all her guns were in action. All Perry needed now was the *Niagara*. With an additional broadside of 32-pounder carronades, the pendulum would inevitably swing to the American side, and the British would find themselves inundated by American metal.

But as Perry glanced astern he was unsure his eyes were focusing properly. Through the dense gunsmoke it appeared *Niagara* had brailed [furled] her jib and backed her main topsail. It was a nightmare. *Niagara* had indeed shortened sail and stalled her forward progress, leaving the unbelieving crew of the *Lawrence* aghast and bewildered.

The actions of *Niagara*'s commander, Jesse Elliott, were unclear at the time and have been further obfuscated over the passing years. In the long run his motives are irrelevant. What mattered was the *Niagara* failed to close *Queen Charlotte* and that by his actions Elliott doomed the *Lawrence* and her beleaguered crew.

With no opponent for her own carronades *Queen Charlotte* swung out of line and pulled forward, leveling her broadside at the *Lawrence*.

Following her lead was *General Hunter*, also blazing away at the *Lawrence*. With *Niagara* timorously shying away and Perry's smaller supporting vessels virtually ignored, the British pinpointed the combined broadsides of their three largest vessels on Perry's isolated flagship. For two endless hours *Lawrence*'s crewmen suffered systematic and excruciating torment while Elliott, aboard *Niagara*, wallowed ineffectually out of range, little more than a spectator.

Shortly after *Queen Charlotte* gathered way and pushed ahead in the British line, *Niagara* again set sail and glided forward. Inexplicably, however, Elliott hugged the wind, sliding away from the British line. His later recollections indicated he was attempting to assault the head of the British line, a redundant goal he was unable to achieve even after a two-hour time span. Elliott was conscious of the terrible destruction suffered by the American flagship, but he made no concerted effort to close with the enemy line as per Perry's specific order.

By 2:30 P.M. the plight of the ravaged *Lawrence* almost defied description. At best she was a defenseless hulk. Pride welled up in Perry's chest at the superb performance and superhuman sacrifice manifested by his incomparable crew, a sacrifice he could not mock by ignominious surrender.

Staring at the proud words emblazoned on his battle standard, still straining against its halyard at the main top, Perry realized he had no choice but to betray its unyielding tenor and abandon his precious ship. Anguished by his decision and feeling the questioning stares of the many wounded and the few sailors still on their feet, Perry ordered the damaged, but usable, small boat prepared and his battle flag hauled down.

Moments earlier Perry had glimpsed the *Niagara* approximately one-half mile to windward, her unseeming serenity a haunting visage compared to the horror of *Lawrence*'s gundeck. Anger and frustration sparked the image of a plan. Rounding up four unwounded seamen—no easy task— Perry manned the amazingly intact cutter and pulled for *Niagara*. Straining at the oars the already exhausted sailors were spurred on by the incessant splash of British shot.

It was a simple matter for the British to recognize Perry's strategy. Only a few minutes before, the promise of victory leaned toward the Union Jack; however, if Perry was allowed to engage a fresh battery the day might yet be lost. Every effort was put forth to smother the tiny rowboat skimming over the waves. Again and again sweating British gunners rammed powder, wad, cannonball, another wad, finally touching off the shot they hoped would win the battle. Deafened and dazed by the constant roar and bone-jarring concussion of thunderous cannonading, their actions were nevertheless swift and automatic, the product of training, discipline, and proud British naval tradition.

The little skiff disappeared in the splash of British cannonballs, only to reappear unscathed, its oarsmen and daring commodore soaked to the skin but otherwise unharmed. Again it disappeared, and still again, each time miraculously sculling clear from the storm of shot and funnels of falling water. Finally, after a harrowing and terrifying journey of about fifteen minutes, the frail cutter and its soggy occupants gratefully slipped under the protective sheer of the looming *Niagara*.

The dialogue which ensued after Perry boarded *Niagara* can only be imagined; accounts vary depending on the eyewitness reporter. Regardless of what was said, however, Elliott apparently volunteered to relinquish command of his own undamaged vessel, depart his ship in Perry's small boat, and row back to hurry along the lagging schooners.

Perry, not surprisingly, exerted no effort to defer or delay Elliott's departure. After conducting a brief survey to determine *Niagara*'s fighting capabilities Perry rapped out a string of orders. Sailors scampered up *Niagara*'s ratlines and scurried along the footropes of her giant yards, shaking out the reefed canvas, which instantly bellied out in the freshening wind. The menacing mouths of her cold carronades were each stuffed with two heavy six-inch cannonballs. Soldiers in the fighting tops anxiously fingered the hammers of their muskets. At last the *Niagara*'s earnest and willing crew were about to join the fray.

Eyes widened in shock as British officers and seamen viewed the truculent apparition approaching through the dissolving gunsmoke. After two hours of blood and suffering, they had defeated the American flagship; by rights they should have won the day. The unimpaired brig now running down on their line was like a slap in the face.

Although completely wrecked, the *Lawrence* had nevertheless succeeded in meting out harsh punishment to her opponents. British casualties had been severe. Barclay himself was wounded early in the battle, but he endured the pain and managed to stay the deck. Then, as *Niagara* neared the British line Barclay suffered a second wound, this one serious enough to force him below to the surgeon. In fact, by the time *Niagara* bore down on the British line the captain and first officer of every British ship had been either killed or wounded. Inexperienced junior officers now commanded these complex vessels of war. Certainly they were brave men, but they were uninitiated and untutored in directing complex fighting vessels in a complicated naval engagement.

The British were all too aware that only one tactic might preserve them from *Niagara*'s fresh broadsides. If they could manage to wear ship—turn the vessels 180 degrees—then the guns on their starboard [right] sides, not yet engaged, could be brought to bear. Far too many of their larboard [left side] guns had been disabled; a successful repulse of the enemy was entirely dependent on those unused starboard broadsides.

Haste was imperative, *Niagara* was rapidly bearing down on the British line. Orders were prescribed and British sailors strained at the braces. The ravaged British flagship slowly turned with the wind—all too slowly.

Having borne the brunt of *Lawrence*'s guns, *Detroit*'s sails, spars, and rigging were heavily damaged. Mistiming the evolution, the confused junior officer commanding the *Queen Charlotte* failed to judge *Detroit*'s sluggish movements and pressed on too much canvas. Before any remedial action could be initiated, *Queen Charlotte*'s bowsprit plunged squarely into *Detroit*'s mizzen rigging, creating a tangled mess that would require precious minutes to hack away, minutes that would cost the British dearly. Now, at the most critical phase of the battle, the two largest British ships were locked together and helpless.

Perry thrust the *Niagara* mid-point between the British battle line—three "sail" to starboard, three to larboard. Twenty gun captains jerked twenty lanyards and *Niagara* was instantly shrouded in acrid smoke. A mind-numbing blast rippled the dispassionate water as forty heavy cannonballs sped on their destructive mission. Sponge, load, fire! Sponge, load, fire!

Dozens of jagged holes abruptly disfigured the flanks of Barclay's ships. Masts quivered like trees feeling the axe; loud tearing noises presaged the shredding of blossoming canvas; hundreds of deadly wood splinters purged the disarrayed decks; British and Canadian blood flowed freely.

After turbulent minutes of hacking and slashing, with many of those wielding the axes cut down in the process, *Detroit* and *Queen Charlotte* cleared the discordant clutter of entangled rigging and eased apart. But by then it was too late. Too few guns were capable of firing, too few gunners remained standing. Other than death and total destruction only one option was left. *Detroit*, her imposing ensign prominently nailed to the mast, fired a gun off her disengaged side, signaling her surrender. Moments later a white flag slowly ascended from *Queen Charlotte*'s deck, while *General Hunter* and *Lady Prevost* similarly signified their surrender. The two smallest British vessels, *Chippewa* and *Little Belt*, shook out their sails to make a run for it, closely pursued by two American ships. It proved a short chase. A shot across their bows impressed upon the British the futility of flight and the last two enemy vessels soon capitulated. The entire British fleet had been captured.

At first the silence, after three hours of earsplitting pandemonium, was perplexing; but after a few minutes Perry began to grasp the enormity of his success. His victory proved to be the first time in all of British naval history that an entire fleet of warships had been captured. Harrison must be informed! Finding an old letter Perry hastily scribbled on the back of the envelope,

Dear General:
We have met the enemy and they are ours. Two ships, two brigs, one schooner, and a sloop.

Yours with great respect and esteem,

O. H. Perry

At long last Lake Erie was in American hands. William Henry Harrison now possessed the crucial component necessary to transport men and supplies rapidly and simply across the lake, the precise factor required to launch his long delayed invasion. Oliver Hazard Perry achieved what he set out to do, and in the process immortalized himself in American naval lore.

III

Evolution of the American Military, 1815–1860

Officers and Politicians: The Origins of Army Politics in the United States before the Civil War

William B. Skelton

One of the marks of the American military establishment has been civilian control of the armed forces. This pattern was set between independence and the Civil War and basically followed thereafter. However, as William B. Skelton of the University of Wisconsin–Stevens Point argues in this essay, while open and direct intervention in partisan politics was generally rejected even then, military officers, while being nonpartisan, have not been apolitical. They have used political means to pursue professional goals, specifically for individual advancement, for the promotion of the interests of certain branches (especially the Corps of Engineers), and for the welfare of the military as a whole. Although political activities in the interest of goals outside these parameters have sometimes been pursued, the pattern set in the early nineteenth century has been maintained to the present.
Reprinted by permission of Transaction Publishers. "Officers and Politicians: The Origins of Army Politics in the United States Before the Civil War," by William B. Skelton, Armed Forces and Society, *6/1 (Fall 1979). Copyright © by Transaction Publishers.*

One of the most cherished of America's political ideals is civilian control of the military establishment. At least until the involvement of the armed forces in national policy making during the Cold War era, army and navy officers overwhelmingly accepted the supremacy of their civilian superiors. The only major exception to this pattern was the so-called Newburgh Conspiracy at the end of the Revolution, but that was a brief and ambiguous affair, manipulated by civilian leaders and eventually contained within the army itself. Its failure left the fabric of civil supremacy intact. Perhaps the most important characteristic separating the American pattern of political "modernization" from those of developing nations in the twentieth century was the peripheral role of the professional officer corps in that process.

Given the significance of civil supremacy in United States history, it is surprising that historians have devoted so little attention to its origins and development. However, a variety of influences seems to have contributed to civil control. One was the long-standing distrust of standing armies in Anglo-American political culture, deriving from the bitter controversies surrounding the army in seventeenth century England and reinforced in America by the militia tradition and the experience of British occupation before and during the Revolution. The founding fathers only reluctantly accepted the government's power to maintain permanent armed forces and wrote into the Constitution elaborate checks on military authority. Antimilitarism became a staple of American political ideology, periodically renewed in the democratic reform movements of the nineteenth century and only temporarily submerged after World War II.

A second influence was the general stability of American political life: the absence of the bitter class and tribal conflicts which plague many developing nations; the long experience with the electoral process; and the density and perceived legitimacy of civilian institutions. In contrast to events in Third World societies, the United States armed forces have neither seen the necessity nor been offered the opportunity for political intervention to restore order in time of upheaval or to arbitrate irreconcilable political controversies. Even the extraordinary conditions of the Civil War did not deprive the rival governments of broad popular support or create power vacuums for the exploitation of a "man on horseback." Also, civil supremacy arose in part from the internal character of the military establishment. American officers have always derived from a relatively broad spectrum of society; thus the armed forces have not been the preserve of a single social class or geographical region which might use military power to acquire or defend a privileged position. Finally, the permanent armed forces were small and geographically isolated until the mid-twentieth century, lacking the power to dominate civilian institutions even if they had been so inclined.

However, the interplay of these factors merely defined the outer boundaries of civil-military relations in the United States, precluding direct and open intervention in the civilian political process. Within this framework, much latitude existed for less direct and less threatening types of political involvement. Concentrating on the twentieth century, social scientists have analyzed a complex variety of political activities by military men: lobbying for weapons systems and for strategic and foreign policy doctrines; pushing service interests; aligning with local and private groups for mutually beneficial spending programs; propagandizing a strong military posture generally. As Samuel P. Huntington has shown, the constitutional separation of powers actually encourages such behavior, as it blurs the civilian chain of command and permits officers to play one branch of the government against others. American officers have usually been nonpartisan, but they have been anything but apolitical.

Although most visible and controversial in recent years, the basic patterns of military politics emerged in the first half of the nineteenth century. During that period, professional army officers began to work out for the first time their collective role in relationship to politics. While professional ideology rejected partisanship and discouraged taking sides on purely civilian issues, officers eagerly embraced political means to pursue goals defined as *professional*: individual advancement within the military hierarchy; the interests of particular branches of the service; the welfare of the army as a whole. Frequently, they rationalized personal or group interest on the basis of national security. Military politics have grown more complex in the twentieth century, but their basic outlines have not significantly changed. Thus, the development of officers' political attitudes and activities before the Civil War had a major impact on the conduct of civil-military relations in the United States.

From the formation of the regular army in 1784 to the end of the War of 1812, no clear pattern marked officers' political relations. The dominant characteristic of the army during this period was instability. No consensus existed in Congress or the nation as a whole as to the size or specific functions of the military establishment. Reductions, expansions, and reorganizations of the army were frequent and kept the officer corps in a continual state of flux. Military careers were short: only 17% of the men on the 1789 army list and 12% of those on the 1797 army list served twenty years or longer. The army lacked uniform regulations, systematic administrative procedures, and effective institutions to educate aspiring officers and instill group values. Except for a small minority of careerists, the officer corps consisted of a mass of individuals, still closely linked to civilian life, whose brief military experiences did not produce consistent, professionally defined patterns of thought or behavior.

Political conditions in the early republic blurred the distinction between civil and military affairs. During the Revolution, state and regional jealousies and the ill-defined powers of the Continental Congress created a tangle of command problems which, at times, threatened to disrupt the Continental Army. Military appointments, promotions, and assignments became highly charged political issues, as commanders maintained local bases of support and freely maneuvered for advancement. Under the Articles of Confederation, initiative in military matters rested mainly with the states.

Congress lacked the power to raise revenue, and the constitutionality of a permanent army remained in doubt. Officers found it necessary to lobby continually both in Congress and in the states for pay, benefits, and even decisions on relative rank. While the Constitution gave the federal government the clear authority to raise an army, the development of political parties during the 1790s added another complication. Political leaders viewed the army as a source of patronage and, at least in the case of certain Federalists, as a potential tool to quell internal opposition. Because of the lateral appointment policy—the practice of appointing citizens directly to high rank—political considerations continued to influence the chain of command. During the Quasi-War with France, the size and character of the military establishment became central issues in national politics. The struggle between John Adams and Alexander Hamilton over the "New Army" of 1798—in the opinion of one historian, the "only completely political army in American history"—divided the Federalist party and contributed to its defeat in 1800.

Although the Jefferson administration inherited a predominantly Federalist officer corps, it made no concerted attempt to purge its opponents. However, the Democratic Republicans continued to use military appointments for patronage purposes and hoped to make the army a bastion of the administration. When Congress expanded the army in 1808, the War Department consulted prominent Republicans on appointments. "As we have quite a sufficient number of our opponents political now in the Army," the Secretary of War wrote a Connecticut Republican, "it may be advisable to pay some attention to the political feelings of the Candidates." The army's role in enforcing the controversial Embargo Act increased administration interest in the political orthodoxy of the officer corps. By the War of 1812, lateral appointments had given the high ranks of the army the appearance of a Democratic Republican political caucus: of the thirty-five men who served as general officers between 1808 and 1815, eight had supported the administration in Congress, four had been Republican state or territorial governors, and at least five others had been Republican state legislators. The middle rungs of the officer corps included scores of former officeholders and journalists, overwhelmingly Jeffersonian in their politics.

Under these circumstances, military and political life interpenetrated at all levels. Not all officers engaged in politics, of course; much depended on the individual's family and social standing. The Articles of War, the basic code of military justice, prohibited officers from openly criticizing the president or Congress. However, officers demonstrated little awareness of military life as a separate realm of endeavor, distinct from the political forum and guided by its own code of values. Military men appealed to their political friends for redress on professional matters, publicized personal quarrels in the press, cultivated ties in the regions where they were stationed, and took open stands on general political issues. During the 1790s, for example,

General James Wilkinson carried on a complex intrigue in both Congress and the army to replace Anthony Wayne as commander of the army. Officers in the Trans-Appalachian West participated in that region's web of expansionist and secessionist schemes; perhaps more than twenty regulars, General Wilkinson among them, were involved in the Burr Conspiracy. At St. Louis, New Orleans, Mackinac, and other army stations, military men exercised civil as well as military authority, serving as judges, postmasters, customs collectors, and even territorial governors. Inevitably, civil-military intimacy prevailed, and officers plunged into local political affairs. Before and during the War of 1812, the appointment of Republican politicians and editors intensified the overlap between politics and the army. In one of the most flagrant cases, William Duane of Philadelphia continued to publish his Republican newspaper and advise the administration on political matters while holding a regular army commission.

The years following the Peace of Ghent marked no abrupt change in the traditionally confused patterns of army politics. The euphoric nationalism of the postwar period briefly submerged popular antimilitarism; scores of returning veterans received heroes' welcomes and mingled in prestigious political circles. Most high-ranking officers had entered the army as recently as 1808 or 1812 and few were, in the strict sense, careerists. The senior generals, Andrew Jackson and Jacob Brown, established their headquarters at their personal residences, where they mixed military administration with farming and political interests. The complex political infighting of the Era of Good Feelings absorbed the attention of many regulars. The candidacy of Secretary of War John C. Calhoun was particularly popular in the army; several officers supported him in the press, and General Brown served as intermediary when Calhoun agreed to run for vice president under John Quincy Adams in 1824.

Beneath the surface, however, the changing circumstances of army life led officers to view their relationship with politics in a somewhat different light. Most basically, the period after 1815 brought a new stability to the military profession. In 1821, the last major peacetime reduction and reorganization of the army in the nineteenth century occurred. From that point forward, the trend was toward a gradual, though uneven, expansion of the officer corps—from 532 in 1823 to 1108 in 1860. With the sporadic encouragement of the executive branch of the government, officers worked out a common conception of their professional role, emphasizing the development of expertise and organizational efficiency in preparation for a future conflict with a major European power. The introduction of tactical manuals, standardized regulations, and uniform administrative procedures brought regularity to all phases of the military establishment. Under the supervision of Sylvanus Thayer, the United States Military Academy emerged as the most important entry point into the officer corps and an effective means of socializing young men into military life.

Perhaps the most significant change of the period after the War of 1812 was the stabilization of military careers. No longer were officers faced with imminent disbandment. The decreasing use of lateral appointments, except in wartime, assured young men entering the army as second lieutenants of gradual upward mobility within the military hierarchy. Although officers continued to complain about low pay, slow promotion rates, and the lack of public esteem for their profession, more and more of them found military life sufficiently attractive to make a long-term career commitment. The median career length for officers on the 1797 army register, for example, was ten years; for those on the 1830 list, it was twenty-two years. The percentage of officers who would serve twenty or more years rose from 12% of the 1797 total to 59% of the 1830 total.

The interaction of these trends—the regularization of military procedure, the emergence of West Point as a socializing institution, the lengthening of military careers—gave the profession of arms a cohesion and a permanence which it had previously lacked. Increasingly, military men manifested common patterns of thought and behavior, determined more by their experiences as cadets and officers than by their social backgrounds or their contacts with the civilian world. Political attitudes reflected this transition. By the 1820s and 1830s, officers had begun to distinguish between military and political life. As military professionals, their principal responsibility was to the nation as a whole, rather than to a particular section, faction, or party. Their involvement in a centralized, restrictive bureaucratic institution led them to emphasize hierarchical values—order, obedience, discipline—which set them apart from the rough-and-tumble egalitarian flavor of contemporary political life. West Point administrators stressed the Academy's national image and tried to isolate cadets from civilian politics.

Officers' perception of the political environment reinforced their tendency to separate the military from the civilian sphere. The regular army enjoyed considerable prestige immediately after the War of 1812. By the early 1820s, however, antimilitary sentiment was resurfacing in Congress. The initial stimulus was rivalry between Secretary of War Calhoun and Secretary of the Treasury William H. Crawford, both candidates for the presidency in 1824. To embarrass Calhoun and cut back government expenditures, Crawford's congressional supporters sponsored a series of investigations into the War Department and led the struggle to reduce the army in 1821. Congressional hostility, or at least indifference, continued through the Adams administration. While specific military programs fared better under the Jacksonians, the regular army was continually a target for congressmen, state legislators, and editors, who found its authoritarian structure and reliance on specialized expertise incompatible with egalitarian values. Antimilitary rhetoric peaked during the depression years of the early 1840s, as economy-minded congressmen considered reductions of the army and the abolition of West Point. The danger was more apparent than real: the expanding frontier and threats of foreign war brought periodic increases in military strength. Officers exaggerated the extent of public hostility, however, and came to see politicians as adversaries. Immersion in the world of civilian politics might provoke the wrath of Congress, threatening both the army as an institution and their personal careers with it.

Though seldom expressed in theoretical form, officers developed a conception of the army as an apolitical instrument of public policy. As servants of the nation, they should stand aloof from party and sectional strife and avoid taking sides on civilian political issues. Colonel Henry Atkinson favored Andrew Jackson for the presidency in 1824 but felt himself "too delicately situated (being an officer in the army) to take an active part." Colonel Duncan L. Clinch stated in 1829 that he had "always deprecated the practice of officers of the Army interfering in elections, either of a general or local character, except so far as respects an honest and moderate expression of their opinions—and have never approached the polls, or given a vote, since I have been in the Army." Brigadier General Edmund P. Gaines opposed partisan allegiances by officers: "In war we must serve our country with all our hearts, and with all our soul, and with all our strength; we are thus rendered incapable of serving a political party." According to a correspondent of a military periodical, officers' political attachments might turn the army into "an armed mob, dangerous in its nature to the vital interests of the government, and subversive of the honor belonging to the profession of arms." By accepting a commission, an officer voluntarily surrendered his rights of political action.

A corollary of officers' distinction between political and military life was a negative view of politicians. In contrast to the discipline and devotion to duty which allegedly typified the military profession, politicians appeared shifty, divisive, self-serving, and too willing to compromise principles. They were "loafers" and "demagogues" who courted the "mob" and failed to appreciate the sacrifices of the army. They placed sectional and party welfare above the national interest. Individual officers privately questioned the desirability of democratic government. "I am no longer a democrat," wrote Lieutenant John Sedgwick on learning of disorders among volunteer troops in the Mexican War. "I go for an empire, governed by a strong hand, reserving the right of revolutionizing—when opposition becomes too hard." Captain Thomas Williams blamed the secession crisis on universal manhood suffrage and favored "an hereditary Executive, an hereditary Senate, property qualifications for voters; property qualifications for Representatives."

It would be misleading to take at face value officers' professions of political neutrality. After both the War of 1812 and the Mexican War, senior commanders harbored political ambitions; General Winfield Scott desperately pursued the presidency through his long career. As earlier, civil-military intimacy often prevailed at frontier posts. However, the dissociation of the military profession from politics was not entirely rhetorical. By the 1830s, most career officers were demonstrating little interest in political issues not directly relevant to the army. When they expressed a preference for a particular candidate or party, they usually did so on the basis of *professional* considerations—the potential impact on military programs or their personal careers. Officers' private correspondence rarely mentioned such staple issues of the Jacksonian Era as the tariff, the national bank, or even sectional controversies. National elections frequently passed unnoticed or were dismissed with comments similar to that of Colonel Abraham Eustis in 1840, who thought life "not long enough to devote any portion of it to reading long speeches, pro & con, on Log-cabins & Hard Cider." This tendency is especially striking when compared to the overwhelming popular interest in politics which marked the 1830s and 1840s.

Officers' political energies were not lacking but were channeled into the pursuit of professional goals. These goals were of three general types: personal career advancement; the interests of particular branches of the service (often reflecting intraservice rivalries); the army interest as a whole. In seeking these goals, officers institutionalized patterns of political behavior which would survive into the twentieth century.

The most widespread variety of political activity by military men was advancement of their personal careers. Matters of rank and promotion took on special significance in the United States Army. First, American culture generally emphasized competition and individual advancement, never more strongly than in the mid-nineteenth century. Secondly, the officer corps was recruited from a relatively broad social base. In contrast to contemporary European armies, officers did not derive from an aristocratic ethos which could afford them secure status independent of the army; instead, they tended to come from middle-class farming and professional families, often in declining economic circumstances. Most of them identified with military rank as the principal determinant of both their status and their financial well-being, an inclination reinforced by lengthening career commitments. In the opinion of one correspondent of a military journal, rank constituted "the substance of all [the military men] can hope of advancement in the scale of social being." Captain Orlando B. Wilcox stated the same sentiment more dramatically in his novel based on military life: "Promotion! promotion! give men promotion or they die!"

The regularization of military administration after the War of 1812 somewhat restricted the scope of political patronage. Lateral appointments to high rank became rare in peacetime; seniority strictly governed regular promotions through the grade of colonel. However, the army's personnel system included important areas where political sponsorship could further an officer's career. Congressmen determined most appointments to West Point, by far the most common entry point to the officer corps, and political considerations influenced the granting of direct citizens' commissions, especially when new regiments were raised. More important to the internal functioning of the army was the use of political influence in such matters as assignments to detached service, leaves of absence, transfers from line regiments to desirable staff positions, and the issuance of brevet rank—honorary rank above an officer's regular grade, awarded for gallant or meritorious conduct or for ten years service in one grade. In addition, promotions to the rank of general lay outside the seniority system, as did the periodic bonanzas of irregular promotions caused by expansions of the army.

To obtain these advantages, officers suppressed their generalized disdain for politicians and cultivated influential supporters. The nature of the political system facilitated their efforts. The army was a national bureaucracy existing in a decentralized, community-oriented social order. Officers retained ties in their former localities and often knew their congressmen personally; many extended their contacts through marriage or through prolonged service in a particular region. Although the War Department denied that political pressure affected its personnel decisions, each reorganization or expansion of the army and each death of a general officer brought a rush of officers' claims which the government could ignore at its own risk. Under this pressure, army administrators usually tried to strike a rough geographical balance in distributing favors, with political patronage playing a significant role. A veteran of War Department bureaucracy explained the facts of military life to a candidate for a staff appointment in 1857:

> You have enough of army recommendations, you want some political ones. Do not let this word deter you, from using in your own defence lawful weapons, which have been already turned against yourself. . . . Virginia influence is now in the ascendency, and that, through your wife's relatives you can command. By all means, use it. . . . Request your friends, to watch for a vacancy, and, on the occurrence of one, to *lose no time*, in pressing your claim, in person, if they can, if not by letter.

Examples of such activity abound. The reduction and reorganization of the army in 1821 created a tangle of politically charged claims which disrupted military administration for years. Officers and their sponsors aired their cases in the press; controversy over appointments kept the Adjutant General's Office without a permanent chief until 1825 and the Second Artillery Regiment without a colonel until 1832. When the commanding general of the army died in 1828, a bitter struggle ensued over succession to his office. The political implications of choosing among rival candidates led John Quincy Adams to favor abolishing the office altogether. When Adams did make a decision, one of the disappointed candidates openly defied the administration and appealed for redress to Congress. Similar controversy surrounded the appointment of officers to the newly formed Ordnance

Department in 1832 and First Dragoons in 1833; the selection of a brigadier general to replace Winfield Scott after his promotion to commanding general in 1841; the granting of brevet promotions for Mexican War service; and the nomination of officers to the four new regiments added in 1855. Of course, political intervention for leaves, transfers, and favorable assignments was continual. In 1833, the beleagured Secretary of War prohibited officers from visiting the capital except on official business. This order was soon rescinded, however, probably because officers charged that it interfered with their rights. Captain Samuel P. Heintzelman expressed a common opinion in 1855: "I must get to Washington & try to get promotion. . . . There is nothing like being on the spot."

The use of political support for individual career advancement mainly continued and confirmed practices common before the War of 1812. The second category of officers' political action—pushing the interests of particular branches of the army—marked a significant new development. The principal source of this trend was the period of military reform after the War of 1812, which brought a greater degree of specialization within the officer corps. In place of the previously fluctuating organization, a stable regimental structure emerged in the line or "combat" portion of the army, consisting of four artillery and seven (by 1860, ten) infantry regiments. The reintroduction of mounted regiments in the 1830s added a third combat arm. Most importantly, staff and support functions earlier performed by civilians or by officers scattered through the geographical commands were concentrated in separate general staff departments, or bureaus, headquartered at Washington. These bureaus—quartermaster, ordnance, medical, pay, engineers, and others—were largely autonomous within the army, responsible in most matters directly to the secretary of war. They were headed by high ranking chiefs and staffed by relatively permanent cadres of officers who identified strongly with departmental interests.

The result of this internal segmentation was a great deal of intraservice rivalry—perhaps the most distinguishing characteristic of nineteenth century military administration. The line branches and staff bureaus frequently fought among themselves: infantry officers, for example, envied the desirable seaboard posts of the artillery, while the Corps of Engineers quarreled sporadically with the Corps of Topographical Engineers over politically popular internal improvements projects. However, the principal divisions were between staff and line. Staff officers wished to perpetuate and expand their departmental jurisdictions; line officers resented the size and independence of the bureaus and tried to curb the alleged privileges in pay, promotion, and stations enjoyed by their staff colleagues. Of course, personal ambition interacted with group interest—virtually any change in military organization would affect individual careers. Much intraservice friction was contained within the army, taking the form of angry exchanges of official correspondence and appeals to the War Department for redress. However, all sides frequently resorted to political channels. The staff departments had obvious advantages: their headquarters were in Washington and their chiefs had easy access to the president, secretary of war, and congressional committees. Line officers, scattered at small posts along the frontier and coastline, looked to the commanding general as their spokesman and made use of local political connections.

Political activity in pursuit of branch objectives took several forms. Most common were appeals by individual officers to their congressmen or their influential friends and relatives. Another important channel was the press. For example, two of the principal adversaries of intraservice feuding, the artillery regiments and the Ordnance Department, carried on an acrimonious pamphlet war during the 1840s and 1850s, the artillery pushing for a merger of the two branches, the ordnance seeking to preserve its independence. Other intraservice quarrels were aired in newspapers, military periodicals, and even literary magazines. Officers used circular letters and memorials to win congressional support and actively lobbied in Washington. When possible, they established ties with regional and local interests in a civil-military version of log-rolling. Most successful in this respect was the Corps of Topographical Engineers, the department in charge of army exploration and many internal improvements projects. Beginning in the 1820s, topographical officers worked on a wide variety of canals, railroads, harbor and river improvements, and other civil works which brought them into contact with businessmen and politicians. They aligned with powerful southern and western leaders in support of territorial expansion and a southern route for the transcontinental railroad. While sometimes a center of controversy, the corps profited from these relationships. Between 1830 and 1860, it achieved independent bureau status, improved promotion opportunities, and nearly a four hundred percent increase in personnel. Individual topographical officers, as well as many from other branches, used contacts made through civil projects to obtain lucrative positions on leaving the service.

Perhaps the most politically oriented branch of the army was the Corps of Engineers. Since its formation in 1802, this corps had enjoyed an elite status within the military establishment. Its duties were defined as "the most elevated branch of military science" and each year it drew the top graduates of West Point. As with the topographical engineers, the army engineers supervised various civil works and thus benefitted from local political alliances. However, the engineers had responsibility for two programs on which there was no public consensus. One was the Military Academy itself, frequently under attack during the Age of the Common Man as a seedbed of elitism and authoritarianism. The second was the construction of seacoast fortifications. The government had begun a systematic program of coastal fortification after the disastrous experiences of the War of 1812. In the absence of a strong foreign threat, however, congressional skeptics constantly criticized its expense and sometimes reduced or delayed appropriations. Moreover, developments in military technology—rifled artillery, explosive shells, steam-powered naval vessels, railroads which could concentrate large forces at threatened spots—raised questions as to the military effectiveness of the entire system. In defending its vulnerable programs, the engineers could not expect united support from the army as a whole. While the artillery and the Ordnance Department had a vested interest in the fortification program, all branches resented the corps' elite position, especially its exclusive control of West Point, and frequently lobbied against it.

The Corps of Engineers countered these threats by developing an array of political weapons. Senior officers in Washington kept in close contact with the executive branch and Congress, promoting and even drafting bills which might benefit the corps. Lower-ranking engineers looked after the corps' interests in the areas where they were stationed. When the Connecticut legislature passed resolutions in 1842, calling for the abolition of West Point, Captain George W. Cullum rushed to repair the damage: "I spent a day or two spouting to the loafers and trust I have put some right ideas in their heads." The chief engineer attempted to stifle internal dissent potentially harmful to engineer programs and encouraged his subordinates to write articles for the civilian press, designed to convince the public of the vital importance of coastal fortifications and formal military education.

The most elaborate political campaign waged by the Corps of Engineers before the Civil War occurred during the early 1850s. In 1851, the House of Representatives tabled the annual appropriation bill for fortifications, in part because of the unsettled state of military technology, in part because of western suspicions that the program was a useless pork barrel scheme to benefit the coastal states. At the same time, junior officers in several staff departments favored legislation to speed promotion in their branches. An ambitious young engineer officer stationed at the Coast Survey Office in Washington, Lieutenant Isaac I. Stevens, coordinated a lobbying campaign to push the two programs. Stevens and other officers at the capital personally solicited the support of scores of congressmen. They raised funds from the corps to print memorials and reports bolstering their case which they distributed to prominent men in the federal government and the states. On Stevens' advice, engineer officers lobbied in the districts where they were stationed, published articles in local newspapers, and mobilized their influential friends and relatives. The campaign succeeded; the army appropriation bill for 1853 restored the funds for fortifications and, much to the resentment of the line, provided engineer, topographical, and ordnance lieutenants with automatic promotion to captain after fourteen years service. Stevens hoped that "our officers hereafter will realize their responsibilities as American Citizens, and will discharge, what I consider their bounden duty to enlighten the public mind."

A variation on the theme of intraservice friction was the occasional attempt by an individual officer, who differed with his branch or with the administration on policy questions, to take his case directly to Congress or the public. Through the 1830s and 1840s, for example, Brigadier General Edmund P. Gaines urged the War Department to adopt a military program based on mobile "floating batteries" for harbor defense and a federally constructed railway system, radiating from the interior states to the seacoast and capable of concentrating masses of militia to repel an invasion. When the administration showed little interest, Gaines doggedly pushed his ideas through his influential friends, the press, public lectures, and even memorials to Congress. Another military gadfly, Major William H. Chase of the Corps of Engineers, clashed with the leadership of his branch on a variety of issues and did not hesitate to appeal to higher authority. In his opinion, unquestioning obedience to the chief engineer would make every officer "but a paid hireling, bound to do all or any work required of him no matter how injurious it may be to the commonwealth." Among other things, Chase publicly attacked pay differentials favoring staff over line officers, lobbied against a bill to form a company of engineer troops, and criticized the orthodox fortification program during the 1850s.

In common with such twentieth century mavericks as General William Mitchell and Admiral Hyman Rickover, service critics irritated their superiors. However, there were few disciplinary means at their disposal, short of potentially embarrassing courts-martial. The seniority rule protected critics from the subtle pressures of "merit" evaluations; prolonged service in particular areas allowed them to develop local ties and enjoy a considerable degree of autonomy.

The third area of officers' political activity—the pursuit of general army interests—was of only limited importance before the Civil War. Military men were certainly aware that they constituted a group distinct from the rest of society; they frequently portrayed themselves as a devoted band of brothers, serving an ungrateful and rather degenerate public. However, this identity only sporadically found expression through political channels. In contrast to the immediate, tangible nature of individual and branch interests, the army interest was poorly defined. Antimilitary rhetoric notwithstanding, a general consensus usually existed in the government that the regular army should be retained and even increased occasionally to meet the demands of westward expansion. Army-navy rivalry was not yet a significant incentive to internal service solidarity. The two services had relatively clear, mutually exclusive functions; service appropriations were determined by separate congressional committees and had little bearing on one another. The navy occasionally crossed swords with the Corps of Engineers on the perennial issue of coastal fortifications, but many line officers were indifferent to that program and viewed it as a branch rather than a service matter. In other words, few political issues compelled army officers as a group to close ranks. Moreover, regulars were wary of actions which might appear to challenge civil control and thus provoke congressional retaliation.

Nevertheless, officers occasionally did evoke general service interests. The desire of high commanders to enhance the army's public image subtly influenced decisions on troop distributions, the opening and closing of military posts, and army participation in transportation projects. In 1820, for example, Major General Jacob Brown suggested stationing additional troops in Maine in order to make that state's congressional delegation more favorable to the army. He also hoped that regulars would, through military road building, "achieve a victory over some of the prejudices of the country by their useful labours, in peace if they could not by their deeds of arms in War." Officers lobbied almost continually for higher pay and other economic benefits. They pushed for a retirement and pension system, intended both to increase military efficiency and speed promotion for junior officers. Military humanitarians supported bills to improve the condition of enlisted men, especially the establishment of "military asylums" for old soldiers. The congressional economy drive following the Depression of 1837 caused some activity in defense of general service interests, though intraservice squabbling was a more typical reaction. The officer corps as a whole favored the addition of new regiments in 1855.

The Mexican War briefly intensified service solidarity. That conflict followed a period of demoralization within the officer corps, caused by the frustrating, controversial Second Seminole War and the pressures of the congressional retrenchment campaign. Even officers with misgivings about Manifest Destiny greeted the outbreak of fighting with an enthusiasm bordering on euphoria. Dreams of glory and rapid promotion infatuated subaltern and gray-haired veteran alike. Moreover, the war provided an opportunity to prove the professional skills of the regular army and permanently silence its civilian critics.

Battlefield experience confirmed the army's hopes, both individual and institutional. However, the seemingly partisan direction of the war effort by the administration of James K. Polk soon produced dissatisfaction. Officers resented the large-scale call-up of volunteers, the appointment of citizens to the temporary "regular" regiments created for the emergency, and the commissioning of prominent Democrats as generals. No opinion was as pervasive within the officers corps as contempt for citizen soldiers, and the administration's reliance on "mushroom generals" and its promotion of "partisans lawyers and quacks" over regulars and West Point graduates seemed a conscious plan to degrade the army. Captain William H. T. Walker predicted that every regular officer "with one spark of chivalry" who could make a living outside the army would resign after the war. "I would rather serve as a private in a foreign army than to be a captain in an army which is trodden upon as ours is by its government." The ultimate insult was Polk's suspension of General Winfield Scott from command of the forces in Mexico City early in 1848, after his spectacular conquest of the enemy capital. Although the outgrowth of factional conflict which involved regular as well as volunteer officers, the "martyrdom" of Scott appeared to many regulars the epitome of the army's suffering. The simmering resentment of politicians came to the surface. Lieutenant Francis Collins, who "was not ignorant of the foul workings of a contemptible scheme of political partyism," found Polk's action beyond belief. Lieutenant Colonel Ethan Allen Hitchcock considered the army in Mexico, aside from a small clique of dissidents, universally opposed to Scott's suspension. "We all see the enormity of the conduct of the President—deplore and abhor it."

However, this upsurge of army solidarity was short lived. Temporarily isolated in Mexico, officers could take little immediate action beyond writing indignant letters home. The briefness and the overwhelming success of their campaign rapidly defused resentment. The budding militance of the officer corps dissipated as veterans returned to heroes' welcomes, saw their most popular commander elected president, and scrambled for individual rewards, especially brevet promotions. The Mexican War left an important legacy for the regular army in the form of professional pride. It did not create an alienated praetorian class, prepared to use united political action on behalf of group interests.

Another characteristic of officers' political behavior working against a unified army interest was the relatively bipartisan—or perhaps nonpartisan—nature of the officer corps. In contrast to the pre-War of 1812 army, regulars appear to have favored neither political party consistently. Although it is risky to generalize from the limited evidence available, a sampling of officers' preferences during the period of the second party system (approximately 1828 to 1852) reveals a nearly even division: thirty Democrats; thirty-two National Republicans or Whigs (or at least anti-Jacksonians). In addition, officers' party identifications were remarkably "soft" when compared to the intense partisanship in the larger society. Even in private correspondence, they usually expressed their allegiances obliquely, even apologetically, and tended to view their party as the lesser of two evils. Presidential candidates with military backgrounds inspired surprisingly little enthusiasm. During the 1820s, a number of influential officers supported John C. Calhoun, Monroe's popular secretary of war, but Andrew Jackson and William Henry Harrison drew only mixed responses from the army. While many regulars favored Zachary Taylor in 1848, partly as a rejection of the Polk administration, the similar Whig candidacy of Winfield Scott four years later aroused little noticeable support within the officer corps and even some active opposition.

Several factors help explain the absence of a strong partisan bias in the antebellum army. The first is ideological. As Richard Hofstadter has demonstrated, Americans by the 1830s were moving toward a conception of parties and party conflict as legitimate and even beneficial institutions—necessary to check the concentration of power, to publicize important issues, and generally to structure political conflict in a sprawling, heterogeneous society. On the other hand, the emerging professional ideology of the officer corps, with its emphasis on service to a unified nation, perpetuated the older view of partisanship as divisive and potentially disruptive. Officers might use party connections to pursue professional goals, but they saw such ties as a necessary evil—a compromise with an imperfect world—rather than as a virtue.

Secondly, the military appointment process tended to divide and weaken the officer corps' party allegiances. Before the War of 1812, the executive branch controlled all appointments and inevitably favored its supporters. Thus the political coloration of the officer corps reflected the party in power: largely Federalist through the early 1800s; overwhelmingly Republican after 1808. By the 1820s, however, the War Department had adopted the practice of appointing most West Point cadets on the recommendation of congressmen, a procedure confirmed by law in 1843. Military commissions continued to be a form of patronage, of course, but mainly congressional rather than executive patronage. Thus, the political allegiances which officers brought to the army—blurred in most cases by four years at West Point—resembled the party composition of Congress, and presumably of the nation as a whole. Beginning in 1832, the use of professional examining boards to determine medical appointments weakened political patronage in the Medical Department.

A final factor softening officers' partisanship was the relative insignificance of military policy as an issue in party conflict. From the 1790s to the reduction of the army in 1821, military affairs had frequently inspired intense political debate. After 1821, however, the size and organization of the army aroused only occasional interest in Congress. Although there has been no detailed analysis of congressional voting on military questions, neither Democrats nor Whigs seem to have consistently supported or opposed army interests. On six House of Representatives roll calls involving relatively well-defined army interests, for example, Whigs voted in favor of the army position by a 56.9% majority while Democrats did so by a 52.6% majority. The expansionist foreign policy of national Democratic leaders, especially in the 1840s, appealed to officers' hopes for action and promotion; the usual Democratic control of the federal government eased the passage of certain military bills. On the other hand, many regulars disliked the egalitarian flavor of Democratic political rhetoric, which they associated with opposition to West Point and the regular army, and felt more comfortable with the seemingly conservative Whigs. Divisions on some military issues tended to follow regional rather than party lines: the eastern seaboard usually supported coastal fortifications while western states were more likely to favor expansions of the infantry and mounted regiments and the appointment of citizens directly to the army. At any rate, military policy remained a secondary issue through the antebellum period, subordinated to debates over foreign policy, government expenditures, and other more controversial matters. Thus, officers principally interested in professional objectives saw little consistent basis for choice between the major parties.

By the 1850s, regular army officers had come to manifest consistent patterns of thought and behavior in their relationship with the political world. The most important influence had been the emergence of a distinct military profession after the War of 1812. Regulars developed a professional ideology which distinguished clearly between military and political life. While the army was dedicated to politically neutral national service, politicians and especially parties seemed divisive and self-serving. Although officers continued to engage in political activity, both ideology and the quest for career security channeled their energies almost exclusively toward professional goals: individual career advancement; branch objectives; and, to a limited extent, the general interest of the army. In the process, the more politically oriented regulars grew familiar with such common strategies of the second party system—and of interest group politics generally—as congressional lobbying, the manipulation of patronage, and the use of the press to gain public support.

The sectional crisis of the late 1850s and 1860s temporarily disrupted these patterns. As politics polarized North against South, military men found it increasingly difficult to concentrate on professional matters to the exclusion of the general political environment. Although the army contained both abolitionists and ardent secessionists, most officers were moderate in their views and genuinely alarmed by the sectional split. Not only did the crisis threaten the national unity so central to their professional ideology, but also the army itself and their personal careers within it. Predictably, they tended to blame the nation's troubles on political leaders, whom they accused alternately of self-serving opportunism and blind fanaticism. "Most [congressmen] are more interested in making sensation speeches for their immediate constituents than in working for the good of the country," wrote a Virginia-born officer late in 1860. "I have heretofore thought them to be harmless; but they have finally succeeded in bringing the country to the verge of dissolution." A Pennsylvanian attributed the crisis to "fanatics who regard the principles (?) of a political party as paramount to the interests of their country and the welfare of a few miserable negroes of more importance than the perpetuity of the American Union." With the emergence of the Republican party in the late 1850s, the bipartisanship of the officer corps temporarily declined, as regulars looked to the Democrats, whatever their flaws, as the best hope for national unity.

Secession split the officer corps. Forced to choose between their budding professional identities and older sectional, state, and especially family loyalties, most southern-born officers and a few northerners with ties in the

South resigned and joined the Confederacy. The Civil War and Reconstruction confronted military men with unprecedented problems—organizing and commanding mass armies of volunteers, "nation building" in the South—which further eroded the line separating the army from the civilian world. As the sectional crisis receded, however, prewar patterns of political behavior reemerged and continued into the twentieth century. With the rise of efficiency reports and other methods of evaluating "merit," outside political support for career advancement became less conspicuous, though it did not disappear. The growth of interservice rivalry added a strong incentive to internal service solidarity. By the mid-twentieth century, the vast size of the armed forces and their symbiotic relationship with the industrial economy made military politics more complicated than they had been in the days of the old army. Nevertheless, nonpartisan pressure group action in pursuit of professionally defined objectives continues to characterize the officer corps' relationship to the political world.

The nature of officers' political behavior suggests an additional explanation for the strength of the American tradition of civil control. On one hand, the conditions mentioned at the start of this essay—the historical suspicion of standing armies, the general stability of the political system, the small size and relatively broad recruitment base of the professional officer corps—placed constraints on regular army officers, discouraging them from forming an exclusive praetorian elite. On the other hand, military men enjoyed rather free access to political channels. Rather than standing haughtily aloof or attempting as a group to dominate the political process, regulars entered politics at a number of levels and for a variety of often competing objectives. Thus, the "military interest" did not constitute a united front but an array of interests—individual, intraservice, service—which tended to diffuse the impact of officers' political action. In their political behavior, regulars were both military professionals and American citizens. Professional concerns shaped the goals they sought, but the methods which they adopted lay very much in the mainstream of political life. In other words, American political culture in the nineteenth century both coerced and coopted army officers into accepting the principle of civil control.

The Veracruz Expedition of 1847
K. Jack Bauer

Amphibious landings played a major role in Allied operations during World War II in both the European and Pacific Theaters of Operation and at Inchon during the Korean War. During the Mexican-American War, however, General Winfield Scott's landing at the Gulf of Mexico port of Veracruz in March 1847 preparatory to a march on Mexico City was an untried operation requiring unrehearsed cooperation between the Army and the Navy. The landing, America's first large-scale amphibious operation, was a resounding success, but, as the late Jack Bauer of Renssalear Polytechnic Institute argues, it was not without its logistical and tactical difficulties. Still, it stands as an early example of interservice cooperation in wartime to overcome obstacles in order to attain an essential goal. This essay was originally printed in Military Affairs *(20/3 [Fall 1956], 162–69) and is reprinted with permission.*

The failure of President James K. Polk to secure a negotiated peace with Mexico during the summer and fall of 1846 led to the November 17 decision in favor of an advance on Mexico City. After canvassing possible invasion routes only one was found practicable: a landing at Veracruz followed by an advance overland to the Mexican capital. The projected expedition was not only the most ambitious military operation yet undertaken by the United States but also involved America's first large scale amphibious operation.

During the middle of the nineteenth century amphibious operations were still a *terra incognita*. No operational doctrine yet existed and special purpose landing craft were all but unknown. Nearly all previous landings had taken place in protected waters from ship's boats. Such protected waters did not exist around Veracruz.

Veracruz was considered by many to be the strongest fortified point in North America. A walled town of about 15,000 people, it lay on a sandy strip of coast about 450 miles south of the mouth of the Rio Grande. About half a mile offshore, in front of the town, Gallegos Reef broke the swell and formed a small but insecure harbor. On the inshore tip of the reef stood the massive fortress of San Juan de Ulloa commanding both the town and harbor. Veracruz lay in the midst of the yellow fever belt, forcing an invading army to seize Veracruz and Ulloa in time to move inland before the arrival of the disease season in late April or early May.

The command of this very ambitious and extremely difficult undertaking went to Major General Winfield Scott. Although he was without a doubt America's ablest and most distinguished soldier, his choice was not a congenial one to Polk who distrusted Scott as a professional soldier and as a Whig. But, no other general of sufficient stature or ability was acceptable either. To Polk's credit, it must be said that once appointed he supported Scott fully.

Before leaving for the south Scott outlined his requirements for the coming campaign: 14,000 men, 140 surfboats to land his army, a large siege train, and fifty transports to lift his force. Although the bulk of the men could be drawn from General Zachary Taylor's army in Northern Mexico part of the men and nearly all the material and transport had to come from the States. These were the responsibility of Secretary of War William L. Marcy and the War Department. Scott believed that with reasonable luck he could have his expedition afloat by the middle of January 1847.

Scott's flatboats, or surfboats, are of some interest. They were the first specialized landing craft built in the United States. Built in three sizes, thirty-five to forty feet long they were double-ended, flat-bottomed craft carrying thirty-five to forty-five men. Although slow and cumbersome they served their purpose well.

Scott left Washington for the south November 23, 1846, travelling via New York, and reached New Orleans December 19. While at New Orleans Scott fixed the island of Lobos, off the Mexican coast between Tampico and Veracruz, as point of rendezvous for his forces and set early February as target date for beginning the expedition. He ordered 2500 of the men from Taylor's army to embark at the Brassos Santiago at the mouth of the Rio Grande and 5500 to embark at the newly captured port of Tampico. The additional troops (newly raised volunteers) and material from the States were to proceed directly to Lobos. The troops at Brassos Santiago and Tampico were ready to embark by the last of January but a shortage of transports delayed their embarkation for nearly a month. The troops and material from the States were equally slow in arriving. When Scott reached Lobos on February 21, 1847, he found only parts of his five new volunteer regiments had arrived and when the bulk of the troops from the Brassos Santiago and Tampico arrived a week later he had less than 9,000 of his expected 14,000 men. Even more critical was his shortage of ordnance and the absence of half his surfboats. These shortages were due to a number of reasons. Bad weather and a shortage of crews held up many of the transports for almost a month; ten transports were cancelled through a misunderstanding between Scott and the War Department; and some of the shortages appear to have been caused by dilatory actions in Washington.

The advent of the yellow fever season loomed large in Scott's plans for he must complete his campaigning in the Veracruz area before the scourge's arrival around the first of May. Already his expedition was a month late. "Indeed," Scott wrote the Secretary of War on the last day of February, "the season has already advanced, in reference to the usual return of the yellow fever on this coast, that I can only wait a day or two longer for . . . any body [of troops] . . . or for anything behind; and two thirds of the ordnance and ordnance stores, and half the surfboats, are yet unheard of." Two days later Scott led his transports south towards the navy's base at Anton Lizardo south of Veracruz.

Meanwhile Commodore David Conner, commanding the American naval forces in the Gulf of Mexico, strengthened his squadron for the descent. Although none of the promised reinforcements from the States had arrived he called in every possible vessel from his blockade of the long Mexican coast. By stripping his blockading forces Conner was able to concentrate two frigates, three sloops-of-war, one large steamer, a brig, three steam gunboats and five schooner gunboats off Veracruz. In expectation of Scott's arrival Conner stationed vessels off the entrance to Anton Lizardo to furnish pilots and instructions to the incoming transports. Scott's transports, scattered by a gale, began arriving during the morning of March 4.

During March 5 Scott arrived and immediately conferred with Conner. They agreed on the importance of an early landing, "it being important that we should effect a landing before a norther should come on, as this would delay us two or three days." The following morning Scott with his generals and staff joined Conner on board the small steamer *Petrita* for an inspection of the possible landing beaches. Following the shoreline north towards Veracruz they came within range of the guns of Ulloa which bracketed the frail steamer before Lieutenant Samuel Lockwood could haul out of range unscathed. Scott and Conner agreed that the best landing place would be on Collado Beach about two and a half miles southeast of Veracruz where Sacrificios Island offered some protection for the transports and landing craft. A curving sandy beach with a gentle sloping approach and a range of low sand hills about 150 yards inland, Collado appeared undefended.

Scott's original plan for the landing called for transferring his men from their transports directly to the landing craft off the landing beach while the navy stood by to give gunfire support. However, the anchorage behind Sacrificios was too small to hold both the transports and the naval covering force. Therefore, Scott, of necessity, accepted Conner's suggestion that the men be embarked on the naval vessels and the army's few steam transports for the trip to Sacrificios. At the same time Conner agreed to man the surfboats and superintend the landings.

Scott organized his army into three brigades: about 2595 regulars under Brigadier General William J. Worth constituted the first; about 2465 regulars under Brigadier General David E. Twiggs the second; and about 3530 volunteers made up of the third under command of Major General Robert Patterson. Worth's First Brigade, strengthened by the marines from Conner's squadron, formed the first landing wave; Patterson's brigade the second; while Twigg's regulars remained in reserve.

Conner had the responsibility of assigning the vessels to carry Scott's force from Anton Lizardo to the anchorage off Sacrificios. He distributed Worth's brigade between the frigate *Raritan*, the screw sloop *Princeton*, and the army steamer *Edith*; Patterson's among the frigate *Potomac* and the army steamers *Virginia* and *Alabama*; and the reserve among the sloops of war

Albany and *St. Mary's*, the brig *Porpoise*, the small steamer *Petrita*, and the army steamers *Massachusetts* and *Eudora*.

The landings were set for March 8 but a falling barometer during the evening before caused Conner to postpone the landings for fear that a norther was approaching. As the norther did not appear he rescheduled the landings for the following day, March 9—the thirtieth anniversary of General Scott's reaching flag rank.

At daylight on the ninth the surfboats began the ferrying of troops from their transports to the warships and steamers. Completing their mission about 10:00 A.M. the empty surfboats then made fast to the steamers for the tow to Sacrificios. At 9:45 the schooner-gunboats *Reefer, Bonita, Petrel, Tampico,* and *Falcon* of the inshore covering force hoisted anchor and stood up for the landing area. About an hour and three quarters later the remainder of the attack force, led by Conner in the *Raritan* and Scott in the *Massachusetts*, exited in single file through the narrow entrance to Anton Lizardo and stood north towards the landing area.

The schooner-gunboats anchored off Collado Beach at about 12:15 P.M. and soon afterward the rest of the expedition began arriving. It was nearly 3 o'clock before the last of the vessels had taken its assigned place. At 3:30 the schooner-gunboats and the light draft steamers *Spitfire* and *Vixen* shifted their positions to form a line about ninety yards off the beach. At the same time Scott hoisted the signal to commence loading the surfboats. As the boats filled they attempted to form a line abreast of the *Princeton*, about 450 yards offshore, but the strong current setting in around Sacrificios threw the heavily laden boats into confusion. In an attempt to remedy the situation the *Princeton* at about four o'clock threw out a hawser to which the surfboats made fast. The surfboats were hopelessly confused and rather than delay the landings to reform his boats General Worth contented himself with arranging his regimental colors in the line of battle and instructing the surfboats to form on them when cast off for the landing.

The confusion among the surfboats took on a greater significance when the lookouts in the squadron reported a large cavalry patrol in the dunes behind the beach—a seemingly certain indication that the Mexicans would oppose the landings.

At 5:30 the *Massachusetts* fired a gun as the signal for the surfboats to cast off and pull for shore. After some confusion while the boats found their proper places the line swept in towards the sandy shore. As it neared the beach a gig pulled ahead on the left of the line, grounded on the beach, and a lone figure leaped out and waded ashore, his gold braid glistening in the sun. It was General Worth. Quickly the rest of the boats grounded and their passengers waded ashore. To the complete surprise of the Americans, the Mexicans fired not a shot. The first Americans to reach the top of the range of sand hills learned the reason. There were no Mexicans in sight; even the cavalry patrol had disappeared.

The reasons for General Juan Morales' failure to oppose the landing is difficult to understand. He had not been surprised and even a small force should have been able to make the landing very costly. Apparently Morales believed his poorly trained men could not stand up under a bombardment by naval guns and would be so demoralized by it that he would be unable to salvage a sufficient number to man the defenses of the city. Morales had barely enough troops to man his defenses and the loss of more than a very few would have made the defense of Veracruz extremely difficult if not impossible. Apparently also, Morales' strategy was to hold out as long as possible in the defenses of Veracruz in the hope that a relief force could fight its way through to him.

Once the first wave had landed the surf boats returned to load Patterson's men. Since there had been no opposition no attempt was made to keep a line of battle, or even much order, as the surfboats shuttled back and forth individually, carrying the rest of Scott's men. The whole army of more than 8600 men was ashore without loss by midnight. Even today this would be no insignificant achievement, but in 1847 it was magnificent.

As soon as the army was ashore the landing of its supplies began. Conner rushed the landing of supplies because the appearance of a norther would seriously delay further unloading. Subsequently, a series of northers lasting from the twelfth to the seventeenth did seriously hamper the landing of supplies.

Under cover of a brief diversionary bombardment of Ulloa by Commander Josiah Tattnall in the light draft steamer *Spitfire* Scott began his encirclement of Veracruz on the morning of March 10. Three days later it was complete.

Scott's first siege batteries were ready by March 22. They opened fire the same day in conjunction with a bombardment of the town by the light draft steamers and gunboats of the squadron. The absence of a large part of the army's siege train left Scott without sufficient heavy artillery to breach the walls of the town. To remedy this defect he requested the loan of some heavy guns from the navy. Commodore Matthew C. Perry, who had just relieved Commodore Conner, agreed provided the navy should man its guns. Scott concurred.

The navy sent ashore six guns, three eight-inch shell guns and three thirty-two pounders. Emplaced in a battery laid out by Captain Robert E. Lee of Scott's staff, these first fired during the morning of March 24. After three days of action the navy's heavy guns had nearly breached the western wall of the town.

With the bombardment beginning to show effect General Scott and Commodore Perry readied an assault which never occurred. General Morales called a council of war of his principal officers during the evening of the twenty-fifth. The council advised surrender to save further bloodshed, as the town and its inhabitants had suffered heavily from the pounding of the army's heavy mortars and howitzers. Morales opposed surrender and resigned his command to General José Juan Landero. The next day Landero opened the negotiations which led to the signing of Articles of Capitulation on March 27. To the pleasant surprise of the Americans, Landero included the Castle of San Juan de Ulloa in his surrender, thereby removing Scott's greatest obstacle. On March 29, a full month before the onset of the yellow fever season, the Americans marched into their prize.

Even if Veracruz was not resolutely defended, and it was not, Scott's success should not be minimized. He conducted a well planned and well executed operation in spite of disheartening shortages of nearly everything except drive and resourcefulness on the part of the commanding general. He was ably assisted and supported by Commodore Conner whose relief during the siege was unfortunate and has robbed him of the recognition he deserves.

IV

The Civil War,
1861–1862

Civil War Weapons and Tactics

John K. Mahon

Despite the continuing historical interest in the Civil War, its battles, and its outcome, few readers, professional or nonprofessional, have an adequate understanding and appreciation of how the battles were actually fought, i.e., of Civil War land tactics. In this essay the author, now Professor Emeritus of History, The University of Florida, explains exactly how infantry, artillery, and cavalry units were employed and why this was so. He stresses the impact of improved weapon technologies on combat and how these changed the mode of warfare offensively and defensively during the fratricidal conflict and thereafter. This essay first appeared under the title "Civil War Infantry Assault Tactics" in Military Affairs (25/2 [Summer 1961], 57–68) and is reprinted with permission.

In 1848 Claude Etienne Minié, a captain in the French Army, perfected a bullet which revolutionized warfare. Napoleon III, recognizing his accomplishment, conferred on the Captain both money and honor. Minié's new bullet was conoidal and hollow at the base instead of round. When fired from a gun it acquired horizontal spin because the explosion of the propellant expanded the hollow base so as to engage the rifling of the barrel. In consequence a soldier could drop the Minié ball down the muzzle of his shoulder arm almost as easily as if it had been round, yet fire it in the opposite direction with horizontal spin imparted to it. Such spin, unobtainable with a round ball in a musket (all muskets were smoothbores, hence without rifling) meant additional range, velocity and accuracy. Indeed, because of it infantry tactics may be labeled "before Minié (BM) and "after Minié" (AM). BM infantrymen had had to carry muskets because such rifles as existed were too slow to load; AM they could graduate to rifles. BM the footsoldier could reach out about 100 yards to injure his foe with some degree of accuracy, AM he could be accurate at two or two and one-half times that distance.

The United States Army adopted the Minié principle in 1855 and the government arsenals soon began to manufacture weapons incorporating it. By 1861 the arsenals had standardized a muzzleloading shoulder arm with a rifled barrel known as a "rifle musket." Four feet, eight inches in length, nine pounds one ounce in weight, .58 caliber in bore, it was fired by means of a percussion cap. Because of the conoidal bullet with the hollow base, loading was simple, at least compared to earlier muskets. The soldier took in his hand a paper cartridge in which powder and ball were wrapped together, bit the end off it, poured the contents into the barrel via the muzzle, stroked a couple of times with his ramrod, then fitted a small copper cap loaded with fulminate onto a nipple outside the barrel. Now he was ready to fire. A trained soldier could get off two or three rounds a minute. The greatest disadvantage was that none but a contortionist could load the weapon lying down. You had to roll over on your back and virtually wrestle with it. But once loaded this weapon was able to stop an attack at 200 to 250 yards, and kill up to 1,000 yards.

The story of infantry assaults in the American Civil War must begin with Captain Minié; for it was his improvement of shoulder arms which conditioned tactics. Because of Minié's innovation bullets dominated the battlefields where Johnny Reb fought Billy Yank.

By no means did every infantryman have so fine a weapon as the standard product of the government arsenals. No less than eighty-one different types of shoulder arms were used by the Union forces, generous numbers of them obsolete. Agents of both sides scoured Europe for guns and picked up the castoffs of every army. Consequently all sorts of firing mechanisms were represented in the American armies from flintlock to rimfire; all sorts of loading systems from muzzleloading singleshot to breechloading repeater. Calibers were legion; small wonder that ammunition supply was tangled.

Better shoulder weapons existed than the best muzzleloaders issued to the bulk of the infantry. Among them were good breechloaders, Sharp's, Henry's, and Spencer's; and good repeaters, notably the Henry and the Spencer. The former carried sixteen charges, the latter seven. Men fortunate enough to be armed with repeaters naturally had a great advantage over others armed with singleshot muzzleloaders. Troops who had once used them were never thereafter satisfied with the old style. But only a few on either side had a chance to try the new ones. Around six and one-third muzzleloaders were issued to Union soldiers for every breechloader. Most of the latter went to the cavalry, becoming for that branch the standard arm in 1864.

Responsible latter day students, and some contemporaries, have claimed that the Union could have armed enough of its men with repeaters to have ended the war in 1862. What stood in the way was a conservative point of view in certain high places. Brigadier General James W. Ripley, Chief of Ordnance, who occupied the key position, disapproved both Spencer and Henry in December 1861. They were too heavy, he said, required special ammunition which had not been proved, were constructed of untested parts that might malfunction, and were far too high priced (roughly $36.00 as compared to $20.00 for the standard Springfield muzzle-loader). Only when President Lincoln himself overruled the Chief of Ordnance were repeaters put into production. It ought to be added in defense of Ripley that he was in distinguished company. Robert E. Lee himself did not favor repeaters because he thought they encouraged poor fire discipline.

To place American weapons-conservatism in context one must remember that no important nation had unqualifiedly adopted a breechloader. Prussia came closest with her needle-gun (loaded at the breech), but she issued it only to one battalion in each regiment and to one or two elite corps. Neither had any nation adopted a repeating shoulder arm. Now, when one remembers that America had always leaned heavily upon Europe in military matters, it is not at all surprising to find the nation entering the war virtually without breechloaders and repeaters. Three years of war, and a change of chiefs of ordnance, reversed this initial position, but it was too late then to supply the improved rifles to more than a few infantrymen.

Even granting that the rifle musket was not the best shoulder weapon available, it was good enough to alter tactics. It enforced the following vital changes: (1) Stretched battle lines, (2) obliged armies to form for combat much farther apart, (3) reduced the density of men in the battle zone, and (4) made battles into firefights with shock action decidedly subordinate. Still more important it caused battles to be at once much longer in time and less decisive in outcome. There were to be no more Waterloos. Finally, it made defense a good deal stronger than offense. For this last result there were two principal reasons: the new firepower literally drove men to throw up temporary earthworks; and behind these they could gather in greater density and be better supplied with ammunition than their attackers. Nowhere was the superior power of the defense better illustrated than at the Battle of Fredericksburg. Here, at the foot of Marye's Hill Confederate infantry, protected by a stone wall, stood four ranks deep to blast their assailants. Inasmuch as the front rank stepped to the rear to load after firing, the fusillade never slackened. This spelled carnage for the Federals, relatively minor losses for their foes.

General J. F. C. Fuller contends that the bullet and the trench, due to heightened firepower, dominated the battlefields of the Civil War, and continued to do so at least through World War I. Their power deprived the combat arms of true mobility. It does not detract from his thesis to point out that excessive numbers of bullets were required to achieve this domination. One scholar has estimated that 900 pounds of lead propelled by 240 pounds of powder were required to drop every Confederate who was killed. This was a somewhat worse record than Napoleon's soldiers had scored. But it was a better record than the bayonet made. Throughout the bloody struggles in the wilderness north of Richmond during May, June, and July of 1864—where there was more hand to hand fighting than usual—33,292 Union men received treatment for bullet wounds, only thirty-seven for bayonet thrusts. Nor are there any grounds to suppose that most of the bayonet casualties were lying dead on the battlefield. Heros von Borcke, a German soldier of fortune serving with the South, took the trouble to ride over battlefields examining corpses, and he reported finding very few that displayed thrust wounds. Generally speaking the physical damage done by bayonet attacks was inflicted by bullets, and the issue decided before the two fighting lines closed with each other. In short, it was the threat of being run through, coupled with firepower, not the act itself that made attacks with the bayonet effective.

There is no intent to contend here that bayonet attacks were invariably ineffective. On the contrary, to pick some notable examples, they were significant at Malvern Hill, Seven Pines, and Mill Springs (all in 1862), and at Missionary Ridge in 1863. But more critical than their occasional effective use was the impact which the tradition of bayonet assaults had on tactics. Civil War attack formations were arranged with the idea that the bayonet would decide the outcome. This is one of the reasons why assault formations were so dreadfully at the mercy of defending troops. General Fuller, by the way, claims that the same mistaken theory underlay tactics as late as World War I.

Bullets worked their greatest execution against bodies of men advancing to the assault. The fact is that the firepower of the rifle musket was relatively modern whereas the formations used in attacks were obsolete. One reason for this has just been presented: attack formations were based upon the outmoded theory that bayonets would win. In the second place, shoulder arms had outpaced artillery in rate of development. Because of the drawing apart of armies, enforced by heightened firepower, attacking infantry was obliged to pass across extended areas scourged by fire, in the case of Pickett's charge about 1,400 yards. Supporting cannon had not the capability either to do the defenders great harm or to follow the attacking lines and aid them efficiently. After all, the zone of attack was sprayed by three times as many bullets as had been the case during the American Revolution only eighty-five years before. In contrast, defending artillery was at its deadliest just in the zones where supporting artillery fire could not go. At 400 yards the defenders opened with grapeshot, at 200 they switched to canister. Both being scattershot, wreaked havoc.

What were the human blocks of which assaulting formations were composed. In general they were divisions of four brigades, brigades of four regiments, and regiments of ten companies. The authorized number of officers and men in a full-strength regiment totaled 1,046. Of course the number actually on the field varied widely from this norm, witness the average figures for six important battles:

Shiloh	6 and 7 April, 1862	560
Fair Oaks	31 May to 1 June 1862	650
Chancellorsville	1–5 May, 1863	530
Gettysburg	1–3 July 1863	375
Chickamauga	19 and 20 September, 1863	440
Wilderness	5–7 May 1864	440

General Lee wasted fewer men in obsolete assault formations than Grant. This may have been because his strategic problem was fundamentally a defensive one. He could afford to hold his ground and let the Federals try to dislodge him. According to General Augur, a perceptive French observer writing in the 1880's, Lee had a typical tactic which reflected the defensive character of his strategy. He habitually sought a vital plot of ground where the enemy could not afford to leave him, threw up earthworks, taking care to open avenues through which to take the offensive, and awaited the attack. Once it came he blasted it with devastating fire, and at the proper moment issued from his works upon its flanks, or, if possible, its rear. When he could not do this, but stumbled into battle instead, as at Gettysburg, the result was unhappy for the Confederacy.

Obsolete though they were in the 1860's, attack formations had changed many times during the hundred years since Frederick II. Density of men on a battlefield had shrunk from eight per unit of ground to one, while the rising firepower had followed about the same ratio in reverse, that is from one to eight. Within the decade just passed the Crimean War had demonstrated the terrible effect of gunfire on great masses of men such as Russia had employed. But it also had revealed weaknesses in the thin line. The latter, two ranks deep, was the basic line formation for American troops. When in drillbook formation men stood side by side with an interval of twenty-one to twenty-four inches between them while the distance from the back of a man to the face of the one behind him was no more than thirty-two inches. Before the war, American drill manuals had given promise of the increasing use of extended order, that is of increased distance and interval between men in a battle line. This promise was not fulfilled. Neither was the wider use of platoons, sections, and squads implied in the drill manuals of the 1850's. Whence came these lapses? For one thing, it was easier to instruct green recruits to fight in close order than otherwise. And drill masters of the Civil War were forced to work with little else, especially at the beginning.

In general it may be said that attack formations were more apt to be irregular in the early years of the war than at the end. For instance at the Battle of Belmont, 7 November 1861, Grant's initial combat command (not counting the earlier war with Mexico), the First Illinois Infantry advanced from tree to tree Indian fashion. Likewise, formal battle formations rarely developed during the Peninsular Campaign in the spring of 1862; rather the men took advantage of cover and advanced in short rushes. In contrast, there are examples of line actions in the first two years as formal as if directed by Frederick the Great himself. For instance, in the opening engagements of Second Bull Run, August 1862, two lines which happened upon each other stood in close order and blazed away in the style of half a century earlier. At Corinth, 3 October 1862, the Confederate line advanced at a slow step which could not be maintained without the strictest discipline and training. Finding the delay hard to bear the Federals lay down. At thirty yards they rose and fired point blank; then when Confederates were a musket length away, they fired again. So quick a refire indicates that part of the line did not join the first volley.

Even if men started in good formation, withering fire drove them to seek cover. There is the case of the Ninth New York charging Confederates behind a stone wall at Antietam. Forced to lie down, the soldiers reformed by crawling into place. Still the fire sought them out and killed so many that they were glad to get to their feet and resume the assault.

A skirmish line in advance of the main force was by no means new with the Civil War. It had been developed, at least in modern form, in the time of Frederick II and perfected during the American Revolution. The armies of the Napoleonic Wars had also made extensive use of skirmishers. But until close to the middle of the nineteenth century skirmishing had been the special mission of light troops who took little part in line fighting. Thereafter improvements in firearms (and other changes) had increased the importance of skirmishing so much that by the time of the Civil War all soldiers, Union and Confederate, were given light as well as line training.

Skirmishers assaulted in an irregular line of one rank, taking advantage of the terrain. They also invariably fired at will. Nevertheless they were subject to the control of the officer commanding their line, and when well trained could display impressive cohesion. Their purpose was to prepare the way for the main battle line by throwing the enemy off balance and by drawing his fire. After the war there was a brisk argument among students as to the relative efficiency of line and skirmish line. Statistics showed that aimed fire delivered by the latter made twice as many hits as the volley fire of the line. On the other hand it was claimed that skirmishers had retreated upon suffering two percent losses while lines had held even with forty percent of their men down. Naturally, a skirmish line suffered fewer casualties than a battle line because the interval between the men was much wider and because it had no depth. At Antietam the battle line of the Sixth Wisconsin lost fifty-four percent while one of its companies acting as skirmishers lost only five percent. With the benefit of perspective it may be said that the skirmish line was the assault formation of the future. If anyone saw this at the time it was General Sherman, who in some cases used a line or lines of skirmishers instead of the battle line of two ranks. Obviously skirmish formations thrust added responsibility upon junior officers.

G. F. R. Henderson, one of the most perceptive students of the War, credits Americans with having devised two assault techniques to meet the threat of annihilative firepower. One of these became the typical assault formation, if any can be said to have been typical. This was a succession of lines, containing two ranks each, with a prescribed distance of thirty-two inches separating ranks. The lines varied greatly in width and in the distance at which they followed one another. Some were as wide as a whole brigade lined up in two ranks, others only as wide as a company. If there was a usual width it was that of a brigade, and the resulting formation, although in reality it was a succession of lines, was called a division in column of brigades. When a division attacked in this formation it had as many lines as there were brigades in it, with each brigade forming a line of two ranks. Distance between lines ranged up to 300 yards and down to 50, but the commonest was 150. If the lines were three hundred yards apart they were likely to be beaten in detail. The intervals between men and the distance between ranks and lines were almost identical with those Napoleon had used. Unfortunately the rifles which played upon attackers were by no means comparable to the muskets of Napoleon's time.

When a company of volunteers was at full strength it occupied about twenty-seven yards in the line of battle. Thus, a regiment of ten full companies, with an interval of three yards between the companies, took up three hundred yards, and a brigade of four regiments close to 1,300 yards. This meant that a division attacking in a column of brigades advanced on a front nearly three-quarters of a mile wide.

If the successive lines were under good control they stopped in the midst of the assault to fire. On rare occasions the fire was by volley, that is the whole company, or some large subdivision of it, fired together at a command. If the fire was by file, the right file, being the two men at the right end of each rank, shot first; then the fire passed down the line by file from right to left. Most of the time, however, individual soldiers fired when they were ready. But it was customary for the two soldiers of a file to work together, one of them loading while the other fired.

Officers on foot led a charge while mounted officers were supposed to follow the line. Whether before or behind, their lives were precarious, for sharpshooters among the defenders preferred them as targets.

As might be expected, the successive lines ran together and approached the defenders bunched into vulnerable crowds. Yet if they held a semblance of their formation they could keep the enemy reeling by striking him with recurring waves of fire and shock. The best officers understood this advantage and sought to have the benefit of it. For example General George H. Thomas trained his troops so well that they even climbed Kenesaw Mountain in formal lines which did not bunch. In contrast, though equally well trained, General James McPherson's Army of the Tennessee went up more or less Indian style. Brigadier General Emory Upton undertook to prevent bunching, by giving detailed orders. At Spotsylvania on 10 May 1864 he required the first line of his brigade to break to the flanks when within the enemy position to try for envelopment. The second line was ordered to halt at the enemy works and fire straight to the front, while the third lay down farther to the rear. The fourth was directed to remain at the edge of a wood two hundred yards distant until sent forward.

Pickett's charge at Gettysburg was a succession of lines with a front about 500 yards wide. It had to cross 1,400 yards under severe fire, in the course of which it became bunched, and was then vulnerable to the cannon fire raking it from Little Round Top. General Longstreet said he watched one shell time and again knock over five or six of Pickett's men.

The second innovation which G. F. R. Henderson credited to the Americans of the Civil War was the attack by a succession of rushes. This type of assault doubtless occurred many times by chance, but Arthur Lockwood Wagner contends that it was first used formally at the Battle of Ft. Donelson, 15 February 1862. General Morgan L. Smith's brigade of two regiments was advancing in a succession of lines. Under heavy fire the two lines lay down, the second forming on the left of the first. All the while the skirmishers plied the enemy with an effective fire. When the foe's fire abated, the brigade rose again, rushed forward, absorbed its skirmishers, and again lay down and opened fire. Taking cover when the enemy's fusillade was hottest and dashing forward in slack periods, the brigade at length reached and carried the hostile position with but slight loss. Such tactics were far in advance of the time. Indeed, concerning the tactics of the war as a whole, Henderson claims that they were more modern than those of the Austro-Prussian War which began after the Civil War ended and was waged by two of the great military powers of Europe.

The basic dilemma which commanders had to resolve in assault tactics was whether to use a column or a line. Both formations had shown strengths and weaknesses during the recent Crimean War. The advantage of the column was that it had great penetrating power. Furthermore, it was sanctified by the fact that Napoleon had used it (heavy versions of it) during his later campaigns. His most frequent attack formation had been a line of battalions in close column by division at deploying distance. Roughly explained, this was a group of battalions side by side with an interval of one hundred or one hundred and fifty yards between them. Each battalion was massed nine or twelve ranks deep. The line of battalion masses advanced abreast, striking the enemy every hundred yards or so along his entire front. It was the mission of the skirmishers to protect the gaps between battalions and to shake the aim of the enemy at the easy targets the masses presented. Usually lines of battalions followed each other in succession, and the masses of the second struck the places in the enemy line missed by the first. This formation, or something approximating it, was later adopted by nearly every European power.

The weaknesses of mass formations sprang from firepower, or the lack of it. Only the first rank or two of a column could shoot; the rest were neutralized. But when it came to receiving the enemy's fire, all ranks were nakedly vulnerable, particularly to scattershot from cannon. Lines in contrast had been developed to allow every soldier to shoot, but possessed of course much less penetrating power than columns. The American succession of lines was in reality an unconscious attempt to avoid the two horns of the dilemma. It allowed full expression of firepower, yet also was capable of some of the shock impact of a column.

But the succession-of-lines technique did not eliminate heavy columns from the Civil War tactical repertory. It was during Grant's hammering north of Richmond in the spring of 1864 that the tendency to use masses reached its peak. This stemmed partly from the thickly wooded nature of the country and partly from Grant's determination to break the Army of Northern Virginia at whatever cost. The heaviest mass formation of all appears to have been used by Winfield Scott Hancock's Second Corps at Spotsylvania on 12 May 1864. Here 20,000 Union infantrymen in close order formed almost a solid rectangle. The Federals knew that the Confederate artillery had been shifted away from the point they meant to attack, and this influenced the formation. The huge body advanced through thicket and in fog. It was made up, as were most Civil War mass formations, of regiments (synonymous with the battalions of Napoleon's time) in Napoleonic masses, that is in close column by division. (The term division as here used designated two companies.) In it the two companies of a division were in line side by side, but in two ranks instead of the three still used in Europe. The regiment, then, was in five lines of two ranks each (unless a company or two had been detached as skirmishers) with thirty-two inches' distance between the ranks and a distance of three yards between the lines. The interval between the men in the ranks was one foot. In summary, if the regiment was full strength, its attacking mass was eighty-two men wide and ten deep. When the regiments of a brigade were side by side in close column by division, the interval between them was usually sixty yards.

But Hancock's divisions at Spotsylvania were not all formed in column. David Birney's Third Division was arranged in two deployed lines. Francis Barlow's First Division, in contrast, was solid, forty ranks deep. The men under Barlow were ordered to uncap their guns and rely on shock action. Nelson Miles serving in the massed division recorded that he saw bayonets crossed for the first time in the war, although he had been in it since the beginning. Whatever the cause, Barlow's Division suffered more than the others. For the two weeks 8-21 May it lost 2.393 casualties while Birney suffered

1,015. As for the defending Confederates, they were able to pour three volleys into the Corps before it struck them. So intense was their fire that it cut down big trees. The Corps' casualty list from 8-21 May totalled 6,642, probably about twenty-five per cent of those present for duty.

Apparently General Barlow had had enough of mass formations, for at Cold Harbor on 3 June he formed his division into two deployed lines, two brigades per line. But this time John Gibbons commanding the Second Division assumed a mixed formation. His first wave comprised two brigades in two lines of two ranks each, but his second line was in close columns.

The use of mixed formations was not confined to Grant's army struggling through the Wilderness. General Thomas in his successful assault on Hood at Nashville, 15 and 16 December 1864, used a deployed front line and a second in close column by division. It may be asserted that his was the more hazardous use of this vulnerable formation, for in Grant's 1864 campaign the terrain prevented the full effect of artillery while in Thomas's that destructive arm was uninhibited.

It took seventeen months of war for the deadly firepower of the rifle musket to oblige men defending a position regularly to dig like badgers. But after Antietam in September 1862 nearly every force which defended against an assault usually protected itself with temporary earthworks. Hereafter the armies seldom came together without digging entrenchments. Foreign observes were amazed at the speed and completeness of their burrowing. For example, a brigade in the spring of 1865 was observed to have erected a breastwork across its entire front in forty minutes. Reverting to Barlow's division at Cold Harbor, when it had advanced as far as possible, it quickly switched to the defensive and erected earthworks, in some places no more than thirty yards from the enemy lines. There it stayed. Such habitual use of hasty field fortifications was one of the innovations in the craft of war contributed by Americans during the Civil War. Thus was achieved the use of the trench which shared with the bullet the domination of the battlefield, and which, General Fuller contended, had not changed when the First World War broke out half a century later.

If only indirectly, the soldiers' load affected assaults. The Confederate infantrymen began the war lightly loaded and remained so. Stonewall Jackson exploited their lightness so well that he set records in the swift movement of foot troops. In contrast the Union forces had to achieve lightness by discard. Very early they began to throw away the issue knapsack and, as the Confederates did, roll their extra things up in their blankets and sling these in a horseshoe over the shoulder. The custom was to pile the bedrolls in a heap before an action, but since there was not time, the bedrolls often went into battle too. Weapons were not exempt from discard; indeed there are many records of men throwing away their bayonets, especially in the western armies.

Hardly anyone will deny that infantry was "queen of battles" during this war. But naturally she relied heavily on the other combat arms, for example the artillery. That arm had not advanced apace, and as a result its fire was very little more destructive than during the Mexican War fifteen years before. This was because no such revolution had touched cannon as had transformed the infantryman's shoulder weapon from musket to rifle in the interlude. It is true there were rifled artillery pieces with twice the range and accuracy of any employed against Mexico, but they did not become the chief reliance during the Civil War. Instead the twelve pounder Napoleon, a smoothbore, was preponderant. Firing shells at 1,200 yards, grapeshot at 400, and canister at 200, this piece decimated attacking infantry. Yet, marvellous to tell, it was not equal to the infantrymen's rifle as a killer. For example the Medical Director of the Army of the Potomac reported for the two weeks from 8 May to 21 May 1864 that 749 wounds from artillery projectiles were treated as compared to 8,218 from bullets, that is one-tenth as many. To complete the figures only 14 bayonet cuts and one from a sword entered the report.

Like the artillery of World War I (carrying out General Fuller's parallel), the artillery of the Civil War could not solve its problems. As previously noted, it had not the range, precision or elevation to give assaulting infantry the supporting fires needed in the critical area just in front of the enemy's lines. In other words it could not deliver what are now called effective preparations. For example, although 150 guns pounded the Union lines to prepare the way for Pickett's charge, they did little damage. The defenders calmly lay down until the preparation had spent itself. Nor could the cannon successfully aid assaulting troops by following closely after them. Fifteen or sixteen pieces followed Pickett's charge, but were not able to distract the defenders. The latter ignored them and poured destruction upon the infantry. All in all artillery was useful primarily as a defensive weapon, one which added materially to the superiority of the defense over the offense.

In defense, artillery was sometimes decisive. One factor that made it so was in increasing tendency to use it in masses. At Malvern Hill during the Peninsular Campaign in the spring of 1862 the Federals massed many cannon (Henderson said 300) in a commanding position and repulsed what could have been a fatal Confederate thrust. Half the Southern casualties in this engagement were from artillery fire, a very rare circumstance. Again, twenty-five cannon along Plum Run at Gettysburg held the Federal line without infantry support. Later at Atlanta General O. O. Howard united sixteen batteries behind his threatened right wing and thus prevented almost certain envelopment. On the morning of 18 May 1864 twenty-nine of his cannon, firing spherical and case shot, held 12,000 infantry at bay. He here demonstrated the technique which had developed for defensive use; namely to concentrate pieces behind the portion of the line which had been penetrated and with them drive the invaders out. At Pea Ridge, Arkansas, in March 1862 General Franz Sigel even made good use of artillery to cover his retreat.

Of course there were unusual uses of artillery. For example it sometimes moved forward with the skirmishers. Also, General Thomas at Nashville, not being able to rely on green infantry to hold the enemy in position, pinned them by means of cannon fire.

In contrast to artillery, cavalry, since it had greater mobility than the other arms, played an offensive role, albeit a different one than had been traditional in Europe. On the battlefield it rarely made mounted charges against coherent infantry. Indeed to do so was a last desperate resort. Nevertheless there are some notable instances of this use. For instance Union Major General John Buford led a mounted attack at Gettysburg which the Confederate infantry repulsed by forming the square just as Wellington's troops would have done fifty years earlier. Again, when it was necessary to delay Stonewall Jackson's infantry column at all cost in May 1863, Alfred Pleasanton's cavalry struck it at right angles to its front. The price in lives was high, but the vital delay was achieved. Later at Winchester on 19 September 1864, a mounted charge was successful against Confederate infantry.

Neither side in the American war supported heavy cavalry of the sort Napoleon had used to clinch his victories. When that great captain had seen that a portion of the enemy's line was wavering he had often ordered his heavy horse to hurl themselves at it and by the power of shock break the position and win the day. In contrast, when American cavalrymen assailed the enemy's line they usually did so as infantry. They were in reality dragoons, the forerunners of armored infantry. They used their horses to reach the scene of an action with speed, then dismounted and fought on foot. In spite of their lack of infantry training they gave a good account of themselves, and when they were armed with Spencer repeaters, as most of the Union cavalry was by mid-1864, they were as good as the best infantry.

The habit of fighting on foot was reflected in armament. At the start a horse soldier had sword or sabre, pistol, and carbine. As time passed many discarded the cutting weapon and relied more heavily on firepower At least one unit of Union cavalry started the war armed with lances, but in its earliest actions the lances slowed down a precipitate retreat. After that they were soon discarded.

In summary, if cavalry affected infantry assaults—which by the way were the principal assaults of the war—it did so, except in rare cases, acting as infantry.

The study of Civil War tactics is a dwarf compared to strategy, and probably justly so. There is doubtless little of a practical nature to be learned in the thermonuclear-missile age from the way men advanced against fire one hundred years ago. Antiquarian though the pursuit be, perhaps some readers will feel enriched by a more perfect knowledge of how their forbears assaulted their enemies. The one clear lesson that emerges—and it seems to have modern application—is that Civil War assault formations were obsolete in comparison to the fire against which they were launched.

The Bloodiest Day:
The Battle of Antietam

Stephen W. Sears

The Battle of Antietam, or Sharpsburg, of September 17, 1862, was, indeed, the bloodiest day of the Civil War. In this extended essay (edited and abbreviated for this reprinting) illustrating the frenzied horror of Civil War combat, Stephen W. Sears, the author of Landscape Turned Red: The Battle of Antietam (1983), *describes the events leading up to this climactic battle around that Maryland hamlet, the contests of arms that took place that day (from north to south, from the Cornfield to Bloody Lane to Burnside's Bridge to the arrival of A. P. Hill's troops from Harpers Ferry), and the aftermath of that day's bloodletting. As Sears makes clear, the blame for the Union lack of success at Antietam must be placed on the head of General George B. McClellan, the Union commander. The laurels of victory belong to General Robert E. Lee. This essay in its original form was first published in* Civil War Times. *From* Civil War Times, *April 1987, by Stephen W. Sears. Copyright © 1987 by* Civil War Times. *Reprinted by permission of PRIMEDIA Enthusiasts Publications (History Group).*

Major General George B. McClellan had never taken more pleasure from his military accomplishments. It was 9:30 on the morning of September 15, 1862, and he was writing a hurried note to his wife. The Army of the Potomac had "gained a glorious & complete victory; every moment added to its importance," he told her. ". . . How glad I am for my country that it is delivered from immediate peril. I am about starting with the pursuit & must close this. . . . If I can believe one tenth of what is reported, God has seldom given an army greater victory than this. . . ."

He telegraphed the good tidings to Washington, D.C. His information was "perfectly reliable," he announced, that the enemy was fleeing "in a perfect panic, & that Genl Lee last night stated publicly that he must admit they had been shockingly whipped." A report just in, he wrote in a second telegram, "completely confirms the rout & demoralization of the rebel Army. . . . It is stated that Lee gives his loss as fifteen thousand."

The subject of General McClellan's euphoria was the Battle of South Mountain, Maryland, fought the day before. His pursuit was undertaken to drive the Confederates out of Maryland and across the Potomac River back into Virginia. For more than a week he had tried to track the invaders across some 600 square miles of western Maryland on a military chessboard that extended from Harper's Ferry, Virginia, on the Potomac River, northward to Hagerstown, near the Pennsylvania line, and from Frederick westward across South Mountain to the Maryland village of Sharpsburg. With this one victory, he thought, he had won the campaign. As was his habit, however, McClellan was indulging in a good deal of wishful thinking. He furnished the Lincoln administration with more overheated rumor than fact. Confederate General Robert E. Lee had not lost anything close to 15,000 men at South Mountain, nor did he say publicly (or privately) that he had been "shockingly whipped." Nor was his Army of Northern Virginia fleeing "in perfect panic."

General Lee marched for Sharpsburg that day (September 15) because it was the most convenient spot on the Maryland side of the Potomac to concentrate his widely scattered army. It offered good defensive ground and was a position not easily turned. Lee was puzzled by General McClellan's unexpected aggressiveness, which had brought on the fighting at South Mountain, but he was unwilling to give up his campaign because of it. A primary rationale behind his entire plan of operations in Maryland was the fact that McClellan commanded the Federal army. The events of the past thirty-six hours had not changed Lee's opinion that his opponent put caution ahead of all other military considerations.

As Lee suspected, whatever had suddenly impelled McClellan to go on the offensive, it was not due to a change of character. It was pure chance. Two days earlier, on the morning of September 13, McClellan had been handed what became famous as the "Lost Order." It was lost, apparently, through the carelessness of a Southern courier or staff officer, and found by Corporal Barton W. Mitchell of the 17th Indiana in a meadow near Frederick, Maryland, where Mitchell's regiment was making camp. Headed "Special Order No. 191, Headquarters Army of Northern Virginia" and dated September 9, it was a copy of Lee's field order for his complex operation against the Federal garrison at Harper's Ferry. Here, in full detail, was listed every major command in the Confederate army, the objectives and routes of march for each, and a timetable. When McClellan telegraphed the president at noon that day, "I have all the plans of the rebels," he was not exaggerating. It was the intelligence coup of the Civil War.

Fresh from his victory at the Second Battle of Bull Run on August 29 and 30, 1862, General Lee had every intention of retaining the strategic initiative but no intention of attacking Washington's strong fortifications. He invaded Maryland for a number of reasons—to forestall another Federal offensive into Virginia, to provision his army, to put pressure on the Lincoln administration's shaky political coalition, among them. But above all Lee was looking to pull McClellan far from his Washington base for a showdown fight on a field of his own choosing. He wanted him out of his lines so he "could get at him." Lee had intended the battlefield of his choice to be somewhere in the Cumberland Valley of Maryland and Pennsylvania. Moving that far west meant running his supply line through the Shenandoah, and to protect that line something would have to be done about the Federals at Harper's Ferry. Instead of simply masking the garrison there, obstructing its view of his operations, he devised a plan to divide his army to surround and capture it—men, supplies, ordnance, and all. In drawing up "Order

191" he assigned six of his nine divisions to the task, under the overall command of Major General Thomas J. Jackson—the famous "Stonewall," renowned for his mastery of independent operations.

In carrying out the Harper's Ferry movement, the Confederates maneuvered for several days behind the northern barrier of South Mountain in ways that McClellan could not fathom. But by noon on September 13 McClellan had the "Lost Order" and understood all these movements, and he promised Lincoln "no time will be lost" in catching Lee in his own trap and punishing him severely. A swift advance across South Mountain would put his forces squarely between the widely scattered elements of the Rebel army. "My general idea is to cut the enemy in two & beat him in detail," he told one of his generals. For George McClellan, however, losing no time meant starting the first thing next day. It was eighteen hours before any Federals marched in response to the finding of the "Lost Order."

The Battle of South Mountain on September 14 would be fought for the two main passes through the mountain—Turner's Gap to the north, where the National Road from Frederick crossed the range, and Crampton's Gap to the south, where a road crossed into Pleasant Valley and went on to Harper's Ferry. Had McClellan lost no time and ordered strong forces to advance to within striking distance of the passes during the afternoon of September 13 (seven hours of daylight were available in which to march the ten or twelve miles to the foot of the mountain), the next morning he would have met only slight opposition at Turner's Gap and nothing but a cavalry screen at Crampton's Gap. A vigorous offensive begun at first light on September 14 would have put the Federals across South Mountain by midday and in position to divide and conquer Lee's army—and to rescue the Harper's Ferry garrison.

At it happened, it was late afternoon on the 14th before a full-fledged attack was mounted at either pass. By then the Confederates had enough troops on the scene to make a fight of it, and when darkness ended the firing the Federals had reached no farther than the crest of the mountain. In the meantime, Stonewall Jackson drew his noose tightly about Harper's Ferry. He notified Lee that he expected to capture it in the morning. At daylight on September 15 the ranks of Jackson's guns surrounding Harper's Ferry resumed their bombardment, and at 8:00 a.m. the garrison raised the white flag of surrender. The closest rescue force was half a dozen miles away and a day late. Jackson's spoils included 11,500 men, 13,000 small arms, 73 pieces of artillery, and a huge stock of supplies.

The march of the Federals toward Antietam that morning was badly directed, with units delayed, getting in one another's way, and no one from headquarters straightening out the tangles. It was only a six- or seven-mile march to Antietam Creek, but it was two o'clock in the afternoon before the first Yankee infantry reached the scene. McClellan did not appear until an hour later. He made what he described as a "rapid examination" of Lee's position and decided (as he reported to Washington) that "it was too late in the day to attack." McClellan was a prudent man by nature, but what activated his almost unnatural caution in military matters was the picture of the enemy he carried in his head. It dominated his every action. In contemplating the situation on September 15, he based his calculations on the belief that Lee had invaded Maryland with 120,000 men, an army 25 percent larger than his own. Even after he knew from the "Lost Order" that the Army of Northern Virginia was widely scattered, he remained preoccupied with the odds he might face. ". . . I have the mass of their troops to contend with," he told Union General-in-Chief Major General Henry W. Halleck in announcing his find, "& they outnumber me when united." He had almost 60,000 troops under his immediate command that day. As McClellan reckoned it from the "Lost Order," Lee had opposed him at Turner's Gap with 30,000 men. Consequently, there ought to be only that number at Sharpsburg, less whatever losses (substantial losses, by his count) were suffered in the Turner's Gap fight. Yet here was his opponent standing defiantly in line of battle, apparently perfectly willing to resume the fight. Whatever the numbers, McClellan concluded there was not time enough left that day to launch a coordinated, fully manned, carefully planned attack. To attempt anything less would be a dangerous improvisation. Tomorrow would be soon enough to act.

Unaware that his opponent knew all the workings of his Harper's Ferry operation, Lee was running a substantial bluff that day. He had scarcely 15,000 men in the line of battle, McClellan observed in his hurried inspection. Lee had his gunners put every piece of artillery they had in the line, with orders to fire on any Federals they saw. Then, about noon, a courier brought Lee confirmation of the capture of Harper's Ferry, along with the welcome news that Jackson would have his troops on the road by evening and be at Sharpsburg the next day. But even when the army was reunited, Lee would have less than 40,000 fighting men of all arms. Robert E. Lee did not stand and fight at Sharpsburg because he was cornered and forced to it. He might have continued his retreat from South Mountain on September 15 and very likely could have crossed the Potomac into Virginia before the Federal pursuit caught up. He could certainly have made the crossing safely under the cover of darkness. Instead, he stood his ground north of the river and dared McClellan to attack him.

Gambling on a Timid General

To fight at Sharpsburg was the boldest and most hazardous decision of any that Lee made during the Civil War. Some would term it foolhardy; not until the final doomed hours at Appomattox Court House in April 1865 would he again stand so great a chance of losing his entire army. And only in those last days of the war would the Army of Northern Virginia be as small as it was at Sharpsburg.

Lee and his generals had good enough intelligence sources, and they had seen enough of the Federals at Turner's Gap and as they arrived before Antietam Creek to estimate the size of McClellan's force. They figured rightly that they were outnumbered by as much as two to one. And they knew it was not even certain that all Confederate commands could be reunited in time to meet a Federal attack. But on this last point, General Lee felt secure in his judgment of his opponent's caution and how much that timidity would benefit him. The battlefield Lee chose at Sharpsburg was fairly good for defense but by no means strong. Its greatest weakness was that there were too few men to defend it; the Army of Northern Virginia promised to be stretched very thin trying to hold its lines from flank to flank. Another serious drawback was the fact that the Potomac River was only three miles to the rear. The bridge at Shepherdstown had long since been burned, and the only crossing was Boteler's Ford, deep, rocky, and not easily negotiated. Should the two-to-one odds be too much for the Rebels and force them to retreat under fire, chances were poor that many would escape across the river in the face of vigorous pursuit. It was for just this reason that the military textbooks warned against an army fighting with a river at its back, yet here was Lee risking the utter destruction of his army on the banks of the Potomac if McClellan's offensive succeeded. Considering the weakness of his army, Lee could hardly count on the decisive victory he had originally hoped for, but a victory of whatever sort might buy time and set back Federal plans for the rest of the year.

And there was more to Lee's decision than that. After cataloguing all the disadvantages of making a fight at Sharpsburg, E. Porter Alexander listed the advantages: "There is a single item, but it is an important one." General McClellan brought an army superior in numbers and equipment to the field, he wrote, "but he brought *himself* also. Perhaps the anticipation of that fact encouraged Lee to risk the odds. . . ." To Lee's way of thinking, that was the equalizer. He was sure beyond doubt that he could defeat George McClellan on any field of battle.

At dawn on Tuesday, September 16, a thick ground fog blanketed the hollows and woods around Sharpsburg and hid the Confederate positions from the Federals east of Antietam Creek. McClellan telegraphed General Halleck in Washington that the fog "had thus far prevented our doing more than to ascertain that some of the enemy are still there. Do not yet know in what force. Will attack as soon as situation of the enemy is developed." To Major General William B. Franklin of VI Corps in Pleasant Valley he telegraphed: "If the enemy is in force here, I shall attack him this morning."

These promises to bring Lee to battle promptly were straightforward enough, but there was no substance to them. McClellan had not yet completed a plan for an offensive, nor had he moved troops into attack position. When at mid-morning the fog burned off and revealed the Confederate army still in place, the pretense ended. "It became evident from the force of the enemy and the strength of their position that desperate fighting alone could drive them from the field, and all felt that a great and terrible battle was at hand," he explained. The day would be devoted to preparation— "obtaining information as to the ground, rectifying the position of the troops, and perfecting arrangements for the attack."

Up to that time, McClellan had gained remarkably little profit from his possession of "Lee's Order 191." The engagements at South Mountain cost him 2,300 men, including one of his ablest corps commanders, Major General Jesse Reno, killed by a Rebel sharpshooter. And fighting there failed to put him in position to crush Lee's scattered commands one by one. The badly managed pursuit of September 15 gave further life to the Army of Northern Virginia. On the morning of September 16 McClellan could put four times as many men on the firing line as his opponent, but once again the opportunity for an overwhelming victory slipped away.

It was not until midday on September 16 that Jackson and the vanguard of his force reached Sharpsburg. They had made what Jackson admitted was "a severe night's march," and the exhausted men continued to straggle in throughout the afternoon. Lee could now count six of his nine divisions, and the lack of activity across the valley of the Antietam made it obvious that he would not have to face a serious attack that day. He put Jackson in command of the left of the line and Major General James Longstreet in command of the right. Lee also sent orders to Major Generals Lafayette McLaws and Richard H. Anderson with their two trailing divisions south of the Potomac to resume their march in time to be at Sharpsburg early on the 17th. Another courier galloped off to Harper's Ferry with orders for Major General A. P. Hill, whose division Jackson had left to manage the details of the surrender, to set off first thing in the morning to rejoin the army. Lee had concluded that McClellan would grant him no more gifts of time. Gunners were told to hold their fire and save their ammunition for a battle the next day.

Antietam Creek was an important battlefield feature, for it was just wide enough and deep enough to complicate Federal movements in any offensive, particularly for the artillery and the ammunition trains. Three arched stone bridges crossed the Antietam in the vicinity of Sharpsburg: the Rohrbach Bridge to the south (soon to be made famous as the "Burnside Bridge"), the Middle Bridge almost due east of Sharpsburg, and the Upper Bridge to the north. As Lee posted his men that day, his line of infantry and artillery extended some four miles. From north to south it ran along the face of a ridgeline and generally parallel to and in front of the Hagerstown turnpike, covered Sharpsburg, and ended on high ground overlooking Antietam Creek below the Rohrbach Bridge.

From his first look at the field on September 15, General McClellan decided to throw the main weight of his offensive against the northern flank. Not only did the ground on the Confederate left seem best suited for maneuver, but also the approach to it by the Upper Bridge was beyond the reach of the enemy's artillery. Another inspection of the field on the 16th made him comfortable with this decision, and by noon that day he was ready to order the movement. It would be the first time in his Civil War career that he planned and directed an offensive battle, and the first battle of any kind that he directed, or even witnessed, from start to finish. But he issued no written order outlining his plan and called no meeting of his generals to explain it. With the possible exception of his confidant and unofficial second-in-command, Major General Fitz John Porter, McClellan seems to have discussed his plans for the fight with no one but Major General "Fighting Joe" Hooker. As Major General Ambrose E. Burnside and Brigadier General Jacob Cox understood it, upon orders from headquarters in the morning they were simply to mount a diversion at the Rohrbach Bridge to prevent the Confederates from withdrawing troops from their right to meet the main attack on their left. For such a diversion to succeed it would have to be made when Hooker and his I Corps opened their attack on the northern flank or soon afterward, but there was no certainty about McClellan's actual intentions on this point.

For equally vague reasons, McClellan held Franklin's corps in Pleasant Valley throughout the day on September 16, and only that evening sent orders for it to march the next morning to rejoin the main army. Then he directed Major General Darius N. Couch from Franklin's corps to Harper's Ferry, an errand he never explained and perhaps could not explain. As a result, of Franklin's 19,000 men, only 12,000 (two of his three divisions) arrived on the battlefield on September 17, and only when the battle was half over. Couch's troops were removed to a distance from where they could be of little help—and when that help did come, it was too late. And normally cavalry scouted the terrain and developed the enemy's positions and observed their movement. On the evening of September 16 Confederate Major General "Jeb" Stuart was doing precisely that, locating the new posting of Hooker's I Corps. Lee would be informed and fully prepared to meet the morning's opening assault. The Federal cavalry, however, performed no such role at Antietam. McClellan placed Brigadier General Alfred Pleasonton's 4,300-man cavalry division alongside Porter's corps at the center of his line, intending it to deliver the finishing blow if there was to be one. This was a tactic of an earlier day, and quite out of touch with the reality of the 1860s. During the Napoleonic Wars mass cavalry charges had their place against infantry armed with short-ranged, inaccurate smoothbore muskets. Against Civil War infantry with rifled muskets it was a hopeless, murderous tactic, yet McClellan proposed just such a charge to Pleasonton on September 17. (Pleasonton ignored the suggestion.) Of more significance, in this posting the cavalry ceased to act as the eyes of the army. On the night of September 16 McClellan announced: "To-morrow we fight the battle that will decide the fate of the republic."

Slaughter in the Cornfield

At first light on Wednesday, September 17, Joe Hooker rode forward to his picket line on the Joseph Poffenberger farm to examine the ground he would be fighting for. Looking due south along the Hagerstown turnpike, he could see about a mile from where he was standing a small, white-washed brick building in a fringe of woods alongside the turnpike. Many soldiers that day thought it was a schoolhouse, but it was actually a church of the German Baptist Brethren, a pacifist sect that believed church steeples to be an expression of vanity and whose practice of baptism by total immersion caused them to be known as Dunkers (or Dunkards). Just across the turnpike from the church was an open plateau-like area crowded with Confederate guns. Hooker concluded that if he could seize that area he would be in a fair way toward rolling up the enemy flank. Apparently his instructions from McClellan were no more specific than to assault the Confederate left; how and in what strength was left to him. He understood, he later testified to Congress, that attacks on the enemy right and center would be made "simultaneous with my attack." Hooker would prove that day to be a hard fighter but a cautious planner. He determined to open his attack with only his own three divisions—8,600 fighting men in all—and leave Major General Joseph K. F. Mansfield's XII Corps well to the rear, to be called up should he need help.

In narrowly focusing on his intent to take the Dunker church and the area around it, Hooker did himself a disservice. He gave no thought to seizing the Nicodemus Hill, high ground off to his right that dominated both the Federal and Confederate positions. Jeb Stuart's guns on that hill played a major part in the first few hours of fighting, but neither Hooker, nor the other Federal generals on the scene, nor McClellan back at headquarters, took any action against this key site beyond ordering Union artillery to fire back. Had the Federals captured Nicodemus Hill and posted batteries on it, an observer wrote, Jackson's position "could not have been held fifteen minutes."

Alerted to the main thrust of McClellan's design by the movement of Hooker's corps across Antietam Creek on September 16, Stonewall Jackson had squared off the Confederates' left flank so that the Union I Corps would be making what amounted to a frontal attack, three Union divisions against three Confederate divisions. Brigadier General Alexander R. Lawton had one brigade of his division in the pasture south of farmer David Miller's 30-acre cornfield—soon to win grim fame as *the* Cornfield—and a second brigade in line beyond it, facing the East Woods, on the farm of Samuel Mumma. Jackson posted Lawton's remaining two brigades, as well as the two-brigade division of Brigadier General John B. Hood, in reserve in the West Woods. Jackson's third division, under Brigadier General John R. Jones, was positioned a quarter-mile north of the Dunker church, partly in the West Woods and partly in a meadow alongside the turnpike. Jackson's 7,700 men numbered some 900 fewer than Hooker could put into action.

The Battle of Antietam opened almost spontaneously at 5:00 in the morning as the artillerists in Jackson's and Hooker's commands began banging away at each other the moment it was light enough to see targets. The day dawned overcast and a patchy ground fog lingered in the hollows and woodlots, hampering visibility for a time. Soon the Rebel batteries under Colonel Stephen D. Lee (no relation to the commanding general) posted on the plateau near the Dunker church joined in, and were promptly answered at long range by Federal guns east of Antietam Creek. Musketry added to the din as Major General George Gordon Meade's brigade in the East Woods, under Brigadier General Truman Seymour, resumed the brief fight that darkness had interrupted the night before. Seymour's Pennsylvanians pushed ahead through the woods to the Smoketown road, a country lane that angled off the Hagerstown turnpike at the Dunker church, and engaged the Rebel brigade of Colonel James Walker on the Mumma farm.

Meanwhile, Joe Hooker was putting Brigadier General Abner Doubleday's division on the right and Brigadier General James B. Ricketts' division on the left into line of battle, and at 6:00 they marched into the Cornfield. In the pasture south of the Cornfield, Colonel Marcellus Douglass had his brigade of Georgians laying down behind poles of fence rails and in hollows. He told his men to each take aim at his "own corn row," and when the Federals came out of the corn the Georgians stood up and delivered a surprise blast of fire that shattered the Yankees' first rank. In what would become a characteristic scene on this bloody day, the two battle lines stood facing each other in the open, less than 250 yards apart, and fired as fast as they could load their rifles. Finally neither side could take the losses any longer and found what shelter they could and continued the firing. Colonel Walker brought most of his brigade over from the Mumma farm to a rock ledge in the pasture to join the fight, catching the Federals in a converging arc of fire, then taking heavy losses in return. Walker ordered the veteran 12th Georgia Regiment to work around the enemy's flank, but only a few men responded. He went forward to urge the others on personally and found none but dead and wounded behind the ledge. The regiment began the day with 100 men. Already it had lost 60 of them.

At least in piecemeal fashion Ricketts' remaining brigades pushed through the Cornfield to the killing ground at its southern edge. To meet this new Yankee advance General Lawton sent in a brigade of Louisianans under Brigadier General Harry T. Hays, and along with the Georgians they pressed a counterattack right up to the edge of the Cornfield and the East Woods. Then it was the Confederates' turn to be raked by a converging arc of gunfire, and their counterattack floundered. Finally the two brigades fell back to their starting points in the pasture. Although the fire did not slacken, the contest in the eastern half of the Cornfield and in the East Woods was stalemated.

At the same time, fighting erupted immediately to the west where Brigadier General Abner Doubleday's division launched the other half of the I Corps' attack. The spearhead of this advance was Brigadier General John Gibbon's brigade of westerners, recently dubbed the Iron Brigade by Hooker for its fight at South Mountain. As they appeared on the field, Doubleday's forces came under a deadly artillery crossfire from Colonel Stephen Lee's batteries near the Dunker church and Jeb Stuart's guns on Nicodemus Hill. Despite the Federals' overall three-to-one advantage in artillery, here as elsewhere this day the Army of Northern Virginia's skillfully managed field artillery gained the edge in firepower at the actual point of contact between the two armies. Hooker felt obliged to divert four of his batteries to protect his open right flank and duel with Stuart's gunners, and in these early morning hours his remaining five batteries were overmatched by Stephen Lee's and Stuart's batteries and Jackson's divisional artillery. Taking its losses, the Iron Brigade pushed southward on both sides of the Hagerstown turnpike, half the line passing through farmer Miller's peach orchard and into the Cornfield, the other half into the field of clover running along the other side of the pike.

The Iron Brigade's fame as one of the Army of the Potomac's best combat outfits was just beginning—Antietam was its third battle—and on this morning it tangled with one of the best-known units in Lee's army, the Stonewall Brigade, now led by Colonel Andrew Grigsby. As the Yankees came within range Grigsby's men rose up and delivered a sudden volley that riddled the right flank of the advance. General Gibbon sent over strong reinforcements and the two battle lines slugged it out until finally the greater weight of the Federal force began to tell. With more than half the men casualties, Grigsby's command fell back behind the cover of rock ledges in the West Woods. The rest of the Iron Brigade meanwhile advanced through the Cornfield to meet a surprise blast of gunfire from the pasture beyond.

This engagement was taking place at the same time the fighting along the edge of the Cornfield to the east reached its peak. As the Federals advanced with the storm of musketry and cannon fire echoing across the battlefield Confederate Colonel William E. Starke met the crisis by personally leading a counterattack with his two remaining brigades, charging at the double-quick out of the West Woods and angling toward the turnpike and the Cornfield. The Yankees turned to meet this threat, and in places the battle lines were scarcely thirty yards apart. This was pointblank range; even in the blanketing battle smoke a shot could hardly miss. The counterattack halted the Federal advance, but at fearful cost. The progress of the I Corps offensive was being communicated to headquarters two miles behind the

Cornfield by flag signal, and a little before 7:00 a.m. General McClellan was heard to remark, "All goes well. Hooker is driving them."

According to McClellan's stated design for the battle, this sign of progress from the front ought to have been the signal to order Burnside to move against the enemy's other flank and for Major General Edwin V. Sumner's II Corps to push forward and capitalize on Hooker's gains. However, except for sending a message to Burnside to be prepared to advance, McClellan did nothing. When no order came to cross the Antietam to be in position, General Sumner went to headquarters to find out about it. McClellan would not see him, and the old general paced back and forth while Hooker's battle raged. Meanwhile, General Lee was anticipating events. Observing that the Federals opposite his right flank at the Rohrbach Bridge were making no threatening movements, he called on Longstreet to dispatch the brigade of Colonel George "Tige" Anderson from its posting in front of Sharpsburg to aid Jackson. The divisions of McLaws and Richard Anderson were now on the scene to serve as his reserve. Soon afterward Lee also ordered Brigadier General John G. Walker's division to march from the right to Jackson's aid on the left.

Confederate Major General A. P. Hill received Lee's order at Harper's Ferry at 6:30 a.m. He was to march to the scene of the fighting and had his men on the road within an hour, driving them unsparingly toward the battlefield. Darius Couch's division of the Union's VI Corps, which set off early that morning toward Harper's Ferry on McClellan's order, had marched perhaps five miles when a courier caught up with it in Pleasant Valley; McClellan had changed his mind and Couch was to turn around and join the main army. He was called on to make a march that day no longer than A. P. Hill's, and if anything he had a headstart. The noise of battle reached the ears of both Couch and Hill; presumably their orders were of equal urgency. Yet Couch set a pace so undemanding that everyone could keep up and no one straggled, and they all arrived five hours after they were needed.

Even before Colonel Starke's counterattack bought time for the embattled left flank, it was clear to Jackson that he would have to commit his last reserves to prevent a breakthrough by the I Corps. The call went out to Major General John B. Hood's division waiting in the West Woods behind the Dunker church. At 7:00 a.m. Hood led his 2,300 soldiers out of the woods in a counterattack. Hood's troops took the place of the embattled fragments of Lawton's division fighting in the meadow south of the Cornfield. Hood's men raised the Rebel yell and opened fire on the Federals. The right wing of Hood's assault overpowered those of Ricketts' men who were still in the East Woods and the eastern half of the Cornfield, sending them flying for the rear. When it was over, Ricketts admitted that of his 3,150 men who began the battle, he doubted just then if there were 300 still with the colors. But Yankee resistance stiffened, and under a hail of rifle and cannon fire Hood's drive in the western half of the Cornfield was finally blunted. The 1st Texas, meanwhile, charged ahead unsupported and out of control. Brigadier General George G. Meade's men were waiting, rifles resting on the rails of the fence at the northern edge of the Cornfield, and when the Texans came into their sights they simply tore them apart. Two companies were wiped out to the last man. Those few minutes cost the 1st Texas 186 of its 226 men, a loss rate of over 82 percent.

It was 7:30 a.m. now, and the opposing commands of Jackson and Hooker were spent and shattered. The I Corps had lost 30 percent of its numbers. More than three-quarters of its 2,600 casualties were in the divisions of Ricketts and Doubleday that had experienced the worst of the combat. In the contest against the I Corps, Jackson's casualties came to 3,000 men. Lawton's division had lost almost half its men. The regiments in the Divisions of Generals John R. Jones and Hood had lost 40 and 60 percent of their numbers, respectively.

Chaos and Clouds of Smoke

The sight of Hood's division swarming to the attack from behind the Dunker church had finally impelled McClellan to action, and at 7:20 a.m. orders went to Major General Sumner and the II Corps to cross the Antietam and march to Hooker's support. Not the entire corps, however; one of the three divisions was held back east of the creek for defensive purposes until Major General George W. Morell's division of Major General Fitz John Porter's corps came up from its camp a mile to the rear to replace it. Morell, yet another Federal officer of dull ability, required ninety minutes to make his one-mile march. By contrast, Sumner moved with all possible speed, but even with his best efforts he was starting from so far to the rear that it would be some time before he could reach the scene of the fighting. And McClellan still issued no orders to Burnside and the IX Corps. Except for sporadic shelling, the rest of the field remained silent.

Both sides were feeding fresh troops into the contest on the Confederate left. Major General D. H. Hill commanded the center of Lee's line, and when he saw Hood launch his counterstroke he advanced one of his own brigades to the pasture south of the Cornfield in support. Hood's assault was driven home with such speed, however, that it had reached its furthermost gain and was already falling back before the brigade reached the scene. But these new troops did arrive in time to drive back the Yankees who came through the Cornfield on the heels of Hood's retreating men. At the same time Mansfield's XII Corps was approaching the battlefield from the north. The XII Corps was the smallest in McClellan's army and seemingly the most unpromising for the work facing it. Fully half the 7,200 effectives were going into battle for the first time, including five regiments of new troops mustered in less than a month before. Mansfield's lead brigade contained three new regiments of raw troops (and their equally raw officers) with virtually no training. Then, while Mansfield was personally positioning some regiments in the East Woods he was struck by a Rebel bullet in the chest. He died the next day, having commanded the XII Corps just 48 hours. Brigadier General Alpheus Williams took over command of the XII Corps after Mansfield was hit.

A buildup of Rebel strength could be seen to the south, beyond the Cornfield, and Hooker, on the scene in the middle of the melee, told Generals Gibbon and Meade, "Gentlemen, you must hold on until Williams's men get up." These threatening forces were three brigades of 3,400 men under D. H. Hill. As the XII Corps took over from the I Corps the battle flared up once more. Hill had posted Colonel D. K. McRae's brigade in the East Woods as a guard against any Yankee flanking movement, and when, after furious fighting, it broke and ran, it opened the door wide to just that possibility. Under the command of sixty-one-year-old Brigadier General George Sears Greene, commanding the XII Corps' second division, the Yankees broke though and drove the Rebels from the East Woods. All three of D. H. Hill's brigades were soon in full retreat, pressed hard by the Yankees.

It was close to 9:00 a.m., and the XII Corps had turned the battle in the Union's favor. If it was called into action too late to reinforce Hooker's force, it was at least in time to rescue them. But like the I Corps, indeed, like every Federal corps that day, the XII Corps made its fight unsupported by the rest of the army. Still, it set the stage for a great victory. In three hours of combat the Rebels had finally been driven from all of the battlefield east of the Hagerstown turnpike—the Cornfield and the East Woods, and the pasture and the Mumma farmstead to the south of them—at a cost of some 8,000 men. This was a loss about equally divided between North and South. Hooker would say he had never seen "a more bloody, dismal battle-field." The Cornfield had been at the center of the maelstrom, and among the trampled stalks and around its four sides the dead and severely wounded carpeted the ground. Along the Hagerstown turnpike the bodies lay in heaps, so torn and covered with dust by the incessant artillery fire, a man wrote, that "you were obliged to look twice before recognizing them as human beings." Men were reminded that day of the tale of the Kilkenny cats, who in the savagery of their battle devoured each other.

Sumner's Wild Advance

It became clear that D. H. Hill could not stem the XII Corps advance. With the 125th Pennsylvania at the Dunker church and Greene's division within supporting distance, Joe Hooker could sense victory within his reach. Then chance intervened. Riding his eye-catching white horse, Hooker came right up to the front to personally position batteries for a renewed offensive, and a Confederate sharpshooter in the West Woods put a bullet through his foot.

Losing consciousness from loss of blood, he had to be taken from the field. His last order was to the XII Corps' spearheads: "Tell them to carry those woods and hold them—and it is our fight." General Sumner took over command of the XII Corps. When he at last arrived in the East Woods with his leading II Corps division, under Major General John Sedgwick, the guns were suddenly stilled. Sumner dressed his lines and prepared to advance. General Williams reported that General Greene was awaiting ammunition resupply and advised Sumner to take precautions in the advance. Sumner brushed him off. Somehow Sumner got the idea that since the only Federal troops he could see were Greene's men several hundred yards to his left in front of the Dunker church, they must mark the army's flank—and the Rebels' flank as well. He need only march straight ahead—due west, through the West Woods—then wheel left and (in the words of the corps historian) "sweep down the Confederate line, driving it before him through Sharpsburg, and heaping it up in disorder before Burnside, who, crossing the lower bridge, will complete the victory." Accordingly, he elected to march in deployed brigades, advancing on a front some 500 yards wide, the three brigades in parallel lines only 30 yards apart. There was absolutely no preparation for facing to the right or left in case either of their exposed flanks should be attacked.

On the other side, when Hood's counterattack was repulsed, Jackson's force holding the Confederate left had been reduced to perhaps 1,400 infantry. But by the time Sumner reached the field Colonel Tige Anderson's brigade from the right and three brigades under Major General Lafayette McLaws from the reserve gave Jackson 3,000 fresh men to counter the new offensive. With 5,400 men in Sedgwick's division, and the 125th Pennsylvania at the Dunker church, the Federals had an edge in manpower, but the Rebels more than offset this by having the advantages of position, of artillery, and of surprise.

It was shortly after 9:00 a.m. when Sumner ordered the advance without waiting for his second division, commanded by Brigadier General William H. French, to catch up. And his third division, commander Major General Israel B. Richardson, was only just then being released by General McClellan to cross the Antietam. When French arrived in the East Woods Sumner was already gone. Whether French misunderstood his orders, or had none, is not clear; at any rate, he did not follow. General Sumner's array of misfortune was now complete. Sedgwick's division would enter a deadly ambush alone and unsupported. When the Yankees began their advance Jeb Stuart's artillery lobbed shells over the West Woods into their ranks with deadly effect. Taking losses, Sedgwick's men pushed through the Cornfield, crossed the Hagerstown turnpike and the clover field beyond, and entered the West Woods. Suddenly there was an outburst of firing some 250 yards off to their left and rear, near the Dunker church. As the 125th Pennsylvania advanced toward the church a hail of gunfire opened on them and rapidly spread until it was striking them from front and flank. The raw troops did the best they could, but the fire was overwhelming and they broke and ran. Just then two strayed regiments from Sedgwick's division turned up at the church, in time to catch the next Confederate volleys. They were veteran troops and stood the fire longer, but finally they too had to fall back. Jackson now directed the full force of his concentration on the exposed left flank of Sedgwick's division in the West Woods. In their formations deployed to the front the Federals were helpless against this devastating fire, and almost equally helpless to react to it. The result was chaos. The regiments forming the left of each brigade took the worst of the hammer blows, and the right and left of the Rebel battle line curled forward until its fire was striking the Yankees from three directions. The only escape was to the north, past the Miller and Nicodemus farms. Regiments or companies would try to make a stand at a fence line or behind a rock outcropping, only to be outflanked or overrun by the tide of fugitives. After a half-mile or so the fight finally ended at a makeshift line of artillery and I Corps troops. In the face of this the Confederates broke off pursuit and retired to the West Woods. Sedgwick's division, together with the 125th Pennsylvania, had suffered 2,355 casualties in Jackson's attack, by far the largest share of them in the opening minutes of the fighting. Jackson's losses came to less than a thousand men. Sumner's conspicuous bravery in the heat of the action was much admired by his men, yet his blundering tactics had turned the course of the battle once again in the Confederates' favor.

It was shortly after 10:00 a.m., and after more than four hours of the most savage fighting either army had ever experienced, McClellan's design for the battle appeared no closer to success (except for Greene's sortie) than when Hooker opened the fighting at sunrise. Of the 75,000 troops McClellan could have put on the firing line that morning—had he ordered all his forces to the battlefield as promptly as possible—just 21,200, considerably less than a third, had been committed to what he termed his "main attack." Furthermore, he put these troops into action "in driblets" (in Sumner's words), with neither timely support nor reinforcement. The Confederates had faced this series of attacks with two-thirds as many men, yet they fought the Federal offensive to a standstill. To this point, McClellan had had the initiative, however imperfectly it was managed. With Sedgwick's repulse, though, he lost control of events. The Battle of Antietam would now follow its own bloody logic to a conclusion beyond his ability to manage. He became totally preoccupied with guarding against defeat instead of seeking victory.

"The Consuming Blast" at "Bloody Lane"

Despite McClellan's later claim that he sent Burnside's orders at an early hour, it was in fact not until 9:10 that morning that he directed him to advance with the IX Corps. Only when he could be assured that the VI Corps was arriving from Pleasant Valley to replenish the tactical reserve would he commit additional troops to the battle.

When William French and his division reached the East Woods at 9:15 a.m., he found no sign of Sedgwick's division, which they had been following. Rather than waiting for some word from Sumner or sending back to army headquarters for orders, French determined to go to the front without delay. At 9:30 a.m., as Sedgwick was being routed in the West Woods, French set off in a direction that would take him into action three-quarters of a mile to the south. Both Lee and Longstreet were with D. H. Hill, the Rebel commander in this sector, watching French's advance. Hill's position, dictated by the nature of the ground, was in the form of a large salient at the center of the Confederate line. Six hundred yards south of the Dunker church a farm lane ran eastward from the Hagerstown turnpike for something over a quarter of a mile, turned southeasterly for another quarter-mile, then angled southward to meet the Boonsboro turnpike halfway between Sharpsburg and Antietam Creek. Over the years heavily loaded farm wagons on their way to a gristmill on the creek had worn the lane down until for much of its length it was several feet below the level of the field on either side. It was in effect a long, naturally formed trench, and would be marked on the military maps as the Sunken Road. Over the next few hours it would earn another name: Bloody Lane. Hill's 2,600 men were outnumbered better than two to one by French's Federals, but the Sunken Road was an extremely strong position, and Hill's men added to its strength by throwing up a breastwork of fence rails. General Lee sent back orders for his last reserves, Richard Anderson's division, to move up to Hill's support.

French's division was led by a general who, like Sumner, went into battle on September 17 with no clear idea of what he was facing or how best to meet it. French would be as surprised as his men by the reception he met. Running along in front of the Sunken Road and fifty to eighty yards from it was a low ridge, and as the Yankees approached the crest they fixed bayonets and charged forward at a run. It was like the earlier slaughter at the Cornfield and the Hagerstown turnpike: an aimed shot could hardly miss at this range. The charge was stopped cold, and in those few moments 450 men, a quarter of a brigade were lost. Next to be thrown into the fight were three regiments of new troops, the 14th Connecticut, 108th New York, and the 130th Pennsylvania. Their reception was equally bloody. The rest of the brigade crowded up to the ridgeline to try to continue the fight and were shot to pieces. Soon they could take no more of it and fell back behind the ridge. It was soon obvious that the Federal troops could make no headway against the formidable Sunken Road position. French's division was finished as an offensive weapon. Its losses on September 17 would total 1,760, second only to Sedgwick's division, by far the largest share of them coming in the first half-hour of its assault on the Sunken Road. Israel Richardson's division arrived on the scene after the last of French's men fell back in defeat. Richardson's 4,000 II Corps veterans might well have been used to exploit the foothold George Greene had won at the Dunker church, but Greene's sortie seems to have had little impression on headquarters. Mc-Clellan still made no effort to direct operations or shape the action toward his original design, and consequently Richardson moved southward to join French's battered force in front of the Sunken Road.

At the same time, there was a brief flurry of gunfire from the south, in the direction of the Rohrbach Bridge. McClellan's courier had reached Burn-side's headquarters shortly before 10:00 a.m. with the order to open the attack on Lee's right, and Brigadier General Jacob Cox immediately set about putting the IX Corps into action. The plan here was to test the Rebel defenses at the bridge with a straight-ahead charge by Colonel George Crook's brigade of the Kanawha Division. At the same time, the division of Brigadier General Isaac P. Rodman, reinforced by a second Kanawha brigade, would set off downstream to cross the Antietam two-thirds of a mile below the bridge at a ford McClellan's engineers had picked out the day before, so as to take the bridge defenders in the flank. The remaining two IX Corps divisions would exploit the opening. It seemed a sound enough basic plan, yet nearly everything went wrong.

There was no doubting that the bridge would be exceedingly difficult to seize. The Rohrbach Bridge road came down from Sharpsburg through a ravine to reach the creek upstream, ran along the bank before turning sharply to cross the bridge, and then ran southward again, close by the Federals' side of the creek, for a quarter of a mile before angling off to Pleasant Valley. On both banks were steep hills, those on the Confederate side slanting right down to the water's edge. The bridge itself was a three-arch stone structure 125 feet long and 12 feet wide. Although there were 12,500 men in the IX Corps, only a small fraction of them could try to cross this narrow bottleneck at any one time. Defending the Rohrbach Bridge were 400 men of the 2d and 20th Georgia under Colonel Henry L. Benning. His men were well dug in and commanded every approach to the bridge at a range of no more than 100 yards. Five batteries backed them up on high ground to the rear. The Georgians formed their line on a hillside in an old quarry and behind a stone wall, improving these positions with piles of fence rails and logs, and it was obvious that a great deal of firepower would be needed to dislodge them.

The high command of the IX Corps was afflicted by a seeming mental paralysis on September 17, beginning at the top with General Burnside. Not a single reconnaissance was carried out in this sector by the corps. Rodman's flanking column had not been advanced to its fording side to be ready to cross the moment the signal was received. Only the skirmishers of the 11th Connecticut actually carried out their part of the attack plan, and they discovered soon enough that the closer they approached to the Rohrbach Bridge the more vulnerable they became. General Rodman's

3,200-man flanking force experienced equally embarrassing difficulties. It discovered that the ford where it was supposed to cross was unusable for artillery and even infantry, with high banks and a 160-foot bluff blocking the approach. When the Federals first arrived in front of Sharpsburg, local citizens told them of Snavely's Ford, a good crossing downstream from the bridge, but no one in the IX Corps had made any effort to locate it. This was normally a matter for the cavalry, but with McClellan holding Pleasonton's troops in his reserve, they had not been available, and the engineers sent in their place muddled the reconnaissance. Snavely's Ford was finally located, but it was a hard two-mile march from Rodman's starting point, and a quarter of the corps was going to be some time getting to the scene of action.

While they waited for some evidence of progress by Rodman, Burnside and Cox could think of nothing better to do than order the bridge to be stormed a second time. With bayonets fixed, the men of the 2d Maryland charged down the road toward the bridge 250 yards away. There was not a shred of cover against the murderous flanking fire from across the creek, and in perhaps a minute and a half they lost 45 percent of their number. In this torrent of musketry and artillery fire there was no chance they could reach the bridge, and finally they could take no more and broke for cover. At was about 11:00 a.m.

The sounds of Burnside's feeble efforts died away and the Sunken Road once more became the central focus of action. As Richardson's division joined the fight, the Confederates under Major General Richard H. Anderson came up in support of D. H. Hill. Anderson's division was the last of Lee's reserves on the field; with the exception of A. P. Hill's division on the march from Harpers Ferry, the entire Army of Northern Virginia was now committed. The first of Richardson's Federal units to arrive was the celebrated Irish Brigade, going into battle under its emerald banners. Brigadier General Thomas F. Meagher had recruited his three Irish regiments in New York City; they were now reinforced by the 29th Massachusetts. Meagher put his men in on the left of what remained of French's division. Heavily fortified with drink, he ordered a bayonet charge. Resting their rifles on the fence-rail breastworks, Hill's men shot the attack to shreds. More than half the Irish Brigade was shot down in these few minutes; Meagher himself was spared when the whiskey proved too much for him and he fell off his horse and had to be carried from the field. Like French's troops before them, the Irish Brigade survivors fell back behind the crest of the ridge and lay down to maintain a fire against the Sunken Road's defenders. With hardly a pause, Richardson put in Brigadier General John C. Caldwell's brigade on Meagher's left. Fresh troops appeared on the Confederate side as well, as more of Dick Anderson's men came onto the field. It was close to noon. Anderson's 3,400 fresh troops appeared to insure solid support for D. H. Hill's men holding the Confederate center, but paradoxically they produced exactly the opposite effect. The ground behind Hill's line, the farm of Henry

Piper, sloped upward toward the Hagerstown turnpike and was in plain view and well within range of the Federal infantry stymied at the Sunken Road, and when Anderson's reinforcements appeared they drew a heavy fire. And Anderson went down with a bad wound almost the moment he reached the field. The reinforcements milled around in Piper's cornfield and orchard without direction, and those who did try to crowd into the Sunken Road caused only confusion. Abruptly and without warning the entire Confederate center fell apart. Casualties mounted among the reinforcements pushing into the crowded lane and continued behind the Sunken Road. Suddenly men by the hundreds began to clamber out of the road and run for the rear. A similar mix-up in orders caused the Confederate left to collapse at almost the same moment. When the 6th Alabama's commander, Colonel John B. Gordon, went down with his fifth wound of the day, the lieutenant colonel replacing him misunderstood Brigadier General Robert Rodes' order to withdraw the regiment's right wing from an exposed angle. Instead, he ordered the 6th Alabama to about face and forward march. Hearing this clear implication of retreat, the commander of the next regiment asking if it was meant for the whole brigade. He was assured it was, so all five of Rodes' regiments promptly scrambled out of the Sunken Road and ran for the rear. As a consequence, the entire center of Lee's line was shattered. A blue tide of Federals rushed across the Sunken Road into the Piper cornfield beyond. The breakthrough was clearly visible from Army of the Potomac headquarters at the Pry house. McClellan exclaimed as he viewed the blue wave surge forward, "By George, this is a magnificent field, and if we win this fight it will cover all our errors and misfortunes forever."

Praying for Nightfall

Confederate officers worked desperately to dam the break in the center of the line and to re-form broken units to meet Richardson's continuing assault. To gain time, they sent in counterattacks that were little more than forlorn hopes. During the hottest of the Sunken Road fighting, when George B. Anderson's brigade was being hard pressed, Longstreet had sought to relieve the pressure with an attack on the opposite Federal flank, held by French's division. With Colonel John R. Cooke of the 27th North Carolina in command, it was intended that the left wing in the Sunken Road, Robert Rodes' Alabamans, join the counterstroke, but by the time the advance was made, Rodes' line had collapsed. That left Cooke to make the assault with fewer than 1,000 men. The little force made a wide swing to the north of the Sunken Road and struck the II Corps' flank in Samuel Mumma's cornfield. There they got into a slugging match in the corn, with the battle line barely 200 yards apart. The Federals pushed in reinforcements and finally Cooke had to fall back to his starting point behind the Hagerstown turnpike. More than half his men were casualties.

Almost unnoticed during this new explosion of musketry was the collapse of the hard-won Union foothold at the Dunker church. For two hours George Greene had clung to this salient deep within the enemy lines; now, shortly after noon, he was driven out in a matter of minutes. Meanwhile, on the Piper farm behind the Sunken Road, D. H. Hill was also seeking to buy time with counterattacks. He and his officers rallied a mixed lot of troops and directed them against the II Corps' southern flank. The objects of the attack, the 5th New Hampshire, crouched among the heaped corpses in the Sunken Road to take the charge. The attackers came at them through the Piper cornfield shrilling the Rebel yell. The 81st Pennsylvania came up in support of their New Hampshire comrades, and finally the flank attack was repulsed. Soon afterward, D. H. Hill picked up a rifle and personally led 200 men in a second charge. Each of these doomed charges gained time for more Confederate guns to come up and form a second line behind the shattered front. After casualties and straggling, hardly 2,000 infantrymen remained to hold the Confederate center, and they were almost entirely without organization. But now there were twenty guns supporting them. In the face of their artillery fire Richardson's advance lost momentum and finally came to a halt. The men were fought out and short of ammunition. So Richardson pulled them back across the Sunken Road to the shelter of the ridgeline.

At the same time, on the Confederate right flank, the IX Corps also gained the upper hand. While waiting for some sign of progress from Rodman's flanking column Cox had organized a third assault on the Rohrbach Bridge. Two regiments were sent straight down the hillside facing the bridge, this time with more fire support from infantry and artillery. They were hardly halfway down the slope when Benning's Georgians met them with a savage fire, and the Federal company commanders saw that the column would never make it across the bridge in this one rush. In the meadow at the foot of the hill they turned the men off to the right and left along a stone wall along the river bank above the bridge and along a split-rail fence bordering the road downstream, there to engage the Georgians in heavy fire. Under the unceasing barrage, the Georgians' fire began to weaken. They had been holding this spot for three hours and their ammunition was running out. As they were seen leaving their line and running for the rear, a charge was ordered and the Yankees stormed across the span. It was 1:00 p.m. and the Rohrbach Bridge was finally, and literally, "Burnside's Bridge."

It was at 1:00 p.m., too, that Israel Richardson went down with a mortal wound from a Confederate artillery shell, and McClellan was confronted with a critical decision. There were ample numbers of both guns and men at hand with seven batteries of artillery a few hundred yards north of the Sunken Road, the divisions of Major Generals William F. Smith and Henry W. Slocum had arrived from Pleasant Valley and were on the field, and Fitz John Porter's V Corps had not been engaged in the morning's fighting. McClellan had 20,500 fresh troops to throw into the fight. He revealed his decision when he personally gave instructions to Richardson's replacement, Brigadier General Winfield Scott Hancock. Presently, Hancock galloped onto the battlefield at the head of his staff and rode the length of the Federal line facing the Sunken Road and cried out, "Now, men stay there until you are ordered away; this place must be held at all hazards!" General McClellan at this decisive moment was haunted by a fear of "a great defeat" at the hands of the Rebel host; as he said in a dispatch to General-in-Chief Halleck, "I have great odds against me." Following the rout of Sedgwick's division in the West Woods, his every action that day would be directed at saving the Army of the Potomac. He did not resume the offensive against the Confederate center. He would not initiate a new offensive anywhere on the field. No report of success, or the prospect of success, would persuade him to commit a single man for reinforcement. The situation at midday was a "remarkable case of a battle won without the victor's knowing it." McClellan sent a member of his staff to Burnside with positive orders to continue his advance (saying nothing about his having promised him reinforcements) and told the staff member that if he was not satisfied that his instructions to Burnside to advance would be carried out he was to deliver an order relieving Burnside of command. But Burnside was delayed by Brigadier General Orlando B. Willcox's division replacing that of Brigadier General Samuel Davis Sturgis, whose division had put forth the most effort storming the bridge, and by Brigadier General Rodman's flanking column having to be brought into position after its long detour. All in all, two hours passed before everything was ready. It was 3:00 p.m. when the IX Corps was ordered forward.

In those two hours after McClellan refused to resume the assault on the Confederate center, fighting on that front had died down to a scattering of rifle fire and random shelling. Major General Henry W. Slocum, totally demoralized by Sedgwick's defeat, refused to authorize an attack on the Confederate left in the West Woods, and McClellan refused to override his decision not to go on the offensive again.

The lull in the fighting was broken at 3:00 p.m. when the IX Corps at last moved forward. There were some 8,500 troops in the three attacking divisions. Thanks to the fumbling leadership at headquarters and in the IX Corps, this attack was beginning four or five hours late, but even so, four hours of daylight remained in which to drive the Army of Northern Virginia into final defeat. The plan worked out by Burnside and Cox was to attack in two parallel thrusts on a broad front three quarters of a mile across. But with the Rebel defenders making a stand at every fence line and farm building, the advance was slow and difficult. Rather than one great battle, it was a series of small, bitter struggles for possession of a stone wall and an apple orchard and a farmer's house and mill. Cavalryman Pleasonton crossed the Middle Bridge and detected what he termed "the embarrassing condition of the enemy" defending Sharpsburg and sent back a request for more of Porter's corps to exploit the opening. Instead, the regulars were recalled to their station guarding the guns at the Middle Bridge and told to stay there. Word came from headquarters that McClellan "has no infantry to spare for this sector." The IX Corps would make its fight unsupported by the rest of the army. At a ridgeline south of Sharpsburg a major confrontation took place with the opposing lines too close for the Confederate artillery to fire without fear of hitting their own men, and the guns fell silent. When the two lines of infantry were fifty yards apart they opened fire, and at this pointblank range—a rarity on most Civil War fields but a grim commonplace at Antietam—men went down by the score. The Yankees and Rebels came together in a brief flurry of hand-to-hand combat, then the outmanned Confederates broke and ran for the rear.

The collapse of this line put the entire Confederate right flank in immediate danger of final collapse. Retreating troops and batteries crowded into Sharpsburg's narrow streets, pursued by Union shell fire that smashed through houses and splintered storefronts. The Federal infantry crowded closer, with their skirmishers dodging among the houses on the outskirts of town. Lee was on the scene, ordering up every artillery piece still serviceable to throw against the attackers. He then rode to a commanding knoll outside of town for a better view of the situation. Off to the south he could make out a column of troops. He called on a passing artillery officer for his telescope. Lee's hands were bandaged from a fall some days earlier and he could not use the glass, but he told the officer to focus on the distant column. "What troops are those?" he asked. After a moment came the answer: "They are flying the Virginia and Confederate flags." As if he had expected no other answer, Lee remarked calmly, "It is A. P. Hill from Harper's Ferry." Something over two days after taking his stand at Sharpsburg, his army was finally united. Hill was coming on the battlefield at precisely the right place—and at the last possible moment.

"This Is the Battle of the War"

A. P. Hill left Harper's Ferry the morning of the 17th with 3,300 men, but straggling on the hard march and the delayed arrival of his trailing brigades cut the number he actually put into action to about 2,000. Yet their impact was multiplied by the elements of position and surprise. That Hill reached the battlefield undetected was the direct consequence of McClellan's mishandling of his cavalry. It was one of the most basic rules of war to post cavalry on an army's flanks to guard against sudden and unexpected attacks. Even this lapse might have been of less consequence had General Couch marched his VI Corps division from Pleasant Valley to Burnside's front with even a fraction of the energy A. P. Hill displayed. Instead, Hill was spared a fight with Couch's veterans and encountered the wide open and poorly-manned left flank of the IX Corps.

The 8th Connecticut Regiment was pushing on in a bold dash at a Rebel battery near the Harper's Ferry road and in the process of capturing it when it was hit front and flank by a vicious counterattack that killed or wounded half the regiment and drove the rest out of the fight. The raw 16th Connecticut a half mile to the rear in the cornfield of John Otto was hit by surprise volleys from two directions by the lead brigade from Hill's division. The attack threw the green troops into a panic. They tried to return fire, but they had loaded their rifles for the first time only the day before, and in the excitement many forgot the complicated procedures. The regiment's organization collapsed in a moment. From their high ground the South Carolinians under Brigadier General Maxcy Gregg poured an equally destructive fire into the 4th Rhode Island. In the meantime Gregg worked his men around to the Yankees' flank, and their line began to unravel. Just then the Connecticut men broke in complete rout, carrying the Rhode Islanders with them. It was nearly 4:30 p.m., and the entire left flank of the IX Corps was swept away.

A. P. Hill's successful counterattack left the Federal forces that had reached as far as the outskirts of Sharpsburg in sudden isolation. With no support from the V Corps on the right, both their flanks were wide open, so Cox ordered them to pull back. They went back cursing, furious at having to give up such hard-won gains. Lee had supplemented the divisional batteries of A. P. Hill and Brigadier General David R. Jones with guns scavenged in ones and twos from battlescarred batteries involved in earlier fighting north of Sharpsburg. As Hill's counterstroke picked up momentum it was supported by forty-three fieldpieces collected from no fewer than fifteen batteries. Against their fire the Federal artillery west of the creek was badly outgunned and forced to withdraw. General Cox was now working desperately to assemble a last-ditch line to hold the Burnside Bridge crossing. Meanwhile McClellan was viewing the decaying situation on the Federal left but refused to send to Burnside's relief Fitz John Porter's V Corps held in reserve. As the sky began to darken, McClellan told the courier who had come from Burnside to request more men and guns to hold his position, "Tell General Burnside this is the battle of the war. He must hold his ground till dark at any cost. I will send him Miller's battery. I can do nothing more. I have no infantry."

On that note of melodrama for all practical purposes the Battle of Antietam came to an end. The IX corps would finally hold the Burnside Bridge on its own; the Confederates on this part of the field were simply too few to drive them into the Antietam, although in the day's fighting they inflicted 2,350 casualties on the Federals at a cost to themselves of barely a thousand. The stalemate continued on the northern part of the field as well. The sun, glowing blood-red in the smoky twilight, went down and as the light faded the battlefield quieted.

By the best estimate, casualties in the Army of Northern Virginia on September 17 came to 1,546 dead, 7,752 wounded, and 1,018 missing, for a total of 10,316. General Lee would say shortly after the battle that had put no more than 35,000 men into action. The count on the Union side came to 2,108 dead, 9,540 wounded, and 753 missing, a total of 12,401. Ninety-six percent of that toll came in four army corps—I, II, IX, XII. Of McClellan's 75,000 effectives, fully a third did not fire a shot that day. The casualties on the two sides, inflicted in those fourteen hours of daylight, totalled 22,719. The Civil War would have many terrible days, but none more terrible than this. The figures have an even darker dimension. It is certain that of the 1,771 marked down as missing, a great many were in fact dead, buried in unrecorded graves. It is possible that the actual count of the dead was many hundreds greater than the 3,654 listed.

And so it happened. There was a truce on September 18 to bury the dead and collect the wounded. The day passed peacefully, and that night the Army of Northern Virginia withdrew unchallenged across the Potomac and into the Shenandoah Valley. Limited attempts were made on September 19 to attack the withdrawing Confederates, but these proved futile. Of all the Civil War battles General Lee fought, it was said, he took the most pride in the contest at Sharpsburg. At no other time did he face longer odds or greater risks, yet at the end of the day his lines were unbroken and he had inflicted one-fifth more casualties than he suffered. In that narrow sense he could claim a tactical victory, and in defiantly facing down his opponent on September 18, he could perhaps claim a moral victory as well. McClellan's contemporaries, by contrast, were highly critical of virtually every aspect of his conduct of the battle. His refusal to fight on September 18 drew particular censure. But McClellan would take a pride in Antietam equal to Lee's. As he saw it, his great achievement on September 17 was to stave off defeat against great odds and thus preserve his country by preserving its principal army. He had no intention on September 18 of running that risk a second time. That Antietam was a unique opportunity to gain a truly decisive victory—a victory his army repeatedly very nearly won in spite of him—was something he would not, and perhaps could not, acknowledge.

If Antietam was not as decisive a battle as it might have been, it proved to be a decisive event. Lee's gamble for a major victory on Northern soil had failed. That was sufficient cause for President Lincoln to feel his position was at last strong enough to announce his policy of emancipation. Emancipation, in turn, made it impossible for any European nation to intervene in America's war; no power dared recognize the Confederacy now that it was clear the South stood for slavery and the North for freedom. Antietam thus changed the war's course, linking the abolition of slavery with the preservation of the Union as Northern war aims. That was a turning point of incalculable importance and a fitting enough consequence of what one soldier described as "a great enormous battle, a great tumbling together of all heaven and earth. . . ."

V

The Civil War, 1863–1865

Shutting the Gates of Mercy: The American Origins of Total War, 1860–1880

Lance Janda

In this extended essay the author contends that the Civil War introduced the tactic of "total war," that is, war not only against enemy combatants but also against the civilian population that sustains them. As he argues, this outlook on warfare grew out of the stubborn resistance and tactics of the Confederates and their supporters, thereby convincing Ulysses S. Grant, William T. Sherman, Philip Sheridan, and even "old school" Henry Halleck that such measures were necessary to break the will of the South and preserve the Union. Further, Janda, of Cameron University, argues that these tactics were subsequently applied in the Army's campaigns against the Native Americans. This article was first published in The Journal of Military History *(59/1 [Jan. 1995], 7–26) and is reprinted with permission.*

To robbery, slaughter, plunder they give the lying name of empire; they make a desert and call it peace.

—Cornelius Tacitus (c. 55–117 A.D.)

Library shelves groan with works pointing to the Civil War as a harbinger of "total war" in its modern form, a kind of macabre prelude to the world wars of the twentieth century. And if total war refers to technology, they seem to be correct, as the Civil War represents the first mass conflict of the industrial age.

Union and Confederate forces became dependent on modern implements like railroads, the telegraph, armored battleships, repeating rifles, and mass-produced weapons and uniforms.

In a more profound way, however, the real significance of the Civil War lies in its tactics, not its technology. The weaponry of total warfare did not originate in the Civil War, and it came to maturity only on the Western Front in Europe in 1914. But if "total war" is defined as using "military force against the civilian population of the enemy," then the Civil War stands as a watershed in the American evolution of total war theory. The application of force against an enemy's noncombatants and resources, the central tenet of total war, had been used since the dawn of civilization when it suited political and military ends. But Union Army commanders were the first in American history to use these tactics on a widespread scale, and they played a crucial role not only in the subjugation of the South, but in the conquest of Native Americans as well. A doctrine that was anathema in 1860 emerged from the Civil War as the weapon of choice on the frontier, and by 1880 total war theory dominated the mainstream of American military thought.

To early Civil War leaders, these destructive tactics seemed revolutionary, for they contradicted codes of behavior developed during the Enlightenment; codes which attempted to spare civilians the travesties of war. Northern commanders, however, faced with a defiance unprecedented in American history, turned to total war because no other strategy held the promise of ultimate victory. As one pillaging soldier explained in South Carolina: "Here is where treason began, and, by God, here is where it shall end!" Union generals did not invent the tactics or the rationale behind total war; these had been present for centuries. But they did rediscover them in their own time, and lent to them vigorous prosecution and eloquent justification. They shaped, and were shaped by these methods, which came to dominate the American practice of war throughout the late 1800s.

Yet historians have devoted little attention to the continuity in tactics and strategy between the Civil War and the frontier wars with Native Americans. Survey histories of "total" or "modern" war theory usually focus on the twentieth century, or connect the Civil War with the Franco-Prussian conflict and World War I. And works on Native American or Civil War campaigns often ascribe to their subjects a uniqueness which allows no comparison. Only a handful recognize that the similarity between methods used to defeat the South and those used against Native Americans was no accident; that Army leaders took lessons from the Civil War and applied them to the frontier. And because even that small body of literature probes the connection only superficially, a deeper understanding of those "lessons," and their application on the frontier is required.

I

The nineteenth-century origins and applications of total war theory began with the Union Army and the trinity of generals who led the North to victory during the Civil War. Ulysses S. Grant, William T. Sherman, and Philip H. Sheridan were not only fervent and eloquent advocates of total war, they were among the most successful commanders of their generation. As victors they defined American military thought and policy for the rest of the century, and each played a key role in the Indian wars from 1865 to 1880, when the refined tactics of total war reached their nineteenth-century zenith. Their careers illustrate the evolution of total war in American military thought, from birth in the Civil War to late nineteenth-century dénouement.

Grant, Sherman, and Sheridan received their formal military training at the United States Military Academy. Although it might seem reasonable to assume the seeds of total war theory were planted during their days at West Point, such was not the case. Instead, their curriculum focused on the study of engineering and fortifications rather than grand strategy or tactics, and reflected Superintendent Sylvanus Thayer's belief that West Point would flourish only if cadets were trained to be useful in nonmilitary ways.

Further, that portion of the curriculum which did focus on the art of war generally mirrored European philosophies and made no allowance for wars against the resources or civilian population of an enemy. Certainly attacks on resources were implicit objectives of naval blockades and sieges, for they represented an indirect way of defeating an opposing army. Starving an enemy army of supplies, however, was altogether different from starving civilians, and the restraints that eighteenth- and early nineteenth-century states placed on their armies were reflected at West Point.

European leaders had concluded that warfare against noncombatants was morally and ethically wrong. This view was shared by American military thinkers, who announced in the Articles of War of 1806: "Any officer or soldier who shall quit his post or colors to plunder and pillage shall suffer death or other such punishment as shall be ordered by sentence of a general court martial." U.S. Army officers adhered to this philosophy, at least in principle, until the early 1860s. Even as late as April of 1863, the Union Army issued General Order One Hundred, which specifically upheld the notion of sparing civilians the devastation of war. Article Twenty-Two of that order stated:

> as civilization has advanced during the last centuries, so has likewise steadily advanced, especially in war on land, the distinction between the private individual belonging to a hostile country and the hostile country itself, with its men in arms. The principle has been more and more acknowledged that the

unarmed citizen is to be spared in person, property, and honor as much as the exigencies of war will admit.

There was no inkling of the wholesale destruction that was to follow; indeed, there was dedicated resolution to avoid it.

Some authors argue that the teachings of Dennis Hart Mahan contained early references to total war and represented a departure from orthodox nineteenth-century theories. Mahan joined the West Point faculty in 1832. A Thayer protégé and an outstanding instructor, he was the primary teacher of engineering and warfare for cadets. Mahan wrote the standard text used in his classes and included a summary of the strategic ideas of Antoine Henri, Baron de Jomini. Although Mahan differed in many instances with Jomini's teachings, the latter was considered the leading interpreter of Napoleonic warfare and studied by all fourth-year cadets.

Yet Jomini never advocated total war as Grant, Sherman, and Sheridan would later define it in practice. He was conservative, emphasized fortifications, and "abhorred indiscriminate bloodshed." Jomini even disapproved of "armies living off the country through which they marched," a tactic that became standard practice during the latter stages of the Civil War. And though Mahan argued that "carrying the war into the heart of the assailants' country" was critical, there is sparse evidence he ever conceived of systematic warfare against civilians.

Even during Mahan's tenure, West Point continued virtually to ignore the serious study of warfare by cadets. Few tactics were learned, and drill was kept at a minimum; instructors taught just enough so that cadets could maneuver on the parade ground. The emphasis instead was on mathematics, engineering, and science, with the formal study of tactics and strategy relegated to curricular insignificance. Mahan's lectures on warfare were crammed within a course on fortifications, which was offered only to seniors and lasted less than a semester. Finally, very few of the principal actors of the Civil War even mentioned Mahan in their memoirs or letters, and none credited him with sparking their notions of total war. There is little reason, therefore, to believe he played any sort of significant role in their embrace of total war concepts.

The American reluctance to involve noncombatants was clearly outlined by Henry Wager Halleck, who went on to become Chief of Staff during the Civil War. A Mahan disciple, Halleck published a number of works during the 1840s which rehashed Jomini and emphasized fortifications. More importantly, he shrank from the idea of armies living off the land or waging war on the general population. Halleck carried these views into his role as Chief of Staff, and they were shared by officers throughout the Union Army. Grant, Sherman, and Sheridan found their inspiration elsewhere.

II

Ultimately, that inspiration stemmed from the nature of the Civil War itself. Bringing the Southern states back into the Union required the complete subjugation of the Confederate people, a fact which Union officers were slow to recognize. There could be no limited peace, no negotiated settlement if the Confederacy had to accept the supremacy of the U.S. Constitution. As nineteenth-century historian Adam Badeau wrote: "It was not victory that either side was playing for, but for existence. If the rebels won, they destroyed a nation; if the government succeeded, it annihilated a rebellion."

Such annihilation required offensive warfare, which was hampered in the early years by ferocious guerrilla activity behind the lines. Guerrillas disrupted Northern supply lines and communications, requiring inordinate numbers of Union troops to be garrisoned in rear areas. Union commanders needed a two-fold strategy to carry the war into Dixie: one that freed them from vulnerable supply lines and which promised to shorten the war by breaking the will of the Southern people. In the early months of fighting, they had none.

Among the first Northern commanders to find his preconceptions of warfare inadequate was John Pope, an early commander of the Union Army of the Potomac. Frustrated by guerrillas who harassed his supply lines, Pope asked President Lincoln in 1862 for limited permission to begin living off the land. Lincoln, also tiring of conciliation and mildness towards the Southern people, authorized Pope to requisition livestock and foodstuffs from civilians. This was mild retribution, however, lasting only a few weeks before Pope was replaced by George B. McClellan.

The Army of the Potomac's new commander frowned upon any kind of warfare directed at civilians. McClellan summed up his views while apologizing to a Virginia gentleman for destruction caused by the Union Army in 1862: "I have not come here to wage war upon the defenseless, upon non-combatants, upon private property, nor upon the domestic institutions of the land."

Yet while McClellan clung tenaciously to the past, U. S. Grant waged the war of the future in Tennessee and Mississippi, quickly abandoning archaic notions of warfare which seemed at variance with reality. After the war, Grant wrote that his views radically changed after witnessing tenacious Southern resistance at the battle of Shiloh, 6–7 April 1862.

> I gave up all idea of saving the Union except by complete conquest. Up to that time it had been the policy of our army, certainly of that portion commanded by me, to protect the property of the citizens whose territory was invaded, without regard to their sentiments, whether Union or Secession. After this, however, I regarded it as humane to both sides to protect the persons of those found at their homes, but to consume everything that could be used to support or supply armies.

Grant's views on total war began to change after he gauged the depth of Southern resolve and found it so stalwart that new means would be necessary to ensure victory. Grant continued to evolve these ideas, molding them to fit circumstances even during his tenure as Commanding General of the Union Army.

The key, as Grant saw it, was that the destruction of enemy supplies "tended to the same result as the destruction of armies," and he continued the policy throughout the war. It was a policy born of the necessity to completely subjugate an entire people, something no American army had previously been asked to do. Grant correctly saw that no contemporary doctrine answered the question of how to force millions of people, both civilian and military, into submission; yet that was what he and other Union leaders were required to accomplish. His solution was to wage war on resources, molding European tactics to fit American tasks.

These tactics allowed greater freedom of maneuver than ever before, as Grant would demonstrate in the brilliant campaign against Vicksburg. From the first to the nineteenth of May 1863, forces under Grant's command marched 180 miles, fought in five major engagements, split the Confederate forces opposing them, and laid siege to the city of Vicksburg, whose fall in July would signal the end of serious Southern opposition along the Mississippi. The pillar of his campaign was the decision to cut loose from his base of supplies and live off the land, practicing total war against the civilians of the South.

In later orders to subordinates Sherman and Sheridan, Grant would demonstrate his commitment to even harsher forms of warfare. Sherman was to "get into the interior of the enemy's country as far as you can, inflicting all the damage you can upon their war resources." And prior to unleashing Sheridan's juggernaut upon the Shenandoah Valley in 1864, Grant declared, "If the war is to last another year, we want the Shenandoah Valley to remain a barren waste."

If the blast furnace of war produced a Grant cleansed of restraint, it also kindled the righteous fury of William Tecumseh Sherman, whose name would become synonymous with destruction throughout the South. His famous March to the Sea and the March through the Carolinas have become infamous through tales of wanton and complete destruction. These legends have much basis in fact, though ironically Sherman began the Civil War convinced of the need for law and order. His transformation in 1862 was similar to Grant's, as he explained to a friend in 1864.

> I would not let our men burn fence rails for fire or gather fruit or vegetables though hungry. . . . We at that time were restrained, tied by a deep-seated reverence for law and property. The rebels first introduced terror as part of their system. . . . Buell had to move at a snail's pace with his vast wagon trains . . . Bragg moved rapidly, living on the country. No military mind could endure this long, and we were forced in self-defense to imitate their example.

Sherman thus argued that the switch to more brutal warfare came out of military necessity; defeating the South required imitating their tactics. Coupled with Grant's focus on guerrillas, which Sherman soon came to share, these ideas were rooted in the belief that Southern forces brought war and vengeance upon themselves. This became a theme throughout Sherman's writings, and it echoed a belief shared by much of the Union Army. He wrote:

> I know that in the beginning, I, too, had the old West Point notion that pillage was a capital crime, and punished it by shooting. . . . This was a one sided game of war, and many of us . . . ceased to quarrel with our own men about such minor things, and went in to subdue the enemy, leaving minor depredations to be charged up to the account of the rebels who had forced us into the war, and who deserved all they got and more.

This idea that the Southern people deserved their fate was of crucial importance to Northern commanders, especially Sherman. The notion that there were no noncombatants in the South, that every man, woman, and child contributed to the prolonging of the war, made it easier to justify attacks on civilians. As he wrote: "we are not only fighting hostile armies, but a hostile people, and we must make old and young, rich and poor, feel the hard hand of war, as well as the organized armies."

By the fall of 1864 Sherman also shared Grant's alarm at the destruction caused by rebel guerrillas, and was reluctant to show mercy towards a Southern population which displayed few signs of weakening. He wrote in his memoirs that garrisoning captured Southern cities was "crippling our armies in the field by detachments to guard and protect the interest of a hostile population." Guerrilla warfare and the collective responsibility of the South were inextricably linked in the Northern rationale for total war.

Sherman went even further, arguing that without popular support Southern armies would collapse not just from want of supplies, but from want of spirit. His marches became "campaigns of terror and destruction," aimed at defeating the South psychologically as well as militarily. To avoid garrisoning the city of Atlanta, for example, Sherman ordered the entire civilian population evacuated and set fire to warehouses, railroads, factories, and foodstuffs. He later explained: "I knew that the people of the South would read in this measure two important conclusions: one, that we were in earnest; and the other, if they were sincere in their common and popular clamor to 'die in the last ditch,' that the opportunity would soon come." This war against the hearts and minds of the Southern people had enormous importance for Sherman. In messages pleading with Grant for permission to march from Atlanta to the sea, he maintained that such a demonstration of Northern power constituted "statesmanship," because it would lead inexorably to the deterioration of Southern morale. Failing that, Sherman was eager to teach the people of the South a lesson in the horrors of war, believing that a harsh war would ensure a lasting peace. He wished to "make them so sick of war that generations would pass away before they would again appeal to it."

Sherman never doubted his conviction that responsibility for the war, as well as the power to end it, lay solely with the South. "If they want peace," he stated, "they and their relatives must stop the war." This belief carried with it the knowledge that his armies left desolation and despair in their wake, but always he returned to the notion of responsibility. In a letter to the citizens of Atlanta he declared: "Now that the war comes home to you, you feel very different. You deprecate its horrors, but did not feel them when you sent car-loads of soldiers and ammunition . . . to carry war into Kentucky and Tennessee." By this juncture, Sherman had resigned himself to the necessities of total war. "You cannot qualify war in harsher terms than I will," he wrote in the same letter. "War is cruelty and you cannot refine it."

Savannah fell in December of 1864, in time for Sherman to present the city to Lincoln as a Christmas present. On 1 February of the following year, he turned northward for an even more destructive assault on the Carolinas. Aware of his army's unique hatred for the state where secession began, Sherman dreaded unleashing his legions upon South Carolina. As he wrote: "the whole army is burning with an insatiable desire to wreak vengeance upon South Carolina. I almost tremble at her fate, but feel that she deserves all that seems in store for her." The march was as terrible as Sherman anticipated, climaxing with the infamous burning of Columbia only weeks before the end of the war. In his writings Sherman again noted the three tenets of his philosophy of total war. The first was military necessity, for he believed that destruction of civilian property and supplies shortened the war by depriving Southern armies of material support. Closely related was the notion of psychological warfare, depriving the Southern people of their spirit, and dousing their enthusiasm for war. Finally, there was the idea of collective responsibility, the belief that whatever happened, the South deserved it. For Sherman, defeating the Confederate Army and its leaders was not enough; every person in the South was seen as part of the war effort, and only total war held the prospect of defeating them all.

Just as Sherman came to share Grant's concept of total war, so did Philip Sheridan. After the Civil War Sheridan would put these lessons to use in the Indian campaigns of 1868 to 1883, sealing the fate of America's native population on the frontier. Unlike Sherman and Grant, Sheridan never clearly spelled out the origins of his belief in total war. He did, however, serve with Grant from 1863 to 1865, first in Tennessee, and eventually as cavalry commander of the Army of the Potomac. It seems reasonable to conclude that Sheridan, much like Sherman, came to share Grant's conviction that breaking the Southern people required the abandonment of more established forms of warfare. He eagerly embraced the new ideas: "I do not hold war to mean simply that lines of men shall engage each other in battle. This is but a duel, in which one combatant seeks the other's life; war means much more, and is far worse than this." His experience convinced him that "reduction to poverty brings prayers for peace more surely and more quickly than does the destruction of human life."

Such views were well suited to the kind of destructive warfare envisioned by Grant when he ordered Sheridan into the Shenandoah Valley in the fall of 1864. Charged with turning the Shenandoah into a "barren waste" to deny Confederate armies a major source of supplies, Sheridan destroyed everything of military value. On 7 October, he proudly informed Grant:

> I have destroyed over 2,000 barns filled with wheat, hay, farming implements; over seventy mills filled with flour and wheat; have driven in front of the army over 4,000 head of stock, and have killed and issued to the troops not less than 3,000 sheep. . . . the Valley, from Winchester up to Staunton, ninety two miles, will have but little in it for man or beast.

Confidently, Sheridan later notified Grant that "I will soon commence on Loudoun County, and let them know there is a God in Israel." In this, his first independent Army command of the war, Sheridan showed a penchant for total war that would become his trademark during the Indian wars of the latter half of the nineteenth century.

Grant, Sherman, and Sheridan were far from alone in their enthusiasm for total war. In his own way even Chief of Staff Halleck approved, discarding the staunch disapproval of total war he learned from Mahan at West Point. In a book written before the Civil War, Halleck denounced the practice of living off the land, declaring: "The inevitable consequences of this system are universal pillage and a total relaxation of discipline . . . and the ordinary peaceful and noncombatant inhabitants are converted into bitter and implacable enemies."

By 1864, however, Halleck had joined the righteous clamor for total war, especially for vengeance against the South. In a letter to Sherman, who was campaigning in Georgia, Halleck outlined his wrathful suggestions for Southern noncombatants.

> Let the disloyal families of the country, thus stripped, go to their husbands, fathers, and natural protectors, in the rebel ranks; we have tried three years of conciliation and kindness without any reciprocation; on the contrary, those thus treated have acted as spies and guerrillas in our rear and within our lines. . . . I would destroy every mill and factory within reach which I did not want for my own use.

When Sherman's forces reached the Carolinas, and appeared headed for the city of Charleston, Halleck was even more specific. "Should you capture Charleston, I hope that by some accident the place may be destroyed, and if a little salt should be sown upon its site it may prevent the growth of future crops of nullification and secession."

Halleck's transformation to a hesitant Cato the Elder resonated with the depth of commitment found among the more ordinary members of Sherman's army. The enlisted men called Sherman "Uncle Billy," and they enthusiastically agreed with the necessity of a war against resources and civilians. Most noncombatants escaped with their lives, but with little else. And for many soldiers, the march through Georgia was a gigantic pleasure excursion. As one Union soldier wrote: "we had a gay old campaign. . . . Destroyed all we could not eat, stole their niggers, burned their cotton and gins, spilled their sorghum, burned and twisted their R. Roads and raised Hell generally."

But to say that many Union soldiers enjoyed their rampage is not to suggest the destruction lacked military value. Atrocities and outrages certainly occurred, but for Sherman and his men only a thin line separated these excesses from the destruction needed to bring an end to the war. Even an Alabama-born major attached to Sherman's staff came to believe the whirlwind of devastation was vital, even merciful, because it aimed at shortening the war. He wrote in his diary:

> It is a terrible thing to consume and destroy the sustenance of thousands of people . . . while I deplore this necessity daily and cannot bear to see the soldiers swarm as they do through fields and yards . . . nothing can end this war but some demonstration of their helplessness. . . . This Union and its Government must be sustained, at any and every cost; to sustain it, we must war upon and destroy the organized rebel forces, must cut off their supplies, destroy their communications . . . produce among the people of Georgia a thorough conviction of the personal misery which attends war, and the utter helplessness and inability of their "rulers," State or Confederate, to protect them. . . . If that terror and grief and even want shall help to paralyze their husbands and fathers who are fighting us . . . it is mercy in the end.

The crushing effect of this campaign on the morale of Southern soldiers was summed up eloquently, even sadly, in the almost illiterate prose of a Confederate private.

> i hev conkluded that the dam fulishness uv tryin to lick shurmin Had better be stoped. we hav bin gettin nuthin but hell & lots uv it ever sinse we saw the dam yankys & I am tirde uv it. . . . Thair thicker an lise on a hen and a dam site ornraier.

Sherman's engine of destruction was having the desired effect on Southern spirits, though it created animosity and bitterness among the people of the South for generations. Yet Grant, Sherman, and Sheridan consistently argued that total war was necessary to bring about an early end to the war, and the tactics of terror were forced on the Union by the ferocity of Southern resistance. The destruction, they contended, seemed poetic justice for a people who brought war on themselves. This entry of total war into the mainstream of American military thought was evident in the *United States Service Magazine* in 1865:

> It will be different when it is realized that to break up the rebel armies is not going to bring peace, that the people must be influenced. . . . They must feel the effects of war. . . . They must feel its inexorable necessities before they can realize the pleasures and amenities of peace.

By the time of Lee's surrender at Appomattox, an entire generation of Army officers had been exposed to the philosophy of total war. It was this generation that would battle Native Americans in the decades to come, and it is no accident that with Grant as their Commander in Chief, Sherman as General of the Army, and Sheridan in command of the frontier, they would use the same terrifying tactics to achieve the same devastating results.

III

In the years following the Civil War, U. S. Grant became president, and Sherman rose to command the entire American army. Removed from the field by the demands of Washington, Sherman passed the torch to Sheridan, who from 1867 to 1883 took the lessons of total war and applied them to the frontier. The forces under his command fought over 619 engagements, completing the conquest of the American West from its native population.

Sheridan's odyssey in the west, and his refinement of the tactics of total war to suit the frontier, began in 1867 when he assumed command of the Department of the Missouri. Composed of Missouri, Kansas, Indian Territory, and the territories of Colorado and New Mexico, Sheridan's new command was garrisoned by only 6,000 men. This minuscule force reflected the astonishing reduction of the American army in the aftermath of the Civil War; from 1869 until the war with Spain in 1898, total strength averaged no more than 25,000. Sheridan would later write that "no army in modern times has had such an amount of work put upon the same number of men."

The army was responsible for protecting freedmen and preserving law and order in the South, as well as garrisoning frontier forts, defending the railroads, and escorting settlers on their treks westward. The acute shortage of men helped shape Sheridan's tactics during the Indian wars, for it was vital that campaigns end swiftly and decisively. To achieve total victory in short periods of time Sheridan waged war on resources, by striking in winter when Indians were most vulnerable. He drew on Civil War experiences to justify his actions, as he explained in an 1873 letter to Sherman:

> In taking the offensive, I have to select that season when I can catch the fiends; and, if a village is attacked and women and children killed, the responsibility is not with the soldiers but with the people whose crimes necessitated the attack. During the war did any one hesitate to attack a village or town occupied by the

enemy because women or children were within its limits? Did we cease to throw shells into Vicksburg or Atlanta because women and children were there?

Sheridan was hardly the first to launch winter attacks on the frontier. Christopher "Kit" Carson and Patrick Connor conducted similar campaigns against the Navajo and Shoshonis in 1863 and 1864, and General John Sullivan used assaults on resources as part of his Revolutionary War battles with the Iroquois. But there is little evidence Sherman or Sheridan drew exclusively on those experiences after the Civil War. They relied primarily on their wartime experience to serve as a guide for future frontier wars, and no doubt agreed with Carson and Connor's methods because they reinforced total war concepts conceived in the South. As Robert Utley wrote, "Sherman and Sheridan were of a single mind on strategy. Atlanta and the Shenandoah Valley furnished the precedents." Sherman and Sheridan also expanded the aim of total war by fighting for strategic victory rather than simple tactical advantage. Their system of war aimed at subjugating entire races of people. Earlier generals often attacked resources inconsistently and only as a means of defeating Native Americans in the field and pushing them westward, not as a means of subjugation on the Civil War model.

Ironically, the Civil War was generally a poor model for fighting on the frontier. Ponderous supply lines and slow-moving columns were both vulnerable to attack and easy to avoid, but most officers were unwilling to challenge tactics that had been so successful against the South. They reflected the mind-set at West Point and among senior commanders, who were concerned with future wars against conventional foreign armies, not with counter-guerrilla warfare in the west. And though there were exceptions like George Crook and Nelson Miles who threw away the book and fought Native Americans on their own terms, Army doctrine did not change. Sherman and Sheridan remained unrepentant advocates of total war, which alone among Civil War lessons proved extraordinarily successful on the frontier.

Just as in the South, responsibility was placed on the shoulders of noncombatants, who presumably deserved their fate for supporting enemies of the army. Sheridan's case was less than plausible in the Indian wars, where the army rather than the enemy was often the aggressor. The general realized this, writing to the War Department in 1878 that: "we took away their country and their means of support, broke up their mode of living, their habits of life, introduced disease and decay among them, and it was for this and against this they made war. Could any one expect less?"

Yet these inner notions did not deter Sheridan from waging relentless and aggressive campaigns against Native Americans. In the fall of 1868 it was the Southern Cheyenne, Arapaho, Kiowa, and Comanches who fell victim to winter attacks, in campaigns throughout northern Texas and the western portions of Indian Territory.

In 1869 Sheridan was elevated to command of the Division of the Missouri, an enormous expanse of American territory stretching from Chicago to western Montana, and from Canada to the Texas border. Within the over one million square miles under his command lived most of the native population of North America: Sioux, Northern and Southern Cheyenne, Kiowas, Comanches, Arapahos, Utes, Apaches, and many others. No precise figures for their population can ever be known, though the estimate in 1882 was approximately 175,000.

To these tribes Sheridan brought the same kind of ferocious attacks that had proven successful in earlier campaigns. Writing to Ranald S. Mackenzie prior to launching a campaign against the Kickapoo in 1873, Sheridan ordered: "I want you to be bold, enterprising, and at all times full of energy, when you begin, let it be a campaign of annihilation, obliteration, and complete destruction." That these tactics were supported by his superiors, Grant and Sherman, was never in doubt. Responding to an increase in the number of attacks on emigrant wagon trains in 1868, Grant vowed to protect settlers, "even if the extermination of every Indian tribe was necessary to secure such a result." And in response to the Fetterman massacre of 21 December 1866, in which eighty soldiers were killed by Sioux along the Bozeman Trail, Sherman proclaimed: "We must act with vindictive earnestness against the Sioux, even to their extermination, men, women, and children." Despite the ferocity of their language, it is unlikely that Grant, Sherman, or Sheridan ever intended extermination. Theirs was rhetoric meant for consumption by a public terrified by images of bloodthirsty attacks on settlers. But it is clear they were determined to act decisively, and Sheridan's assaults on Indian resources promised success.

The key to this success was the high vulnerability of Native-American families and their resources. To a much greater degree than the Confederate Army, Native-American raiding parties depended on tenuous sources of supplies. In warm months their superior mobility and knowledge of the terrain made them almost impervious to attack. But in winter their custom was to pitch camp and wait for spring, and Sheridan found these stationary camps to be easy targets. Winter attacks destroyed shelter and foodstuffs, forcing Native Americans to surrender or attempt escape through the snow, where most died of starvation and exposure. This was true of war ponies as well. Their destruction eliminated mobility for those warriors that survived until spring, and without mobility they were doomed.

Despite the success of these tactics, other nations ignored the American example, believing it to be isolated and too rare for general instruction. Yet Sheridan was convinced. During the Franco-Prussian War of 1870 he accompanied the Prussian Army as an observer, and was amazed at the limited attacks made on civilians and resources. In a conversation with Bismarck while Paris lay under siege, Sheridan summed up his philosophy of war by declaring: "The proper strategy consists in the first place in inflicting as telling blows as possible upon the enemy's army, and then causing the inhabitants so much suffering that they must long for peace, and force their government to demand it. The people must be left nothing but their eyes to weep with over the war."

Upon his return to America Sheridan had ample opportunity to put these ideas into practice, fighting a number of wars designed to keep the Indians on closely guarded reservations. In the Red River War of 1874–75, he returned to winter attacks in ruthless campaigns against the Southern Cheyenne, who were further weakened by disintegration of the great southern buffalo herd. Indeed, elimination of the buffalo became economic warfare of the first order, and Sheridan actively encouraged their extermination. When the Texas state legislature was considering a bill to protect buffalo in 1875, he portrayed bison hunters as vital components of the war against Native Americans:

> These men have done in the last two years, and will do more in the next years, to settle the vexed Indian question, than the entire regular army has done in the last thirty years. . . . They are destroying the Indians' commissary; and it is a well known fact that an army losing its base of supplies is placed at a great disadvantage. Send them powder and lead, if you will; but for the sake of a lasting peace, let them kill, skin, and sell until the buffaloes are exterminated.

As the last of the southern herd vanished, Sheridan turned to the great northern herd, writing to the Adjutant General in 1881:

> If I could learn that every buffalo in the northern herd were killed I would be glad. . . . The destruction of this herd would do more to keep Indians quiet than anything else that could happen.

Though a handful of buffalo were saved, Sheridan was proven correct. From his military perspective, buffalo were only an economic resource of the Plains Indians, one that played a role of critical importance in their way of life. In that sense, they were no different than railroads or foodstuffs in the Shenandoah in 1864; their elimination promised an end to the fighting. The slaughter of buffalo helped settle the "vexed Indian question," and the "domination and thorough destruction of a flowered culture" was complete.

The defeat of the northern Plains Indians in 1876–77, and the annihilation of the buffalo, ended serious resistance on the frontier. There were trials in 1877 with the Nez Perce and in the 1880s with the Apache, but the outcome of these duels remained a foregone conclusion. Given superior resources, and ultimately superior tactics, the army was bound to prevail. That it succeeded with so small a force in so short a time was due to Sheridan's relentless energy and commitment to total war. As Oglala Sioux holy man Black Elk sadly wrote: "Wherever we went, the soldiers came to kill us, and it was all our own country."

IV

In hindsight the tactics of the Indian wars bear a remarkable similarity to methods employed during the Civil War. Given the continuity represented by Grant, Sherman, and Sheridan, this is no surprise, though it must be remembered that each struggled to find a doctrine that worked. Like other Union officers, they began the Civil War as prisoners of their education and previous experience. When the war ended, however, they were accustomed to a form of warfare uniquely suited to changing national policy towards Native Americans. An old cliché holds that the Army always prepares to fight the last war; if so, Sheridan was fortunate that his "last war" accustomed him to a style of warfare also suited to the frontier.

In their desperate search for success during the early years of the Civil War, Grant, Sherman, and Sheridan abandoned the limited tactics of their training to seek victory with more methodical, destructive methods. They waged war on the physical and spiritual infrastructure of the Confederacy, matching the South's frightening resolve with equally frightening tactics. The battlefields of the Civil War were classrooms in which American officers learned the tactics they would apply with devastating effect against Native Americans. Faced with an implacable foe on the frontier, the Army completed the evolution of a strategy born of necessity into the dominant doctrine of the era.

The generals who introduced the strategy of total war to American military thought were memories before their tactics earned a formal title. Though their writings make no mention of the phrase "total war," they clearly understood the meaning of the idea, and its potential for subsequent generations of warriors. Grant, Sherman, and Sheridan were hardly the first to wage war on civilians or resources, and if history is any guide they will not be the last. They were, however, prophets of their era, just as Shakespeare's Henry V was a prophet of his own.

> . . . for, as I am a soldier . . . I will not leave the
> half-achieved Harfleur
> Till in her ashes she lies buried.
> The gates of mercy shall be all shut up,
> And the fleshed soldier, rough and hard of heart,
> In liberty of bloody hand shall range
> With conscience wide as hell . . .

The Military Leadership
of North and South

T. Harry Williams

Convinced that great generalship is decisive in warfare, the late T. Harry Williams of Louisiana State University in this essay evaluates the leaders of the Union and Confederate armies during the Civil War. After examining the qualities inherent in great generalship and the Jominian principles by which the generals fought the war, he dismisses as lacking in one way or another almost all the major military commanders on both sides and concludes that only three deserve to be ranked as "great": Robert E. Lee for the Confederacy and Ulysses S. Grant and William T. Sherman for the Union. Lee, he argues, was an outstanding theater commander; Grant was able to rise above traditional concepts of war to fight a modern war; and Sherman grasped the importance of economic and psychological warfare. This essay was originally published in David H. Donald, ed., Why the North Won the Civil War *(Touchstone. New York: Simon & Schuster, 1996), 38–57, and is reprinted with permission.*

Generals and their art and their accomplishments have not been universally admired throughout the course of history. Indeed, there have been some who have sneered at even the successful captains of their time. Four centuries before Christ, Sophocles, as aware of the tragedy of war as he was of the tragedy of life, observed: "It is the merit of a general to impart good news, and to conceal the bad." And the Duke of Wellington, who knew from experience whereof he spoke, depreciated victory with the bitter opinion: "Nothing except a battle lost can be half so melancholy as a battle won."

Civil War generals were, of course, not considered sacrosanct—were, in fact, regarded as legitimate targets of criticism for anyone who had a gibe to fling. Senator Louis T. Wigfall was exercising his not inconsiderable talent for savage humor, usually reserved for the Davis administration, on the military when he said of John B. Hood: "That young man had a fine career before him until Davis undertook to make of him what the good Lord had not done—to make a great general of him." One can understand Assistant Secretary of War P. H. Watson's irritation when the War Department could not locate so important an officer as Joe Hooker on the eve of Second Manassas while also noting Watson's patronizing attitude toward all generals in a letter to transportation director Herman Haupt stating that an intensive search for Hooker was being conducted in Willard's bar. "Be patient as possible with the Generals," Watson added. "Some of them will trouble you more than they will the enemy."

And yet in the final analysis, as those who have fought or studied war know, it is the general who is the decisive factor in battle. (At least, this has been true up to our own time, when war has become so big and dispersed that it may be said it is managed rather than commanded.) Napoleon put it well when he said, perhaps with some exaggeration: "The personality of the general is indispensable, he is the head, he is the all of an army. The Gauls were not conquered by the Roman legions, but by Caesar. It was not before the Carthaginian soldiers that Rome was made to tremble, but before Hannibal. It was not the Macedonian phalanx which penetrated to India, but Alexander. It was not the French Army which reached the Weser and the Inn, it was Turenne. Prussia was not defended for seven years against the three most formidable European Powers by the Prussian soldiers, but by Frederick the Great." This quotation may serve to remind us of another truth about war and generals that is often forgotten: That is that tactics is often a more decisive factor than strategy. The commander who has suffered a strategic reverse, Cyril Falls emphasizes, may remedy everything by a tactical success, whereas for a tactical reverse there may be no remedy whatever. Falls adds: "It is remarkable how many people exert themselves and go through contortions to prove that battles and wars are won by any means except that by which they are most commonly won, which is by fighting."

If, then, the general is so important in war, we are justified in asking, what are the qualities that make a general great or even just good? We may with reason look for clues to the answer in the writings of some of the great captains. But first of all, it may be helpful to list some qualities that, although they may be highly meritorious and desirable, are not sufficient in themselves to produce greatness. Experience alone is not enough. "A mule," said Frederick the Great, "may have made twenty campaigns under Prince Eugene and not be a better tactician for all that." Nor are education and intelligence the touchstones to measure a great general. Marshal Saxe went so far as to say: "Unless a man is born with a talent for war, he will never be other than a mediocre general." And Auguste Marmont, while noting that all the great soldiers had possessed "the highest faculties of mind," emphasized that they also had had something that was more important, namely, character.

What these last two commentators were trying to say was that a commander has to have in his make-up a mental strength and a moral power that enables him to dominate whatever event or crisis may emerge on the field of battle. Napoleon stated the case explicitly: "The first quality of a General-in-Chief is to have a cool head which receives exact impressions of things, which never gets heated, which never allows itself to be dazzled, or intoxicated, by good or bad news." Anyone who knows the Civil War can easily tick off a number of generals who fit exactly the pattern described next by Napoleon: "There are certain men who, on account of their moral and physical constitution, paint mental pictures out of everything: however exalted be their reason, their will, their courage, and whatever good qualities they may possess, nature has not fitted them to command armies, nor to direct great operations of war." Karl von Clausewitz said the same thing in a slightly different context. There are decisive moments in war, the German pointed out, when things no longer move of themselves, when "the machine itself"—the general's own army—begins to offer resistance. To overcome this resistance the commander must have "a great force of will." The whole inertia of the war comes to rest on his will, and only the spark of his own purpose and spirit can throw it off. This natural quality of toughness of fiber is especially important in measuring Civil War generalship because the rival generals were products of the same educational system and the same military background. As far as technique was concerned, they started equal, and differed only in matters of mind and character. It has been well said: "To achieve a Cannae a Hannibal is needed on the one side and a Terentius Varro on the other." And one may add, to achieve a Second Manassas a Robert E. Lee is needed on the one side and a John Pope on the other.

When Marshal Saxe enumerated the attributes of a general, he named the usual qualities of intelligence and courage, and then added another not always considered in military evaluations—health. It is a factor that deserves more attention than it has received. Clifford Dowdey has recently reminded us of the effects of physical and mental illness on the actions of the Confederate command at Gettysburg. A comparison of the age levels of leading Southern and Northern officers in 1861 is instructive. Although there are no significant differences in the ages of the men who rose to division and corps generals, we note that, of the officers who came to command armies for the South, Albert Sidney Johnston was fifty-eight, Joseph E. Johnston and Lee were fifty-four, John C. Pemberton was forty-seven, Braxton Bragg was forty-four, and P. G. T. Beauregard was forty-three. Of the Union army commanders, Hooker was forty-seven, Henry W. Halleck and George G. Meade were forty-six, George H. Thomas was forty-five, D. C. Buell was forty-three, William S. Rosecrans was forty-two, William T. Sherman was forty-one, U. S. Grant was thirty-nine, Ambrose Burnside was thirty-seven, and George B. McClellan was thirty-four. Hood and Philip H. Sheridan at thirty represent the lowest age brackets. Youth was clearly on the side of the Union, but obviously it cannot be said, with any accuracy or finality, that the generals in one particular age group did any better than those in another. Nevertheless, when Grant thought about the war in the years after, he inclined to place a high premium on the qualities of youth, health, and energy, and doubted that a general over fifty should be given field command. He recalled that during the war he had had "the power to endure" anything. In this connection, it may be worthy of mention that during the Virginia campaign of 1864 Lee was sick eleven of forty-four days, while Grant was not indisposed for one.

The Civil War was pre-eminently a West Pointers' fight. Of the sixty biggest battles, West Point graduates commanded both armies in fifty-five, and in the remaining five a West Pointer commanded one of the opposing armies. What were the men who would direct the blue and gray armies like in 1861? How well trained were they for war? What intellectual influences had formed their concepts of war and battle? A glance at the Point curriculum reveals that it was heavy on the side of engineering, tactics, and administration. The products of the academy came out with a good grounding in what may be termed the routine of military science. They knew how to train and administer a force of troops; or, to put it more accurately and to apply it specifically to the Civil War, they had the technical knowledge that enabled them to take over the administration of a large force without imposing too much strain on them or their men. It should be emphasized, however, that none of the West Pointers had had before 1861 any actual experience in directing troops in numbers. Not a one had controlled as large a unit as a brigade, and only a few had handled a regiment. Except for a handful of officers who had visited Europe, the men who would lead the Civil War hosts had never seen an army larger than the fourteen thousand men of Winfield Scott or Zachary Taylor in the Mexican War.

One subject which was taught but not emphasized at West Point was strategy, or the study of the higher art of war. The comparative subordination of strategy may be explained by the youth of the cadets and the feeling of the school's directors that it was more important to impart a basic knowledge of tactics and techniques to the boys. Nevertheless, many of the graduates enlarged their knowledge of the topic by reading books on military history while stationed at army posts. The strategy that was presented at the Point and studied by interested graduates came from a common source and had a common pattern. It was the product of the brilliant Swiss officer who had served with Napoleon, Antoine Henri Jomini, universally regarded as the foremost writer on the theory of war in the first half of the nineteenth century. Every West Point general in the war had been exposed to Jomini's ideas, either directly, by reading Jomini's writings or abridgments or expositions of them; or indirectly, by hearing them in the classroom or perusing the works of Jomini's American disciples. The influence of Jomini on the Civil War was profound, and this influence must be taken into account in any evaluation of Civil War generalship. There is little exaggeration in General J. D. Hittle's statement that "many a Civil War general went into battle with a sword in one hand and Jomini's *Summary of the Art of War* in the other."

Here it is impossible to attempt more than a summary of Jomini's ideas and writings. Essentially his purpose was to introduce rationality and system into the study of war. He believed that in war rules prevailed as much as in other areas of human activity and that generals should follow these rules. He sought to formulate a set of basic principles of strategy for commanders, using as his principal examples the campaigns and techniques of Napoleon. The most convenient approach to Jomini is through the four strategic principles that he emphasized, the famous principles that many Civil War generals could recite from memory:

1. The commander should endeavor by strategic measures to bring the major part of his forces successively to bear on the decisive areas of the theater of war, while menacing the enemy's communications without endangering his own.
2. He should maneuver in such a way as to engage the masses of his forces against fractions of the enemy.
3. He should endeavor by tactical measures to bring his masses to bear on the decisive area of the battlefield or on the part of the enemy's line it was important to overwhelm.
4. He should not only bring his masses to bear on the decisive point of the field but should put them in battle speedily and together in a simultaneous effort.

It is, perhaps, unnecessary to remark that much of this was not new. Xenophon had said about the same thing to the Greeks, and the definition of strategy as the art of bringing most of the strength of an army to bear on the decisive point has been fairly constant in the history of war. But it should be noted that Jomini envisioned the decisive point as the point where the enemy was weakest. This is often true but not always. There are occasions in war when the decisive point may be the strongest one, as Epaminondas demonstrated at Leuctra and the American strategists in the cross-Channel attack of World War II.

To explain how his principles should be applied in war, Jomini worked out an elaborate doctrine based on geometrical formations. He loved diagrams, and devised twelve model plans of battle; some Civil War generals actually tried to reproduce on the field some of these neat paper exercises. In all Jomini's plans there was a theater of operations, a base of operations, a zone of operations, and so forth. The smart commander chose a line of operations that would enable him to dominate three sides of the rectangular zone; this accomplished, the enemy would have to retire or face certain defeat. Jomini talked much of concentric and eccentric maneuver and interior and exterior lines, being the first theorist to emphasize the advantage of the former over the latter.

At times, especially when he discussed the advantage of the offensive—and he always stressed the offensive—Jomini seemed to come close to Clausewitz's strategy of annihilation. But a closer perusal of his writings reveals that he and the German were far apart. Although Jomini spoke admiringly of the hard blow followed by the energetic pursuit, his line of operation strategy allowed the enemy the option of retiring. In reality Jomini thought that the primary objectives in war were places rather than armies: the occupation of territory or the seizure of such "decisive strategic points" as capitals. He affected to be the advocate of the new Napoleonic ways of war, but actually he looked back instead of forward. It has been rightly said of him (in R. A. Preston, S. F. Wise, and H. O. Werner, *Men in Arms*): "By his emphasis on lines of operation Jomini, in effect, returned to the eighteenth-century method of approaching the study of war as a geometric exercise. . . . In emphasizing the continuance of traditional features he missed the things that were new. There can be no doubt that this interpreter of Napoleonic warfare actually set military thought back into the eighteenth century, an approach which the professional soldiers of the early nineteenth century found comfortable and safe."

Jomini confessed that he disliked the destructiveness of the warfare of his time. "I acknowledge," he wrote, "that my prejudices are in favor of the good old times when the French and English guards courteously invited each other to fire first as at Fontenoy. . . ." He said that he preferred "chivalric war" to "organized assassination," and he deplored as particularly cruel and terrible what he called wars of "opinion," or as we would say today, of "ideas." War was, as it should be, most proper and polite when it was directed by professional soldiers and fought by professional armies for limited objectives. All this is, of course, readily recognizable as good eighteenth-century doctrine. This could be Marshal Saxe saying: "I do not favor pitched battles . . . and I am convinced that a skillful general could make war all his life without being forced into one." Eighteenth-century warfare was leisurely and its ends were limited. It stressed maneuver rather than battle, as was natural in an age when professional armies were so expensive to raise and maintain that they could not be risked unless victory was reasonably certain. It was conducted with a measure of humanity that caused Chesterfield to say: "War is pusillanimously carried on in this degenerate age; quarter is given; towns are taken and people spared; even in a storm, a woman can hardly hope for the benefit of a rape." Most important of all, war was regarded as a kind of exercise or game to be conducted by soldiers. For the kings war might have a dynastic objective, but in the thinking of many military men it had little if any relationship to society or politics or statecraft.

Many West Pointers—McClellan, Lee, Sherman, and Beauregard, among others—expressed their admiration of Jomini and usually in extravagant terms. Halleck devoted years to translating Jomini's works, and his own book on the elements of war was only a rehash of Jomini, in parts, in fact, a direct steal. William Hardee's manual on tactics reflected Jominian ideas. But the American who did more than any other to popularize Jomini was Dennis Hart Mahan, who began teaching at West Point in 1824 and who influenced a whole generation of soldiers. He interpreted Jomini both in the classroom and in his writings. At one time Jomini's own works had been used at the academy but had been dropped in favor of abridgments by other writers. In 1848 Mahan's book on war, usually known by the short title of *Outpost*, became an official text. Most of the Civil War generals had been Mahan's pupils, and those older ones who had not, like Lee, were exposed to his ideas through personal relationships or through his book. Probably no one man had a more direct and formative impact on the thinking of the war's commanders.

Mahan, of course, did little more than to reproduce Jomini's ideas. He talked much of the principle of mass, of defeating the enemy's fractions in succession, and of interior lines. But it should be emphasized that his big point, the one he dwelt on most, was the offensive executed by celerity of movement. Mahan never tired of stressing the advantage of rapidity in war—or of excoriating "the slow and over-prudent general" who was afraid to grasp victory. "By rapidity of movement we can . . . make war feed war," he wrote. "We disembarrass ourselves of those immense trains." There was one operation that could change the face of a war, he said. When one's territory was invaded, the commander should invade the territory of the enemy; this was the mark of "true genius." (This passage makes us think immediately of Lee and Stonewall Jackson.) Jominian strategy as interpreted by Mahan then was the mass offensive waged on the battlefield, perhaps with utmost violence, but only on the battlefield. It cannot be sufficiently emphasized that Mahan, like his master, made no connection between war and technology and national life and political objectives. War was still an exercise carried on by professionals. War and statecraft were still separate things.

The Jominian influence on Civil War military leadership was obviously profound and pervasive. But before considering its manifestations, it may be helpful to dispose of a number of generals who do not meet the criteria of greatness or even of acceptable competence. This perhaps too brutal disposal will be performed by means of some undoubtedly too sweeping generalizations. These generals fell short of the mark partly because, as will be developed later, they were too thorough Jominians, and partly because they lacked the qualities of mind and character found in the great captains of war. Of the generals who commanded armies we can say that the following had such grave shortcomings that either they were not qualified to command or that they can be classified as no better than average soldiers: on the Union side—McClellan, Burnside, Hooker, Meade, Buell, Halleck, and Rosecrans; on the Confederate side—Albert Sidney Johnston, Beauregard, Bragg, Joe Johnston, and Edmund Kirby Smith.

McClellan will be discussed later, but here we may anticipate by saying that he did not have the temperament required for command. Burnside did not have the mentality. Hooker was a fair strategist, but he lacked iron and also the imagination to control troops not within his physical vision. Meade was a good routine soldier but no more, and was afflicted with a defensive psychosis. Buell was a duplicate of McClellan without any color. Halleck was an unoriginal scholar and an excellent staff officer who should never have taken the field. Rosecrans had strategic ability but no poise or balance; his crack-up at Chickamauga is a perfect example of Napoleon's general who paints the wrong kind of mental picture. A. S. Johnston died before he could prove himself, but nothing that he did before his death makes us think that he was anything but a gallant troop leader. Beauregard probably was developing into a competent commander by the time of Shiloh, but his failure to win that battle plus his personality faults caused him to be exiled to comparatively minor posts for the rest of the war. Bragg, the general of the lost opportunity, was a good deal like Hooker. He created favorable situations but lacked the determination to carry through his purpose; he did not have the will to overcome the inertia of war. Kirby Smith made a promising start but seemed to shrink under the responsibility of command and finally disappeared into the backwash of the Trans-Mississippi theater. The stature of Joe Johnston probably will be argued as long as there are Civil War fans to talk. But surely we can take his measure by his decision in the Georgia campaign to withdraw from a position near Cassville that he termed the "best that I saw occupied during the war" merely because his corps generals advised retiring. A great general, we feel, would have delivered the attack that Johnston originally planned to make. Johnston undoubtedly had real ability, but he never did much with it. It is reasonable to expect that a general who has sustained opportunities will sometime, once, achieve something decisive. Certainly Johnston had the opportunities, but there is no decisive success on his record.

Of the lesser generals, it is fair to say that James Longstreet and Stonewall Jackson were outstanding corps leaders, probably the best in the war, but that neither gave much evidence of being able to go higher. Longstreet failed in independent command. Jackson performed brilliantly as commander of a small army but probably lacked the administrative ability to handle a large one. In addition, he was never fairly tested against first-rate opposition. Thomas and W. S. Hancock stand out among Union corps generals. Thomas also commanded an army, but his skills were of a particular order and could be exercised only in a particular situation. He excelled in the counterattack delivered from strength. J. E. B. Stuart, Sheridan, N. B. Forrest, and J. H. Wilson were fine cavalry leaders, but we cannot say with surety that they could have been anything else. On the one occasion when Sheridan directed an army he displayed unusual ability to handle combined arms (infantry, cavalry, artillery), but he enjoyed such a preponderant advantage in numbers over his opponent as to be almost decisive. He was never really subjected to the inertia of war. In the last analysis, the only Civil War generals who deserve to be ranked as great are Lee for the South and Grant and Sherman for the North.

We can now turn to an examination of the influence of Jominian eighteenth-century military thought on Civil War generalship, first directing our attention to the first Northern generals with whom Abraham Lincoln had to deal. It is immediately and painfully evident that in the first of the world's modern wars these men were ruled by traditional concepts of warfare. The Civil War was a war of ideas and, inasmuch as neither side could compromise its political purposes, it was a war of unlimited objectives. Such a war was bound to be a rough, no-holds-barred affair, a bloody and brutal struggle. Yet Lincoln's generals proposed to conduct it in accordance with the standards and the strategy of an earlier and easier military age. They saw cities and territory as their objectives rather than the armies of the enemy. They hoped to accomplish their objectives by maneuvering rather than by fighting. McClellan boasted that the "brightest chaplets" in his history were Manassas and Yorktown, both occupied after the Confederates had departed, because he had seized them by "pure military skill" and without the loss of life. When he had to lose lives, McClellan was almost undone. The "sickening sight" of the battlefield, he told his wife after Fair Oaks, took all the charms from victory. McClellan's mooning around the field anguishing over the dead may seem strange to the modern mind, but Jomini would have understood his reactions. Buell argued, in the spirit of Marshal Saxe, that campaigns could be carried out and won without engaging in a single big battle. Only when success was reasonably certain should a general risk battle, Buell said, adding: "War has a higher object than that of mere bloodshed." After the Confederates retired from Corinth, Halleck instructed his subordinates: "There is no object in bringing on a battle if this object can be obtained without one. I think by showing a bold front for a day or two the enemy will continue his retreat, which is all I desire." Meade, who confessed shame for his cause when he was ordered to seize the property of a Confederate sympathizer, thought that the North should prosecute the war "like the afflicted parent who is compelled to chastise his erring child, and who performs the duty with a sad heart."

With an almost arrogant assurance, Lincoln's first generals believed that war was a business to be carried on by professionals without interference from civilians and without political objectives. It is no exaggeration to say that some of the officers saw the war as a kind of game played by experts off in some private sphere that had no connection with the government or society. Rosecrans gave a typical expression of this viewpoint when he resisted pressure from Washington to advance before the battle of Stone's river: "I will not move until I am ready! . . . War is a business to be conducted systematically. I believe I understand my business. . . . I will not budge until I am ready." But, as might be expected, the classic example is McClellan. He refused to retain General Charles Hamilton in his army when Lincoln requested him to, even after, or more accurately, especially after the President emphasized that there were weighty political reasons for assigning Hamilton a minor position. When McClellan conceived his Urbanna plan, he did not tell Lincoln about it for months. He did not seem to know that it was his job to counsel his political superior on his plans; in fact, he did not seem to know that there was any relationship between war and politics. In the winter of 1861–1862 Lincoln implored McClellan to make a move, even a small or diversionary one, to inspire public opinion with the belief that more decisive action was contemplated later. McClellan refused on the grounds that he was not yet completely prepared. That the public might become so discouraged that it would abandon the war impressed McClellan not at all. With him the only question was when the professionals would be ready to start the game.

Lincoln's early generals also accepted blindly the Jominian doctrine of concentration. As they interpreted it, it meant one big effort at a time in one theater. McClellan's proposal to mass 273,000 troops in the eastern department in 1861, a physical and military impossibility at that time, was a typical piece of Jominian thinking. Of course, each commander was convinced that the one big push should be made by him, and each one demanded that other departments be stripped of troops to strengthen his own army. It would be possible to argue that the apparent caution of every Union general in the first years of the war, and the consequent inaction of Union armies, was the result of each commander's conviction that he did not possess enough strength to undertake the movements recommended by Jomini. But this feeling of the generals brought them into conflict with their commander in chief, who was no Jominian in his strategic notions, and their differences with Lincoln will be discussed later.

When we examine the psychology of the Northern generals, the thought immediately occurs that the Southern generals were not like this, and inevitably we ask, why not? Had the Southerners freed themselves from Jomini's dogma? Were they developing new ways of war? The answer to both questions is no. The Confederates were, if possible, more Jominian than the Federals. They simply gave a different emphasis to the traditional pattern of strategic thought. Whereas the Federals borrowed from Jomini the idea of places as objectives, the Confederates took from him the principle of the offensive. Moreover, the Southern generals were fortunate in being able to make enemy armies the object of their offensives because Confederate policy did not look to the acquisition of enemy territory. The influence of Mahan, with his doctrine of celerity and the headlong attack, is also apparent in Confederate strategy, especially as it was employed by Lee. In addition, the poverty of Southern resources had the effect of forcing Southern generals to think in aggressive terms. They could not afford to wait for a big build-up in men and equipment, but had to act when they could with what they had. Paradoxically, the Industrial Revolution, which would have so much to do with bringing about the advent of total war with all its destructiveness, had the immediate consequence of making the Northern generals less inclined to deal out destruction. They could secure material so easily that they refused to move until they had received more than they needed—after which they were often so heavily laden they could not move.

Far from departing from Jomini, the Confederates were the most brilliant practitioners of his doctrine. If we look for successful applications of the principles that Jomini emphasized—the objective, the offensive, mass, economy of force, interior lines, and unity of command—we find them most frequently in the Confederate campaigns and most particularly in the Virginia theater. Lee, the Confederacy's best general, was also its greatest Jominian. Probably it is because Lee embodied so precisely the spirit of traditional warfare that he has been ranked so high by students of war. Military historians are likely to be as conservative as generals. The English writers, who have done so much to form our image of the war, have been especially lavish in their praise. It may be suspected that their attitude stems largely from a feeling that Lee was a gentleman, English style, although for a long while the British, when they faced a possible combination of superior continental powers, studied Lee's strategy because of its application of the principle of interior lines. Cyril Falls said that Lee was a master combination of "strategist, tactical genius, leader of the highest inspiration, and technician in the arts of hastily fortifying defensive positions superbly chosen." Falls added: "He must stand as the supreme figure of this survey of a hundred years of war." Colonel A. H. Burne was more restrained, but spoke admiringly of Lee's audacity, his use of the offensive, and his skill at concentration. The opinions of G. F. R. Henderson and G. J. Wolseley are so well known as not to require quotation.

Let us concede that many of the tributes to Lee are deserved. He was not all that his admirers have said of him, but he was a large part of it. But let us also note that even his most fervent admirers, when they come to evaluate him as a strategist, have to admit that his abilities were never demonstrated on a larger scale than a theater. Cyril Falls, after his extravagant eulogy of Lee, falls on his face in attempting to attribute to his subject gifts for "large-scale strategy": the only example he can find is Lee's redeployment of forces between the Shenandoah Valley and Richmond during the Peninsula campaign! Lee was pre-eminently a field or a theater strategist, and a great one, but it remains unproven that he was anything more or wanted to be anything more. "In spite of all his ability, his heroism and the heroic efforts of his army," writes General J. F. C. Fuller, "because he would think and work in a corner, taking no notice of the whole, taking no interest in forming policy or in the economic side of the war, he was ultimately cornered and his cause lost." For his preoccupation with the war in Virginia, Lee is not to be criticized. He was a product of his culture, and that culture, permeated in its every part by the spirit of localism, dictated that his outlook on war should be local. Nevertheless, it must be recognized that his restricted view constituted a tragic command limitation in a modern war. The same limitation applied to Southern generalship as a whole. The Confederates, brilliant and bold in executing Jominian strategy on the battlefield, never succeeded in lifting their gifts above the theater level.

In many respects Lee was not a modern-minded general. He probably did not understand the real function of a staff and certainly failed to put together an adequate staff for his army. Although he had an excellent eye for terrain, his use of maps was almost primitive. He does not seem to have appreciated the impact of railroads on warfare or to have realized that railroads made Jomini's principle of interior lines largely obsolete. His mastery of logistics did not extend beyond departmental limits. In February, 1865, he said that he could not believe Sherman would be able to move into North Carolina. The evidence of Sherman's great march was before him, and yet he was not quite sure it had really happened.

The most striking lack of modernity in Lee was his failure to grasp the vital relationship between war and statecraft. Here the great Virginian was truly a Jominian. Almost as much as McClellan, he thought of war as a professional exercise. One of his officers said admiringly that Lee was too thorough a soldier to attempt to advise the government on such matters as the defense of Richmond. When late in the war a cabinet member asked Lee for his opinion on the advisability of moving the capital farther south, the general replied: "That is a political question . . . and you politicians must determine it. I shall endeavor to take care of the army, and you must make the laws and control the Government." And yet what could be a more strategic question than the safety of the capital? Lee attained a position in the Confederacy held by no other man, either in civil or military life. There was little exaggeration in the statement General William Mahone made to him: "You are the State." But Lee could not accept the role that his eminence demanded. He could never have said as Pitt did: "I know that I can save the country and that no one else can." It has been suggested that Lee did not try to impose his will on the government because of his humility of character, and this may well be true. But it would also seem to be true that he did not know that a commander had any political responsibility.

Lincoln's first generals did not understand that war and statecraft were parts of the same piece. But none of the Confederate generals, first or last, ever grasped this fact about modern war. The most distinguishing feature of Southern generalship is that it did not grow. Lee and the other Confederate commanders were pretty much the same men in 1865 that they had been in 1861. They were good, within certain limits, at the beginning, and they were good at the end but still within the original limits. They never freed themselves from the influence of traditional doctrine. The probable explanation, David Donald has suggested, is that the Confederates won their first battles with Jominian strategy and saw no reason to change and that the Southern mind, civil and military, was unreceptive to new ideas. The North, on the other hand, finally brought forward generals who were able to grow and who could employ new ways of war. Even so doctrinaire a Jominian as Halleck reached the point where he could approve techniques of total war that would have horrified the master. But the most outstanding examples of growth and originality among the Northern generals are Grant and Sherman.

The qualities of Grant's generalship deserve more analysis than those of Lee, partly because they have not been sufficiently emphasized but largely because Grant was a more modern soldier than his rival. First, we note that Grant had that quality of character or will exhibited by all the great captains. (Lee had it, too.) Perhaps the first military writer to emphasize this trait in Grant was C. F. Atkinson in 1908. Grant's distinguishing feature as a general, said Atkinson, was his character, which was controlled by a tremendous will; with Grant action was translated from thought to deed by all the force of a tremendous personality. This moral strength of Grant's may be news to some present-day historians, but it was overpoweringly apparent to all who were thrown into close association with him. Charles Francis Adams, Jr., like all his family not disposed to easy praise, said that Grant was really an extraordinary person, although he did not look it. In a crisis, Adams added, all would instinctively lean on Grant. Lincoln saw this quality in Grant clearly: "The great thing about Grant, I take it, is his perfect coolness and persistency of purpose. I judge he is not easily excited,—which is a great element in an officer." But the best tribute to Grant's character was paid by the general who knew him best. In a typical explosive comment to J. H. Wilson, Sherman said: "Wilson, I am a damn sight smarter than Grant. I know a great deal more about war, military history, strategy, and administration, and about everything else than he does. But I tell you where he beats me, and where he beats the world. He don't care a damn for what the enemy does out of his sight, but it scares me like hell." On the eve of the great campaigns of 1864 Sherman wrote to Grant that he considered Grant's strongest feature was his ability to go into battle without hesitation, doubts, or reserve. Characteristically Sherman added "It was this that made me act with confidence."

In this same letter Sherman confessed to a reservation that he had had about Grant: "My only points of doubt were as to your knowledge of grand strategy, and of books of science and history; but I confess your common sense seems to have supplied all this." Common sense Grant had, and it enabled him to deal with such un-Jominian phenomena as army correspondents and political generals. Unlike Sherman, Grant accepted the reporters—but he rendered them harmless. "General Grant informs us correspondents that he will willingly facilitate us in obtaining all proper information," Junius Browne wrote S. H. Gay, then added significantly that Grant was "not very communicative." Unlike McClellan, who would not accept General Hamilton for political considerations urged by Lincoln, Grant took John A. McClernand at the President's request. He could not imagine why Lincoln wanted a command for McClernand but assumed that there must be some reason important to his civil superior. He put up with McClernand until he found a way to strike him down to which Lincoln could not object. In this whole affair Grant showed that he realized the vital relation between politics and modern war.

It was Grant's common sense that enabled him to rise above the dogmas of traditional warfare. On one occasion a young officer, thinking to flatter Grant, asked his opinion of Jomini. Grant replied that he had never read the master. He then expressed his own theory of strategy: "The art of war is simple enough. Find out where your enemy is. Get at him as soon as you can. Strike at him as hard as you can and as often as you can, and keep moving on." After the war Grant discussed more fully his opinion of the value of doctrine. He conceded that military knowledge was highly desirable in a commander. But he added: "If men make war in slavish observance of rules, they will fail. No rules will apply to conditions of war as different as those which exist in Europe and America. . . . War is progressive, because all the instruments and elements of war are progressive." He then referred to the movement that had been his most striking departure from the rules, the Vicksburg campaign. To take Vicksburg by rules would have required a withdrawal to Memphis, the opening of a new line of operations, in fact, a whole new strategic design. But Grant believed that the discouraged condition of Northern opinion would not permit such a conformity to Jominian practice: "In a popular war we had to consider political exigencies." It was this ability of Grant's to grasp the political nature of modern war that marks him as the first of the great modern generals.

The question of where to rank Sherman among Civil War generals has always troubled military writers. He is obviously not a Jominian, and just as obviously he is not a great battle captain like Grant or Lee. Colonel Burne points out that never once did Sherman command in a battle where he engaged his whole force and that he never won a resounding victory. Conceding that in the Georgia campaign Sherman displayed imagination, resource, versatility, broadness of conception, and genuine powers of leadership—all fundamental traits of a great commander—Burne still contends that Sherman exhibited two serious failings: that of pursuing a geographical rather than a military objective and that of avoiding risk. B. H. Liddell Hart, on the other hand, depicts Sherman as the greatest general of the war because more than any other commander he came to see that the object of strategy is to minimize fighting. Part of this evaluation can be written off as an attempt by Liddell Hart to glorify through Sherman the British strategy of the "indirect approach." And yet he is right in saying that Sherman had the most complete grasp of the truth that the resisting power of a modern democracy depends heavily on the popular will and that this will depends in turn on a secure economic and social basis. Sherman, a typical Jominian at the beginning of the war, became its greatest exponent of economic and psychological warfare. Nobody realized more clearly than Sherman the significance of the techniques he introduced. Describing to Grant what he meant to do on his destructive march, he said, "This may not be war, but rather statesmanship." At the same time we must recognize that Sherman's strategy by itself would not have brought the Confederacy down. That end called for a Grant who at the decisive moment would attack the enemy's armed forces. As Burne puts it: "Sherman might help to prepare the ground, but it was Grant who struck the blow." The North was fortunate in finding two generals who between them executed Clausewitz's three objectives of war: to conquer and destroy the enemy's armed forces, to get possession of the material elements of aggression and other sources of existence of the enemy, and to gain public opinion by winning victories that depress the enemy's morale.

It remains to touch on the military leadership of the North and the South at the highest levels where strategy was determined—at the rival Presidents and the command systems they headed. In supreme leadership the Union was clearly superior. Lincoln was an abler and a stronger man than Davis. The Northern President illustrated perfectly the truth of Clausewitz's dictum that "a remarkable, superior mind and strength of character" are the primary qualifications of a director of war. The North developed at an early date an over-all plan of strategy, and it finally devised a unified command system for the entire military machine. The South was unable to accomplish either one of these objectives. But its failure should not be set down as the result of a shortage of brains among its leaders. Here again we need to remind ourselves that ways of making war are always the product of cultures. For the nationalistic North it was comparatively easy to achieve a broad view of war. Conversely, it was natural for the localistic South to adopt a narrow view and to fight a conservative war. Confederate strategy was almost wholly defensive, and was designed to guard the whole circumference of the country. In military jargon, it was a cordon defense. Probably the South's best chance to win its independence by a military decision was to attempt on a grand strategic scale the movement its generals were so good at on specific battlefields—the concentrated mass offensive. But the restrictions of Southern culture prevented any national application of the one Jominian principle that might have brought success.

Just as a cordon defense was the worst strategy for the South, a cordon offense was the best strategy for the North. This was the strategy that Lincoln had pressed upon his generals almost from the beginning of the war—to make enemy armies their objective and to move all Federal forces against the enemy line simultaneously. An offensive along the entire circumference of the Confederacy would prevent the enemy from moving troops from one threatened point to another and would inevitably achieve a breakthrough. It was an eminently sensible strategy for the side with the greater numbers and the superior lines of transportation and for a war fought over such a vast theater. When Lincoln proposed his plan to general after general, it met with polite scorn. It violated the Jominian principle of concentration in one theater for one big effort. It was the product of a mind that did not know the rules of war.

Not until he found Grant did Lincoln find a general who was original enough to employ his strategy. Grant's master design for 1864 called for an advance of Federal armies all along the line. It was the operation that broke the back of the Confederacy. When Grant explained his plan to the President, he remarked that even the smaller Federal forces not fighting would help the fighting by advancing and engaging the attention of the enemy. We have dealt much with maxims here, and we may fittingly conclude with one. Lincoln grasped Grant's point immediately and uttered a maxim of his own. At least for the Civil War it had more validity than anything written by Baron Jomini. "Those not skinning can hold a leg," said the commander in chief.

VI

❦

Military Arm of an Expanding Nation

No More Cold Harbors: Issues in Tactics, 1865–1880

Perry D. Jamieson

It was obvious to some military leaders in the post–Civil War years that the tactics utilized during the war would have to be reexamined in view of the improved weaponry now available to armies. Accordingly, such questions as the continued use of two-rank advances against a well-entrenched enemy, the best use of artillery, the reliance on the offensive, the adoption of breech-loading rifles and the Gatling gun, and the use of the bayonet for infantry and the sabre by cavalry were debated in Army circles in the post-war decades. But leading reformers such as Emory Upton, William T. Sherman, and the members of various boards called into being to discuss these issues of tactics met with stolid resistance from military traditionalists. Still, the issues were raised, and the Army groped for solutions through the closing decades of the 19th century. This essay is the opening chapter of Jamieson's Crossing the Deadly Ground: United States Army Tactics, 1865–1880 *(Tuscaloosa & London: University of Alabama Press, 1994), 1–21, and is reprinted with permission. Jamieson is the staff historian, United States Air Force Office of History, Bolling AFB.*

The chaplain of the First Massachusetts discerned a pattern in the confused, back-and-forth fighting that he saw during the Battle of the Wilderness. "Wherever the Federal troops moved forward," he observed, "the Rebels appeared to have the advantage. Whenever they advanced, the advantage was transferred to us." This New England clergyman, who witnessed several attacks during the gruesome combat that opened the Virginia campaign of 1864, had identified the fundamental tactical problem of the Civil War:

defending troops usually held the upper hand over attackers. The introduction of rifled shoulder arms, the power of artillery on the defensive, and the use of field entrenchments, which became more sophisticated during the course of the war, all weighed heavily on the side of the defense. Civil War attacks, frontal assaults in particular, often ended in bloody failures. The most famous Confederate leader, General Robert E. Lee, suffered his worst defeats while fighting on the tactical offensive, at Malvern Hill and at Gettysburg. One of the Union's most inept commanders, Major General Ambrose E. Burnside, lost more than 12,000 soldiers during a single day of senseless attacks at Fredericksburg, and one of its greatest heroes, Lieutenant General Ulysses S. Grant, sent nearly 14,000 of his men to slaughter in two days at Cold Harbor.[1]

The strengths of the tactical defensive and the large size of Civil War armies made them extremely resilient, able to absorb hard blows, withstand heavy casualties, and still keep their cohesion. An army, or part of it, might be routed from a battlefield, the fate at First Bull Run of Brigadier General Irvin McDowell's collection of poorly trained divisions or at Chancellorsville of Major General Oliver O. Howard's ill-starred Eleventh Corps. But during the entire four years of the Civil War, only one large field force can be said to have been destroyed in combat. At the Battle of Nashville on December 15, 1864, well-executed Union attacks drove in both flanks of the Army of Tennessee. Its survivors fled to Mississippi and never again formed an effective army.

This lone exception to the resilience of Civil War armies is readily explained by events two weeks earlier at the Battle of Franklin, where General John Bell Hood, the most aggressive of Southern army commanders, sacrificed the Army of Tennessee in a mindless frontal assault that provided another tragic example of the power of the tactical defensive. In a single heroic advance, the Confederates suffered total casualties of 7,000 troops, at least a third of their attacking infantry, losses that included six generals killed or mortally wounded and an untold number of experienced company and regimental officers. It was hardly remarkable that Hood's army met the fate that it did at Nashville, half a month after its calamity at Franklin. After the end of the Civil War, thoughtful soldiers foresaw that the tactical defensive would become even stronger, and armies even more resilient, as breech-loading arms—if not repeaters—became more common and that as firepower increased, the value of the bayonet and saber would diminish.[2]

These developments suggested that the post–Civil War army needed new ideas about how to fight its future battles, and some officers concluded that it should develop tactics of its own, independent of European influence. "Now that the war is ended," the *Army and Navy Journal* editorialized in November 1865, "some of our officers evidently fancy it to be the proper time to start a new school of warfare which, no doubt, they would call the 'American School.'" Earlier that autumn one Civil War veteran had declared: "We are a practical people. . . . Let us leave show and useless, brain-confusing evolutions to monarchial Europe." After the reformer Emory Upton published in 1867 the first tactical manual authorized after the Civil War, the commanding general of the army, Ulysses S. Grant, emphasized to the secretary of war that this work, unlike its predecessors, was "purely American" and not a translation. When the long-tenured veteran Brigadier General John Pope enumerated some of the United States Army's problems in 1873, he included the "feeble imitation of foreign systems."[3]

An "American school" of tactics probably had no stronger advocate in the post–Civil War army than its commanding general, William T. Sherman. In 1874 Sherman reminded his old comrade Stephen A. Hurlbut that throughout their careers the United States military had been shaped by the "principles and practices" of its counterpart in France. "In 1840 the French nation stood preeminent as a military people," Sherman recalled, "and it was natural and proper that we should in a measure be influenced by their example; but the Institutions of every country should harmonize with the genius & tone of the mass of the people. Our People are not French but American, and our Army should be organized and maintained upon a model of our own, and not copied after that of the French, who differ from us essentially." Sherman's nationalism also was evident when, later in the 1870s, he made some suggestions for the curriculum of the Artillery School at Fort Monroe, Virginia, which, since its revival in 1868, had required students to give presentations on military history to their classmates and staff. The commanding general recommended that every artilleryman should research, write, and read to his class a paper on the strategy and tactics of a campaign from American history. Sherman proposed a list of such topics, beginning with the Brandywine campaign of George Washington, the nation's premier military hero, and ending with the operations then still in progress against the Plains Indians. (He also modestly included two case studies from his own career.) At the end of the 1870s, the content of the Artillery School's ten-week course in military history and geography was as nationalistic as the commanding general's recommendations for its student papers. Although the curriculum gave a nod to Marlborough and Frederick the Great, it concentrated on the American Civil War.[4]

Another senior army officer, Lieutenant General Philip H. Sheridan, doubted that Americans could gain much from studying European tactics, an opinion he formed while observing the Franco-Prussian War. "I find that but little can be learned here to benefit our service," he wrote from France during the Sedan campaign. "We are far ahead in skill and Campaign Organization." On another occasion Sheridan reported that he saw "many things of great interest . . . but not much in this Old World which should be taken as a standard for the New World." The peppery American general said of the Franco-Prussian conflict in his memoirs: "I saw no new military principles developed, whether of strategy or grand tactics."[5]

In addition to nationalist pride like Sheridan's, there was at least one practical reason for the United States Army to develop its own tactics in the late 1860s: the likelihood that, at least for the foreseeable future, it would train and fight on American, and not European, terrain. Foreign war was thought so unlikely that the late nineteenth-century army rarely expended its meager funds on training regiments as full units. The *Army and Navy Journal* wondered in 1865 if the time had arrived for the service to embrace tactics tailored to "the nature of our country." When Emory Upton's first tactical manual appeared two years later, it carried the subtitle, "Adapted to American Topography and Improved Fire-Arms."[6]

An "American school" of tactics was also promoted by the belief that the translations of European manuals by William J. Hardee and Silas Casey used during the Civil War had proven inadequate. "We are beginning to overhaul our Scott, our Hardee, our Casey," the *Army and Navy Journal* observed in November 1865, "and to question whether, after all, the officers who edited these tactics did not follow the original too closely." G. K. Warren, who had been a corps commander in the Army of the Potomac, was quoted after the war as complaining that Casey's manual left "the Army in some situations virtually without any tactics at all." Time and again during the war, frontal assaults in the close-ordered lines of Hardee and Casey, against defenders armed with rifles and protected by entrenchments, had ended in disaster. Long after the Civil War, in 1890, one veteran who remembered these bitter experiences passed on this warning: "We can never again march solid first lines to the attack under heavy fire, as at Fredericksburg or Cold Harbor."[7]

No officer of the postwar army was more convinced of the need for new ideas than Emory Upton, who had been critical of the leadership and tactics he had seen during the Civil War[8] and had become one of the conflict's most innovative tacticians. Looking for an alternative to the close-ordered linear tactics of Hardee and Casey, Upton experimented with light-column formations at Rappahannock Station on November 7, 1863, and at Spotsylvania Court House on May 10, 1864.[9] The following April he helped plan, then lead, an assault of dismounted cavalrymen armed with Spencer repeaters that carried an entrenched Confederate position at Selma, Alabama. Before the war ended, this intense officer from New York began developing a tactical system of his own, and in January 1866 he wrote to the assistant adjutant general, asking that his tactics be considered by the secretary of war or by a board of officers.[10]

Two such panels studied Upton's system and recommended that it become the army's authorized tactics. The first was a board of officers chaired by Colonel Henry B. Clitz,[11] and the second, larger and more prestigious, was presided over by the commanding general of the army, Ulysses S. Grant. Acting on the endorsements of these committees, the War Department on August 1, 1867, adopted Upton's work as the official tactics for the

United States Army. The author published his effort at his own expense, under the title *A New System of Infantry Tactics, Double and Single Rank.*[12]

Within two years of the publication of this manual, Upton assumed the leading role in the army's effort to develop what nineteenth-century soldiers called an "assimilated" tactics, a system with commands and formations that were compatible among infantry, artillery, and cavalry. A board of officers chaired by a distinguished Union veteran, Major General John M. Schofield, undertook this project in 1869. Upton, who had gained experience with all three arms of the service during the Civil War, proposed to the Schofield Board early in its deliberations that his 1867 infantry manual could serve as the basis for an assimilated system. The committee never formally accepted this offer, but the board's findings, presented to the War Department in 1871, included an infantry tactics similar to Upton's.[13]

The War Department did not endorse the results of the Schofield Board. One contemporary observer alleged that complacent reviewers had filed the panel's report in one of the bureaucracy's "pigeon holes." There may have been sound reasons for the War Department's failure to accept the Schofield Board's efforts. One officer claimed that Philip St. George Cooke, a Union trooper who had written a cavalry manual of his own, raised enough criticisms to discredit the panel's mounted tactics. It was also suggested that the Schofield Board's infantry drill was so similar to Upton's that its adoption would infringe his copyright.[14]

This might well have been the end of the assimilation project, but the army's senior officer intervened. William T. Sherman served as a mentor to Upton, encouraging his work on tactics and other reforms. In the case of the assimilated manuals, Sherman had confidence in the studious New Yorker's knowledge of the subject and perhaps also believed that the best resolution of the copyright issue was the adoption of Upton's own work. The commanding general directed his enterprising subordinate and three other officers to prepare an assimilated tactics, based on Upton's own system.[15]

The War Department authorized the results of their efforts, which were published in 1874 in three volumes, one for each arm of the service. These books were not a combined-arms tactics, advising, for example, a battery commander how best to cooperate with infantry. They were, instead, manuals whose commands and formations were compatible among the three arms, so that an officer could move, for instance, from the artillery service to a cavalry regiment and quickly learn the drill of his new unit. Upton and his comrades did not produce a combined-arms tactics, but they were the first board of officers in the army's history to study the three arms together and design a system applicable to all of them. Eight years after the publication of these assimilated volumes, General Sherman pronounced them "all sufficient for my day and generation."[16]

In both the assimilated tactics and his 1867 work, Upton tried to move troops more efficiently than the Civil War manuals had allowed. Looking for more flexibility than he found in Hardee and Casey, Upton made groups of four men, "fours," the basic units of his infantry system, using them to replace the platoons and sections of earlier drill books. Upton's scheme allowed foot soldiers to march in columns composed of "fours," deploy from column into fighting line by "fours," and use this same primary unit to march by the flank, to wheel, or to perform other movements before or during contact with an enemy. A regiment of ten companies, the basic infantry unit, could align and maneuver by collections of "fours," blocks of eight or twelve men.[17]

Upton's other significant innovation was his introduction of single-rank tactics. He expected breechloaders, and repeating breechloaders in particular, to increase the firepower of an infantry regiment so greatly that in some cases it could be deployed in a single, rather than a two-line, formation. Upton pointed to the wartime successes won by dismounted Union cavalrymen armed with seven-shot Spencer rifles, examples that he believed proved "that one rank of men so armed is nearly, if not quite, equal in offensive or defensive power to two ranks armed with the Springfield musket. If this be admitted, a one-rank tactics becomes necessary for a certain proportion of troops, especially those designed to turn or operate on the enemy's flank." Many years after Upton's single-rank tactics were adopted, one infantry officer reflected that with the advent of breechloaders and Gatling and Hotchkiss guns, footsoldiers deployed in the two-line formations of the Civil War became "simply food for gunpowder. The single rank formation is now and will be the only one used in battle, unless, indeed, the line shall become still more attenuated by the introduction of an open order system."[18]

Upton's innovative 1867 manual was well received in some quarters. The Grant Board gave it a strong endorsement, commending its provision for single-line tactics. The *Army and Navy Journal* devoted two lead articles, in September 1866 and February 1867, to favorable publicity for the work. The year after the manual had been adopted as the army's authorized tactics, one Civil War veteran praised the efficiency of Upton's system of "fours," asking rhetorically: "What is simpler than this?"[19]

Despite his innovations, or perhaps because of them, Upton attracted many critics. William H. Morris, who had published a *Field Tactics for Infantry* of his own in 1864, raised the specter that his rival's new tactics were too novel, and Major General Thomas W. Sherman, a veteran of both the Mexican and Civil Wars, warned that Upton's system contained major, perhaps fatal, flaws. One stubborn soldier declared in 1868: "I remain a staunch adherent of the dethroned Casey."[20]

Whether an officer criticized or praised the new tactics depended in part on his beliefs about the relative merits of firepower and shock. Upton introduced his "fours" and single-line tactics in response to the deadly volleys he had experienced on Civil War battlefields and in the expectation that infantry fire would become even more powerful in the future. An implied corollary was that shock tactics, the use of close-ordered lines or heavy columns to overpower a defender with a sudden bayonet charge, would become increasingly dangerous. In 1874 George B. McClellan, who was an unsuccessful field general but an astute observer of military affairs, warned that these traditional formations could not survive the long-range, rapid, and accurate fire delivered by the latest weapons.[21]

Given the dominance of firepower over shock, some officers concluded that the bayonet had lost most of its value. One soldier complained in 1868: "The trouble with the admirers of the bayonet is that they do not reflect on what the breech-loader can accomplish. . . . There is but one way to oppose breech-loaders, namely, with breech-loaders." Discussing weapons with Philip H. Sheridan in 1878, William T. Sherman suggested that the army should recognize that the bayonet and the noncommissioned officer's sword had lost their utility in combat and exchange them for more practical armaments. Sheridan's chief ordnance officer agreed with Sherman and recommended that the bayonet, along with the saber, "be replaced by a more useful weapon and tool."[22]

In spite of such statements, the sentiment persisted that the infantry should not abandon the bayonet. None of the weapon's proponents were more vigorous than Francis J. Lippitt, a veteran of the Mexican and Civil Wars who published a book on tactical theory just after Appomattox. Suggesting tactics for all three arms of the service, Lippitt's recommendation to foot soldiers was that "the proper mode of attack by infantry on infantry is with the bayonet." He ignored the contrary evidence from Civil War experience and declared: "The bayonet is usually more effective than *grape, canister*, or *bullets*." Although few officers were so zealously in favor of the bayonet as Lippitt, the edged weapon did not lack defenders. A lieutenant of the Third Infantry wrote, early in the 1870s: "Nobody . . . would . . . for a moment think of depriving the Infantry arm of half its force by taking away the bayonet." William T. Sherman seemed to retreat from his earlier statement to Sheridan when, in October 1879, the conqueror of Atlanta acknowledged that the army would have to retain its traditional edged weapon in some form.[23] If the commanding general of the army appeared to put himself on both sides of this question within two years, the soldier and lawyer Alfred H. Terry straddled the issue in the course of a single report that he signed in 1872. "I think the day of the bayonet has passed away," Terry offered at one point but later on the same page added: "While, however, this is my belief, I do not think it prudent to definitely abandon the weapon until actual practice in war shall demonstrate that it is no longer of use." The army's reluctance to give up this traditional armament was also evidenced when it issued ten thousand trowel bayonets in 1874. Designed by Lieutenant Edmund Rice, this accessory was both an entrenching tool and a close combat weapon. The trowel bayonet allowed infantry to prepare fieldworks more quickly—an important benefit when defending against fire from breechloaders—and at the same time retain the traditional edged weapon of the foot soldier.[24]

While infantrymen discussed the bayonet, cavalrymen debated the saber. Critics of edged weapons contended that rifled shoulder arms had made mounted charges against infantry too dangerous. They could point out that Civil War saber attacks against foot soldiers had been rare and successful ones rarer still. The prospects darkened further when the infantry gained breechloaders. In 1868 the *Army and Navy Journal* declared the day of the saber had ended, arguing that in nine cases out of ten, infantry massacred horsemen who relied on it. Faced with breechloaders, William T. Sherman predicted, "the bold Sabreur must disappear."[25] The Schofield Board, which studied weapons and accoutrements as well as tactics, recommended that cavalrymen be armed with carbines and revolvers, rather than sabers, and a captain of the Sixth Cavalry commented in 1880 that if the troopers practiced well with these firearms, they would have little need of their edged weapons, for either conventional or Indian warfare.[26]

The defenders of the saber, some of whom seemed to regard any criticism of the weapon as an attack on the entire cavalry service, were as adamant as those of the bayonet. In 1871 Major William R. Parnell of the First Cavalry prepared a saber manual that was based on another one published thirty years earlier. A Union cavalry veteran wrote to contradict the *Army and Navy Journal*: "The days of the sabre are *not* over, and never will be, except for those who have no love for horses and no faith in steel; and for such the days of the sabre never dawned." One volunteer cavalryman disparaged the Schofield Board's findings, citing what he believed was an important lesson of the Franco-Prussian War. "If the recommendations of the St. Louis Board are enforced," this trooper predicted, "our regular cavalry will soon become as useless as the French cavalry proved in the war of 1870, always ready to run away. The sabre is as valuable for its moral effect as for its actual execution." Four months after the army's worst defeat during the Indian wars, another cavalryman claimed that George Armstrong Custer would have "given millions" for a hundred sabers at the Little Big Horn.[27] Wesley Merritt, a highly regarded veteran of the Union cavalry, recommended in 1879 that the cavalry keep its carbines and, "above all," its sabers. One of the army's most conscientious students of weapons and tactics, Colonel John C. Kelton, commented the following year that cavalrymen remained divided over the issue, with "perhaps" a majority in favor of the saber over firearms.[28]

Some horse soldiers concluded that the fault was not the weapon itself but its maintenance: the troopers must keep their sabers well honed. Generals David S. Stanley and William W. Averell believed that sharp blades had raised the morale of their soldiers during the Civil War. "Give our troopers the sabre," advised one cavalryman in the mid-1870s. "Sharpen it and teach them its use." George Custer's biographer Frederick J. Whittaker argued in

1871 that dull weapons were among the mounted arm's worst problems. "Sabres are issued blunt enough to ride on to San Francisco . . . ," he complained from his home in New York. "The men lose confidence in the weapon, and prefer the revolver." Whittaker recommended that cavalrymen carry "razors three feet long."[29]

A cavalryman's opinion as to whether he needed a saber or not depended in part on his answer to the larger question of whether he was more likely to fight mounted or dismounted. During the course of the Civil War, troopers had increasingly left their saddles to fight on foot. James H. Wilson, drawing on his extensive experience during that conflict, advised a board of officers on cavalry tactics in 1868 that they give their main attention to the dismounted drill. The commanding general of the army suggested, ten years later, that horses served chiefly to bring cavalrymen rapidly to the battlefield, where the troopers would fight on foot with their infantry comrades.[30]

Traditionalists continued to champion the idea that cavalry should fight from the saddle. Gilbert E. Overton of the Sixth Cavalry, who won a brevet by leading a charge on a Cheyenne village in 1874, described in 1880 what he considered the ideal mounted unit. "In a charge," Overton wrote, "it would rival the Mamelukes, who did fire from their horses; it would prove a wonder to the Indians of the plains, who invariably dismount to deliver their fire." One soldier grumbled in 1875 that the Civil War had made troopers too enamored with dismounted cavalry fighting, and John Bell Hood's 1880 memoirs harshly criticized this style of combat. The aggressive Southerner contended: "A cavalryman *proper* cannot be trained to fight, one day, mounted, the next, dismounted, and then be expected to charge with the impetuosity of one who has been educated in the belief that it is an easy matter to ride over infantry and artillery, and drive them from the field."[31]

In addition to the mounted-dismounted debate, the saber was a consideration in the controversy over whether the cavalry's standard formation should be single or double rank. The War Department had authorized and published a two-rank tactics in 1841. The work proved popular with Civil War commanders and enjoyed several printings during the conflict. In 1861 the War Department also authorized Brigadier General Philip St. George Cooke's *Cavalry Tactics*, a single-rank system. The two schools competed for decades, until the official cavalry manual of 1891 resolved the issue in favor of the single-rank tactics. It is significant that debaters on each side of this question emphasized how well the formation they favored would contribute to the shock of mounted tactics rather than to the firepower of dismounted fighting.[32]

While cavalrymen debated these issues, artillerymen considered a few tactical questions that were unique to their arm. Some observers judged that rifled shoulder arms had brought a decline in artillery's power, relative to infantry. The autumn after the Civil War one correspondent of the *Army and*

Navy Journal offered the opinion that field gunnery had "lost its terrors." Six years later, another writer expanded on the point: "The glory of the field artillery has in a measure departed. Batteries lean more heavily on the infantry for support than of old, and there is no longer the scope there once was for 'the judgment, the dash and enterprise, which, in the days of short-ranged and muzzle-loading small arms, went so far in making up the character of the model battery commander.'" A British military observer concluded in the late 1870s that infantry skirmishers could sweep artillerymen from their pieces, while field or even siege guns could make little impression against earthworks staunchly defended by breech-loaders.[33]

Still other soldiers believed that the artillery was gaining in importance. George B. McClellan predicted in 1874 that as field batteries replaced their muzzle-loading pieces with breech-loading ones, they would be able to operate with minimal support from the infantry and that their commanders would thus become more independent. Francis J. Lippitt's *A Treatise on Intrenchments*, published in 1866, assigned artillery a significant role in attacks on fieldworks. A year later the *Army and Navy Journal* emphasized rifled cannon, which had greater accuracy and range than smoothbore pieces, among the factors that were forcing infantry to adopt looser formations.[34]

One of the sharpest artillery debates began with the appearance of the earliest machine guns, which were initially considered fieldpieces rather than infantry weapons because, like cannon, they were mounted on carriages and worked by crews. (The examination for commissioned officers at the Artillery School in 1878 included exercises with "Field guns, including Gatlings.") The first of these new arms were the French Montigny mitrailleuse and the American Ager[35] and Gatling guns. Patented in 1862, the initial model of Richard J. Gatling's weapon had six barrels that were rotated by a hand crank. A later version, tested in January 1865, fired twenty rounds from four barrels in eight seconds.[36] Only a few Civil War officers, all of them Northerners—David D. Porter, Winfield S. Hancock, Benjamin Butler, and John W. Geary—took any interest in the new, rapid-firing weapons.[37] President Abraham Lincoln gave the Ager gun both its nickname, the "Coffee Mill" gun, and his hearty support.[38] But the interest taken by these senior officers and the president was outweighed by resistance from the Union chief of ordnance, James W. Ripley, and the machine gun saw little service during the Civil War.[39]

After Appomattox inventors continued to improve these rapid-firing weapons, and some soldiers welcomed this new ordnance. George B. McClellan found "good grounds for believing" in 1874 "that for the defence of works, of defiles, or of a position of limited extent[,] the mitrailleuse, or, still better, the Gatling gun, will prove to be a very reliable adjunct." Frederick Whittaker predicted that the new weapons would be "invaluable" on the defensive against close-in assaults. William F. Barry, an accomplished artillerist in both theaters of the Civil War, chaired a board of officers that prepared a new artillery tactics in 1868 and 1869. The Barry Board's work included a Gatling gun drill, which was incorporated into the 1874 assimilated artillery manual.[40]

The Gatling gun raised questions about its organization and employment that the army debated for years.[41] Many officers were reluctant to accept the rapid-firing weapons. The most famous example occurred on the eve of the Battle of the Little Big Horn, when George Custer declined Alfred Terry's offer of a platoon of three Gatlings to accompany the Seventh Cavalry. Custer had a sensible reason for refusing the machine guns: mobility was vital in Indian warfare, and the Gatlings were ill suited to the rough terrain of the West. The guns that Custer left to Terry indeed proved a hindrance. Lieutenant James H. Bradley, who marched with the Montana column to the Little Big Horn, recorded that one evening "the cry did go up: ' The battery is missing!' A halt was made, and after some racing and hallooing the missing guns were set right again, having lost the human thread and so wandered a mile or so out of the way." Lieutenant Edward J. McClernand recalled "descending a long and precipitous hill, where it was necessary to fasten many lariats together, tie them to the Gatling gun carriages and then lower the latter by hand." McClernand also remembered that later during Terry's march, "the battery, especially, had great difficulty in keeping up. Several times it was lost and only brought back by repeated trumpet calls."[42]

The questions that the Gatling gun raised for the artillery were part of a larger dilemma. In the late 1860s and 1870s, rapid improvements in weapons had left every arm of the service in a quandary about its tactics. Thoughtful veterans remembered the hideous losses suffered by attacking infantrymen at Malvern Hill, Gettysburg, Cold Harbor, Franklin, and elsewhere and lost confidence in close-ordered assaults. Perceptive soldiers also foresaw that, with defenders gaining breechloaders and improved artillery, attacks would become even more dangerous in future combats than they had been on the dismal battlefields of the Civil War. One veteran of that conflict, Nelson A. Miles, had come up through the ranks to command a division during the Petersburg campaign, when rifle-and-trench warfare came to its culmination in the eastern theater. Miles wrote a letter in 1877 that envisioned future improvements in weapons and logistics but, significantly, said nothing about any corresponding progress in tactics. "In the next war," he predicted, "the breech-loading rifle will give place to the magazine gun, the old models of artillery will disappear and the science of equipping, supplying & muniting a command will be better understood." William T. Sherman was well aware that his army must be willing to change its tactics to keep up with improvements in weapons. He estimated that the American soldier of 1880 could deliver twelve times the firepower of his counterpart of 1779 and imagined that, "if Baron Steuben were to arise, he would doubtless attack one of Upton's thin lines with his old column of attack doubled on the center and would learn in a single lesson that the world has advanced in science, if not in patriotism, courage, and devotion to duty."[43]

It was far easier for the commanding general to declare that new tactics were needed than it was for his subordinates to agree on what those tactics should be. There were several reasons for this. One was that the army's thinking about strategy and tactics continued during the 1870s and 1880s to stress the importance of taking the offensive. Sir Edward Bruce Hamley's *Operations of War*, which Sherman praised as an excellent book,[44] became a text at West Point in 1870 and was taught at the Artillery School in the early 1870s and at the School of Application for Infantry and Cavalry, established at Fort Leavenworth, Kansas, in 1881. Hamley balanced his discussions of the advantages of offense and defense,[45] but his strongest words warned against fighting solely on the strategic and tactical defensive. "To pursue such a course, then," he admonished, "even when very inferior in force, is suicidal in a defender." American commanders continued to regard taking the offensive as a principle of war, and they recognized that, even though attacks had become more dangerous, some situations would require them. "The fact that breech-loading rifles [have] made comparatively easy the defense of any building or intrenchment by a small force against a large one," Sherman noted in 1879, "does not alter the fact that such points must be defended, or must be carried[,] according to the object aimed at."[46]

A second issue was the practical matter of a small-unit commander's ability to control his men. Emory Upton made a case for his system of "fours" and single rank tactics, hoping that loose order and flexibility would help attackers regain parity with defenders. Until the invention of the field radio, however, an officer could not disperse his men far and still communicate orders to them. Alexander S. Webb, a brigade commander during the Battle of the Wilderness, calculated that if the Union force in that engagement had been "properly disposed for battle" in two ranks, with a third of its numbers in reserve, the Federals would have occupied a front of twenty-one miles. If nineteenth-century soldiers were deployed in loose formations across such distances, their officers could not control them. Upton himself acknowledged that "the safety of an army cannot be intrusted to men in open order with whom it is difficult to communicate."[47]

Still another problem was that some officers refused even to consider new tactics. At least one soldier concluded within four years of Appomattox that the army already had given too much study to the question. "After 'cramming' through Scott, Hardee, Casey and Upton," he said wearily, "we hoped that all would join in the exclamation, *Ohe! jam satis* (O! now, there is enough)." William H. Morris believed that there were officers who in 1866 still preferred Scott's old, Mexican War–era musket tactics to Hardee's rifle tactics or, for that matter, to any other system. Morris identified the opponents of tactical innovation as "the old prejudiced fogies" and those who wanted "to preserve the difficulties of the profession—as doctors stick to their prescriptions in latin and hyerogliphics." Another Federal veteran, T. C. H. Smith, believed the resistance came from "the bulk of the old officers aware of having to learn new things."[48]

While some officers resisted new tactics, many others ignored the subject altogether, once they had left West Point. During the late nineteenth century, military science became more complex, requiring soldiers to devote more time to staying current with professional developments, and many did not make the effort. Charles D. Parkhurst, who graduated with the Academy's class of 1868, worried in 1892 that a cadet "is filled with mathematics but not grand tactics. He learns the drill of the three arms of the service, but the drill only; study and labor for years after graduation, are necessary to keep him up to the progress made in the art of war shown by modern battles." During the early months of the Civil War, the volunteer soldier Jacob D. Cox had observed that most career army officers spent little time reading about tactical theory after they left West Point, and he asked Gordon Granger, a regular, about this. " 'What would you expect,' [Granger] said in his sweeping way, 'of men who have had to spend their lives at a two-company post, where there was nothing to do when off duty but play draw-poker and drink whiskey at the sutler's shop?' " Cox believed his comrade's remarks were "picturesquely extravagant, but [they] hit the nail on the head, after all." The commanding general of the army, William T. Sherman, expressed concern that after young officers left West Point, they were not likely to give much more thought to the science of war. "My experience has been," he reflected in 1881, "that Graduates after leaving the Academy, if studiously inclined, are more apt to rest content with the knowledge [they have] already acquired of Tactics without further study, than of mathematics, mechanics, chemistry, geology, &c, which are more attractive." Four years later, one soldier disparagingly claimed that few captains could drill their companies properly and that still fewer officers knew how to drill a battalion.[49]

Those officers who were interested in studying tactics had trouble finding books on the subject. The soldiers assigned to the Department of Missouri during the 1870s and early 1880s could not have read very much about the science of war: their commander, Brigadier General John Pope, complained that the libraries on every post in his jurisdiction had "disappeared" during the Civil War and had not been replaced. The cadets at the United States Military Academy fared only somewhat better. "At the close of the [Civil War]," Jacob D. Cox wrote of West Point, "there was no instruction in strategy or grand tactics, in military history, or in what is called the Art of War. The little book by [Dennis Hart] Mahan on Out-post Duty was the only text-book in Theory, outside the Engineering proper." A cavalryman complained in 1873: "It is well known that we have had breech-loading arms for the last ten years, yet never a line from any competent authority as to how they shall be used." As for the third arm of the service, the artillery,

Inspector General Randolph B. Marcy examined the textbooks available in 1880 and found only one that he considered satisfactory. He dismissed the others as, "for the most part, obsolete" because they included "nothing regarding the improvements and changes in guns, carriages, &c., for the past fourteen years."[50]

If a soldier managed to collect a few books on tactics, he probably had little chance to read them. The army of the late 1860s and 1870s, a small organization that had to contend with Reconstruction, Indian warfare, and daily routine, could not spare much time for professional studies. M. C. Meigs, a well-seasoned officer, acknowledged the press of day-to-day business when he advised in 1879 that it was more useful for a soldier to study "the duties of a Company officer" than "grand strategy." The commanding general of the army expressed his concern the same year that "less time is given to drills and professional instruction than should be the case." Colonel John Gibbon, a perceptive veteran of the Civil and Indian wars, toured the Department of Dakota at the time of these comments and heartily agreed with them. Dissatisfied with the drill and target practice of the troops he inspected, Gibbon blamed "the small size of the companies and the large drafts made upon them for working parties to keep up the ordinary routine labor of the posts." John Pope complained that a similar situation prevailed in his Department of the Missouri, where the "constant work imposed on" his infantrymen "both as laborers and soldiers in the field" left them with "little of the time possessed by [the] more favored arms of [the] service for drills or other military exercises." Pope advocated assembling "a large number" of companies "for purposes of discipline and instruction."[51]

It would be unreasonable to expect the post–Civil War army to have arrived at what twentieth-century officers would consider a body of tactical doctrine. The nineteenth-century army had no permanent process for creating and revising an officially authorized set of tactical principles, recognized and taught throughout the service. Those few officers who were inclined, and were able to find the time, to study tactics could pursue the subject on their own, and they might—or might not—eventually get their ideas before a board of their peers.[52]

The small group of soldiers who evidenced an interest in tactics disagreed among themselves over several fundamental questions of theory, and the army entered the 1880s without a consensus about its tactics. In the late 1860s some officers began to envision grim days when breechloaders, Gatling guns, and improved artillery would create future battlefields even more dangerous than Antietam and Chickamauga. But other soldiers found inspiration in an earlier time, before the Civil War, when leveled bayonets and sharpened sabers had prevailed. These disagreements did not dismay the army's commanding general, who accepted them as part of the natural order of things. Writing in 1881, Sherman recalled the debates of the late 1860s and early 1870s and calmly reflected: "New arms, new habits, and new ideas were engendered by [the Civil War], and good men, skillful officers differed then as now and always."[53]

Endnotes

1. The chaplain of the First Massachusetts is quoted by Edward Steere, *The Wilderness Campaign* (Harrisburg, Pa., 1960), 226, citing W. H. Cudworth, *History of the First Massachusetts Infantry* (Boston, 1886), 460. On the dominance of the tactical defensive during the Civil War, see Grady McWhiney and Perry D. Jamieson, *Attack and Die: Civil War Military Tactics and the Southern Heritage* (University, Ala., 1982), and Edward Hagerman, *The American Civil War and the Origins of Modern Warfare: Ideas, Organization, and Field Command* (Bloomington and Indianapolis, 1988). For Burnside's and Grant's losses, see Thomas L. Livermore, *Numbers and Losses in the Civil War in America, 1861–65* (Boston and New York, 1900), 96, 114.

2. On the resilience of Civil War armies, see Herman Hattaway and Archer Jones, *How the North Won: A Military History of the Civil War* (Urbana, Ill., 1983), 47, 168, 200, 229, 384, 454, 692, 720. Hood's losses at Franklin are discussed in James Lee McDonough and Thomas L. Connelly, *Five Tragic Hours: The Battle of Franklin* (Knoxville, 1983), 157. On the importance of the breech-loading rifle, see Perry D. Jamieson, "The Development of Civil War Tactics" (Ph.D. diss., Wayne State University, 1979), 186, 188, 193–195; on the diminished value of the bayonet and saber, 186, 213–214. Although American soldiers readily understood the advantages of the breechloader, the U.S. Army was slow to adopt a repeating breechloader as its standard arm. See Richard I. Wolf, "Arms and Innovation: The United States Army and the Repeating Rifle" (Ph.D. diss., Boston University, 1981).

3. *Army and Navy Journal* (hereinafter *ANJ*) 3 (November 4, 1865), 169; "Veteran," "Change of Tactics," *ANJ* 3 (September 23, 1865), 76; Ulysses S. Grant to Edwin M. Stanton, February 4, 1867, Roll 680, Grant Board Papers, Adjutant Generals Office (AGO) File 312 A 1869, M-619, National Archives; John Pope, Address to the Army of the Tennessee, October 16, 1873, Roll 19, General Correspondence, William T. Sherman Papers, Library of Congress.

4. William T. Sherman to Stephen A. Hurlbut, May 26, 1874, Roll 46, Letterbooks, Sherman Papers; Annual Reports of the War Department, 1822–1907, M-997, National Archives, Report of the Artillery School, September 12, 1871, Roll 18, 1:79–80 (hereinafter AR, used to mean vol. I only); William T. Sherman to George W. Getty, January 10, 1878, Roll 45, Letterbooks, Sherman Papers; AR, Report of the Artillery School, October 18, 1879, Roll 33, 180–181, (quotation, 180). Founded in the 1820s and active until 1860, the Artillery School was revived in 1868. Russell F. Weigley, *History of the United States Army* (Bloomington, Ind., 1984), 273.

5. Philip H. Sheridan to William T. Sherman, August n.d. and August 20, 1870, Roll 15, Correspondence, Sherman Papers; Philip H. Sheridan, *Personal Memoirs of P. H. Sheridan*, 2 vols. (New York, 1888), 2:451. See also Philip H. Sheridan to William T. Sherman, December 26, 1870, Roll 16, Correspondence, Sherman Papers.

6. Weigley, *History of the Army*, 290; *ANJ* 3 (November 4, 1865), 169; Emory Upton, *A New System of Infantry Tactics, Double and Single Rank, Adapted to American Topography and Improved Fire-Arms* (New York, 1867).

7. *ANJ* 3 (November 4, 1865), 169; "Veteran," "Change of Tactics," 76; McWhiney and Jamieson, *Attack and Die*, 81–88; H. S. Hawkins, quoting Colonel

Robert Home, in "Outline of a Manual of Infantry Drill," *Journal of the Military Service Institution of the United States* (hereinafter *JMSIUS*), II (1890), 361.

8. Emory Upton to Dear Brother, November 6, 1863, and to My Dear Sister, June 4, 1864, and June 5, 1864, in Peter S. Michie, *The Life and Letters of Emory Upton* (New York, 1885), 80, 108, and 109.

9. Michie, *Life and Letters of Upton*, 189–190; U.S. War Department, *The War of the Rebellion: A Compilation of the Official Records of the Union and Confederate Armies*, 128 vols. (Washington, D.C., 1880–1901), ser. 1, 29, pt. 1:576, 586, 588, 589; 36, pt. 1:667–668.

10. Michie, *Life and Letters of Upton*, 156, 191; Emory Upton to Edward D. Townsend, January 13, 1866, ibid., 191–193. On Upton's ideas about tactics, see also Stephen E. Ambrose, *Upton and the Army* (Baton Rouge, 1964), 22, 60–64.

11. "Upton's Tactics," *ANJ* 4 (September 29, 1866), 85; Henry B. Clitz to Edward D. Townsend, January 14, 1867, Roll 680, Clitz Board Papers, AGO File 312 A 1869, M-619, National Archives. Before it considered Upton's tactics, the Clitz Board had reviewed and rejected a system proposed by William H. Morris. Henry B. Clitz to Edward D. Townsend, January [n.d.] 1867, ibid.

12. Special Orders No. 300, June 11, 1867, Edward D. Townsend to Edwin M. Stanton, February 6, 1867, Ulysses S. Grant to Edwin M. Stanton, February 4, 1867, and Proceedings of the Grant Board, Roll 680, Grant Board Papers; Michie, *Life and Letters of Upton*, 197, 198; Upton, *A New System*, ii, iii–iv; William T. Sherman to Philip St. George Cooke, March 7, 1876, Roll 46, Letterbooks, Sherman Papers.

13. AR, Report of the General of the Army, November 10, 1870, Roll 17, 5–6; Special Orders No. 60, August 6, 1869, Roll 682, Schofield Board Papers, AGO File 312 A 1869, M-619, National Archives; Russell F. Weigley, "Emory Upton," *Dictionary of American Military Biography* (Westport, Conn., 1984), 3:1123–1124; Emory Upton to John M. Schofield, September 13, 1869, Roll 682, and William T. Sherman to William W. Belknap, January 18, 1871, Roll 685, Schofield Board Papers; "New Cavalry Tactics," *ANJ* 11 (June 27, 1874), 730; Emory Upton to Thomas M. Vincent, July 11, 1873, Roll 685, Schofield Board Papers.

14. "Where Are the Tactics?," *ANJ* 10 (September 7, 1872), 55; "New Cavalry Tactics," 730.

15. William T. Sherman to Emory Upton, January 3, August 18, and September 23, 1873, Roll 45, and May 21, 1873, Roll 46, Letterbooks, Sherman Papers.

16. Emory Upton, *Infantry Tactics, Double and Single Rank* (New York, 1874); U.S. War Department, *Cavalry Tactics, United States Army, Assimilated to the Tactics of Infantry and Artillery* (New York, 1874), and idem, *Artillery Tactics, United States Army, Assimilated to the Tactics of Infantry and Cavalry* (New York, 1874); William T. Sherman to William H. Morris, August 17, 1882, Roll 47, Letterbooks, Sherman Papers. On the "assimilated" tactics, see also Ambrose, *Upton and the Army*, 76–81.

17. Upton, *A New System*, 1, 48–49, 57–59, 59–63, 83–87. Upton's first manual and his later "assimilated" one both assumed a regiment of ten companies. Ibid., 1–2, and Upton, *Infantry Tactics*, 149.

18. Upton, *A New System*, 92–96; Emory Upton to Edward D. Townsend, January 13, 1866, in Michie, *Life and Letters of Emory Upton*, 192; "Line Officer," "A Tactical Necessity," *ANJ* 23 (January 16, 1886), 488.

19. Upton, *A New System*, iii, iv; "Upton's Tactics," *ANJ* 4 (September 29, 1866), 85, and (February 2, 1867), 421; "Advantages of Upton's Tactics," *ANJ* 5 (May 23, 1868), 634.

20. William H. Morris to Edwin M. Stanton, January 4, 18[6]7, Roll 680, Clitz Board Papers; T. W. Sherman to Lorenzo Thomas, March 26, 1867, Roll 680, Grant Board Papers; "Atlanta," "Upton's and Casey's Tactics," *ANJ* 5 (June 27, 1868), 714. On Upton's critics, see also Jamieson, "Development of Civil War Tactics," 204–207.

21. George B. McClellan, "Army Organization," *Harper's New Monthly Magazine* 49 (1874):409.

22. "Bayonet and Breech-loader," *ANJ* 6 (November 14, 1868), 200; William T. Sherman to Philip H. Sheridan, February 20, 1878, and J. W. Reilly to Philip H. Sheridan, April 2, 1878, Roll 45, Letterbooks, Sherman Papers.

23. Francis J. Lippitt, *A Treatise on the Tactical Use of the Three Arms: Infantry, Artillery, and Cavalry* (New York, 1865), 5, 24 for quotations, and see also 4, 8, 27, 51; Board of Officers, *Reports of Experiments with Rice's Trowel Bayonet, Made by Officers of the Army, Pursuant to Instructions from the War Department* (Springfield, Mass., 1874), 17; William T. Sherman to Francis V. Greene, October 20, 1879, Roll 45, Letterbooks, Sherman Papers.

24. Board of Officers, *Rice's Trowel Bayonet*, 34, 39.

25. McWhiney and Jamieson, *Attack and Die*, 131–132; "Rifle and Sabre," *ANJ* 6 (October 31, 1868), 131; William T. Sherman to Philip H. Sheridan, February 20, 1878, Roll 46, Letterbooks, Sherman Papers.

26. John M. Schofield to William T. Sherman, October 12, 1869, Roll 15, Correspondence, Letterbooks, Sherman Papers; Ordnance Memoranda No. 11, June 10, 1870, Roll 685, Schofield Board Papers; "Small Arms and Accoutrements," *ANJ* 8 (June 17, 1871), 700; Report of Captain E. C. Hentig, August 14, 1880, Roll 94, Recommendations of Lt. Col. James W. Forsyth, AGO File 1558 AGO 1882, M-689, National Archives.

27. William R. Parnell, "Sabre Practices—Cavalry Tactics—1841," *ANJ* 8 (April 22, 1871), 571; "Caballo," "Rifle and Sabre," *ANJ* 6 (January 9, 1869), 326; "A Volunteer Cavalryman," "The St. Louis Board," *ANJ* 8 (July 1, 1871), 735; "Sabre of the Regulars," "Sabres for the Cavalry," *ANJ* 14 (October 14, 1876), 154. See also C. C. C. Carr, "Discussion," *Journal of the United States Cavalry Association* (hereinafter *JUSCA*) 1 (1888), 53–54.

28. Wesley Merritt, "Our Cavalry," *ANJ* 16 (July 5, 1879), 873; John C. Kelton to the Adjutant General, May 24, 1880, Roll 94, Recommendations of Lt. Col. James W. Forsyth.

29. McWhiney and Jamieson, *Attack and Die*, 130; "Sabre of the Regulars," "Sabres for the Cavalry," 154; "A Volunteer Cavalryman," "The Lessons of the Decade," *ANJ* 8 (January 21, 1871), 366.

30. McWhiney and Jamieson, *Attack and Die*, 135–136; James H. Wilson to William H. Emory, July 27, 1868, Roll 680, Emory Board Papers, AGO File 312 A 1869, M-619, National Archives; William T. Sherman to Philip H. Sheridan, February 20, 1878, Roll 46, Letterbooks, Sherman Papers.

31. Francis B. Heitman, *Historical Register and Dictionary of the United States Army*, 2 vols. (Washington, D. C., 1903), 1:763; Report of First Lieutenant Gilbert E. Overton, May 31, 1880, Roll 94, Recommendations of Lt. Col. James W. Forsyth; *ANJ* 13 (October 16, 1875), 153; John B. Hood, *Advance and Retreat* (Bloomington, Ind., 1959), 132.

32. Jamieson, "Development of Civil War Tactics," 218; U.S. War Department, *Cavalry Drill Regulations, United States Army* (Washington, D.C., 1891), 10.

33. "American Infantry Tactics," *ANJ* 3 (October 28, 1865), 149; "A Few Thoughts on Artillery," *ANJ* 8 (July 15, 1871), 768; "The Modern Breechloader," *ANJ* 15 (April 13, 1878), 571. See also "Modern Infantry Fire," *ANJ* 17 (January 3, 1880), 427.

34. McClellan, "Army Organization," 409, 410; Francis J. Lippitt, *A Treatise on Intrenchments* (New York, 1866), 109, 126, 127, 135, 136; "Rank Formation with Breech-Loaders," *ANJ* 4 (February 23, 1867), 421.

35. General Order No. 7, Headquarters Artillery School, March 25, 1878, quoted in AR, Report of the Commanding Officer of the Artillery School, November 4, 1878, Roll 30, 200; David A. Armstrong, *Bullets and Bureaucrats: The Machine Gun and the United States Army, 1861–1916* (Westport, Conn., and London, 1982), 14–22, 60–61.

36. "Tactics for Field Artillery," 11, Roll 682, Proceedings and Report of the Barry Board, AGO File 312 A 1869, M-619, National Archives; "The Gatling Gun," *ANJ* 8 (July 8, 1871), 752–753; Armstrong, *Bullets and Bureaucrats*, 32, 36.

37. Robert V. Bruce, *Lincoln and the Tools of War* (Indianapolis, 1956), 290–291; Armstrong, *Bullets and Bureaucrats*, 18–19.

38. Armstrong, *Bullets and Bureaucrats*, 17–18.

39. Ibid., 14, 15–19, 24–25, 33; Bruce, *Lincoln and the Tools of War*, 120, 196–197, 200, 249–251, 290.

40. McClellan, "Army Organization," 409; "A Volunteer Cavalryman," "The Lessons of the Decade," *ANJ* 8 (April 15, 1871), 558; "Tactics for Field Artillery," 167–170, Roll 682, Proceedings and Report of the Barry Board; Emory Upton to Henry A. DuPont, February 25, 1875, in Michie, *Life and Letters of Emory Upton*, 212; War Department, *Artillery Tactics Assimilated*, 74–79.

41. See David A. Armstrong's thorough study, *Bullets and Bureaucrats*.

42. Robert M. Utley, *Frontier Regulars: The United States Army and the Indian, 1866–1891* (New York and London, 1973), 259, 265; Edgar I. Stewart, *Custer's Luck* (Norman, Okla., 1955), 178, 246; James S. Brisbin to E. S. Godfrey, January 1, 1892, quoted in E. A. Brininstool, *Troopers with Custer: Historic Incidents of the Little Big Horn* (London and Lincoln, Nebr., 1989), 279–280; James H. Bradley, *The March of the Montana Column: A Prelude to the Custer Disaster*, ed. Edgar I. Stewart (Norman, Okla., 1961), 150; Edward J. McClernand, *With the Indian and the Buffalo in Montana, 1870–1878* (Glendale, Calif., 1969), 49 and 50. McClernand believed Custer "could have taken the [Gatling] guns as easily as [John] Gibbon [and Alfred Terry], for the latter crossed a more difficult country." Ibid., 47. Whether the Gatlings would have saved Custer is another matter. See Armstrong, *Bullets and Bureaucrats*, 82.

43. Nelson A. Miles to William T. Sherman, January 4, 1877, Roll 23, General Correspondence, Sherman Papers; William T. Sherman, Address to the Class of 1880, U.S. Artillery School, April 28, 1880, Roll 45, Letterbooks, Sherman Papers.

44. Robert Wooster, *The Military and United States Indian Policy, 1865–1903* (London and New Haven, Conn., 1988), 57–58; William T. Sherman to Emory Upton, January 3, 1873, Roll 44, Letterbooks, Sherman Papers.

45. Wooster, *The Military and Indian Policy*, 57; William T. Sherman to Emory Upton, January 3, 1873, Roll 44, Letterbooks, Sherman Papers; AR, Orders No. 127, Post of Fort Leavenworth, Kansas, May 28, 1884, Roll 47, 192; Edward Bruce Hamley, *The Operations of War* (Edinburgh and London, 1866), 41–45, especially 44–45.

46. Ibid., 44; William T. Sherman to Francis V. Greene, October 20, 1879, Roll 45, Letterbooks, Sherman Papers. It should be acknowledged that while American

soldiers were unable to solve the problem of the dominance of the defensive, neither were European military men, many of whom failed to grasp the tactical lessons of the Civil War. See Jay Luvaas, *The Military Legacy of the Civil War: The European Inheritance* (Chicago, 1959), especially 46, 49, 73–74, 115, 123, 140–142, 150, 166–168, 179.

47. Alexander S. Webb, "Through the Wilderness," Robert U. Johnson and Clarence C. Buel, eds., *Battles and Leaders of the Civil War*, 4 vols. (New York, 1956), 4:152; Upton, *Infantry Tactics*, viii.

48. "Uniform Tactics," *ANJ* 7 (September 18, 1869), 66; William H. Morris to George H. Thomas, June 8, 1866, Roll 680, Clitz Board Papers; T. C. H. Smith to Philip St. George Cooke, November 4, 1866, Roll 680, Grant Board Papers.

49. Charles D. Parkhurst, "Field Artillery: Its Organization and Its Role," *Journal of the United States Artillery* (hereinafter *JUSA*) 1 (1892), 262; Jacob D. Cox, *Military Reminiscences of the Civil War*, 2 vols. (New York, 1900), 1:175; William T. Sherman to the Secretary of War, August 20, 1881, Roll 47, Letterbooks, Sherman Papers; H., "Ignorance of Tactics in the Army," *ANJ* 22 (January 3, 1885), 451. This opinionated letter sparked a lively debate in the *Army and Navy Journal*. See: G. N. Whistler, "Ignorance of Tactics in the Army," *ANJ* 22 (January 17, 1885), 480; "Ignorance of the Tactics," *ANJ* 22 (January 24, 1885), 515; and "Knowledge of Tactics," *ANJ* 22 (February 21, 1885), 597.

50. AR, Report of the Department of Missouri, September 15, 1877, Roll 28, 65; Cox, *Military Reminiscences*, 1:177; "Cavalry," "Cavalry Tactics," *ANJ* 10 (February 8, 1873), 410; AR, Report of the Inspector General, October 9, 1880, Roll 35, 50.

51. M. C. Meigs to William T. Sherman, July 9, 1879, Roll 26, General Correspondence, Sherman Papers; AR, Report of the General of the Army, November 1, 1879, Roll 33, 14; AR, Report of the Acting Inspector General, Department of Dakota, October 3, 1879, 67; AR, Report of the Department of the Missouri, October 3, 1879, 84. On the army's experience with Reconstruction, see James E. Sefton, *The United States Army and Reconstruction* (Baton Rouge, 1967), and Edward M. Coffman, *The Old Army: A Portrait of the American Army in Peacetime, 1784–1898* (New York and Oxford, 1986), 234–246.

52. The post–Civil War army's lack of "doctrine," in the formal way that twentieth-century officers defined the term, is discussed in the third chapter of this work and in Larry D. Roberts, U.S. Army Combat Studies Institute, "Strategy, Doctrine, and the Frontier Army" (MS in possession of P. D. Jamieson).

53. William T. Sherman to Philip St. George Cooke, May 10, 1881, Roll 46, Letterbooks, Sherman Papers.

Our First Southeast Asian War

David R. Kohler and James Wensyel

Almost totally forgotten in American history is the four-year war fought by the Army against Filipino guerrillas in the aftermath of the Spanish-American War. Before it was over some 126,000 U.S. troops had been committed and 4,000 lives had been lost. And as many as 200,000 Filipinos had also perished from wounding, sickness, and starvation. For the Army, drastic changes in strategy and tactics had to be learned and put into practice to overcome stubborn Filipino resistance in a war marked by brutality on both sides. Unfortunately, the lessons learned in this colonial war were soon forgotten, only to be relearned in blood in Vietnam six decades later. David Kohler is a retired Navy officer, and James Wensyel is a retired Army officer. From American History Illustrated, *Jan./Feb. 1990 by David R. Kohler and James Wensyel. Copyright © by American History Illustrated. Reprinted by permission of PRIMEDIA Enthusiasts Publications (History Group).*

Guerrilla warfare . . . jungle terrain . . . search and destroy missions . . . benevolent pacification . . . strategic hamlets . . . terrorism . . . ambushes . . . free-fire zones . . . booby traps . . . waning support from civilians at home. These words call forth from the national consciousness uncomfortable images of a war Americans fought and died in not long ago in Southeast Asia. But while the phrases may first bring to mind America's painful experience in Vietnam during the 1960s and '70s, they also aptly describe a much earlier conflict—the Philippine Insurrection—that foreshadowed this and other insurgent wars in Asia.

The Philippine-American War of 1898–1902 is one of our nation's most obscure and least-understood campaigns. Sometimes called the "Bolo War" because of the Filipino insurgents' lethally effective use of razor-sharp bolo knives or machetes against the American expeditionary force occupying the islands, it is often viewed as a mere appendage of the one-hundred-day Spanish-American War. But suppressing the guerrilla warfare waged by Philippine nationalists seeking self-rule proved far more difficult, protracted, and costly for American forces than the conventional war with Spain that had preceded it.

America's campaign to smash the Philippine Insurrection was, ironically, a direct consequence of U.S. efforts to secure independence for other *insurrectos* halfway around the world in Cuba. On May 1, 1898, less than a week after Congress declared war against Spain, a naval squadron commanded by Commodore George Dewey steamed into Manila Bay to engage the Spanish warships defending that nation's Pacific possession. In a brief action Dewey achieved a stunning victory, sinking all of the enemy vessels with no significant American losses. Destroying the Spanish fleet, however, did not ensure U.S. possession of the Philippines. An estimated 15,000 Spanish soldiers still occupied Manila and the surrounding region. Those forces would have to be rooted out by infantry.

President William McKinley had already ordered a Philippine Expeditionary Force of volunteer and regular army infantry, artillery, and cavalry units (nearly seven thousand men), under the command of Major General Wesley Merritt, to "reduce Spanish power in that quarter [Philippine Islands] and give order and security to the islands while in the possession of the United States."

Sent to the Philippines in the summer of 1898, this limited force was committed without fully considering the operation's potential length and cost. American military and government leaders also failed to anticipate the consequences of ignoring the Filipino rebels who, under Generalissimo Don Emilio Aguinaldo y Famy, had been waging a war for independence against Spain for the past two years. And when American insensitivity toward Aguinaldo eventually led to open warfare with the rebels, the American leaders grossly underestimated the determination of the seemingly ill-trained and poorly armed insurgents. They additionally failed to perceive the difficulties involved in conducting military operations in a tropical environment and among a hostile native population, and they did not recognize the burden of fighting at the end of a seven-thousand-mile-long logistics trail.

Asian engagements, the Americans learned for the first time, are costly. The enterprise, so modestly begun, eventually saw more than 126,000 American officers and men deployed to the Philippines. Four times as many soldiers served in this undeclared war in the Pacific as had been sent to the Caribbean during the Spanish-American War. During the three-year conflict, American troops and Filipino insurgents fought in more than 2,800 engagements. American casualties ultimately totaled 4,234 killed and 2,818 wounded, and the insurgents lost about 16,000 men. The civilian population suffered even more; as many as 200,000 Filipinos died from famine, pestilence, or the unfortunate happenstance of being too close to the fighting. The Philippine war cost the United States $600 million before the insurgents were subdued.

The costly experience offered valuable and timeless lessons about guerrilla warfare in Asia; unfortunately, those lessons had to be relearned sixty years later in another war that, despite the modern technology involved, bore surprising parallels to America's first Southeast Asian campaign.

Origins

America's war with Spain, formally declared by the United States on April 25, 1898, had been several years in the making. During that time the American "yellow press," led by Joseph Pulitzer's *New York World* and William Randolph Hearst's *New York Journal*, trumpeted reports of heroic Cuban *insurrectos* revolting against their cruel Spanish rulers. Journalists vividly described harsh measures taken by Spanish officials to quell the Cuban revolution. The sensational accounts, often exaggerated, reminded Americans of their own uphill fight for independence and nourished the feeling that America was destined to intervene so that the Cuban people might also taste freedom.

Furthermore, expansionists suggested that the revolt against a European power, taking place less than one hundred miles from American shores, offered a splendid opportunity to turn the Caribbean into an American sea. Businessmen pointed out that $50 million in American capital was invested in the Cuban sugar and mining industries. Revolutions resulting in burned cane fields jeopardized that investment. As 1898 opened, American relations with Spain quickly declined.

In January 1898 the U.S. battleship *Maine* was sent to Cuba, ostensibly on a courtesy visit. On February 15 the warship was destroyed by a mysterious explosion while at anchor in Havana harbor, killing 262 of her 350-man crew. The navy's formal inquiry, completed on March 28, suggested that the explosion was due to an external force—a mine.

On March 29, the Spanish government received an ultimatum from Washington, D.C.: Spain's army in Cuba was to lay down its arms while the United States negotiated between the rebels and the Spaniards. The Spanish forces were also told to abolish all *reconcentrado* camps (tightly controlled areas, similar to the strategic hamlets later tried in Vietnam, where peasants were regrouped to deny food and intelligence to insurgents and to promote tighter security). Spain initially rejected the humiliation of surrendering its arms in the field but then capitulated on all points. The Americans were not satisfied.

On April 11, declaring that Spanish responses were inadequate, President McKinley told a joint session of Congress that "I have exhausted every effort to relieve the intolerable condition . . . at our doors. I now ask the Congress to empower the president to take measures to secure a full and final termination of hostilities in Cuba, to secure . . . the establishment of a stable government, and to use the military and naval forces of the United States . . . for these purposes. . . ."

Congress adopted the proposed resolution on April 19. Learning this, Spain declared war on the 24th. The following day, the United States responded with its own declaration of war.

The bulk of the American navy quickly gathered on the Atlantic coast. McKinley called for 125,000 volunteers to bolster the less than eighty-thousand-man regular army. His call was quickly oversubscribed; volunteers fought to be the first to land on Cuba's beaches.

The first major battle of the war, however, was fought not in Cuba but seven thousand miles to the west—in Manila Bay. Dewey's victory over Spanish Admiral Patricio Montojo y Pasarón (a rather hollow victory as Montojo's fleet consisted of seven unarmored ships, three of which had wooden hulls and one that had to be towed to the battle area) was wildly acclaimed in America.

American leaders, believing that the Philippines would now fall into America's grasp like a ripe plum, had to decide what to do with their prize. They could not return the islands to Spain, nor could they allow them to pass to France or Germany, America's commercial rivals in the Orient. The American press rejected the idea of a British protectorate. And, after four hundred years of despotic Spanish rule in which Filipinos had little or no chance to practice self-government, native leaders seemed unlikely candidates for managing their own affairs. McKinley faced a grand opportunity for imperialistic expansion that could not be ignored.

The debate sharply divided his cabinet—and the country. American public opinion over acquisition of the Philippines divided into two basic factions: imperialists versus anti-imperialists.

The imperialists, mostly Republicans, included such figures as Theodore Roosevelt (then assistant secretary of the navy), Henry Cabot Lodge (Massachusetts senator), and Albert Beveridge (Indiana senator). These individuals were, for the most part, disciples of Alfred Thayer Mahan, a naval strategist who touted theories of national power and prestige through sea power and acquisition of overseas colonies for trade purposes and naval coaling stations.

The anti-imperialists, staunchly against American annexation of the Philippines, were mainly Democrats. Such men as former presidents Grover Cleveland and Rutherford B. Hayes, steel magnate Andrew Carnegie, William Jennings Bryan, union leader Samuel Gompers, and Mark Twain warned that by taking the Philippines the United States would march the road to ruin earlier traveled by the Roman Empire. Furthermore, they argued, America would be denying Filipinos the right of self-determination guaranteed by our own Constitution. The more practical-minded also pointed out that imperialistic policy would require maintaining an expensive army and navy there.

Racism, though demonstrated in different ways, pervaded the arguments of both sides. Imperialists spoke of the "white man's burden" and moral responsibility to "uplift the child races everywhere" and to provide "orderly development for the unfortunate and less able races." They spoke of America's "civilizing mission" of pacifying Filipinos by "benevolent assimilation" and saw the opening of the overseas frontier much as their forefathers had viewed the western frontier. The "subjugation of the Injun" (wherever he might be found) was a concept grasped by American youth— the war's most enthusiastic supporters (in contrast to young America's opposition to the war in Vietnam many years later).

The anti-imperialists extolled the sacredness of independence and self-determination for the Filipinos. Racism, however, also crept into their argument, for they believed that "protection against race mingling" was a historic American policy that would be reversed by imperialism. To them, annexation of the Philippines would admit "alien, inferior, and mongrel races to our nationality."

As the debate raged, Dewey continued to hold Manila Bay, and the Philippines seemed to await America's pleasure. President McKinley would ultimately cast the deciding vote in determining America's role in that country. McKinley, a genial, rather laid-back, former congressman from Ohio and one-time major in the Union army, remains a rather ambiguous figure during this period. In his Inaugural Address he had affirmed that "We want no wars of conquest; we must avoid the temptation of territorial aggression." Thereafter, however, he made few comments on pacifism, and, fourteen weeks after becoming president, signed the bill annexing Hawaii.

Speaking of Cuba in December 1897, McKinley said, "I speak not of forcible annexation, for that cannot be thought of. That, by our code of morality, would be criminal aggression." Nevertheless, he constantly pressured Madrid to end Spanish rule in Cuba, leading four months later to America's war with Spain.

McKinley described experiencing extreme turmoil, soul-searching, and prayer over the Philippine annexation issue until, he declared, one night in a dream the Lord revealed to him that "there was nothing left for us to do but to take them all [the Philippine Islands] and to educate the Filipinos, and uplift, and civilize, and Christianize them." He apparently didn't realize that the Philippines had been staunchly Roman Catholic for more than 350 years under Spanish colonialism. Nor could he anticipate the difficulties that, having cast its fortune with the expansionists, America would now face in the Philippines.

Prosecuting the War

Meanwhile, in the Philippine Islands, Major General Wesley Merritt's Philippine Expeditionary Force went about its job. In late June, General Thomas Anderson led an advance party ashore at Cavite. He then established Camp Merritt, visited General Aguinaldo's rebel forces entrenched around Manila, and made plans for seizing that city once Merritt arrived with the main body of armed forces.

Anderson quickly learned that military operations in the Philippines could be difficult. His soldiers, hastily assembled and dispatched with limited prior training, were poorly disciplined and inadequately equipped. Many still wore woolen uniforms despite the tropical climate. A staff officer described the army's baptism at Manila: ". . . the heat was oppressive and the rain kept falling. At times the trenches were filled with two feet of water, and soon the men's shoes were ruined. Their heavy khaki uniforms were a nuisance; they perspired constantly, the loss of body salts inducing chronic fatigue. Prickly heat broke out, inflamed by scratching and rubbing. Within a week the first cases of dysentery, malaria, cholera, and dengue fever showed up at sick call."

During his first meeting with Dewey, Anderson remarked that some American leaders were considering annexation of the Philippines. "If the United States intends to hold the Philippine Islands," Dewey responded, "it will make things awkward, because just a week ago Aguinaldo proclaimed the independence of the Philippine Islands from Spain and seems intent on establishing his own government."

A Filipino independence movement led by Aguinaldo had been active in the islands since 1896 and, within weeks of Dewey's victory, Aguinaldo's revolutionaries controlled most of the archipelago.

Aguinaldo, twenty-nine years old in 1898, had taken over his father's position as mayor of his hometown of Kawit before becoming a revolutionary. In a minor skirmish with Spanish soldiers, he had rallied the Filipinos to victory. Thereafter, his popularity grew as did his ragtag but determined army. Aguinaldo was slight of build, shy, and soft-spoken, but a strict disciplinarian.

As his rebel force besieged Manila, Aguinaldo declared a formal government for the Philippines with himself as president and generalissimo. He proclaimed his "nation's" independence and called for Filipinos to rally to his army and to the Americans, declaring that "the Americans . . . extend their protecting mantle to our beloved country. . . . When you see the American flag flying, assemble in numbers: they are our redeemers!" But his enthusiasm for the United States later waned.

Merritt put off Aguinaldo's increasingly strident demands that America recognize his government and guarantee the Filipinos' independence. Aguinaldo perceived the American general's attitude as condescending and demeaning.

On August 13, Merritt's forces occupied Manila almost without firing a shot; in a face-saving maneuver the Spanish defenders had agreed to surrender to the Americans to avoid being captured—and perhaps massacred—by the Filipino insurgents. Merritt's troops physically blocked Aguinaldo's rebels, who had spent weeks in the trenches around the city, from participating in the assault. The Filipino general and his followers felt betrayed at being denied a share in the victory.

Further disenchanted, Aguinaldo would later find his revolutionary government unrepresented at the Paris peace talks determining his country's fate. He would learn that Spain had ceded the Philippines to the United States for $20 million.

Officers at Merritt's headquarters had little faith in the Filipinos' ability to govern themselves. "Should our power . . . be withdrawn," an early report declared, "the Philippines would speedily lapse into anarchy, which would excuse . . . the intervention of other powers and the division of the islands among them."

Meanwhile, friction between American soldiers and the Filipinos increased. Much of the Americans' conduct betrayed their racial bias. Soldiers referred to the natives as "niggers" and "gu-gus," epithets whose meanings were clear to the Filipinos. In retaliation, the island inhabitants refused to give way on sidewalks and muscled American officers into the streets. Men of the expeditionary force in turn escalated tensions by stopping Filipinos at gun point, searching them without cause, "confiscating" shopkeepers' goods, and beating those who resisted.

On the night of February 4, 1899 the simmering pot finally boiled over. Private William "Willie" Walter Grayson and several other soldiers of Company D, 1st Nebraska Volunteer Infantry, apprehended a group of armed insurgents within their regimental picket line. Shots were exchanged, and three Filipino *insurrectos* fell dead. Heavy firing erupted between the two camps.

In the bloody battle that followed, the Filipinos suffered tremendous casualties (an estimated two thousand to five thousand dead, contrasted with fifty-nine Americans killed) and were forced to withdraw. The Philippine Insurrection had begun.

Guerrilla Warfare

The Americans, hampered by a shortage of troops and the oncoming rainy season, could initially do little more than extend their defensive perimeter beyond Manila and establish a toehold on several islands to the south. By the end of March, however, American forces seized Malolos, the seat of Aguinaldo's revolutionary government. But Aguinaldo escaped, simply melting into the jungle. In the fall, using conventional methods of warfare, the Americans first struck south, then north of Manila across the central Luzon plain. After hard marching and tough fighting, the expeditionary force occupied northern Luzon, dispersed the rebel army, and barely missed capturing Aguinaldo.

Believing that occupying the remainder of the Philippines would be easy, the Americans wrongly concluded that the war was virtually ended. But when the troops attempted to control the territory they had seized, they found that the Filipino revolutionaries were not defeated but had merely changed strategies. Abandoning western-style conventional warfare, Aguinaldo had decided to adopt guerrilla tactics.

Aguinaldo moved to a secret mountain headquarters at Palanan in northern Luzon, ordering his troops to disperse and avoid pitched battles in favor of hit-and-run operations by small bands. Ambushing parties of Americans and applying terror to coerce support from other Filipinos, the insurrectionists now blended into the countryside, where they enjoyed superior intelligence information, ample supplies, and tight security. The guerrillas moved freely between the scattered American units, cutting telegraph lines, attacking supply trains, and assaulting straggling infantry-men. When the Americans pursued their tormentors, they fell into well planned ambushes. The insurgents' barbarity and ruthlessness during these attacks were notorious.

The guerrilla tactics helped to offset the inequities that existed between the two armies. The American troops were far better armed, for example, carrying .45-caliber Springfield single-shot rifles, Mausers, and then-modern .30-caliber repeating Krag-Jorgensen rifles. They also had field artillery and machine guns. The revolutionaries, on the other hand, were limited to a miscellaneous assortment of handguns, a few Mauser repeating rifles taken from the Spanish, and antique muzzle-loaders. The sharp-edged bolo knife was the revolutionary's primary weapon, and he used it well. Probably more American soldiers were hacked to death by bolos than were killed by Mauser bullets.

As would later be the case in Vietnam, the guerrillas had some clear ad-vantages. They knew the terrain, were inured to the climate, and could gen-erally count on a friendly population. As in Vietnam, villages controlled by the insurgents provided havens from which the guerrillas could attack, then fade back into hiding.

Americans soon began to feel that they were under siege in a land of en-emies, and their fears were heightened because they never could be sure who among the population was hostile. A seemingly friendly peasant might actually be a murderer. Lieutenant Colonel J.T. Wickham, commanding the 26th Infantry Regiment, recorded that "a large flag of truce enticed officers into ambushes . . . Privates Dugan, Hayes, and Tracy were murdered by town authorities . . . Private Nolan [was] tied up by ladies while in a stupor; the insurgents cut his throat . . . The body of Corporal Doneley was dug up, burned, and mutilated . . . Private O'Hearn, captured by apparently friendly people was tied to a tree, burned over a slow fire, and slashed up . . . Lieu-tenant Max Wagner was assassinated by insurgents disguised in American uniforms."

As in later guerrilla movements, such terrorism became a standard tac-tic for the insurgents. Both Filipinos and Americans were their victims. In preying on their countrymen, the guerrillas had a dual purpose: to discour-age any Filipinos disposed to cooperate with the Americans, and to demon-strate to people in a particular region that they ruled that area and could destroy inhabitants and villages not supporting the revolution. The most fa-vored terroristic weapon was assassination of local leaders, who were usu-ally executed in a manner (such as beheading or burying alive) calculated to horrify everyone.

By the spring of 1900 the war was going badly for the Americans. Their task forces, sent out to search and destroy, found little and destroyed less.

The monsoon rains, jungle terrain, hostile native population, and a determined guerrilla force made the American soldiers' marches long and miserable. One described a five-week-long infantry operation: ". . . our troops had been on half rations for two weeks. Wallowing through hip-deep muck, lugging a ten-pound rifle and a belt . . . with 200 rounds of ammunition, drenched to the skin and with their feet becoming heavier with mud at every step, the infantry became discouraged. Some men simply cried, others slipped down in the mud and refused to rise. Threats and appeals by the officers were of no avail. Only a promise of food in the next town and the threat that if they remained behind they would be butchered by marauding bands of insurgents forced some to their feet to struggle on."

News reports of the army's difficulties began to erode the American public's support for the war. "To chase barefooted insurgents with water buffalo carts as a wagon train may be simply ridiculous," charged one correspondent, "but to load volunteers down with 200 rounds of ammunition and one day's rations, and to put on their heads felt hats used by no other army in the tropics . . . to trot these same soldiers in the boiling sun over a country without roads, is positively criminal. . . . There are over five thousand men in the general hospital."

Another reported that the American outlook "is blacker now than it has been since the beginning of the war . . . the whole population . . . sympathizes with the insurgents. The insurgents came to Pasig [a local area whose government cooperated with the Americans] and their first act was to hang the 'Presidente' for treason in surrendering to Americans. 'Presidentes' do not surrender to us anymore."

New Strategies

Early in the war U.S. military commanders had realized that, unlike the American Indians who had been herded onto reservations, eight million Filipinos (many of them hostile) would have to be governed in place. The Americans chose to emphasize pacification through good works rather than by harsh measures, hoping to convince Filipinos that the American colonial government had a sincere interest in their welfare and could be trusted.

As the army expanded its control across the islands, it reorganized local municipal governments and trained Filipinos to take over civil functions in the democratic political structure the Americans planned to establish. American soldiers performed police duties, distributed food, established and taught at schools, and built roads and telegraph lines.

As the war progressed, however, the U.S. commanders saw that the terrorism practiced by Aguinaldo's guerrillas was far more effective in controlling the populace than was their own benevolent approach. Although the Americans did not abandon pacification through good works, it was thereafter subordinated to the "civilize 'em with a Krag" (Krag-Jorgensen rifle) philosophy. From December 1900 onward, captured revolutionaries faced deportation, imprisonment, or execution.

The American army also changed its combat strategy to counter that of its enemy. As in the insurgents' army, the new tactics emphasized mobility and surprise. Breaking into small units—the battalion became the largest maneuver force—the Americans gradually spread over the islands until each of the larger towns was occupied by one or two rifle companies. From these bases American troops began platoon- and company-size operations to pressure local guerrilla bands.

Because of the difficult terrain, limited visibility, and requirement for mobility, artillery now saw limited use except as a defensive weapon. The infantry became the main offensive arm, with mounted riflemen used to pursue the fleeing enemy. Cavalry patrols were so valued for their mobility that American military leaders hired trusted Filipinos as mounted scouts and cavalrymen.

The Americans made other efforts to "Filipinize" the war—letting Asians fight Asians. (A similar tactic had been used in the American Indian campaigns twenty years before; it would resurface in Vietnam sixty years later as "Vietnamization.") In the Philippines the Americans recruited five thousand Macabebes, mercenaries from the central Luzon province of Pampanga, to form the American-officered Philippine Scouts. The Macabebes had for centuries fought in native battalions under the Spanish flag—even against their own countrymen when the revolution began in 1896.

Just as a later generation of American soldiers would react to the guerrilla war in Vietnam, American soldiers in the Philippines responded to insurgent terrorism in kind, matching cruelty with cruelty. Such actions vented their frustration at being unable to find and destroy the enemy. An increasing number of Americans viewed all Filipinos as enemies.

"We make everyone get into his house by 7 P.M. and we only tell a man once," Corporal Sam Gillis of the 1st California Volunteer Regiment wrote to his family. "If he refuses, we shoot him. We killed over 300 natives the first night. . . . If they fire a shot from a house, we burn the house and every house near it."

Another infantryman frankly admitted that "with an enemy like this to fight, it is not surprising that the boys should soon adopt 'no quarter' as a motto and fill the blacks full of lead before finding out whether they are friends or enemies."

That attitude should not have been too surprising. The army's campaigns against the Plains Indians were reference points for the generation of Americans that took the Philippines. Many of the senior officers and noncommissioned officers—often veterans of the Indian wars—considered Filipinos to be "as full of treachery as our Arizona Apache." "The country won't be pacified," one soldier told a reporter, "until the niggers are killed off like the Indians." A popular soldiers' refrain, sung to the tune of "Tramp, tramp, tramp, the boys are marching," began, "Damn, damn, damn the Filipinos," and again spoke of "civilizing 'em with a Krag."

Reprisals against civilians by Americans as well as insurgents became common. General Lloyd Wheaton, leading a U.S. offensive southeast of Manila, found his men impaled on the bamboo prongs of booby traps and with throats slit while they slept. After two of his companies were ambushed, Wheaton ordered that every town and village within twelve miles be burned.

The Americans developed their own terrorist methods, many of which would be used in later Southeast Asian wars. One was torturing suspected guerrillas or insurgent sympathizers to force them to reveal locations of other guerrillas and their supplies. An often-utilized form of persuasion was the "water cure," placing a bamboo reed in the victim's mouth and pouring water (some used salt water or dirty water) down his throat, thus painfully distending the victim's stomach. The subject, allowed to void this, would, under threat of repetition, usually talk freely. Another method of torture, the "rope cure," consisted of wrapping a rope around the victim's neck and torso until it formed a sort of girdle. A stick (or Krag rifle), placed between the ropes and twisted, then effectively created a combination of smothering and garroting.

The anti-imperialist press reported such American brutality in lurid detail. As a result, a number of officers and soldiers were court-martialed for torturing and other cruelties. Their punishments, however, seemed remarkably lenient. Of ten officers tried for "looting, torture, and murder," three were acquitted; of the seven convicted, five were reprimanded, one was reprimanded and fined $300, and one lost thirty-five places in the army's seniority list and forfeited half his pay for nine months.

Officers and soldiers, fighting a cruel, determined, and dangerous enemy, could not understand public condemnation of the brutality they felt was necessary to win. They had not experienced such criticism during the Indian wars, where total extermination of the enemy was condoned by the press and the American public, and they failed to grasp the difference now. Press reports, loss of public support, and the soldiers' feeling of betrayal—features of an insurgent war—would resurface decades later during the Vietnam conflict.

Success

Although U.S. military leaders were frustrated by the guerrillas' determination on one hand and by eroding American support for the war on the other, most believed that the insurgents could be subdued. Especially optimistic was General Arthur MacArthur, who in 1900 assumed command of the seventy thousand American troops in the Philippines. MacArthur adopted a strategy like that successfully used by General Zachary Taylor in the Second Seminole War in 1835; he believed that success depended upon the Americans' ability to isolate the guerrillas from their support in the villages. Thus were born "strategic hamlets," "free-fire zones," and "search and destroy" missions, concepts the American army would revive decades later in Vietnam.

MacArthur strengthened the more than five hundred small strong points held by Americans throughout the Philippine Islands. Each post was garrisoned by at least one company of American infantrymen. The natives around each base were driven from their homes, which were then destroyed. Soldiers herded the displaced natives into *reconcentrado* camps, where they could be "protected" by the nearby garrisons. Crops, food stores, and houses outside the camps were destroyed to deny them to the guerrillas. Surrounding each camp was a "dead line," within which anyone appearing would be shot on sight.

Operating from these small garrisons, the Americans pressured the guerrillas, allowing them no rest. Kept off balance, short of supplies, and constantly pursued by the American army, the Filipino guerrillas, suffering from sickness, hunger, and dwindling popular support, began to lose their will to fight. Many insurgent leaders surrendered, signaling that the tide at last had turned in the Americans' favor.

In March 1901, a group of Macabebe Scouts, commanded by American Colonel Frederick "Fighting Fred" Funston, captured Aguinaldo. Aguinaldo's subsequent proclamation that he would fight no more, and his pledge of loyalty to the United States, sped the collapse of the insurrection.

As in the past, and as would happen again during the Vietnam conflict of the 1960s and '70s, American optimism was premature. Although a civilian commission headed by William H. Taft took control of the colonial government from the American army in July 1901, the army faced more bitter fighting in its "pacification" of the islands.

As the war sputtered, the insurgents' massacre of fifty-nine American soldiers at Balangiga on the island of Samar caused Brigadier General Jacob W. "Hell-Roaring Jake" Smith, veteran of the Wounded Knee massacre of the Sioux in 1890, to order his officers to turn Samar into a "howling wilderness." His orders to a battalion of three hundred Marines headed for Samar were precise: "I want no prisoners. I wish you to kill and burn, the more you kill and burn the better it will please me. I want all persons killed who are capable of bearing arms against the United States." Fortunately, the Marines did not take Smith's orders literally and, later, Smith would be court-martialed.

On July 4, 1902 the Philippine Insurrection officially ended. Although it took the American army another eleven years to crush the fierce Moros of the southern Philippines, the civil government's security force (the Philippine Constabulary), aided by the army's Philippine Scouts, maintained a fitful peace throughout the islands. The army's campaign to secure the Philippines as an American colony had succeeded.

American commanders would have experienced vastly greater difficulties except for two distinct advantages: 1) the enemy had to operate in a restricted area, in isolated islands, and was prevented by the U.S. Navy from importing weapons and other needed supplies; and 2) though the insurgents attempted to enlist help from Japan, no outside power intervened.

These conditions would not prevail in some subsequent guerrilla conflicts in Asia.

In addition to the many tactical lessons the army learned from fighting a guerrilla war in a tropical climate, other problems experienced during this campaign validated the need for several military reforms that were subsequently carried out, including improved logistics, tropical medicine, and communications.

The combination of harsh and unrelenting military force against the guerrillas, complemented by the exercise of fair and equitable civil government and civic action toward those who cooperated, proved to be the Americans' most effective tactic for dealing with the insurgency. This probably was the most significant lesson to be learned from the Philippine Insurrection.

Lessons for the Future

Vietnam veterans reading this account might nod in recollection of a personal, perhaps painful experience from their own war.

Many similarities exist between America's three-year struggle with the Filipino *insurrectos* and the decade-long campaign against the Communists in Vietnam. Both wars, modestly begun, went far beyond what anyone had foreseen in time, money, equipment, manpower, casualties, and suffering.

Both wars featured small-unit infantry actions. Young infantrymen, if they had any initial enthusiasm, usually lost it once they saw the war's true nature; they nevertheless learned to endure their allotted time while adopting personal self-survival measures as months "in-country" lengthened and casualty lists grew.

Both wars were harsh, brutal, cruel. Both had their Samar Islands and their My Lais. Human nature being what it is, both conflicts also included acts of great heroism, kindness, compassion, and self-sacrifice.

Both wars saw an increasingly disenchanted American public withdrawing its support (and even disavowing its servicemen) as the campaigns dragged on, casualties mounted, and news accounts vividly described the horror of the battlefields.

Some useful lessons might be gleaned from a comparison of the two conflicts. Human nature really does not change—war will bring out the best and the worst in the tired, wet, hungry, and fearful men who are doing the fighting. Guerrilla campaigns—particularly where local military and civic reforms cannot be effected to separate the guerrilla from his base of popular support—will be long and difficult, and will demand tremendous commitments in resources and national will. Finally, before America commits its armed forces to similar ventures in the future, it would do well to recall the lessons learned from previous campaigns. For, as the Spanish-born American educator, poet, and philosopher George Santayana reminded us, those who do not learn from the past are doomed to repeat it.

VII

World War I, 1914–1918

Iron General

Thomas Fleming

The name of General John J. "Black Jack" Pershing is synonymous with the American Expeditionary Force that sailed to France in 1917 and fought beside its allies until the armistice of November 1918. Pershing was a man of strong ideas and will who insisted that his Doughboys be allowed to fight on the Western Front only as an independent American army. In this essay Thomas Fleming tells the story of this iron-willed leader both as a man and as a military commander in "The Great War," in the process telling the larger story of the AEF and its contribution to Allied victory. From MHQ: The Quarterly Journal of Military History, *Winter 1995, by Thomas Fleming. Copyright © 1995 by* MHQ: The Quarterly Journal of Military History. *Reprinted by permission of PRIMEDIA Enthusiasts Publications (History Group).*

On February 5, 1917, the rear guard of the 11,000-man Punitive Expedition to Mexico recrossed the Rio Grande to American soil. With them was John J. Pershing, the lean, grim-lipped, jut-jawed major general who had managed to pursue Pancho Villa around northern Mexico for nearly eleven months without starting a war. Although he had not captured the guerrilla chieftain, Pershing had scattered Villa's army and killed a number of his lieutenants—and silently swallowed his frustration when President Woodrow Wilson ordered a withdrawal. Within hours of his return to the United States, Pershing called a conference of the newspapermen who had followed him into Mexico. "We have broken diplomatic relations with Germany," he said. "That means we will send an expedition abroad. I'd like to command it. . . . Tell me how I can help you so that you can help me."

It was neither the first nor the last time Pershing would reveal the shrewd self-promotion that lay behind the image of the "Iron General." When he had invaded Mexico, he had obligingly posed on horseback fording the Rio Grande with his staff. Actually, he had traveled across the inhospitable Chihuahuan desert in a Dodge touring car. In many surprising ways, large and small, Pershing was a very modern major general. In other ways, he was a man of his own time.

Pershing had graduated from West Point in 1886 as first captain of the cadet corps, a coveted title that testified to an aptitude for things military. Scholastically he was in the middle of his seventy-seven-man class. Post–Civil War West Point was intellectually moribund, turning out men who learned by rote what little was taught. If they acquired anything from their four-year indoctrination, it was a ferocious dedication to discipline and military minutiae.

Robert Lee Bullard, who graduated a year ahead of Pershing and would later serve under him, admired his ability to give orders, which seemed to come naturally to him. The Alabama-born Bullard also noted that Pershing inspired admiration and respect, but not affection. There was something impersonal, almost detached, in his style of command. With women, on the other hand, a different man emerged, full of wit and charm. He was a "spoony" cadet, with a pretty girl on his arm for every hop. Later, as a cavalryman on the western frontier and a guerrilla fighter in the Philippines, he gravitated inevitably toward the prettiest woman in sight.

Another large factor in his life soon emerged—what some people called "Pershing luck." Others called it an uncanny ability to ingratiate himself with men in high places. Having watched Pershing in action during the last of the Indian Wars, Nelson Miles selected the young man as his aide after he became commanding general of the army. In 1896, Miles sent Pershing to New York to represent him at a National Guard tournament in Madison Square Garden. Avery Andrews, a classmate who had retired from the army to go into business, invited Pershing to share his box. Another guest was Theodore Roosevelt, on his way to becoming President William McKinley's assistant secretary of the navy. An avid western buff and admirer of soldiers, TR was fascinated by Pershing's skirmishes with Sioux who were part of the Ghost Dance cult, his knowledge of Indian dialects, his Missourian enthusiasm for the West's potential. A friendship was born that became a pivot of Pershing's career.

In the West, Pershing had served with the black troopers of the 10th Cavalry. Posted to West Point in 1897, he became the most unpopular tactical officer in recent memory—an accomplishment in itself. In retaliation for his uncompromising discipline, the cadets nicknamed him "Nigger Jack"— a reference to his service with the 10th and a sad commentary on the racism of the era. (It was later softened to "Black Jack"—a name that stuck, largely because most people thought it had something to do with the potentially deadly nature of the instrument of the same name.) When the Spanish-American War broke out in 1898, Pershing rejoined the regiment and went up San Juan Hill with the dismounted black regulars, proving himself "as cool as a bowl of cracked ice" against Spanish sharpshooters who killed or wounded 50 percent of the regiment's officers.

In 1902, while serving in the Philippines, Captain Pershing pacified much of Mindanao with 700 troops, cajoling Moro *dattus* out of their forts whenever possible, demolishing them in short, savage attacks when necessary. His exploits won headlines in many newspapers. His friend Theodore Roosevelt, now ensconced in the White House, tried to promote Pershing to brigadier general. But not even the president could alter the rigid, seniority-based promotion system.

A military celebrity, back in Washington for service on the General Staff, Pershing in 1905 married a vivacious Wellesley graduate, Helen Frances Warren, the daughter of the wealthy Wyoming senator who headed the Military Affairs Committee. Confronted with subtle threats to their annual budgets, the army's higher ranks became more amenable to Pershing's promotion. In 1906, Roosevelt vaulted him over 862 senior officers to brigadier, making most of these gentlemen instant enemies. They retaliated with a smear campaign about his sex life in the Philippines, claiming he had had a series of native women as mistresses and had sired several children. He denied everything, but the scandal stained his reputation so badly that, six years later, newspapers howled when he was proposed as superintendent of West Point.

Marrying influential daughters was an old army custom. Nelson Miles had married the daughter of Senator John Sherman, who was the brother of General William Tecumseh Sherman and the most powerful senator of his day. In Pershing's case, surviving letters and diaries make it clear the marriage was loving. As his honeymoon ended, Pershing confided to his diary that he was "the happiest man in the world." Four children, three girls and a boy, were born to Jack and "Frankie."

On August 27, 1915, while Pershing was patrolling the restive Mexican border against guerrilla incursions, an excited reporter called headquarters and got the general himself. Without realizing to whom he was talking, the newsman blurted out that Pershing's wife and three daughters had been killed in a midnight fire at their quarters in the Presidio in San Francisco. Only his six-year-old son, Warren, had survived, saved by a courageous orderly. A devastated Pershing wrote a friend: "All the promotion in the world would make no difference now."

Pershing seemed to deal with his sorrow through work, responsibility, the grinding details of duty. That is one explanation of his pursuit of the command of the American Expeditionary Force (AEF). Another is the very strong probability that he thought he was the best man for the job. One of Pershing's characteristics was his matter-of-fact assumption of his ability.

He courted Woodrow Wilson with a fulsome letter praising the president's speech of April 2 before Congress, calling for a war to make the world safe for democracy. He wrote a similar letter to Secretary of War Newton D. Baker. Senator Warren worked hard on Pershing's behalf, telegraphing him at one point to ask about his knowledge of French. Pershing had barely passed the subject at West Point, but he replied that he could easily acquire "a satisfactory working knowledge" of the language.

There was only one other major general who could compete with Pershing for the job: Frederick Funston. He had won instant fame by capturing rebel leader Emilio Aguinaldo and crippling the Philippine insurrection in 1901. On February 19, 1917, Funston dropped dead in the lobby of a San Antonio hotel—perhaps another instance of Pershing luck.

In early May, Pershing got the job—leaping over five major generals senior to him. What he found in Washington, D.C., would have daunted a less confident man. The U.S. Army had little more than 11,000 combat-ready regulars. The 122,000-man National Guard was a joke. Fully half its members had never fired a rifle. Hugh Scott, the aging chief of staff, frequently fell asleep at meetings with his officers. The only plan Scott had on his desk was the brainchild of Wilson and Secretary Baker—to send Pershing at the head of a 12,000-man division to France as part of a "flexible" response to the war.

French and British missions swarmed to American shores to deluge the War Department and the president with frantic pleas for men. Instead of Wilson and Baker's symbolic 12,000, they wanted 500,000 men immediately—and they did not particularly want John J. Pershing, or any other American general. The British suggested that the half-million recruits be shipped directly to depots in England, to be trained there and sent to France in British uniforms, under British officers. The French were a bit more polite, but it came down to the same thing: They wanted American soldiers to become part of their army.

From the day he heard the idea, Pershing opposed amalgamation of forces. He had no intention of becoming superfluous in France. For the time being, Wilson, Baker, and General Tasker H. Bliss—the large, slow-moving military politician who soon succeeded Scott as chief of staff—agreed with him. Not without some conflict, Pershing also opposed a proposal by his friend Theodore Roosevelt to raise 50,000 volunteers and lead them himself to Europe to bolster the Allies' sagging morale. As an observer in Manchuria during the Russo-Japanese War in 1904, Pershing had seen a modern battlefield, and he did not think there was room on it for amateurs like TR. He may also have sensed, with his finely honed instinct for command, that there could be only one American leader in Europe.

Pershing saw himself not only as that American leader but as the general who could win the war. He thought he had the answer to breaking the bloody stalemate on the Western Front—"open warfare." This idea was a variation on the doctrine taught at West Point by Dennis Hart Mahan, the man who dominated the academy for much of the nineteenth century. Speed, fire, and movement were the essence of Mahan's ideas, along with seizing and holding the initiative. Pershing believed the American soldier's natural gifts as a marksman and wielder of the bayonet would shock the German army—and the Allies' armies—out of their trenches.

Three weeks after his appointment, Pershing sailed for Europe with a 191-man staff. In London, people liked what they saw. One American reporter, Heywood Broun, opined, "No man ever looked more like the ordained leader of fighting men." Another, Floyd Gibbons, called him "lean, clean, keen." But even as he was charming the newsmen, Pershing was requesting from Washington the power to impose rigid censorship on everything they wrote in France.

In Paris the population went berserk, chanting the "Marseillaise" and pelting Pershing and the staff with flowers as they rode to the Hotel Crillon. On the balcony overlooking the place de la Concorde, when the wind whipped a tricolor toward him, Pershing reverently kissed its folds. The crowd screamed its approval. Inside, he got a very different reception. The American ambassador, William Sharp, said: "I hope you have not arrived too late." The writer Dorothy Canfield Fisher, an old friend, told Pershing the French were beaten: They had had 2 million casualties, and "there is a limit to what flesh and blood . . . can stand."

Pershing learned even worse news from General Henri Pétain, the French commander in chief. In April, after a disastrous offensive on the Aisne River that cost 120,000 casualties, the French army had mutinied. Most of it was still in a state of "collective indiscipline," as Pétain put it. Russia, with its immense reservoir of manpower, was even closer to military collapse. The March revolution, which ousted the czar, had failed to add vigor or coherence to their army. More bad news soon arrived from the British front, where Field Marshal Sir Douglas Haig was in the process of squandering 300,000 men on futile attacks in the Ypres salient. An appalled Pershing told his military censor, Major Frederick Palmer, that he feared the worst: "Look at what is expected of us and what we have to start with! No army ready and no ships to bring over an army if we had one."

Pershing soon decided he could not rely on the General Staff in Washington for anything; it took weeks to get a reply from anyone. Tasker Bliss was still writing orders with the stub of a pencil and hiding urgent telegrams under his blotter while he made up his mind what to do about them. Pershing set up his own general staff in France—a far more efficient one than the fumbling team in Washington.

For his chief of staff, Pershing chose Major James Harbord. Neither a West Pointer nor a close friend, but extremely intelligent, Harbord had caught Pershing's eye in the Philippines. He was his commander's opposite in many ways—genial, warm, a man with first-class diplomatic instincts.

Harbord kept a voluminous diary, from which we get a good picture of Pershing on the job.

> He thinks very clearly . . . and goes to his conclusions directly when matters call for decision. He can talk straighter to people when calling them down than anyone I have ever seen. . . . He loses his temper occasionally, and stupidity and vagueness irritate him more than anything else. . . . He develops great fondness for people whom he likes . . . but . . . is relentless when convinced of inefficiency. . . .
>
> He does not fear responsibility. . . . He decides big things much more quickly than he does trivial ones. Two weeks ago, without any authority from Washington, he placed an order . . . for $50,000,000 worth of airplanes . . . and did not cable the fact until too late for Washington to countermand it. . . . He did it without winking an eye, as easily as though ordering a postage stamp.

Alfred Thayer Mahan, Dennis Mahan's son, was fond of saying that war is business. As commander of the AEF, Pershing proved it. Until he took charge, each army bureau and department had its own supply officer with its own budget, a system that caused immense confusion and duplication of effort and expense. (For example, the various bureaus had ordered a total of 30 million pairs of shoes when 9 million were needed!) Pershing organized the AEF's purchases around a single man, an old friend and future vice president, Charles Dawes. A canny businessman, Dawes had absolute authority to buy anything and everything the army needed from the French and British at the best possible price.

The decisions Pershing and his staff made to prepare the AEF for battle were awesome. Along with French planes for their newly created independent air force, they bought French .75s for their artillery; the English Enfield rifle and steel helmet and the French light machine gun, the Chauchat, for their infantry; and the French light tank, the Renault, for George S. Patton's embryonic tank corps. Pershing also decided to make an AEF division, an entity that did not exist in the prewar American army, of 28,000 men, twice the size of an Allied or German division. He wanted an organization large enough to mount a sustained attack under the command of a single general. Unfortunately, he did not double the size of the new division's artillery, the first symptom of his inability to appreciate the lethal increase in firepower that had transformed warfare on the Western Front.

Pershing also strove to put his own stamp on the spirit of the AEF. In October 1917, he announced: "The standards for the American Army will be those of West Point. The . . . upright bearing, attention to detail, uncomplaining obedience to instruction required of the cadet will be required of every officer and soldier of our armies in France." To have every private behaving like a Pershing was an impossible dream, but the Iron General never wavered in his insistence. To improve the appearance of the officer corps, he ordered them to wear the British Sam Browne belt and authorized the use of canes. The first item was hated by many officers, the second mocked by enlisted men, but they became part of the dress code nonetheless.

Heywood Broun, who followed Pershing around France for a while, was bewildered by the general's appetite for details. He climbed into haylofts where soldiers were quartered and discussed onions with cooks, to make sure men were being billeted in reasonable health and comfort. Broun derided this attention to detail, sneering that Pershing thought he could read a man's soul "through his boots or his buttons." The reporter quoted a junior officer who thought Pershing's favorite biblical figure was Joshua, "because he made the sun and moon stand at attention." Broun's candor got him kicked out of France; Pershing's AEF censors had a low tolerance for such negative remarks. The rest of the press corps remained firmly in Pershing's corner.

One man who never succumbed to the system was Charles Dawes. Pershing made him a brigadier general to give him some weight with his French counterparts, but Dawes remained a civilian. His shoes went unshined, and his uniform was usually a rumpled mess. Pershing would frequently button Dawes's shirt or coat before they would appear together in public. Once, when he walked into a Dawes conference, everyone rose and saluted. But Dawes neglected to take a large cigar out of his mouth. "Charlie," Pershing said, "the next time you salute, put the cigar on the other side of your mouth."

Although he could relax that way with close friends, and make visual gestures for photographers or admiring crowds, the one thing Pershing could not do was inspire soldiers or civilians with a ringing phrase. He was astute enough psychologically to trace this limitation to a boyhood episode, in which he forgot a speech during an elocution performance. A speech his staff wrote for him to make at Lafayette's tomb on July 4, 1917, ended with the oratorical high note, "Lafayette, we are here." Pershing crossed it out and wrote "not in character" beside it. He let one of his staff officers who spoke good French say it instead.

Another flaw, which drove Harbord and the rest of his staff to near distraction, was a complete lack of a sense of time. Pershing constantly arrived late to dinners or receptions, leaving kings, queens, prime ministers, and Allied generals impatiently tapping their VIP feet. The explanation was his appetite for detail. Devouring a report on weapons procurement or shipping schedules, Pershing would lose touch with the external world.

The euphoria of Pershing's arrival soon vanished: The promise of American aid remained unfulfilled. In the fall, the Germans and Austrians wrecked the Italian army at Caporetto. The Bolsheviks, having seized power in Moscow, took Russia out of the war, freeing an estimated seventy-seven German divisions for service on the Western Front. As a handful of American divisions trickled into Saint-Nazaire on their way to training areas in Lorraine, the Allies put more and more pressure on Pershing to give them control of his army.

The French and British generals summoned political reinforcements. Premier Paul Painlevé and Prime Minister David Lloyd George assailed

Washington, D.C., with warnings of disaster and grave doubts about Pershing's capacity—simultaneously arranging for Pershing to be made aware of these fires being ignited in his rear. The only reinforcement Pershing got from Wilson was Bliss, an Anglophile who immediately sided with the British on amalgamation. Bliss said they should cable their opposing views to Washington and let the president decide. Pershing responded with some very straight talk. "Bliss," he said, "do you know what would happen if we did that? We would both be relieved from further duty in France and that is exactly what we should deserve." Bliss capitulated for the time being, a tribute not to the inferiority of his ideas but to the force of Pershing's personality.

The amalgamation pressure hardened Pershing's determination to make the AEF the best army in Europe. He was particularly tough on the 1st Division, which arrived in time to march through Paris on July 4—without the precision he expected. He took an instant dislike to the division's commander, Major General William Siebert, an engineering officer with little field experience. In October, inspecting the division, Pershing blasted Siebert in front of his officers. A young staff captain, George C. Marshall, stepped forward and launched a passionate defense of the general and the division, which was hampered by shortages of everything from motor transport to ammunition. The rest of the staff watched, wide-eyed, certain that Marshall and his military career were about to be obliterated. Instead, Pershing studied him for a long thoughtful moment and more or less apologized for his bad temper. It was the beginning of Marshall's rise to a colonel's rank and a dominant role on the AEF staff.

But Marshall did not change Pershing's opinion of Siebert. "Slow of speech and of thought . . . slovenly in dress . . . utterly hopeless as an instructor or tactician" were among his comments. Within a month, Bullard had replaced Siebert as commander of the 1st Division. Pershing was equally unrelenting about most of the other generals who were shipped to Europe to survey the Western Front while their divisions were training in the United States. "Too old," "very fat and inactive," "could not begin to stand the strain" were some of the judgments he made of them. Washington ignored his criticisms and sent almost all of these losers back to France, giving Pershing the unwelcome job of relieving them—a task he performed with grim efficiency.

Ironically, one of the few who escaped Pershing's lash was the fattest general in the army, Hunter Liggett. Pershing kept him because Liggett, former head of the Army War College, had a brain. The Pershing within the Iron General had enough humor to like Liggett's defense of his bulk: There was nothing wrong with fat as long as it was not above the collar.

In the fall of 1917, Pershing moved AEF headquarters to Chaumont, a hilly town of 20,000, some 140 miles east of Paris. There, he and the staff were less exposed to the temptations of the *guerre de luxe*, as more cynical types called service in the City of Light. But Pershing had already succumbed. In September he had begun a liaison with a twenty-three-year-old Romanian artist, Micheline Resco, who had been commissioned by the French government to paint his portrait. He visited her by night in her apartment on the rue Descombes, sitting up front with his chauffeur on his way there and back, the windshield signs with the U.S. flag and his four stars flat on the dashboard, out of sight. Contrary to appearances, it was another love match, and it lasted, without benefit of clergy, for the rest of his life.

The Germans gave him other things to think about. In November they raided the 1st Division just after it entered the lines, killing three Americans, wounding five, and taking twelve prisoners. When Pershing heard the news he wept—not with grief for the dead, but with the humiliation of even a small defeat, which he knew would lead to more French and British condescension and demands for amalgamation. When the 1st Division planned a retaliatory raid of its own, the AEF commander supervised it personally. It was a humiliating flop. The infantry and the engineers failed to meet in no-man's-land and, without the latter's bangalore torpedoes, no one could get through the German barbed wire.

Eventually the division pulled off a successful raid, led by Theodore Roosevelt's oldest son, Ted, but these trivial skirmishes only intensified Allied disillusion with Pershing. The new French premier, Georges Clemenceau, locally known as the Tiger, bared his claws and remarked that Pershing's chief preoccupation seemed to be having dinner in Paris.

As 1918 began, Pershing had only four divisions in France, and three of them were short a total of 20,000 men. None but the 1st had fired a shot at the Germans. Wilson complicated Pershing's life by issuing his own peace terms, the Fourteen Points, infuriating the French and English with the president's blissful ignorance of political realities. The Germans ignored Wilson and continued to shift divisions to the Western Front—with new tactics designed to create their own version of open warfare.

The tactics had been developed by the German General Staff and first used in Italy and on the Eastern Front. They depended heavily on surprise. German artillerists had solved the problem of aiming guns accurately at night without registering fire, which had previously announced offensives on both sides. The key troops were elite *Sturmtruppen* with mission-oriented orders—rather than the detailed timetables that had hobbled earlier offensives. Instead of being assigned a particular objective, the storm troopers were told to penetrate as deeply as possible and disrupt the enemy rear areas. Commanders would commit additional infantry only at breakthroughs, leaving enemy strongpoints isolated and eventually vulnerable to assault from the rear.

On March 21, 1918, the Germans unleashed these innovations on the British Fifth Army, guarding the hinge between the two Allied forces in Picardy. In three days, 90,000 Tommies surrendered, and another 90,000 became casualties. The Fifth Army ceased to exist, and the Germans menaced Amiens, the key rail hub connecting the British and French armies. The frantic Allies convened a conference at Doullens, to which they did not even bother to invite Pershing or any other American. The only general who seemed interested in fighting was Ferdinand Foch, until recently in disgrace for squandering his men in suicidal attacks. The politicians persuaded Haig and Pétain to accept Foch as the supreme commander, to coordinate the collapsing battle line.

Instead of sulking over being ignored, Pershing made his only grand gesture of the war. He drove to Foch's headquarters outside Paris and, in reasonably good French, declared: "I have come to tell you that the American people would consider it a great honor for our troops to be engaged in the present battle. I ask you for this in their name and my own." Everyone applauded the performance. It made headlines. But Pershing soon learned he had embraced a rattlesnake.

Instead of taking the four available American divisions and putting them into line as an army corps, which was what Pershing wanted, Foch assigned them to quiet sectors, piecemeal, after the battle for Amiens subsided. Next, behind Pershing's back, Foch dispatched a cable to Wilson telling him that unless 600,000 infantrymen were shipped to Europe in the next three months, unattached, for use as replacements in the French and British armies, the war was lost.

Pershing fought the Frenchman with his only weapon: an immense stubbornness and rocklike faith in his vision of an independent American army. Even when the secretary of war was cajoled into backing Foch by the devious Bliss, who seized the first opportunity to revoke his capitulation to Pershing, the Iron General clung to his determination. In May, soon after a second German offensive had come perilously close to smashing through the northern end of the British line and seizing the Channel ports, the Allies convened another conference at Abbeville. Pershing faced Lloyd George, Clemenceau, and Italian prime minister Vittorio Emanuele Orlando, plus Haig, Foch, and a half-dozen other generals and cabinet officers. Bliss said not a word in his support. The others raged, screamed, cursed, and pleaded—but Pershing would not change his mind. He absolutely refused to let the Americans fight in units smaller than a division—and he insisted that even this concession would be temporary, pending the formation of an American army.

"Are you willing to risk our being driven back to the Loire?" Foch shouted.

"Gentlemen," Pershing said after another forty minutes of wrangling, "I have thought this program over very deliberately and I will not be coerced."

Pershing was taking one of the greatest gambles in history. On May 27, the Germans struck again, this time at the French along the Chemin des Dames ridge northeast of Soissons. Once more, the German artillery's fiendish combination of high explosives and poison gas tore apart the front lines, and the storm troopers poured through the gaps. The French Sixth Army evaporated. In a week Soissons and Château-Thierry fell, and the Germans were on the Marne, only fifty miles from Paris.

This time, American divisions were not diverted to quiet sectors. The 2nd and 3rd divisions went into line around Château-Thierry as *poilus* streamed past them shouting, "La guerre finie." Except for some lively skirmishing, the Germans did not attack. Their infantry went on the defensive, while the generals brought up their artillery and tried to decide what to do with the huge salient they had carved in the French lines between Soissons and Reims.

The French commander of the sector, General Jean-Marie-Joseph Degoutte, was, like Foch, an apostle of the school of frontal attack—which had done little thus far but pile up Allied bodies in front of German machine-gun emplacements. Finding himself in possession of fresh American troops, he went on the offensive, ordering an attack on Belleau Wood. He found a willing collaborator in Colonel Preston Brown, the 2nd Division's chief of staff. Brown—who dominated the overage and incompetent division commander, Omar Bundy—was burning to demonstrate American prowess. He accepted at face value French reports that the Germans held only the northern corner of the wood. In fact, they occupied it to the last inch with infantry supported by machine guns set up for interlocking fields of fire.

On June 6, without sending out a single patrol to find more information, Brown and Harbord, recently reassigned to the division as commander of the 4th Marine Brigade, ordered their men forward in a frontal assault. The marines advanced in massed formations unseen on the Western Front since 1914. Incredulous German machine gunners mowed them down in windrows. The slaughter revealed the limitations of Pershing's doctrine of open warfare. As Liggett later mournfully remarked, no one, including Pershing, had thought it out.

The marines eventually captured Belleau Wood, after the French pulled them back and treated the Germans to a fourteen-hour artillery barrage that smashed the place flat. Pershing rewarded Harbord for his incompetence (there were 50 percent casualties) by making him commander of the 2nd Division in place of Bundy, who had stood around during the battle without saying a word while Harbord and Brown made their bloody blunders.

The desperate French trumpeted Belleau Wood as a major victory in their newspapers, and reporters around the world followed suit. Pershing went along because he was even more desperate for proof that his men could stand up to the Germans. The battering he had taken from Foch, Haig, and others had broadened his definition of what constituted a battlefield success. Henceforth, Pershing would countenance the pernicious idea that high casualties were proof of a commander's fighting ability.

Beginning on the night of July 14, seven American divisions (troops were starting to arrive in ever-greater numbers) played crucial roles in smashing the next German offensive, code-named Friedensturm—the "peace assault." Casualties were relatively light because the Allies, perhaps borrowing a bit of Pershing luck, discovered the exact day and hour of the attack from a captured German officer. Ignoring Foch's senseless order to hold every inch of sacred soil, General Pétain created an elastic defense that inflicted enormous losses on the *Sturmtruppen*. Pershing was only a spectator at this three-day clash, his divisions being temporarily under the orders of French generals.

Foch, an apostle of attack, at last became the right general in the right place at the right time. He threw the American 1st and 2nd divisions and a French colonial division into the soft left flank of the German Marne salient around Soissons. The first day, July 18, was a sensational success, but on the second day the Germans recovered from their surprise. Their machine guns sprouted everywhere, and casualties mounted. Again and again, Americans advanced across open ground without concealment or cover—with predictable results. The 1st and 2nd had 12,000 casualties. The 2nd, already bled by Belleau Wood, collapsed and was withdrawn after two days. The 1st, equally battered (the 26th Infantry Regiment lost 3,000 out of 3,200 men), was withdrawn the following day. This was hardly the staying power Pershing had envisioned for his double-sized divisions. But he ignored the danger signs and told Harbord that even if the two divisions never fired another shot, they had made their commanders "immortal."

Having seized the initiative, Foch was determined not to relinquish it. For the next six weeks, he ordered attacks all around the Marne salient. In the vanguard were American divisions, fighting under French generals. This little-studied Aisne-Marne offensive proved the courage of the American infantrymen—and the limitations of their open-warfare tactics. Before it ended in early September, over 90,000 Americans were dead or wounded.

Inept tactics were not the only problem. Too often, Americans found their flanks exposed by the failure of a French division to keep pace with their attack. Bullard, who by then was supposed to be supervising American operations as commander of the III Corps, fretted about the murderous casualties but did little else. There is no record of Pershing saying anything.

The climax of this messy operation was on August 27, when an isolated company of the 28th Division was annihilated in Fismette, on the north bank of the Vesle River. Bullard had tried to withdraw the soldiers—they were the only Americans on that side of the river, surrounded by some 200,000 Germans—but Degoutte, now commander of the Sixth Army, had revoked the order. When Bullard reported the episode a few days later, Pershing asked, "Why didn't you disobey the order?"

"I did not answer. It was not necessary to answer," Bullard wrote in his memoirs.

By this time, five other American divisions were training with the British army. On August 8, the British had made a successful attack on the western flank of the salient that the Germans had created when they routed the Fifth Army in Picardy. Pershing had permitted these divisions to go directly into British training areas when they arrived in Europe—an example of the partial surrenders of control extracted from him by Foch and Haig, with the help of the German army. But Pershing stubbornly discounted the possibility that perhaps this was the best way to use the Americans finally flooding into France—brigading them with British or French armies, who already had sophisticated staffs and supply systems in place.

Instead, the Iron General never stopped insisting on a totally independent army. On August 10, he opened First Army headquarters; five days later, he handed Foch a plan for an attack on the Saint-Mihiel salient, another huge bulge into the French lines, south of Verdun. He withdrew three of his five divisions from a choleric Haig, and all that were under French control.

On August 28, as the Americans moved into the lines, Foch descended on Pershing with one last attempt to utilize the AEF in—from the viewpoint of the supreme commander—a more rational way. He announced a master plan he had conceived while visiting Haig. The whole German battlefront, he said, was one huge salient that should be attacked from the north, the south, and the center. He therefore wanted Pershing more or less to abort the Saint-Mihiel operation, limiting it to a few divisions, and transfer the rest of his army back to French control for attacks in the Aisne and Argonne theaters.

A vehement argument ensued. At one point, both men were on their feet screaming curses at each other. "Do you wish to take part in the battle?" Foch shrilled, the ultimate insult one general could throw at another. For a moment, Pershing seriously thought of flattening the little Frenchman with a roundhouse right. "As an American army and in no other way!" he replied.

"I must insist on the arrangement!" Foch shouted.

Pershing squared his jaw. "Marshal Foch, you may insist all you please, but I decline absolutely to agree to your plan. While our army will fight wherever you decide, it will fight only as an independent American army."

After another week of wrangling, Pershing accepted a dangerous compromise. He would attack the Saint-Mihiel salient on September 12, as planned, then transfer the bulk of his 500,000-man army west of the Meuse to attack north through the Argonne as part of the overall Allied offensive on September 26. It was an ambitious assignment for a general who had never commanded more than 11,000 men in action and a staff that had yet to fight a single battle. Only a man with Pershing's self-confidence would have tried it. To compound his potential woes, he accepted a battle plan from Foch that gave French generals command east of the Meuse and west of the Argonne Forest, violating a primary military maxim: An attacking army should be responsible for both sides of a natural obstacle such as a forest or a river.

On September 5, Pershing, disturbed by AEF casualties in the Aisne-Marne offensive, made a stab at defining open warfare. In a general order issued to the First Army, he contrasted it to trench warfare, which he claimed was "marked by uniform formations, the regulation of space and time by higher commands down to the smallest details and little initiative." Open warfare had "irregular . . . formations, comparatively little regulation of space and time . . . and the greatest possible use of the infantry's own fire-power to enable it to get forward . . . [plus] brief orders and the greatest possible use of individual initiative." It was much too late for such complex ideas to filter down even to division staffs, much less to the captains and lieutenants leading companies. Nor did this inchoate rhetoric offer a clue to how to deal with the primary defensive weapon on the Western Front—the machine gun.

At first, Pershing luck seemed to hold. The Saint-Mihiel offensive was the walkover of the war. The Germans were in the process of withdrawing from the salient when the Americans attacked. Resistance was perfunctory. The bag of prisoners and captured guns was big enough to make headlines, although the take was not nearly as large as originally hoped. Pershing and his staff now tried to imitate the Germans and achieve surprise in the Argonne. He left most of his veteran divisions in Saint-Mihiel and shifted largely green units west. No significant snafus developed on the roads, thanks to the planning genius of George C. Marshall, who was nicknamed the Wizard for managing the sixty-mile transfer in wretched rainy weather.

On September 26, after a German-style, 4,000-gun artillery barrage, Pershing threw 250,000 men in three corps at an estimated 50,000 unprepared German defenders in the twenty-mile-wide Argonne valley. A massive hogback ran down the center, forcing the attackers into defiles on both sides. It was, Liggett said, a natural fortress that made the Virginia Wilderness seem like a park. Yet Pershing's plan called for no less than a ten-mile-abreast advance the first day to crack the Kriemhilde Stellung, the main German defensive line.

Five of Pershing's nine divisions had never been in action before. Even experienced divisions such as the 77th, which had been blooded under the French, were full of green replacements. The 77th received 2,100 men who had never fired a rifle the day before they attacked. Everything imaginable proceeded to go wrong with Pershing's army. The Germans fell back to well-prepared defenses and began machine-gunning charging Americans. Massive amounts of enemy artillery on the heights east of the Meuse and along the edge of the Argonne Forest, which loomed a thousand feet above the valley floor, exacted an even heavier toll.

Rigid orders, issued by Pershing's own staff, held up whole divisions at crucial moments. The 4th Division could have captured the key height of Montfaucon the first day, but it stood still for four hours, waiting for the green 79th Division, assigned the objective, to come abreast of it. By the time

Montfaucon fell the following day, the Germans had poured in five first-class divisions, and the American advance had stumbled to a bloody halt.

In the north, where the British and French were attacking, the Germans could give ground for sixty or a hundred miles before yielding anything vital. But only twenty-four miles from the American jumping-off point in the Argonne was the Sedan–Mézières four-track railroad, which supplied almost all the food and ammunition to the Germans' northern armies. They were fighting to protect their jugular in the Argonne. By October 4, they had elements of twenty-three divisions in line or local reserve.

Withdrawing his green divisions, Pershing replaced them with the veteran units he had left in Saint-Mihiel and tried to resume the attack. He was on the road constantly, visiting corps and division headquarters, urging generals and colonels to inject their men with more "drive" and "push." But Pershing was discovering that rhetoric could not silence a machine gun.

His men bled, and also began to starve. Food did not get forward, as monumental traffic jams developed on the few roads into the Argonne. Wounded lay unevacuated. Clemenceau, caught in a jam while visiting the front, lost half a day and departed vowing to get rid of Pershing. Stragglers were another problem. Liggett estimated that at the height of the battle, 100,000 fugitives were wandering around the First Army's rear areas. One division reported an effective frontline strength of only 1,600 men. Early in October, Pershing authorized officers to shoot down any man who ran away—proof of his growing desperation.

Worsening Pershing's woes, while the Americans were withdrawing the wreckage of the green divisions, was a visit from Foch's chief of staff, who informed Pershing that the generalissimo thought he had too many men in the Argonne. Foch proposed shifting six divisions to nearby French armies. Recent historians have been inclined to think Foch was probably right. The French on Pershing's right and left were making little progress and could have used some help. But by now, Pershing hated Foch too much to take his advice about anything. He told the supreme commander to go to hell. Foch retaliated with a formal on-the-record letter ordering him to attack continuously "without any [further] interruptions."

Killing fire from the guns east of the Meuse stopped the veteran divisions when they jumped off on October 4. German counterattacks drove them back again and again. Only the 1st Division, under the Cromwellian Charles Summerall, gained some ground, plunging up the left defile for a half-dozen miles—at a cost of 9,387 casualties. On October 8, Pershing sent two divisions east of the Meuse to join the French in an attempt to silence the artillery. The attack faltered and collapsed into a pocket on the banks of the Meuse, deluged by gas and shellfire.

Pershing drove himself as hard as he did his men. He sat up until three or four in the morning reading reports and pondering maps. Rumors drifted into headquarters that Foch and Clemenceau were urging Wilson to replace him with Bliss. One day, in his car with his favorite aide, Major James Collins, a played-out Pershing put his head in his hands and, speaking to his dead wife, moaned: "Frankie . . . Frankie . . . my God, sometimes I don't know how I can go on."

Outwardly, no one else saw anything but the Iron General, still in charge. "Things are going badly," he told Major General Henry Allen, commander of the 90th Division. "But by God, Allen, I was never so much in earnest in my life, and we are going to get through." Marshall thought this was Pershing's finest hour. More critical recent historians, pointing to the substantial gains being made, and the huge numbers of prisoners and guns being captured, by French and British armies on other fronts, suggest Pershing was hopelessly out of his depth but was refusing to admit it.

There may be some truth to this assertion—except for the last part. On October 12, tacitly admitting he did not have the answer to the Argonne, Pershing gave Liggett command of the First Army and created a Second Army, under Bullard, to operate east of the Meuse. Pershing became the commander of the army group—chairman of the board instead of chief executive officer. The First Army continued to attack for another seven days, finally breaching the Kriemhilde Stellung on October 19. It had taken three weeks and 100,000 casualties to achieve what Pershing and his staff had thought they could do in a single day.

At this point, the First Army was, in the opinion of one staff officer, "a disorganized and wrecked army." Liggett promptly went on the defensive. When Pershing persisted in hanging around headquarters, talking about launching another attack, Liggett told him to "go away and forget it." Pershing meekly obeyed.

It was just as well, because he soon had a more serious topic on his mind. Early in October, the Germans had announced they were willing to accept peace on the basis of Wilson's Fourteen Points. As Wilson began negotiating with them, Pershing came perilously close to making the president look foolish by issuing a public statement that he favored unconditional surrender.

The Wilson administration was infuriated. Many people assumed Pershing's statement was the opening salvo of a run for the presidency. On the contrary. Pershing was motivated by two things. His political mentor, Theodore Roosevelt, was savaging Wilson back in the United States with a similar call for unconditional surrender. The Iron General was also seething because Haig, the British commander, had recommended an armistice, arguing that the British and French were close to exhaustion and the American army was too inept to bear any substantial share of another offensive. Pershing wanted more war to make Haig eat those words.

Under fierce pressure from Wilson, Pershing accepted the idea of armistice. But he remained convinced it was a mistake. When the First Army resumed the offensive on November 1, he urged it forward with ferocious intensity, hoping it could smash the Germans before negotiators agreed on terms. Rested and reorganized, imbued with new tactics that urged infiltration and flank attacks rather than piling men against enemy strongpoints, the Americans were sensationally successful. They stormed across the Meuse, cutting the Sedan–Mézières railroad and threatening the German armies in the north with imminent starvation and collapse. At Pershing's insistence, they kept attacking until the armistice went into effect at 11:00 A.M. on November 11. "If they had given us another ten days," Pershing said, "we would have rounded up the entire German army, captured it, humiliated it." There are strong reasons to doubt this postwar Pershing boast, however. In the final days, replacements had become a major AEF problem. The German army was still a formidable fighting force—and a policy of unconditional surrender might have inspired them to resist with desperate ferocity, as they demonstrated in World War II.

In these same final days, Pershing, still fuming over Foch's condescension and Clemenceau's sneers, attempted to retaliate with a ploy that seriously endangered the fragile alliance. He decided the Americans would capture Sedan, the city where the French had ingloriously surrendered to Bismarck's Germans in 1870. Ignoring a boundary drawn by Foch that placed Sedan in the zone of the French Fourth Army, he ordered the First Army to capture the city and deprive the French of this symbolic honor. The order—which directed the I Corps, spearheaded by the 42nd Division, to make the main thrust, "assisted on their right by the V Corps"—was so vague that it encouraged General Summerall, by then the commander of the V Corps, to march the 1st Division across the front of the 42nd Division to get there first. In the darkness and confusion, the 1st Division captured Douglas MacArthur, one of the 42nd's brigadiers, who looked like a German officer because of his unorthodox headgear. It was a miracle that the two divisions did not shoot each other to pieces. If the German army had been in any kind of fighting shape, a counterattack would have wreaked havoc. The episode suggests Pershing's limitations as a practitioner of coalition warfare. In the end, the French Fourth Army was permitted to capture Sedan. Liggett wanted to court-martial Summerall, but Pershing dismissed the whole affair.

When the bells rang out across France and the people erupted into mad joy, not even Pershing could resist the emotions of victory. In perhaps his most significant summary of the war, he said several times, "The men were willing to pay the price." Perhaps this was as close as the Iron General came to admitting he had made some mistakes.

For the rest of his long life—he did not die until 1948—Pershing spent a good deal of his time fostering the career of the man who would lead America's armies in World War II. Marshall served as his aide when he was chief of staff after the war, they became close friends, and Pershing was best man at Marshall's wedding in 1927. When MacArthur, then the army chief of staff, tried to short-circuit Marshall's advancement by appointing him senior instructor to the Illinois National Guard in 1933, Pershing visited him in Chicago, creating headlines for the obscure young colonel. The next chief of staff, a Pershing man, brought Marshall back to Washington as his assistant. In 1939, Pershing persuaded FDR to make Marshall the chief of staff.

In his private life, Pershing was a dutiful father to his only son, Warren. He made no objection when Warren chose a civilian rather than a military career. Pershing remained devoted to Micheline Resco, but he was frequently linked romantically to other women. He once remarked that if he married all the women he was reported to be romancing, he would have to start a harem.

Trying to sum up Pershing, almost everyone found him full of contradictions. Secretary of War Baker wondered how a man could combine such large views with an obsessive concern for buttons. "If he was not a great man," wrote the newsman Frank Simonds, "there were few stronger." The British military thinker B. H. Liddell Hart said no other man could have built the AEF, and "without that army the war could hardly have been saved and could not have been won." Perhaps his unmilitary friend Charles Dawes came closest to the Iron General's inner secret: "John Pershing, like Lincoln, recognized no superior on the face of the earth." Unquestionably, Pershing left something to be desired as a field commander. But without him, American doughboys might have become cannon fodder for French and British generals—a development that would have caused a huge political backlash on the home front. Meanwhile, he and his men learned the bitter lessons of how to fight on the Western Front. Fortunately for Pershing, the doughboys were willing to pay the price.

The Unreal City: The Trenches of World War I

Robert Cowley

Persons of even limited exposure to the history of the Western Front in World War I are aware of the trench line that developed in 1914 with the failure of Germany's Schlieffen Plan and eventually stretched from the North Sea to the Swiss border. It was the scene of incredible slaughter for four long years. Few, however, are aware of how extensive these trenches were and, as such, how difficult they were to penetrate offensively on the stalemated front. The trenches were, in fact, extensive "unreal cities" in which men lived and died by the thousands in a seemingly endless chronicle of carnage. In this essay Robert Cowley, the editor of American Historical Publications, outlines the history of military trenching before presenting a detailed and engaging description of the "strip city" trenches that graphically characterized the Western Front and remain as negative memories of twentieth-century attritional warfare. This essay was originally published under the title "The Unreal City." From MHQ: The Quarterly Journal of Military History, *Winter 1994, by Robert Cowley. Copyright © 1994 by* MHQ: The Journal of Military History. *Reprinted in edited form by permission of PRIMEDIA Enthusiasts Publications (History Group).*

1   As They Saw It

We live in an age defined by its fierce boundaries, military and political: Has any affected our lives more conclusively than the Western Front? The Great War trench line that stretched from the North Sea to the Swiss border gave us a modern metaphor for senseless slaughter, for stalemate without hope. It added indelible words and phrases to our language: the trenches, over the top, no-man's-land, three on a match. Here was the barrier on which were shattered traditions of humanism and refinement nurtured over centuries—not just a physical presence but one of the genuine dividing lines of history.

At a time when urbanization was becoming the dominant mode of civilization, was it an accident that the Western Front adhered to that mode and even turned into something of a paradigm for its rise and decline? "Unreal city under the brown fog," T. S. Eliot wrote in *The Waste Land*. He was describing London just after the war, but his words might have fit another recent unreal city just as well. Aviators flying along the Western Front were struck by the brown haze compounded of mist and dust, an inversion caused by constant shellfire, that reached a height of several thousand feet above the trenches.

The Western Front. The name evokes an image of physical devastation, surpassed only by Hiroshima. It is the obsessive landscape of our night-mares, the apparition of hell on earth. The English artist Paul Nash captured the stylized essence of horror that it has come to represent:

> No glimmer of God's hand is seen anywhere. Sunset and sunrise are blasphe-mous, they are mockeries to man, only the black rain out of the bruised and swollen clouds all through the bitter black of night is fit atmosphere in such a land. The rain drives on, the stinking mud becomes evilly yellow, the shell-holes fill up with green-white water, the roads and tracks are covered in inches of slime, the black dying trees ooze and sweat and the shells never cease. . . . anni-hilating, maiming, maddening, they plunge into the grave which is this land; one huge grave, and cast upon it the poor dead.

Those who experienced the Western Front strained to find comparisons, as they rang the sour changes on the wasteland that confronted them. There were intimations of biblical calamity in the words of an Irish subaltern, who saw it as "an ocean floor suddenly exposed and tensed for a crashing re-engulfment." Sometimes men resorted to noisome similes. The front after a rainstorm, a French aviator commented, looked like "the humid skin of a monstrous toad." The comparisons could be remarkably similar. The front was like "a man's face after smallpox or a telescopic view of the moon," wrote Lance Corporal Roland Mountfort in 1916. Wilfred Owen merged the same image in verse: "Grey, cratered like the moon with hollow woe, / And pitted with great pocks and scabs of plagues."

An American named James McConnell, flying with the Lafayette Es-cadrille, was reminded of "Gustave Doré's picture of the fiery tombs of the arch-heretics in Dante's 'Hell.' " In a letter home, written before his own death, he spoke of "that sinister brown belt, a strip of murdered nature. It seems to belong to another world. Every sign of humanity has been swept away. The woods and roads have vanished like chalk wiped from a black-board; of the villages nothing remains but gray smears. . . ." A German in-fantryman, Alfred Hein, added (about the same Verdun sector): "A cold mathematical monstrosity had usurped the place of nature." You might call the Western Front, in the scientific jargon of doomsday, a premature ecologi-cal sink—and, indeed, I have seen photographs of places like Passchendaele used to conjure the image of coming environmental disaster. The Western Front always seemed larger than the life it denied.

2   A Capsule History of Trenches

There was nothing new about trenches. They were as old as city sieges. Ar-chaeologists recently found evidence of one outside the walls of ancient Troy; it dates back to the thirteenth century B.C., when the Trojan War is sup-posed to have taken place. Its function may have been more to impede at-tackers and their siege engines than to protect defenders, but it was a trench nonetheless. Caesar's legions dug trenches, and they were incorporated into Hadrian's Wall. Approach trenches, which sheltered besieging troops from cannon fire, were common in the 1500s, if not earlier. The first notable continuous defensive line in which trenches were a significant feature was the so-called Great Wall of the Dutch Republic. A combination of wooden redoubts and earthen ramparts, it was built in 1605 in an effort to hold off an expected Spanish invasion; the Spanish broke through it anyway. When Swedish armies invaded Poland in the 1620s, Polish propagandists scoffed at their siege techniques as "mole's work" and manifestations of a "grave-digger's courage"—while Polish military engineers hastened to copy them.

As that violent century progressed, continuous trench lines became something of a military fashion, spreading over large areas of France and the Low Countries. "Such lines," the military historian John A. Lynn tells us, "used river and canals as wet-dike barriers whenever possible, buttressing these barriers with redoubts and where necessary running between water courses with entrenchment representing a high state of military engineering."

They were mainly single-line affairs, and their purpose was not to repel invading armies but to protect valuable territory from raiders. "It is almost impossible that the enemy parties could carry out their designs beyond these entrenchments," wrote Sébastien Le Prestre de Vauban, that supreme artist of siegecraft, in 1678. Time and again he tightened a noose of trenches around a citadel or city, and he also oversaw the digging of numerous extended lines. It was one of those coincidences of history that so many crossed the Flanders plain south of Ypres—and to compound the irony, Vauban also built the walls of Ypres and the fortress of Verdun. His handiwork would have done the Western Front proud.

Not until the Great War would the pick and shovel earn more prominence than they did in the War of the Spanish Succession (1701–14). The lines of Brabant, which the French dug at the beginning of the war, stretched 130 miles from Antwerp to the Meuse River. The French proclaimed another extended fortification (much of it aboveground, but so were parts of the Western Front) as Ne Plus Ultra—"Nothing further is possible." Begun in the winter of 1710–11, it passed close to Vimy Ridge, Arras, and Cambrai—household names two centuries later—and reached the English Channel. It was about as long as the lines of Brabant, but its undoing made it better known. With linked entrenchments, fortifications, and inundations, all backed by a system of lateral roads, this most elaborate of the continuous lines of the period was designed to block not just marauders but the duke of Marlborough's army. Call it the Maginot line of the eighteenth century, which may explain the consternation in Paris when he breached its supposedly impenetrable defenses. English politics may have saved France that time: Marlborough was recalled, and his innovative campaign sputtered.

Increasingly, maneuver became the rule and digging the exception. Though we do not think of the shovel as a primary implement of the

Napoleonic Wars, it did figure in one notable episode: the defense of the Torres Vedras lines. In 1810 in Portugal, the future duke of Wellington's outnumbered army constructed a triple line of 114 redoubts connected by trenches. The strongpoints were about a mile apart and allowed for crossing fire by artillery—what might be called one of the earliest experiments with defense in depth. Torres Vedras worked: The French retreated, without even an attempt at Marlborovian dazzle. At the beginning of the Civil War, the defenses around Washington, D.C., were a copy of Torres Vedras, as were those that Robert E. Lee dug around Richmond in 1861. For his efforts he earned the nickname "King of Spades." Digging was considered unmanly.

That attitude did not long survive the unprecedented range and intensity of Civil War battlefield fire. During the 1862 Peninsula campaign, fully one-third of General George McClellan's Union army was engaged in digging. By the final year of the war there could be no doubt about it: As the saying went, "Spades were trumps." The defenses of Petersburg, the historian Gerald R. Linderman writes, "were so complex as to seem permanent." The mortar, with shells weighing up to 300 pounds, became a favorite weapon, and the threat of high-explosive underground mines kept the Confederate defenders on edgy alert. The lament of one Virginian officer was already an old one: "This mole-like existence was killing the men."

Trenches were everywhere in the Civil War, in all theaters of operations, and they should have been an omen. They were an omen disregarded. So were the futile Russian charges against the Turks dug in along the ridges of Plevna and the suicidal, if ultimately successful, Japanese attacks at Port Arthur. Positional warfare had returned with a vengeance. But the message most Western observers brought home from Manchuria was that the Japanese had won by a fanatic reliance on the offensive. It seemed beside the point that the losers, badly generaled as they were, had exacted an enormous price with weapons that would become basic to the Western Front: hand grenades, machine guns, mines and countermines, barbed wire, and even some primitive experiments with poison gas.

While some of those observers went around counting bayonet wounds in corpses to prove the efficacy of the attacker's cold steel, at least one group, the combat engineers of the German Pioneer Corps, recognized the Russo-Japanese War for the dress rehearsal it was. They began to prepare for the kind of large-scale siege warfare they believed to be inevitable. By 1913, as the tactical historian Bruce I. Gudmundsson has pointed out, contractors were developing improved grenades, trench mortars, and flamethrowers.

It is true that none of the belligerents, including the greater part of the German army, were prepared for trench warfare. Both sides at the beginning of August 1914 expected that a decision would be reached in a month or so—"before the leaves fell," as the saying went. But it is also true that before many days of the war had passed, men were digging trenches. They were meant only for temporary protection, but they were trenches nonetheless. Many of the more offense-minded officers disdained them. On August 21, the French general Charles Lanrezac ordered his troops to dig in before the Battle of Charleroi; some officers simply disregarded the order or had their men throw up a token parapet. The British army had not been involved in siege warfare since Sevastopol, in the Crimean War, sixty years earlier.

But the Germans' edge in siege warfare may have been their undoing. Instead of regrouping after the reverses of the Marne and resuming the drive for Paris, large parts of their army simply burrowed in the earth and waited for the enemy to come at them, while the rest headed north in an attempt to seize the Channel ports, leaving windrows of new trenches to mark the limits of their final surge, the "race to the sea." For the record, the last gap in the Western Front seems to have closed on October 15, when patrols of the Royal Scots Greys and the English 3rd Cavalry Division met at Kemmel, a few miles south of Ypres.

By that time the Western Front had congealed into what was in effect a solid line. Soldiers on both sides began to connect rifle pits and scattered lengths of shallow freestanding trench. The digging not just of front-line trenches but of reserve trenches signaled that something different was happening. A *system* was taking shape, and one that soon had marks of permanence. Parapets were built up with sandbags—which rarely contained sand—and rough shelters appeared. So, on the German side, did steel observation plates. The first wire was strung up, often as an obstacle in the empty spaces between trenches. "We did not yet have American barbed wire, only a plain strand without points, such as was used in the country to hang doorbells or to train wires up walls." The writer was a historian turned soldier, Sergeant Marc Bloch of the French 272nd Reserve Infantry Regiment. At the beginning of October, Bloch (who was serving in the Argonne) noted that quartermasters were handing out woolen underwear to the men in the trenches. Now they knew the truth: They would not be home before the leaves fell.

3   Twice around the Earth

It was hardly as if the phenomenon that was the Western Front had emerged spontaneously, going in a single leap from mud-hut cluster to metropolis without intermediate experiments in military urbanization. What was different about this new world-class city was its length, depth, and variety, as well as its complexity of military and social organization.

The length of "that sinister brown belt" was about 470 miles—the most trustworthy estimates of the line that was established by midautumn range from 466 to 475 miles. Even with detailed trench maps, a finite reckoning is well-nigh impossible. What date would you pick for the measurement? Would it be before or after this major offensive or that series of raids? Would you measure from the German or the Allied side? Protuberances did not always correspond with indentations. Attacks inevitably produced (the words are those of the marvelously dogged Australian official historian C. E. W. Bean) "here or there a slight local bulge, or a hardly perceptible dint." Through 1916, the largest bulge, the result of the Battle of the Somme, would be just seven miles deep. But essentially the line might as well have been cast in concrete—and in places it was.

The Western Front would contract by about 25 miles in March 1917, when the Germans made their premeditated withdrawal to the Hindenburg line—and would expand considerably when they made their gamble for victory in the spring and early summer of 1918. During those months the Western Front would briefly reach a maximum length of some 600 miles, as mobility (though not true maneuver) returned to the war.

More numbers: On the average, 200 to 300 yards separated the opposing trenches, though that mean distance narrowed to 150 yards in Flanders. The exceptions to the average were too numerous to be considered curiosities. Near the North Sea, the polders that the Belgians had inundated in the autumn of 1914 kept the lines as much as three miles apart. In other sectors, the dead zone of no-man's-land could be a mile wide or more.

That gap could shrink to ten yards or less, about the width from sidewalk to sidewalk of an ordinary city street. It was not unheard-of for the two sides to share the same trench, with only a barricade of barbed wire and sandbags keeping them apart. At Lingekopf in the Vosges, there were only a few yards between the opposing trenches, which were protected by antigrenade screens angled acutely: Grenades burst upward. (The Germans finally resorted to flamethrowers to dislodge the French.) A young English officer, Edwin Campion Vaughan, told of returning in the spring of 1917 to a trench he had occupied some months earlier at Biaches, just south of the Somme. He discovered that at one point only a cellar wall had separated him from a German dugout. The saying went that the adversaries were close enough to shake hands—or to cross bayonets. But the following exchange, which Bloch recorded, may put the situation somewhat more in perspective: "The Germans are only thirty meters away from us," cries a panic-stricken soldier. "Well," a noncom answers, "we are only thirty meters from the Germans."

Accident, as well as determination not to give up an inch more of ground, initially accounted for the narrowness of no-man's-land. It was as if men in the midst of an open rural landscape were engaged in the sort of close combat normally associated with cities. Too, tacticians thought that an abbreviated interval between lines would make possible an assault in a single bound. But in the early months of the Western Front, that interval was a measure of an enthusiasm and intensity, a hankering for sacrifice, that amounted to a generational death wish. Once the grenade was introduced in quantity and became the infantryman's weapon of choice, the trenches tended to retreat beyond throwing range. But it was also difficult to shell an enemy trench if it was hard by. As the war grew longer, so did the distances.

The basic frontline systems ordinarily consisted of three trenches. The outer one was called the fire trench. Ideally, it was a ditch deep enough for a man of normal height to stand erect, and wide enough for him to pass another man without difficulty. Laziness or local conditions did not always permit the ideal: In part of Flanders you could not dig down more than a couple of feet without striking water. Parapets built up with prodigious heaps of sandbags made up the height difference. (A parapet had to be 20 inches wide to stop a rifle bullet fired from a trench 200 yards away.) By the end of 1915 the British army estimated that it needed 30 million sandbags per month.

Neither fire trenches nor the ones behind them ever ran as straight as they look on most military maps. The French favored a saw-toothed pattern to their trenches; the British and Germans, a crenellated one, like teeth on a jack-o'-lantern. The teeth were called firebays, and the brief backward stretches, traverses. Their purpose was to prevent an attacker who had gained a foothold from shooting down a long, unobstructed alley—enfilade fire. (It was a principle of self-protection already old when Vauban employed it.) The fire trench was actually not the most forward extension of the system, for narrow saps were thrust out into no-man's-land, like suckers sprouting from a gnarled branch. At their ends were listening posts, often uncomfortably close to the enemy wire (and to his own saps). They were usually occupied only at night.

A support trench formed the second line, although sometimes a so-called travel trench would intervene. Counterattacks would issue from the support trench if the first line was overrun. Support trenches were sited from 70 to 100 yards behind the fire trench. Military doctrine ordained that distance early in the war: The first two lines should be dug far enough apart so that they could not be bombarded at the same time. The murderous sophistication of the artillery took care of that illusion before long. Still, support trenches were relatively safe, and the real life of the front was spun out along their winding, jagged thoroughfares. Field kitchens were located there, as well as the deep dugouts that housed command posts, supplies, and sleeping quarters.

Finally, several hundred yards to two miles back, was a reserve trench. Reserve trenches were in fact not always trenches but loosely connected lines of dugouts and sandbagged shelters, preferably situated behind a hedge to hinder enemy observation; regimental aid posts were generally located here. (Even farther back, there might be another vague line, to be deepened and garrisoned in an emergency, and at key points such as river crossings there might be a last line of posts, also ungarrisoned.)

Communication trenches—*boyaux*—completed the effect of a demented spider's web. They zigzagged cross-country, roughly at right angles to the frontline system; some were miles long. The busiest never stopped being busy, especially at night, as fresh troops and supply and work parties moved up in them, passing weary detachments returning from the front, and the wounded and the dead being carried back. Between the first two lines, the communication trenches were even more numerous, dug at intervals of about seventy-five yards. Again, if an attack captured a length of the first trench, it could be contained within a pocket formed by two communication trenches and the support line. With a little help from machine guns, this was one theory that generally did work.

By the end of the first year of trench warfare, the average combined width of the frontline systems, including no-man's-land, was between one and two miles. Yet the belt that constituted the Western Front was still more green than brown, eerily so. A German soldier standing on the ridgeline of Passchendaele—to pick a spot later swept famously clean of nature—could see beyond pleasantly wooded slopes an undomesticated vista of deserted cottages and barns, a bit battered perhaps but still standing, underbrush discreetly creeping up on them, and fields now sown with shell holes and plowed by erratically spaced furrows of upturned earth that crisscrossed a widening band of new wilderness in which not a single human being was visible. Those trenches concealed thousands of men, and under cover of darkness they would come alive. It was only in the latter half of the war, when artillery became a contagion, that the shattered trees that became associated with the Western Front began to dominate. Even in 1918 you could find stretches of the line that had been roughed up but not ravaged.

In places, peasants continued to farm almost to the reserve lines. When their children went out to play, they carried gas masks and seemed oblivious to the shells bursting a couple of fields away. The fall of 1915 was mild, and men would crawl "into the long grass of no-man's-land, when off duty," a former English subaltern remembered, "to smoke and read their home letters undisturbed." This was near the end of what you might call the Arcadian period of the war, and one day late in December another English officer, an artilleryman named P. H. Pilditch, looked out from an observation post at "the almost green strip . . . sloping up" toward the "high chalk German parapet." He noted what looked like "a flock of sheep grazing all over" the no-man's-land of the recent battlefield of Loos. "It seemed very weird, but with a telescope I saw clearly what they were. They were hundreds of Khaki bodies . . . destined to remain there between the trenches till one side or the other advanced, which seemed unlikely for years." Pilditch was more prescient then he probably imagined.

Gradually the front grew broader, and the brown—or the dead white of upturned chalk—spread across the landscape. The excavating intensified. Side trenches accommodated kitchens, latrines, trench mortars, and stacks of duckboards. Wired-in defensive strongpoints, connected to the main system by diagonal switch lines, were constructed to the rear, as well as added trench lines in case of future emergencies. You have the feeling that sometimes all this compounded effort was just digging for digging's sake, to keep thousands of men occupied. (British military engineers estimated that 450 men needed six hours to dig 250 yards of frontline trench; the factories of the empire rose to the challenge by providing the army with 10,638,000 spades and shovels during the fifty-one months of the war.) Both the French and the British experimented with gasoline-powered trench-digging machines. But these noisy and conspicuous devices were apparently used only in back areas, out of sight of enemy artillery. Manpower was still more reliable.

The German trench system tended to be far more intricate than the Allied one, and it was known to reach a depth of ten lines. It was not just that the Germans were better prepped in siege-warfare techniques; as long as they had to fight a two-front war, they were at a numerical disadvantage. By nature and necessity they became more defense-minded than their adversaries—whose staffs insisted that trenches that looked too permanent detracted from the spirit of attack. But the habits of the mole were hard to shake. When the Germans made their retreat to the Hindenburg line in 1917, the Allied pursuers who emerged from the trenches were so bewildered by their first taste of open warfare, and so overcautious, that they let the enemy slip clean away.

As much as anything, continuous fighting, concentrated in a single sector, accounted for the growing width of the Western Front. The French might take two lines; the Germans would dig three more—and then the process would start afresh. No one remembered who, or which side, had dug some of the oldest trenches: They seemed as ageless as the war itself.

Pilditch, in July 1917, took in the view from the summit of the Flanders hill called, somewhat grandiloquently, Mont Kemmel (it was barely 500 feet high). Below, a "hideous six-mile-broad scar" stretched "brown and loathsome" as far as his eye could see. (That was before the Passchendaele offensive, which widened the scar in the crescent around Ypres by another five miles.) The sector that could probably boast the greatest width of trenchworks was in Champagne, roughly between two geographic nonentities, the village of Tahure and the Ferme de Navarin fields. There, the combined width of the opposing systems reached twelve miles. On the Somme at the beginning of 1917, the trench lines approached a similar width—and if you add to that desert the intentional devastation bequeathed by the Germans retreating to the Hindenburg line, you have a band of wasteland more than thirty miles across.

Henri Barbusse's *Le Feu* takes these figures a step further. (*Le Feu* meant "the front" or "up front," a bit of soldier slang that the translator of the English version, *Under Fire*, was either ignorant of or chose to ignore.) In the Barbusse novel, played out during the Artois offensives of 1915, one of his soldier characters, Cocon, makes some calculations—and provides a memorable picture of the trench system in the process. Barbusse's "Man of Figures" begins:

> In the sector occupied by our regiment, there are fifteen lines of French trenches. Some are abandoned, invaded by grass, and half leveled; the others solidly upkept and bristling with men. These parallels are joined up by innumerable galleries which hook and crook themselves like ancient streets. The system is much more dense than we believe who live inside it. On the twenty-five kilometers'

width that forms the army front, one must count on a thousand kilometers of hollowed line—trenches and saps of all sorts.

He goes on to estimate that on the French front alone there are about 10,000 kilometers—6,250 miles—of trenches, "and as much again on the German side"—12,500 miles in all. He doesn't add in the totals for the British and Belgians and their German opponents, facing one another on what was that year the final tenth of the front. Tack on another 2,500 miles—which gives the Western Front something like 15,000 miles of trenches, an extraordinary figure.

But it would seem that Cocon/Barbusse may have vastly underestimated: At the end of 1915, French army statisticians calculated that there were twenty miles of trench for every mile of front. By summer's end, 1916, that had increased to thirty miles. Can we believe the figures? It would mean that there were almost 15,000 miles of trenches just on the Allied side of the Western Front. But we can't simply accord the Germans, those consummate moles, an equivalent 15,000 miles. A reasonable estimate might credit them with a third again as many trenches—5,000 miles—at least. That would bring the total to perhaps 35,000 miles of "hollowed lines"—and the war was only half over.

What was the final total? We can make a reasonable guess. In an address delivered on June 19, 1920, the president of France, Raymond Poincaré, estimated that "265,000,000 cubic meters of trenches had to be filled up" on French soil alone. Since the average trench was dug down about a meter and a half (and then thick parapets of sandbags or raised earth were thrown up), with a mean width from top to bottom of a couple of meters, it seems safe to calculate three cubic meters for every meter of trench—and that would include deep fire trenches as well as connected shell holes and the hen scratchings that passed for reserve lines. You come up with a kilometric figure that translates to about 55,000 miles. Add to that the intensely entrenched Belgium, and the total for the entire Western Front might have been 60,000 miles—almost two and a half times the circumference of the earth!

4 Strip City

Think of the Western Front as the first strip city in history—not as long, as wide, or as thickly populated as what urbanologists call Bosnywash on the East Coast of the United States; still, immense enough. This perception came to me independently some years ago, but I have discovered since that I hold no monopoly on the urban analogy. "That strange over-populated city," John Keegan called it. "After all, the Western Front was genuinely a *place*, however suddenly settled, however swiftly depopulated, with its own street plan, place-names, backwaters, dangerous turnings, local patriotisms, and emotional geography"—sectors such as the Ypres salient or Verdun having a heightened emotional charge for both sides. C. E. W. Bean spoke of a system where men lived "as in the streets of a city":

> The elaborately constructed machine-gun and trench-mortar positions, headquarters, observation and sniping posts, and dumps were the industrial establishments, and the nightly fatigue parties, dodging the light of flares and the stream of machine-gun bullets along the trench tramways, were the transport.

These "workers of war" (the phrase was coined by one of them, the German novelist Ernst Jünger) were the proletariat of a true revolution. War in its modern incarnation required a vast work force recruited to meet the needs of the assembly lines of mass destruction set up along the entire extent of the Western Front. Indeed, by 1916, military commentators were speaking of the "material battle." But the millions of men and the machines they serviced could exist only in a concentrated urban setting, a martial version of the Ruhr or the Midlands.

Unreal the Western Front may have been—its total maleness, if nothing else, made it so. But a city it surely was. It had its boroughs and arrondissements (the army sectors), its distinct neighborhoods that ran the gamut from serene to perilous, from slummy to plush (but that were apt to go downhill precipitously), its suburbs in the rear areas, including those ultimate bastions of privilege, the châteaus where the staffs had their rooms at the top. (The peculiarly rigid urban design of the trenches encouraged a social and command structure that was hierarchical in the extreme, one that increasingly insulated the captains of this vast military industry from the workaday world they presided over.)

The strip city had its "avenues," the communication trenches which could extend for miles, with side streets and cul-de-sacs branching off. They took on names that were alternately picturesque—Dead Dog Avenue, Panama Canal, Queer Street—or grandly prosaic—Devon Avenue, Savile Row, Boyau d'Evian, Unter den Linden—names that recalled places that so many would never see again. The strip city had its long and intricate underground systems: One that the British occupied was an elaboration of existing coal mines and ran some twelve miles from Loos to Arras. It had dugouts up to forty feet deep that could be for officers like the London clubs of St. James's or for enlisted men like the Berlin tenements of Neükolln. The German writer Ludwig Renn described one tunnel on the Somme front where tiers of wooden bunks lined a narrow passageway seventy yards long: "Down below there hung a cold damp fog of wet clothes, tobacco smoke, and soot, making the candles burn reddish-brown. . . ." But the German dugouts could also exhibit a degree of luxury unknown on the Allied side of the line, with electric lights and ventilation pumps, water tanks, stoves and ovens, and varnished wood paneling, wallpaper, and rugs for the officers' quarters.

The strip city had its distinctive nighttime illumination, not neon but the rockets called Verey lights. Those were the hours when the activity of the trenches became positively bazaarlike. It had its nearby and all-but-built-in entertainment centers—towns like Lille and Laon and, until 1916, Verdun, where you could find cinemas, restaurants, and bordellos. (Directly behind the lines off Armentières, the British army had converted a brewery into a bathhouse, and once they emerged from the vats turned hot tubs, soldiers could wander back to browse in shops that were, in the first year of the war, still brightly lit.) The diseases of filth and exposure that men suffered from were the urbanlike maladies endemic to their way of life: trench foot (mud and wet and cold), trench fever (lice), scabies (nits), the liver ailment called Weil's disease (rats). For every two men brought into casualty clearing stations with battle wounds, three reported in with serious illness.

There was an undeniably cosmopolitan quality about the Western Front experience, and one that only great cities possess. In 1917, my father, an American Field Service volunteer, billeted behind the lines in the Chemin des Dames sector, observed a sight that he would recall to me seventy years later:

> Sometimes for three days at a time, a column of men and guns wound through the village where we were quartered. Chasseurs slouching along in their dark-blue uniforms, canteens and helmets banging against their hips; a regiment of Senegalese, huge men with blue-black faces . . . Behind them, dust rose from an interminable line of seventy-fives drawn by great bay horses, with very blond Flemish artillerymen riding the caissons. . . . Then, in horizon blue, an infantry regiment from Provence, three thousand men with sullen features.

Looking on with the American college boys like my father were Annamite road menders—as the laborers from the French colony of Indochina were then called. "The long parade of races was a spectacle which it was our privilege to survey, a special circus like the exhibition of Moroccan horsemen given for our benefit on the Fourth of July. . . ."

How many men populated this strip city? Erich von Falkenhayn, the German chief of staff, estimated that early in July 1916 the combined total for both sides was 6.1 million. That would have made the Western Front the largest metropolis in the world.

· ·

During the 1,563 days of fighting on the Western Front, the average *daily* loss for all combatants in killed, wounded, captured, or missing was 8,000—a total of about 12.5 million men. That figure exceeds the combined 1914 populations of London, Paris, and Berlin.

As the dark satanic mills of the Western Front shut down, the skeletons in the weeds waited to be collected. They were the true products of a new industrial revolution, an industrial revolution of war, and the ultimate reality of that unreal city.

VIII

The Interwar Years, 1919–1939

Innovation in the U.S. Army, 1917–1945

David E. Johnson

In this essay David E. Johnson, a senior policy analyst at The Rand, ponders the question as to why the Army during the interwar period neglected the potential of armor and accepted the potential of air power (especially strategic bombing), as clearly revealed in the National Defense Act of 1920, which abolished the Tank Corps yet created the Army Air Service. The answer, he asserts, lies not in external factors (such as a lack of funds and outside support) but in internal factors, specifically in the myopic dominant military culture, prevailing paradigms, and bureaucratic politics. His conclusion is clear: "The Army, in short, was responsible for its own unpreparedness [for World War II]." This essay was originally published as the conclusion to Johnson's Fast Tanks and Heavy Bombers: Innovation in the U.S. Army, 1917–1945 *(Ithaca & London: Cornell University Press, 1998), 218–29, and is reprinted text only with permission.*

The sober realities of combat revealed the serious flaws in the technological assumptions underpinning the U.S. Army's tank and airplane doctrines. American tanks had to fight superior German tanks, and unescorted heavy bomber formations could not defend themselves against enemy fighter attacks without incurring unacceptable losses. Both doctrines had to be adapted to the realities of war, and the decisiveness expected by American planners from the tank and the heavy bomber was never fully realized. Instead, each machine simply became another weapon in America's arsenal of attrition. Unfortunately, the Army's tank and bomber crews paid the price for the doctrinal failures.

199

Why did the Army make its decisions about tanks and airplanes? Why were American armor and air doctrines mutually exclusive, even in the face of an apparently successful model, the German blitzkrieg, that emphasized cooperation between air and ground forces? Answers to these questions are elusive. Clearly, many external factors influenced the Army's development of tanks and airplanes. Both weapons evolved during the interwar period, when the Army was struggling to adapt to the changing nature of war in a period of constrained budgets and rapid technological change. Nevertheless, the airplane enjoyed a number of advantages over the tank. The airplane had more clearly demonstrated its potential during World War I than the tank had. It was also a "dual-use" technology that had an important civilian dimension that the tank did not. In the years following World War I industrial and research organizations achieved further developments in aviation—developments that relied heavily on requirements from the Army's air arm. Quite simply, the tank technology lacked this commercial utility, because it "could not be used in civilian life. . . . Therefore, armored warfare was technologically feasible but not technologically necessary." Finally, largely because of its commercial utility, the airplane had a substantial congressional constituency that pushed for its advance.

The domestic and international conditions between the wars also influenced the development of tanks and airplanes. In the aftermath of World War I, there was no immediate threat to U.S. national security. American defense policy focused on disarmament and isolation. Consequently, military preparedness received little emphasis from an economy-minded Congress. Given this absence of civilian interest in the Army, Edward Katzenbach's conclusion about the cavalry, perhaps the most traditional branch in the Army, rings true:

> When there was no interest in the military, as in the United States, there was no pressure to change, and the professional was given tacit leave to romanticize an untenable situation. Thus the U.S. Horse Cavalry remained a sort of monument to public irresponsibility in this, the most mechanized nation on earth.

Ironically, this absence of civilian interest in anything related to the military during the interwar period also influenced the development of American strategic bombing doctrine. In contrast to the ground army, in which civilian ambivalence supported conservatism, in the air arm this disinterest and the absence of oversight created a permissive environment within which an offensive doctrine, focused on bombing industrial targets and clearly at odds with the isolationist policies of the United States, could be developed.

During the Great Depression the United States faced a domestic economic crisis. To meet domestic needs Congress trimmed already-slim military budgets. In the late 1930s, when the international situation presented a threat to national interests, the War Department began to receive more adequate budgets. Even then the airplane maintained its advantage over the tank. When military policies focused on hemispheric defense, heavy bombers could augment the Navy in defending the nation and its possessions from enemy attack. Finally, when the United States entered the war, the Eighth Air Force was the only way to take the war directly to the German homeland.

These interwar conditions explain what on the surface seems to be a compelling justification for any failures by the War Department. Major General John S. Wood, a wartime armored division commander, stated the argument eloquently:

> Back to normalcy was the post-war slogan, and back to normalcy the post-war Army went, struggling to keep alive a flickering flame and faltering spirit of national preparedness, struggling to maintain and modernize its arms and equipment, and struggling for its very life to obtain the funds necessary for its meager existence. Back it went to promotions few and far between, to small posts and small units, and to the apathy that follows periods of high endeavor.

Though the essence of Wood's argument was that the Army did the best it could under austere conditions, the evidence indicates otherwise. When the United States entered World War II, budgetary constraints were no longer an issue, but Army leaders apparently saw no reason to analyze tank and airplane technologies and doctrines. Instead, existing designs were rushed into mass production to support already-sanctioned doctrines.

Internal arrangements—culture, prevailing paradigms, and bureaucratic politics—exercised the most pervasive influence on how the War Department responded to the potential of tanks and airplanes and exacerbated the effects of external factors. Ironically, the Army had faced these same weaknesses before World War I. Major General Johnson Hagood, a member of the War Department General Staff before World War I, argued in 1927: "Our unpreparedness did not come from lack of money, lack of soldiers, or lack of supplies. It came from lack of brains, or perhaps it would be fairer to say, lack of genius." Hagood also noted the difficulty in addressing the Army's deficiencies: "Why, seeing these things did I not do something to correct them? The answer is that I did not see them, or seeing them did not understand. Hindsight is better than foresight."

Hagood was unable to gauge events accurately because of the culture surrounding his career. The challenge he faced before World War I was similar to the one his successors encountered during the interwar period: immersion in the day-to-day realities of an Army making the difficult cultural and institutional transitions from frontier constabulary to modern army, from absolute faith in man and animal to reliance on machines and science.

The prevailing internal dynamics of the post–World War I Army were perpetuated in the National Defense Act of 1920. This legislation, reflecting the perspectives of the Army's ranking officers, abolished the wartime Tank Corps, thus submerging the tank within the infantry until 1931, when the cavalry was allowed to experiment with mechanization. The act also created the Air Service as a branch within the War Department hierarchy. Quite simply, the act engendered a constituency for the airplane within the Army— one vitally interested in its advancement—and abolished the structure that might have nurtured the tank. The future of U.S. Army aviation was in the hands of advocates; the potential of the tank was controlled by traditionalists, largely satisfied with the existing doctrines and technologies.

The decisions in the Defense Act were not, in the context of the times in which they were made, particularly surprising. The airplane had demonstrated its immense potential in World War I; the tank had not. The airplane had vocal champions during the congressional hearings on Army reorganization after the war, many of whom pressed for a separate aviation service equivalent to the Army and Navy; most of the proponents for the continuance of the Tank Corps believed, as did officers in other branches, that it was an adjunct of the infantry. Therefore, the decision to place the Infantry in charge of tank development was not particularly contentious. It went largely unchallenged.

Still, little should be presumed about the impact the presence of an independent tank arm might have had within the U.S. Army. The British example is instructive here. Even though an independent Royal Tank Corps existed in the British Army, it still had to contend with the entrenched infantry, cavalry, and artillery branches for constrained resources and acceptance. Consequently, the tank arm remained immersed in the British Army, of which it was clearly a component. Given the ascendance of these same branches in the U.S. Army, the highly decentralized nature of the War Department that sanctioned the prerogatives of the branches, the intense competition for resources within the Army, and the absence of a civilian dimension for the tank, innovation with armor would probably not have been radically different if the Tank Corps had survived World War I as a separate branch. Like the other branches, it would likely have focused on its own parochial interests. Given these dynamics within the U.S. Army, it is doubtful that an independent Tank Corps would have been a catalyst for the combined-arms cooperation at the heart of German effectiveness.

Nevertheless, the National Defense Act of 1920 established the institutional parameters within which the tank would develop in the U.S. Army. From the promulgation of the act until the creation of the Armored Force in July 1940, the tank was viewed as an auxiliary of the infantry or as a way to modernize the cavalry. The biases inherent in these traditional branches shaped American tank doctrines and designs. Infantry tank designs focused on providing a weapon to aid foot soldiers in the assault against enemy machine guns and strong points; cavalry combat cars provided an "iron horse" to conduct traditional cavalry missions.

The powerful chiefs of infantry and cavalry repressed officers who advocated a broader role for tanks. Additionally, the last chief of cavalry, Major General John Herr, viewed mechanization as a threat to the continuance of horse cavalry and actively thwarted the expansion of the 7th Cavalry Brigade (Mechanized). The limit of Herr's acquiescence in technology was the formation of horse-mechanized corps reconnaissance regiments. This admixture of horse and machine was reflective of Herr's underlying approach to technology: "As always, Cavalry's motto must remain: When better roller skates are made, Cavalry horses will wear them." Retention of the horse remained his absolute goal.

When the War Department created the Armored Force in response to the German blitzkrieg, the officers who controlled the organization brought their biases with them. Major General Adna Chaffee designed the armored division to conduct traditional cavalry missions. Concurrently, the General Headquarters (GHQ) tank battalions remained in the Army, perpetuating the traditional tank role of supporting infantry. The debate within the Armored Force focused largely on organizational arrangements—the proper mix of light tanks, medium tanks, infantry, and artillery—not the appropriateness of the existing tanks or the doctrine for their employment. Further complicating doctrinal and technological decisions about tanks was Lieutenant General Lesley McNair's dogmatic support of the tank destroyer as an antitank panacea. He was a powerful man, and tank destroyers proliferated in the Army.

The creation of the Air Service provided an institution vitally concerned with the airplane's exploitation. Air officers, led at first by Brigadier General Billy Mitchell, believed that World War I proved the potential of independent air power and that only airmen could realize the full implications of military aviation. The fight to gain independence for the air arm politicized the technology and radicalized its proponents. These insurgents struggled tenaciously to wrest control of the aerial weapon from the War Department hierarchy, whom they believed repressed the potential of air power.

In the early 1930s a doctrine that would ostensibly prove the decisiveness of air power began to evolve—unescorted, high-altitude, daylight precision bombing of the industrial infrastructure of an enemy nation. Crucial to this concept was the assumption that heavy bomber formations could defend themselves during long-range penetrations to attack the enemy's centers of production. The B-17 seemed to offer the technology to realize this goal.

By World War II the bomber advocates, having gained control of the air arm, had simply overwhelmed any air officers critical of their doctrine. Since prevailing military authority believed that the success of bombardment was not contingent on long-range escort fighters, the development of this type of airplane received low priority. Additionally, since the bomber proponents viewed air power as a decisive, independent force, they paid little attention to the support of ground forces. They feared that this role could restrict their hard-won autonomy, because ground officers would almost certainly control such a mission.

Consequently, the Army Air Forces entered World War II with an institutional imperative to prove the decisiveness of strategic bombing. If it failed, there could be no justification for the long-cherished goal of an independent air force. Therefore, the Army Air Forces focused on building the Eighth Air Force, and General Henry Arnold placed enormous pressure on Lieutenant General Ira Eaker to make the air campaign against Germany succeed.

The structure of the War Department itself, codified in the National Defense Act of 1920, as well as the attitudes of the officers who controlled the institution, also influenced the development of tanks and airplanes. During the interwar years the War Department became a cumbersome, decentralized bureaucracy. The powerful branch chiefs were allowed to develop doctrines and technologies for their arms with little direction from above or integration with the other branches. They proved largely incapable of critical self-analysis, consistently interpreting reports from the Spanish civil war, the invasion of Poland, the fall of France, and the Battle of Britain in ways that supported their predilections. To the chief of infantry the lesson was clear—tanks were most effective as infantry support weapons. The chief of cavalry concluded that the horse was still a vital factor in war. The head of the Armored Force saw German blitzkrieg tactics as validation of mechanized cavalry concepts. And air officers saw aerial successes as validation of their views and elected to see failures as incorrect applications of fundamental air power principles. The War Department provided little leadership, critical or otherwise, to sort out these matters; the nominal head of the institution was not in control of the component parts. Thus, innovation in the interwar Army was constrained by unquestioned faith in ruling paradigms—paradigms that shaped perceptions of external experiences.

The Army school system, rather than serving as an agent for change, focused almost completely on accepted doctrine. In the absence of practical opportunities in the field, officers learned the intricacies of maneuvering and supporting large units through exercises, mainly in Army schools. The Command and General Staff School trained officers for duty at division, corps, and army level and "dealt exclusively with professional military subjects." The Army War College prepared its students for command and staff at and above the army level and for service on the War Department General Staff. Finally, the Army Industrial College opened in 1924 to school officers in wartime procurement and industrial mobilization. Collectively, the schools focused on developing officers who could supervise the mobilization, fighting, and supplying of a mass army along World War I lines. As one scholar of the Army War College noted, the institution failed to produce a Clausewitz, Mahan, Liddell Hart, or Quincy Wright. It contributed only marginally to any body of theory on the phenomenon of war. But that had not been its aim. Its aim had been utilitarian—to produce competent, if not necessarily brilliant, leadership that could prepare the Army for war and fight a war successfully if it came.

The same purpose applied generally to all of the Army's schools during the interwar era—the production of "able military practitioners," not "military theoreticians." Nevertheless, the schools were a reflection of the institution they served, one dominated by senior officers who "looked with satisfaction on the achievements of World War I, and were cautious and conservative in their outlook." Although the Command and General Staff School at Fort Leavenworth was generally viewed as the "source of Army doctrine and procedure," it was clearly a captive of the Army's sanctioned doctrine. Instruction remained riveted on conservative doctrines, largely ignoring emerging, competitive perspectives such as mechanization and air power.

The curriculum of the 1938–39 regular course is a good example of the conservatism reigning at Leavenworth. It contained 198 hours of instruction on the World War I–vintage four-regiment, "square" infantry division. The study of mechanized units and tanks merited only 29 hours and aviation a mere 13 hours of the students' time—small wonder many air officers believed "it was silly to send air officers to the Command and General Staff School for 2 years to learn the minutia of ground officers' duties." In April 1939 the War Department sent Brigadier General Lesley J. McNair to Leavenworth to modernize the course of instruction. McNair accomplished little. Before he could significantly change the regular course at Leavenworth, the War Department curtailed it, as well as the courses at the War and Industrial Colleges. The Army needed officers in units, not classrooms, as war approached.

The Command and General Staff School at Fort Leavenworth also reflected the cultural mores of an Army imbued with the upper middle class traditions of the gentleman soldier. Although the notion of the "indefinable social prestige which the man on horseback, the cavalier, the hidalgo, the gentleman" possessed was perhaps most evident within the cavalry branch, the social routine at Fort Leavenworth, like that of many Army posts, revolved around horse shows, polo matches, and the hunt. The course of study at the Command and General Staff School reflected and reinforced the cultural importance of the horse; as late as 1939, officers still participated in thirty-one hours of equitation. Air Corps officers could substitute flying for equitation, but on the days they did not fly they had to join their classmates in learning the "proper adjustment of the saddle and bridle and to riding at all gaits with a comfortable seat." Most students had little problem with the requirement. A survey of the class of 1939 showed that more than half of the respondents favored equitation in the curriculum, an indication of the importance of horsemanship in officer culture.

Army culture had another pervasive influence over the officer corps. Throughout the interwar era, the values of an American society caught up in "the business liberalism of the 1920's and the reform liberalism of the 1930's" was bothersome to Regular Army officers. That the country was seemingly "abandoning its moral anchor and venturing out into a chaotic sea of pragmatism and relativism" was anathema to a conservative officer corps wedded to a belief in the moral superiority of the military life. The result of this conflict of values was "the isolation forced upon the military by the hostility of a liberal society" and "a renewed emphasis upon military values, and a renewed awareness of the gulf between military values and those values prevalent in American society." One officer wrote in 1936 that "if a man cannot find satisfaction in living a purely military life, he should get out of the army. . . . The soldier and the civilian belong to separate classes of society."

Of all the military values, one ranked the highest: loyalty. Loyalty was the "cardinal military virtue" stressed during the interwar years, a trait clearly at odds with the prevailing societal value of individualism. Loyalty placed bounds on initiative, since it required "loyal identification with, and understanding of, the desires of the superior." At the heart of this emphasis on loyalty was "a feeling that as the officer corps came to think alike, to adhere to the same body of doctrine, subjective cohesion would replace objective restraints."

The Army was also largely isolated in American society, because its ethos stressed loyalty to the organization. Denied a voice in any debate over national policy, the Army turned inward. There was little tolerance within the Army for dissent. The system repressed those who agitated for change, and early advocates of a larger role for tanks quickly abandoned their cause. There were no Harts, Fullers, de Gaulles, or Guderians in the U.S. Army. The air arm was different, though. Air officers transferred their loyalty from the Army to the concept of an independent air force. The means to effect this ideal was the development of air power as a decisive, war-winning instrument independent of ground combat. In pursuit of this goal, the air arm developed its own institutional orthodoxy, to which it demanded loyalty. Bomber advocates dominated the air arm and marginalized air officers who did not share their views.

When the United States entered the war, the War Department had to be turned upside down to make it function. The new institutional arrangements that created the Army ground forces and air forces resulted in an army that was prepared to fight two separate wars—one on the ground and one in the air. Much of the basis for this internal dichotomy was the result of another factor that had determined the War Department's approach to technology and doctrine. During the interwar years the War Department and its branches, except the air arm, were in the firm grasp of a succession of ground officers bent on protecting the Army's personnel strength. When tight budgets seemingly forced a decision between men and machines, the War Department inevitably opted to cut its modernization programs to preserve its personnel. When war came, and the Army's tanks proved inferior to those of the Germans, the failure was not critical to the success of ground operations. Hence, the rapid development and fielding of a replacement for the M4 tank was not a priority. There were enough Sherman tanks to aid the infantry and armored divisions in overwhelming the Germans, although the cost to American tank crews was unnecessarily high.

Air officers viewed machines differently. They embraced technology as the crucial factor in warfare. Using machines to attack the enemy's means of producing machines was their way of war. In the quest to realize their vision, the air officers invented a doctrine that hinged on the ability of their bomber technology to meet their expectations. When, in the autumn of 1943, the Germans proved that heavy bomber formations could not survive without fighter escorts, the Army Air Forces faced a technological crisis. When the institution responded by providing escort fighters, losses were reduced to an acceptable level and the doctrine, albeit modified, was saved.

One result of the unresolved intraservice dispute over how to wage war was the U.S. Army's failure to develop a coherent doctrine to combine ground and air forces to achieve the synergy demonstrated by the Germans. A postwar review of operations in the European theater asserted that the Army's failure to develop air-ground doctrine meant that means of cooperation had to be invented extemporaneously in the field. In the combat theaters, ground and air commanders were forced to create ad hoc procedures for tactical air power because their superiors provided no centralized direction. Indeed, by the end of the war, American armored doctrine had come to resemble the German blitzkrieg in that it stressed the importance of coordinating ground and air tactical operations. The final after-action report of General Omar Bradley's 12th Army Group emphasized that "the air-armor team is a most powerful combination in the breakthrough and in exploitation. . . . The use of this coordinated force, in combat, should be habitual." Thus, although air support of ground operations played an important role in the Allied drive into Germany and procedures were continually improved, the initiative came from below. In the combat zones, where Americans were dying, intraservice agendas were discarded and field expedients were devised to overcome institutional inertia.

At the end of the war a general board convened to assess the performance of the U.S. forces in the European theater. Its conclusions about American armored forces were telling. Although the board's various reports declared that the doctrine in existing field manuals was essentially correct for the missions and employment of the armored division and the separate tank battalions, the board recognized that changes were necessary. Its recommendations generally reflected the lessons learned about the importance of close cooperation between tanks and infantry, stressing the integration of tanks and infantry, both in armored divisions and infantry divisions. Furthermore, the board recognized that tactical air power was a necessary, and often critical, component of successful ground operations.

The General Board, however, judged existing tanks inadequate to execute American armored doctrine. Fundamental to the board's analysis of American armored vehicle performance was the premise that "the European campaign demonstrated that tanks fight tanks." The board thus recommended that the Army adopt as the "*minimum* standard for future [tank gun] development . . . [f]or exploitation tanks of an armored division, a 'gun capable of penetrating the sides and rear of any enemy armored vehicle and the front of any but the heaviest assault tank,' at normal tank fighting ranges." Even reconnaissance (light) tanks required a gun able to penetrate the "sides and rear of any enemy armored vehicle." The board also specified the protection required for future infantry support tanks: "Frontal armor and armor over ammunition stowage must be capable of withstanding all foreign tank and anti-tank weapons at normal combat ranges."

The acknowledgment that "tanks fight tanks" led ineluctably to the conclusion that tank destroyers were unnecessary. Armored division commanders believed that given "the trend to tanks with high velocity weapons capable of destroying other tanks," there was no requirement for tank destroyer units in the armored division. Infantry division commanders confirmed this view: "If a tank is given to the Infantry with a proper anti-tank gun, the division commanders favor the replacement of the tank destroyer with a tank."

The American strategic bombing effort was also assessed. The U.S. Strategic Bombing Survey, after conducting exhaustive analyses of the air war against Germany, concluded that the use of air power in the war in Europe, although important, "might have been employed differently or better in some respects." Although "it brought the economy which sustained the enemy's armed forces to a virtual collapse . . . the full effects of this collapse had not reached the enemy's front lines when they were overrun by Allied forces."

This inability of the Army Air Forces to independently end the war was due in large measure to "battle conditions," the resilience of German industry, and the fact that formation flying resulted in bomb patterns in which "only a portion [of the bombs] could fall on small precision targets." The survey surmised that during bombing operations over Germany, "only about 20% of the bombs aimed at precision targets fell within this target area [within 1,000 feet of the aiming point]."

In the blinding flash of the nuclear detonation in Hiroshima, Japan, the criticisms of the bombing campaign in Europe became largely irrelevant.

With the advent of the atomic bomb, air power seemed to become the decisive force envisioned by a generation of American bomber advocates. The destructive capability of air power no longer hinged on precision bombing or large formations of bombers fighting their way to enemy industrial centers. Instead, a single aircraft could deliver an overwhelming blow against virtually any target, as the *Enola Gay* had done at Hiroshima. The Strategic Bombing Survey asserted that "the atomic bomb . . . raises the destructive power of a single bomber by a factor of somewhere between 50 and 250 times, depending upon the nature and size of the target." The survey also postulated that "given an adequate supply of atomic bombs, the B-29s based in the Marianas had sufficient strength to have effectively destroyed in a single day every Japanese city with a population in excess of 30,000 people."

Air officers quickly grasped the implications of this revolution in destructive power. In the aftermath of the bombing of Hiroshima, Army Chief of Staff General George Marshall sent a message to General Carl Spaatz, commanding general of U.S. Army Strategic Air Forces in the Pacific, asking him to refrain from commenting on the implications of the bomb. Marshall told Spaatz that he was "being widely quoted in [news]papers . . . regarding results of such a bomb on landings on Normandy, to the effect that our present Army is not necessary for the further prosecution of the war in the Pacific and tha[t] an invasion will be unnecessary." Spaatz apologized to Marshall for any possible embarrassment he may have caused but added that he had told the press that "if such a bomb had been available early in the European War it might have shortened the war by about six months."

Ironically, the atomic bomb fundamentally reframed the debate between air and ground officers: one of the points Marshall had specifically asked Spaatz to stop raising was "that the future of Armies has been decidedly curtailed." The Strategic Bombing Survey, although not seeing an end to the need for armies, predicted that "the context in which they are employed [has changed] to such a degree that radically changed equipment, training, and tactics will be required." In the future, the ground army would struggle to justify its existence in the context of a nuclear world largely dominated in the American defense structure by an independent U.S. Air Force. As the historian Russell Weigley has observed, "the Army in the late 1940's seemed almost irrelevant. . . . To the extent Americans saw the Communist threat as a military threat, their answer to it was simply the American atomic monopoly. . . . The United States would win such a war with air-atomic power."

The story of the Army's development of the tank and the airplane between the wars has implications beyond either the technologies or the times. Although internal arrangements were the most important factor in how the Army developed these weapons, a central paradox lurks in this conclusion. The tank was developed in an environment in which its advocates were suppressed and the technology itself was subordinated to the traditional arms. In contrast, the aims of the air power advocates were fulfilled largely because of the nurturing climate within the air arm. Nevertheless, neither weapon met its supporters' prewar expectations. In the case of the tank, innovation was stifled by traditional biases. The development of the airplane, relatively free of any constraints imposed by tradition, was guided by a generation of insurgents who viewed strategic bombing as a means to achieve their freedom from the Army. Their zealousness blinded them to the flaws inherent in the technology and the doctrine they designed around it.

In the final analysis, the U.S. Army that entered World War II was a reflection of the biases and institutional arrangements that existed in the War Department throughout the interwar era. Branch parochialism, a largely powerless War Department General Staff, tension between air and ground officers, a conservative culture, and disparate views about technology all conspired to inhibit innovation and intraservice cooperation. Although the War Department's focus on personnel enabled it to create and deploy a mass army in World War II, it constrained weapons research and development throughout the interwar period.

How valid, then, is the traditional interpretation of the Army's unpreparedness for World War II? Were congressional penury and public malaise responsible for the Army's deficiencies? What the Army would have done if it had been more generously funded can only be answered by speculation. Nevertheless, given the internal dynamics of the Army during the interwar period, more resources would probably have resulted in more of the same. The ground Army, focused on personnel mobilization, would almost surely have used any additional resources to fill the 280,000-man structure authorized by the National Defense Act of 1920. If it had achieved that number it probably would have pressed for more. The air arm, bent on achieving autonomy, just as certainly would have invested any increased funds in strategies that would have facilitated its long-cherished goal of independence. In short, the ground Army would have bought more personnel, and the air Army would have bought more bombers.

The Army, in short, was responsible for its own unpreparedness. Tight budgets and an isolationist-minded Congress and public were powerful constraints, but the Army would not have been ready even with adequate resources.

The "Industrial-Military Complex" in Historical Perspective: The InterWar Years

Paul A. C. Koistenen

The "military-industrial complex" and its economic-political-military impact on the nation has been the subject of considerable debate—if not rancor—since the 1950s and the onset of the Cold War. In this essay the author, of the History Department at California State University–Northridge, argues that World War I amply illustrated the necessity of cooperation between industry and the military in an all-out war effort. Accordingly, steps were taken during the interwar years to assure such cooperation, but not without considerable friction between the economic sector and the military as to which would dominate and not without opposition by antiwar groups. The Nye Committee was also involved in the debate as to the ends and means of wartime mobilization. Thus, contrary to dominant opinion that the military-industrial complex was the product of World War II and the Cold War, Koistenen makes clear that it arose out of World War I and the technological-economic realities of modern warfare, the interwar decades being the time in which a concerted effort was made to come to grips with these realities. This essay was originally published in The Journal of American History *(LVI/4 [Mar. 1970], 819–39) and is reprinted with permission.*

Scholars and journalists have limited their analyses of the "industrial-military complex" to the years of World War II and the Cold War. This focus is quite natural, for it is during this period that the multibillion-dollar war and defense budgets have had the most dramatic effects upon the nation's institutional structure. Nevertheless, to neglect the years prior to 1940 greatly limits an understanding of the "complex" which has resulted from the military's expanded role in the federal government and its elaborate ties with the industrial community.

The "industrial-military complex" of World War II and after is an outgrowth of economic mobilization for World War I, of interwar planning by the armed forces and the business community for future emergencies, and of defense spending during the 1920s and 1930s. Almost all practices currently ascribed to the "complex" arose before 1940.

During World War I, as during World War II, federal agencies, largely controlled by industry and the military, regulated the economy. World War I differed from World War II, however, in that the army, the largest wartime military service, was a reluctant participant in the civilian mobilization agencies. Relatively isolated within the federal government and the nation before hostilities, the army was suspicious of, and hostile toward, civilian institutions. It was also unprepared for the enormous wartime responsibilities.

Congress and the Wilson administration had to force the army to integrate its personnel into the War Industries Board (WIB). This integration was essential for coordinating army procurement with the Board's regulatory functions in order to maintain a stable economy.

After the war, Congress authorized the army to plan for procurement and economic mobilization in order to insure its preparation for future hostilities. The navy also joined the planning process. The interwar planning was guided by thousands of industrialists, and by the late 1930s the armed services were not only prepared for wartime operations but also in full agreement with prominent industrial elements on plans for economic mobilization. Those plans, based on World War I mobilization, provided the guidelines for regulating the World War II economy.

Interwar planning was inseparable from defense spending. Many of the businessmen who participated in the planning were associated with firms that were actual or potential military contractors. Despite the relatively small defense budgets of the 1920s and 1930s, the pattern of industrial-military relations during those years foreshadows in many striking ways what developed after World War II.

The American economy was mobilized for World War I by federal agencies devised and staffed primarily by businessmen. In the Army Appropriations Act of August 1916, Congress provided for a Council of National Defense, which consisted of six cabinet members, to serve as the President's advisory body on industrial mobilization. It was assisted by a National Defense Advisory Commission (NDAC), composed largely of businessmen serving for a dollar-a-year or without compensation; most of the members surrendered neither their positions nor incomes as private citizens. When the nation declared war, NDAC assumed responsibility for mobilizing the economy. In July 1917 a more effective mobilization agency, WIB, took over NDAC functions; the former agency, like the latter, was controlled by business elements. Until March 1918, neither NDAC nor WIB had legal authority to enforce its decisions; both were subordinate to the Council of National Defense, and it could only advise the President.

During 1917, businessmen perfected the mobilization agencies and devised the means for curtailing civilian production and converting industry to meet governmental needs. In addition, they developed price, priority, allocation, and other economic controls. By the end of the year, WIB had created the organization and the controls essential for regulating a wartime economy.

Through WIB, industry largely regulated itself during World War I. Key to WIB's operations were major subdivisions called commodity committees, which served under the chairman and his lieutenants. These committees, which made policy for and administered the various industries, were staffed by businessmen who often came from the industries they directed. Assisting the commodity committees were war service committees which were trade associations or councils elected by the national industries. Since the war service committees were neither organized nor financed by the government, they officially only "advised" the commodity committees. But in practice the commodity committees relied heavily upon industry representatives to formulate and execute all policy decisions.

Even without legal authority to enforce its decisions, WIB had industry's cooperation because businessmen dominated it. Industry's cooperation, however, was not enough to maintain a stable wartime economy. WIB required some control over procurement by the war and navy departments and other agencies. Throughout 1917 it attempted to coordinate procurement with its own operations in order to prevent the various departments and agencies from competing among themselves and to insure uniform prices and the distribution of contracts according to availability of facilities, resources, and transportation. Economic stability depended upon such coordination, since wartime demand always exceeded supply. With only advisory powers, WIB relied upon the procurement agencies' voluntary cooperation. While most of these proved to be reasonably cooperative, the war department—the largest, most powerful procurement agency—undermined WIB's regulatory efforts by acting independently and purchasing billions of dollars worth of munitions. As a result, industrial plants in the Northeast were overloaded with contracts; prices skyrocketed; critical shortages of fuel, power, and raw materials developed; and the railway and shipping systems became hopelessly congested.

The war department was both unwilling and unable to cooperate with WIB—unwilling, because it feared that the civilian agency would try to take over army procurement functions; unable, because the department could not control its own supply operations, let alone coordinate them with WIB. As many as eight supply bureaus, such as the Quartermaster Corps and the Ordnance Department, purchased independently for the army. Competing with one another and other purchasing agencies, the bureaus let contracts indiscriminately, commandeered facilities without plan, and hoarded supplies. Cooperation between WIB and the war department was also thwarted by the fact that WIB was organized along commodity lines while the army's supply network was structured by function (such as ordinance and quartermaster). Before army procurement could be coordinated with WIB, the war department had first to accept the need for cooperating with the civilian mobilization agency and then to centralize its supply network along commodity lines. For months, the department would do neither, not only because it was suspicious of WIB but also because it was torn by internal dissension.

In theory, the war department was under the centralized control of the chief of staff, aided by the General Staff. Serving as the secretary of war's principal military adviser, the chief of staff supervised the entire army, including the supply bureaus as well as the combat troops. This system never worked in practice. The bureaus resisted control by the chief of staff. Conflict between the General Staff and the bureaus rent the war department before the war; it paralyzed the department during hostilities.

Unable to regulate the economy without war department cooperation, WIB during 1917 sought the authority to impose its will on the department. But Secretary of War Newton D. Baker, reflecting army suspicion of the Board, squelched the efforts to give it more than advisory powers. He managed to do so because he served as chairman of the Council of National Defense, under which WIB functioned, and as Woodrow Wilson's chief adviser on industrial mobilization.

By the winter of 1917–1918, with WIB stalemated by the war department and the latter virtually collapsing under burgeoning munitions requirements, the economy had become critically dislocated. The business community and Congress demanded that the crisis should be resolved by placing military procurement under a civilian munitions ministry. Adamantly opposed to such a drastic remedy, Wilson headed off the critics in March 1918 by separating WIB from the Council of National Defense and placing it directly under his control. He granted it broad powers for regulating the economy, including a measure of authority over the procurement agencies. To avoid losing control of procurement and to facilitate coordination with WIB, the war department also began reforming its supply system. In December 1917, the department began to consolidate the bureaus into one agency under General Staff control. The new organization was structured to match WIB's commodity committee system.

From March 1918, the strengthened WIB, under the chairmanship of Bernard M. Baruch, effectively used the organization and economic controls developed over the past year to regulate the economy. Procurement was coordinated with WIB activities by integrating war department representatives and those of the other purchasing agencies into WIB. Once the department reorganized its system and adopted a cooperative attitude, members of the army commodity committees joined WIB committees and shared equally in making decisions. Working together, industrial and military personnel learned that WIB could function for their mutual interests. Through WIB's operations, the foundation for the "industrial-military complex" was laid.

The collaboration of industry and the military continued during the 1920s and 1930s and took the form of procurement and economic planning for future wars. This planning was authorized by Congress in the National Defense Act of 1920, which reorganized the war department's system of supply and procurement. To insure that the army did not disrupt economic mobilization in a future emergency, the act placed the supply bureaus under an assistant secretary of war. It was assumed that he would be an industrialist. The assistant secretary would supervise the bureaus and, through planning, prepare them for wartime procurement. Since the assistant secretary was made the chief of staff's equal, the secretary of war had two principal advisers instead of one, as had been the case before 1920.

Congress based the legislation upon the recommendations of Assistant Secretary of War Benedict Crowell, various industrial consultants, several bureau chiefs, and other military personnel. Crowell, a Cleveland business-man who had been involved in military procurement since 1916, believed that World War I demonstrated that industrial production was as important to military success as were tactics and strategy. He felt that supply and procurement must receive the same emphasis in war department affairs as did the traditional military functions. That would not take place, he maintained, under the old system in which the chief of staff, aided by the General Staff, served as the secretary of war's principal adviser. The General Staff would neglect supply and procurement because it knew little about those subjects. Only by placing the bureaus under a qualified civilian who was equal to the chief of staff, he argued, would the army be prepared for future hostilities. Crowell and his associates intended that the assistant secretary of war should plan only for army procurement. Congress went further. The National Defense Act empowered the assistant secretary, though in an ambiguous way, to plan for an entire wartime economy. Why Congress authorized the more comprehensive planning is obscure.

J. Mayhew Wainwright, the first assistant secretary of war under the act, set up an Office of the Assistant Secretary of War (OASW) with personnel drawn from the bureaus. In 1922 an Army-Navy Munitions Board was created in order to include the navy in the planning and to coordinate the supply systems of the two services. And, in 1924 the war department supply planners organized an Army Industrial College to facilitate their work.

At first, OASW concentrated upon wartime military procurement, but it soon became obvious that this planning was futile without also planning for economic mobilization. Though authorized to draft such plans, war department officials, civilian and military alike, hesitated to assume what they considered to be civilian responsibilities. It took the influence of Baruch to convince the war department that economic planning was not exclusively a civilian matter. After World War I, he and other architects of wartime mobilization insisted that the nation's security depended upon constant preparation for war. They favored joint industry-military planning for economic mobilization in order to avoid confusion and delay. Baruch pleaded with the department to draw up full-scale plans for mobilization based on World War I. After years of hesitation, OASW began to plan for economic mobilization as well as procurement. Under Baruch's critical eye, the supply planners between 1929 and 1931 drafted the first official economic blueprint for war—the "Industrial Mobilization Plan" of 1930.

This plan amounted to little more than a proposal for using the methods of World War I to regulate a wartime economy. The key to OASW's blueprint was a War Resources Administration. Comparable to the War

Industries Board, the War Resources Administration would rely upon a commodity committee-war service committee system for economic control. The military services would also organize their procurement networks along commodity lines and integrate their personnel into the War Resources Administration. In a future war, the economy would be mobilized by new federal agencies largely dominated by industrial and military personnel. In 1933, 1936, and 1939, the war department published revised editions of the plan. With each revision, the proposed mobilization apparatus was simplified and patterned more explicitly after the World War I model.

The fact that the war department wrote the 1930 plan is of the greatest significance. After ten years of planning, OASW recognized that modern warfare required a totally planned economy; the armed services would have to adapt themselves to the civilian mobilization agencies during hostilities. The Industrial Mobilization Plan did not mean, however, that the army as a whole had accepted the new conditions of warfare. Before that could take place, the supply planners had to convert the chief of staff and the General Staff to their point of view. Throughout the 1920s and into the 1930s, the army's command structure refused to recognize that supply and procurement set limits for tactics and strategy; and the General Staff's war plans provided for raising and fielding an army at rates that exceeded the economy's capacity. The General Staff insisted that supply had to adjust to strategy. OASW and the supply bureaus adamantly opposed such thinking. Both the economy and the military mission, they argued, would be threatened. The admonition went unheeded for years.

The General Staff turned a deaf ear to OASW because, knowing little about procurement, it could not gauge the effects of industrialized warfare on the army or the economy and, therefore, continued to view civilian and military responsibilities as if they were unrelated. In addition, the General Staff and OASW were rivals for power. The General Staff resented the 1920 reorganization which deprived it of control of the bureaus. It was intent upon keeping the supply side of the department subordinate to itself. If the General Staff granted the importance of supply and procurement in military affairs, it would strengthen the hand of its rival. Relations between the two groups in the war department became so embittered in the 1920s that communication broke down almost completely. In the 1930s, however, the strife began to wane. As relations improved, the General Staff gradually became more receptive to OASW ideas.

A major turning point occurred in 1935–1936, when General Malin Craig became chief of staff and Harry W. Woodring, secretary of war. Woodring, who had served as assistant secretary of war from 1933 to 1936, was convinced of the need for practical war plans. Craig agreed. Under their combined influence, the General Staff's Mobilization Plan of 1933 was scrapped and the Protective Mobilization Plan drawn up and perfected between 1936 and 1939. It was the first war plan based on the nation's industrial potential. A radical change had taken place in the thinking of the army's command structure. It had finally accepted army dependence on the civilian economy in order to fulfill the military mission. Woodring observed: "I believe the reduction of our mobilization program to sensible workable proportions to be one of the highest attainments of the War Department since the World War."

OASW planning naturally led to numerous war department contacts with the business community. Thousands of industrialists, most of whom had participated in wartime mobilization, guided and assisted the department's efforts in various ways. When the Army Industrial College was organized, it had an Advisory Board graced with such prominent business figures as Baruch, Elbert H. Gary, and Walter Gifford. The various procurement districts also set up civilian advisory boards composed of army contractors to review the department's supply operations. In 1925 the department organized a Business Council, which included members from the nation's largest corporations, to help introduce modern business techniques into army operations and to familiarize the industralists with army procurement and planning methods.

Most contacts between the war department and industry involved representatives from trade associations and interested corporation executives. Often these men were or became reserve officers assigned to OASW. By 1931 about 14,000 individuals served in such a capacity. They aided in the drafting of procurement and mobilization plans and sought to further cooperative relations between the military and business.

Mixed motives explain industry's participation in war department planning. Firms contracting with the army obviously welcomed the opportunity of working closely with OASW in order to secure or advance their special interests. Some business elements assisted the army so that they could identify their products or materials with national defense in order to enhance their chances for tariff protection, government assistance, or other special privileges. Also, their firms received free publicity of a "patriotic" nature. But reasons other than immediate economic concerns must be considered in assessing industry's role in army planning. Industrial preparedness became almost an ideological crusade for some business executives after the war. That was the case with Baruch and his coterie; with Howard E. Coffin, a prominent industrialist and leading participant in wartime mobilization; and with businessmen associated with the American Legion. They participated in army planning as a means of preparing the nation for war. The business community in general was not so disposed. Without being committed to industrial preparedness *per se*, many businessmen were willing to assist in the planning at the war department's request because it helped the department to adjust its structure and thinking to modern warfare.

The general trend of the interwar political economy is also significant for measuring the response of business to army planning. World War I greatly strengthened the cooperative ethic within the business community and between it and the government. Before World War II, both business and the government experimented with official and unofficial attempts at economic control through industrial cooperation. The National Recovery Administration was only the most formal example. The army's economic planning accurately reflected this cooperative trend. For that reason, among others, the planning received the endorsement of interested businessmen.

OASW did not confine itself simply to planning for industrial mobilization. It also sought legislative authority for implementing the "Industrial Mobilization Plan" in an emergency.

During the 1920s the department's drive for industrial preparedness was carried on in conjunction with the American Legion. The Legion rank and file seethed with resentment about alleged wartime profiteering and the unequal burden shouldered by the fighting forces. In order to remove the promise of riches as an inducement to war and to distribute the burdens of warfare more equitably, the returning veterans demanded a total draft of manpower and capital in any future emergency. Ironically, the Legion's peace movement, which originated in dissent over the economics of World War I, was ultimately converted into support for the "Industrial Mobilization Plan" based on the wartime model. Legion leadership and its special relationship with the war department explains why. Substantial business elements and former military officers dominated Legion affairs; throughout the 1920s the secretaries and assistant secretaries of war were usually active Legionnaires. When acting on the proposal for a total draft that was favored by the rank and file, the Legion leaders turned to the war department for assistance. In 1922, OASW drafted for the Legion a bill that in general terms would have granted the President almost unlimited authority over the nation's human and economic resources in the event of war. The Legion consistently referred to the bill as a "universal draft," as a measure for promoting peace, and as a proposal for "equalizing wartime burdens." That was scarcely the case. The bill was so vague that it could be used for many different purposes. Its grant of authority was so great and its power so general that it could sanction a presidential dictatorship. Once the economic planning of OASW was fully underway, the war department and the Legion leadership clearly intended the bill to be a general grant of authority for implementing the "Industrial Mobilization Plan."

Beginning in 1922, the Legion-sponsored bill was repeatedly introduced in Congress. Despite Legion lobbying and war department support, each Congress sidetracked the proposed legislation. Unable to get its bill through Congress, the Legion asked for a bipartisan commission to study and recommend policies for industrial mobilization. An active campaign by congressmen who were also Legionnaires soon led to action. By a joint resolution in June 1930, Congress created the War Policies Commission (WPC), which consisted of eight congressmen and six cabinet members. Six of the fourteen commissioners were Legionnaires. The Commission was to study and make recommendations for equalizing war burdens and preventing war profiteering, and it was to formulate "policies to be pursued in event of war."

WPC, like the Legion's drive for a "universal draft," quickly became a means for furthering military preparation. Because the war department dominated the proceedings, WPC emphasized how to mobilize the economy for war and not how to equalize war burdens and eliminate war profits. Secretary of War Patrick J. Hurley, an active Legionnaire, served as WPC's chairman. WPC's staff came almost exclusively from the war department. The department's presentation of its 1930 "Industrial Mobilization Plan" and Baruch's testimony on the economics of World War I were the highlights of WPC's public hearings. After extended deliberations, WPC, with only one dissenting vote, directly endorsed the department's planning and indirectly endorsed the "Industrial Mobilization Plan." WPC efforts were more impressive as an attempt to popularize and legitimize department planning than as a serious study of wartime economics.

Despite a friendly Commission, the department was unable to drum up much overt support for its plans. In addition to the department itself, the principal advocates of the planning before WPC were the American Legion and some wartime mobilization leaders like Baruch, Gifford, and Coffin. The business community in general was either unconcerned about or unwilling to commit itself publicly on issues involving economic mobilization. Of the thousands of businessmen participating in the army planning, only a few came forward to testify.

Although support for department planning was weak, the opposition was vociferous. Witnesses like Norman Thomas, several congressmen, and spokesmen for some peace societies and humanitarian groups were hostile to WPC and the department's plans. Some advocates of peace detected inherent dangers in the department's work. According to their analyses, the promise of wartime riches, while not a major cause of war, was a contributing one that had to be eliminated. The army's plans would not do this. Moreover, the opponents feared that the industrial-military ties resulting from department planning could endanger the nation's future. But the critics—among them a member of WPC, Representative Ross A. Collins of Mississippi—were weak on analysis. Their critique of the department's plans and planning was often nebulous, contradictory, or incomplete. Seymour Waldman, a journalist covering the hearings, articulated more clearly and precisely what appeared to alarm Collins and some witnesses before WPC:

> The hearings revealed a gigantic machine, whose intricate parts touch the entire nation, which is being constructed by the War Department and industrial magnates for use in the event of war. . . . They reveal the dangers inherent in a

militarization of industry, an industrialization of the military forces, or a combination of the two. . . .

I would feel rewarded and gratified if this book should be the precursor of a much needed diagnosis of the whole problem, a study of the interlocking of our war mechanism and our economic system. . . . Such a work . . . is imperative if we are to be effective in preventing more national and international bloodshed.

Opposition to the department's plans and proposed legislation for implementing them increased after WPC's hearings as the peace and isolationist movement gained in strength. The most formidable challenge came from the Senate's so-called Nye Committee. In addition to the munitions makers, the Nye Committee's purview included economic mobilization for World War I, interwar military procurement policies, and the "Industrial Mobilization Plan." In a fragmentary manner, the Committee disclosed the dynamics of an emerging "industrial-military complex." The elements were presented in the Committee hearings and reports, but they were not fitted together. Senator Gerald P. Nye and his colleagues still saw only through a glass darkly.

The Nye Committee clearly perceived that industrialized warfare created qualitatively new and ominous problems for the nation. To fight a modern war, even to prepare for one, eroded the barriers between private and public, civilian and military institutions. The Committee observed that during hostilities "[p]ractically every important industry in the country is necessary for the supply of the armed forces." "[E]ven in time of peace," the Committee reported, "the line of demarkation between the munitions industry and other industries is not clear and fixed."

From its investigation of interwar defense spending, the Committee established that various industries depended upon military contracts for profitable operations and that the military services depended upon them for developing and producing weapons. There were many prime examples. Shipbuilding indirectly included "the steel companies, the electrical manufacturing groups, the boiler producers, the instrument people," and "the biggest banking interests in the Nation." Du Pont and other munitions producers were virtual adjuncts of the war department. Industrialists and military leaders regarded their interests as mutual. Industry favored and worked for increased military appropriations; the armed services granted industry special favors, encouraged monopoly where it served their interests, financed research, and, despite legislation to the contrary, displayed little concern about profit restraints. Committee members were shocked to find that the war and navy departments, and even the commerce and state departments at times, cooperated with munitions firms in a manner that compromised national policies for disarmament, arms limitation, arms sales, and arms embargoes. The fact that Public Works Administration funds, intended to stimulate industrial recovery, went to the armed services and that some businessmen favored defense spending as an antidote to the depression also disturbed Nye and his colleagues.

The Nye Committee found a web of personal as well as contractual ties binding industrial-military elements. Retired army and navy officers often joined firms contracting with the services. Frequently, officials of corporations supplying the armed services became reserve officers. A society like the Army Ordnance Association, organized in 1919, combined in its membership actual or potential military contractors and retired and active army officers. The Association lobbied for the army, participated in the industrial mobilization planning, and attempted to influence war department policies and the selection and promotion of personnel.

The Nye Committee carefully avoided charges of conspiracy. It pointed out that plausible reasons existed for what was done and stated that it was not drawing a one-to-one correlation between expenditures for defense and the causation of war. Nevertheless, argued the Committee,

> any close associations between munitions and supply companies . . . and the service departments . . . , of the kind that existed in Germany before the World War, constitutes an unhealthy alliance in that it brings into being a self-interested political power which operates in the name of patriotism and satisfies interests which are, in large part, purely selfish, and that such associations are an inevitable part of militarism, and are to be avoided in peacetime at all costs.

In order to check the growth of an "unhealthy alliance," a majority of the Committee favored nationalizing the munitions facilities. Congress never seriously considered the proposal. Upon the advice of the Roosevelt administration, Congress even refused to strengthen regulations governing military procurement as the Committee minority recommended.

The army's economic planning for war also disturbed the Nye Committee. The planning, argued the Committee, assured that industry and the military would function more effectively as a team than they had in World War I; but, because the "Industrial Mobilization Plan" was patterned after wartime methods, it would not eliminate the "economic evils of war." According to the Committee's analysis, World War I mobilization was accompanied by "shameless profiteering" and extravagant waste. The war left a legacy of inflation, debt, and increased concentration of economic power. Similar results would occur in a future war if industry, in conjunction with the armed services, virtually regulated itself.

In order to secure the nation's economic future and to remove the promise of riches as an inducement to war, the Nye Committee maintained that wartime "economic evils" had to be eliminated. That required radical changes in the economic system during hostilities, not the preservation of the status quo as proposed by the "Industrial Mobilization Plan." The profit motive and the prerogatives of private property would have to be modified. To accomplish that purpose, the Committee supported legislation drafted under the direction of John T. Flynn. In an emergency, profits would be limited to 3 percent and personal annual income to $10,000. No individual with direct or indirect interests in an industry could serve in a government capacity involving that industry. Moreover, the President would be granted vast authority over the economy to the point of conscripting capital and management if necessary. Although vague at many points, the Flynn legislation amounted to a proposal for state capitalism during wartime with the industrial managers removed from the seats of power.

The war department opposed the Committee's major recommendations. It viewed with alarm any taxation proposals that threatened production. It maintained that conscripting management would not work and insisted that economic mobilization was impossible without the assistance of managers of the industries to be regulated. Baruch responded to the proposed bill with undisguised hostility. Attempting to change the economic system during a war, he argued, was an invitation to disaster.

In its most impressive reports, the Nye Committee curiously agreed with both the war department and Baruch. The Committee's support of the Flynn proposals ignored its own findings. Without constitutional amendments that could be "far worse than the situation of profiteering in a national emergency," the Flynn legislation could not be enforced. The Committee recognized that, even if the bill and the necessary amendments were adopted, they would probably be repealed or ignored in an emergency. The only men qualified to administer a wartime economy were industrialists themselves. It was inconceivable that they would attempt to enforce laws they considered detrimental to the economy and to the war effort.

The Flynn bill was introduced into Congress in 1935. For a time, Franklin D. Roosevelt seemed disposed toward the bill. Ultimately, he joined Baruch, the war department, and, with reservations, the Legion in backing competing legislation that would have granted the President authority for mobilizing the economy, but with few safeguards against abuse. That bill would have sanctioned what the "Industrial Mobilization Plan" proposed. The administration let it be known that it, too, believed that curtailing the profit motive during a war would jeopardize any mobilization program. No legislation was passed.

After the Nye Committee investigation, the nation knew more about the political economy of warfare; but short of avoiding war and excessive spending for defense, there was no viable way to prevent close and compromising relations between business and the armed services. Military spending in the American industrial system inevitably drew industrial and military elements together, and the threat of an "unhealthy alliance" was always present.

War department planning entered its final and most important phase after the Nye Committee investigation. With the approach of war and the growing American preparedness movement, the department launched a drive for the appointment of a joint industry-military board to review and ultimately to implement the "Industrial Mobilization Plan."

The proposal for a joint board originated with civilians who were concerned about a major flaw in the "Industrial Mobilization Plan." Because of a continuing distrust of civilian institutions, the army determined to dominate the wartime mobilization agencies. To insure that OASW plans were realistic and to keep the nation ready for war, Baruch and others repeatedly recommended that industrialists officially meet each year with the war department. They would review the department's plans and prepare themselves for the eventuality of official duty.

The war department resisted suggestions for officially sharing its planning authority with industrialists until Louis Johnson, a past American Legion commander, became assistant secretary of war in June 1937. With international relations deteriorating, Johnson was determined to prepare both the army and the nation for war. He arranged for Baruch, some former WIB members, and younger talent to serve as an advisory board to OASW. For Johnson, that was the first essential step for instituting the "Industrial Mobilization Plan." But the President refused to sanction the scheme. Despite the setback, Johnson was determined to create an advisory board. He was stealthily maneuvering to achieve that end in mid-1939, when Roosevelt, fearing that war was imminent and that the nation might become involved, authorized Johnson to set up a mobilization advisory group called the War Resources Board (WRB). Roosevelt chose Edward R. Stettinius, Jr., of the United States Steel Corporation as chairman and left the selection of other members to the war department. With Stettinius serving as an intermediary, Johnson, Acting Secretary of the Navy Charles Edison, Army Chief of Staff George Marshall, and two senior members of OASW selected the others. In addition to Stettinius, WRB included Gifford, president of American Telephone and Telegraph; John Lee Pratt of General Motors Corporation; Robert E. Wood, chairman of Sears, Roebuck, and Company; Karl T. Compton of the Massachusetts Institute of Technology; and Harold G. Moulton, president of the Brookings Institute. The membership was cleared with the President. Why Baruch was excluded is still unclear. He was described as being "sore as hell" about being passed over. WRB did not get his blessing until his close associate, John Hancock, was appointed to it in September. Hancock played a prominent role in WRB proceedings.

Assistant Secretary of War Johnson announced to the nation that WRB would review the "Industrial Mobilization Plan" of 1939, revise it if necessary, and implement it in an emergency. Key to the plan was the War Resources Administration, organized along commodity committee-war service committee lines with military representatives integrated into it. Unlike earlier plans, the 1939 edition moderated proposed military influence in the civilian agencies.

Working hand in hand with the armed services, WRB, while still reviewing the "Industrial Mobilization Plan," began preparing to institute it. In sharp contrast to its attitude toward WPC, the business community was eager to cooperate with WRB. The National Association of Manufacturers and the United States Chamber of Commerce rushed forward to volunteer their services. Through conferences with these organizations, former WIB members, the commerce department, and other private and public sources, WRB drew up an industrial who's who to staff the War Resources Administration and also made provisions for the use of war service committees. The most daring move was a memorandum drafted for the President's signature that would have granted the WRB and the Army-Navy Munitions Board authority to mobilize the economy and that instructed all government agencies to cooperate with those two boards.

Roosevelt suddenly cut the ground from under WRB shortly after its creation because the war scare had waned and because of widespread opposition within the administration and the nation to it. Liberal Democrats were aghast at the dominant position held by the major banking and industrial interests in WRB. They identified Stettinius, Gifford, and Pratt with J. P. Morgan. The anti-Morgan banking elements on Wall Street who were sympathetic to the administration were bitterly disappointed. Labor and agriculture were irate over their exclusion.

The President waited until WRB had completed reviewing the "Industrial Mobilization Plan" and had submitted a final report in November 1939 before dismissing it. In its final report, WRB indirectly endorsed the war department plan and fully accepted its basic assumptions. A wartime economy should be regulated by federal agencies largely controlled by industry and the military services. In circumscribed terms, WRB recommended the suspension of the antitrust laws and also suggested that domestic reform would be a casualty of a mobilized economy. It further proposed that the Army-Navy Munitions Board, through consultation with industry, continue to explore the yet unresolved issues of industrial mobilization. It concluded by offering its advisory services for the future. Roosevelt thanked WRB members and never called on them again.

WRB's fate did not negate the years of planning. Because of this planning, the war department adjusted to emergency conditions during World War II with relative ease. In the late 1930s the department began a gradual transition from planning for, to participating in, a mobilization program. Starting in 1937–1938, Congress, after years of departmental advocacy, authorized educational orders and the stockpiling of essential and strategic raw materials and slowly modified peacetime restraints on military contracting. As the army and military budgets grew, OASW expanded its staff and activities proportionately until the mobilization stage was reached in 1940–1941. Writing in mid-1940, Assistant Secretary of War Johnson observed: "Without the benefit of plans perfected by 20 years of study the successful and timely execution of this [expanded munitions] program would have been virtually impossible."

When the war department began the transition to mobilization in 1937–1938, it also launched the drive for implementing the "Industrial Mobilization Plan"; it had been convinced by the years of planning that civilian mobilization agencies were essential for fulfilling the military mission. During 1940–1941, the Army-Navy Munitions Board played a more active role in mobilizing the economy than the army plans had envisaged. But that was the case principally because the civilian agencies were weak. After WRB's demise, the Roosevelt administration relied upon the resuscitated NDAC and other agencies that were totally inadequate for mobilization. War department officials were in the vanguard of those working for more effective civilian agencies until the creation in early 1942 of the War Production Board.

Throughout the years 1940–1941, the war department, and the navy department as well, sided with industry on most major policies involving economic mobilization. After war was declared, the nation's largest corporations and the armed forces ultimately dominated the War Production Board through an alliance of mutual interests. Though officially rejected in 1939, the principal proposals concurred in by WRB and the military were adopted during World War II. As foreseen by the Nye Committee and others, relations between the business community and the armed services during World War I and the interwar period prepared the way for the full-blown "industrial-military complex" of World War II and the Cold War years.

IX

World War II: European Theater, 1939–1945

Imperfect Victory at Falaise
Flint Whitlock

One of the most contentious arguments regarding the Allied drive across France and into Germany after the breakout from the Normandy beaches in 1944 remains their failure to close the Falaise Gap and destroy German Army Group B, perhaps thereby ending the war sooner. In this essay Flint Whitlock, historian and author of Soldiers on Skis *and* Rock of Anzio, *explains in detail why the Gap was not closed more expeditiously, concentrating not only on the battles fought but also on the command decisions that led to only a partial victory for the Allies rather than a crushing and perhaps fatal defeat of the Germans. He concludes that the major blame must fall on Field Marshal Bernard Law Montgomery, the commander of 21st Army Group, rather than on other field commanders, especially Lieutenant General Omar Bradley. From* World War II, *May 1997 by Flint Whitlock. Copyright © 1997 by* World War II. *Reprinted by permission of PRIMEDIA Enthusiasts Publications (History Group).*

In the long and bloody history of warfare, for sheer horror there was perhaps nothing to equal the Allied attempted encirclement of the Germans at Falaise. For the Germans, jammed into a narrow killing zone barely five miles wide, it was like a nightmare in which one tries to run away from a terrible fate, only to find one's legs leaden, unable to move. But this was no dream.

Into this panicked river of humanity that once was Germany's formidable Army Group B fell every conceivable munition in the Allied arsenal: artillery shells, mortar bombs, machine-gun and rifle bullets, and rifle-propelled grenades. In the air above the corridor, Allied fighters turned and wheeled and dove into the masses, unleashing their rockets and bombs and napalm, strafing the helpless enemy with their machine guns and cannons.

Bombs and shells exploded with terrible fury in the midst of tightly packed men. Men roasted to death in tanks and trucks, bullets slammed into men and horses, and the agonized screams of men and animals intermingled. And still the killing went on, unrelenting, unpitying, unstoppable.

Had it been a boxing match, the referee would have stepped in and stopped it, so thoroughly were the Germans beaten. But it was no boxing match, and the carnage went on, the Allies paying the Germans back in spades for all the death and suffering Adolf Hitler's forces had inflicted upon the world for nearly five years.

The killing ground—a once peaceful area of farms and placid French villages—was called the Falaise Gap, or, to those who were there, the Corridor of Death. The one-sided battle, as horrible as it was, would have been far worse had it not been for the feuding among the Allies, who, with victory nearly in their grasp, committed one blunder after another in August 1944.

The German army in France was still reeling from the effects of Operation Overlord, the mightiest combined air, sea and land battle ever fought. While they grudgingly gave up ground yard by yard, they could not, as Hitler had demanded, throw the Allies back into the sea. Indeed, the German soldiers could not even keep the Allies from slowly and inexorably pushing them back to the borders of Germany. By clinging to his belief that Normandy was merely a diversionary operation, and by failing to respond quickly and correctly to the threat, Hitler had sealed the fate of the Third Reich, now being pummeled from east and west, as well as from the south in Italy. Furthermore, by directing his battered troops in France to thrust westward in an ill-considered counterattack at Mortain, Hitler had doomed Army Group B to near annihilation.

During the early months of Allied planning for the invasion of France, no one knew where the decisive battle might be fought. Would it be on the beaches, in the fields and villages, in the major cities, or along the rivers? One thing was certain: In the days immediately following a successful invasion, securing airfields for the support of further operations would be imperative. With the British and Canadian invasion beaches located farther east and closer to Paris, it was logical that the British and Canadians would have the task of securing existing airfields and ground suitable for conversion into airfields. The Americans, landing farther west, most likely would be tied up contending with German forces on the Cotentin Peninsula and in Brittany before they could swing eastward and join the British and Canadian forces in a push toward the Seine River.

Britain's Field Marshal Bernard Law Montgomery, commander of 21st Army Group and overall Allied ground commander, was always more comfortable with a well-planned, set-piece battle in which all the participants—

even, and especially, the enemy—did exactly what he had scripted them to do. The Americans, on the other hand, seemed to adapt more easily to the unexpected, using Yankee ingenuity to react to rapidly changing situations. The post-Normandy plan, then, seemed ideal for both sides. Monty would engage his forces in a set-piece assault on Caen and the nearby Carpiquet airfield, while the Americans would roam freely, mopping up German forces in northwestern France.

The first problem came when the British and Canadians, after brilliant *coup de main* airborne/glider operations on the eastern flank of the beachhead, failed to take Caen, only 12 miles inland, by sundown on June 6 as they had expected to do. In fact, Monty's men—the Second British Army under Lt. Gen. Sir Miles Dempsey—did not set foot in Caen's rubble-strewn streets until July 9, more than a month after D-Day.

Meanwhile, the American First Army, under Lt. Gen. Omar Bradley, had swung west and north, up the Cotentin, and had taken Cherbourg by the end of June. The Yanks, spearheaded by superior air power and the VII Corps' aggressive commander, Lt. Gen. Joseph L. "Lightning Joe" Collins, then reversed course, driving southward into Brittany and mopping up German forces under the aegis of Operation Cobra.

Hitler, still shaken by the July 20 attempt on his life at Rastenburg, felt he could no longer trust his generals and took an even more direct hand in commanding his forces. He saw the American drive near Mortain as a dangerous threat to Germany's entire war effort in the west. Field Marshal Hans von Kluge, who had succeeded Gerd von Rundstedt as commander in chief in the west, was ordered to counterattack Collins' VII Corps at midnight on August 6 and threw the weight of his troops at the U.S. 30th Division, which had recently occupied Mortain. Kluge's order of the day said, "The decision in the battle of France depends on the success of the attack." Bolstered by 70 panzers, the 2nd SS Panzer Division and 2nd Panzer Grenadier Division attacked the 30th Division, dug in on the key terrain feature, Hill 317, which separated the U.S. First and Third armies. The Americans suffered heavy casualties but held off the Germans in a desperate battle.

The valiant American defense broke the back of the German counterattack. Moreover, the Germans' westward push had created a dangerous salient that, to Supreme Allied Commander General Dwight D. Eisenhower and Bradley, appeared to be an invitation to encirclement and annihilation of those German forces. Lieutenant General George Patton, commanding the recently activated Third Army, was sent dashing off toward the east, along the southern flank of the salient. It was during this drive, while surveying the smoldering remains of a tank battle, that Patton remarked to his aide-de-camp, Colonel Charles Codman: "Just look at that, Codman. Could anything be more magnificent? Compared to war, all other forms of human endeavor shrink to insignificance. God, how I love it!"

Phoning Montgomery on August 8, Bradley told the British commander about the opportunity being presented to the Allies. If the bulk of the

American Twelfth Army Group were to push eastward along the German salient's southern boundary while other U.S. divisions kept the Germans busy along its perimeter, and then turn northward at Argentan to meet the Canadians heading south through Falaise, the Allies had a chance for a massive encirclement that would surely, as Bradley said, "destroy an entire hostile army." Montgomery agreed to the idea.

The ambitious plan, however, depended on the Canadians being able to break through German lines north of Falaise. Under Lt. Gen. Sir Henry Crerar (in whom Montgomery had no confidence), the Canadians had already launched their attack—Operation Totalize—toward Falaise the previous night, August 7.

Lieutenant General Guy Simonds' II Canadian Corps, consisting of three infantry divisions, two armored divisions and two armored brigades with hundreds of tanks, moved off under cover of darkness. Confused by the smoke and dust of a heavy Allied artillery and aerial bombardment, the Canadians lost their way and only managed to advance three miles. Initially caught off guard, the Germans reacted savagely, knocking out many tanks.

Yet, the Canadians enjoyed some success and seemed on the verge of breaking through the German lines. Tragically, however, RAF bombers miscalculated their release points the next day and dropped bombs on both the 4th Canadian Division and the 1st Polish Armored Division (attached to the Canadian II Corps), killing 65 and wounding 250. Although the enemy force was numerically weaker—two understrength divisions with only 60 tanks—the Canadian-Polish attack faltered. The next day, coming up against Colonel Kurt Meyer's fanatical 12th SS Panzer Division, the Canadian drive lost its momentum and petered out.

Farther west, the battle around Mortain finally waned on August 9, the day before Maj. Gen. Wade Haislip's U.S. XV Corps launched its attack northward from Le Mans through Alençon and Argentan to Falaise. On August 11, Alençon fell to the Americans. Haislip then received two armored divisions from Patton's Third Army—Lunsford Oliver's 5th U.S. Armored and Jacques LeClerc's 2nd French Armored—and he placed them side by side on the front lines.

A fervently patriotic and able armored commander, LeClerc (whose forces would be given the honor of being the first Allied troops to liberate Paris) had his own ideas as to how his tanks should be used and how the battle should be fought. Flagrantly disobeying Haislip's order, LeClerc trespassed onto the Alençon–Argentan road, which had been reserved for the 5th Armored, and managed to botch what started out to be an easy operation. The ensuing six-hour traffic jam on August 12 disrupted the American attack and allowed the Germans to reinforce their lines. The delay enabled Kluge to rush three armored divisions from Mortain—the 1st SS, 2nd and 116th Panzer divisions—into position.

The Germans sensed what was about to befall them. A *Kesselschlacht*—a battle of encirclement—was becoming a very real possibility. As the sides of the bag closed around them, they realized that their only means of escape was eastward, through the open neck between Falaise and Argentan, a narrow gap of only about 10 miles. Josef "Sepp" Dietrich, commander of the Fifth Panzer Army, declared that it was imperative for the German forces to begin at once to extricate themselves from the closing jaws of the trap. "If every effort is not made to move the forces toward the east and out of the threatened encirclement," he wrote to his superiors, "the army group will have to write off both [the Fifth Panzer and Seventh] armies."

Meanwhile, General Simonds was putting the finishing touches on Operation Tractable, the successor to Operation Totalize, which he hoped would prevent the Germans from holding the roads through Falaise. However, a senior Canadian officer of the 8th Reconnaissance Regiment, who was carrying the plans for Tractable, strayed into Kurt Meyer's lines and was captured. Armed with information about the Canadians' intentions, the Germans covered the routes of attack with 88mm fire to foil the Canadian advance.

The Allies, on the other hand, did not need to rely on capturing enemy officers to discern German plans. The top-secret Ultra device enabled Allied cryptographers to decipher and read encoded German communiqués, so Eisenhower, Montgomery and Bradley knew what the Germans were going to do almost before the Germans did. Knowledge, however, was one thing—actually being able to react and respond was quite another.

On the 12th, Haislip, worried that his own drive was now creating a salient that could be attacked by the Germans as they retreated eastward from Mortain, asked Patton if he should continue northward once Argentan was taken. Patton told Haislip to press on with his drive and link up with the Canadians to close the neck of the bag. At this moment, the space between the Yanks and Canadians was only about 18 miles wide. However, that night when Patton informed his boss what he had authorized Haislip to do, Bradley pulled the reins up short. "Don't go beyond Argentan," Bradley ordered. "Stop where you are and build up on that shoulder." Bradley had already received Ultra intercepts indicating that the Germans were planning to hit Haislip's flank.

Although disappointed and chafing at the order, Patton, who was in the doghouse for past indiscretions and breaches of orders, dutifully obeyed and told Haislip to stop where he was. Even Montgomery's staff was shocked and surprised at Bradley's directive, and they urged Monty to overrule the American and let Haislip cross the British-American boundary drawn on the maps. Incredibly, Monty declined.

No records exist to indicate what happened, but during the night Bradley changed his mind, or Patton changed it for him, for, shortly after midnight on the 13th, Patton directed Haislip to resume his advance toward Falaise, crossing the imaginary boundary line between the two Allied armies. That morning, Haislip tried to comply, but his men were halted by stiff German resistance in and to the east of Argentan. Then Bradley issued another order not to go any farther. Patton was furious but incapable of countermanding the order.

In his diary, General Patton wrote: "Haislip's XV Corps could easily advance to Falaise and completely close the gap, but we have been ordered to halt because the British sowed the area with a number of time bombs [supposedly to hinder German movement]. I am sure this halt is a great mistake, as I am certain that the British [meaning the Canadians] will not close on Falaise." Three days later, he added: "I believe that the order [to halt] emanated from [Montgomery's] 21st Army Group, and was either due to jealousy of the Americans or to utter ignorance of the situation or a combination of the two. It is very regrettable that the XV Corps was ordered to halt, because it could have gone on to Falaise and made contact with the Canadians northwest of that point and definitely and positively closed the escape gap."

In the half-century since the war ended, much controversy has swirled around the decision not to close the gap until tens of thousands of German troops had been allowed to escape. Some have blamed Montgomery, some have blamed Bradley, who was worried about an attack on Haislip's flank, while others have blamed Eisenhower—who could easily have ordered the two Allied armies to complete their pincers movement—for his "hands-off" leadership policy.

Simmering resentments held by some high-ranking British officers—especially Montgomery and General Sir Alan Brooke, chief of the Imperial General Staff—began to boil over into undisguised hostility. They still harbored petty envy of the Americans. To the British it seemed that there were too many young, brash Yanks who had everything and who had been given the starring role to play in Overlord while still newcomers to the war. Their battle-worthiness was, to Montgomery's mind, still in question. Worst of all, according to Monty, was the ascendency of Eisenhower, who had never commanded troops in combat, to supreme commander.

Montgomery was also furious with Eisenhower for another reason. Confidence in Montgomery's leadership capabilities was crumbling at Supreme Headquarters Allied Expeditionary Forces. The supreme commander, concerned with Monty's slow, methodical buildup and—from Eisenhower's point of view—leisurely, overcautious approach to the battle, had met with Churchill in late July to get the prime minister to pressure the British commander "to get on his bicycle and start moving."

In addition, General George C. Marshall, the U.S. Army chief of staff, had met with Montgomery on July 24 and was so alarmed by the British commander's sense of self-importance and his army's snail-like pace while Americans were dying by the thousands in western France that he was ready to request that Churchill dismiss him. As ever, when the Americans were demanding his head, Monty managed to persuade the prime minister to ignore them. However, Churchill posted a War Cabinet liaison officer at Montgomery's headquarters to send back unvarnished status reports.

Although stung by the reproach, Montgomery put his anti-American feelings into temporary abeyance to give at least the appearance of movement. On August 13, Montgomery, Bradley and Dempsey met to decide on a course of action for trapping the Germans. The Canadians would renew their efforts to take Falaise, then drive on toward Trun and Argentan. Dempsey's British Second Army would head east for Falaise, while Courtney Hodges' U.S. First Army would provide flank security as Haislip's XV Corps pushed toward Argentan from the south. Already, a recon unit from LeClerc's 2nd Armored Division was nearing the outskirts of Falaise. Patton was to send Walton Walker's XX Corps to Dreux, and Gilbert Cook's XII Corps to Chartres, to provide for a deeper envelopment. The attacking forces would be supported by Allied air power, which enjoyed the advantage of clear skies and virtually no *Luftwaffe* interference.

At noon on the 14th, the Canadians and Poles, supported by 800 bombers, crossed their line of departure, only to be hit once again by bombs from friendly aircraft; more than 500 casualties were reported among the Canadian and Polish units, and the operation quickly halted amid the confusion. Luckily, things got sorted out and the attack resumed; by the end of the day, the Canadians and Poles had advanced four miles and were within four miles of Falaise.

By this time, however, a great many Germans had already made their escape. The troops were rapidly heading eastward by any means possible— by truck, tank, civilian vehicle, horse, bicycle and shoe leather—and the Allied commanders were beginning to worry that the enemy was going to elude the trap. In a message to Bradley on the 14th, Montgomery wrote: "It is difficult to say what enemy are inside the ring and what have got out to the east. A good deal may have escaped. . . . We want to head off the Germans, and stop them breaking out." Monty recommended that the Allies prepare to head off the Germans farther east of Falaise and Argentan, as he worried the "short hook" that had already begun would be akin to closing the barn door behind the fleeing horse.

Complying with this directive, Bradley ordered Patton to send half of Haislip's XV Corps to Dreux, while the XX Corps was redirected toward Chartres and the XII Corps was ordered to move farther on to Orleans. While setting the stage for a deeper envelopment, these moves weakened American strength near Argentan and called into question Haislip's ability to firmly slam shut the jaws of the trap.

Meanwhile, the strain between the British and Americans, who were chafing under British control, was becoming palpable. Eisenhower had moved his headquarters onto the Continent and was preparing to take over command of ground operations from Montgomery, a preplanned arrangement. Montgomery, however, was dreading the day. In a report to Brooke (who shared his contempt for the Americans), Monty wrote: "Ike is actually here in Normandy, which is too bad. His ignorance of everything about war is total. He is so amiable that it is difficult to be irritated with him. But I am firm on one point: never will I permit him to be at a conference between me, my army commanders, and Bradley." Leonard Gerow had just replaced Hugh Gaffey as head of V Corps—further delayed the start of the operation.

Finally, on the 17th, Monty ordered the gap closed, and that afternoon Bradley lifted the order halting Patton's forces at Dreux, Orleans and Chartres; Patton then directed the troops to continue rolling eastward to cut off Germans who had slipped through the trap. Meanwhile, Hodges' First Army was to drive northward toward Chambois and Trun and meet up with the Canadians, who were already running into more tough opposition outside Trun.

Patton, it seems, had a good, clear plan for wiping out the Germans in France: he proposed sending the XX, XII and XV corps all the way to the Seine, then turning northward to provide a solid roadblock against which even more fleeing Germans would have to crash. But Bradley and Montgomery rejected the idea; to them, the Germans in France were as good as finished. Their focus was now on how and where to enter the Ruhr, Germany's industrial heartland. With Montgomery's and Bradley's rejection of the Patton plan, many believe the opportunity to end the war in 1944 slipped away from the Allies.

On the 17th, Field Marshal Walter Model arrived to take command of Army Group B from Kluge, whom Hitler had blamed for the debacle in the west, and who had been under suspicion since the July 20 attempt on the *Führer*'s life. That night, more German units in the western end of the pocket slipped farther east.

Also on the 17th, the U.S. Ninth Air Force, along with the British and Canadian Second Tactical Air Force, which had been effectively bombing and strafing the enemy, received an astonishing order. They were prohibited from bombing enemy targets within the pocket. This order ostensibly sprang from the short-bombing incidents that had caused friendly casualties earlier. Other reports suggest it was to avoid hitting German vehicles with Red Crosses displayed on them; it was feared that if their ambulances were attacked, the Germans might retaliate against Allied prisoners and wounded.

The no-attack order enabled the Germans, in a bold move, to load 45 cargo planes with thousands of gallons of fuel and deliver them to the ground troops to help continue their withdrawal.

The next day, Gerow's V Corps launched its attack, only to be met fiercely by the Germans around Argentan and Chambois, stalling the move. Northward, however, the Canadians finally broke through—the Canadian 4th Armored Division took Trun, and the Polish 1st Armored Division advanced nearly to Chambois. The desperate Germans knew their only escape route was at stake and fought like tigers. Under cover of darkness, the Germans pushed more men from the west toward the shrinking gap.

The Allies blasted the remnants of some 15 German divisions compressed into the six-mile width of the "neck of the bag" with a tremendous volume of artillery and—after a daylong pause—air attacks. Once the no bomb/no strafe order was lifted, Allied fighter pilots reported that the massed German units in the pocket presented perfect and stationary targets for their bombs, rockets, cannons and machine guns. On August 18, 1,471 sorties were flown against the retreating Germans.

The artillery spotter planes brought more death and destruction, giving uncannily accurate coordinates to Allied guns that spared neither man nor beast. Low on fuel and motorized transport, the Germans had relied on horses to pull supply wagons and artillery pieces. Now those same horses, crazed with fear, trampled through ranks of men, or got tangled in their harnesses, or plunged screaming into streams and ravines while the bombs and shells burst around them, killing them along with the soldiers.

Trying to dispel the growing pessimism of his men as Allied bombs and shells crashed into their ranks, Lt. Gen. Richard Schimpf, commander of the German 3rd Parachute Division, told his troops there was "no reason for a paratrooper, who is specially trained to jump into the midst of the enemy, to feel depressed. He who thinks or talks otherwise will be slapped across the mouth."

Kluge, on the other hand, was in deep depression. In a letter to Hitler following his removal from command, Kluge wrote: "When you receive these lines, I shall be no more. I cannot bear the accusation that I sealed the fate of the West by taking wrong measures. . . . I have steadfastly stood in awe of your greatness, your bearing in this gigantic struggle, and your iron will. . . . If Fate is stronger than your will and your genius, that is Destiny. You have made an honorable and tremendous fight. History will testify this for you. Show now that greatness that will be necessary if it comes to the point of ending a struggle which has become hopeless. I depart from you, my *Führer*, having stood closer to you in spirit than you perhaps dreamed, in the consciousness of having done my duty to the utmost." Near Metz, on his way back to Germany, Kluge committed suicide by swallowing cyanide.

On the morning of the 19th, the neck of the bag was finally closed from Le Bourg-St. Leonard to Chambois and St. Lambert when men of the U.S. 90th Division linked up with a company of Polish troops. The barrier was less than formidable; German troops continued to slip through in large numbers for the next two days. In fact, the eastward rush of escaping German troops threatened to overrun the Polish 1st Armored Division troops that were directly in their path atop 800-foot-high Mont Ormel. Wave after wave of Germans charged up the slopes, threw themselves in suicidal fury against the entrenched Poles and were cut down. In the town of St. Lambert, the Canadians, too, were in danger of being trampled in the Germans' rush to escape, but fought off one attack after another.

The carnage of war is never a pleasant sight, but the horror of the battlefield at Trun, St. Lambert and Chambois was enough to sicken even the most jaded, battle-hardened veteran. Mangled corpses of men and horses were strewn everywhere, their bodies bloated, the wounds alive and crawling with the maggots of blowflies. The U.S. First Army operations report detailed the grim scene: "The roads and fields were littered with thousands of enemy dead and wounded, wrecked and burning vehicles, smashed artillery pieces, cars laden with the loot of France overturned and smoldering, dead horses and cattle swelling in the summer's heat."

An American officer, a veteran of the carnage of World War I, also described what he saw: "I stood in a lane, surrounded by twenty or thirty dead horses or parts of horses, most of them still hitched to their wagons and carts . . . As far as my eye could reach on every line of sight, there were vehicles, wagons, tanks, guns, prime movers, sedans, rolling kitchens, etc., in various stages of destruction."

A French lieutenant colonel remarked: "Chambois will remain in our memory as a kind of vast graveyard. To open a passage for our vehicles, the Americans had to sweep the corpses aside with a bulldozer."

Even Eisenhower was appalled at the enormity of the destruction. Touring the battleground on August 23, he wrote, "I was conducted through it on foot, to encounter scenes that could be described only by Dante. It was literally possible to walk for hundreds of yards at a time, stepping on nothing but dead and decaying flesh."

No exact accounting of the casualties is possible. Out of some 400,000 German troops in the pocket, some estimates say that 10,000 German soldiers died, while another 50,000 were taken prisoner. No one knows for certain. A Canadian chaplain recalled seeing some 5,000 corpses buried in a mass grave 75 feet deep. Remains of soldiers were still being unearthed decades after the battle ended. As for the horses, some 2,000 were killed, with another 3,000 wounded. Estimates of the number of Germans who escaped vary widely—perhaps as many as 250,000. What is known is that the bulk of the German Seventh Army and Fifth Panzer Army escaped to fight again another day in a war that continued for another eight months.

There are still too many imponderables and unanswered questions that taint the victory. What if the French had not gotten in the way of 5th Armored? What if Bradley had not halted Patton's drive to close the gap? What if Allied planes had not accidentally bombed Canadian positions twice? What if Allied air power had not been ordered to refrain from bombing the troops in the pocket? And the most important question of all: Who was responsible for leaving the trap door open for so many days and allowing tens of thousands of Germans to escape?

While Bradley seemed inordinately eager to "take the rap" (in his autobiography, he stated that "the decision to stop Patton was mine alone"), the circumstantial evidence points elsewhere. Bradley contended that, had he allowed Haislip to advance northward from Argentan to the Canadian positions at Falaise, there might have been an accidental clash of friendly armies rushing toward each other. This argument seems specious when one considers that Bradley knew the Canadian-Polish forces had been checked by the Germans north of Falaise and showed no signs of breaking through anytime soon. Therefore, the danger of two Allied armies rushing headlong into each other like runaway trains was negligible, if not nil.

A more plausible reason for not ordering Haislip's men northward was the boundary line that Montgomery had established between the U.S. and British armies south of Argentan. Bradley needed Monty's permission to allow American troops to cross the line and, for whatever reason, he was reluctant to ask for that permission. On the 16th, Monty allowed the Americans to cross the boundary line but did not move it northward as he easily could have done.

That Montgomery delayed in allowing the troops to cross must be attributed to the fractious relationship between him and the American high command. Still smarting from Marshall's and Eisenhower's July attempts to get him moving—or removed from command—and embarrassed by the Americans' rapid, headline-grabbing advances during and following Operation Cobra, it seems logical that the vindictive Montgomery did not want to give the Americans the credit for closing the gap and coming to the rescue of his stalled forces. With the clear hindsight of history, it seems obvious now that Monty delayed giving the order for the closure as long as possible, hoping that, by some stroke of luck, the Canadians and Poles could break through the German lines and drive south to effect the linkup.

Perhaps, in their attempt not to embarrass Montgomery further, and to maintain the patina of American-British solidarity, both Bradley and Eisenhower chose to smooth over the incident by clinging to the illogical argument that the Americans delayed in their drive northward from Argentan to avoid an accidental head-on collision with a Canadian-Polish force that was unable to move.

Whatever the reason, the battle of the Falaise Gap could have been counted as one of the great Allied victories of the war; instead, it has become tainted as a situation that was bungled at the highest levels, as an opportunity that went begging, and as a short-sighted blunder that let far too many German troops escape to regroup and fight again, prolonging the war in the west.

Evolution of U.S. Strategic Bombing of Urban Areas

Conrad C. Crane

As Carl von Clausewitz pointed out in his classic Vom Kriege (On War), *wars tend to escalate in violence in an attempt to force the enemy to bow to one's will. An outstanding modern example of this escalation can be found in American strategic bombing of urban areas, including the acceptance of high civilian casualties, during World War II. As Conrad Crane, Research Professor of Military Strategy, United States Army War College, Carlisle Barracks, points out in this essay, the lack of effectiveness of preferred American high-altitude precision bombing, the support of public opinion, and the grim necessity of ending the war expeditiously led to an acceptance of the bombing of populated urban areas despite the troubling moral and ethical questions involved. The bombing of German and Japanese cities culminated in the firebombing of Japanese urban areas in 1945 and, finally, in the dropping of atomic bombs on Hiroshima and Nagasaki to end the Pacific war. This essay was originally published in* The Historian (50/1 [Winter 1987], 14–39) *and is reprinted with minor modifications by permission of the author. The author's ideas are more fully developed in* Bombs, Cities, and Civilians: American Airpower Strategy in World War II (University Press of Kansas, 1993).

Dear Hap;

Last month my son Ted won his wings at Randolph Field. He is now going through a bombardment school, and in a short time expects to go to the front.

Will you tell me—has he become what our enemies call him, "A Hooligan of the Air?" Is he expected to scatter death on men, women, children—to wreck churches and shrines—to be a slaughterer, not a fighting man? . . .

I remember so well when you and Frank Lahm, and Tommy Milling won your wings. We all thought it was a new day in chivalry, bravery, manhood. What do Air Force wings mean today? In winning his wings, has Ted lost his spurs? Please tell me.

This letter from a concerned mother in Massachusetts in May 1943 to General Henry H. Arnold, Army Air Forces chief of staff, raised questions about the role of American strategic bombing in World War II—questions that historians are still debating. During the war, the United States Army Air Forces (AAF) enunciated a policy of avoiding indiscriminate attacks on population centers in favor of pinpoint assaults on industrial or military targets. This seems to differentiate U.S. policy from that of Germany, Great Britain and Japan, all of which resorted to intentional terror attacks on enemy cities throughout the war. Scholars who have cited the official AAF history emphasize the intention of American leaders to resist bombing noncombatants in Europe, both for moral and strategic reasons. U.S. airmen regarded civilian casualties as an unintentional and regrettable side effect of bombs dropped on military or industrial objectives; in contrast, the intention of the Royal Air Force campaign was to destroy the cities themselves and kill or dislocate their inhabitants.

British writers have for some time criticized the claimed ethical superiority of AAF strategic bombing, and recently American scholars such as Ronald Schaffer and Michael Sherry have expressed similar objections. In a 1980 article, Schaffer examines the statements of AAF leaders as well as numerous wartime bombing documents in Europe and concludes that ethical codes "did little to discourage air attacks on German civilians." In fact, "official policy against indiscriminate bombing was so broadly interpreted and so frequently breached as to become almost meaningless." He argues that both the policy against terror bombing and ethical support for that policy among AAF leaders were "myths." In his recent study which also examines strategic bombing in the Pacific, Schaffer examines the issue in even more detail and concludes that while "virtually every major figure concerned with American bombing expressed some views about the moral issue . . . moral constraints almost invariably bowed to what people described as military necessity," another disputed concept. Sherry deals primarily with the American firebombing of Japan, which he sees as a result of a prewar willingness to kill civilians. Strategists adopted this policy after precision bombing against military and industrial targets proved only marginally effective in 1944. Firebombing became the inadvertent but inevitable product of an anonymous "technological fanaticism" of Allied bombing. The American press accepted such measures as retribution for war crimes or as preparation for invasion. The decision to firebomb, like that to drop the atomic bomb, may have been made on the assumption that using everything available would lead to eventual victory.

There are elements of truth in both arguments, but also inaccuracies. Morale and terror attacks did have a place in AAF strategy, though only as part of a vaguely defined final blow to end the war. Contrary to Schaffer's conclusions, an examination of the record indicates a fairly consistent American policy against indiscriminate bombing in Europe, especially when compared with the practices of the RAF Bomber Command, although World War II technology never allowed AAF operational policy to match stated claims. Technological limitations also influenced the British campaign. Aircraft capabilities and German countermeasures made early RAF daylight precision attacks unprofitable, but public pressure demanded that the RAF strike back at Germany. Night raids on urban areas seemed the only viable alternative. While General Arnold and many on his staff in Washington maintained an "open mind" about such terror attacks, field commanders almost always considered civilian casualties a by-product rather than a goal of bombing. They viewed terror bombing as ineffective or unpopular with the American public, while morality constituted a key concern for some leaders and planners. The primary objective was to win the war with the most efficient use of resources and the fewest possible American casualties. Mission requirements usually prevented any sense of morality from being "an overriding criterion" on aerial operations, although one planner stated that his group "took some comfort that our proposals would be much less costly in terms of the lives of civilians." The need for Allied cooperation also tended to mute ethical arguments because the British so strongly supported morale attacks and the Americans did not want to cause a rift or aid German propaganda. While it is difficult to differentiate between moral positions and official records and correspondence, ethical restraints were probably not the most important reason for limiting United States Strategic Air Forces terror bombing. Nevertheless, the role of such considerations should not be discounted.

*

One cannot deny that a significant shift in American policy occurred during the war. In 1939 President Roosevelt pleaded with belligerents to refrain from the "inhuman barbarism [of] bombardment from the air of civilian populations or of unfortified cities," but by 1945 *Impact* magazine, published by the assistant chief of air staff, Intelligence, stated U.S. objectives in the incendiary bombing of Japan "basically . . . were the same as those of British area bombing." However AAF operations in the Pacific differed from those in Europe. Less allegiance was given to restrictions against attacks on civilians during the strategic air campaign against Japan, but this did not stem from any prewar inclination to kill Japanese civilians. As in the European theater, the primary bombing objective remained the destruction of the enemy's military and industrial capacity. Beliefs and practices that had evolved in the war against Germany, combined with different perceptions of Japanese society and severe operational limitations, produced the fire raids. Michael Sherry is correct in seeing the decision to drop the A-bomb as a natural product of the evolution in American strategic bombing, but he does not give adequate credit to wartime exigencies in that development process. Also neither he nor Schaffer deals in much detail with the reaction of the public to these allegedly immoral acts of total war, or tries to explain why few citizens wrote letters such as the one from the Massachusetts mother to General Arnold. Public opinion constituted another ingredient in the formula that produced AAF bombing theory, and the public's acquiescence can be just as revealing as resistance. Understanding this air power equation is essential in order to gain a clear picture of the evolution of American air warfare in World War II, along with what seems to be an increasing acceptance of civilian casualties as a result of strategic bombing.

A progression of theorists influenced the development of American air doctrine before the war. Giulio Douhet, an Italian often called the "Father of Airpower Doctrine," viewed the airplane as an invincible weapon capable of shattering civilian morale by the indiscriminate bombardment of cities.

"Billy" Mitchell may have incorporated some of Douhet's ideas, but he tailored his concepts to the American situation. He considered cities attractive targets which did not have to be destroyed, just disrupted. "It will be sufficient," he wrote, "to have the civilian population driven out so they [sic] cannot carry on their usual vocations. A few gas bombs will do that."

By 1923 Army Air Corps schools had access to Douhet's writings but they did not widely accept his theories on mass area bombing of civilians. Air Corps maneuvers in 1929 impressed observers with the "invincibility of the bomber" and accurate daylight bombardment began to receive increased emphasis. Many factors combined to produce a precision bombing doctrine: public opposition to mass civilian bombings, intense congressional debates on the legality of aerial bombardment, a traditional American respect for marksmanship dating back to frontier days; technological developments such as accurate bombsights and the B-17; and the belief that bombardment of specific industrial targets constituted the most effective and economical way to wage war. Daylight was essential for accuracy, just as high altitude and tight formations were essential for defense. In short, moral, legal, cultural, technical, strategic and tactical reasons shaped the theory and tactics of precision industrial bombing in the 1930s.

Other air forces of that period did not espouse the precision doctrine, and terror attacks occurred in China, Ethiopia and Spain. The League of Nations and the U.S. government condemned such acts as "contrary to principles of law and humanity." The attacks led to public outrage and American newspaper editors cried that the "laws of war are becoming just scraps of paper." Military strategists questioned the value of these terror tactics, noting that they tended to harden civilian resolution, nurture hatred and often led to reprisals and destruction of the attackers' cities.

After Mitchell's death in 1936, emigré aircraft designer Alexander P. de Seversky became the dominant theorist. Because civilians did not panic under air bombardment, Seversky concluded that precision bombing of carefully selected targets must replace indiscriminate bombing of cities. He based his reasoning more on efficiency than morality. "The will to resist can be broken in a people," he argued, "only by destroying effectively the essentials of their lives—the supply of food, shelter, light, water, sanitation, and the rest." Morale could be a target without the indiscriminate slaughter of civilians. His ideas widely circulated among Air Force officers and in numerous journals. Walt Disney even made Seversky's influential book, *Victory Through Air Power* (1942) into a movie.

In August 1941, with U.S. involvement in World War II imminent, American Air Force leaders in the Air War Plans Division drew up guidelines in a key document, "Munitions Requirements of the AAF for the Defeat of our Potential Enemies," known as AWPD/1 [Air War Plans Division/1]. The plan, which influenced operations throughout the war, accepted the "Germany First" policy of overall strategic direction and adhered to the precision bombing doctrine. German power, transportation and oil industries became the main target objectives. Area bombing of civilian concentrations would only commence as a final blow when German morale began to crack. The plan did not define whether this would be a single assault or a series of attacks. Leaders sanctioned this one-time exception to general policy on the grounds that it would save lives on both sides by ending the war. Late in the war this concept of an aerial *Todesstoss* (death blow) would prove a potent lure for American leaders and help sanction the use of the atomic bomb.

*

Pearl Harbor transformed American public opinion about terror attacks on civilians. A poll on December 10, 1941, revealed that sixty-seven percent of the population favored unqualified and indiscriminate bombing of Japanese cities, while only ten percent gave an outright "no." The same justification of "tit for tat" that motivated earlier *Luftwaffe* and RAF raids on London and Berlin seemed to be evident here. Subsequent surveys produced similar results. A vast majority of Americans favored urban bombing even if it brought Axis retaliation. This implied a deep commitment or resignation to total warfare and reflected the intense anxiety about a war that appeared to be going so disastrously.

The only significant flurry of U.S. protest against strategic bombing came in response to a pamphlet, "Massacre by Bombing," written by an English citizen, Vera Brittain, and published in America by the Fellowship of Reconciliation, a small pacifist group. When the *New York Times* reprinted excerpts along with an introductory petition signed by twenty-eight prominent clergymen, educators and professionals in the spring of 1944, reaction was intense. The public condemned Brittain in over two hundred articles and the *New York Times* reported receiving letters at a fifty-to-one ratio against her. Most letters agreed with author MacKinlay Kantor who deplored the "softheartedness" of those who worry about " . . . socking the rapacious German nation with every pound of high explosives available." A rabbi declared that "The Germans must reap the fruits of their own wicked deeds." Other clergy echoed his sentiments, citing Nazi precedents as the final justification for American bombing. Editorial comment in general disclaimed moral questions and recognized the raids as a "revolting necessity." Even more acidic comments towards the Japanese reflected racial and cultural bias.

These reactions, which ranged between avid support and resigned acceptance, probably represented the majority of public opinion on killing enemy civilians. The average American may not have been aware of the extent of the destruction bombing wreaked on cities; posters depicted Allied bombers attacking factories instead of people, and periodicals described B-17s dropping explosives down industrial smokestacks. Even if they had known the exact results of bombing, it would not have made much difference. Most American families had experienced the deaths of loved ones, friends or neighbors; if bombing enemy civilians would speed victory and save American lives it had to be done.

The belief that the AAF avoided indiscriminate killing of civilians whenever possible comforted many Americans. In turn, AAF leaders perceived a public opinion in line with the position of publications like the *New Republic*, which stated that it did not approve of terror bombing but added that, to the best of its knowledge, most bombardment was directed at military objectives. A subtle, important interaction existed between public perceptions of American strategic bombing and the attitudes of the leaders carrying it out. Air Force planners interpreted public opinion as favoring precision attacks on industrial and military targets without indiscriminate civilian casualties. Military reports and news releases designed to demonstrate the accuracy and effectiveness of pinpoint bombardment in turn shaped public attitude.

*

Government decisions in war might be limited by the perceived tolerance of public opinion, but at least some leaders privately opposed the intentional killing of enemy noncombatants. Secretary of War Henry L. Stimson represented a school of thought repulsed by the barbarism of indiscriminate attacks on civilians. He had been instrumental in U.S. government protests against such raids during the 1930s and tried to keep a close watch on American strategic air operations during World War II. Stimson's diary is filled with references to atrocities and war crimes and the conviction that the Nazi leaders and secret police, not the German people, caused the war. Reports of the fire raids against Japan evoked a strong reaction; Stimson felt he had been misled by Lovett, assistant secretary of war for air, and AAF leaders who had promised to restrict operations there to "the precision bombing which it (the AAF) has done so well in Europe." He explained, "I am told it is possible and adequate. The reputation of the United States for fair play and humanitarianism is the world's biggest asset for peace in the coming decades." Discussing the topic later with President Truman, Stimson realized the validity of Air Force arguments that the omnipresence of Japanese industry made it difficult to prevent area bombing, but he "did not want to have the United States get the reputation of outdoing Hitler in atrocities." He often agonized over signing orders for bombing raids and wondered about the lack of public protest.

Although ethical considerations often did not limit other leaders, command pressure from Stimson, fear of hostile public opinion or belief in the inefficiency of area bombardment sometimes served the same purpose; all three at one time or another had an impact on the AAF chief of staff. In 1941 Arnold wrote in a book he co-authored with Colonel Ira C. Eaker that "bombing attacks on civil populace are uneconomical and unwise" because "bombers in far larger numbers than are available today will be required for wiping out people in sufficient numbers to break the will of a whole nation." Arnold kept his options for future civilian bombardment open, and his memoirs reveal even more flexibility on this subject. The damage a relatively small number of *Luftwaffe* bombers caused London impressed him and he envisioned great results from larger fleets of American planes. The idea of pilotless flying bombs like the German V-1s also fascinated him and he considered abandoning strategic bombers in favor of much cheaper radio-controlled "Bugs," remotely piloted craft capable of dropping bombs on the enemy.

In public Arnold called terror bombing "abhorrent to our humanity, our sense of decency," a policy he did not believe in. In private he told his air staff that "this is a brutal war and . . . the way to stop the killing of civilians is to cause so much damage and destruction and death that the civilians will demand that their government cease fighting." He added, however, "This doesn't mean that we are making civilians or civilian institutions a war objective, but we cannot 'pull our punches' because some of them may get killed." In order to support his desire for a postwar independent air service he had to maintain the proper public image, but he also needed impressive results to prove the effectiveness of air power. His main goal was to make the largest possible contribution to winning the war, and to ensure that the AAF received credit for it through proper publicity. His pressure for more raids despite bad weather led to increased use of less accurate radar-directed bombardments in Europe, and his demand for increased efficiency in Japan inspired the resort to fire raids. Arnold also liked to glean ideas from the minds of experts; gadgets and "hot ideas" fascinated him. He commented favorably on plans to bomb volcanoes around Tokyo and schools of fish off Japan, and he wanted to retaliate for German booby traps in North Africa by dropping explosive devices in fountain pens and pocketbooks onto German territory. There seemed to be little consideration for ethics in most of Arnold's decisions, but he did espouse the traditional moral position of airpower theory which claimed that bombing would cost fewer lives than land warfare and end the war more quickly.

The policies of General Carl Spaatz, commander of the United States Strategic Air Forces (USSTAF) and an officer most historians credit with continuing to raise the moral issue in opposition to British attempts to enlist American participation in terror attacks, fell somewhere between the positions of Stimson and Arnold. He did express fear of an ethical backlash when he stated to Arnold, "There is no doubt in my mind that the RAF want very much to have the U.S. Air Forces tarred with the morale bombing aftermath which we feel will be terrific." Yet in a questionable interview in 1962 he said, "It wasn't for religious or moral reasons that I didn't go along with urban area bombing." Nonetheless, his resistance to terror attacks provided an important limiting factor, whatever its motivation.

Many of Spaatz's subordinates shared his view, believing that both ethics and efficiency justified precision bombing. Major General Frederick L. Anderson, eventually USSTAF deputy commander for operations, was one of the AAF's leading bombardment experts before the war and a staunch advocate of precision bombing. His papers include a suggested reply to the Massachusetts mother's letter that emphasized that air warfare only differed from more traditional forms in its massive potential for destruction. "Law cannot limit what physics makes possible," it said. "We can depend for moderation only upon reason and humane instincts when we exercise such a power." It pointed out that "the precision which is the keynote of America" was more efficient than terror bombing, and at the same time more humane. By allowing reason and humanity to curb the "bestial instincts" released by "the awful weapon at our disposal," the AAF showed "that humanity pays and that Air Power is the most powerful urge for peace." (This reply was probably written by someone on Arnold's staff in Washington, but accurately reflected Spaatz's and Anderson's views as well.)

Anderson wrote another letter which illuminated additional aspects of the American position on strategic bombing. In replying to Sir Charles Portal, Britain's chief of air staff, about undesirable civilian casualties from attacks on targets in enemy-occupied countries, Anderson admitted the imperfection of precision bombing and resultant incidental casualties. He agreed with Portal's contention that the Allies had to do everything possible to avoid unnecessary civilian casualties and to limit objectives in occupied countries to key factors in Axis strategy, but differed with his view in regard to the status of workers. Anderson considered all civilians employed "willingly or otherwise" in Axis industry as assisting the enemy and thought they should accept the risks "which must be the lot of any individual who participates directly in the war effort of a belligerent nation." This policy applied to German workers as well as French, and showed a consistency in thought independent of any political considerations. Axis employees were no longer viewed as noncombatants, an important step in escalation to total war. Yet it must be noted that this combatant status applied only to workers in factories being bombed; the AAF strategic campaign, unlike that of the RAF, did not aim to kill laborers in their homes.

*

In order to get a true picture of American strategic bombing policy, it is important to examine its aerial operations. Schaffer claims that radar bombing, special operations like Thunderclap and Clarion, assaults on marshalling yards and transportation targets, and "war-weary" bomber projects all exemplified indiscriminate bombing. It is important to differentiate, however, between the intent of American tactics and the actual effect. A closer look at these examples shows much more restraint than Schaffer would admit.

This is especially evident in the use of "non-visual" navigation to bomb through European cloud cover, a practice Schaffer calls "tantamount to urban area attacks." Such methods employed devices ranging from radio direction finders to radar sets that enabled bombardiers to identify targets on the ground. Planners realized that these techniques involved some compromise with precision tactics and required a careful choice of targets. At first they selected objectives in city areas on coastlines or estuaries because of the verifiable distinction between water and land on radar screens. The technique allowed a large increase in raids during the testing period in late 1943 and early 1944, and thereby relieved much of the intense pressure Arnold applied for maximum bombing.

The first non-visual mission on Wilhelmshaven in October 1943 proved a resounding success, and in December the Eighth Air Force announced the "development of a new day bombardment technique employing latest scientific devices enabling bombing through solid cloud cover." It added:

> While accuracy is not equal to that usually attained in high altitude attacks when the target can be seen, . . . accuracy is satisfactory and gives promise of improvement. It was explained that the new technique is regarded as a logical outgrowth of American bombardment doctrine made possible by scientific advances and does not involve any basic change in the American conception of bombardment.

It can be assumed that a public which seldom questioned such military pronouncements accepted this position, which also seemed to represent USSTAF beliefs accurately. The first missions on recognizable docks and shipyards in cities like Wilhelmshaven and Kiel served to encourage believers in radar bombing and to convert doubters, but the early successes turned out to be beginner's luck. They "gave an unfounded hope of potential accuracy; and it may therefore have contributed to an unfortunate tendency to treat H2X (radar) as a rival of visual bombing rather than a supplement to it." It may also have helped to make the Eighth Air Force complacent about the increased rate of operations which the new equipment made possible through the winter. By early 1944 it became evident that new training and equipment would be necessary to achieve acceptable accuracy.

In the last quarter of 1944, approximately seventy-five percent of AAF strategic missions in Europe involved some use of blind-bombing techniques. Despite the implementation of new equipment only a little over one-third of the bombs fell within 1000 feet of the target. Leaders knew about the results, but felt the effort must be continued to prevent important sectors of German industry from getting a respite. The AAF would continue to improve and perfect its techniques through experience. AAF accuracy was still better than the RAF's record for area raids at this time. Civilian casualties from radar attacks were incidental rather than planned. An important distinction must be made between American intent and effect. Spaatz continued to seek more accurate radar sets, and lamented late in 1944 that "our air war is becoming a radar war." The AAF held so much confidence in these non-visual techniques that the tactical Ninth Air Force employed them for close-support missions while work continued to lessen the danger to Allied positions when targets were very close. Development also continued on strategic uses, with eventual success. Equipped with new Eagle radars and special training in the last seven weeks of the war, the 315th Wing managed to obtain results with radar bombings on Japanese oil refineries that were ninety-eight percent as accurate as visual means.

Close cooperation with the British, a growing lack of industrial targets, pressure for greater results, and the lure of *Todesstoss* all made area bombing more attractive to American airmen as the war continued. But most still believed it was not as efficient as precision bombing and did not have public support. Some leaders feared terror bombing would tarnish the Air Force image, while Stimson's and Lovett's pressure against such raids influenced others.

All these elements affected air operations after the invasion of Europe. By mid-July 1944 Arnold began to feel that a well-timed strike by ground or air units would destroy the "increasingly shaky structure" of German resistance. Although he and General Laurence S. Kuter, assistant chief of air staff for plans, saw some promise of weakening German morale with air attacks concentrated on one or two cities, Spaatz and Anderson envisioned widely dispersed raids on many targets to impress civilians in rural towns with Allied might. About the same time the British Air Ministry prepared a memorandum which proposed attacking German civilian morale with a massive RAF/AAF assault on Berlin. At AAF headquarters this idea produced "diverse reactions," most of them negative. Kuter echoed Spaatz's fears when he wrote to Anderson, "we should consider whether the recent buzz-bomb attacks have not instilled in the British government a desire for retaliation in which American air units will be called upon to share with RAF Bomber Command the onus for the more critical features of night area bombing." He reiterated that American policy had been to bomb military and industrial targets. Apathy and discouragement created by morale bombing "are not the qualities to pressure revolt," and people in the Nazi police state were not in a position to influence national will as much as in a democracy. "Furthermore," he added, "it is contrary to our national ideals to wage war against civilians." AAF headquarters found several other aspects of the British plan unacceptable. Contrary to Anderson's opinions, Kuter thought that "attacks against impressed labor of non-German origin are unsound." In regard to strikes against civilians, he added: "We do not want to kill them—we want to make them think and drive them to action."

During this period AAF leaders seemed to feel that although a contingency plan was preferable, the time had not yet come for *Todesstoss*. The supreme allied commander, General Dwight D. Eisenhower, no doubt influenced by the British air chief marshall, Sir Arthur Tedder, overruled them. "While I have always insisted," Eisenhower told Spaatz on August 28, 1944, "that U.S. Strategic Air Forces be directed against precision targets, I am always prepared to take part in anything that gives real promise to ending the war quickly." Despite Spaatz's protests, Eisenhower ordered plans for a large RAF/AAF raid on Berlin, which the Psychological Warfare Division of SHAEF (Supreme Headquarters Allied Expeditionary Forces) later denounced as too terroristic. American air crews shared Spaatz's disdain for the long and dangerous Berlin missions. Typical complaints in a June survey included that the city "is not a military target," and "I don't believe in spite bombing." In mid-September the Combined Chiefs of Staff deferred a British proposal to endorse morale bombing after Admiral William Leahy, Roosevelt's chief military advisor, said it would be a mistake to "record" such a decision. This appeared to be a diplomatic way to avoid both offending the British and endorsing a distasteful proposition. These recommendations and a lack of fighter escorts postponed any such assault on Berlin until 1945. By then AAF planners had redefined American targets to include transportation facilities and government areas more susceptible to precision tactics. The density of the city resulted in high civilian casualties and since the raid occurred close to the one on Dresden, it contributed to the ensuing controversy over whether the AAF was adopting terror tactics.

At the time the Berlin attack, Operation Thunderclap, was being formulated, Spaatz wrote Lovett in early October that he had "started the development of a plan for the full-out beating up of Germany with all the Air Forces at our disposal." "To my mind," he stated, "it represents the only means of terminating the war this year with our forces." The concept of one massive daylight effort to end the war coincided with Arnold's and Eisenhower's desires, and sought "to impress the German high command with the might and destructive power of Allied air power." Although Spaatz still believed that oil was the most critical and vulnerable target system in Germany, limited capabilities of the RAF Bomber Command and the Tactical Air Forces diverted attention to the German transportation system.

The shift to targeting transportation facilities signified a change in AAF priorities, more than a change in doctrine. Although transportation systems had been low on the list of precision bombardment objectives, many in SHAEF believed that widespread attacks might collapse the German economy and assist the tactical situation as well. The final operation based on Spaatz's plan, Clarion, also incorporated earlier USSTAF ideas on morale attacks. A memo submitted to General Kuter in early September summed up these positions: "It is believed that a great many comparatively small attacks in relatively virgin areas of Germany would have more of the desired effect than a series of annihilation attacks on a few communities." It was recommended that small numbers of aircraft attack precision targets such as machine shops and communications facilities in rural areas. Because of more scattered defenses in those areas, bombers could fly at lower altitudes, allowing greater accuracy, better visibility and a chance for most of the population to see the invincibility of Allied air power. The memo ended: "Though it will be regrettable if circumstances force the adoption of civilian morale as a primary target, the form of attack advocated herein will be both the most acceptable and the one most likely to succeed." These tactics were acceptable because they would limit civilian casualties and increase the effect on morale.

This morale bombing reflected the philosophy of Seversky more than Douhet; it is much different to terrorize a civilian by attacking a nearby train or bridge than to purposefully try to kill him. While morale loss remained a secondary objective, the primary focus was to cripple transportation. Nonetheless, many AAF officers strongly opposed the operation. Eaker feared that civilian casualties would convince the German people that Americans were the barbarians portrayed by Nazi propaganda. He told Spaatz: "You and Bob Lovett are right and we should never allow the history of this war to convict us of throwing the strategic bomber at the man in the street." General Charles Cabell, the USSTAF director of plans, penciled on his copy of the plan for Clarion, "This is the same old baby killing plan of the get-rich-quick psychological boys, dressed up in a new kimono." But Spaatz decided to give the plan a try even though, unlike most other AAF leaders, he had given up "following the chimera of the one air operation which will end the war." He told General Arnold that he expected the attack to paralyze German transportation for several days. On February 22 the weather cleared enough to leave most of Germany vulnerable, and for two days strategic and tactical bombers pummelled German railroads. The heavy bombers could fly at lower altitudes and in smaller groups which allowed them to pinpoint attacks in a broader area with more accuracy and fewer civilian casualties. But the lack of serious damage to either morale or the economy caused Portal and the Joint Intelligence Committee to recommend total suspension of the operations. Tedder and Spaatz disagreed and to this day studies differ radically in their assessments of Clarion. Schaffer argues vehemently that Clarion was a terror attack, citing, among other items, instructions to a briefing officer which emphasized that the attack, striking throughout Germany, would provide "a deterrent for the initiation of future wars." Yet even this was considered a side effect. The reports from participating units concentrate on the destruction of railways and rolling stock; none mention morale targets or effects.

AWPD/1 recognized that large transportation objectives such as marshalling yards, because of their dispersed nature and easy reconstruction, required repeated area bombing. Area bombardment differed from attacks on major urban zones. Still, the selection of such an objective within a city usually resulted in increased civilian casualties. In American formation bombing techniques all planes dropped their loads simultaneously with the lead bombardier, covering a wide zone. While this tactic maximized defensive capabilities and chances of hitting the objective, it also produced a bomb pattern as dispersed as the formation. Strategists reasonably expected that most bombs would fall on or near the target, but results were never as precise as articles on the home front claimed. An example of the deadly effect of formation bombing on a target within a major city occurred a week prior to Clarion during the American raid on Dresden, planned in conjunction with massive British night area bombardments. Poor visibility over the target, in part due to smoke from the many fires started by the RAF, compounded errors. Melden Smith provides a detailed study of the decision-making process leading to the raid, laying much of the blame on Churchill and the confusion over Russian requests for support, in addition to the fact that Dresden coincided with other Thunderclap proposals. Despite later reports to the contrary, the city did contain important industrial and transportation targets. Newspaper accounts emphasized the communications and industrial characteristics of Dresden and the support the attack gave to the Russians. They did not mention civilian casualities; the American press did not gloat over such figures the way British reporters sometimes did.

At a press conference after the raid, however, an Associated Press reporter misinterpreted the remarks of the briefing officer, and the ensuing dispatch caused nationwide headlines like "Terror Bombing gets Allied Approval as Step to Speed Victory." Arnold called Spaatz immediately when he saw it because the release contradicted previously announced policies. Anderson explained that the report had exaggerated the briefing officer's statements and had never been cleared by censors. He reiterated that the USSTAF's mission remained to destroy Germany's ability to wage war, and the Air Force did not consider attacks on transportation centers terror attacks. "There has been no change in policy," he added. "There has been only a change of emphasis in locale."

Despite AAF fears of U.S. public reaction to the terror bombing announcements, none came. Americans at home accepted such tactics if they would help end the war. In reality, while the new policy showed no change in the USSTAF commitment against direct bombing of civilian areas, the AAF no longer selected targets to assure minimum casualties. With the lack of good industrial targets and the lure of *Todesstoss*, U.S. military opposition to area bombing weakened as the war dragged on.

Another supposed sign of this change came from growing AAF support for use of "war-weary" B-17s, stripped of armor and armament, and loaded with ten tons of explosives. Not surprisingly, Arnold was the primary advocate of this project; he saw no difference between these robot planes and British night area bombing. But field commanders used more caution and discrimination in their use of radio-controlled bombers. Hardened V-1 sites provided the initial objective; priority later shifted to submarine pens. The

AAF also conducted tactical tests to assist ground forces with attacks on fortified areas. This utilization of the aircraft persuaded Admiral Leahy, who had earlier considered them "an inhuman and barbarous type of warfare with which the United States should not be associated," to change his mind. There appears to have been little enthusiasm for the project outside the Joint Chiefs of Staff. Air commanders thought the war-wearies too vulnerable and ineffective for strategic missions. Their ground counterparts expressed reservations about safety on tactical missions, as war-wearies endangered friendly troops along the robots' flight path. British fear of German retaliation called a final halt to the project; USSTAF and SHAEF showed little resistance to that decision.

*

As the strategic air campaign in Europe drew to a close, the focus moved to the Pacific. The same forces and precedents involved in the assault on Germany influenced aerial bombardment of Japan, but more than just distance separated the two theaters of operations. Americans held disparate perceptions of the Japanese and Germans. President Roosevelt thought American troops felt more hatred toward the Japanese than the Germans. At one point he even approved a project to attack Japan with bats carrying small incendiary bombs; planners thought this approach would be effective against bamboo houses as well as the superstitious natures of their occupants. Fighting in the Pacific theater was particularly ferocious. Japanese soldiers and civilians committed hari-kari rather than surrender, and thought it just as shameful for their enemies to surrender. Americans retaliated when the Japanese mutilated and killed captives; "not since the French and Indian War had American troops been so brutal." While combatants offered no truces in combat, American troops committed no atrocities against civilians. General MacArthur had the most restrictive policy anywhere on air attacks in the Philippines. Bombing of any target "located within inhabited areas of cities and barrios or sufficiently close thereto to endanger such areas by the operations contemplated" had to be cleared through his headquarters.

Air strategy against the Japanese homeland was to be the same as in Europe. Brigadier General Haywood Hansell, one of Arnold's top planners and a prime advocate of precision bombing doctrine, took command of the Twenty-first Bomber Command and set out to put his theories into practice. The results were dismal. Atrocious weather, poor visibility and the two-hundred-mile-an-hour jet stream between B-29 bases in the Marianas and Tokyo made navigation and storms unpredictable. The winds exceeded the limitations of both bombardiers and bombsights. Many of the B-29 crews arrived believing in the effectiveness of radar bombing techniques supposedly perfected in Europe, but they soon reached new conclusions. The bombing had little effect on Japanese production due to the dispersion of cottage industries as well as the woeful inaccuracy of high-explosive bombs. Some experimental fire bombing raids which Arnold ordered on dock areas showed success, but Hansell refused to abandon his belief in precision doctrine. Arnold relieved him from command in February 1945 and replaced him with Major General Curtis LeMay.

Initially LeMay also tried daylight precision attacks, hoping that better organization and training would improve results. Many planners on Arnold's staff, wishing to exploit the psychological effects of the loss of the Philippines and further demoralize the Japanese people, recommended an incendiary assault on industrial centers. Even precision advocates like Anderson could see no alternative to area raids. But pinpoint attacks on aircraft engine factories retained first priority in Arnold's directives; LeMay alone decided to switch methods. He took a great gamble with revolutionary tactics and did not even inform Arnold of the new plans until the day before the first fire mission. He stripped his planes of defensive armament to allow them to carry a heavier bomb load and brought them in at night for surprise and at low altitude for accuracy. Results were spectacular and soon Arnold's staff constructed a new list of industrial sectors within cities for priority targets. LeMay still used some precision attacks on small targets like isolated aircraft factories, but emphasis changed to the more productive area raids.

Newspaper reports of the raids, like Air Force intelligence on bombing results, concentrated on the physical damage from the attacks rather than on civilian deaths. Articles on the first Tokyo raid are typical. They note the heavy population density of the area but emphasize that in the fifteen square miles destroyed, "eight identifiable industrial targets lie in ruins along with hundreds of other industrial plants." One LeMay quote mentions thousands of "home industries" destroyed. Accounts do not estimate civilian casualties but proclaim that the many thousands made homeless posed an immense refugee problem for the Japanese government. Deaths are not mentioned, and of course there are no pictures of the destruction, just maps of the destroyed zone.

Fire raids marked another stage in the evolution of total war and represented the culmination of trends started in the air war against Germany. Although target selection late in the European campaign showed less effort taken to avoid civilian casualties, LeMay's planning ignored such considerations altogether. His intelligence officers advised him that massive fires were essential in order to jump the fire breaks around factories. Noncombatant deaths were unavoidable in order to destroy Japanese industry and forestall an invasion of Japan, which LeMay feared would cost half a million American lives. While areas of industrial concentrations remained primary targets, the concept of workers as belligerents which had surfaced in European combat once again justified civilian casualties. American leaders did not view Japanese society as a police state or one containing impressed workers. All Japanese participated in manufacturing for the war effort, often in their homes. LeMay defended his raid on Tokyo by writing:

We were going after military targets. No point in slaughtering civilians for the mere sake of slaughter. Of course, there is a pretty thin veneer in Japan, but the veneer was there. It was their system of dispersal of industry. All you had to do was visit one of those targets after we'd roasted it, and see the ruins of a multitude of tiny houses, with a drill press sticking up through the wreckage of every home. The entire population got into the act and worked to make those airplanes or munitions of war . . . men, women, children. We knew we were going to kill a lot of women and kids when we burned that town. Had to be done.

LeMay also emphasized that, whenever possible, populations were warned to evacuate. The intent was to disrupt industry without killing everyone. Refugees clogged roads and caused the Japanese government immense relocation problems. One successful psychological warfare operation involved dropping leaflets which named a number of Japanese towns as potential bomb sites and recommended that they be evacuated. "At the height of the campaign, more than six and one-half million Japanese were involved in leaving their cities—many from cities never touched."

This aspect of morale exploitation incorporated a plan that had been rejected for use in Europe, another sign of the intensification of the Japanese campaign. When Spaatz transferred to the Pacific theater after V-E Day, he was appalled by the fire bombing. He confided in his diary, "I never have favored the destruction of cities as such with all inhabitants being killed."

LeMay wrote in April that he believed that he had the resources to destroy the enemy's ability to wage war within six months. Other airmen envisioned a swift *Todesstoss* to demoralize the enemy. Some AAF leaders, amazed when the bombings failed to force Japan's collapse, could no longer estimate when the war would terminate. In Europe it had been fairly obvious when the end of war approached and targets disappeared, but in Japan attacks had to continue in preparation for the invasion of the home islands. Resistance remained fanatic and the Japanese people seemed prepared to die for the emperor. American battle casualties dramatically increased as the average monthly rate of loss quadrupled to nearly 13,000. The desperate fighting on Okinawa during the spring and early summer foreshadowed the consequences of invasion. Leaders pursued any idea that held hope of speeding victory and reducing losses. Generals Marshall and MacArthur favored the use of poison gas and the Joint Chiefs of Staff advocated destruction of the Japanese rice crop. The results of fire raids did not look as unconscionable when compared to projections of American casualities during an invasion. Indeed the incendiary attacks seemed a "revolting necessity." That very effort may have been decisive. Prince Konoye later claimed, "Fundamentally, the thing that brought about the determination to make peace was the prolonged fire bombing by the B-29s."

The incendiary bombings of Japanese cities set the stage for the use of the atomic bomb—the culmination of "the slide to total war" of the American strategic bombing campaign. Precision bombing practices, especially in

Europe, must be seen as an attempt to halt, or at least slow, the rush to unlimited warfare. Although efficiency more than ethics provided the basis of AAF doctrine, a limitation on the "uncurbed bestial instincts" of warfare emerged. It also resulted from a subtle interplay between military and public perceptions of strategic bombing, affected by newspaper reports, press releases and bombing assessments. The desired accuracy, which many believed achievable, could not yet be attained with the tactics and equipment available. American airmen did the best they could with what they had, but theory exceeded technology. Objective observers could still detect a definite difference between AAF strategic bombing and the British area raids on cities or the German "Blitz" on London.

Sanctions restricting the bombing of civilians eroded as the war entered its complex final phases, and pressure increased for the Allies to achieve their stated aim of winning the war "as decisively and speedily as possible." This was especially evident in the campaign against Japan, when AAF leaders increased the intensity of the fire raids in the belief that they provided the best chance to end the war quickly and cheaply, demonstrate a true "victory through airpower," and secure a strong position to bargain for postwar status as an independent service. Civilian deaths were never a direct objective of AAF attacks, but avoiding such casualties became less and less a consideration. Perhaps the culmination of this trend is best exemplified by the message Gen. Lauris Norstad sent to Spaatz in the Pacific on August 8, 1945:

> It is understood that the Secretary of War in his press conference tomorrow will release a map or photostat of Hiroshima showing the aiming point and the general area of greatest damage. . . . It is believed here that the accuracy with which this bomb was placed may counter a thought that the CENTERBOARD (A-Bomb) project involves wanton, indiscriminate bombing.

If an atomic bomb dropped on a city is construed as a method of precision bombing, then precision bombing no longer took civilian casualties into account. Yet we should not make hasty moral judgments on the men who firebombed Tokyo and dropped the atomic bomb. As distinguished British historian Michael Howard has observed, when statesmen and their generals deal with the ethical issues of a war threatening their people and nation "the options open to them are likely to be far more limited than is generally realized." And leaders' problems are much more complex in an era of total war and nuclear weapons. The issues of law, physics and airpower ethics which men like Anderson and Arnold expressed and every AAF leader faced, are all part of what Bill Moyers has called "the great unresolved dilemma of our age: Will we go on doing what our weapons make possible?"

X

World War II: Pacific Theater, 1939–1945

The Dorn Report

(Memorandum of December 15, 1995, to Deputy Secretary of Defense John M. Deutch from Edwin Dorn, Under Secretary of Defense, and submitted to Congress recommending against advancement of Major General Walter C. Short and Rear Adm. Husband E. Kimmel to three- or four-star rank posthumously.)

In the immediate aftermath of the Japanese surprise attack on Pearl Harbor on December 7, 1941, in which 2,403 persons died and 18 warships were sunk or damaged, blame fell on the heads of General Short, Commanding General, Hawaii Department, and Admiral Kimmel, Commander in Chief, Pacific Fleet, for the disaster. They were relieved of command, reduced in rank, and retired. Since that time a debate has raged involving historians, politicians, military figures, and the families of the men over these commanders' responsibility for what occurred that Sunday morning. In the aftermath of the attack various official inquiries were conducted that placed all or at least partial blame on these officers, but the issue continued to be debated. In 1995 Senator Strom Thurmond again raised the question of their responsibility, and Edwin Dorn chaired an investigation as to whether or not the actions taken by these officers 50 years before were excessively harsh and whether posthumous advancement in rank for each would be appropriate. The Dorn Report concluded that Kimmel and Short shared partial responsibility and recommended that advancement was not merited. Agitation continued, however, and Congress passed legislation in October 2000 advancing Kimmel to four-star rank and Short to three-star rank on the retired list, and President Bill Clinton signed it into law on October 30 of that year. Despite this political decision, the debate over the culpability of these two officers for the tragedy at Pearl Harbor will undoubtedly continue in the years to come.

This report is available online at http:/sunsite.unc.edu/pha/pha/dorn/dornmemo.

UNDER SECRETARY OF DEFENSE
4000 DEFENSE PENTAGON
WASHINGTON, D.C. 20301-4000

[Stamped: Dec. 15 1995]

MEMORANDUM FOR THE DEPUTY SECRETARY OF DEFENSE

SUBJECT: Advancement of Rear Admiral Kimmel and Major General Short

This review was undertaken in response to a commitment that former Deputy Secretary Deutch made to Senator Thurmond in April 1995. You assigned me to conduct it. In essence, you asked me to advise you whether actions taken toward General Short and Admiral Kimmel some 50 years ago were excessively harsh, and if so, whether posthumous advancement to three- and four-star rank is the appropriate remedy.

These issues are immediate and highly emotional to the descendants of Admiral Kimmel and General Short. Family members feel that the Pearl Harbor commanders were scapegoats for a disaster that they could neither prevent nor mitigate, and that others who were blameworthy escaped both official censure and public humiliation. They argue that advancement (or, as they put it, restoration to highest rank held) is the best way to remove the stigma and obloquy.

More is at stake here than the reputations of two officers and the feelings of their families. The principle of equity requires that wrongs be set right. In addition, we owe it to posterity to ensure that our history is told correctly.

With support from a small team of DoD civilians and military officers, I studied the performance of the two commanders, the procedures that led to their relief and retirement and the reports of the several Pearl Harbor investigations. I also tried to understand the basis for the families' claim that General Short and Admiral Kimmel were unfairly denied restoration to three-star and four-star rank when that action became legally possible in 1947. The team reviewed thousands of pages of documents, read a number of secondary sources, visited Pearl Harbor and interviewed members of the families.

My findings are:

1. Responsibility for the Pearl Harbor disaster should not fall solely on the shoulders of Admiral [Husband E.] Kimmel and General [Walter C.] Short; it should be broadly shared.

a. The United States and Japan were pursuing policies that were leading inexorably to war. Japan had occupied Manchuria, was threatening much of Asia and had joined in a tripartite alliance with Italy and Germany. The US reaction was to stop selling Japan strategically important materials including oil (Japan bought most of its oil from the US) and, in the summer of 1941, to freeze Japanese assets in the US. Negotiations in the summer and fall of 1941 failed to break the impasse. By late November 1941, civilian and military leaders in the US had concluded that conflict was imminent; the only questions were when and where it would occur.

b. Admiral Kimmel and General Short were both sent "war warning" messages on November 27. They were advised that negotiations were stalemated and that Japan might take hostile action at any moment. Admiral Kimmel was ordered to execute a "defensive deployment" consistent with the US war plan in the Pacific; General Short was ordered to undertake "reconnaissance and other measures . . .", but his instructions were muddied somewhat by advice to avoid actions that would "alarm [Hawaii's] civil population or disclose intent."

c. Admiral Kimmel and General Short discussed the November 27 war warning, but concluded that an attack would occur in the Western Pacific, not in Hawaii. Indeed, the November 27 messages had mentioned the likelihood that the attack would occur in "the Philippines, Thai or Kra Peninsula or . . . Borneo." Washington also did not expect Hawaii to be attacked. Further, it appears that Admiral Kimmel and General Short were depending on timely tactical warning from Washington, should Hawaii become a target. Military leaders in Washington, on the other hand, appear to have felt that the November 27 war warning would lead Admiral Kimmel and General Short to heighten their vigilance, and failed to examine closely what they actually were doing.

d. Officials in Washington did not send Admiral Kimmel and General Short other information, derived from the *Magic* project that broke the Japanese code, that might have given them a greater sense of urgency and caused them to surmise that Hawaii was a likely target. For example, Washington did not tell them that Japanese agents in Hawaii had been instructed to report on the precise location of ships at Pearl Harbor. (The Japanese attacked Hawaii, the Philippines and several other targets on the same day.)

e. Information-sharing and operational cooperation were hampered by bureaucratic rivalries. The Army and Navy were separate executive departments reporting directly to the President, and only the President could ensure that they were working together. Admiral Kimmel and General Short had cordial personal relations, but felt it inappropriate to inquire into one another's professional domains. This apparently was the standard at the time. General Short's mission was to defend the fleet in Hawaii; Admiral Kimmel apparently never asked in detail about General Short's plans. Admiral Kimmel's mission was to prepare for offensive operations against Japan. Early in 1941 the Navy also had assumed from the Army responsibility for conducting long-range aerial reconnaissance. Even after receiving the war warning, General Short apparently did not ask Admiral Kimmel whether the Navy actually was conducting long-range air patrols. Nevertheless, General Short assumed that he would receive the advance warning needed to launch Army Air Corps fighters, which were on four-hour alert, and to ready his antiaircraft guns, whose ammunition was stored some distance from the batteries. Just as Washington did not provide the Hawaii commanders with all the intelligence that was derived from *Magic*, so it also appears that Admiral Kimmel had more intelligence than he chose to share with General Short. For example, Admiral Kimmel learned on December 2 that several Japanese carriers were "lost" to US intelligence; their radio signals had not been detected for more than two weeks. He did not tell General Short.

    f. The run-up to Pearl Harbor was fraught with miscommunication, oversights and lack of follow-up. In his November 27 war warning message, Army Chief of Staff Marshall directed General Short to "undertake such reconnaissance and other measures as you deem necessary . . ." General Short assumed this order was misworded, because he believed General Marshall knew that the Navy had taken over the reconnaissance responsibility from the Army. He also assumed that the Navy was doing it. General Short's response to General Marshall described plans to defend against sabotage, but said nothing about reconnaissance. Apparently, no one in the War Department took note of the omission. The November 27 war warning from Admiral Stark, the Chief of Naval Operations (CNO), instructed Admiral Kimmel to undertake a "defensive deployment preparatory to carrying out the tasks assigned in WPL 46; [the war plan]." Exactly what Admiral Stark intended is not clear. Admiral Kimmel interpreted the CNO's guidance to mean that he (Admiral Kimmel) should continue what he had been doing for several weeks—sending submarines and planes to patrol around Wake and Midway, and patrolling outside Pearl Harbor for Japanese submarines. Carrier task forces en route to Wake and Midway were doing aerial reconnaissance as part of their normal training, thus covering a portion of the Pacific west and southwest of Hawaii. "Deployment" also could have meant to sortie the fleet from Pearl Harbor. Admiral Kimmel did not do that. Instead, he kept his ships in port, but pointed their bows toward the entrance so that they could leave quickly if the need arose. Moving several dozen warships through Pearl Harbor's narrow channel and into fighting posture on the high seas would have taken several hours. No one in the Department of Navy took issue with Admiral Kimmel's interpretation of the CNO's instructions.

    g. Resources were scarce. Washington didn't have enough cryptologists and linguists to decode all the Japanese message traffic, so the analysts gave priority to diplomatic traffic over military traffic. The Navy in Hawaii was short of planes and crews. The Army in Hawaii was short of munitions.

    h. Finally, the Japanese attack was brilliantly conceived and flawlessly executed. It involved a bold new use of carriers. It required crossing four thousand miles of ocean undetected, which meant taking the storm-tossed northern route where there was little commercial shipping. It required new technology—torpedoes that could be used in the shallow, narrow confines of Pearl Harbor. And the attack required extraordinarily well trained air crews with commanders capable of coordinating more than 150 planes in each wave of attack. US Naval exercises during the 1930s and the British Navy's 1940 raid on the Italian fleet at Taranto had demonstrated the feasibility of carrier-based attacks. But the scale and complexity of the Japanese attack greatly exceeded anything envisioned before. American military experts underestimated Japanese capability.

2. To say that responsibility is broadly shared is not to absolve Admiral Kimmel and General Short of accountability.

a. Military command is unique. A commander has plenary responsibility for the welfare of the people under his or her command, and is directly accountable for everything the unit does or fails to do. When a ship runs aground, the captain is accountable whether or not he/she was on the bridge at the time. When a unit is attacked, it is the Commander and not the intelligence officer or the sentry who is accountable. Command at the three- and four-star level involves daunting responsibilities. Military officers at that level operate with a great deal of independence. They must have extraordinary skill, foresight and judgment, and a willingness to be accountable for things about which they could not possibly have personal knowledge. Today, for example, the senior Commander in Hawaii is responsible for US military operations spanning half the world's surface—from the West coast of the United States to the east coast of Asia. His fleets sail the Pacific, the Indian Ocean, the China Sea, the Sea of Japan, the Arctic and the Antarctic. This, in the understated language of military law, is "a position of importance and responsibility."

b. It was appropriate that Admiral Kimmel and General Short be relieved. In the immediate aftermath of the attack, their relief was occasioned by the need to restore confidence in the Navy and Army's leadership, especially in the Pacific, and to get going with the war. Subsequently, investigations concluded that both commanders made errors of judgment. I have seen no information that leads me to contradict that conclusion.

c. The intelligence available to Admiral Kimmel and General Short was sufficient to justify a higher level of vigilance than they chose to maintain. They knew that war was imminent, they knew that Japanese tactics featured surprise attacks, and Admiral Kimmel (though not General Short) knew that the US had lost track of Japan's carriers. Further, they had the resources to maintain a higher level of vigilance. Admiral Kimmel believed that the optimum aerial reconnaissance would require covering 360 degrees around Hawaii for a sustained period. The Navy clearly did not have enough planes for that. This does not mean, however, that Admiral Kimmel had to choose between ideal aerial reconnaissance and no aerial reconnaissance. The fleet also had cruisers and destroyers that could have been used as pickets to supplement air patrols, but were not.

d. Different choices might not have discovered the carrier armada and might not have prevented the attack, but different choices—a different allocation of resources—could have reduced the magnitude of the disaster. The Navy and the Army were at a low level of alert against aerial attack. Shipboard anti-aircraft guns were firing within five minutes. The Army was not able to bring its batteries into play during the first wave of the attack and only four Army Air Corps fighters managed to get airborne. US losses included 2,403 dead (1,177 of whom are entombed in the Arizona), 1,178 wounded, eight battleships, ten other vessels and more than 100 aircraft. Japanese losses were 29 aircraft, one large submarine and five midget submarines.

3. The official treatment of Admiral Kimmel and General Short was substantively temperate and procedurally proper.

a. Admiral Kimmel and General Short were the objects of public vilification. At least one Member of Congress demanded that they be summarily dismissed, stripped of rank and denied retirement benefits. They received hate mail and death threats. The public and Congress were clamoring for information about Pearl Harbor. The news media went into a feeding frenzy, gobbling up tidbits of blame and punishment. Under the circumstances, it is not surprising that information very hurtful to Admiral Kimmel and General Short—information implying that they would be court martialed, for example—was given to the press. These things happen, often not for the most honorable of reasons. This does not mean, however, that Admiral Kimmel and General Short were victims of a smear campaign orchestrated by government officials.

b. In contrast to their treatment by some of the media, their official treatment was substantively temperate. They were relieved, they reverted to two-star rank, and under the laws in force at the time, their retirements were at the two-star Level. Although there was mention of court martial, no charges were brought. Indeed, official statements and investigations seemed purposely to avoid wording that would lead to court martial. For example, the Roberts Commission used the phrase "dereliction of duty"—a stinging rebuke, but at the time not a court martial offense. The Roberts Commission avoided other phrases, such as "culpable inefficiency" and "neglect of duty", that were court martial offenses. Later investigations such as the Joint Congressional Committee report eschewed "dereliction" in favor of "errors of judgment."

c. Admiral Kimmel requested a court martial in order to clear his name, but the request was not acted on. There is an allegation that the government feared bringing charges because a court martial would have put other senior military and civilian leaders in a bad light. This is possible. But it is equally possible that there simply were not sufficient grounds to sustain a successful prosecution. A court marital almost certainly would have revealed the existence of *Magic*, a key US intelligence asset.

d. I do not find major fault with the procedures used in the investigations. Family members have complained that Admiral Kimmel and General Short were denied "due process"; that is, they were not allowed to call their own witnesses or to cross-examine witnesses. But the calling and cross-examination of witnesses is characteristic of trials, not of investigations. Some of the investigations may have been more thorough than others, but I do not see a convincing basis for concluding that Admiral Kimmel and General Short were victims of government scapegoating or of a government-inspired smear campaign.

4. History has not been hostile to Admiral Kimmel and General Short.

a. None of the official reports ever held that Admiral Kimmel and General Short were solely responsible for the Pearl Harbor disaster, although the Roberts Commission came close. Later reports exchewed [sic] the stinging "dereliction of duty" rebuke in favor of "errors of judgment."

b. Historians who write about Pearl Harbor seem to be divided into three camps: those who hold Admiral Kimmel and General Short partly (but not solely) responsible; those who believe they were scapegoats; and those who lay much of the blame on bureaucratic factors such as the lack of coordination between the Army and the Navy. National Park Service guides at the Arizona Memorial, for example, focus on the factors that led to war and on the tactics used in the attack, not on individual military leaders. A 30-minute film produced exclusively for use at the Arizona Memorial mentions Admiral Kimmel and General Short only once, and not at all disparagingly. Admiral Kimmel and General Short are not discussed prominently or disparagingly in history classes at West Point, Annapolis and the Air Force Academy. Of eight US history texts in use at the service academies today, one is critical of Admiral Kimmel. Thus, while their reputations may have been damaged in the years immediately following Pearl Harbor, the passage of time has produced balance.

5. There is not a compelling basis for advancing either officer to a higher grade.

a. Their superiors concluded that Admiral Kimmel and General Short did not demonstrate the judgment required of people who serve at the three- and four-star level. That conclusion may seem harsh, but it is made all the time. I have not seen a convincing basis for contradicting it in the instant case. It also is important to keep in mind that retirement at the two-star grade is not an insult or a stigma. Very few officers rise to that level of distinction.

b. Retirement at three- and four-star level was not a right in 1947 and is not today. Officers are nominated for retirement at that level by the President at the President's discretion and based on his conclusion that they served satisfactorily at the temporary grades. His nomination is subject to the advice and consent of the Senate. A nominee's errors and indiscretions must be reported to the Senate as adverse information.

In sum, I cannot conclude that Admiral Kimmel and General Short were victims of unfair official actions and thus I cannot conclude that the official remedy of advancement on the retired list in order. Admiral Kimmel and General Short did not have all the resources they felt necessary. Had they been provided more intelligence and clearer guidance, they might have understood their situation more clearly and behaved differently. Thus, responsibility for the magnitude of the Pearl Harbor disaster must be shared. But this is not a basis for contradicting the conclusion, drawn consistently over several investigations, that Admiral Kimmel and General Short committed errors of judgment. As commanders, they were accountable.

Admiral Kimmel and General Short suffered greatly for Pearl Harbor. They lost men for whom they were responsible. They felt that too much of the blame was placed on them. Their children and grandchildren continue to be haunted by it all. For all this, there can be sadness. But there can be no official remedy.

I recommend that you provide a copy of this memorandum and attachment to Senator Thurmond, the families of Admiral Kimmel and General Short, the secretaries of Army and Navy and other interested parties.

/S/ Edwin Dorn

The Epic Battle of Leyte Gulf, 1944
Thomas J. Cutler

The Battle of Leyte Gulf of October 1944 was the largest naval battle involving more ships and men and the largest field of combat than any other sea battle in history. At its end the Imperial Japanese Fleet had been eliminated as a force in the Western Pacific and the invasion of the Philippines could go forward. In this essay the author, Lieutenant Commander Thomas J. Cutler, U.S. Navy (Retired), author of The Battle of Leyte Gulf *(2000), places the battle in its historical-military context before taking the reader step by step through the various facets of the battle that spelled the end of effective Japanese naval power—although introducing into warfare the dreaded Japanese kamikaze suicide planes. This essay was originally titled "Greatest of All Sea Battles" when published in* Naval History *(8/5 [Sept.–Oct. 1994], 10–18. Copyright © 1994 by United States Naval Institute/www.navalinstitute.org. Reprinted with the permission of the publisher.*

The Battle of Leyte Gulf was the biggest and most multifaceted naval battle in history. It involved hundreds of ships, nearly 200,000 participants, and spanned more than 100,000 square miles. Some of the largest and most powerful ships ever built were sunk, and thousands of men went to the bottom of the sea with them. Every facet of naval warfare—air, surface, subsurface, and amphibious—was involved in this great struggle, and the weapons used included bombs of every type, guns of every caliber, torpedoes, mines, rockets, and even a forerunner of the modern guided missile.

But more than mere size made this battle significant. The cast of characters included such names as Halsey, Nimitz, MacArthur, even Roosevelt. It introduced the largest guns ever used in a naval battle and a new Japanese tactic that would eventually kill more U.S. sailors and sink more U.S. ships than any other used in the war. It was the last clash of the dreadnoughts and the first and only time that gunfire sank a U.S. aircraft carrier. It was replete with awe-inspiring heroism, failed intelligence, sapient tactical planning and execution, flawed strategy, brilliant deception, incredible ironies, great controversies, and a plethora of lessons about strategy, tactics, and operations.

If all this is true, why is Leyte Gulf not a household word—like Pearl Harbor? Why have fewer Americans heard of it than the Battle of Midway or the Normandy invasion of Europe? The answer lies in timing. Leyte Gulf occurred late in the war, after several years of conflict, when great battles had become commonplace. Tales from such places as Midway, Stalingrad, Guadalcanal, and Normandy were by then frequent fare. More significant, however, was that the Battle of Leyte Gulf happened when most of the United States had accepted ultimate victory as merely a matter of time rather than as a debatable question. Midway was accepted widely as the turning point of the war in the Pacific, a dramatic reversal of what had been a losing trend. The D-Day invasion at Normandy was seen as the true beginning of the end of war in Europe. But many saw Leyte Gulf as the continuation of a normal and inevitable trend. Lacking the drama of earlier battles, Leyte Gulf was then eclipsed by later events—a near-reversal at the Battle of the Bulge, ferocious fighting at Iwo Jima and Okinawa, and the cataclysmic dropping of atomic bombs on Hiroshima and Nagasaki.

But the Battle of Leyte Gulf was indeed pivotal. It represented the last hope of the Japanese Empire and the last significant sortie of the Imperial Japanese Navy. It was vastly important to millions of Filipinos and thousands of Allied prisoners of war whose liberation from Japanese oppression depended upon it. And, while a U.S. victory in the battle may have been viewed as somewhat mundane by that stage of the war, a defeat would have been disastrous.

Prelude

On 11 March 1942, a U.S. Army general stood at the water's edge and surveyed his wilting domain. Where lush vegetation and vibrantly colored tropical flowers had flourished, all that remained was the shattered remnants of an army on the verge of capitulation. Trees had been reduced to mere jagged stumps. Buildings that had housed a proud garrison lay in ruin. General Douglas MacArthur, 25 pounds lighter than he had been three months earlier, removed his gold-encrusted khaki cap and raised it in a final salute to Corregidor, the island-fortress he had been ordered to abandon.

In the gathering darkness of those early days of the war, when defeat had followed defeat, the brave but futile stand that MacArthur's forces had made on the fortified peninsula of Bataan had been a welcome ray of light. MacArthur had been elevated to heroic proportions not equaled since Admiral George Dewey had defeated the Spanish Fleet in these same Philippine waters at the close of the last century. To allow him to fall into the hands of an enemy whose propagandists predicted that they would see him hanged publicly in the Imperial Plaza in Tokyo was simply unthinkable. So President Franklin D. Roosevelt had ordered the general to leave.

This was no simple order. First, there was the natural reluctance of the general to abandon his command. Then came the realization that escape from the Philippines was more easily ordered than carried out. Japanese forces virtually controlled the air and sea approaches such that only a bold and clandestine move had any hope of success. And finally, there were MacArthur's special ties to the Philippines. His father, General Arthur MacArthur, had been both war hero and military governor there, and young Douglas's first assignment after graduating from West Point had been a tour of duty in the Philippines as a second lieutenant in the elite Corps of Engineers. He returned there several more times during his career, and by the time the Japanese landed troops at Lingayen Gulf in December 1941, MacArthur had become a field marshal of the Philippine Army and commander of U.S. Army Forces in the Far East.

As evening darkness descended upon Manila Bay and rain-laden clouds erased the moon, Lieutenant John D. Bulkeley's *PT-41* threaded its way through the defensive minefield and headed for the blackened waters of Mindoro Strait, where enemy ships were known to prowl. On board, General MacArthur vowed to recover from this ignominious moment, to avenge the inevitable defeat, to come back as soon as possible with the forces necessary to drive out the invading Japanese, and to restore the honor of the United States—and his own. In a few days he voiced this determination to the world, capturing the imagination of those Americans and Filipinos who had placed their faith in him with three small but powerful words: "I shall return."

The Return

The course of the war dictated that two years would pass before MacArthur could make good on his promise. By the time U.S. forces were poised to recapture the Philippines, the Battle of Midway had turned the tide of battle in the Pacific, amphibious assaults on Japanese island strongholds had become almost commonplace, and the most powerful fleet in U.S. history roamed the Pacific in search of a final showdown with the Imperial Japanese Navy.

But at last, in October 1944, MacArthur was able to make his promised return, bringing a huge invasion force to land on Leyte Island on the eastern side of the Philippine archipelago. In support of that momentous invasion, the Joint Chiefs of Staff had assigned Vice Admiral Thomas C. Kinkaid to command the naval forces that would actually carry out the assault. Kinkaid's forces were designated the Seventh Fleet. Admiral William F. Halsey, in command of the awesome striking power of the Third Fleet—consisting of four powerful task forces containing 14 aircraft carriers and more than 1,000 aircraft—lurked nearby in case the Japanese Navy showed up to contest the landing.

On 20 October, a landing craft crunched up onto the shore of Leyte Island, and the bow-door rattled down into the surf. The craft was still some distance from the dry sand of the beach, so General MacArthur and his entourage had to step off into knee-deep water and wade the rest of the way in. It was one of those moments that carved a graven image in the American heritage.

MacArthur strode across the sand to a waiting microphone and transmitter. He took the handset and held it close to his lips.

"People of the Philippines," MacArthur said in his resonant voice. "I have returned."

The gray skies above opened suddenly, and rain cascaded from the clouds like tears so fitting to this emotional moment.

"By the grace of Almighty God," MacArthur continued. "Our forces stand again on Philippine soil—soil consecrated in the blood of our two peoples."

With the sounds of mortal combat still thundering around him, soldiers of both sides dying not far away, this man, whom many characterized as an egotistical demagogue and others worshipped as a military saint, sent his words out over the Philippine archipelago to a people who had long awaited his return. "The hour of your redemption is here," he intoned, and countless numbers of Filipinos rejoiced. "Your patriots have demonstrated an unswerving and resolute devotion to the principles of freedom that challenge the best that is written on the pages of human history."

In the years that followed, MacArthur's detractors panned this moment. They accused him of "grandstanding," which is undeniable. They criticized his use of the first-person, which is certainly questionable. Some even characterized his speech as trite and overblown, which is arguable. But an objective observer would recognize that this was truly an important moment in history. Just as General Dwight D. Eisenhower had spoken on the shores of Normandy to a people long-suffering under the boot of Adolf Hitler's tyranny, so General MacArthur had given new hope to a people who had trusted in the United States to free them from Japanese domination.

"Rally to me," MacArthur challenged. And many did. In the months following the landing at Leyte, many Filipinos laid down their lives, fighting as guerrillas in the Japanese rear as U.S. troops pushed on inexorably through the islands. These people, at least, had listened when MacArthur said, "Let the indomitable spirit of Bataan and Corregidor lead on. As the lines of battle roll forward to bring you within the zone of operations, rise and strike. Strike at every favorable opportunity. For your homes and hearths, strike! For future generations of your sons and daughters, strike! In the name of your sacred dead, strike!"

The Response

Just after midnight on 18 October 1944, the sound of anchor chains rattling in hawsepipes drifted across the still waters of the Lingga Roads [in Borneo] anchorage as seven battleships, 15 cruisers, and 20 destroyers of the Imperial Japanese Navy prepared to get under way. Deep in the bellies of these great steel whales, young sailors, firing their boilers, turned huge valve-wheels to regulate the flow of the oil, which at the moment was more precious than gold to the Japanese Empire.

Most of these vessels were combat-hardened veterans of the Pacific War, many still pocked with the scars of battle, some partially debilitated by the ravages of war and long ocean transits. The cruiser *Mogami* had endured a horrific pounding at Midway. Yet there she was, still afloat, still able to inflict great harm, under way for the Philippines and a chance for revenge. The battleship *Haruna*, which had struck a German mine in World War I and had been reported sunk time and again in this one, steamed out of the Lingga anchorage, her shadowy form hauntingly vague in the subdued light of the distant stars. The destroyer *Shigure*, veteran of the Coral Sea, Solomons, and New Guinea campaigns, had been the sole Japanese survivor at the battle in Vella Gulf. As her crew worked to bring her anchor into short stay, some of them surely wondered if their luck would continue through the coming engagement.

Of all the ships making up this powerful force, the most formidable were the gigantic battleships *Yamato* and *Musashi*. At the time, these two 862-foot-long, 70,000-ton behemoths were the largest surface warships ever built.

This formidable task force, under Vice Admiral Takeo Kurita, was the most powerful element in a multifaceted operation the Japanese had dubbed *Sho Go*, Operation Victory. This complex plan relied heavily upon both timing and surprise and called for Kurita to hit the U.S. forces from two different directions in what is traditionally called a pincer attack. After refueling in [nearby] Brunei, the larger of the two elements, including the superbattleships *Yamato* and *Musashi*, would remain in Kurita's tactical command and proceed northward, then cut through the Philippine archipelago using the Sibuyan Sea as passage. Once across this rather narrow inland waterway, this force would pass through San Bernardino Strait, proceed south along the coast of the island of Samar and attack the U.S. landing forces at Leyte Gulf from the north.

Meanwhile, the other, smaller element, consisting of the battleships *Yamashiro* and *Fuso*, the heavy cruiser *Mogami*, and four destroyers, was placed under the command of Vice Admiral Shoji Nishimura. It would sortie from Brunei after Kurita's force and take the shorter but more hazardous route through the Philippines via the Sulu and Mindanao seas. With proper timing, Nishimura would pass through Surigao Strait and enter Leyte Gulf from the south at about the same time Kurita's force was attacking from the north.

Complexity and the need for near-perfect timing were obvious disadvantages to the plan, but the biggest problem facing the Japanese was that the United States had such an overwhelming advantage in available forces. Japanese intelligence reports, though not perfect, were providing a reasonably accurate assessment of what was waiting at Leyte. The Japanese were aware of the large amphibious fleet (Kinkaid's Seventh) that was spearheading the invasion. If this were the only force to contend with, Kurita thought his two-pronged attack would have an excellent chance for success. But the Japanese knew that Halsey's forces were also lurking about, spoiling for a fight, and they also knew that they had no hope of surviving a battle with such a gargantuan agglomeration of naval striking power. Halsey and Kinkaid together had more than enough forces available to take on any number of pincer elements, coming from any number of directions. How then could the Japanese hope to contend with such overwhelming odds?

The answer lay in an age-old weapon that served inferior forces for as long as there has been warfare. Deception was to be the offsetting element that might negate some of the preponderant U.S. advantage. Although the Japanese knew that their carrier striking forces had been rendered impotent by their lack of trained pilots, they reasoned that the U.S. forces might not fully appreciate this fact and might still consider the carriers a force to reckon with. So the Japanese command had decided that Admiral Jisaburo Ozawa's role in the forthcoming battle would be to serve as a decoy. His carrier striking forces had been rendered virtually useless by catastrophic losses of pilots and aircraft at the Battle of the Philippine Sea the previous June (known popularly as the "Marianas Turkey Shoot"). These carriers had been operating in Japanese home waters since the June battle, trying desperately but hopelessly to train new pilots and effect repairs.

Hoping that the United States was not fully cognizant of how limited these carriers were, the Japanese plan called for Ozawa to approach from the north in a straightforward manner, hoping to be detected in order to lure some portion of the U.S. forces away from Leyte Gulf. With luck, it would be the U.S. carrier striking forces that would be lured away, giving Kurita's powerful surface ships a fighting chance of carrying out their mission against the amphibious forces at Leyte. The success of the plan depended upon how much the Japanese could draw off the U.S. Navy's air power to chase Ozawa. Except for the support land-based air forces stationed in the Philippines could provide, Kurita would be very vulnerable to air attack once he moved within range of U.S. aircraft. Operation Victory was a long shot. But the plan was workable.

Sibuyan and Sulu Seas

On the morning of 24 October 1944, Admiral Halsey initiated the first phase of the Battle for Leyte Gulf when he picked up a radio handset and ordered the aircraft squadrons of his powerful Third Fleet: "Strike! Repeat: Strike!" Earlier that morning his reconnaissance aircraft had spotted Kurita's force on the western side of the Sibuyan Sea [in the center of the archipelago] and had discovered Nishimura's force starting to cross the Sulu Sea [farther to the south]. Hundreds of U.S. aircraft took to the skies to intercept these oncoming Japanese forces.

Aircraft from the USS *Enterprise* (CV-6) reached Nishimura's force in the Sulu Sea and launched a coordinated but largely ineffective attack that caused minor damage to the battleship *Fuso* and the destroyer *Shigure*. Undaunted, Nishimura's force continued to Surigao Strait.

In the Sibuyan Sea, lookouts in Kurita's force had spotted the earlier reconnaissance planes from Halsey's force. Kurita had increased speed immediately to 24 knots and prepared for battle. Tense minutes ticked by as the Japanese waited for the attack. The night before, Kurita's ships had been attacked by two U.S. submarines in the Palawan Passage west of the Philippines. Two cruisers had been sunk, one of them Kurita's flagship, and the admiral had been rescued from the sea by one of his destroyers and later transferred to the superbattleship *Yamato*.

Two hours passed before radar finally detected the anticipated U.S. aircraft, and at 1025 they roared in off the starboard beam. This first engagement lasted only 24 minutes, but it was intense and not without consequence to both sides. Extra antiaircraft guns had been added to Kurita's ships when it had become clear that Japanese air power would lend little support, making these ships very prickly prey. Battleships, cruisers, and even the destroyers bristled with hundreds more 25-mm guns than they had ever had before, and the effect was noticeable. Several of the torpedo bombers were splashed in the early moments of the attack and a Hellcat fighter soon joined them. But a number of the U.S. aircraft penetrated the wall of heavy fire, and great geysers leaped skyward from the water close aboard Kurita's flagship, *Yamato*. The heavy cruiser *Myoko* was damaged severely and began to limp, soon falling behind Kurita's formation.

Kurita's lookouts spotted the second wave of U.S. aircraft at a little past noon. The planes went for the Japanese force like angry bees out of the hive. In just minutes, three of the torpedo planes had left their stingers in the superbattleship *Musashi*, which set a pattern as subsequent attack waves began concentrating on the same ship.

All day the attacks continued. Wave after wave of U.S. aircraft descended upon Kurita's hapless force. With no air cover, Kurita's ships had no hope of victory and little for survival. Although U.S. aircraft were falling from the sky and airmen were dying, the virtually endless supply of planes and pilots pouring forth from Halsey's great fleet ensured the outcome. As the day wore on, the incoming strikes grew larger in number, and proportionately fewer aircraft succumbed as more and more Japanese antiaircraft batteries fell silent.

As the day wore on, the *Musashi*—a vessel once proclaimed unsinkable by her Japanese designers—began to list. The great battleship had absorbed 19 torpedo hits and nearly as many bombs. Most of her bow was under water. Her crew had tried to run her aground rather than sink—at least that way her great guns could remain in service as a gigantic shore-battery—but damage to her steering equipment relegated her to slow circles in the

Sibuyan Sea, and it seemed only a matter of time before she would succumb. As evening approached, the *Musashi* began to roll slowly to port, gaining momentum as she went. Sailors ran along the rotating hull in the opposite direction like lumberjacks at a log-rolling contest, trying to stay on the upward side of the ship. Many of them were barefooted in preparation for the anticipated swim, and the barnacles encrusted along what had been her underwater hull lacerated their feet as they ran. Some dived into the sea only to be sucked back into the ship through gaping torpedo holes. Within minutes, the battleship was standing on end, her gigantic propellers high in the evening sky, her bow already deep in the dark sea. She paused there for a moment; then there was a convulsive underwater explosion, and the *Musashi* plunged into the deep, taking half of her 2,200-man crew with her.

Despite his serious losses and a temporary turn back to the west, Admiral Kurita's force had shown incredible stamina in the face of the aerial onslaught. The remainder of his force, still potent by any standard, continued on across the Sibuyan Sea toward San Bernardino Strait, the passage that would take him to Leyte Gulf.

Midwatch in Surigao Strait

As darkness descended over the Philippines and Kurita's force pressed on toward San Bernardino Strait, Rear Admiral Jesse B. Oldendorf, Kinkaid's subordinate in command of Seventh Fleet's Bombardment and Fire Support Group, prepared to meet Nishimura's force approaching Leyte Gulf from the south through Surigao Strait. Partly because of a geographical accident and partly because of sensible planning, Oldendorf had prepared quite a reception for Nishimura.

Approaching through the confined strait would force the Japanese to maintain a narrow formation. Oldendorf's disposition of forces would put the oncoming Japanese force into the jaws of several succeeding pincers, as PT boats and destroyers gnawed at his flanks along the way. This alone would have been a difficult gauntlet to run. But the array of battleships and cruisers across the northern end of the strait was something out of the oldest textbooks on naval tactics, known as "capping the 'T' " and giving the U.S. ships a tremendous advantage in firepower by placing Oldendorf at the advantageous cap and the unfortunate Nishimura forming the vulnerable base of the T.

With the moon and stars blanketed by clouds, ensuring total darkness in the strait, Nishimura headed for the southern end of the strait that Ferdinand Magellan had once sailed in his famed circumnavigation of the earth. The U.S. PT boats attacked valiantly but were driven off, suffering more damage than they were able to inflict. Although these diminutive craft had little effect on the oncoming Japanese, their radio reports provided Oldendorf with valuable information on the enemy's progress up the strait.

The next phase of the battle began when U.S. destroyers charged down the strait, sowing the blackened waters with torpedoes while withholding gunfire so as not to reveal their positions. This time the damage to Nishimura's ships was severe.

Toward the end of the midwatch in one of the U.S. destroyers retiring from the fray, a young torpedoman peered into the darkness and said, "Would you look at that?" His voice was full of wonder. "Over there. Off the starboard side. In the sky." Several crimson streaks of light flashed across the sky from north to south like meteors. Several more followed almost immediately. A throaty rumble like distant thunder, felt more than heard, rolled in from the north. "The heavies are shooting," someone said.

Oldendorf's cruisers and battleships had indeed begun their barrage. On board one of the destroyers still pressing the attack down in the strait, a squadron commodore heard a strange sound overhead and looked up. In the black sky above he saw the tracer shells of the cruisers and battleships arcing their way southward, adding to the damage inflicted by the destroyers. "It was quite a sight," he later said. "It honestly looked like the Brooklyn Bridge at night—the tail lights of automobiles going across Brooklyn Bridge."

The Battle of Surigao Strait proved to be an epoch of history. In those brief and terrible minutes, surface ships fought surface ships without the intrusion of those interlopers from the sky that had stolen the show from the gunships in this war. Battleships at last unleashed the havoc they were designed for. Yet it was not the grand show long dreamed about. Despite their frightful destructive power, in this showdown in Surigao Strait their little brothers, the destroyers, outdid these leviathans. The torpedo that—for all of its early-war development problems and in spite of its inability to measure up to the pyrotechnic glamor of gunfire—had done the most damage in that last night surface action. The great guns spoke in anger that night, not merely at an enemy with whom they had a score to settle, but also in frustration at their own untimely impotence, in one final gasp of pent-up fury that would serve as a ceremonial salute to their own passing.

As the sun rose next morning, several columns of thick black smoke towered into the brightening sky like remnants of the black shroud that had engulfed Surigao Strait the night before. The morning light revealed clusters of men clinging to debris littering the waters of the strait, and large smears of oil stretched for miles. As U.S. destroyers moved in to pick up the Japanese survivors, most of them swam away or disappeared beneath the oily water, shunning rescue in one last great act of noble defiance.

Far to the north, in Leyte Gulf, U.S. sailors in the amphibious transports had spent the night watching with fascination and some dread as the flashes of gunfire had reflected off the clouds to the south. They need not have worried. The scorecard for this battle was an impressive one, and notably one-sided. All told, the Japanese had lost two battleships, three cruisers, and four destroyers as a result of this last of the great gun and torpedo battles. By comparison, one U.S. destroyer and several PT boats had been damaged in the action. One of the PTs was sunk, but no other U.S. ships had been lost. Exact personnel casualty figures for the Japanese are unknown, but they were in the thousands. The United States had lost but 39 men, with another 114 wounded.

As 25 October 1944 got under way, the U.S. Navy had dealt another devastating blow to its Imperial Japanese counterpart. But the Battle of Leyte Gulf was not yet over. What naval historian Samuel Eliot Morison later dubbed "the main action" had not yet occurred. Only a few more hours were left to this greatest of all sea battles, but before they were over, many more ships and men would perish.

"Charge of the Light Brigade"

Despite the one-sided victory in Surigao Strait, the potential for disaster loomed rather large on the morning of the 25th. The day before, Third Fleet reconnaissance aircraft had detected Ozawa's decoy force coming down from the north, and Halsey had taken the bait. Mistakenly believing that his earlier strikes in the Sibuyan Sea had eliminated Kurita's fleet, the aggressive Admiral Halsey took his entire fleet northward in pursuit of Ozawa's carrier forces, leaving the entrance to San Bernardino Strait unguarded. With Halsey's massive striking power lured northward and Kinkaid's Seventh Fleet punch drawn southward to cover Surigao Strait, the landing forces in the gulf were left virtually unprotected and would be easy pickings for a marauding force of gunships such as the one on its way through San Bernardino Strait. Confused communications caused by an awkward command structure and by some unwarranted assumptions on the part of both Halsey and Kinkaid had exacerbated the situation.

Thus, the only element left between Kurita and the vulnerable transports in the gulf were the Seventh Fleet escort carriers (CVEs) and their accompanying destroyers. Any tactician worth his salt could see that this was no great obstacle. The CVEs were, after all, merely cheap imitations of the larger and more potent CVs and CVLs, brought to Leyte Gulf to provide air support to the troops on shore and to hunt for submarines. They were ill prepared for a surface battle of any description, much less one with a force of Kurita's size and power.

So, by a combination of clever tactical deception and dogged determination on the part of the Japanese, and poor communications and some misjudgment on the part of the U.S. Navy, the greatly outclassed Japanese fleet had managed to set itself up for what just days before had seemed impossible. Despite the costly setbacks in Palawan Passage, the Sibuyan Sea, and Surigao Strait, the Japanese had achieved the main objective of their elaborate plan. The door was open to Leyte Gulf.

Admiral Kurita steamed through that open door during the night of 24–25 October, emerging from San Bernardino Strait into the Philippine Sea with the expectation of running headlong into waiting U.S. forces. All he found was an empty sea.

Expecting to be pounced on at any moment, Kurita headed south. For the next six-and-a half hours anxious Japanese eyes scanned the surface for ominous shadows, while weary ears listened to the strange chorus echoing in the ocean's depths, trying to discern manmade sounds from the natural ones residing there. As the sky brightened in the east, the tension level increased. Soon the skies, too, would be potentially hostile as U.S. warbirds left their nocturnal roosts to begin their diurnal search for prey.

Finally, just before 0630, lookouts spotted several masts piercing the horizon to the southeast. They were the telltale thin masts of U.S. ships, and as Kurita turned his formation toward them, more masts appeared on the horizon. It soon became clear that a sizable U.S. force lay ahead. Probably because the Japanese were expecting to encounter Halsey's powerful Third Fleet, the lookouts began mistakenly reporting the U.S. ships as full-size carriers, cruisers, and even battleships, instead of the Seventh Fleet CVEs and escorts that they actually were. By this error the Japanese forfeited a great psychological advantage, entering the battle with a fatalistic feeling of sacrifice and little hope of victory rather than with the confidence that should have accompanied this tremendous tactical advantage.

Nevertheless, Kurita did not hesitate to attack, and he ordered his fleet to engage the enemy. Within minutes, the *Yamato*'s mighty 18.1-inch guns were firing for the first time at enemy shipping. The Battle of Samar was under way.

Ironically, this was the anniversary of the Crimean War's Battle of Balaclava, in which a much inferior British cavalry unit charged against the heavy artillery of the Russians, inspiring Alfred Lord Tennyson to write his immortal poem, "The Charge of the Light Brigade." In a similar act of suicidal courage, the U.S. destroyers and destroyer escorts of the vulnerable escort carriers came about and charged headlong at the giant Japanese attackers. Furthermore, although they were not equipped to fight heavily armored ships, the escort carriers' aircraft also attacked the oncoming Japanese battleships and cruisers.

What followed was one of the wildest melees in naval history, marked by errors of judgment, innovative tactics, terrible carnage, and selfless valor. The U.S. escort ships and aircraft had no hope of defeating, nor even inflicting serious damage upon their Japanese adversaries. Yet they attacked with a tenacity that rivals the awe-inspiring feats of John Paul Jones, Stephen Decatur, and David Farragut. By their sacrificial actions and the confusion that resulted among the Japanese forces, the day was saved. Kurita, still believing he was fighting far more powerful forces, broke off the engagement at the critical moment and retired. In his wake were the sunken remains of four U.S. ships and their noble crews: two destroyers, one destroyer escort, and one aircraft carrier—a terrible loss in human terms; an incredible achievement in terms of the cold calculus of war. By all rights, many more U.S. ships should have been at the bottom of the Philippine Sea.

> When can their glory fade?
> O the wild charge they made!
> All the world wondered.
> Honour the charge they made!
> Honour the Light Brigade,
> Noble six hundred!

Epitaph

Far to the north, Halsey's powerful Third Fleet was engaging Ozawa's force at about the same time the wild melee was proceeding off Samar. The magnitude of the battle of Leyte Gulf comes better into perspective when one considers that this northernmost engagement—in which four aircraft carriers, a cruiser, and two destroyers were sunk—can be reasonably described as anticlimactic. With no insult intended toward those who fought there, this Halsey-Ozawa showdown remembered as the Battle of Cape Engaño was almost mundane in comparison to the other actions associated with Leyte Gulf. It was unquestionably one-sided, yet it was indecisive. It was fought by unquestionably brave men, yet there were no unusual feats of bravery recorded. It was the result of a successful diversion on the part of Ozawa, yet Kurita's failure to press his advantage at Samar robbed the diversion of its real impact.

Particularly frustrating was the missed chance for Halsey's battleships to get into the fray. In response to desperate calls for help in the south once Kurita had begun his attack, Halsey had broken off his battleships from the carrier force and headed south in a hopeless chase that served only to place those powerful gunships in a frustrating limbo between battles. Although Halsey would never admit his mistake in going north after Ozawa's decoy force, he would later lament his decision to take his battleships south, saying "I consider this the gravest error I committed during the Battle of Leyte Gulf."

In the final analysis, the battle was not decisive in the same sense that the Battle of Midway had been. What occurred there in Philippine waters did not alter the course of the war. But, perhaps just as significant, the result of the Leyte Gulf battle permitted the course of the war to continue. This has less dramatic appeal than a reversal, but from the U.S. point of view it was no less important. Had the Japanese prevailed in their fairly modest goal of disrupting the landings, the impact on the U.S. conduct of the war could have had some far-reaching consequences.

In trying to convince President Roosevelt of the importance of recapturing the Philippines, MacArthur had warned the president earlier about the postwar ramifications of by-passing this important archipelago, pointing out that U.S. prestige in the Far East would suffer a serious blow if the Philippines were not liberated. A similar loss of credibility could well have resulted from defeat.

This gargantuan sea battle, ensuring the recapture of the Philippines, cut Japan's oil supply lines once and for all. Without oil, it would only be a matter of time before the once-powerful Japanese war machine would grind to a halt.

At battle's end, Japan had lost four aircraft carriers, three battleships (including one of her super-dreadnoughts), nine cruisers, a dozen destroyers, hundreds of aircraft, and thousands of airmen and sailors. It was a tremendous defeat by any standard, and it ensured that the Imperial Japanese Navy had finally been eliminated as a meaningful threat in the Pacific.

XI

❧❧❧

Cold War and Korea, 1945–1960

The Korean War: A Fresh Perspective

Harry G. Summers, Jr.

Long referred to as "the forgotten war," the Korean War of 1950–1953 is now being reexamined in light of the various conflicts in which the American military has been involved during the last half-century. One of these reexaminations was undertaken by the late Colonel Harry G. Summers, Jr. (U.S. Army, Retired), author of On Strategy, *a classic work on the Vietnam War, and founding editor of* Vietnam *magazine. In this essay Summers not only gives a broad overview of the conflict but also discusses how governmental and military strategy was affected by the war both then and since, lamenting the fact that lessons learned are too often soon forgotten. From* Military History, *April 1996, by Harry G. Summers, Jr. Copyright © 1996 by* Military History. *Reprinted by permission of PRIMEDIA Enthusiasts Publications (History Group).*

Dismissed as the "forgotten war," Korea was in actuality one of America's most significant conflicts. Although born of a misapprehension, the Korean War triggered the buildup of U.S. forces in the North Atlantic Treaty Organization (NATO), began American involvement in the Vietnam War, and, although seen as an aberration at the time, now serves as the very model for America's wars of the future.

One reason the importance of the Korean War is not better appreciated is that from the very start the conflict presented confusing and contradictory messages. Historian and Korean War combat veteran T.R. Fehrenbach wrote in his classic *This Kind of War*: "Americans in 1950 rediscovered something that since Hiroshima they had forgotten: you may fly over a land forever; you may bomb it, atomize it, pulverize it, and wipe it clean of life—but if you desire to defend it, protect it, and keep it for civilization, you must do this on the ground the way the Roman legions did, by putting your young men into the mud."

Fehrenbach concluded: "By April 1951, the Eighth Army had again proven Erwin Rommel's assertion that American troops knew less but learned faster than any fighting men he had opposed. The tragedy of American arms, however, is that having an imperfect sense of history, Americans sometimes forget as quickly as they learn." Those words proved to be only too true.

Two years later, as the war came to an end, Air Force Secretary Thomas K. Finletter declared that "Korea was a unique, never-to-be-repeated diversion from the true course of strategic air power." For the next quarter century, nuclear weaponry dominated U.S. military strategy. As a result, General Maxwell D. Taylor, the Eighth Army's last wartime commander (and later chairman of the Joint Chiefs of Staff during the Vietnam War), complained that "there was no thoroughgoing analysis ever made of the lessons to be learned from Korea, and later policy makers proceeded to repeat many of the same mistakes."

The most damning mistake those policy-makers made was to misjudge the true nature of the war. As Karl von Clausewitz, the renowned Prussian philosopher of war, wrote in 1832: "The first, the supreme, the most far-reaching act of judgment that the statesman and the commander has to make is to establish . . . the kind of war on which they are embarking. . . . This is the first of all strategic questions and the most important."

As President Harry S. Truman's June 27, 1950, war message makes evident, the U.S. assumption was that monolithic world communism, directed by Moscow, was behind the North Korean invasion. "The attack upon Korea makes it plain beyond all doubt," said Truman, "that Communism has passed beyond the use of subversion to conquer independent nations and will now use armed invasion and war."

That belief, later revealed as false, had enormous and far-reaching consequences. Believing that Korea was a diversion and that the main attack would come in Europe, the United States began a major expansion of its NATO forces. From 81,000 soldiers and one infantry division stationed in Western Europe when the war started, by 1952 the U.S. presence had increased to six divisions—including the National Guard's 28th and 43rd Infantry divisions—503 aircraft, 82 warships and 260,800 men, slightly more than the 238,600 soldiers then in combat in Korea.

Another critical action was the decision to become involved in Vietnam. In addition to ordering U.S. military forces to intervene in Korea, Truman directed "acceleration in the furnishing of military assistance to the forces of France and the Associated States in Indo-China and the dispatch of a military mission to provide close working relations with those forces."

On September 17, 1950, Military Assistance Advisory Group (MAAG) Indochina was formed, an organization that would grow to the half-million-strong Military Assistance Command Vietnam (MACV) before U.S. involvement in that country came to an end almost a quarter century later. As in Korea, the notion that monolithic world communism was behind the struggle persisted until almost the very end.

The fact that such an assumption was belied by 2,000 years of Sino-Vietnamese hostility was ignored, and it was not until Richard Nixon's diplomatic initiatives in 1970 that the United States became aware of, and began to exploit, the fissures in that so-called Communist monolith. By then it was too late, for the American people had long since given up on Vietnam.

The fact that the U.S. response to both the Korean War and the Vietnam War was built on the false perception of a Communist monolith began to emerge after the dissolution of the Soviet Union in December 1991. At a July 1995 conference I attended at Georgetown University, Dr. Valeri Denissov, deputy director of the Asian Department of the Russian Foreign Ministry, revealed the true nature of the Korean War's origins.

Drawing from the hitherto secret documents of the Soviet Foreign Ministry, Denissov revealed that far from being the instigator of the war, Soviet Premier Josef Stalin was at best a reluctant partner. In September 1949, the Politburo of the Soviet Communist Party rejected an appeal from North Korea's Kim Il Sung to assist in an invasion of the South. But in April 1950, says Denissov, Stalin changed his mind and agreed to provide assistance for an invasion of the South. For one thing, Kim had convinced Stalin that the invasion was a low-risk operation that could be successfully concluded before the United States could intervene.

"Thus," said Denissov, "the documents existing in Russian archives prove that . . . it was Kim Il Sung who unleashed the war upon receiving before-hand blessings from Stalin and Mao Zedong [Mao Tse-tung]."

Why did Stalin change his mind? The first reason lay in Mao Tse-tung's victory in the Chinese Third Civil War. Denissov asserted that "Stalin believed that after the U.S.A. deserted Chiang Kai-shek 'to his own fortunes' in the internal Chinese conflict they would not risk a participation in a Korean-Korean war as well." Another factor, Denissov believed, was that "the Soviet Union had declared the creation of its own nuclear bomb, which according to Stalin's calculations deprived Americans of their nuclear monopoly and of their ability to use the 'nuclear card' in the confrontation with the Soviet Union."

Another Russian Foreign Ministry official at the conference, Dr. Evgeny Bajanov, added yet another reason for Stalin's change of heart—the "perceived weakness of Washington's position and of its will to get involved militarily in Asia."

That perception was well-founded. Dispatched to Korea at the end of World War II to disarm the Japanese there, the U.S. military was not too fond of the country from the start. When I arrived at the replacement depot at Yongdungpo in November 1947, our group was addressed by Lt. Gen. John R. Hodge, commander of the XXIV Corps and of U.S. forces in Korea. "There are only three things the troops in Japan are afraid of," he said. "They're gonorrhea, diarrhea and Korea. And you've got the last one."

After a year with the 6th Infantry Division in Pusan—a time spent mostly confined to barracks because of the civil unrest then sweeping the country—I was only too glad to see the division deactivated in December 1948 and myself transferred to the 24th Infantry Division in Japan. In 1949, the 7th Infantry Division, the only remaining U.S. combat unit in Korea, was also transferred to Japan, leaving only the several hundred men of the Korean Military Advisory Group (KMAG).

"In Moscow," Denissov said, "American military presence in South Korea in 1945–1949 was viewed as a 'deterring factor' which became defunct after America's withdrawal from the South." Yet another sign of lack of American will was Secretary of State Dean Acheson's public statement in January 1950 that Korea was outside the U.S. defense perimeter in Asia. Finally, Moscow must have been well aware of the drastic cuts made in America's defenses by the false economies of Truman and Louis Johnson, his feckless secretary of defense.

While Stalin's and Kim Il Sung's perceptions of U.S. lack of resolve may have been well-founded, they were also wrong. During a Pentagon briefing in 1974, General Vernon Walters, then deputy director of the Central Intelligence Agency (CIA), was asked about the unpredictability of U.S. reaction. "If a Soviet KGB spy had broken into the Pentagon or the State Department on June 25, 1950, and gained access to our most secret files," Walters said, "he would have found the U.S. had no interest at all in Korea. But the one place he couldn't break into was the mind of Harry Truman, and two days later America went to war over Korea."

In taking the United States to war in Korea, Truman made two critical decisions that would shape future military actions. First, he decided to fight the war under the auspices of the United Nations, a pattern followed by President George Bush in the Persian Gulf War in 1991 and, currently, by President Bill Clinton in Bosnia. Second, for the first time in American military history, Truman decided to take the nation to war without first asking Congress for a declaration of war. Using the U.N. Security Council resolution as his authority, he said the conflict in Korea was not a war but a "police action."

With the Soviet Union then boycotting the U.N. Security Council, the United States was able to gain approval of U.N. resolutions labeling the North Korean invasion a "breach of the peace" and urging all members to aid South Korea.

The United States was named executive agent for the conduct of the war, and on July 10, 1950, Truman appointed General of the Army Douglas MacArthur as commander in chief of the U.N. Command. In reality, however, the U.N. involvement was a facade for unilateral U.S. action to protect its vital interests in northeast Asia. The U.N. Command was just another name for MacArthur's Far East Command in Tokyo.

At its peak strength in July 1953, the U.N. Command stood at 932,539 ground forces. Republic of Korea (ROK) army and marine forces accounted for 590,911 of that force, and U.S. Army and Marine forces for another 302,483. By comparison, other U.N. ground forces totaled some 39,145 men, 24,085 of whom were provided by British Commonwealth Forces (Great Britain, Canada, Australia and New Zealand) and 5,455 of whom came from Turkey.

While the U.N. facade was a harmless delusion, Truman's decision not to seek a declaration of war set a dangerous precedent. Claiming their war making authority rested in their power as commanders in chief, both Presidents Lyndon B. Johnson and Richard M. Nixon refused to ask Congress for approval to wage war in Vietnam, a major factor in undermining support for that conflict. It was not until the Gulf War in 1991 that then President Bush rejected suggestions that he follow the Korean precedent and instead, as the Constitution provides, asked Congress for permission to wage war.

All those political machinations, however, were far from the minds of those of us then on occupation duty in Japan. We were as surprised as Stalin and Kim Il Sung at Truman's orders to go into action in Korea. For one thing, we were far from ready. I was then a corporal with the 24th Infantry Division's heavy tank battalion, only one company of which was activated—and that unit was equipped not with heavy tanks but with M-24 Chaffee light reconnaissance tanks, armed with low-velocity 75mm guns, that proved to be no match for the North Koreans' Soviet-supplied T-34 85mm-gun medium tanks.

Also inadequate were the infantry's 2.36-inch anti-tank rocket launchers. Radios did not work properly, and we were critically short of spare parts. Instead of the usual three rifle battalions, the infantry regiments had only two. And our field artillery battalions had only two of their three authorized firing batteries. Although our officers and sergeants were mostly World War II combat veterans, we were truly a "hollow force."

The 24th Infantry Division was the first U.S. ground combat unit committed to the war, with its initial elements landing in Korea on July 1, 1950. We soon found ourselves outgunned by the advancing North Korean People's Army (NKPA). All of our tanks were lost to the NKPA T-34s, and our commander was killed for want of a starter solenoid on our tank retriever. Going into action with some 16,000 soldiers, the 24th Division had only 8,660 men left by the time it was relieved by the 1st Cavalry Division on July 22.

The shock of those initial disasters still reverberates throughout the U.S. Army more than four decades later. After the end of the Cold War in 1991, the watchwords of Army Chief of Staff General Gordon Sullivan were

"Remember Task Force Smith," a warning not to let the Army again become the hollow force of 1950 that paid in blood for America's unpreparedness.

Task Force Smith was the first of the 24th Infantry Division's units to be committed. Named after its commander, Lt. Col. Charles B. "Brad" Smith, the task force consisted of the 1st Battalion, 21st Infantry, and "A" Battery, 52nd Field Artillery Battalion. The task force came under attack by the infantry columns of the NKPA 4th Infantry Division and the T-34s of the 209th Armored Brigade at Osan on July 5, 1950. Outnumbered and unable to stop the NKPA tanks, it was forced to fall back toward Taejon. There, the remainder of the 24th Infantry Division made a stand until July 20, before being pushed back into the Naktong Perimeter—losing the commander, Maj. Gen. William F. Dean (captured by the NKPA), in the process. Although at a terrible price, it had bought time for the remainder of the Eighth U.S. Army (EUSA) to move from Japan to Korea. Contrary to Kim Il Sung's calculations, America had been able to intervene in time. North Korea's attempt to conquer South Korea in one lightning stroke had been thwarted.

Wars are fought on three interconnected levels. At first, the United States was on the operational (i.e., theater of war) and tactical (i.e., battlefield) defensive, but at the strategic (i.e., national policy) level, it was still pursuing the same policy of "roll-back and liberation" that it had followed in earlier wars. That policy called for temporarily going on the defensive to buy time to prepare for a strategic offensive that would carry the war to the enemy in order to destroy his will to resist.

While EUSA held the Naktong River line against a series of North Korean assaults, General MacArthur laid plans to assume the strategic, operational and tactical offensive with a landing behind enemy lines at Inchon.

In a brilliant strategic maneuver, MacArthur sent his X Corps ashore on September 15, 1950. Consisting of the Army's 7th Infantry Division and the Marine 1st Division, it rapidly cut the enemy's lines of supply and communication to its forces besieging the Naktong Perimeter to the south, forcing them to withdraw in disarray. While X Corps pressed on to recapture Seoul, South Korea's capital city, EUSA broke out of the Naktong Perimeter and linked up with X Corps near Osan on September 26. Seoul fell the next day.

"After the Inchon landing," Secretary of State Acheson told the Senate in May 1951, "General MacArthur called on these North Koreans to turn in their arms and cease their efforts; that they refused to do, and they retired into the North, and what General MacArthur's military mission was, was to pursue them and round them up [and] we had the highest hopes that when you did that the whole of Korea would be unified."

On Korea's western coast, EUSA crossed the 38th parallel dividing North and South Korea and captured the North Korean capital of Pyongyang on October 19, 1950. EUSA continued to drive north against light opposition, and on November 1, 1950, it reached its high-water mark when the village of Chongdo-do, 18 air miles from the Yalu River separating

Korea and the Chinese province of Manchuria, was captured by the 21st Infantry Regiment.

Meanwhile, on the opposite coast, X Corps had moved into northeastern Korea. The 1st Marine Division occupied positions around the Chosin Reservoir, while on November 21, elements of the Army's 7th Infantry Division's 17th Infantry Regiment reached the Yalu River near its source at Hyesanjin in eastern Korea. It seemed as though the war was over.

But disaster was at hand. On October 4, 1950, Chairman Mao Tse-tung had secretly ordered "Chinese People's Volunteers" into action in Korea. Those Chinese Communist Forces (CCF) consisted of some 380,000 soldiers, organized into two army groups, nine corps-size field armies and 30 infantry divisions.

From October 13 to 25, the 130,000-man CCF XIII Army Group covertly crossed the Yalu River in the western sector opposite EUSA. Two weeks later, the 120,000-man CCF IX Army Group also moved surreptitiously into the eastern sector in Korea, opposite X Corps. Because of intelligence failures, both in Washington and in Korea, the Chinese managed to achieve almost total surprise. Their intervention would change not only the battlefield conduct of the war but also its strategic nature.

According to the Soviet archives, in May 1950, Mao had agreed to join with the Soviet Union and support the North Korean invasion of South Korea. As the Russian Foreign Ministry's Evgeny Bajanov noted at the 1995 Georgetown conference, Chinese Foreign Minister Chou En-lai "confirmed [on July 2, 1950] that if the Americans crossed the 38th parallel, Chinese troops disguised as Koreans would engage the opponent" and that Chinese armies had already been concentrated in the area of Mukden in Manchuria. "In August-September 1950 on a number of occasions," said Bajanov, "Mao personally expressed concerns over the escalation of American military intervention in Korea and reiterated the readiness of Beijing to send troops to the Korean peninsula 'to mince' American divisions." But when Stalin sent a message to Mao on October 1, asking him to "come to the rescue of the collapsing Kim regime," Mao refused, instead suggesting "the Koreans should accept defeat and resort to guerrilla tactics."

Under intense Soviet pressure, however, on October 13, "the Chinese, after long deliberation, did agree to extend military aid to North Korea," said Bajanov. "Moscow in exchange agreed to arm the Chinese troops and provide them with air cover. According to the available information, it was not easy for Beijing to adopt that military decision. Pro-Soviet Gao Gang and Peng Dehuai [who would later command the CCF in Korea] finally managed to convince Mao to take their side. Their main argument was that if all of Korea was occupied by the Americans, it would create a mortal danger to the Chinese revolution."

In any event, after feints in early November against EUSA at Unsan and against X Corps at Sudong, both of which were ignored by Far East

Command intelligence officers, the CCF launched its main attack. On November 25, the XIII Army Group struck the EUSA, driving it out of North Korea and retaking Seoul on January 4, 1951. Meanwhile, on November 27, the CCF IX Army Group struck X Corps, and by December 25, 1950, had forced its evacuation from North Korea as well.

At first, both Moscow and Beijing were elated. On January 8, 1951, Bajanov reported, Stalin cabled Mao, "From all my heart I congratulate Chinese comrades with the capture of Seoul." But Bajanov added, "By the end of January 1951 . . . the euphoria of Communists started to decline and quite soon it disappeared and was replaced with worries, fear, confusion and at times panic."

What made the difference was Lt. Gen. Matthew B. Ridgway, who took command of EUSA on December 26, 1950, replacing Lt. Gen. Walton H. Walker, who had been killed in a jeep accident. Ridgway turned EUSA from dejection and defeat into a tough, battle-ready force within a matter of weeks. "The Eighth Army," wrote Fehrenbach, "rose from its own ashes in a killing mood. . . . By 7 March they stood on the Han. They went through Seoul, and reduced it block by block. . . . At the end of March, the Eighth Army was across the parallel."

Attempting to stem that tide, on April 22, 1951, the CCF launched its great spring offensive, sending some 250,000 men and 27 divisions into the attack along a 40-mile front north of Seoul. It was the largest battle of the war, but by May 20 the CCF, after some initial gains, had been turned back with terrible losses. As *Time* magazine put it, "The U.S. expended ammunition the way the Chinese expended men." After that success, the United States was in good position to retake the offensive and sweep the CCF from Korea. But Washington ordered EUSA to maintain its defensive posture, for U.S. military policy had changed from rollback and liberation to containment. That ruled out battlefield victory, for the best possible result of defensive operations is stalemate.

On July 10, 1951, armistice talks began between the U.N. Command and the CCF/NKPA. After the front line stabilized in November 1951, along what was to become the new demarcation line, the fighting over the next 20 months degenerated into a bloody battle for terrain features like Old Baldy, Heartbreak Ridge and Pork Chop Hill. The U.S. forces suffered some 63,200 casualties to gain or retain those outposts. With victory no longer in sight, public support for the war plummeted, and in 1952 Truman decided not to run for re-election rather than risk almost certain defeat. With the signing of the armistice agreement on July 27, 1953, the war finally came to an end.

Dwarfed by the total U.S. victory in World War II, the negotiated settlement in Korea seemed to many observers to be a defeat and at best a draw. Certainly it seemed no model for the future.

As indicated previously, it was Eisenhower's strategy of massive nuclear retaliation that dominated the immediate postwar era. Conventional forces, like the Korean War itself, were dismissed as irrelevant. Even when the atomic war strategies were challenged by the John F. Kennedy administration's policy of flexible response, conventional forces were still ignored in favor of the "new" counterinsurgency war. Vietnam would be its test case.

The Vietnam War, like the Korean War, was pursued on the strategic defensive—the United States still not realizing that the best result possible was stalemate. In Korea, U.S. forces kept the external enemy at bay while giving local forces responsibility for counterguerrilla operations. But in Vietnam, this strategy—the only one with any hope of success—was regarded as ineffective, even though the Korean War objective of preserving South Korea's independence had been attained.

Only in the wake of an unqualified failure in Vietnam, where Saigon fell not to guerrilla attack but to a Korea-style cross-border blitzkrieg by the North Vietnamese army, did the limited validity of both nuclear war and counterinsurgency operations become evident. The most probable future conflict was still a war fought with conventional weapons in pursuit of limited political goals—in short, another Korea.

That was exactly what happened in the 1990–91 Persian Gulf War, and what the Pentagon is now prepared for with its policy of being able to fight two regional conflicts almost simultaneously.

One of those potential regional conflicts is Korea. As President Bill Clinton told the Korean National Assembly in July 1993, "The Korean peninsula remains a vital American interest." As proof of U.S. resolve, almost a half century after it was decimated at Kunu-ri protecting EUSA's withdrawal from North Korea, the 2nd U.S. Infantry Division currently sits astride the Seoul invasion corridor as a tripwire guaranteeing certain U.S. involvement in any future conflict there.

Truman Fires MacArthur
David McCullough

Two strong personalities—the imperious General Douglas MacArthur and the flinty President Harry S. Truman—came to a spectacular clash in April 1951 in the midst of the Korean War over American political and military strategy and presidential prerogatives regarding that conflict. Truman won. In this essay David McCullough, Truman's distinguished biographer, gives a full and balanced account of the president's firing of one of the nation's top military icons from command, arguing that Truman was correct in relieving the US-UN Far East commander despite the temporary political fallout from his action. From MHQ: The Quarterly Journal of Military History, *Autumn 1992, by David McCullough. Copyright © 1992 by* MHQ: The Quarterly Journal of Military History. *Reprinted by permission of PRIMEDIA Enthusiasts Publications (History Group).*

In the history of American arms, few personal showdowns have been quite so freighted with consequence as the confrontation between Harry S. Truman and Douglas MacArthur. How often do two such major figures find themselves on a collision course, from which neither is willing to veer? On the one hand, there was Truman, the artillery captain of World War I, the accidental president, the surprise election victor of 1948, whose decisions at the start of the cold war would define the West's diplomatic and military policies for forty years. On the other, there was MacArthur, twice a Medal of Honor winner, the supreme commander of Allied forces in the southwest Pacific during World War II, the sometimes brilliant strategist turned benevolent autocrat who had presided over the reconstruction—and democratization—of Japan. This American Kitchener was a genuine hero; but then (although people did not recognize it at the time), so was Truman. The two men distrusted each other at long distance—they would meet only once. "Mr. Prima Donna, Brass Hat, Five Star MacArthur," Truman had once noted in his diary. "Don't see how a country can produce such men as Robert E. Lee, John J. Pershing, Eisenhower, and Bradley and at the same time produce Custers, Pattons, and MacArthurs." The feeling was mutual.

It was the crisis of the Korean War that brought on the confrontation. On June 24, 1950, North Korean tanks had crossed the 38th parallel into the Republic of South Korea, in a blitzkrieglike attack. The United States had persuaded the United Nations to intervene, and MacArthur was given overall command. Meanwhile, the outnumbered and outgunned South Korean forces, along with contingents of American troops airlifted from Japan, tried vainly to delay the onslaught of the North Korean "People's Army." In the next months, as disaster changed to triumph and then disaster again, and a third world war loomed, Truman would come to one of the most difficult decisions of his presidency. What follows is excerpted from a book that is already being recognized as one of the signal American biographies of recent years, David McCullough's Truman, *just published by Simon & Schuster.*

It was, in many respects, one of the darkest chapters in American military history. But MacArthur, now in overall command of the U.N. forces, was trading space for time—time to pour in men and supplies at the port of Pusan—and the wonder was the North Koreans had been kept from overrunning South Korea straightaway. Despite their suffering and humiliation, the brutal odds against them, the American and Republic of Korea units had done what they were supposed to, almost miraculously. They had held back the landslide, said Truman, who would rightly call it one of the most heroic rearguard actions on record.

In the first week of July, MacArthur requested 30,000 American ground troops, to bring the four divisions of his Eighth Army to full strength. Just days later, on July 9, the situation had become so "critical" that he called for a doubling of his forces. Four more divisions were urgently needed, he said in a cable that jolted Washington.

The hard reality was that the army had only ten divisions. In Western Europe there was but one, and as former British prime minister Winston Churchill noted in a speech in London, the full allied force of twelve divisions in Western Europe faced a Soviet threat of eighty divisions. The NATO allies were exceedingly concerned lest the United States become too involved in distant Korea. Years of slashing defense expenditures, as a means to balance the budget, had taken a heavy toll. For all its vaunted nuclear supremacy, the nation was quite unprepared for war. But now, in these "weeks of slaughter and heartbreak," that was to change dramatically and with immense, far-reaching consequences.

On Wednesday, July 19, first in a special message to Congress, then in an address to the nation, Truman said the attack on Korea demanded that the United States send more men, equipment, and supplies. Beyond that, the realities of the "world situation" required still greater American military strength. He called for an emergency appropriation of $10 billion—the final sum submitted would be $11.6 billion, or nearly as much as the entire $13 billion military budget originally planned for the fiscal year—and announced he was both stepping up the draft and calling up certain National Guard units.

"Korea is a small country thousands of miles away, but what is happening there is important to every American," he told the nation, standing stone-faced in the heat of the television lights, a tangle of wires and cables at his feet. By their "act of raw aggression . . . I repeat, it was raw aggression," the North Koreans had violated the U.N. Charter, and though American forces were making the "principal effort" to save the Republic of South Korea, they were fighting under a U.N. command and a U.N. flag, and this was a "landmark in mankind's long search for a rule of law among nations."

As a call to arms it was not especially inspirational. Nor did he once use the word *war* to describe what was happening in Korea. But then neither was there any question about his sincerity, nor was he the least evasive about what would be asked of the country. The "job" was long and difficult. It meant increased taxes, rationing if necessary, "stern days ahead." In another televised address at summer's end, he would announce plans to double the armed forces to nearly 3 million men. Congress appropriated the money—$48.2 billion for military spending in fiscal 1950–51, then $60 billion for fiscal 1951–52.

Was he considering use of the atomic bomb in Korea, Truman was asked at a press conference the last week of July. No, he said. Did he plan to get out of Washington anytime soon? No. He would stay on the job.

That Truman was less than fond or admiring of his Far Eastern commander, Douglas MacArthur, was well known to his staff and a cause of concern at the Pentagon. Truman's opinion in 1950 seems to have been no different from what it had been in 1945, at the peak of MacArthur's renown, when, in his journal, Truman had described the general as "Mr. Prima Donna, Brass Hat," a "play actor and bunco man." The president, noted his press aide Eben Ayers, expressed "little regard or respect" for MacArthur, calling him a "supreme egotist" who thought himself "something of a god." But working with people whom one did not like or admire was part of life—particularly the politician's life. Firing the five-star Far Eastern commander would have been very nearly unthinkable. John Foster Dulles told Truman confidentially that MacArthur should be dispensed with as soon as possible. Dulles, the most prominent Republican spokesman on foreign policy and a special adviser to the State Department, had returned from a series of meetings with MacArthur in Tokyo convinced the seventy-year-old general was well past his prime and a potential liability. Dulles advised Truman to bring MacArthur home and retire him before he caused trouble. But that, replied Truman, was easier said than done. He reminded Dulles of the reaction there would be in the country, so great was MacArthur's "heroic standing." Nonetheless, at this stage Truman expressed no doubt about MacArthur's ability. If anything, he seems to have been banking on it.

By the first week in August, American and ROK forces, dug in behind the Naktong River, had set up the final defense line to be known as the Pusan Perimeter, a thinly held front forming an arc of 130 miles around the port of Pusan. On the map it looked like a bare toehold on the peninsula. On the ground the fighting went on as savagely as before. But the retreat was over. At his briefing for the president on Saturday, August 12, in his customary, dry, cautious way, Omar Bradley, the chairman of the Joint Chiefs of Staff, described the situation, for the first time, as "fluid but improving."

Truman's special assistant Averell Harriman, meanwhile, had returned from a hurried mission to Tokyo, bringing the details of a daring new MacArthur plan. Harriman had been dispatched to tell the general of Truman's determination to see that he had everything he needed, but also to impress upon him Truman's urgent desire to avoid any move that might provoke a third world war. This was Truman's uppermost concern, and there must be no misunderstanding. In particular, MacArthur was to "stay clear" of Chiang Kai-shek. Truman had instructed Harriman to tell MacArthur that the Chinese Nationalist leader, now on Formosa, must not become the catalyst for a war with the Chinese Communists.

MacArthur had no reservations about the decision to fight in Korea, "absolutely none," Harriman reported to Truman at Blair House. MacArthur was certain neither the Chinese Communists nor the Soviets would intervene. MacArthur had assured Harriman that of course, as a soldier, he would do as the president ordered concerning Chiang Kai-shek, though something about his tone as he said this had left Harriman wondering.

Of greater urgency and importance was what Harriman had to report of a plan to win the war with one bold stroke. For weeks there had been talk at the Pentagon of a MacArthur strategy to outflank the enemy, to hit from behind, by amphibious landing on the western shore of Korea at the port of Inchon, 200 miles northwest of Pusan. Inchon had tremendous tides—30 feet or more—and no beaches on which to land, only seawalls. Thus an assault would have to strike directly into the city itself, and only a full tide would carry the landing craft clear to the seawall. In two hours after high tide, the landing craft would be stuck in the mud.

To Bradley it was the riskiest military proposal he had ever heard. But as MacArthur stressed, the Japanese had landed successfully at Inchon in 1904, and the very "impracticabilities" would help ensure the all-important element of surprise. As Wolfe had astonished and defeated Montcalm at Quebec in 1759 by scaling the impossible cliffs near the Plains of Abraham, so, MacArthur said, he would astonish and defeat the North Koreans by landing at the impossible port of Inchon. But there was little time. The attack had to come before the onset of the Korean winter exacted more casualties than the battlefield. The tides at Inchon would be right on September 15. Truman made no commitment one way or the other, but Harriman left Blair House convinced that Truman approved the plan.

By early August, General Bradley could tell the president that American strength at Pusan was up to 50,000, which, with another 45,000 ROKs and small contingents of U.N. allies, made a total U.N. ground force of nearly 100,000. Still, the prospect of diverting additional American forces for MacArthur's Inchon scheme pleased the Joint Chiefs not at all. Bradley continued to view it as "the wildest kind" of plan.

Then, on Saturday, August 26, the Associated Press broke a statement from MacArthur to the Veterans of Foreign Wars, in which he strongly defended Chiang Kai-shek and the importance of Chiang's control of Formosa: "Nothing could be more fallacious than the threadbare argument by those who advocate appeasement and defeatism in the Pacific that if we defend Formosa we alienate continental Asia." It was exactly the sort of dabbling in policy that MacArthur had assured Harriman he would, as a good soldier, refrain from.

Truman was livid. He would later say he considered but rejected the idea of relieving MacArthur of field command then and there and replacing him with Bradley. "It would have been difficult to avoid the appearance of demotion, and I had no desire to hurt General MacArthur personally."

But whatever his anger at MacArthur, to whatever degree the incident had increased his dislike—or distrust—of the general, Truman decided to give MacArthur his backing. "The JCS inclined toward postponing Inchon until such time that we were certain Pusan could hold," remembered Bradley. "But Truman was now committed." On August 28, the Joint Chiefs sent MacArthur their tentative approval.

In time to come, little would be said or written about Truman's part in the matter—that as commander in chief he, and he alone, was the one with the final say on Inchon. He could have said no, and certainly the weight of opinion among his military advisers would have been on his side. But he did not. He took the chance, made the decision for which he was neither to ask nor to receive anything like the credit he deserved.

In the early hours of September 15—it was afternoon in Washington, September 14—the amphibious landing at Inchon began. As promised by MacArthur, the attack took the enemy by total surprise; and as also promised by MacArthur, the operation was an overwhelming success that completely turned the tables on the enemy.

The invasion force numbered 262 ships and 70,000 men of the X Corps, with the 1st Marine Division leading the assault. Inchon fell in little more than a day. In eleven days Seoul was retaken. Meantime, as planned, General Walton Walker's Eighth Army broke out of the Pusan Perimeter and started north. Seldom in military history had there been such a dramatic turn in fortune. By September 27 more than half the North Korean army had been trapped in a huge pincer movement. By October 1, U.N. forces were at the 38th parallel and South Korea was under U.N. control. In two weeks it had become an entirely different war.

In Washington the news was almost unbelievable, far more than anyone had dared hope for. The country was exultant. It was a "military miracle." A jubilant Truman cabled MacArthur: "I salute you all, and say to all of you from all of us at home, 'Well and nobly done.' "

For nearly three months, since the war began, the question had been whether U.N. forces could possibly hang on and survive in Korea. Now, suddenly, the question was whether to carry the war across the 38th parallel and destroy the Communist army and the Communist regime of the north and thereby unify the country. MacArthur favored "hot pursuit" of the enemy. So did the Joint Chiefs, the press, politicians in both parties, and the great majority of the American people. And understandably. It was a heady time; the excitement of victory was in the air. Virtually no one was urging a halt at the 38th parallel. "Troops could not be expected . . . to march up to a surveyor's line and stop," said Secretary of State Dean Acheson.

Truman appears to have been as caught up in the spirit of the moment as anyone. To pursue and destroy the enemy's army was basic military doctrine. If he hesitated or agonized over the decision—one of the most fateful of his presidency—there is no record of it.

The decision was made on Wednesday, September 27. MacArthur's military objective now was "the destruction of the North Korean Armed Forces"—a very different objective from before. He was authorized to cross the 38th parallel, providing there was no sign of major intervention in North Korea by Soviet or Chinese forces. Also, he was not to carry the fight beyond the Chinese or Soviet borders of North Korea. Overall, he was free to do what had to be done to wind up the war as swiftly as possible. George Marshall, now secretary of defense, told him to "feel unhampered tactically and strategically," and when MacArthur cabled, "I regard all of Korea open for military operations," no one objected. Carrying the war north involved two enormous risks—intervention by the Chinese, and winter. But MacArthur was ready to move, and after Inchon, MacArthur was regarded with "almost superstitious awe."

At the end of the first week of October, at Lake Success, New York, the United Nations recommended that all "appropriate steps be taken to ensure conditions of stability throughout Korea," which meant U.N. approval for proceeding with the war. On October 9, MacArthur sent the Eighth Army across the 38th parallel near Kaesong, and on the following day, Truman made a surprise announcement: He was flying to an unspecified point in the Pacific to confer with General MacArthur on "the final phase" in Korea.

It was the kind of grand, high-level theater irresistible to the press and the American public. Truman and MacArthur were to rendezvous, as was said, like the sovereign rulers of separate realms journeying to a neutral field attended by their various retainers. The two men had never met. MacArthur had been out of the country since 1937. Truman had never been closer to the Far East than San Francisco.

The meeting place was a pinpoint in the Pacific—Wake Island, a minuscule coral way station beyond the international date line. The presidential expedition was made up of three planes: the *Independence* with Truman and his staff, physician, and Secret Service detail; an Air Force Constellation carrying Harriman, Dean Rusk, and Philip Jessup from the State Department, Army Secretary Frank Pace, Jr., and General Bradley, plus all their aides and secretaries, as well as Admiral Arthur Radford, commander of the Pacific Fleet, who came on board at Honolulu; and a Pan American Stratocruiser with thirty-five correspondents and photographers. General MacArthur flew with several of his staff, a physician, and John Muccio, the American ambassador to South Korea.

As a courtesy, Truman had let MacArthur choose the place for the meeting, and for the president, Wake Island meant a flight across seven time zones, a full round trip from Washington of 14,425 miles, while MacArthur had only to travel 4,000 miles from Tokyo and back. Events were moving rapidly in Korea, Truman would explain, "and I did not feel that he [MacArthur] should be away from his post too long."

To many the whole affair looked like a political grandstand play to capitalize on the sudden, unexpected success of the war and share in MacArthur's Inchon glory on the eve of the off-year elections in November. The president had been out of the headlines for some time, it was noted. Now he was back, and for those Democrats in Congress who were up for reelection, it was "the perfect answer to prayer and fasting." MacArthur himself, en route to Wake Island, appeared disgusted that he had been "summoned for political reasons." In fact, the idea for the meeting had originated with the White House staff as "good election year stuff," Charlie Murphy remembered, and at first Truman had rejected it for that very reason, for being "too political, too much showmanship." Apparently it was only after being reminded that Franklin Roosevelt had made just such a trip to meet with MacArthur at Hawaii in 1944 that Truman changed his mind. He appears to have had second thoughts, even as he flew the Pacific. "I've a whale of a job before me," he wrote on the plane. "Have to talk to God's right-hand man tomorrow. . . ."

The importance of the occasion, like its drama, centered on the human equation, the vital factor of personality. For the first time the two upon whom so much depended, and who were so strikingly different in nature, would be able to appraise one another not at vast distance, or through official communiqué or the views of advisers only, but by looking each other over. As Admiral Radford commented at the time, "Two men can sometimes learn more of each other's minds in two hours, face to face, than in years of correct correspondence." Truman, after returning, would remark simply, "I don't care what they say. I wanted to see General MacArthur, so I went to see him."

Also what would be largely forgotten, or misrepresented by both sides in time to come, after things turned sour, was how the meetings at Wake Island actually went, and what the president and the general actually concluded then, once having met.

Truman's plane put down at 6:30 A.M. on Sunday, October 15, just as the sun rose from the sea with spectacular brilliance, backlighting ranks of towering clouds. The single airstrip stretched the length of the island.

MacArthur was there waiting. Later, MacArthur would be pictured deliberately trying to upstage Truman by circling the airstrip, waiting for

Truman to land first, thus putting the president in the position of having to wait for the general. But it did not happen that way. MacArthur was not only on the ground, he had arrived the night before and was at the field half an hour early.

As Truman stepped from the plane and came down the ramp, MacArthur stood waiting at the bottom, with "every appearance of warmth and friendliness." And while onlookers noted also that the general failed to salute the president, and though Truman seems to have been somewhat put out by MacArthur's attire—his open-neck shirt and "greasy ham and eggs cap" (MacArthur's famed, gold-braided World War II garrison cap)—the greeting between them was extremely cordial.

MacArthur held out his hand. "Mr. President," he said, seizing Truman's right arm while pumping his hand, which experienced MacArthur watchers knew to be the number one treatment.

"I've been waiting a long time meeting you, General," Truman said with a broad smile.

"I hope it won't be so long next time, Mr. President," MacArthur said warmly.

Truman was dressed in a dark blue, double-breasted suit and gray Stetson. In Honolulu, he had outfitted his whole staff in Hawaiian shirts, but now he looked conspicuously formal, entirely presidential, and well rested, having slept during most of the last leg of the flight.

For the benefit of the photographers, he and MacArthur shook hands several times again, as a small crowd applauded. Then the two men climbed into the back seat of a well-worn black two-door Chevrolet, the best car available on the island, and drove a short distance to a Quonset hut by the ocean, where, alone, they talked for half an hour.

According to Secret Service Agent Henry Nicholson, who rode in the front seat beside Floyd Boring, the driver, Truman began talking almost immediately about his concern over possible Chinese intervention in Korea. Nicholson would distinctly recall Truman saying, "I have been worried about that."

At the Quonset hut, according to Truman's own account in his *Memoirs*, MacArthur assured him that victory was won in Korea and that the Chinese Communists would not attack. When MacArthur apologized for what he had said in his Veterans of Foreign Wars statement, Truman told him to think no more of it, he considered the matter closed—a gesture that so impressed MacArthur that he later made a point of telling Harriman. What more was said in the Quonset hut is not known, since no notes were taken and no one else was present. But clearly the time served to put both men at ease. Each, to judge by his later comments, concluded that the other was not as he had supposed.

About 7:30 they reemerged in the brilliant morning sunshine and again drove off, now to a flat-roofed, one-story, pink cinderblock shack, a Civil

Aeronautics administration building close to the beach where the Japanese had stormed ashore in 1941. Beyond the beach, blue Pacific rollers crashed over the dark hulks of two Japanese landing boats.

Some seventeen advisers and aides were waiting in a large, plain room. Truman, setting a tone of informality, said it was no weather for coats, they should all get comfortable. He sat in his shirt-sleeves at the head of a long pine table, MacArthur on his right, Harriman on the left, the rest finding places down the table or against the walls. MacArthur, taking out a briar pipe, asked if the president minded if he smoked. Everyone laughed. No, Truman said, he supposed he had had more smoke blown his way than any man alive.

The meeting proceeded without formal agenda, and as MacArthur later wrote, no new policies or war strategies were proposed or discussed. But the discussion was broad-ranging, with MacArthur doing most of the talking, as Truman, referring only to a few handwritten notes, asked questions. As so often before, MacArthur's performance was masterful. He seemed in full command of every detail and absolutely confident. The time moved swiftly.

MacArthur had only good news to report. The situation in Korea was under control. The war, "the formal resistance," would end by Thanksgiving. The North Korean capital, Pyongyang, would fall in a week. By Christmas he would have the Eighth Army back in Japan. By the first of the year, the United Nations would be holding elections, he expected, and American troops could be withdrawn entirely very soon afterward. "Nothing is gained by military occupation. All occupations are failures," MacArthur declared, to which Truman nodded in agreement.

Truman's first concern was keeping it a "limited" war. What were the chances of Chinese or Soviet intervention, he asked. "Very little," MacArthur said.

> Had they interfered in the first or second months it would have been decisive. We are no longer fearful of their intervention. . . . The Chinese have 300,000 men in Manchuria. Of these probably not more than 100,000 to 125,000 are distributed along the Yalu River. They have no Air Force. Now that we have bases for our Air Force in Korea, if the Chinese tried to get down to Pyongyang there would be the greatest slaughter.

The Russians, MacArthur continued, were a different matter. The Russians had an air force in Siberia and could put a thousand planes in action. A combination of Chinese ground troops and Russian air power could pose a problem, he implied. But coordination of air support with operations on the ground was extremely difficult and he doubted they could manage it.

The support he had been given from Washington was surpassing, MacArthur stressed. "No commander in the history of war," he said, looking around the table, "has ever had more complete and adequate support from all agencies in Washington than I have." How soon could he release a division for duty in Europe, Bradley wished to know. By January, MacArthur assured him.

Dean Rusk, concerned that the discussion was moving too fast, passed Truman a note suggesting he slow down the pace. Too brief a meeting, Rusk felt, would only fuel the cynicism of a press already dubious about the meeting. Truman scribbled a reply: "Hell, no! I want to get out of here before we get into trouble."

As to the need for additional U.N. troops, MacArthur would leave that for Washington to decide. It was then, at about 9:05, that Truman called a halt. "No one who was not here would believe we have covered so much ground as we have been actually able to cover," he said. He suggested a break for lunch while a communiqué was prepared. But MacArthur declined, saying he was anxious to get back to Tokyo and would like to leave as soon as possible—which to some in the room seemed to border on rudeness. "Whether intended or not," wrote Bradley, "it was insulting to decline lunch with the President, and I think Truman was miffed, although he gave no sign."

"The communiqué should be submitted as soon as it is ready, and General MacArthur can return immediately," Truman said. The conference had lasted one hour, thirty-six minutes.

In later studies, some historians would write that Truman had traveled extremely far for not much. But to Truman, at the time, it had all been worth the effort. He was exuberant. He had never had a more satisfactory conference, he told the reporters present. Tony Leviero of the *New York Times* described him beaming "like an insurance salesman who had at last signed up an important prospect."

The communiqué, which MacArthur read and initialed, stressed "the very complete unanimity of view" that had made possible such rapid progress at the conference table and called MacArthur "one of America's great soldier-statesmen." At the airstrip, in a little ceremony just before boarding his plane, Truman said still more as he honored MacArthur with a Distinguished Service Medal. He praised MacArthur for "his vision, his judgment, his indomitable will and unshakable faith," his "gallantry and tenacity" and "audacity in attack matched by few operations in history."

The whole spirit of Wake Island was one of relief and exhilaration. The awful bloodshed in Korea, the suffering, was all but over; the war was won. If MacArthur said there was "very little" chance of the Chinese coming in, who, after Inchon, was to doubt his judgment, particularly if what he said confirmed what was thought in Washington? If Truman and MacArthur had disliked or distrusted one another before, they apparently did so no longer. If the conference had accomplished that alone, it had been a success.

They said good-bye in the glaring sunshine of midday at Wake Island, as Truman boarded the *Independence*.

"Good-bye, sir," MacArthur said. "Happy landing. It has been a real honor talking to you."

It was their first and their last meeting. They never saw each other again.

November through December 1950 was a dreadful passage for Truman. Omar Bradley was to call these sixty days among the most trying of his own professional career, more so even than the Battle of the Bulge. For Truman it was the darkest, most difficult period of his presidency.

That Chinese troops had come into the war was by now an established fact, though how many there were remained in doubt. MacArthur estimated 30,000, and whatever the number, his inclination was to discount their importance. But in Washington concern mounted. To check the flow of Chinese troops coming across the Yalu, MacArthur requested authority to bomb the Korean ends of all bridges on the river, a decision Truman approved, after warning MacArthur against enlarging the war and specifically forbidding air strikes north of the Yalu, on Chinese territory.

Another cause of concern was MacArthur's decision, in the drive north, to divide his forces, sending the X Corps up the east side of the peninsula, the Eighth Army up the west—an immensely risky maneuver that the Joint Chiefs questioned. But MacArthur was adamant, and it had been just such audacity, after all, that had worked the miracle at Inchon.

With one powerful, "end-the-war" offensive, one "massive comprehensive envelopment," MacArthur insisted, the war would be quickly won. As always, he had absolute faith in his own infallibility, and while no such faith was to be found at the Pentagon or the White House, no one, including Truman, took steps to stop him.

Bitterly cold winds from Siberia swept over North Korea, as MacArthur flew to Eighth Army headquarters on the Chongchon River to see the attack begin. "If this operation is successful," he said within earshot of correspondents, "I hope we can get the boys home for Christmas."

The attack began Friday, November 24, the day after Thanksgiving. Four days later, on Tuesday, November 28, in Washington, at 6:15 in the morning, General Bradley telephoned the president at Blair House to say he had "a terrible message" from MacArthur.

"We've got a terrific situation on our hands," Truman told his staff a few hours later at the White House, having waited patiently through the routine of the morning meeting. The Chinese had launched a furious counterattack with a force of 260,000 men, Truman said. MacArthur was going over on the defensive. "The Chinese have come in with both feet."

Truman paused. The room was still. The shock of what he had said made everyone sit stiff and silent. Everything that had seemed to be going so well in Korea, all the heady prospects since Inchon, the soaring hopes of Wake Island were gone in an instant. But then Truman seemed to recover himself, sitting up squarely in his high-backed chair. "We have got to meet this thing," he said, his voice low and confident. "Let's go ahead now and do our jobs as best we can."

"We face an entirely new war," MacArthur declared. It had been all of three days since the launching of his "end-the-war" offensive, yet all hope of victory was gone. The Chinese were bent on the "complete destruction" of his army. "This command . . . is now faced with conditions beyond its control and its strength."

In further messages MacArthur called for reinforcements of the "greatest magnitude," including Chinese Nationalist troops from Formosa. His own troops were "mentally fatigued and physically battered." The directives he was operating under were "completely outmoded by events." He wanted a naval blockade of China. He called for bombing the Chinese mainland. He must have the authority to broaden the conflict, MacArthur insisted, or the administration would be faced with a disaster.

That same day, November 28, at three o'clock in the afternoon, a crucial meeting of the National Security Council took place in the Cabinet Room— one of the most important meetings of the Truman years. For it was there and then, in effect, with Truman presiding, that the decision was made not to let the crisis in Korea, however horrible, flare into a world war. It was a decision as fateful as the one to go into Korea in the first place, and stands among the triumphs of the Truman administration, considering how things might have gone otherwise.

General Bradley opened the discussion with a review of the bleak situation on the battlefield. Vice President Alben Barkley, who rarely spoke at such meetings, asked bitterly why MacArthur had promised to have "the boys home for Christmas"—how he could ever have said such a thing in good faith. Army Secretary Pace said that MacArthur was now denying he had made the statement. Truman warned that in any event they must do nothing to cause the commander in the field to lose face before the enemy.

When Marshall spoke, he sounded extremely grave. American involvement in Korea should continue as part of a U.N. effort, Marshall said. The United States must not get "sewed up" in Korea, but find a way to "get out with honor." There must be no war with China. That was clear. "To do this would be to fall into a carefully laid Russian trap. We should use all available political, economic and psychological action to limit the war."

"We can't defeat the Chinese in Korea," said Acheson. "They can put in more than we can." Concerned that MacArthur might overextend his operations, Acheson urged "very, very careful thought" regarding air strikes against Manchuria. If this became essential to save American troops, then it would have to be done, but if American attacks succeeded in Manchuria, the Soviets would probably come to the aid of their Chinese ally. The thing to do, the "imperative step," said Acheson, was to "find a line that we can hold, and hold it." Behind everything they faced was the Soviet Union, "a somber consideration." The threat of a larger war, wrote Bradley, was closer than ever, and it was this, the dread prospect of a global conflict with Russia erupting at any hour, that was on all their minds.

The news was so terrible and came with such suddenness that it seemed almost impossible to believe. The last thing anyone had expected at this point was defeat in Korea. The evening papers of November 28 described "hordes of Chinese Reds" surging through a widening gap in the American Eighth Army's right flank, "as the failure of the Allied offensive turned into a dire threat for the entire United Nations line." The whole Eighth Army was falling back. "200,000 OF FOE ADVANCE UP TO 23 MILES IN KOREA" read the banner headline across the *New York Times* the following day. The two calamities most dreaded by military planners—the fierce Korean winter and massive intervention by the Chinese—had fallen on the allied forces at once.

What had begun was a tragic, epic retreat—some of the worst fighting of the war—in howling winds and snow and temperatures as much as 25 degrees below zero. The Chinese not only came in "hordes" but took advantage of MacArthur's divided forces, striking both on their flanks. The Eighth Army under General Walton Walker was reeling back from the Chongchon River, heading for Pyongyang. The choice was retreat or annihilation. In the northeast the ordeal of the X Corps was still worse. The retreat of the 1st Marine Division—from the Chosin Reservoir forty miles to the port of Hungnam and evacuation—would be compared to Xenophon's retreat of the immortal ten thousand or Napoleon's withdrawal from Moscow.

"A lot of hard work was put in," Truman would remember of his own days in Washington. And, as Acheson would write, all the president's advisers, civilian and military, knew something was badly wrong in Korea, other than just the onslaught of the Chinese. There were questions about MacArthur's morale, grave concern over his strategy and whether on the actual battlefield a "new hand" was needed to replace General Walker. It was quite clear, furthermore, that MacArthur, the Far Eastern commander, had indeed deliberately disobeyed a specific order from the Joint Chiefs to use no non-Korean forces close to the Manchurian border.

But no changes in strategy were ordered. No "new hand" replaced Walker. No voices were raised against MacArthur. Regrettably, the president was ill-advised, Bradley later observed. He, Marshall, the Joint Chiefs, had all "failed the president." Here, in a crucial few days, said Acheson afterward, they missed their chance to halt the march to disaster in Korea.

Acheson was to lament their performance for the rest of his life. Truman would never put any blame on any of them, but Acheson would say Truman had deserved far better.

General Matthew Ridgway would "well remember" his mounting impatience "that dreary Sunday, December 3," as hour after hour in the War Room discussion continued over the ominous situation in Korea. Unable to contain himself any longer, Ridgway spoke up, saying immediate action must be taken. They owed it to the men in the field and "to the God to whom we must answer for those men's lives," to stop talking and do something. For the first time, Acheson later wrote, "someone had expressed what everyone thought—that the Emperor had no clothes on." But of the twenty men who sat at the table, including Acheson, and twenty more along the walls behind, no one else spoke. The meeting ended without a decision.

Why didn't the Joint Chiefs just send orders and tell MacArthur what to do, Ridgway asked the air force chief of staff, General Hoyt Vandenberg, afterward. Because MacArthur would not obey such orders, Vandenberg replied. Ridgway exploded. "You can relieve any commander who won't obey orders, can't you?" he said. But Vandenberg, with an expression Ridgway remembered as both puzzled and amazed, only walked away.

The next day, in another closed session, this time at the State Department, Dean Rusk would propose that MacArthur be relieved of command. But again, no one else commented.

MacArthur, meanwhile, was being taken to task by the press, as he had never been. *Time*, which had long glorified him, charged him with being responsible for one of the worst military disasters in history. An editorial in the New York *Herald-Tribune* referred to his "colossal military blunder." Unused to such criticism, his immense vanity wounded, MacArthur started issuing statements of his own to the press. He denied that his strategy had precipitated the Chinese invasion and said his inability to defeat the new enemy was due to restrictions imposed by Washington that were "without precedent."

Truman did not hold MacArthur accountable for the failure of the November offensive. But he deplored MacArthur's way of excusing the failure, and the damage his statements could do abroad, to the degree that they implied a change in American policy. "I should have relieved General MacArthur then and there," he would write much later.

As it was, he ordered that all military officers and diplomatic officials henceforth clear with the State Department all but routine statements before making them public, "and . . . refrain from direct communications on military or foreign policy with newspapers, magazines, and other publicity media." Dated December 6, the order was widely and correctly seen as directed to MacArthur.

Truman did not relieve the Far Eastern commander, he later explained, because he knew no general could be a winner every day and because he did not wish to have it appear that MacArthur was being fired for failing. What he might have done had Acheson, Marshall, Bradley, and the Joint Chiefs spoken up and insisted that MacArthur be relieved is another question and impossible to answer.

For now the tragedy in Korea overshadowed the rest. If MacArthur was in trouble, then everything possible must be done to help. "We must get him out of it if we can," Truman wrote in his diary late the night of December 2, following an intense session with Acheson, Marshall, and Bradley that had left him feeling desperately low. The talk had been of evacuating all American troops. Marshall was not even sure such an operation would succeed, should the Chinese bring in their own air power. "*It looks very bad*," Truman wrote. Yet bad as it was, there was no mood of panic, and this, as those around him would later attest, was principally because of Truman's own unflinching response.

The bloody retreat in Korea continued. Pyongyang fell "to overwhelming masses of advancing Chinese," as the papers reported. General Walker's Eighth Army was heading for the 38th parallel. But Truman remained calm and steady. He wrote in his diary, "I've worked for peace for five years and six months and it looks like World War III is here. I hope not—but we must meet whatever comes—and we will."

It was Harry Truman's long-standing conviction that if you did your best in life, did your "damndest" always, then whatever happened you would at least know it was not for lack of trying. But he was a great believer also in the parts played by luck and personality, forces quite beyond effort or determination. And though few presidents had ever worked so hard, or taken their responsibilities so to heart in time of crisis as Truman had since the start of the war in Korea, it was luck, good and bad, and the large influence of personality, that determined the course of events time and again, and never more so than in late December 1950, in the midst of his darkest passage.

Two days before Christmas, on an icy highway north of Seoul, General Walton Walker, commander of the Eighth Army, was killed when his jeep ran head-on into an ROK army truck. Walker's replacement—as requested by MacArthur and approved immediately by Truman—was Matthew Ridgway, who left Washington at once, arriving in Tokyo on Christmas Day. At his meeting with MacArthur the next morning, Ridgway was told to use his own judgment at the front. "The Eighth Army is yours, Matt. Do what you think best." MacArthur, wrote Dean Acheson later, "never uttered wiser words."

That afternoon, Ridgway landed at Taegu, and in the weeks following came a transformation no one had thought possible. Rarely has one individual made so marked a difference in so little time. With what Omar Bradley called "brilliant, driving, uncompromising leadership," Ridgway restored the fighting spirit of the Eighth Army and turned the tide of war as have few commanders in history.

Since the Chinese onslaught of November 28, the Eighth Army had fallen back nearly 300 miles, to a point just below the 38th parallel, and for a while Ridgway had no choice but to continue the retreat. Abandoning Seoul, Ridgway withdrew as far as Oswan, near the very point where the first green American troops had gone into action in July. Now, instead of the murderous heat of summer, they fought in murderous cold.

The mood in Washington remained bleak. MacArthur continued to urge a widening of the war—again he proposed bombing and blockading China and utilizing the troops of Chiang Kai-shek—and, as before, his proposals were rejected. Dire consequences would follow, he implied, unless policy were changed. He reported:

> The troops are tired from a long and difficult campaign, embittered by the shameful propaganda which has falsely condemned their courage and fighting qualities . . . and their morale will become a serious threat in their battlefield efficiency unless the political basis upon which they are being asked to trade life for time is clearly delineated. . . .

Truman found such messages "deeply disturbing." When a general complained about his troops' morale, observed Marshall, the time had come for the general to look to his own morale.

MacArthur called on the administration to recognize the "state of war" imposed by the Chinese, then to drop thirty to fifty atomic bombs on Manchuria and the mainland cities of China. The Joint Chiefs, too, told Truman that mass destruction of Chinese cities with nuclear weapons was the only way to affect the situation in Korea. But that choice was never seriously considered. Truman simply refused to "go down that trail," in Dean Rusk's words.

Truman also still refused to reprimand MacArthur. Rather he treated MacArthur with what Acheson considered "infinite patience"—too much infinite patience, Acheson thought, having by now concluded that the general was "incurably recalcitrant" and fundamentally disloyal to the purposes of his commander in chief.

Truman had by now declared a national emergency, announcing emergency controls on prices and wages, and still greater defense spending—to the amount of $50 billion, more than four times the defense budget at the start of the year. He had put Charles E. Wilson, head of the General Electric Company, in charge of a new Office of Defense Mobilization; appointed General Eisenhower as supreme commander of NATO; and, in a radio and television address to the nation on December 15, called on every citizen "to put aside his personal interests for the good of the country." So while doing all he could to avoid a wider war, he was clearly preparing for one. As Marshall later attested, "We were at our lowest point."

But then, on the morning of Wednesday, January 17, Marshall telephoned Truman to read an astonishing report just in from General Joe Collins, who had flown to Korea for talks with Ridgway. "Eighth Army in good shape and improving daily under Ridgway's leadership," Marshall read. "Morale very satisfactory. . . . Ridgway confident he can obtain two to three months' delay before having to initiate evacuation. . . . On the whole Eighth Army now in position and prepared to punish severely any mass attack."

Plainly MacArthur's bleak assessment of the situation, his forecasts of doom, had been wrong—and the effect of this realization was electrifying. As word spread through the upper levels of government that day, it would be remembered, one could almost hear the sighs of relief. The long retreat of the Eighth Army—the longest in American military history—had ended. On January 25, 1951, less than a month after Ridgway's arrival, the Eighth Army began "rolling forward," as he said.

By the end of March, having inflicted immense casualties on the Chinese, the Eighth Army was again at the 38th parallel. Yet Ridgway's progress seemed only to distress MacArthur further. Unless he was allowed to strike boldly at the enemy, he said, his dream of a unified Korea was impossible. He complained of a "policy void." He now proposed not only to massively attack Manchuria, but to "sever" Korea from Manchuria by laying down a field of radioactive wastes, "the by-products of atomic manufacture," all along the Yalu River. As so often before, his request was denied.

Talking to journalists on March 7, MacArthur lamented the "savage slaughter" of Americans inevitable in a war of attrition. When, by the middle of March, the tide of battle "began to turn in our favor," as Truman wrote, and Truman's advisers at both the State Department and the Pentagon thought it time to make a direct appeal to China for peace talks, MacArthur refused to respond to inquiries on the subject. Instead he decried any "further military restrictions" on his command. To MacArthur, as he later wrote, it appeared that Truman's nerves were at a breaking point— "not only his nerves, but what was far more menacing in the Chief Executive of a country at war—his nerve."

Truman ordered careful preparation of a cease-fire proposal. On March 21, the draft of a presidential statement was submitted for approval to the other seventeen U.N. nations with troops serving in Korea. On March 20 the Joint Chiefs had informed MacArthur of what was happening—sending him what Truman called the "meat paragraphs" of the statement in a message that seems to have impressed MacArthur as nothing else had that there was indeed to be no all-out war with Red China. His response so jarred Washington as to leave a number of people wondering if perhaps he had lost his mind. Years afterward Bradley would speculate that possibly MacArthur's realization that his war on China was not to be "snapped his brilliant but brittle mind."

On the morning of Saturday, March 24, in Korea (Friday the 23rd in Washington), MacArthur, without warning, tried to seize the initiative in a manner calculated only to inflame the situation. He issued his own florid proclamation to the Chinese Communists—in effect, an ultimatum. He began by taunting the Red Chinese for their lack of industrial power, their poor military showing in Korea against a U.N. force restricted by "inhibitions." More seriously, MacArthur threatened to expand the war.

> The enemy, therefore, must by now be painfully aware that a decision of the United States to depart from its tolerant effort to contain the war to the areas of Korea, through an expansion of our military operations to his coastal areas and interior bases, would doom Red China to the risk of imminent military collapse.

In conclusion, MacArthur said he personally "stood ready at any time" to meet with the Chinese commander to reach a settlement.

All Truman's careful preparations of a cease-fire proposal were now in vain. MacArthur had cut the ground out from under him. Later MacArthur would dismiss what he had said as a "routine communiqué." Yet his own devoted aide, General Courtney Whitney, would describe it as a bold effort to stop one of the most disgraceful plots in American history, meaning the administration's plan to appease China.

In his *Memoirs*, Truman would write that he now knew what he must do about MacArthur.

> This was a most extraordinary statement for a military commander of the United Nations to issue on his own responsibility. It was an act totally disregarding all directives to abstain from any declarations on foreign policy. It was in open defiance of my orders as President and as Commander in Chief. This was a challenge to the President under the Constitution. It also flouted the policy of the United Nations. . . .
>
> By this act MacArthur left me no choice—I could no longer tolerate his insubordination. . . .

And yet . . . MacArthur was not fired. Truman said not a word suggesting he had reached such a decision. He sent MacArthur only a restrained reprimand, a message he himself dictated to remind the general of the presidential order on December 6 forbidding public statements that had not been cleared with Washington.

Meantime, on March 14, the Gallup Poll had reported the president's public approval at an all-time low of 26 percent. And soon there were appalling new statistics: U.N. forces had now suffered 228,941 casualties, mostly South Koreans but including 57,120 Americans.

Truman was dwelling on the relationship between President Abraham Lincoln and General George B. McClellan during the Civil War, in the autumn of 1862, when Lincoln had been forced to relieve McClellan of command of the Army of the Potomac. Truman had sent one of his staff to the Library of Congress to review the details of the Lincoln-McClellan crisis and give him a report. Lincoln's troubles with McClellan, as Truman knew, had been the reverse of his own with MacArthur: Lincoln had wanted McClellan to attack, and McClellan refused time and again. But then, when Lincoln issued orders, McClellan, like MacArthur, ignored them. Also like MacArthur, McClellan occasionally made political statements on matters outside the military field. Truman later wrote that

> Lincoln was patient, for that was his nature, but at long last he was compelled to relieve the Union Army's principal commander. And though I gave this difficulty with MacArthur much wearisome thought, I realized that I would have no other choice myself than to relieve the nation's top field commander. . . .
>
> I wrestled with the problem for several days, but my mind was made up before April 5, when the next incident occurred.

On Thursday, April 5, at the Capitol, House Minority Leader Joe Martin took the floor to read a letter from MacArthur that Martin said he felt duty-bound to withhold no longer. In February, speaking in Brooklyn, Martin had called for the use of Chiang Kai-shek's troops in Korea and accused the administration of a defeatist policy. "What are we in Korea for—to win or to lose? . . . If we are not in Korea to win, then this administration should be indicted for the murder of American boys." Martin had sent a copy of the speech to MacArthur, asking for his "views." On March 20, MacArthur had responded—and virtually all that he said was bound to provoke Truman, as Martin well knew. Since MacArthur's letter carried no stipulation of confidentiality, Martin decided to make it public.

The congressman was right in calling for victory, MacArthur wrote, right in wanting to see Chinese forces from Formosa join the battle against communism. The real war against communism was in Asia, not in Europe. "There is no substitute for victory."

The letter was on the wires at once. At the Pentagon, Bradley called a meeting of the Joint Chiefs. "I did not know that Truman had already made up his mind to relieve MacArthur," he remembered, "but I thought it was a strong possibility." The Joint Chiefs, however, reached no conclusion about MacArthur.

On Friday, April 6, official Cadillacs filled the White House driveway. Marshall, Bradley, Acheson, and Harriman met with the president for an hour. Saying nothing of his own views, Truman asked what should be done. When Marshall urged caution, Acheson agreed. To the latter it was not so much a problem of what should be done as how it should be done. He later remembered:

> The situation could be resolved only by relieving the General of all his commands and removing him from the Far East. Grave trouble would result, but it

could be surmounted if the President acted upon the carefully considered ad-vice and unshakable support of all his civilian and military advisers. If he should get ahead of them or appear to take them for granted or be impetuous, the harm would be incalculable.

"If you relieve MacArthur," Acheson told Truman, "you will have the biggest fight of your administration."

Harriman, reminding the president that MacArthur had been a problem for too long, said he should be dismissed at once. "I don't express any opin-ion or make known my decision," Truman wrote in his diary. "Direct the four to meet again Friday afternoon and go over all phases of the situation."

He was a model of self-control. For the next several days, an air of un-natural calm seemed to hang over the White House. "The wind died down," remembered Joe Martin. "The surface was placid . . . nothing happened."

On Saturday, Truman met again with Marshall, Acheson, Bradley, and Harriman, and again nothing was resolved. Marshall and Bradley were still uncertain what to do. They were hesitating in part, according to Bradley's later account, because they knew the kind of abuse that would be hurled at them personally—an understandable concern for two such men at the end of long, distinguished careers.

On Monday, April 9, the same foursome convened with the president once more, this time at Blair House. But now the situation had changed. The Joint Chiefs had met the afternoon before and concluded that from a mili-tary point of view, MacArthur should be relieved. Their opinion was unani-mous. Truman, for the first time, said he was of the same opinion. He had made his decision. He told Bradley to prepare the necessary papers.

"Rarely had a matter been shrouded in such secrecy at the White House," reported the Washington *Post* on Tuesday, April 10. "The answer to every question about MacArthur was met with a 'no comment' reply." In Tokyo, according to a United Press dispatch, a member of MacArthur's staff said meetings between the general and Secretary of the Army Pace were "going forward with an air of cordiality"—thus seeming to refute dismissal rumors. A photograph on page 1 of the *Post* showed a smiling MacArthur welcoming an even more smiling Pace at the Tokyo airport.

At the end of a routine morning staff meeting, the president quietly announced—"So you won't have to read about it in the papers"—that he had decided to fire General MacArthur. He was sure, Truman added, that MacArthur had wanted to be fired. He was sure also that he himself faced a political storm, "a great furor," unlike any in his political career. From be-yond the office windows, the noise of construction going on in the White House was so great that several of the staff had to strain to hear Truman. At 3:15 that afternoon, Acheson, Marshall, Bradley, and Harriman reported to the Oval Office, bringing the drafted orders. Truman looked them over, borrowed a fountain pen, and signed his name.

The orders were to be sent by State Department channels to Ambassador Muccio in Korea, who was to turn them over to Secretary Pace, who by now was also in Korea, with Ridgway at Eighth Army headquarters. Pace was to return at once to Tokyo and personally hand the orders to MacArthur—this whole relay system having been devised to save the general from the embarrassment of direct transmission through regular army communications. All aspects of the issue thus far had been kept secret with marked success, but it was essential that there be no leaks in the last critical hours. Announcement of the sensational news about MacArthur was not to be made until the following morning.

The next several hours passed without incident, until early evening. Harriman, Bradley, Rusk, and six or seven of Truman's staff were working in the Cabinet Room, preparing material for release, when Press Secretary Joe Short received word that a Pentagon reporter for the Chicago *Tribune*, Lloyd Norman, was making inquiries about a supposed "major resignation" to take place in Tokyo—the implication being that somehow MacArthur had already learned of Truman's decision and was about to resign before Truman could fire him.

Bradley telephoned Truman at about nine o'clock to report there had been a leak. Truman, saying he wanted time to think, told Bradley to find Marshall and Acheson. Marshall, it was learned, had gone to a movie, but Acheson came to the White House immediately; he thought it would be a mistake to do anything rash because of one reporter's inquiry. As he had from the start, Acheson stressed the importance of the manner in which the general was dismissed. It was only fair and proper that he be informed before the story broke.

Meantime, something apparently had gone wrong with the transmission of the president's orders. Nothing had been heard from Muccio about their receipt. By 10:30, Truman had decided. Short telephoned the White House to have all the orders—those relieving MacArthur, as well as those naming Matthew Ridgway his successor—mimeographed as quickly as possible.

"He's not going to be allowed to quit on me," Truman reportedly said. "He's going to be fired!" In his diary Truman recorded dryly, "Discussed the situation and I ordered messages sent at once and directly to MacArthur."

From a small first-floor study in his Georgetown home, Dean Acheson began placing calls to various officials. At the State Department, Rusk spent a long night telephoning the ambassadors of all the countries with troops in Korea. "Well, the little man finally did it, didn't he," responded the ambassador from New Zealand.

At the White House, switchboard operators began calling reporters at their homes to say there would be an extraordinary press conference at

1:00 A.M. And at 1:00 A.M. on Wednesday, April 11, Press Secretary Joe Short handed out the mimeographed sheets in the White House press-room. Truman, in his second-floor bedroom at Blair House, was by then fast asleep.

General MacArthur learned of his recall while at lunch in Tokyo, when his wife handed him a brown Signal Corps envelope. If Truman had only let him know how he felt, MacArthur would say privately a few hours later, he would have retired "without difficulty." Where the *Tribune* reporter got his tip was never revealed. MacArthur would later testify that he had never given any thought to resigning.

According to what MacArthur said he had been told by an unnamed but "eminent" medical authority, Truman's "mental instability" was the result of malignant hypertension, "characterized by bewilderment and confusion of thought." Truman, MacArthur predicted, would be dead in six months.

TRUMAN FIRES MACARTHUR

The headline across the early edition of the Washington *Post* on April 11, 1951, was the headline everywhere in the country and throughout much of the world, with only minor variations. The reaction was stupendous, the outcry from the American people shattering. Truman had known he would have to face a storm, but however dark his premonitions, he could not possibly have measured what was coming. No one did; no one could have.

The day on Capitol Hill was described as "one of the bitterest . . . in modern times." Prominent Republicans, including Senator Robert Taft, spoke angrily of impeaching the president. The full Republican leadership held an emergency meeting in Joe Martin's office at 9:30 in the morning, after which Martin talked to reporters of "impeachments," the accent on the plural. "We might want the impeachments of 1 or 50." A full-dress congressional investigation of the president's war policy was in order. General MacArthur, announced Martin, would be invited to air his views before a joint session of Congress.

In New York, 2,000 longshoremen walked off their jobs in protest over the firing of MacArthur. A Baltimore women's group announced plans for a march on Washington in support of the general. Elsewhere, enraged patriots flew flags at half-staff, or upside down. People signed petitions and fired off furious letters and telegrams to Washington. In Worcester, Massachusetts, and San Gabriel, California, Truman was burned in effigy. In Houston, a Protestant minister became so angry dictating a telegram to the White House that he died of a heart attack.

In the hallways of the Senate and House office buildings, Western Union messengers made their deliveries with bushel baskets. According to one tally, of the 44,358 telegrams received by Republicans in Congress during the first forty-eight hours following Truman's announcement, all but 334 condemned him or took the side of MacArthur, and the majority called for Truman's immediate removal from office.

A number of prominent liberals—Eleanor Roosevelt, Walter Reuther, Justice William O. Douglas—publicly supported Truman. Further, throughout Europe, MacArthur's dismissal was greeted as welcome news. But most impressive was the weight of editorial opinion at home in support of Truman—including some staunch Republican newspapers—despite vehement assaults in the McCormick, Hearst, and Scripps-Howard papers, as well as the renewed glorification of MacArthur in Henry Luce's *Time* and *Life*.

Nothing had so stirred the political passions of the country since the Civil War. At the heart of the tumult was anger and frustration over the war in Korea. Senator Kenneth Wherry had begun calling it "Truman's War," and the name caught on. People were sick of Truman's War, frustrated, and a bit baffled by talk of a "limited war." America didn't fight to achieve a stalemate, and the cost in blood had become appalling. The country wanted it over. MacArthur at least offered victory.

Except for a brief broadcast from the White House the night after his dismissal of MacArthur, Truman maintained silence on the matter. General MacArthur was "one of our greatest military commanders," he told the nation, but the cause of world peace was far more important than any individual.

MacArthur landed at San Francisco on Tuesday, April 17, to a delirious reception. He had been away from the country for fourteen years. Until now, the American people had had no chance to see and cheer him, to welcome the hero home. Ten thousand were at the San Francisco airport. So great were the crowds on the way into the city, it took two hours for the motorcade to reach his hotel. "The only politics I have," MacArthur told a cheering throng, "is contained in a simple phrase known to all of you—God Bless America."

When Truman met with reporters the next day, at his first press conference since the start of the crisis, he dashed all their expectations by refusing to say anything on the subject. Scheduled to appear before the American Society of Newspaper Editors on Thursday, April 19, the day MacArthur was to go before Congress, Truman canceled his speech, because he felt it should be the general's day and did not wish anything to detract from it.

There would be "hell to pay" for perhaps six or seven weeks, he told his staff and the Cabinet. But eventually people would come to their senses, including more and more Republican politicians who would grow doubtful of all-out support for the general. Given some time, MacArthur would be reduced to human proportions. Meanwhile, Truman could withstand the bombardment, for in the long run, he knew, he would be judged to have made the right decision. He had absolutely no doubt of that. "The American people will come to understand that what I did had to be done."

At 12:31 P.M., Thursday, April 19, in a flood of television lights, Douglas MacArthur walked down the same aisle in the House of Representatives as had Harry Truman so often since 1945, and the wild ovation from the packed chamber, the intense, authentic drama of the moment, were such as few had ever beheld. Neither the president's Cabinet nor the Supreme Court nor any of the Joint Chiefs were present.

Wearing a short "Eisenhower" jacket, without decoration, the silvery circles of five-star rank glittering on his shoulders, MacArthur paused to shake hands with Vice President Barkley, then stepped to the rostrum, his face "an unreadable mask." Only after complete silence had fallen did he begin: "I address you with neither rancor nor bitterness in the fading twilight of life, with but one purpose in mind: to serve my country."

There was ringing applause and the low, vibrant voice went on, the speaker in full command of the moment. The decision to intervene in support of the Republic of Korea had been sound from a military standpoint, MacArthur affirmed. But when he had called for reinforcements, he was told they were not available. He had "made clear," he said, that if not permitted to destroy the enemy bases north of the Yalu, if not permitted to utilize the 800,000 Chinese troops on Formosa, if not permitted to blockade the China coast, then "the position of the command from a military standpoint forbade victory. . . ." And war's "very object" was victory. How could it be otherwise? "In war, indeed," he said, repeating his favorite slogan, "there can be no substitute for victory. There were some who, for varying reasons, would appease Red China. They were blind to history's clear lesson, for history teaches, with unmistakable emphasis, that appeasement begets new and bloodier war."

He was provocative, and defiant. Resounding applause or cheers followed again and again—thirty times in thirty-four minutes. He said nothing of bombing China's industrial centers, as he had proposed. And though he said "every available means" should be applied to bring victory, he made no mention of his wish to use atomic bombs, or to lay down a belt of radioactivity along the Yalu. He had been severely criticized for his views, he said. Yet, he asserted, his views were "fully shared" by the Joint Chiefs—a claim that was altogether untrue but that brought a deafening ovation. Republicans and most spectators in the galleries leaped to their feet, cheering and stamping. It was nearly a minute before he could begin again.

To those who said American military strength was inadequate to face the enemy on more than one front, MacArthur said he could imagine no greater expression of defeatism. "You cannot appease or otherwise surrender to Communism in Asia without simultaneously undermining our efforts to halt its advance in Europe." To confine the war only to Chinese aggression in Korea was to follow a path of "prolonged indecision."

"Why, my soldiers asked of me, surrender military advantages to an enemy in the field?" He paused; then, softly, his voice almost a whisper, he said, "I could not answer."

A record 30 million people were watching on television, and the performance was masterful. The use of the rich voice, the timing, surpassed that of most actors. The oratorical style was of a kind not heard in Congress in a very long time. It recalled, as one television critic wrote, "a yesteryear of the theater," and it held the greater part of the huge audience wholly enraptured. Work had stopped in offices and plants across the country, so people could watch. Saloons and bars were jammed. Schoolchildren saw the "historic hour" in classrooms or were herded into assemblies or dining halls to listen by radio. Whether they had any idea what the excitement was about, they knew it was "important."

"When I joined the army, even before the turn of the century, it was the fulfillment of all my boyish hopes and dreams," MacArthur said, his voice dropping as he began the famous last lines, the stirring, sentimental, ambiguous peroration that the speech would be remembered for.

> The hopes and dreams have long since vanished. But I still remember the refrain of one of the most popular barracks ballads of that day which proclaimed most proudly that "Old soldiers never die. They just fade away." And like the old soldier of the ballad, I now close my military career and just fade away—an old soldier who tried to do his duty as God gave him the light to see that duty.
>
> Good-bye.

A "hurricane of emotion" swept the room. Hands reached out to him. Many in the audience were weeping. "We heard God speak here today, God in the flesh, the voice of God!" exclaimed Republican Representative Dewey Short of Missouri, a former preacher. To Joe Martin, it was "the climaxing" of the most emotional moment he had known in thirty-five years in Congress. Theatrics were a part of the congressional way of life, Martin knew, but nothing had ever equaled this.

It was MacArthur's finest hour, and the crescendo of public adulation that followed, beginning with a triumphal parade through Washington that afternoon, and climaxing the next day in New York with a thunderous tickertape parade, was unprecedented in U.S. history. Reportedly 7,500,000 people turned out in New York, more than had welcomed Eisenhower in 1945, more even than at the almost legendary welcome for Lindbergh in 1927.

In fact, not everybody cheered. There were places along the parade route in New York where, as MacArthur's open car passed, people stood silently, just watching and looking, anything but pleased. In Washington, one senator had confided to a reporter that he had never feared more for his country than during MacArthur's speech. "I honestly felt that if the speech had gone on much longer there might have been a march on the White House."

Truman had not listened to MacArthur's speech, or watched on television. He had spent the time at his desk in the Oval Office, meeting with Dean Acheson as was usual at that hour on Thursdays, after which he went back to Blair House for lunch and a nap. At some point, however, he did read what MacArthur had said. Speaking privately, he remarked that he thought it "a bunch of damn bullshit."

As Truman had anticipated, the tumult began to subside. For seven weeks in the late spring of 1951, the Senate Foreign Relations and Armed Services committees held joint hearings to investigate MacArthur's dismissal. Though the hearings were closed, authorized transcripts of each day's sessions, edited for military security reasons, were released hourly to the press.

MacArthur, the first witness, testified for three days, arguing that his way in Korea was the way to victory and an end to the slaughter. He had seen as much blood and disaster as any man alive, he told the senators, but never such devastation as during his last time in Korea. "After I looked at that wreckage and those thousands of women and children and everything, I vomited. Now are you going to let that go on . . . ?" The politicians in Washington had introduced a "new concept into military operations—the concept of appeasement," its purpose only "to go on indefinitely . . . indecisively, fighting with no mission. . . ."

But he also began to sound self-absorbed and oddly uninterested in global issues. He would admit to no mistakes, no errors of judgment. Failure to anticipate the size of the Chinese invasion, for example, had been the fault of the CIA. Any operation he commanded was crucial; other considerations were always of less importance. Certain that his strategy of war on China would not bring in the Soviets, he belittled the danger of a larger conflict. But what if he happened to be wrong, he was asked. What if another world war resulted? That, said MacArthur, was not his responsibility. "My responsibilities were in the Pacific, and the Joint Chiefs of Staff and various agencies of the Government are working night and day for an over-all solution to the global problem. Now I am not familiar with their studies. I haven't gone into it. . . ." To many, it seemed he had made the president's case.

The great turning point came with the testimony of Marshall, Bradley, and the Joint Chiefs, who refuted absolutely MacArthur's claim that they agreed with his strategy. Truman, from the start of the crisis, had known he needed the full support of his military advisers before declaring his decision about MacArthur. Now it was that full support, through nineteen days of testimony, that not only gave weight and validity to the decision, but discredited MacArthur in a way nothing else could have.

Never, said the Joint Chiefs, had they subscribed to MacArthur's plan for victory, however greatly they admired him. The dismissal of MacArthur, said all of them—Marshall, Bradley, the Joint Chiefs—was more than warranted; it was a necessity. Given the circumstances, given the seriousness of MacArthur's opposition to the policy of the president, his challenge to presidential authority, there had been no other course. The fidelity of the military high command to the principle of civilian control of the military was total and unequivocal.

Such unanimity of opinion on the part of the country's foremost and most respected military leaders seemed to leave Republican senators stunned. As James Reston wrote in the *New York Times*, "MacArthur, who had started as the prosecutor, had now become the defendant."

The hearings ground on and grew increasingly dull. The MacArthur hysteria was over; interest waned. When, in June, MacArthur set off on a speaking tour through Texas, insisting he had no presidential ambitions, he began to sound more and more shrill and vindictive, less and less like a hero. He attacked Truman, appeasement, high taxes, and "insidious forces working from within." His crowds grew steadily smaller. Nationwide, the polls showed a sharp decline in his popular appeal. The old soldier was truly beginning to fade away.

Truman would regard the decision to fire MacArthur as among the most important he made as president. He did not, however, agree with those who said it had shown what great courage he had. (Harriman, among others, would later speak of it as one of the most courageous steps ever taken by any president.) "Courage didn't have anything to do with it," Truman would say emphatically. "General MacArthur was insubordinate and I fired him. That's all there was to it."

But if the firing of MacArthur had taken a heavy toll politically, if Truman as president had been less than a master of persuasion, he had accomplished a very great deal and demonstrated extraordinary patience and strength of character in how he rode out the storm. His policy in Korea—his determined effort to keep the conflict in bounds—had not been scuttled, however great the aura of the hero-general, or his powers as a spellbinder. The principle of civilian control over the military, challenged as never before in the nation's history, had survived, and stronger than ever. The president had made his point and, with the backing of his generals, he had made it stick.

XII

*Cold War and Vietnam,
1960–1975*

The Vietnam War, 1964–1969:
A Chinese Perspective
Xiaoming Zhang

*That aid from the People's Republic of China was a significant factor in North Viet-
nam's defeat of the United States and South Vietnam in the Vietnam War has clearly
been established. Why China was willing to grant that aid in the form of weaponry, air
defense capabilities, and even full-scale intervention if North Vietnam was attacked by
U.S. ground forces has not been fully understood and appreciated. In this essay Xiao-
ming Zhang of Texas A&M International University explains that China was fearful of
the actions of the South Vietnamese government with U.S. backing and with bases on its
southern border (as had been true regarding Korea and also in reference to Taiwan). This
was a major factor in its support of North Vietnam. China also saw itself as a major
player in an Asiatic and world proletariat movement. Perceiving American escalation of
the war as a direct threat to itself, it cooperated throughout the war as a communist
comrade to Hanoi and was prepared for all-out war with the United States if necessary
to protect what it saw as its national security and ideological interests. This essay was
originally published in* The Journal of Military History *(60/4 [Oct. 1996], 731–62)
and is reprinted with permission.*

Why did the United States lose the Vietnam War? Various explanations have
come from scholars with American perspectives. One popular interpretation
is that American leaders feared direct Chinese entry into the war and that
this concern precluded full-scale use of U.S. military power against North
Vietnam. Although Beijing's support of the Democratic Republic of Vietnam
(DRV) against the United States has been recognized, that facet of the conflict

has been under-researched and little understood. Numerous studies, using information from contemporary newspapers and intelligence reports, attempt to provide detailed and plausible interpretations of the attitudes and policies of the People's Republic of China (PRC) with regard to the war, but they fail to give a comprehensive picture of China's support for the DRV.

Because of the lack of Chinese sources of information on the Vietnam War, the PRC's role has been discussed only marginally or largely neglected. Limited understanding of China's role in the Vietnam War has led scholars to overlook the possibility of Chinese intervention. Colonel Harry G. Summers argues that American leaders' lack of appreciation of the relationship between military strategy and national policy was the major cause of U.S. defeat in the war. Such a mistake was born of Washington's fear of Chinese intervention in Vietnam to the extent that the United States limited the conflict with Hanoi. Believing that the possibility of Chinese intervention was just "a matter of conjecture," Summers urged American military leaders to adopt a total war strategy based on Carl von Clausewitz's classic, *On War*, in any future commitment of U.S. armed forces. Summers's thesis received favorable comments from military professionals and was further reinforced by the Gulf War victory in 1991.

Recent Chinese sources regarding PRC policy toward the Vietnam War suggest that China had been extensively involved in the Vietnam War throughout this period. However, China's involvement in North Vietnam did not cause a direct confrontation between Beijing and Washington as had happened in Korea in the early 1950s. This essay examines how China supported Hanoi's drive to unify all of Vietnam and defended North Vietnam against U.S. attacks between 1964 and 1969. It analyzes the circumstances under which China most probably would have gone to war with the United States if the strategy advocated by Summers had been implemented. But, as will be revealed, China also had reasons for doing everything possible to avoid a Sino-American confrontation.

China and Vietnamese National Liberation

Hanoi's official histories have minimized China's role in the war in South Vietnam. American scholars have believed that China did not want to deal with a strong unified Vietnam under Hanoi leadership; that China preferred to deal with two independent Vietnamese states instead of a unified Vietnam, fifty million strong and with a long history of antipathy toward China. China thus relied on the United States to serve its interests by preventing a decisive military victory by Hanoi. A protracted war meant continued commitment of North Vietnamese men and resources toward the South, away from China.

Chinese Communist Party (CCP) leaders had paid attention to the Vietnamese Communist revolution from the beginning. Mao Zedong, Zhou Enlai, and other Chinese leaders had developed close relationships with Ho Chi

Minh. Mao especially felt a rapport with Ho because they not only shared beliefs and values, but they also experienced comparable hardships during their revolutionary careers. China's determination to offer material and manpower support for the DRV was based on a mixture of strategic and ideological considerations. Chinese leaders comprehended Vietnam's strategic importance to the security of China's southern border. Beijing regarded Vietnam along with Korea and Taiwan as the most likely places where the United States might establish bases and possibly initiate military hostilities. In the meantime, the Beijing leadership was anxious to see the model of the Chinese revolution implemented in Indochina. During the first Indochina war, between 1950 and 1954, Chinese leaders offered moral and material support for Ho Chi Minh and his Viet Minh. After the 1954 Geneva conference, Beijing continued to anticipate possible U.S. intervention in the region that would turn Indochina into a U.S. military base from which to threaten China.

The great unfinished task of the Vietnamese revolution, as defined by Hanoi in the aftermath of the 1954 Geneva Conference, was to unify all of Vietnam under its rule. By 1958, it seemed apparent to Hanoi that this goal could not be achieved except by military force against the southern regime, and domestic and international conditions appeared propitious for a resumption of the armed struggle in the South, with the socialist North serving as a base of support. Thus, beginning in 1959, Hanoi's strategy of armed struggle went forward in South Vietnam.

Beijing's advice to Hanoi was based on the CCP's own experiences during the Chinese revolution. The CCP leaders suggested that Hanoi conserve its military forces while maintaining close contact with the populace and awaiting opportunities for local uprisings. When Hanoi's leaders consulted with their Chinese counterparts concerning resumption of the armed struggle in the South, the CCP leaders argued that such action was premature and dangerous; it was too early to expose Hanoi's strength in the South. In 1960, revolutionary prospects in South Vietnam looked good, and Chinese leaders agreed to give Hanoi full support. Beijing's reassessment of the situation in South Vietnam may have led to this shift, but Beijing had its own reasons for supporting Hanoi's new strategy for the liberation of South Vietnam.

The growth of U.S. military involvement in South Vietnam, culminating in the formal establishment of the U.S. Military Assistance Command in Vietnam (MACV) in February 1962, caused Chinese leaders deep concern. They believed that the United States, which in their view had failed in Korea and Taiwan in the 1950s, was now expanding the war against China into Vietnam. From the Chinese perspective, Beijing's support for Hanoi's war of national liberation would serve to break "the ring of encirclement" by U.S. imperialism and thus increase the security of China.

The Chinese perception of internationalism also determined Beijing's support for Hanoi's drive to liberate South Vietnam. Beijing perceived Ho's war of national liberation as a vital part of a world proletarian revolutionary movement. According to Mao Zedong, the success of "national revolution-ary" struggles was the key to the defense of socialist states from imperialist attack and to the ultimate success of the global revolutionary struggle. Achievement of world revolutionary objectives in the 1960s required the overthrow of the U.S.-dominated international order. U.S. military interven-tion in Vietnam in the early 1960s put Hanoi at the center of what could become a global revolution following the Chinese model. Thus, Chinese leaders believed it was their duty to assist Ho and his party in order to pro-mote an Asia-wide or even world-wide revolution.

Deteriorating Sino-Soviet relations may also have affected Beijing's policy of supporting Hanoi's war of national liberation. Mao appeared to re-sent Stalin's role in dividing countries at the end of World War II, and Khrushchev's lukewarm support of Ho Chi Minh and his struggle for Viet-namese unification. We still know little about how the ideological schism between China and the Soviet Union in the early 1960s affected China's role in Vietnam. Nevertheless, victory in North Vietnam's war of national libera-tion could have demonstrated Mao's political correctness in adopting a more militant approach toward the United States, in contrast to the Soviet policy, which favored peaceful coexistence with what China viewed as U.S. imperialism. Furthermore, resolute Chinese support for the Vietnamese struggle against the U.S. could ensure that Hanoi in turn would stand at Beijing's side.

Under the terms of the 1954 Geneva Agreements, the DRV could not augment its military forces. Nevertheless, Beijing continued to supply sig-nificant quantities of arms and ammunition to Hanoi. As Hanoi developed its army (the People's Army of Vietnam, or PAVN) into a fully professional modern force in the late 1950s, China stepped up its efforts to equip and train North Vietnamese soldiers. Between 1955 and 1963, China provided the DRV with 247 million yuans' worth of military aid, including 240,000 guns, 2,730 pieces of artillery, 15 planes, 28 naval vessels, 175 million rounds of ammunition, and other military equipment and supplies. In 1962 alone, Beijing supplied 90,000 rifles and machine guns to North Vietnam, for up-grading Hanoi's drive to liberate South Vietnam. These weapons were enough to equip 230 infantry battalions.

In the early 1960s, when Soviet policy toward Indochina was equivocal at best, Ho Chi Minh and the North Vietnamese government regarded China as the only reliable source of military supplies for their revolutionary cause. Even though, under Brezhnev and Kosygin, Moscow adopted a more active policy of support for the DRV, Ho Chi Minh continued to look to China for ways to achieve unification and independence. Western analysts have long believed that there was conflict between Hanoi and Beijing over the question of united Sino-Soviet assistance in support of Hanoi. Ho was disheartened by the Beijing-Moscow dispute. He regarded the Soviet Union and China as Vietnam's big brother and big sister, and he hoped for united Sino-Soviet support for his revolutionary cause in Vietnam. Although divergent opinions toward China most likely existed within Hanoi's elite, Ho Chi Minh continued to seek a special relationship with China. He characterized the Vietnamese and Chinese peoples as "comrades and brothers" who go through thick and thin together.

Ho and other North Vietnamese leaders traveled frequently to Beijing, where they consulted with Chinese leaders concerning nearly every major development in their war of national liberation in South Vietnam. North Vietnamese leaders' determination to fight against U.S. aggression deeply impressed Mao and Zhou. China's leaders had great esteem for those Vietnamese leaders who were in charge of the armed struggle in the South. Appearing well-informed and following the events in Vietnam closely, Mao and Zhou showed sincere concern for Hanoi's drive to unite all of Vietnam. It was Mao's view that China must provide whatever Hanoi needed for the war in the South. He carefully studied Hanoi's request for aid from China, and even ordered mosquito nets for all North Vietnamese soldiers because he thought that the hot and humid south of Vietnam must be infested with mosquitoes and ants. When a food products factory in Shanghai began to manufacture food especially for Vietnamese soldiers, Mao ordered that the hardtack must be light and nutritious. Zhou, too, repeatedly emphasized that China's aid to Hanoi's war in the South was the most important job for the Chinese. In March 1965, he personally went to Hanoi to arrange for shipments of supplies. Believing that the United States would blockade South Vietnam, he urged that Chinese supplies be shipped to Vietnam as quickly as possible. Because supplies for the most part were carried by Vietnamese soldiers and women, Zhou directed that each package of supplies should weigh less than thirty kilograms.

In order to meet Hanoi's urgent needs, Beijing gave highest priority to supplying arms and military equipment to Hanoi. Between 1961 and 1972, China supplied Hanoi with 280 122-mm howitzers, 960 57-mm antiaircraft guns, and 20,237 mortars, while the People's Liberation Army (PLA) received 200 howitzers, 2,000 antiaircraft guns, and 17,000 mortars. The Chinese version of the Soviet-designed AK-47 automatic rifle, which was manufactured in China after 1956, was provided to nearly all the regular PAVN soldiers even before the PLA soldiers had been equipped. Often, when Hanoi's requests exceeded China's production capability, Beijing transferred arms and equipment directly from the PLA to Hanoi's inventory. In 1969 Hanoi badly needed 107-mm rocket launchers, but they were no longer produced in China. Beijing then consigned all of the PLA's stock to Vietnam.

Several western studies argue that China never actually supported Hanoi's decision to employ an offensive strategy in South Vietnam; that Beijing feared expansion of the fighting into China, and thus desired only that Hanoi continue an extended war of attrition. Recently released Chinese records do not support these views. In April 1967, both Chinese and Vietnamese leaders agreed that 1968 was a year of crucial importance because Hanoi would probably defeat the enemy during that year's dry season and force the Americans to withdraw from Vietnam. During Ho's medical treatment at Beijing that year, Mao met him, urging Hanoi to move away from guerrilla tactics toward big-unit warfare in the South. Ho promptly relayed Mao's views to the other leaders in Hanoi. At its fourteenth plenum in December, the Central Committee of the Lao Dong Party (North Vietnamese Workers' Party) made the final decision to launch the Tet offensive in early 1968. To what extent Beijing's advice influenced Hanoi's decision remains unknown. Recent scholarship on the Vietnam War emphasizes that the key to Hanoi's victory was the employment of a military strategy that always reflected local realities in Vietnam and essentially differed from the strategic doctrine of the Chinese revolution. However, few recognize that the two countries' revolutionary situations were different in one critical aspect: Beijing's support for Hanoi significantly contributed to the ultimate success of Vietnamese national liberation, whereas the CCP received no assistance from foreign countries, including the Soviet Union, during the Chinese revolution. In 1968, even though Beijing's leaders resented Hanoi's negotiations with the Americans, they continued to provide North Vietnam with offensive weapons, hoping that Hanoi would continue the military struggle. Between 1970 and 1972, while the pace of American withdrawal from the South accelerated, China supplied more than 300 tanks and 204 130-mm field guns, along with 450,000 artillery shells, to enable Hanoi to continue offensive warfare. The Chinese munitions industry manufactured 20-mm antiaircraft artillery specifically for Hanoi's troops to counter U.S. helicopter warfare on the battlefields of the South.

Chinese sources suggest that Beijing did not unquestioningly give Hanoi everything it requested. In October 1965, during negotiations between PLA Chief of Staff Luo Ruiqing and PAVN Chief of Staff Van Tien Dung, the Vietnamese side requested that China provide 140 million rounds of ammunition immediately. Luo questioned Dung about whether Hanoi was able to ship that amount of ammunition to the South, and he advised Dung to make a more reasonable demand. However, Beijing's close relationship with Hanoi, as well as its revolutionary ideology, ensured that China would remain a major supporter of North Vietnam in spite of differences about strategy and aid. Hanoi's drive for national liberation put both Mao's world revolutionary strategy and China's own national security at stake.

China's Response to the U.S. Threat from the Air

In the mid-1960s, Chinese leaders were concerned about a possible Sino-American war over Vietnam. American misjudgment of Beijing's warning in Korea in 1950 remained fresh in Chinese minds. The 1964 Tonkin Gulf Incident convinced Chinese leaders that Beijing needed to deploy Chinese military forces to counter possible U.S. expansion of the war into North Vietnam. On 5 August, a few hours after American bombers attacked six North Vietnamese naval bases and associated facilities, Zhou Enlai and Luo Ruiqing sent a message to President Ho Chi Minh, Premier Pham Van Dong, and Chief of Staff Van Tien Dung advising them to investigate the situation and prepare strategies and policies for action. They also proposed military collaboration between the two nations to meet the mounting U.S. threat. Beijing was seriously concerned about Vietnam's situation. One incident that might be closely related to China's concern about Hanoi's situation was the arrival of a Chinese IL-18 aircraft (the kind used for travel by Chinese leaders), at Gia Lam airport on that same day, possibly for a meeting between North Vietnamese and Chinese leaders about the U.S. air attack.

Also, on the evening of 5 August an emergency war meeting was convened at the Headquarters of the General Staff of the PLA. The meeting, presided over by Deputy Chief of Staff Yang Chenwu, continued into the morning of the next day. Participants included the principal commanders of the Air Force, Navy, other armed services, and the Beijing Military Region. They studied the situation in Vietnam, and concluded that U.S. bombing of North Vietnamese naval bases did not signal an immediate war in North Vietnam, but that the threat had increased. Thus, Chinese military leaders recommended that Air Force, Navy, and Army troops in Guangzhou and Kunming Military Regions be on the alert against possible invasion. Chinese commanders decided to immediately strengthen China's air power in Guangxi and Yunnan.

In 1964 China had few planes and airfields in the areas close to North Vietnam. At an Air Force war meeting on the evening of 6 August, Commander of the Chinese Air Force Liu Yalou recommended that the 7th Air Corps headquarters move from Xingning, Guangdong, to Nanning to assume a command role in the Guangxi and Leizhou peninsula areas; and that the 12th Fighter Division and the 3d AAA Division be transferred to Nanning from Quzhou, Zhejiang, and Zhangzhou, Fujian, respectively. He suggested that the Navy also send one of its fighter divisions to Hainan Island, and that additional airfields and radar installations be constructed in Guangxi, Yunnan, and Guizhou. Mao Zedong immediately approved these measures, all of which were carried out within a few weeks.

In addition, the 17th Fighter Division (less the 49th regiment, which was transferred from Tangshan, Hebei, to Kunming) advanced from Kunming to Mengzi, while the 26th Fighter Division at Suixi and the 9th Fighter Division at Guangzhou were ordered to get ready for action at their current positions. Eight other air divisions plus one all-weather fighter regiment were assigned as the second echelon to support the front line. Construction began on three new airfields (Ningming, Tianyang, and Guilin) in Guangxi, while a small airfield near the Laotian border at Simao and one near the Burma border at Xiangyun were extended to accommodate jet fighters. New long-range early warning and ground-control-intercept radar systems were installed. Especially, one radar regiment moved into the airfield at Ningming, twelve miles from the Sino-Vietnamese border. This logically would also enable China and North Vietnam to cooperate in air defense.

The most significant development was the deployment to North Vietnam, on 6–7 August 1964, of a fighter regiment with thirty-six MIGs. These aircraft were based at the newly built airfield at Phuc Yen, twelve miles northwest of Hanoi. Since the DRV had no combat air force at the time, Washington believed that the MIGs were Chinese. Recently released Chinese sources indicate that these MIGs belonged to the DRV's first fighter regiment, which was organized in September 1957 by China and trained in China. During 1963 and 1964, senior officers of the PLA and PAVN held several conferences to discuss military cooperation in case of U.S. invasion. Again, the details of those meetings are unknown, but it is certain that the DRV wanted China to help strengthen its air defense. A group of Chinese air force engineers was sent to help upgrade Noi Bai airfield at Phue Yen. By the summer of 1964, that airfield was ready for use by jet fighters, and the fighter regiment of thirty-six Chinese-made MIGs was based there. Although one regiment of North Vietnamese fighters posed no threat to American air power in Southeast Asia, future U.S. air raids would carry with them the risk of a challenge from the North Vietnamese air force, or even from Chinese fighters.

Although these military moves in China, as American scholar Allen Whiting has argued, were designed to deter further U.S. expansion of the war in the South and bombardment in the North, they also reflected Beijing's perception of the international situation. By the mid-1960s, after the breakdown of the Sino-Soviet alliance, the border conflicts between China and India, Chiang Kai-shek's series of attempts to return to the mainland, and the Tonkin Gulf Incident, Beijing's leaders began to believe that China was surrounded by threats to its security. It seemed to them that a world war was inevitable. On 17 August 1964, Mao, at the CCP's Central Secretariat meeting, stated that the imperialists were planning to start a new war of aggression against China, and that it was therefore necessary for China to prepare for war. In October, Mao stated again that China must be ready for a large, possibly nuclear war. U.S. escalation in Vietnam was viewed as the prelude to such a war. "Preparing for war" became a dominant national theme, penetrating every cell of Chinese society.

In early 1965 the threat was limited mainly to North Vietnam, but the Chinese military did not remain in a passive role. The PLA Air Force and Navy aircraft actively engaged U.S. intruders over Chinese air space throughout the 1960s. Washington had been concerned about a possible large-scale infusion of Chinese military strength in response to U.S. bombing of North Vietnam. U.S. aerial reconnaissance missions increasingly flew over Southwest and South China. Chinese documents reveal that Chinese radar tracked some ninety-seven reconnaissance missions flown over China by BQM-147 Drones (unmanned planes) between August 1964 and the end of 1969. Beijing authorities initially restricted Chinese planes from confronting manned American aircraft that invaded China. They allowed Chinese planes to monitor the intruding American planes only, not to attack them. However, shooting down unmanned reconnaissance planes was not prohibited. Chinese leaders believed that action against U.S. unmanned reconnaissance planes would demonstrate China's readiness to fight U.S. aggression, and might obviate the need to intervene more directly.

During the remainder of 1964 and early 1965, Chinese Air Force and Navy aviation units engaged in a series of actions to intercept unmanned spy planes. Special Jian-6 and Jian-7 (Chinese MIG-19 and MIG-21) combat units were organized and deployed to airfields at Nanning, Suixi, Kunming, Mengzi, and Hainan Island. Despite frustrations in early attempts to shoot down the drones, the Chinese Air Force on 14 November 1964, claimed its first victory. China claimed that twenty U.S. pilotless reconnaissance planes were brought down during the Vietnam War. The Chinese government condemned U.S. aggression while seeking to minimize the possibility of direct action against the United States. But Chinese leaders soon discovered that such restraint did not halt American escalation of the hostilities.

On 8 April 1965, Chinese radar tracked two U.S. Navy F-4Bs over the Yulin naval base on Hainan Island. The Chinese military was alerted, and the intrusion was regarded as a new U.S. provocation against China. The next day when eight U.S. Navy F-4Bs in two groups intruded over Hainan Island, four Jian-5s (MIG-17) of the Navy's 8th Aviation Division were sent up to intercept the second group of F-4Bs, but Chinese pilots were instructed not to fire unless fired upon. In the initial engagement, neither side fired. According to Chinese reports, during the next round an F-4B fired two AIM-7 Sparrow air-to-air missiles, which overshot and hit a Phantom. This account cannot be corroborated in American sources. The U.S. pilots believed that they were flying thirty-six miles southwest of Hainan Island, while the Pentagon insisted that American aircraft were prohibited from flying into China's air space. In any event, the incident forced Beijing to change its policy.

The beginning of sustained U.S. bombing of North Vietnam and the introduction of U.S. combat troops into South Vietnam aggravated Beijing's fear that the United States was on a course of direct confrontation with China. Beijing quickly adopted a strategy whereby China would not stand idly by, but would send its military forces into North Vietnam if the U.S. launched a ground attack against Hanoi. China would not initiate direct military confrontation with the United States, but would make it clear to Washington that a ground attack would risk war with China. In a four-point statement to Pakistan's leader to be forwarded to President Johnson on 2 April 1965, Zhou Enlai expressed China's policy toward U.S. aggression in Vietnam. China would not provoke a war with the United States, he said. But he stressed Beijing's continued willingness to provide aid to any country opposing U.S. aggression. Zhou warned that if the United States imposed war on China, including the use of nuclear weapons, the Chinese would not limit their response, implying that China would carry the war throughout Southeast Asia.

As early as February 1965, Washington had informed China that it had no intention of destroying North Vietnam, nor any desire for a direct confrontation with China. However, U.S. warplanes' intrusion into Hainan Island air space on two consecutive days, along with sustained bombing of North Vietnam, increased Beijing's concerns. On 9 April the PLA General Staff Headquarters made a full report about the incident over Hainan to Zhou Enlai and the Central Military Commission (CMC) of the CCP. The report stated that the American military aircraft's actions constituted a direct threat to China, and requested permission for the PLA air force to attack U.S. warplanes over China's air space. The CMC immediately granted approval. Zhou Enlai pointed out that the existing policy did not suit the current situation. Mao concurred, and ordered that the best units of the Air Force and Navy be sent to southern China to strike relentless blows at any U.S. aircraft that invaded China's air space.

On 12 April the Chinese Air Force stressed that its troops should not only be poised for combat over border areas but should be on standby for a possible large-scale war inside China. Under this new policy, Air Force and Navy aviation units changed their overall military posture in Yunnan, Guangxi, Leizhou peninsula, and Hainan Island. PLA units began deliberately engaging U.S. warplanes that overflew China's air space during their combat operations against the DRV. Beijing records show that between August 1964 and November 1968, U.S. warplanes flew 383 sorties in 155 groups over China's air space. The Chinese Air Force in Guangxi flew more than 2,138 sorties in combat in response to the U.S. threat from the air. China claimed that twelve American warplanes were shot down, with another four reportedly damaged. However, Washington confirmed only five losses.

The change in China's attitude toward incursions by U.S. warplanes reflected Beijing's concern about Washington's intentions in Vietnam. China's responses demonstrated to Washington as well as to Hanoi the seriousness and firmness of Beijing's stand. Later evidence showed that Hanoi's leaders had solicited China's air support, but it is clear that Beijing attempted to keep the military option in low key. Beijing in 1965 drew the line of air defense at the border, hoping to give the Americans no excuse to enlarge the theater of war. When Washington increased its military pressure on Hanoi by extending air bombardments closer to the Chinese border in the spring of 1966, the Chinese began to defend their southern air frontier more vigorously. Warning radar was required to monitor the activities of enemy planes across the border, while PLA planes were ready to take off for military engagement. Throughout the war, the Chinese Air Force was never directly engaged in operations over North Vietnam, although on several occasions Chinese planes crossed the border to engage Americans over North Vietnam. Although these actions remained primarily defensive, the possibility of a Sino-American clash over either North Vietnamese or Chinese air space increased. The situation became even more complicated when all North Vietnamese air bases were destroyed in 1967, forcing North Vietnamese planes to move to bases in China. Chinese records thus far published give no details about China's sanctuary policy toward the PAVN Air Force, but Chinese commanders acknowledged that friendly operations did complicate China's air defense. During the same period (24 April to 21 August 1967), the PLA claimed that seven U.S. planes were shot down over China and one American pilot was captured. However, wreckage of only two American planes was found inside China. This account leaves the record somewhat confused as to whether these engagements occurred over China or North Vietnam.

China's Commitment Against a Possible U.S. Invasion

Although the direct Sino-American confrontation that Chinese leaders feared in the early 1960s did not occur, Chinese leaders remained on the alert to the U.S. escalation in Vietnam. Shortly after the formal establishment of the MACV, Chinese and Vietnamese leaders discussed the seriousness of the situation in the South and concluded that there was a strong possibility of a U.S. invasion of North Vietnam. Beijing agreed to increase its arms supplies to Hanoi. In March 1963, Luo Ruiqing was sent to Hanoi to further discuss the possibility of a U.S. attack on North Vietnam. During his stay, both sides studied the situation, determined the nature and extent of China's assistance to North Vietnam, and planned joint operations to counter a U.S. invasion. During a visit to Hanoi in May, PRC President Liu Shaoqi claimed that the Chinese would stand firmly with the Vietnamese and that China would be Hanoi's rear base if a war erupted. In June 1964, Mao told Van Tien Dung that China would regard Vietnam's problems as her own, and urged close cooperation between China and North Vietnam in order to deal with any U.S. invasion.

The introduction of U.S. combat units into the South in early 1965 heightened the possibility of a U.S. ground attack on North Vietnam. It appeared that Hanoi needed more support. During the first week of April, Le Duan, First Secretary of the Lao Dong Party, and Vo Nguyen Giap, Vice-premier and Minister of Defense, made a sudden and unannounced visit to China. The Vietnamese leaders asked Beijing for more assistance, including the deployment of Chinese military forces to North Vietnam for defense, engineering, and logistics work. This most important development in connection with Le Duan's visit to Beijing did not appear in any public record, leading Western scholars to speculate that Le Duan's trip to Beijing was less successful than his recent visit to Moscow. The most Le Duan received, one study incorrectly concluded, was China's conditional promise to offer volunteers.

On 8 April the North Vietnamese leaders met Liu Shaoqi, who was then handling the daily activities of the party and state. Le Duan told the Chinese leader that the DRV wanted "volunteer pilots, volunteer fighters" and also "engineering units for constructing and repairing railroads, highways, and bridges." He noted that Chinese forces would help defend Hanoi and areas north of Hanoi from U.S. air bombardment, which would also raise the morale of the Vietnamese people. But more important, Le Duan emphasized that the deployment of Chinese troops would allow Hanoi to send its own soldiers to the South, while restricting U.S. bombardment to areas south of the 20th or 19th parallels. Thus, Le Duan's invitation to the Chinese to deploy was primarily aimed at deterring the U.S. escalation of the war in Vietnam. Liu reiterated Beijing's promise that China's aid to Vietnam against the United States was "an unshakable duty of the Chinese people and the Communist Party." The Chinese, Liu continued, would do their best to assist North Vietnam with anything that Hanoi needed and that Beijing could offer. So far as sending Chinese troops was concerned, the Vietnamese leaders had the initiative in deciding what PLA units they wanted to come into Vietnam, and Beijing would send them only at Hanoi's request.

Four days later, the Central Committee of the CCP issued instructions calling upon the party, military, and people of China to make every effort to support the Vietnamese people in resisting U.S. aggression. Meanwhile, a military delegation consisting of forty-five high-ranking officers of the PLA departed for Hanoi in response to a North Vietnamese invitation. Its mission was to prepare for the deployment of Chinese troops in the north of the DRV. On 17 April the CMC ordered the organization of Chinese troops to assist North Vietnam against the United States. Three special division-sized units formed the first Chinese deployment. They were designated as the Corps of the Chinese Rear Services (*Zhongguo houjin budui*).

On 20 and 21 April further discussions were held between Vo Nguyen Giap, Luo Ruiqing, and Yang Chenwu in Beijing. They hammered out the program for the PLA's deployment and mission in North Vietnam. Agreements were subsequently reached between the two sides. China's greatest concern then was that the U.S. would conduct an amphibious assault on the North, replicating Douglas MacArthur's successful Inchon landing in Korea more than a decade earlier. Beijing acceded to Hanoi's urgent request of 17 April, agreeing to send one Chinese military unit immediately to defend the northeast islands and the coast between Haiphong and Hon Gai, while constructing defense works there. Chinese railway engineering troops worked to improve the rail lines between Hanoi and China to handle the increasing flow of Chinese supplies. In accordance with an agreement between the two countries in January 1965, Chinese Air Force engineering units constructed a new airfield, including hangars and parking aprons in mountain caves, at Yen Bai, some 140 kilometers northwest of Hanoi on the rail line running from Kunming to Hanoi along the Red River.

Shortly after Beijing's initial decision to send troops to North Vietnam, Hanoi requested an additional Chinese deployment. On 16 May 1965, Ho Chi Minh himself, accompanied by Xuan Thuy and Le Van Luong, secretly arrived at Changsha. He met with Mao, who was conducting an inspection tour in Hunan, and asked that China help construct roads in North

Vietnam. Ho asserted that in order to step up insurgency in the South to match the U.S. escalation, he needed to build infiltration routes and move his troops south. Ho handed Mao a sketched map of twelve roads he wanted China to build or repair, and Mao immediately telephoned Zhou Enlai in Beijing to make arrangements to do the work.

Prior to 1965, the land route for supplies was secondary to the sea route; 70 percent of Chinese supplies was shipped to the People's Liberation Armed Forces (PLAF) via this sea route. Two ports on Hainan Island were used to handle the south-bound supplies. Chinese vessels traveled to several central Vietnamese off-shore islands, from whence Vietnamese junks and fishing boats transshipped the supplies to the Viet Cong–controlled regions. Since 1965, the U.S. Navy's Operation Sea Dragon had essentially closed this route for Chinese shipments. China then built a special transport line to South Vietnam via Cambodia for supplies to the PLAF. U.S. officials in Saigon in November 1968 believed that one-third of all supplies came through this route. Nevertheless, the rapid build-up of communist forces in the South changed the situation somewhat; the PLAF and PAVN troops in the South could no longer get adequate supplies from the sea route and were forced to rely more on the land routes. Hanoi decided to improve the Ho Chi Minh Trail, which ran from southern North Vietnam via eastern Laos into South Vietnam.

On 25 May the State Council and the CMC called a meeting at the *Zhongnanhai* (the CCP's headquarters) to discuss Hanoi's new request. The chief participants were Luo Ruiqing, Yang Chenwu, and other senior government and military officials from the Headquarters of the General Staff, the Ministry of Foreign Affairs, the Ministry of Communications, and other government agencies. The Headquarters of the General Staff believed that Hanoi's new request would engage another 100,000 troops in North Vietnam. Zhou emphasized that China's involvement in road building should concentrate on projects vital to military operations. After further negotiations between the Chinese and North Vietnamese governments, Beijing decided to send another 80,000 troops to build seven roads in North Vietnam. In June, the Road Construction Headquarters was created, commanding three engineering divisions, antiaircraft artillery units, and other supporting units. In the meantime, Beijing set up a seven-member committee headed by Luo Ruiqing to take charge of all matters regarding assistance and military operations in North Vietnam.

North Vietnamese leaders appeared to be satisfied with China's response to Hanoi's requests. During his visit to Beijing in early June, Van Tien Dung told Luo Ruiqing that the Vietnamese were able to fight the war by themselves, with Chinese military and material support, because the U.S. had involved its ground troops only in the South while bombing the North from the air. However, he wanted China to send two antiaircraft artillery divisions to defend Hanoi and the railroads between Hanoi and the Chinese border. During further discussion, Van Tien Dung laid out Hanoi's need for

Chinese military involvement under other contingencies. He stated that China should provide Hanoi with the services of its Air Force and Navy if the U.S. Air Force and Navy became involved in supporting a South Vietnamese invasion of the North. As to the form that Chinese air support could take, Hanoi believed that: (1) China could send volunteer pilots to fly Vietnamese planes in combat; (2) Chinese pilots and planes could operate from Vietnamese air fields; or (3) Chinese planes could take off from air bases in China to engage Americans over Vietnam. In the event of a U.S. ground attack on the North, Chinese troops were to serve as Hanoi's strategic reserve, ready to assist in defense or to launch a counterattack to take back the strategic initiative. Again, Luo's answer was in the affirmative; Chinese troops would enter the war in the form and at the time Hanoi preferred, and they would be under Hanoi's command.

However, in 1988 Vietnamese scholars told their American counterparts that in June 1965 China had informed Hanoi that it would be unable to provide air cover for North Vietnam despite an earlier promise to do so. The Vietnamese "White Book" of 1979 also revealed that in July 1965 Beijing had refused Hanoi's request to send Chinese pilots to Vietnam because the Chinese believed that "the time was not appropriate." Although the Chinese sources cited above clearly differ from these Vietnamese accounts, there are several points worth noting. Beijing appeared to have made a general promise in 1964 to provide North Vietnam with air cover. The question could be raised as to whether China would have been able to provide the kind of air support that would have been effective against the Americans at a time when the Chinese economy was such that China appeared unable to modernize its own Air Force. But Le Duan's visit to Moscow in the spring of 1965 appeared fruitful. The Soviet Union agreed to aid Hanoi with a sophisticated air defense system, and asked China to allow the Soviet Air Force to use one or two airfields in southern China, on the pretext of providing aid to Hanoi with MIG-21s. Of course, the Chinese turned down the Soviet request. However, this development might have forced Beijing's leaders to take a second look at their promise to provide air cover for Hanoi. Hanoi's conditions for receiving Chinese air support, set out in June 1965, offered Beijing the opportunity to decide the appropriate time for Chinese intervention. Thus, a Chinese decision about military intervention would be based not only upon Hanoi's request, but also upon U.S. actions.

Although China's military commitment to Hanoi was definite, Beijing's leaders had no intention of provoking a direct Sino-American confrontation under the current circumstances. In 1965, Zhou Enlai repeatedly told foreign leaders that China would not initiate war with the United States, but would be ready to fight back if Washington imposed war on China. In order to avoid putting China in a politically and diplomatically disadvantageous position, Beijing did not want the Chinese military involvement in North Vietnam to receive excessive publicity. All troops deployed to North Vietnam were disguised by designating them as the Chinese Rear Services, and Chinese soldiers were dressed in PAVN uniforms, while the railway engineering troops continued to wear their blue work clothes. Hanoi initially wanted the Chinese to provide air defense down to the 19th parallel, but Beijing, in spite of its strong commitment to Hanoi's cause, made it clear that Chinese AAA units in North Vietnam should not be deployed beyond the 21st parallel.

One conclusion that might be drawn is that Beijing did not wish to give America any excuse to exploit the situation, but another view is that Hanoi did not want the outside world to know about North Vietnamese weaknesses in their war against the United States. The North Vietnamese, who had always considered themselves strong and independent, were sensitive about being in a position of dependence upon China's help. Traditional Vietnamese resentment against China's Han chauvinism also prevented Hanoi's leaders from letting Chinese troops remain openly in Vietnam. Indeed, the relationship between the Chinese troops and Hanoi was not always characterized by cordiality and trust. The DRV government often prevented its nationals from fraternizing with Chinese troops during their stay in North Vietnam. Despite the negative effects of the Chinese military presence, the DRV leaders felt it necessary to get China militarily involved at a level sufficient to keep an intensive guerrilla war going in the South, to counter U.S. air attacks on the North, and to deter a U.S. ground invasion of the North. However, Hanoi was careful to set the stage for a minimum of Chinese military involvement in Vietnam.

Chinese leaders were aware of Vietnamese sensitivities. Prior to their deployment to North Vietnam, Chinese troops were instructed about the "traditional friendship" between China and Vietnam and they were reminded of China's international obligations. The Political Department of the PLA issued a "discipline handbook," requiring Chinese soldiers to "respect the Vietnamese government and the People's Army of Vietnam," and "not to contend for triumphs and captures." In short, Beijing would keep Chinese military operations in line with Hanoi's demands. There is little evidence to support the assertion that China's support was conditional or used as a bargaining device in the Sino-Soviet dispute.

Following intensified U.S. bombing of North Vietnam and the introduction of U.S. combat units into South Vietnam, both Hanoi and Beijing were concerned about the possibility of a U.S. invasion of North Vietnam. Few could be under any illusions, especially in light of Washington's misreading of China's signals in the Korean War and Pyongyang's ignoring of China's warnings about a U.S. landing at Inchon in 1950. This time Beijing would move forward more resolutely. On 9 June a special division-size organization of the PLA was deployed to the northeast coast of the DRV. With more than 20,000 military personnel, it consisted of three combat engineering regiments, one artillery regiment, one antiaircraft artillery regiment, one motor transport regiment, one landline communications regiment, one naval transport group, and one submarine cable engineering group. Its mission, according to the CMC's order, was to assist the PAVN in defending the coast, while building defense and security works along the coast and on some major islands.

Despite their engineering mission in North Vietnam, the combat-oriented structure of Chinese troops was a clear indication of their role. The engineering regiment received a reinforcement of one 37-mm antiaircraft artillery battalion, one 85-mm field gun company, one 82-mm mortar company, and other service companies, numbering about 4,000 soldiers. The engineering battalions had a strength of four companies supported by anti-aircraft machine gun, heavy machine gun, recoilless rifle, and signal platoons. From Beijing's standpoint, this deployment would provide first-line defense, along with the railway engineering units, which were also ordered to prepare for combat should the U.S. launch ground attacks.

After the completion of the defense work along the northeast coast in October 1966, the Chinese government continued to help Hanoi build a second defense line in the Red River Delta. That project stretched over hundreds of miles, from Phu Binh in the north to Ninh Binh in the south, and from Vinh Phu in the west to Haiphong in the east. Underground structures and defense works were built at some 121 sites throughout eight provinces of the DRV. The southernmost work site was at Dat Bang Son, only six miles from the 17th parallel. According to Chinese sources, Beijing sent another three engineering regiments, along with several AAA battalions, totaling 16,000 soldiers, to engage in construction work in the Red River Delta. Prior to crossing the Yalu River in mid-October, 1950, no preparations in the form of prepositioned defense works and advance base development had been made for China's intervention in the Korean war. Now, in 1965–66, massive defense works, together with the Chinese deployment of troops, would permit a forceful response to U.S. attacks on North Vietnam.

The Chinese and Rolling Thunder

United States strategy was based on dissuading Hanoi from sending men and materiel into South Vietnam. Bombing the North Vietnamese communications and supply systems appeared to offer a sound deterrent. The Rolling Thunder operations were launched for such purposes. Beginning in April 1965, North Vietnamese railroads, highways, and bridges were key targets for U.S. warplanes. At the request of the DRV government, on 10 April 1965, a Chinese military and railroad delegation departed for North Vietnam to study Vietnamese railroad conditions and to recommend how many Chinese engineering and air defense troops would be needed to keep them operational.

On 27 April 1965, the Chinese and North Vietnamese governments signed an agreement in Beijing that China would undertake some one hundred projects to increase the transportation capacity of the rail lines between

Hanoi and China, including improving existing railroads and facilities, building a new link line between Thai Nguyen and Kep along with new rail yards, and widening and reinforcing bridges. The 2d Railway Engineering Division at Changsha was assigned to take the mission and designated as the 1st Unit of the Chinese Rear Services, with a strength of six engineering regiments and one AAA regiment from the Army 63d AAA Division. On 23 June 1965, the entire unit was deployed along the rail lines between Hanoi, Yunan, and Guangxi.

Hanoi's goal in the war, William Duiker notes, was not to totally defeat the enemy but to foil Washington's war scheme in Vietnam up to the point where the Americans would be willing to "accept a negotiated settlement of the war." However, North Vietnam was one of the world's poorest nations, possessing neither munitions plants nor industry vital to its war effort. Only a large infusion of aid from China could enable the country to survive and achieve this strategic objective. The railroads between Hanoi and China thus not only formed a vital element of North Vietnam's military-industrial complex as a channel for imports, but they substantiated Beijing's pledge that "China provides a vast rear." The existing railroads were meter-gauge track in poor condition, and required transshipment for rail cars at points of entry from the standard gauge of the Chinese rail line. Improvement of the rail system was vital. Thus, the Chinese command concentrated its man-power and resources on the construction of a rail bypass around Hanoi, a rail line between Kep and Thai Nguyen, and on converting much of the track from meter gauge to dual gauge.

Beginning in September 1965, U.S. strategy shifted to interdiction of supplies between the border and Hanoi. Rail cars, bridges, and tracks were among the earliest American targets. Chinese troops were called upon to re-pair the 554 kilometers of railroad between Hanoi and China damaged by U.S. air attacks. In 1967 U.S. bombing of rail lines north of Hanoi reached its peak. In June alone, U.S. warplanes dropped 9.6 tons of bombs on every kilometer of the rail lines, while hitting every meter of major bridges and rail yards with 4.4 tons and 1.3 tons, respectively. The Chinese railway engi-neering troops, having learned from the Korean War, were determined to maintain an uninterrupted transportation line in North Vietnam. The rail complex at Kep, for example, was bombed forty-eight times and suffered se-vere damage from almost every strike, but it was always quickly repaired and remained operational throughout the air war.

Probably the greatest challenge to keeping the North Vietnamese trans-portation system open came when U.S. leaders decided to attack targets within and near Hanoi. In the summer of 1967, the Long Bien Bridge (the ex-Paul Doumer Bridge) became a prime target. Thus, the stage was set for a major effort against U.S. interdiction. The Long Bien Bridge, on the outskirts of Hanoi, served as the rail entry to Hanoi for the east (Haiphong) and the west (Lao Cai) lines, as well as feeder lines from Kep, Thai Nguyen, and

Dong Dang to the north. On 11 August this 1,680-meter bridge was hit by U.S. bombers. One rail span dropped into the water and two highway spans were damaged. Chinese soldiers were ordered to complete its repair within forty days. The next day two Chinese railway engineering battalions threw themselves into the work around the clock, while a rail ferry was established to by-pass the bombed-out bridge. By 30 September the bridge was restored for traffic. Twenty-seven trains passed over the bridge during the first twenty-four hours. The Long Bien Bridge suffered repeated attacks by U.S. warplanes, but it was usually back in use within a month or so. In December two heavy attacks put the bridge out of action for six months, but Chinese engineers used a ferry and a pontoon bridge to provide a by-pass for the traffic across the Red River.

Indeed, U.S. air attacks on the North Vietnamese rail transportation system produced considerable damage. North Vietnamese leaders later acknowledged that the bombing destroyed virtually all transportation and communications facilities built after 1954. However, U.S. bombing failed to coerce Hanoi into suspending its support for the revolution in the South, and the presence of Chinese railway engineering troops significantly reduced the effects of the air strikes. By February 1969, Chinese units had made 1,778 repairs, including 157 kilometers of railroad and 1,420 kilometers of telephone lines. Meanwhile, 3,100 delayed-action bombs had been either removed or defused. By the time Chinese railway engineering units returned to China in July 1970, the rail system in northern North Vietnam had been impressively improved: 217 kilometers of rail lines (including 98 kilometers of lines for military purposes), along with 30 rail bridges and 14 tunnels, had been built; 362 kilometers of existing railroads had been updated; and 20 railway stations and switching yards had been built or repaired. The transportation capacity of the Hanoi-Youyiguan line increased from 1.64 million to 2.80 million tons of goods annually. Improvements and new construction of North Vietnamese railroads had provided a reliable conduit for war supplies.

Since October 1965, 80,000 Chinese troops had also been engaged in improving the road system in northern DRV. They initially concentrated on increasing the transportation capacity of the highway (Route 3) from China to Hanoi via Cao Bang and Thai Nguyen, and on building bypass and alternate lines (Routes 7, 8, and 10) in order to improve movement of North Vietnamese troops in the North. Chinese troops then improved Route 1 from Bien Nghi to Ban Chat in northeast Vietnam, and built two new roads (Routes 11 and 12) to ease traffic flow between the northwest and the Red River Delta. When the U.S. intensified its air interdiction campaign north of Hanoi, Chinese units were also called upon to repair Route 2 between Tuyen Quang and Thanh That. Because of U.S. bombings, most construction was undertaken in extremely difficult conditions; nevertheless, China claimed that by June 1968, Chinese troops had built 1,206 kilometers of highways, including 305 bridges and 4,441 culverts.

Improvements and new construction not only resulted in a substantially increased capacity for moving Chinese supplies to North Vietnam, and from there to the South, but also provided flexibility and better year-round movement. In an assessment of the effect of U.S. air strikes on North Vietnam, the Institute for Defense Analysis stated that the DRV's transportation system by the end of 1967 had become less vulnerable to interdiction than prior to initiation of the Rolling Thunder program. It is most important to note that American policy makers were wrong in believing that bombing North Vietnam would force Hanoi to keep manpower there rather than send it south. Since thousands of Chinese troops were involved in the war against interdiction in North Vietnam, Hanoi was actually able to free up a large number of its own men and thus to embark upon a further expansion of fighting in the South.

Despite early concerns about U.S. ground attack on the DRV, the Chinese troops deployed in North Vietnam were actually engaged in a relentless antiair campaign during the years 1965 to 1968. Rolling Thunder's focus was on strategic persuasion, attempting to coerce the North Vietnamese into abandoning their support of the southern insurgency. Initially, Rolling Thunder strikes concentrated on targets in the southern part of the DRV; after mid-1965, the focus switched from strategic persuasion to interdiction. The bombings were extended to important bridges and segments of rail lines between Hanoi and the Chinese border. On 24 July 1965, the DRV's Military General Staff Directorate formally requested Beijing to send two Chinese antiaircraft artillery divisions to defend North Vietnam not later than 1 August. The next day, Beijing informed Hanoi that two AAA divisions and one regiment would enter Vietnam immediately, and take responsibility for defending two railroads between Hanoi and China.

On 1 August 1965, two army AAA divisions (61st and 63d) of four regiments each (including the 23d regiment from the Air Force) became the first Chinese air defense forces deployed in North Vietnam. They were principally responsible for protecting supply routes and facilities north of Hanoi. Late in 1966, China added a third division (62d), along with five independent battalions, to the defenses around the Thai Nguyen iron and steel complex as a response to heavier attacks on Hanoi, Haiphong, and the border area. By March 1969 (when Chinese forces were withdrawn), sixteen divisions (sixty-three regiments), together with other support units, involving a total of 150,000 Chinese troops, had served in air defense on a six- to eight-month rotation basis.

According to the official history, Chinese air defense units fought their first battle on 9 August 1965 against American planes attacking the Yen Bai area, supposedly downing one F-4C jet. On 23 August another AAA unit also claimed that it had shot down one U.S. plane and damaged another over the Kep area. But the real combat between Chinese AAA units and U.S. planes did not begin until October when Washington escalated its bombing operations in the North.

During the Vietnam War, Chinese AAA units were mainly equipped with outdated 37-mm and 85-mm guns, which were ineffective against modern U.S. aircraft. The Chinese troops developed the strategy of concentrating antiaircraft sites around significant targets. At Yen Bai, where Chinese engineering troops were involved in the construction of a large military complex, including a long runway and cave structures, the 61st Division deployed two regiments to protect the area. Even smaller targets like the Tong Hoa Rail Bridge several miles south of Lang Son bristled with antiaircraft guns. As the air war continued, defenses were intensified around many important targets. For example, during the Air Force 7th AAA Division's tour of duty in North Vietnam, it operated twenty-four batteries around the Kep railroad classification yards.

In North Vietnam, concentrating antiaircraft guns maximized their effectiveness and formed the heaviest AAA environment in all aerial warfare. On 10–11 March 1967, the U.S. military flew 107 sorties in 33 groups against the Thai Nguyen Steel Complex. Chinese antiaircraft emplacements surrounded the steel plant and power plant. In two days of combat, the Chinese claimed that they shot down eighteen U.S. planes and damaged five, while capturing ten American pilots. On the Chinese side, thirteen people died and thirty-five were wounded, but the steel complex was little harmed.

During the battle, Chinese gunners were encouraged to aim at a particular attacker and fire at the closest possible range. According to one Chinese account, on 5 January 1968, when U.S. aircraft made systematic runs against targets along the rail line between Kep and Dap Cau, the Chinese antiaircraft units engaged the U.S. attackers eleven times. Ten times they used three to five or more AAA batteries to fire at one target. At the most intense, twelve batteries poured their fire on a single enemy plane. As a result, they claimed their victory that day, shooting down nine U.S. planes and damaging three others, while only one rail bridge under their protection suffered bombing damage.

Chinese antiaircraft gun batteries shifted position from day to day to increase their effectiveness against attacking planes. Due to Washington-imposed political restraints on air warfare over North Vietnam, throughout the Rolling Thunder operations U.S. planes often used specific air corridors going to and departing from a target. Chinese units adopted a "fire and move" tactic to deceive U.S. crews with dummy sites and thus to ambush attackers. Chinese statistics from nine divisions show that they shot down 125 planes, 20 percent of their total claims, during their move-and-ambush operations. Antiaircraft artillery in North Vietnam provided the most effective air defense. Heavy fire from the ground often prevented U.S. warplanes from attacking their targets from low altitudes. The percentage of hits on the rail system, according to Chinese calculations, dropped from 15.9 percent in 1965 to 9.5 percent in 1968.

The official DRV claim was 4,154 U.S. planes downed during the war. The official number recorded by the United States is 1,096. It is impossible to reconcile this difference. However, factors which led to such disparity deserve to be noted. First, the defending sides, including North Vietnamese and Chinese AAA units, and Soviet SAM units, on occasion might all claim to have shot down the same enemy plane. Second, Hanoi might have lumped all downed and damaged planes together in its claims. Finally, Hanoi and the DRV leaders inflated claims to improve morale. Nevertheless, the Chinese record is impressive. During three years and nine months in North Vietnam, all Chinese antiaircraft artillery divisions, together with those units assigned to protect engineering troops, fought 2,153 engagements. They shot down 1,707 U.S. planes and damaged 1,608, while capturing 42 American pilots.

Between 1965 and 1969 a total of 320,000 Chinese troops served in North Vietnam, and the greatest number at any one time there was 170,000. More than 1,100 Chinese died and 4,300 were wounded in Vietnam. A small number of Chinese sacrifices, as Le Duan once noted, could save two or three million Vietnamese. Hanoi's leaders might not have been completely satisfied with Beijing's support, but they acknowledged that Vietnam could not have succeeded without the vast rear of China and its support.

Conclusion

In the mid-1960s, China's intention to use military force to counter the U.S. in Vietnam was obvious. The fundamental Chinese orientation was a combination of strategic interest and ideological commitment. The history of the People's Republic of China indicated that the U.S. threat to Chinese security was concentrated on three fronts: Korea, Taiwan, and Vietnam. The Chinese leaders had not forgotten that the United States had supported the French during the First Indochina War. They thought that the United States would not easily swallow its setbacks in Korea and its failures in supporting the Nationalists in Taiwan, and thus interpreted U.S. military escalation in Indochina as evidence of actual aggressive action directed toward China. From Beijing's standpoint, the long-anticipated U.S. invasion might actually happen this time, thus China's security seemed at stake. Beijing increased China's support of Hanoi's drive to liberate the South, while at the same time quickly putting its own troops on the alert, and reinforcing its air defense system in south and southwest China. These actions were obviously undertaken with a sense of the potential risk of the conflict escalating into Chinese territory.

Mao Zedong's theory of world revolution determined China's response in aiding Vietnam and resisting the United States. Chinese leaders believed that Hanoi's war of national liberation in the South would tie down U.S. forces, thereby making less likely a military attack on China and other socialist countries. Ho Chi Minh had a close personal relationship with Mao and other Chinese leaders and he shared many of Mao's ideological beliefs. Beijing believed Ho's cause of national liberation was compatible with Mao's rejection of the Soviet "revisionist" orientation toward imperialism. Hanoi was putting Mao's concept of world revolution into practice.

Prior to the summer of 1964, Beijing leaders believed that Vietnamese forces, with China's support, were sufficient to defeat those of the Saigon regime. However, Washington's gradual increase of its air attacks on the DRV and introduction of combat units into South Vietnam in March 1965 convinced both Beijing and Hanoi that Washington was bent on invading North Vietnam and possibly China. Beijing felt it necessary to reinforce China's military power in the regions adjacent to North Vietnam and to take other measures to prepare for a possible war with the United States. The shooting down of U.S. planes became one manifestation of China's support for Hanoi that was also intended to convey warnings to Washington. Issues of overflight did worry American policy makers, who in return repeatedly imposed restrictions on military operations over North Vietnam.

It is impossible to say with certainty what would have happened if the U.S. had followed the Harry Summers approach and invaded North Vietnam. However, the arrival of U.S. ground troops in the South forced Hanoi to seek more concrete evidence of Beijing's pledges to support the Vietnamese struggle for national liberation. If there had been any previous ambiguity in China's commitment to the cause of the DRV's struggle against U.S. invasion, by the spring of 1965, Beijing and Hanoi appeared to have precisely defined the circumstances under which China would send troops to Vietnam. Chinese leaders were under no illusions, especially in view of lessons they had learned from the Korean War, about the implications of agreeing to commit Chinese troops to defend North Vietnam even before any American troops crossed the 17th parallel. Sending Chinese troops for supportive and security purposes was a clear indication of this. Hanoi had counted on Chinese involvement as a deterrent to U.S. intervention in the war. With assurances of military commitment from China, Hanoi had few fears of further escalation by the United States and appeared perfectly capable of defeating the Americans by relying on its own forces. This was obviously the Vietnamese leaders' preference.

Chinese leaders did not devise their Vietnam policy on the basis of hard and fast principles. They shaped China's policy in response to Hanoi's requests and U.S. actions. Chinese leaders were well informed about Hanoi's strategy in the war of national liberation while watching every move of the U.S. in Vietnam closely. There was enough evidence that China would enter the war on North Vietnam's side once Hanoi made its request. China's support of Hanoi's war effort was on a scale substantially greater than that provided to the Viet Minh against the French. If there had been a need for more Chinese troops to defend the North, they would have been sent. Chinese leaders were aware of Vietnamese national pride and their sensitivity about self-sufficiency and self-reliance. Beijing let the DRV leaders take the initiative in deciding whether and when PLA troops should go into Vietnam. Hanoi made it clear that the DRV did not want massive Chinese intervention unless the United States launched a total attack on North Vietnam.

Thus, a U.S. ground invasion would have forced Hanoi (as a last resort) to request that Beijing fulfill China's commitment. Then, China would have had little room to maneuver, but would have been obliged to engage the Americans directly. It is clear now—although it was not at all clear at the time—that Washington's concern about Chinese intervention in North Vietnam saved the U.S. from repeating its Korean War mistake.

Nevertheless, Beijing made every effort to avoid a recurrence of the circumstances of the Korean War. Chinese leaders clearly interpreted Washington's self-imposed restrictions on U.S. bombing in the North as a sign that the United States did not want to expand the conflict with China. By sending Chinese troops to North Vietnam, China probably hoped to deter but not antagonize Washington. Under conditions short of a U.S. ground invasion of the DRV, China's commitment to Hanoi was limited. Beijing never allowed Chinese planes to operate over Vietnamese territory, and unwillingly deployed Chinese AAA units to the areas beyond the 21st parallel. China's weak economy and lack of military modernization may have made Beijing less committed to modern air warfare in Vietnam. However, strategic considerations may have done more to determine the nature of China's involvement in the Vietnam War. The objectives of China's strategy toward the Vietnam War were to support Hanoi with a sizable Chinese military presence in North Vietnam but to avoid a direct confrontation with the United States. This strategy seems to have worked; there was no direct Sino-American confrontation over Vietnam. Hanoi and Washington agreed to negotiate in late 1968, and Beijing began to withdraw Chinese troops from Vietnam in early 1969. Although Beijing's concern about China's security was shifting to the increasing Soviet threat in the north, the Beijing leadership promised that Chinese troops would return if the Americans came back.

During the Vietnam War, China played an important role in Hanoi's victory over the Americans. Unfortunately, since the deterioration of Sino-Vietnamese relations in the late 1970s, Hanoi now attempts to deny China's role in the war. Hanoi's own part in achieving victory has been inflated while China's involvement has been downplayed. Any attempt to comprehend the Vietnam War suffers from this distortion. So also do those who have raised questions concerning the wisdom of American restraint in Washington's conduct of the war. As both past tragedy and future danger lie in contemporary ignorance, today's scholarship must endeavor to construct an objective history of the Vietnam War. Toward that goal, this study offers an evaluation of the Vietnam War from a Chinese perspective.

How We Lost the War
Phillip B. Davidson

Since the United States and South Vietnam lost the Vietnam War over a quarter cen-
tury ago, most citizens who lived through those years have continued to ask "Why?"
Many scholars and military experts have voiced their answers verbally and in print.
Among these is Lieutenant General Davidson, U.S. Army (Retired), former intelligence
officer to General William Westmoreland and General Creighton Abrams. In this chap-
ter from one of his books on the war, Davidson spells out five basic reasons why the
United States lost that prolonged conflict. He ultimately lays the blame on President
Lyndon B. Johnson, but other decision makers, both civilian and military, do not escape
his criticism. His compelling arguments merit close consideration. This essay first ap-
peared as Chapter 8 in Davidson's Secrets of the Vietnam War *(Novato, CA: Presidio*
Press, 1990), 143–65, and is reprinted with permission.

If there is one American foreign policy of the last twenty-five years that commands national unanimity it would be the one enshrined in the slogan "No
More Vietnams." This unanimity is deceptive, for it is held for vastly different
reasons by groups whose views and objectives vary widely. For example, the
true pacifists (a small group) hold to the slogan because they oppose war, period. The leftists and liberals propound it because they detest the idea of the
United States attacking a Socialist (Communist) nation. The isolationists support it because they oppose all entanglements beyond our shores. The minori-
ties and the underclasses embrace it because they believe that the money
spent on such foreign ventures could be better spent on improving their lot at
home. The ordinary American espouses it because the Vietnam War was
costly and unsuccessful. Thoughtful men harbor it because the loss of the war
crippled American foreign policy for a generation. Above all, military men see
it as the symbol of ultimate strategic failure, for they believe that under
proper management, the war could have been won—not only won, but won
at a fraction of the price we paid in lives, wealth, and national unity.

If we are going to understand how we could have won the war, then we
must first comprehend how we lost it. I shall summarize here the five major
causes of our downfall in Vietnam.

The first failing the United States made in fighting the Vietnam War was
that our leadership *never could formulate a clear and measurable objective.* To be
fair, President Johnson and his advisors did take the first step toward a definable objective. In National Security Action Memorandum 288, 17 March 1964,
they set forth as the broad goal, ". . . to preserve South Vietnam as an independent, non-Communist state." But here the process stalled. The president and
his advisors could not translate this pious wish into concrete objectives.

Such a vague statement of national objectives towards Vietnam confused the principal executors of Johnson's policy. General Westmoreland

says that as COMUSMACV, he *deduced* his mission (and the national mission) to be ". . . punishing the Communists until they would come to the conference table." Gen. Maxwell Taylor, in 1966, gave another interpretation of the national objective. Testifying before Congress, he said that we were not trying to "defeat" the North Vietnamese, but only "to cause them to mend their ways."

President Johnson's unwillingness or inability to formulate clear and measurable objectives in the Vietnam War produced supplementary handicaps. First, without definable objectives, the war lost any sense of cohesive logic. Implementing strategies cannot be devised without reference to the one element which gives them their essential direction. In the same sense, alternative strategies cannot be weighed against each other, since if we don't know what we're trying to do, we can't determine the best way to do it.

Second, without a commonly understood and concrete objective, the various parts of the national machine go their own way, uncoordinated, and frequently at cross-purposes. On several occasions, United States bombing attacks in North Vietnam destroyed promising American negotiating ploys. In the South, indiscriminate bombing and artillery fire made the pacification job infinitely more difficult. This ambiguity about objectives spawned interservice battles, as each service followed its own doctrine and biases without means to relate its role to the whole war and how it was to be fought.

Third, the failure to formulate clear objectives resulted in half-measures in pursuit of an unknown goal. Eventually, this ambiguity resulted, not in any desire to win the war, but only in an effort not to lose it "on my watch." Without a clear concept of what had to be done to win the war, the United States leaders found themselves intimidated by the fear of Chinese intervention or a domestic political backlash.

Fourth, without measurable objectives, there was no way to gauge progress toward their attainment, that is, toward winning the war. This ambivalence bred *false* measures of progress, and this helped to create the "credibility gap" into which the Johnson administration fell. The president and his advisors were looking at and reporting the *wrong* indices of progress, indices which were peripheral to the realities of the conflict.

The Nixon administration did have an objective, although not a very heroic one, to withdraw from the Vietnam War while preserving the integrity of American commitments. Nixon and Kissinger camouflaged this withdrawal behind a facade featuring Vietnamization and negotiations. But here again, Nixon and Kissinger refused to convert their broad policy into definable measurable objectives. The policy of Vietnamization was never spelled out in detail, never formalized by treaty or agreement, never controlled by a timetable or schedule, and never provided with concrete objectives. As a result, the American operators of the program were confused as to what was wanted and how to proceed, while the South Vietnamese were hopelessly bewildered. The truth is that this obscurity was intentional, since the pace of Vietnamization and the linked withdrawal of United States forces depended almost entirely on American domestic politics and not on the enhancement of the South Vietnamese armed forces. The program accomplished its primary mission—it camouflaged our withdrawal from Vietnam. But, as the catastrophies of 1975 attest, it failed its broader purpose of preparing South Vietnam to resist North Vietnamese aggression.

Finally, the absence of clear objectives undermined domestic support of the war. From start to finish, the American people were confused and apathetic about the war. They had questions to which no answers were forthcoming: Was the United States in a war or was it not? Why are we in Vietnam? What are we trying to do there? What national purpose does our effort in Vietnam serve? How important is this distant little country to the United States? How do we hope to win the conflict? When? Without answers to these vital national questions, one is surprised, not that the domestic support for the war eventually collapsed, but that it stayed reasonably firm as long as it did.

The second reason we lost the war was our inability to appreciate the strategy the enemy was using against us. This defect was critical because we gave the enemy the strategic initiative, and if we were to counter his strategy, we had to have a firm grasp of the Communists' Strategy of Revolutionary War. Clausewitz stressed the criticality of this, putting it this way: "The first, the supreme, the most far-reaching act of judgment that the statesman and the commander have to make is to establish . . . the kind of war on which they are embarking; neither mistaking it for or trying to turn it into, something which is alien to its nature. This is the first of all strategic questions and the most comprehensive." Beyond that, if the United States was to win the war it had to avail itself of old Sun Tzu's advice given over two millennia ago, "What is of supreme importance in war is to attack the enemy's strategy." This we never did.

A brief recapitulation [of the North Vietnamese strategy for waging revolutionary war] will be helpful here. Revolutionary war is a *political war*, blending political struggle with military struggle, but always seeking to seize control of a nation-state. As waged by the North Vietnamese it was a *total war*, a *protracted war*, carried out with a *total unity of effort*, every element—military, political, psychological—coordinated to achieve the objective. It was a *changing war*, and it was a *"mosaic"* war.

Unfortunately, the inability of American leaders to grasp the enemy's Strategy of Revolutionary War had debilitating consequences. Revolutionary war is a political war, and yet in Vietnam we responded principally by military means. Revolutionary war is total war, yet the United States reacted timidly, by limited half-measures. Against the seamless web of the unity of effort of revolutionary war, the United States responded by disjointed, uncoordinated, often mutually defeating countermeasures. One of the strengths of revolutionary war is its protraction, yet the United States adopted the strategy of limited war, the very concept designed to protract the conflict. Finally, the United States never understood the changing and "mosaic" nature of revolutionary war. Result—confusion: confusion as to concept, countermeasures, organization, strategy, and, above all, confusion of the American people—this last by far the most critical.

The third critical deficiency in the United States prosecution of the Vietnam War rose from the first two noted above—American leadership could not select the appropriate strategies to combat the enemy's Strategy of Revolutionary War. After all, if you don't know what you're trying to do, and if you don't know what the enemy's trying to do (particularly after you've given him the strategic initiative), you don't have much chance of formulating effective counterstrategies to his strategy—and this is what happened in Vietnam.

Without a definable objective and with no comprehensive insight into the enemy strategy, the United States bounded from one strategic concept to another. The selected American strategy at any give time was determined largely by the personal idiosyncrasies of the president and the perceived needs of domestic politics. Never did the American leadership address the real strategic options: seize the strategic initiative from the Communists, or actively combat the enemy's strategy, or get out of the war.

Looking back at the Vietnam War, one can discern some nine different American military strategies by which the United States tried to reach an acceptable end to the war. In chronological order the first of these was the strategy, that, for want of a better name, I call "advise and support." President Eisenhower initiated this strategy in 1954 with the creation in South Vietnam of the Military Assistance and Advisory Group (MAAG). In essence, the MAAG provided advisors and logistic support to the Republic of Vietnam armed forces (RVNAF), while they did the fighting. This strategy, while appropriate to the situation in general, failed in the particulars. From 1955 until 1963, the Communists in South Vietnam carried out a Phase I insurgency, a political-guerrilla type of warfare. The South Vietnamese (and their American advisors) should have concentrated on developing political stability and pacification strategies, along with the development of small units to combat the guerrillas and to clear and hold territory that could then be pacified. Instead, mirror-imaging our own forces, we developed divisions, corps, and air forces.

This "advise and support" strategy held until about 1963, when growing Viet Cong strength and aggressiveness (as well as increased North Vietnamese aid) began to defeat and disintegrate ARVN. In 1964 the deterioration worsened, and by early 1965 the disintegration of the Republic of South Vietnam appeared inevitable. In this dire circumstance, the strategy of "advise and support" collapsed.

The next United States strategy consisted of a combination of an aerial offensive against North Vietnam and the concept of limited war. The concept of air offensive against an enemy's means of making war had been around since pre-World War II. The strategy of limited war was a post-World War II development promulgated by a group of academics. This strategy was one of *gradualism*, ". . . *not* to apply maximum force toward the military defeat of the adversary; rather it must be to employ force skillfully along a continuous spectrum . . . in order to exert the desired effect on the adversary's will." In plain English, it meant that you start operations against an enemy by a limited attack, gradually increasing the pressure until the adversary does what you want him to do. It is, in essence, the use of limited means to attain a limited end.

It was this concept which dominated the aerial offensive against North Vietnam, called ROLLING THUNDER, launched on 13 February 1965. Initially, the program was intended to "signal" the North Vietnamese leadership that the United States was now getting serious about the North Vietnamese aggression against South Vietnam, and that the United States wanted it stopped. Later on, the emphasis of the program shifted, and it was supposed to punish North Vietnam so severely that Ho and company would cease their invasion of the South.

It accomplished neither objective. In keeping with the strategy of limited war, the program was initially so weak and fragmented that the signal Ho Chi Minh got was that the United States was *not* serious about his aggression. By the time the Americans had toughened up ROLLING THUNDER, the North Vietnamese had taken effective countermeasures, dispersing supplies and installations and developing an antiaircraft defense of formidable proportions. The truth was that without a clear, overall objective, nobody had a sure idea what the program was supposed to do. What it *did* do was to create several years of bitter disputes between the military and civilian elements of the United States government who had opposing and irreconcilable views as to the objectives of the program and how it ought to be carried out.

The advent of ROLLING THUNDER brought in its train the third United States strategy, this one the first of the concepts for employment of American ground forces. This was the air base defense strategy. This strategy—and this is an inflated term when applied to the air base defense concept—was a hiccup in the long line of United States strategies. It came about in February 1965, because General Westmoreland was alarmed about the security of the South Vietnamese air fields, particularly Da Nang and Bien Hoa, from which the aircraft of ROLLING THUNDER operated. And he was right, the security furnished by the Army of Vietnam (ARVN) to these bases was abysmal. Westmoreland made a request for two United States Marine battalions to guard the Da Nang base. On 26 February 1965, President Johnson approved the dispatch of the two marine battalions, which landed at the air base on 10 March 1965. They remained in this base defense role until 6 April 1965, when the continued deterioration of ARVN and the military situation forced President Johnson to change their mission ". . . to permit their more active use under conditions to be established and approved by the secretary of defense in consultation with the secretary of state." Of course, this ambiguous wording only increased the confusion. Both Maxwell Taylor, the United States ambassador to South Vietnam, and General Westmoreland begged for clarification.

It came on 20 April 1965, from a high-level conference held in Honolulu. McNamara, Taylor, Westmoreland, Gen. Earle "Bus" Wheeler, the chairman of the Joint Chiefs of Staff, and Admiral Sharp, CINCPAC, attended. A fourth strategy came from this high-level conference, the so-called enclave strategy. It foresaw the establishment of United States enclaves around important coastal areas such as Saigon, Da Nang, Nha Trang, Qui Nhon, Phu Bai (north of Da Nang), and Chu Lai (south of Da Nang). American troops would defend these areas and would be authorized to sally forth not more than fifty miles to assist ARVN troops or to undertake their own counterinsurgency operations. It was a relatively cheap and cautious way to see how United States ground troops would perform in active operations against the Viet Cong.

It was killed shortly by the opposition of Westmoreland and the Joint Chiefs of Staff, because it surrendered the initiative and the tactical offensive to the enemy, and in their opinion these concessions lose wars. The impotence of ROLLING THUNDER also played a part in its demise. The enclave concept was based on the theory that it would deny the Communists victory in the South, while ROLLING THUNDER punished them in the North. When ROLLING THUNDER failed its role, the key assumption of the strategy collapsed.

But the fundamental defect of the enclave strategy lay in its unsuitability to the situation to which the United States tried to apply it. While the enclave concept has some pertinence in a Phase I insurgency, it is a dangerous strategy to apply to a Phase II situation moving toward Phase III, conventional war. It surrenders not only the strategic initiative to the enemy, but the tactical initiative as well. And this is what happened in March–April 1965. The situation deteriorated, ARVN began to unravel, and a total collapse appeared imminent. If South Vietnam was to be saved, the United States ground troops would have to do it. And so, reluctantly, on 26 June 1965 President Johnson approved a JCS plan which gave Westmoreland 44 combat battalions with freedom to use them as he saw fit.

The very next day, Westmoreland conducted an offensive operation into Viet Cong War Zone D northwest of Saigon, using the United States 173rd Airborne Brigade, an Australian battalion, and about five battalions of ARVN infantry. Thus was born the fifth military strategy, called search and destroy, which would govern United States ground operations for three years. This strategy of search and destroy has fueled many smoky fires of controversy. Westmoreland himself described it as "a war of attrition," and this is the sword that his critics have used to attack him and his concept.

Westmoreland's most extreme critics assert that attrition is not a strategy, but a mindless bloodletting without purpose or end. This is nonsense. Attrition is a strategy, and in the right time and place, it is a good one.

Clausewitz wrote that if one could not immediately destroy the enemy's armed forces then one should concentrate on what he calls "wastage" of the enemy (another name for attrition)—making the war more costly to the adversary by laying waste to his territory, increasing the enemy's casualties, and eroding his moral and physical assets. American military history provides a classic example of wars won by attrition. World Wars I and II were wars of attrition. Grant, Sherman, and Sheridan won the Civil War using the strategy of attrition. In fact, Grant utilized pure search and destroy operations. From 1864 on, he focused on Lee's army, attacking it at every chance, and eventually eroding the Confederate force into impotence and surrender. Sherman, meanwhile, laid waste the "breadbasket" of the South, while Sheridan ravaged the Shenandoah Valley of Virginia.

The strategy of attrition has been successful in other than conventional wars. The American Indians, a redoubtable guerrilla force, were subjugated by a series of relentless campaigns designed to erode their strength and means of livelihood. And although it took the American army a century and a half to do the job, they—and the settlers and railroads who followed them—destroyed the Indians as a guerrilla force not by brilliant campaigns, but by grinding attrition.

As we have seen, Westmoreland, who only superficially grasped the enemy's Strategy of Revolutionary War, intuitively devised the combined strategy of search and destroy and clear and hold. The Washington leadership, with even less understanding of the enemy's strategy, was itself bereft of policy, and reluctantly went along. Using his combined strategy, Westmoreland seized the tactical initiative and drove the enemy's main force units into the peripheries of South Vietnam, while his clear and hold operations produced significant gains for pacification.

But Westmoreland's strategy of attrition had its deficiencies. While it gained the *tactical* initiative it could not, due to political restraints, seize the *strategic* initiative. This meant that the Communists could dictate the style and intensity of the ground conflict and thus, their casualties. They fought when they wanted to, and withdrew into their sanctuaries when necessary. And here is where the strategy of attrition failed. To be successful it had to inflict unacceptable punishment on the Communists. While Westmoreland's strategy of attrition could inflict casualties and drive large enemy units from South Vietnam, it could not reach that magical level which was so painful that Ho would cease his aggression. In sum, while Westmoreland's obligatory strategy partially succeeded, it could not meet the fundamental requirements of a winning United States strategy—it could not seize the strategic initiatives nor successfully combat the Strategy of Revolutionary War.

The tactical successes of Westmoreland's 1967 strategy helped bring on the Tet offensive, which in turn panicked the United States governing elite into a search for a new United States strategy. From this search arose a sixth concept called the Demographic Frontier strategy, which appeared in March

1968, shortly after the Tet offensive. This brainchild of a group of OSD civilians proposed that a line be drawn down the Annamite chain, thence west to the border north of Saigon. The area to the *east* of this line, containing the bulk of the population and resources of South Vietnam, would be defended. The rest of South Vietnam would be abandoned to the Communists. The Demographic Frontier strategy was the enclave concept reborn and enlarged.

The violent objections of the military killed the concept, and it was never even proposed to President Johnson. It is significant, however, for two reasons. First, it shows the profound ignorance of American policy-makers about the kind of war they were trying to combat. They were seeking to apply a strategy suitable to a pure insurgency when the conflict after Tet had progressed well beyond that phase of revolutionary war. Second, it foreshadowed a strategy the South Vietnamese president, Nguyen Van Thieu, put into effect in March 1975, a strategy that played a significant role in the final debacle that destroyed the Government of South Vietnam.

The next (seventh) American strategy, military support to pacification was largely forced on the United States by the enemy. The Tet offensive not only largely destroyed the Viet Cong and its political infrastructure, but it dealt a severe blow to the major Communist combat units themselves. As a result the enemy retrogressed from Phase III (conventional war) to Phase II (the combination of insurgency/conventional war), and in some areas even to a Phase I insurgency, but with two significant differences. These new Phase I operations were now carried out not by Viet Cong guerrillas, but by well-trained and highly motivated North Vietnamese sappers, or commandos. The second difference lay in the fact that on the borders of South Vietnam lurked eight to twelve Communist main force divisions, ready to shift the conflict into a conventional war at any moment. General Abrams, who had taken command of MACV in June 1968, when Westmoreland had become chief of staff, United States Army, adjusted to the Communist retrogression by making support to pacification his primary mission. Thus, in late 1968 and into 1969, a new American ground strategy went into operation. Both Abe and his SVN counterpart, General Cao Van Vien, broke their units into small task forces designed to protect the people and to break up enemy preparations for even minor attacks.

In a way this strategy of pacification support proved successful. In the wake of the Tet offensive, pacification made huge gains in 1968–1969, and even greater ones in 1970, so that by the end of 1971, South Vietnam was virtually "pacified." In another way, however, the strategy of support to pacification had serious deficiencies. It was a strategy in which the enemy still held the strategic initiative. It compelled United States forces into modes of warfare in which our advantages of technology and firepower were minimized. It prolonged the war, and this prolongation eroded the domestic support for the conflict within the United States. But given the constraints imposed by popular disillusionment and domestic politics it was the best that could be devised.

This strategy of support to pacification which held from mid-1968 until mid-1969 bridged the gap between the Johnson and Nixon administrations. So, in early 1969, President Nixon and his national security adviser, Henry Kissinger, had to develop *their* strategy for fighting the Vietnam War.

The new strategy would have to consider several factors. First, and most important, a national objective would have to be determined. Any new strategy would have to take into account the suspension of the air attacks on North Vietnam, which Johnson had instituted on 31 October 1968, as well as the ongoing, but stalled, peace negotiations. In Vietnam, as a result of the enemy casualties of the Tet offensive, the armed forces of SVN were stronger, while the Communist forces in the South were much weaker, particularly the Viet Cong. American forces, a half million strong, were at their peak of power.

On the other hand, this encouraging situation in Vietnam was more than offset by the dire perspective at home. Congressional support for the war had all but evaporated as the liberal Democrats, who no longer had to back LBJ, now turned openly against the war. The antiwar protestors, most of academia, and virtually all of the news media raised a shrill crescendo against the continuation of the war. The middle class, left leaderless by Johnson, confused as to the purposes and conduct of the war, reacted with apathy or opposition. Above all, the growing casualties of the war sapped the courage and resolution of the American people.

After some delay, President Nixon and Kissinger came up with the eighth United States strategy. Its primary objective was simply to get the United States out of the war, under conditions as honorable as possible. Its secondary aim was to leave South Vietnam with the capability to defend itself with the American departure. In effect, it was a policy with maximum and minimum objectives. Maximally, the United States gets out of the war, and South Vietnam remains a free, viable nation. Minimally, the United States gets out of the war—period. It was a clear national objective, although not one exalted by either its fidelity or fortitude.

The problem of the Nixon administration came in the next step, the formulation of a military strategy to carry out its national policy. Three options were available. The first option—by a greatly intensified air and naval offensive, the United States could attempt to bludgeon North Vietnam into ceasing, or at least suspending for a long period, its aggression against South Vietnam. Concurrently, the United States would strengthen the RVNAF, so that eventually the GVN could stand alone. This option had several advantages. First, it utilized our great strength (military power) against the enemy's weakness (relative lack of military power). Second, it snatched the strategic initiative from the North Vietnamese, forcing them to play our game. Third, by attempting to force a quick decision, it attacked the enemy's Strategy of Revolutionary War with its emphasis on the protraction of the conflict. Fourth, a quick but heavy air and naval assault, as opposed to a long ground war, would save lives, North and South Vietnamese, as well as American. Fifth, this option would seriously erode, perhaps almost destroy, North Vietnam's war-making potential, leaving South Vietnam in a relatively stronger position and permitting a faster and more secure withdrawal of American forces. Finally, such an all-out offensive would not only punish the North Vietnamese severely, but would heighten their latent fears as to what further escalation the United States would take if the air and naval offensive did not bring the conflict to a satisfactory conclusion—the "other shoe" syndrome.

The disadvantages of this option lay principally in the field of public support for the war. Such an offensive would alarm our European allies, and more crucially, would consternate the American people. By March 1969, John Q. Public didn't want to widen the war; he wanted out of it. Abrogation of Johnson's bombing halt and the air offensive would certainly be seen as an escalation of the war, and rightly so. Congress, the news media, and the antiwar protestors would erupt, particularly since Nixon's electoral campaign and his close victory over Hubert Humphrey gave him no mandate to expand the war in search of peace.

There was one further disadvantage to this option, and it lay in the military field. What would Nixon and the United States do if the air and naval offensive failed? What if Ho and the North Vietnamese people stubbornly refused to even negotiate towards an end to the war? Nixon could continue the assault, bombing North Vietnam "back to the Stone Age," to use Gen. Curtis LeMay's ungenteel expression. Or the administration could bomb the dikes along the Red River, with a resulting deluge which would cause widespread devastation and suffering. Finally, Nixon could use small nuclear weapons in some carefully controlled operation. Any of these acts would bring on worldwide condemnation and the most virulent and widespread opposition and censure within the United States.

In the event of the failure of the air/naval offensive, Nixon could take another tack. He could figuratively shrug his shoulders and say, "Well, we tried, and it didn't work," an admission of defeat which would greatly strengthen Ho's hand and catastrophically weaken Nixon's position, both in negotiations and at home. To use a poker term, if Nixon adopted this option, he would be betting his whole stack of chips on the success of the offensive, a monstrous gamble for his country and for himself.

If Nixon did not elect the bold course embodied in the first option, he had a second course of action open, an option much more timid than the first. It envisioned an extended period of time during which American forces would protect South Vietnam from North Vietnam, while vastly increasing South Vietnam's capability to defend itself. It was the reverse side of the coin to the first option. It surrendered the military advantages inherent in the bolder option. It failed to use United States strength against enemy weakness; it surrendered the initiative to the enemy; its prolongation of the war played to the enemy's strategy of revolutionary and protracted war; it would be more expensive in lives and resources; it would do nothing to erode North Vietnam's war-making capacity, nor would it pose "the other shoe" syndrome.

These military disadvantages would be offset, however, by the great advantages in public support which this option would garner abroad and at home. United States troops would be brought home and American participation in the war curtailed. The increase in the capabilities of the RVNAF, to the so-called "Vietnamization," would provide at least a semantical cloak to cover a United States retreat. It was a cautious course; one designed to gain the minimum objective—to get the United States out of the war.

There was a third option to carry out the Nixon/Kissinger national policy. In 1985 Kissinger described it thusly, ". . . Nixon should have gone to Congress early in his term, outlined his strategy, and demanded an endorsement. Failing that, he should have liquidated the war. Nixon rejected such advice because he felt that history would never forgive the appalling consequences of what he considered an abdication of Executive responsibility. It was an honorable, indeed a highly moral decision."

Before one dismisses this option as summarily as President Nixon did, the observer should note the historical wisdom contained in Kissinger's proposal. What Kissinger now suggests (as I understand it), is that President Nixon do what the United States constitution says he ought to do—ask Congress for a declaration of war or for some other equally binding commitment. If the president can get Congress to commit itself, presumably, Congress thereby commits the American people. If the president can't get congressional approval, presumably he doesn't have the approval of the people. In this latter case the war will eventually be lost. Better get out sooner than later.

We know now that President Nixon chose the second option, Vietnamization, with consequences all too well known. Vietnamization, too, was a flawed strategy. Theoretically, it balanced the withdrawal of American troops by a corresponding enhancement of the South Vietnamese armed forces. This balance was never attained. American forces were withdrawn on a timetable generated, not by RVNAF augmentation, but by the pressure of the antiwar activists and domestic politics. Then, too, Vietnamization contained the same two fundamental deficiencies which doomed the other United States strategies—it left the strategic initiative with the Communists, and it did not attack the enemy's strategy, which during this period saw them waiting out United States withdrawals, while massively increasing their own capabilities.

Even men as astute as Nixon occasionally second-guess themselves, and so it was with this decision. On 10 April 1988 on NBC's TV program "Meet the Press," Nixon said, "I would say the major mistake I made as president was one—this will surprise you—was not doing early in 1969 what I did on May 3 of 1972 and on December 15 of 1972, and that was to bomb and mine North Vietnam. I wanted to do it, I talked to Henry Kissinger about it, but we were stuck with the bombing halt that we inherited from the Johnson administration, with Paris peace talks. . . . if we had done that [the air/naval offensive] then we would have ended the war in Vietnam in 1969 rather than in 1973. *That was my biggest mistake as president.*"

Well, maybe he was right—and again, maybe not. Nobody will ever know what the results would have been if Nixon had done in 1969 what he did in 1972. This is another of those "what if" questions which History never answers.

The all-out aerial assault against North Vietnam of December 1972, called by the news media the "Christmas Bombings," and by the American forces, LINEBACKER II, was the ninth and final American strategy. Its purpose was to force the dilatory North Vietnamese to return to the conference table and conclude the agreement by which the United States would leave the war. From the American viewpoint, the results were spectacular. North Vietnam's military potential, its industry, and its economy lay in ruins. In addition, the raids destroyed North Vietnam's ability to defend itself against further air attacks. Its airfields were destroyed and all its surface-to-air missiles expended. The North Vietnamese promptly returned to the conference table. Although this strategy had a limited purpose, it was the most successful of all. For the first time, it seized the strategic initiative from the enemy. It utilized our strength (air power) against enemy weakness. And above all, it worked.

The fourth failure which contributed to the loss of the war for the United States, was the domestic collapse of support for the conflict. This debacle had many roots, some buried deep in our history and national psyche, others the fallout of the 1960s, still others personality defects of American leaders.

Our history has given Americans a view of war and peace particularly unsuited to the world of the last half of the twentieth century. We view war as the exception in our national life, a cataclysmic break in our customary condition, peace. We do not regard peace as the Soviets do—a continuation of war by other means. To us, a shooting war is an unfortunate occurrence which we end (successfully, of course) as soon as possible, and then get on with our peacetime pursuits. As a nation, we have no stomach for long, drawn-out, twilight struggles mixing war and peace.

The Vietnam War furthered this national confusion about war and peace. This war had no discernable start which might make it comprehensible as an event. With no start, it seemed also to have no finish, no lines on maps nor great victories to indicate progress. It was an undeclared war, and as such, eventually became unacceptable as a war. It became not a national crusade, but a public nuisance.

This feeling that the Vietnam War was something less than a war was intensified by the absence of experiences which modern Americans associate with war. There was no appeal to patriotism, no Liberty Bond drives, no lionizing of American fighting men. There was no sense of shared suffering, no food rationing, no gasoline stamps, no pain to impress on the country that all of us were in a war. Thus, domestic support for the war was built on a fragile foundation, subject to collapse when a load of misfortune fell on it. As Dean Rusk once said, "You can't fight a hot war in cold blood." But he said it *after* the war was over.

Now, a charismatic and assertive president could have taken any number of actions to make the American people aware that a war was going on, and that the national security of the United States was indirectly threatened. President Johnson chose not to do this, and although President Nixon did occasionally rally the American people to the support of the war—as, for example, his "silent majority" speech of 3 November 1969—by the time he came to office, the opportunity to create a solid and lasting foundation of support for the war was gone.

Most critical, neither president understood that part of North Vietnamese revolutionary war strategy, called *dich van*, or action against the enemy (American and South Vietnamese) people, a program aimed at shattering the support of the people for the war. Giap's whole strategy after Tet 1968, was aimed at one decisive objective—the greatest American vulnerability, its will to continue the struggle. The protraction of the war, the propaganda, the inconclusive negotiations, the ambiguities, and the military actions which produced American casualties, were blended and used to strike at this American weakness.

By this strategy, the North Vietnamese not only matched their strength against our weakness, but transferred the principal battlefield from the rice paddies of Vietnam to the streets of the United States. They forced the United States into a no-win strategic dilemma by these same attacks on the American home front. If the American leadership prosecuted the war forcefully, it risked losing domestic support to continue the war. If the United States attempted to assuage its war critics by restraining military initiatives and measures, it had to forego the hope of winning militarily in Vietnam. Any American attempt to walk the fine line between the extremes, or to bound back and forth between them (as Nixon did), only guaranteed eventual defeat.

But Giap must share this triumph with circumstances peculiar to the United States in the late sixties and early seventies. Underlying the American government's failure to maintain the support of its people for the war was a lack of consensus among the intellectuals, the news media, and the political elite. Since at least the 1950s, there has been in America a schism as to what the nation's foreign policy objectives should be, and what place the use of military force should play in attaining them. This lack of unity has been sharpened by ideological extremism, partisan politics, and personal ambition. The gap widened as the war wore on, particularly after Nixon's election. Eventually, this chasm in national unity became so wide and so deep that in the end no rational war policy could bridge it. Only a camouflaged surrender remained.

The news media played their part in demolishing popular support for the war. They misreported the war, sometimes intentionally, more often unintentionally. After all, the media understood the strategy and nuances of revolutionary war even less than the American leaders. In the latter stages of the war, the news media had a bias against the RVN, and since the United States supported the RVN, their own government as well. The media, largely unknowing, were effective practitioners of Giap's *dich van* program within the United States.

Television contributed heavily to the destruction of the American will to prosecute the war. The constant fare of destruction, suffering, and blood brought into American living rooms horrified and dismayed the American people. The Johnson and Nixon administrations never realized until too late that in this age the control of images and information is central to the exercise of political power. The United States government never clearly realized that the hearts and minds of the American people had become the critical battlefield, and that it had to protect the nation here as surely as it did its armed forces in combat.

The greatest erosion of the American resolve to stay the war came from the increasing American casualties as the Vietnam War ground on. In 1983 Professor Lawrence W. Lichty said, "If one does a fairly detailed statistical analysis, the support for the war is a precise, inverted relationship to the number of people getting killed. It was Americans coming home in boxes that tended more than anything else to turn public opinion against the war." This relationship of American casualties to home front support is confirmed by another expert who studied not only the Vietnam War, but the Korean War as well. Daniel Hallin, quoting John E. Mueller, stated that, "Public support for the shorter and less costly limited war in Korea also dropped as its costs rose, despite the fact that television was in its infancy, censorship was tight, and the World War II ethic of the journalist serving the war effort remained strong." The most powerful of all arguments for a short, conclusive war.

The fifth reason for our loss of the war was—*the Communists had a superior grand strategy.* (Grand strategy is defined as the employment of all facets of national power to achieve a political objective.) From the beginning to the end of the Indochina Wars, the Communists had one national objective—the independence and unification of Vietnam, and eventually of all of French Indochina. They achieved this national objective by the conception, development, and implementation of a coherent, long-term, and brilliant grand strategy—the Strategy of Revolutionary War. This strategy was the key ingredient of the Communist victory.

Now, no one strategy is innately better than any other strategy. In some circumstances the strategy of attrition may be the best strategy; under other conditions limited war strategy or revolutionary war strategy may be superior. *The superior strategy is the one which is best fitted to the actual conditions under which the war is waged.* More specifically, *the superior strategy takes advantage of the enemy's vulnerabilities and one's own strengths while neutralizing the enemy's strengths and one's own vulnerabilities.*

This is the sense in which the Strategy of Revolutionary War proved superior to the strategy we used against it. And a superior strategy wins wars. The North Vietnamese have an old axiom they often cite. It is this:

I.   When the tactics are wrong and the strategy is wrong, the war will be quickly lost.

II. When the tactics are right, but the strategy is wrong, battles may be won, but the war will be lost.

III. When the tactics are wrong, but the strategy is right, battles may be lost, but the war will be won.

IV. When the tactics are right, and the strategy is right, the war will be won quickly.

While this obviously oversimplifies a complex subject, it does contain, like most axioms, a solid kernel of truth. Looking at Indochina War II, the American conduct of the war falls into Case II, while the North Vietnamese can be placed in Case III.

This Strategy of Revolutionary War was the key ingredient of the Communist victory. One might argue that crediting the Communist triumph in Vietnam to a superior strategy is overly simplistic. A critic might contend that other factors, such as massive aid from China and Russia, the use of the Cambodian and Laotian sanctuaries, the weakness of the South Vietnamese government and leaders, and the incredible martial spirit of the North Vietnamese soldiers, were significant factors. And this is true, but the factor which welded and focused the Communist effort from first to last was the Strategy of Revolutionary War. Without it, there would have been no Communist victory.

Finally, I conclude this chapter [by] giving the reader my view of the main reason we lost the war—as depressing as that is. Our loss of the war can be laid almost entirely to one man—Lyndon Baines Johnson.

Let me go back to my first book, *Vietnam at War*, where I reported all the accepted explanations why LBJ's war time leadership was so grossly inept and tragically inadequate. Yet, even as I documented these reasons, I was unsatisfied with them as explanations of LBJ's wartime leadership failures. They didn't make sense. All of Johnson's activities prior to the war revealed him to be a dynamic, aggressive, and experienced leader. And there was no question about Johnson's intelligence. Jim Wright, one-time speaker of the United States House of Representatives, said that Johnson was the smartest man he had ever known. So, I had to face the question of why such an able leader could be so abysmally inept in the conduct of military and foreign affairs.

I reviewed the usual explanations of LBJ's inadequacies—his inexperience in foreign affairs, the possibility that his advisors misled him, or overpowered him by their dazzling expertise. The more I researched the matter, however, the more I became convinced that none of these simple explanations held true. LBJ was no neophyte in foreign or military affairs; he was not misled by his advisors or cowed by the self-styled experts.

Finally, the answer came. Johnson's motives became clear, and his actions understandable. While LBJ played the role of an inept and indecisive leader in public, he was an aggressive and effective leader in the privacy of his councils. Lyndon Johnson got the kind of war he wanted, the kind that suited his purposes. *The brutal truth is that Johnson fought the Vietnam War as a secondary adjunct to his domestic political aims.*

These domestic political objectives were twofold. First, he wanted to be reelected in 1968. Second, he wanted to see his Great Society programs brought to their full fruition. The first objective, reelection, requires no comment. As to the second, Johnson intended the Great Society to be his memorial, a monument overarching Roosevelt's New Deal and the more timid social programs which followed, Truman's Square Deal and Kennedy's New Frontier.

But a full-scale war, or even a moderate-scale conflict, endangered these two political objectives. A real war would upset the country, disrupt millions of lives, and cost a lot of money. Such a war would hazard not only his reelection in 1968, but would almost certainly mutilate his Great Society programs as the funds to help the underclass went to pay for the war. And yet, he couldn't just walk away from Vietnam either. He was all too aware of the Republican's [sic] exploitation of Truman's "loss of China," and Johnson knew his "loss" of Vietnam would torpedo his reelection chances.

Now, if Johnson were to fight the war so as to further his two political objectives, his motives had to be camouflaged and his actions carefully crafted. First, he must always steer a middle course. Do something, but not too much. This course placated the Republicans and other hawks on the right and the Democratic doves on the left, either of whom could devastate his Great Society programs. LBJ's real strategy was: don't win the war (and lose the doves), but don't lose it (and lose the hawks). McGeorge Bundy, who in 1965 and early 1966 was National Security advisor to President Johnson, once explained LBJ's real strategy when he said, "(Johnson's) own priority was to get agreement at the lowest level of intensity he could, on a course that would meet the present need in Vietnam and not derail his legislative calendar."

As far as the Congress and the American public were concerned, Johnson hoped to achieve his domestic ends by calculated ambiguities. Here his major thrust was to try to convince Congress and the people by subterfuge and deceit that the conflict in Vietnam was not really a war. Note how he went about this. First, he refused to ask for a declaration of war, an act sure to reveal to the people that we were in a significant conflict. Second, throughout his administration he refused to consider the JCS's recommendations to mobilize the Reserves, a decision Johnson made alone against the unanimous advice of his advisors. Third, he made no effort to reform the draft so as to induct college students and others being unfairly deferred. Fourth, he camouflaged as best he could every troop increase and escalation. Fifth, he was careful never to discuss (or permit discussion) of the cost of the war financially nor the eventual manpower requirement. Sixth, he consistently denied that his Vietnam policies had changed when obviously they had. Seventh, he never spelled out his concrete objectives toward the war, or how he intended to attain these objectives. Finally, he *never,* repeat, *never* made any effort to arouse a sense of patriotism among the American people about the war.

All of the ambiguities served Johnson's political imperatives—reelection and the Great Society programs. They confused the people as to whether the United States was in a war. The refusal to call up the Reserves and amend the draft served two purposes. It maintained the illusion that we were not in a war (or at least, not a major one), and it protected powerful constituencies from the disruption of their lives and the consequent demand that the war be brought to a quick and victorious end. He didn't spell out his objectives and costs because Congress and the people would see through his scheme and demand that the war be funded at the expense of the Great Society. And finally, of course he didn't want to get the American people into a patriotic furor over the war. If he did this, the people and Congress would insist that he do something to win the war, and there would go the Great Society and probably his chances for reelection.

Johnson followed a similar track with his advisors. He carefully engineered the advice he received so that he never got any real analysis or debate about the broad options in the war—all-out victory, limited war, or withdrawal. He refused to consider or be briefed on the war-winning strategy the JCS had drawn up as early as August 1965, and which they constantly tried to force on him over the next two years. He approved ROLLING THUNDER (the bombing of North Vietnam), but intentionally left the details and intensity so vague as to forestall an aggressive and effective air campaign. He used Undersecretary of State George Ball as the "house dissenter." Johnson paraded him before the National Security Council before he made any major decision, but never heeded his advice.

Finally, he never established objectives, costs, or force levels, preferring to approach each decision on an *ad hoc,* short-range basis. Johnson's vacillation and indecision about what strategy to pursue was calculated to further the ambiguities of the situation. This equivocation kept both the hawks and the doves at bay; the hawks thinking that he would escalate to victory; the doves believing he would negotiate his way out of the war. In the words of McGeorge Bundy, Johnson intentionally "put a premium on imprecision."

While LBJ primarily used imprecision to conceal his true aims, he was not above using pure deceit on occasion. He was particularly sensitive to any figures regarding the cost of the war. The true figures would alert the country that we were in a big war, or on our way to a bigger one. Beyond that, Congress would fund the war out of the money he wanted to go to the Great Society. And so, faced with this problem, he had the Defense Department knowingly give the Treasury Department and the Council of Economic Advisors a fallaciously low figure as to the cost of the war. In other words (as David Halberstam put it), "one part of the government was lying to another part."

Finally, look at the skill with which he used the possibility that the Chinese would intervene in the war. Both in public and within his closed councils, he raised this bogeyman of Chinese intervention. It was his most useful tool in turning aside the recommendation of his uniformed advisors to intensify military operations in Vietnam. When the generals and admirals contended that an escalatory action would not bring in the Chinese, Johnson would taunt them with the remark, "That's what MacArthur thought," or "MacArthur didn't think they would come in either." Johnson adamantly rejected all advice from CIA and the JCS that the Chinese would not enter the war and refused even to consider seriously whether Chinese intervention was a real threat. He continued to use this bogeyman after the onset of the Chinese Cultural Revolution when it was obvious that there was no likelihood of Chinese intrusion.

Johnson's real strategy (the protection of his domestic priorities) extended to the actual conduct of military operations. He gave Westmoreland wide latitude in formulating the strategy for the operations within South Vietnam. But Johnson didn't have to worry about Westmoreland's operations getting too bold. He had shackled Westmoreland to the strategic defensive by his decision that no operations could be conducted in Laos, Cambodia, or the DMZ. So, Westmoreland wasn't going to win the ground war, but with the military power available to him, he wasn't going to lose it either. LBJ would keep giving Westmoreland troops (less than Westmoreland wanted), which would placate the hawks, but not enough to win, which would appease the doves.

On the other hand, he rode close herd on the bombing campaign in the north, ROLLING THUNDER. He personally approved almost every target and sometimes even prescribed the armament to be used. In Johnson's "domestic first" strategy, here was the program that could get him in trouble with the doves. He could convince the hawks that the bombing was effective, but if he permitted really devastating attacks (the kind constantly recommended by the JCS) they would bring out the doves in opposition—not only to the bombing escalation, but to the Great Society.

The Tet offensive demolished Johnson's hidden policy of pursuing his domestic objectives at the expense of the war. It showed Congress and the people that we were in a real war. It revealed the deceit and barrenness of his Vietnam strategy. It shocked the Congress and people. And above all, it convinced Johnson that he had no chance to be reelected in 1968.

But he still tried to maintain the facade: After Tet he made a radical change in strategies, but attempted to hide it. He still refused to mobilize the Reserves or reform the draft, and he made no effort to explain the war to the people or to rally them. Finally, on 31 October 1968, he halted all bombing of

North Vietnam, an act of blatant politics to assist the Democratic candidate, Hubert Humphrey.

So, Lyndon Baines Johnson, obsessed by his ambition and his domestic political goals, led the United States into its first defeat in war. True, there were other American actors and other factors contributing to the catastrophe, but he, more than any of them, or the sum of them, brought about the downfall. Professor Larry Berman, the foremost authority on Johnson's decision-making, succinctly summed it up when he said, "Why did it [the American defeat] happen? Because Lyndon Johnson dreamed of a Great Society and not of Asian real estate . . . In the end the [presidential] advisory process mattered only incidentally. Lyndon Johnson mattered a great deal."

It was a tragedy on all fronts. It ruined Lyndon Johnson and denied him the very goals he so hungrily sought, reelection and the Great Society. The impossibility of his reelection has been covered. The Great Society programs were never fully funded and soon fell into failure. Ironically, the programs succeeded in doing the very thing which they had been designed to overcome—the establishment of a permanent underclass. Finally, the Vietnam War was a tragedy for the 58,000 young men who died there and the countless thousands more maimed there. It was a tragedy for the South Vietnamese, above all, it was a tragedy for the United States.

And it need not have been. We could have won the war. And with that victory we could have upheld our solemn commitments to South Vietnam, buttressed our position in the world as a great power and worthy ally, and as a nation could have spared ourselves the paralyzing self-doubts, the domestic divisiveness, and the pusillanimous vacillations in external affairs that have plagued this nation for two decades.

But—as is always the case—the victory would have brought with it onerous problems. If the Korean experience furnishes an example—and it does—the United States would have to keep residual military force in South Vietnam for at least two decades. The American force would have been harassed by minor North Vietnamese forays over the DMZ and by small, but frustrating, ambushes and land mining operations carried out by Communist guerrillas. The needs of the South Vietnamese government for economic and military aid would surely grow into significant fiscal burdens. To paraphrase the old adage—the price of liberty (for a Southeast Asian ally) is not only eternal vigilance, but the assumption of long-term and painful obligations as well.

XIII

❧

Continued Challenges and Commitments, 1976–1991

The Mother of All Battles

Norman Friedman

Desert Shield gave way to Desert Storm, launched on February 24, 1991. Its purpose was to drive Saddam Hussein's Iraqi forces out of neighboring Kuwait, a feat achieved in only 100 hours once the ground war began. The author of this essay, a prominent military historian, discusses the dispositions of the Iraqi and allied forces, the offensive options available to Central Command, the final allied plans, and the reasons why the offensive was so successful. The reader might well note from this essay the complexity of modern coalition warfare and the impact of technology upon it. This essay was reprinted from Friedman, Norman. 1991. The mother of all battles. Chapter 12 in Desert Victory: The War for Kuwait. *(Annapolis: Naval Institute Press) with permission.*

Saddam Hussein repeatedly told his public that the ground contest for Kuwait would be the "Mother of All Battles," that his troops would inflict such heavy casualties that the coalition forces would withdraw in dismay. The reality was, of course, rather different. Saddam's generals were presumably unenthusiastic critics, but Saddam did get some warning from his former patrons, the Soviets. Uncomfortably aware that the ground war would probably be a humiliating disaster, the Soviets tried to broker a cease-fire. They failed because, unwilling to believe what was coming, Saddam Hussein refused to accept the unconditional terms the coalition (led by the United States) demanded. Saddam apparently hoped that he could end the war simply by withdrawing his forces from Kuwait, without either renouncing its annexation or paying for the damage they had done. That was unacceptable to the coalition because it left Saddam's forces intact.

In Saddam's political system, any humiliation might well be fatal. If defeat was inevitable, better to stand and fight and inflict some casualties on the enemy. If Iraq's army put up a good enough resistance, then Saddam might even emerge a sort of hero, having stood against so much of the world. The 100-hour coalition victory was so thorough that Saddam presumably lost even this consolation prize.

The outcome was quite surprising. No one had been able to estimate the degree to which Saddam's army had been broken by air attack. Nor had anyone guessed just how effective the U.S. assaults would be, even when they met serious resistance. Some Iraqi units did stand and fight, but they lost, and lost badly. Readers will recall that throughout the war, the president and senior military officers had constantly cautioned that, although progress up to that point had been very quick, some serious reverses probably lay ahead. These counsels reflected real intelligence data and real skepticism. For example, analysts in Washington, who had their own satellite and other data to hand, were quite doubtful of CentCom's claims of damage inflicted on Iraqi armor and artillery. It is not possible to check now, since so much of the area attacked never fell into allied hands.

Central Command began planning a military campaign to force Saddam out of Kuwait as early as September 1990. As in the case of the air campaign, it was an option, a possibility to be selected if Saddam refused to leave Kuwait. The great issue was always the same. Saddam's troops were digging in. The great equalizer that the United States would wield would be tactical air power, and that air power would be nearly useless against well dug-in troops. The question, then, was always how to force the Iraqis out into the open.

General [Norman] Schwarzkopf's initial plan, in September, was to rush into western Kuwait, coming around the corner at which Kuwait meets Saudi Arabia and Iraq. He had limited forces, but they were reasonably mobile, and he was already building up a large air arm. The wadi forming the western border of Kuwait was a traditional invasion route. The general's hope was that the Iraqis would have to emerge from their bunkers to meet his incoming force, and that their movement would expose them to bombing. In retrospect it is not clear that the Iraqis would have had to come out, since the thrust toward Kuwait City would not necessarily have threatened any vital target. The Iraqis might well have been content to pull the attacking Americans into costly street fighting in Kuwait City itself. Certainly it would have been Saddam Hussein's view that the U.S. forces would have halted rather than risk so gruesome a contest.

Events soon overtook this plan. During the fall, as the force in Saudi Arabia was built up, the Iraqis fortified Kuwait, including the western border. There was no longer an easy way into Kuwait. Planners in XVIII Airborne Corps, the force in place in Saudi Arabia, now argued that it would take at least four divisions just to make the left hook. However, there was an attractive way *around* the Iraqi Army, and that way had the additional advantage of being one the Iraqis could not ignore. They would have to come out and fight or risk having their supply lines cut off. That was the deep left hook General Schwarzkopf chose in October 1990.

The left hook was not, however, the only such option he had. The navy and marines argued forcefully for an amphibious thrust, not (as many imagined) onto the fortified Kuwaiti coast, but up the Shatt-al-Arab toward or beyond Basra. Such an operation would have been altogether feasible, and it would have placed a powerful force deep in the Iraqis' rear. Just like the deep left hook, it would have crushed Iraqi forces between allied armies. Unlike the deep hook, it would not have required as much logistical preparation in the Saudi desert, and so would not have risked betrayal by whatever air reconnaissance Saddam Hussein might have mounted. On the other hand, some form of left hook would still have been needed to cut off the escape of the Iraqis toward Baghdad. General Schwarzkopf vetoed the idea. Before the end of January the marines knew that quite probably they would be fighting mainly as ground troops, and that the amphibious fleet would perform a feint. The debate actually continued up to about a week before the ground war began.

For a time it seemed that the air campaign itself might be decisive. Certainly the daily briefings suggested to many in Washington that Iraq was being damaged so badly that it could not continue to fight. Only those in the field were aware that bomb tonnage was quite limited and that bomb damage assessment was almost impossible in the most crucial cases. As a long-time ground combat veteran, moreover, General Schwarzkopf was well aware that troops almost never surrendered to air attack. They might be badly demoralized, but they would surrender only when armed troops arrived to take over the ground on which they were standing. The air campaign could prepare the battlefield, but it could not end the war.

Through early February, then, Central Command spokesmen stated that the prerequisite for a ground offensive was that half of all Iraqi tanks and artillery pieces be destroyed by air attack. The same spokesmen repeatedly tried to downplay the manifestly pressing time factors. It now seems likely that both efforts were disinformation intended to convince the Iraqis that the battle was not yet imminent.

The enemy force was huge, and it seemed most doubtful that it could be defeated without substantial casualties. Iraqi losses were unknown; it was estimated that up to 545,000 men, in twelve armored and thirty other divisions, were in the Kuwaiti theater of operations. Based on these estimates the 24th Division commander predicted 500 to 2,000 killed and wounded. The XVIII Corps commander thought the marines would suffer 10 to 20 percent losses.

Given the enormous projected human cost of a ground campaign, the actual decision to engage in one had to be made by President Bush. He sent

Secretary of Defence [Richard] Cheney and Chairman of the Joint Chiefs of Staff Gen. Colin Powell to Saudi Arabia to evaluate the situation there. At a meeting on 9 February, General Schwarzkopf recommended an attack between 21 and 25 February. The president approved, and on 14 February General Schwarzkopf set last-minute measures into motion for an attack to be made on 21 February. The offensive was delayed until 24 February so as not to embarrass the Soviets, who were then making a last-minute attempt to broker a cease-fire.

The main problem the coalition commander, General Schwarzkopf, had to solve was the numerical superiority of the Iraqi Army. Classical combat theory requires advantages of 3:1 to advance, and 5:1 to advance into heavy fortifications. Overall, Central Command had to cope with a numerical inferiority of about 4:3 in tanks and worse than 5:3 in artillery. Total numbers of troops were not very different, but the U.S. forces had a much higher ratio of "tail" to "teeth"—that is, support troops to fighting forces (which, incidentally, was why they were so mobile). The only coalition numerical edge, and a heavy one at that, was in aircraft.

These figures were deceptive in a critical way. They were overall totals, not the numbers that would count in any particular engagement. It was the task of Central Command to pin the enemy down in such a way that our forces could be concentrated to achieve the necessary local superiority. Central Command planned conservatively, assuming no particular superiority for the allied troops or their equipment. The combination of strategy (to achieve the sort of numerical edge that would have beaten good troops, albeit at a high cost) and superior equipment and people proved devastating to the Iraqis.

Whatever his private estimate of the quality of Iraqi troops, General Schwarzkopf could not afford to act on an assumption of innate allied superiority. He planned to wear down Iraqi resistance by air attack, and then to win by a deep flanking armored attack. The Iraqi flank was open along the Saudi-Iraqi border to the west of Kuwait, presumably largely because there just were not enough troops to man both the Kuwait land border and the new defenses along the Kuwaiti coast. This type of flanking attack looked so attractive that General Schwarzkopf had to take special measures, such as deep reconnaissance by special forces, to make sure that he was not being lured into a trap.

Achieving local superiority required deception. The main precondition was to deny the Iraqis accurate information as to coalition dispositions. They had lost much of their reconnaissance capacity when their air force was driven from the sky. Other intelligence sources, such as radio direction-finders, were presumably destroyed during the air campaign. That left the Iraqis only whatever they could glean from the news media, and the strict censorship imposed in Saudi Arabia (particularly as to the location of allied units) was crucial. Here the cooperation of the Soviets was extremely valuable. They alone could have supplied the Iraqis with extensive reconnaissance data from their satellites (since the war began it had been obvious that they were observing it with intense interest).

Central Command's own descriptions of the air offensive were an important means of disinformation. The daily briefings suggested that the main weight of the attacks was falling on the Republican Guard divisions, whose importance had been so inflated prewar. Since it is probably nearly impossible for dug-in troops to determine just how badly they have been bombed, the Iraqi command could never really judge the relative weight of air attacks on the Kuwaiti border and farther inland. That denied it an important potential source of intelligence.

In this sense air bombardment offered an important advantage over classical artillery fire. An army planning a breakthrough must concentrate artillery pieces around the point of attack. If that point has been heavily fortified, it generally follows that substantial bombardment is needed, and the target army soon knows where the attack is likely to be made. An enemy particularly strong in artillery might make a dummy bombardment, but resources generally preclude that. Certainly the Iraqis' experience in the war with Iran would have taught the usual lesson.

Aircraft are different. They could attack any part of the Iraqi Army, and once the Iraqi air defenses were gone such attacks carried essentially no cost. They could, then, be used not only for tactically necessary bombardment but also for purposes of suggestion or disinformation. Central Command seems to have been particularly inventive, combining disinformation by action (bombing) with disinformation through its briefings (reinforced by censorship).

Central Command had to destroy large Iraqi units, which it had to assume were still intact (it could never be sure that the bombing had been entirely effective). Both the units in central Kuwait and the Republican Guard were heavily dug in, and direct assaults on their positions could well be costly. Moreover, Central Command could have little enthusiasm for house-to-house fighting in Kuwait City, yet it could not reasonably solve the problem by flattening the place it was fighting to liberate.

The solution was to concentrate on destroying the Iraqi Army rather than seizing Kuwait itself. Once the Iraqis had given up, Kuwait would inevitably fall into allied hands. To accomplish this, the dug-in Iraqi forces had to be forced into the open, where superior coalition tanks and aircraft could destroy them quickly and cheaply. There was, after all, one place the Iraqis absolutely had to move out to defend: Baghdad. Any major offensive into southern Iraq, then, would concentrate Iraqi attention and pull the Republican Guard out of its bunkers. Even if his force did not go all the way to Baghdad, Schwarzkopf would place a powerful allied armored force operating in the Iraqi rear, and capable of encircling (and thus ultimately destroying) them.

For their part, the Iraqis could not cross the destroyed bridges over the Euphrates River, but they could try to cut off the armored thrust by pushing toward the Saudi border behind its spearhead. Thus it was essential that they be forced to deal with simultaneous attacks up from Saudi Arabia. The slower-moving marine and Arab forces near the coast applied the necessary pressure. Depending on the extent to which the border defenses had been wiped out, they could either pin down large Iraqi forces at the border, or they could push inland toward Kuwait City in hopes of forcing the Iraqi defenders out of the city. In the event the Iraqis decided to stay and fight, Kuwait City could be cut off and bypassed, the units moving up from the south closing a trap around the Iraqi regular and Republican Guard divisions.

From the first, the Iraqis had been impressed with the possibility of a Marine Corps amphibious landing. Their countermove had been not only to fortify the Kuwaiti coast but also to mass troops along it. As long as the amphibious threat could be maintained, these divisions would concentrate on the threat from the sea, and they would be unable to move inland to support the other divisions. Moreover, forces concentrating their firepower pointing out to sea might be rolled up by a strong flank and rear attack mounted along the coastal highway.

It was essential that the Iraqi command not sense the preparations for attack. The Iraqis had, unbelievably, left their western flank entirely unprotected. That presented Central Command with an irresistible opportunity, to thrust its large mobile armored force deep into southern Iraq to encircle and destroy the Iraqi forces both inside Kuwait and just north of the Kuwaiti border. Making the thrust, however, required that enormous supply dumps, sufficient for sixty days of combat, be prepared well to the west of the Saudi-Kuwaiti border. Moreover, the armored units had to be moved from positions blocking the Iraqi border forces to their jump-off positions to the west. That took time, and the armored units were vulnerable to flank attacks while they moved west. Moreover, once they had moved, much of the border was no longer protected.

At least three large logistics bases were built in the western Saudi desert, including an ammunition dump covering 40 square miles. General Schwarzkopf deferred construction of the two westernmost bases until after the air war had eliminated most Iraqi air reconnaissance. Once bombing had begun, XVIII Corps moved 500 miles west in twelve days. It left a 100-man deception cell in eastern Saudi Arabia, using inflatable decoys and radio deception measures. The big armored VII Corps began its shorter move only on 16 February. It, too, left behind a deception cell, mainly using electronic measures (a published account cites false Hawk missile radar signals as well as the usual false radio messages).

When the ground offensive began, the French 6th Light Armored Division occupied the extreme western position. To its right, and separated from it, was XVIII Airborne Corps. These units were intended to cover the left flank of the main strike force, VII Corps. To the Corps' right, on the western border of Kuwait, was the U.S. 1st Armored Cavalry Division. On the central part of the Kuwaiti-Saudi border was Joint Forces Command North, the Egyptian-Syrian force. Then came 1st Marine Division. On its right, between the main coastal road and the coast itself, was Joint Forces Command East (five Saudi, Kuwaiti, Omani, and UAE mechanized infantry brigades). The 2d Marine Division began the ground war just to the rear of the 1st Marine Division, and moved up to its left flank.

As in several other cases of coalition success during the war, it was difficult to believe that the Iraqis had not opened their western flank as a deliberate attraction to some sort of allied disaster. General Schwarzkopf cannot have been sure that his own intelligence had detected all of the Iraqi units. He therefore took special precautions. The planned route of the main armored advance was reconnoitered by Special Forces, which ended the war at the Euphrates River. Both XVIII and VII Corps had their own deep-penetration scouts.

Put another way, General Schwarzkopf could not believe that the Iraqis had not seen the same opportunity he had. After the war it was reported that he thought the Iraqis had seen it but had rejected the possibility on the ground that no one could drive that far quickly without losing his tanks. After all, a major reason the Iraqis had not gone into Saudi Arabia after taking Kuwait was that so many of their tanks had broken down. That was, moreover, under relatively benign conditions.

The Iraqis may also have doubted that the massive coalition forces could find their way through the trackless desert to the west. That made the two main tracks especially important, even though the desert itself could easily be crossed for many miles around the inland track to Kuwait City, After all, navigation had presented enormous problems to previous desert campaigners, to the point that the U.S. Army had to do special research on the subject after the formation of the Rapid Deployment Force in 1979. This time new technology, in the form of the GPS (global positioning satellite) system, solved the problem. Using a simple GPS receiver, a vehicle or even an individual soldier can find position within a few tens of feet, anywhere in the world. The Kuwait war was the first combat use of the system, and it was hugely successful. It made possible all the big night maneuvers that in the past would have required numerous scouts and guides along the routes of advance. GPS can be switched to coded transmissions that can be used only by special receivers. In the event, not enough special receivers were available, so the GPS network could not be switched to the coded mode. That meant anyone, including the Iraqis, who had a standard GPS receiver (which is widely available commercially) could use GPS to find his own position. Considerable publicity was given to this apparent lapse in U.S. equipment, but it made little difference, since the GPS itself does not give away the positions of attackers.

GPS made it possible for the attackers to shift their attack plans back and forth virtually up to the moment of attack, since forces using it had no need for fixed markers on the ground. The marines reported that they kept adjusting their breaching point as they received fresh intelligence of Iraqi positions, and as the Iraqis moved their forces.

The Iraqis had placed a large reserve force astride the western Kuwaiti border. The presence of these troops had forced General Schwarzkopf to drop his original attack plan, and in February it appeared that these soldiers could strike at the flank of the advancing VII Corps. The force had to be neutralized. The 1st Armored Cavalry Division was assigned to attack along the Wadi al-Batin, the western border of Kuwait, to pin down the Iraqi force (which VII Corps would eventually overrun from its own flank and rear). Resistance proved lighter than expected, and the division was turned in through the western border of Kuwait, toward Kuwait City.

The attack began at 4 A.M. (local time) on 24 February. Before dawn, the advance elements of the 101st Airborne Division flew into Iraq to set up an advanced base (Objective Cobra), which they needed to leapfrog forward. The assault troops moved out by helicopter, then seized and defended an airhead. The division's 700 trucks linked up with it to provide the fuel and other supplies needed for the next jump forward.

The two key early objectives were Highway 8, the road leading up the Euphrates from Kuwait, and a choke point (between a lake and sand dunes) that any Iraqi reinforcements (or escapees) had to pass, the Iraqi logistics base near Nasiriyah (Orange). General Schwarzkopf could get to Highway 8 before any Iraqis because he had a fast helicopter assault force, the 101st Airborne. Although the helicopter-borne troops could not take much with them, their TOW [antitank] missiles sufficed to hold their position against any early opposition. The follow-up on the ground would seal off any Iraqi attempt to escape from the trap General Schwarzkopf was springing in the Iraqi rear and up out of Kuwait. The first sixty-six troop-carrying Black-hawk helicopters reached Highway 8 on the afternoon of 25 February.

More generally, XVIII Corps was assigned to cut off the Iraqi Army. The early successes of the 101st Airborne and also of the marines advancing into Kuwait were so encouraging that the XVIII Corps' Heavy Division, the 24th Mechanized Infantry, jumped off 15 hours early, at 3 P.M. on the 24th. It reached the Euphrates Valley near Nasiriya on 25 February, turned east toward Basra, and destroyed Iraqi airfields at Talil and Jabilah. Between them it destroyed a large Iraqi logistics center (Objective Gold). As in the other offensives, many of the Iraqis the division found were only too glad to surrender. They had had enough of bombing and short rations due to the air offensive. But others did fight. An Iraqi commando regiment near Talil airfield fought for 4 hours despite the heavy bombing it had withstood. Ultimately the 24th Division encountered the Hammurabi Division near Basra. It stood and fought—and lost. Heavily bombarded by divisional artillery, it broke and fled on the morning of 28 February. The remnants survived only because of the unilateral 28 February cessation of offensive operations.

Further west, the light French division, supplemented by a brigade of the 82d Airborne Division, pressed deep into Iraq toward the Euphrates. It was a vital flank guard against any Iraqi attempt to attack the developing envelopment. This protection was quite necessary. The French destroyed an Iraqi division en route to the Euphrates.

XVIII Corps cut off the Iraqi Army. The heavy armored VII Corps was assigned to destroy it while the marines and the Arab forces in northern Saudi Arabia pushed up to preclude any escape south. The corps was joined by the British 1st Armoured Division. This powerful combination exemplified the size and weight of large ground units. In motion, it covered an area 60 miles wide and 120 miles long, consuming 3 million gallons of fuel each day. The U.S. units alone included 59,000 vehicles and 1,600 aircraft. These figures explain why the buildup in Saudi Arabia had to be accomplished by sea, and why it took so long.

The heavy armored force was the most powerful single unit the U.S. Army had assembled since 1945. The 1st Infantry Division was assigned to make the initial breach through the Iraqi border defense. It conducted a full-scale rehearsal on a replica built in the Saudi desert, the entire British 1st Armoured Division passing through the breach it made. The heavy attack was enormously successful; the initial day's objectives were all met within the first 12 hours. VII Corps crossed the Iraqi border early Sunday morning, and by Monday morning its scouts (2d Armored Cavalry Regiment) were 80 miles into Iraq. By that time this force had already accounted for 270 tanks, including 35 T-72s. The Republican Guard counterattack, led by a column of 80 tanks, failed completely.

The U.S. 1st Infantry Division made the breach on the right flank of VII Corps, and 1st British Division passed through it to deal with the three-division Iraqi operational reserve (12th, 52d, and 17th Armored Divisions) in the Wadi al-Batin. That insured against any flanking attack on the deep strike force (2d Armored Cavalry Regiment leading 2d and 3d Armored Divisions) heading for the Republican Guard.

While VII Corps pushed in behind the Iraqis, the two marine divisions and the Arab units attacked from the south. 1st Marine Division and Saudis and Kuwaitis jumped off at 4:00 A.M., attacking up the coastal road. Next to them the 2d Marine Division and the Saudis approached Kuwait City from the southeast, jumping off at 5:30 A.M. 1st Marine Division took Al Jaber airfield and the Al Burqan oil field the first day; 2d Marine Division destroyed an Iraqi armored column that advanced toward it from Kuwait City. Given these successes, and the weakness of Iraqi resistance, General Schwarzkopf advanced his timetable by 24 hours, and ordered Joint Forces Command North (Egyptians and Syrians) to attack toward the northeast. Initial resistance was surprisingly light. The Egyptians did have to penetrate a burning

Iraqi antitank ditch that had not been disabled (elsewhere these ditches had been burned out), but Iraqi troops on the border did not fight very well.

Most of the Iraqi defenses were somewhat less elaborate than advertised. At least where the marines penetrated, they consisted only of mine fields, trenches, and gun emplacements (the marines saw no antitank trenches and no high berms). The Iraqis did form the multiple defensive lines with which they had been credited.

Considerable effort went into breaching the Iraqi border mine fields. The two marine divisions attacked side by side, with the 1st Marine Division on the right and the 2d on the left. They differed in technique. The 2d Marine Division deployed a light armored infantry battalion (LAVs) the day before the attack to screen it and to ensure a clear passage from the border berm (on the Saudi side) to the first line of Iraqi obstacles. It captured 400 to 500 Iraqis the first night. The division advanced at night with the reinforced 6th Marines in the lead (three battalions on line). The regiment advanced in a straight line until it hit the breach in the first obstacle, then turned and came out at the breach in the third line of obstacles. This sort of navigation, particularly at night, was a considerable feat. It was achieved by using a combination of GPS satellites and PLRS [position location reporting systems].

Typically the first vehicles through the mine field were M60s with anti-mine bulldozer blades, followed by amphibious assault vehicles (AAVs) towing trailers carrying line-charge rockets (MCLCs [mine clearing line charges]). The rockets fired about 150 meters ahead of the lead tanks, and their explosions cleared a path about 10 meters wide. The follow-up plow tanks passed through to test the clearance of the lane. The most effective Iraqi mines turned out to be British-supplied bar mines.

The 1st Marine Division found a gap in the Iraqi mine field and penetrated up to the second Iraqi defensive line on its own right flank. On its left flank, it located the mine field exactly. Thirty hours before the attack was to begin, it infiltrated major elements of two of its regiments. One passed through on the right to seal off the approach lane against possible Iraqi anti-tank missile operators concealed on the ground. The regiment on the left captured an Iraqi who revealed a gap in the mine field. The regiment then passed through, sealed off the gap, and hid itself in preparation for the attack.

Both units expected the Iraqis to use chemicals and antitank missiles in the breaches, as well as counterattacks by the Iraqi immediate mobile reserves. In fact there were no counterattacks until the 2d Marine Division had penetrated about halfway up the coastal road (abreast Al Jaber). Even then, Iraqi attacks were often abandoned after the leading vehicles had been hit. Many of the Iraqi vehicles were no longer threats when they were hit (the advancing marines could not know whether or not they were still manned).

The 2d Marine Division found the going rougher as it advanced because it had to clear Al Jaber. That was an infantry operation, and the advancing force had to stay clear of large numbers of unexploded bombs left over from the air campaign. By the second day, the division was on the escarpment to the west of Kuwait City, on the city's outskirts.

The 1st Marine Division entered Kuwait at an angle to the border and came up alongside the Burgan oil field. The Iraqis counterattacked out of the oil field, and the division had to pass through the smoke from the many fires the Iraqis had set there. The division could not actually penetrate the field, which was filled with above-ground piping and other ground cover behind which enemy troops could hide. Firing into the oil field could easily cause further explosions. The division went up the west side of the oil field, using small infantry units to clear the ground ahead of itself. On its left, it cleared Al Jaber. It was the 1st Marine Division that attacked Kuwait International Airport on 26 February.

By the time the battle was over the division had destroyed 250 T-55/T-62 and more than 70 T-72 tanks. The airport was cleared on the 27th, the division opening its lines to allow Joint Forces Command East, including the Kuwaitis, the honor of entering Kuwait City. The 2d Marine Division stayed near Al Jahra to form the bottom of the box that caught the retreating Iraqi main force. In all, the marines claimed 1,040 enemy tanks, 608 armored personnel carriers, and 432 artillery pieces destroyed or captured, about a quarter of the enemy total.

Several marine amphibious operations were considered. It is not entirely clear at what point they were dropped in favor of the feint. The marines considered a landing on Faylakah Island (eventually such a landing was faked). The landing was dropped only quite late, when the 5th MEB flew its troops ashore to form the operational reserve for the 1st Marine Division. The second major option was a helicopter assault south of Kuwait City to link up with the marines advancing from the south. It was presumably abandoned only when it was discovered that there was no serious Iraqi resistance south of the airport. Even then there was still a possibility that a light force might be inserted by helicopter in the rear of the Iraqi positions. Probably no final decision was made until the last two days of the war. It was to keep these air-assault options alive that the 4th MEB (which had by far the greater helicopter capability) was retained at sea through the ground campaign. Some of its Harrier jets attacked Iraqi positions from their assault carriers (this was the first time Marine Corps Harriers had flown bombing missions from ships).

Disinformation continued as the attack began. Central Command told reporters that the big offshore Kuwaiti islands, Faylakah and Bubiyan, either were under attack or had been taken. In fact no troops had landed, but the amphibious carriers offshore launched Harriers (AV-8Bs) to make ground attacks in support of the spurious reports. There was also radio disinformation, in the form of at least one counterfeit order from a false Radio Baghdad.

As in many other cases of coalition warfare, coordination among the diverse forces presented real problems. The U.S. solution was to attach bilingual Special Forces and tactical air-control personnel to the two Joint Forces Command (Arab) units. Even so, the Arab corps assigned to the left of the marines moved more slowly than expected. For example, even unopposed, it took 4½ hours to breach the main Iraqi defensive line, although that was partly because air preparation had not been as complete as expected. The Egyptians failed to reach their first-day objective, an army barracks about 20 miles inside Kuwait, and the Saudis were also considered slow. Their own armies had never worked together very much, so they were poorly coordinated. At one point the Saudis and the Egyptians exchanged fire (U.S. air liaison officers soon stopped the inadvertent duel).

Iraqi border resistance had largely been crushed by the air bombardment. On the eve of battle, Central Command estimated that the Iraqi divisions on the border were less than 50 percent effective (formations on the coast and farther inland had not been hit nearly as badly). It later turned out that desertion rates throughout the theater ranged from 30 to 60 percent. The passage through the border fortifications was made partly by combat engineers who cleared mines and partly by following the observed paths of enemy patrols. Saddam's oil-filled ditch was burned out, some of its key valves destroyed by laser-guided bombs delivered by F-117s. In one area, however, the Egyptians did have to bridge a burning tank trap.

The Iraqis had indeed laid enormous numbers of land mines, but fortunately they were not as sophisticated as had been feared. For example, there were no reports of casualties to the reported gas mines (although gas mines certainly were found). Allied intelligence was able to plot many of the fields by watching lanes habitually used by enemy soldiers. In one lucky break, the allies captured an Iraqi soldier who had been the driver for a senior officer. Thus he knew just which areas were too dangerous to cross, at least in his sector of the front.

Moreover, many of the mines had been laid either on the surface or buried shallowly. Wind often shifted the sand away from them. Some fields were detonated by light-case 15,000-lb bombs ("daisy cutters" dropped by C-130s), others by fuel-air explosives. Lanes were also cleared using explosive rope trailed by rockets and by mineclearing bulldozers.

The great fear was that troops stalled on the border would be bombarded by Iraqi guns firing chemical shells. In the weeks before the ground war began, there seemed to be considerable evidence of large shipments of 130-mm chemical shells to the border. Great emphasis was therefore placed on physically destroying the dug-in Iraqi guns. Through the period before the ground assault, coalition artillery made nightly attacks on the Iraqi border positions. Iraqi return fire revealed the positions of the long-range Iraqi howitzers. Massed British and U.S. artillery began to shell the Iraqi artillery on 22 February, the day before the planned offensive.

There was also some evidence that Iraqi artillery completely lacked any form of fire control. Reportedly guns were zeroed on particular fixed points, and the Iraqis made no attempt to move the point of aim to hit targets that might reasonably have been expected to move after the first shots. Such tactics recalled World War I experience, when targets were relatively immobile. They did make sense if Saddam expected allied units to become stalled in his border fortifications (on which the guns were presumably zeroed).

Once the dimensions of the disaster were clear, Saddam made one last attempt to extricate his army intact. He announced that his forces were pulling out of Kuwait, a move which fortunately precluded either a house-to-house battle or a siege. However, it was clear that the pull-out would have preserved the Iraqi Army intact. The coalition reply was that Iraqi units moving in military formation would be attacked. Only deserters on foot would be safe.

For example, an Iraqi motorized column was spotted leaving Kuwait City in panic. Attacked by air at either end, it formed a 3-mile traffic jam. Aircraft completely destroyed it. Afterwards it turned out that, even in their final panic, the Iraqis had not been able to resist looting Kuwait. The remains of the column stank of looted perfume.

It is not clear to what extent Saddam's order further demoralized an already unhappy Iraqi Army. There were claims postwar that units who knew that their government was giving up would hardly be willing to fight. Yet the Iraqi tank units did stand and try to fight their way out of the trap. Some surrounded units even tried to fight well after the unilateral cessation of offensive action which effectively ended the war. None succeeded.

Much of this last battle was conducted in weather much too overcast for effective air support. It was a classical tank battle, with a very nonclassical outcome. Thanks to their superior vision equipment (mainly FLIRs), the U.S. tanks spotted their targets well before they were even seen, at ranges beyond 3,800 yds. Their superior ballistic computers insured that they could make killing hits at these ranges. Even when they could engage, the Iraqi tanks were unable to penetrate the M1A1's armor. That was true even of T-72s, which were armed with the best Soviet-made gun, the 125-mm, and which, before the war, had been considered quite impressive.

The sheer speed of the offensive was shocking. Limited Iraqi resistance showed in the small U.S. ammunition expenditure; VII Corps used only 10 to 15 percent of the 70,000 tons it had built up, although some of its units did run short due to the pace of the advance. Perhaps the greatest surprise was that the Iraqis never used gas. There was no question that they had it, and many U.S. officers expected it. On the other hand, they had been heavily leafletted with threats of dire consequences if gas were used. It may also be that, despite Saddam Hussein's public statement that his corps commanders could use gas whenever they wanted to, they still had to wait for specific orders from Baghdad. The word could not come over jammed and destroyed channels. It is also possible that individual Iraqi unit commanders were leery of using gas for fear that their own troops would die if the gas clouds drifted the wrong way or if gas shells burst as they were being loaded (both quite common risks). It turned out that the Iraqis' gas masks were largely worn out (as was first suspected from the condition of masks carried by deserters encountered early in the war).

The ground attack was stunningly successful. Total casualties were ludicrously low: eighty-eight Americans killed in action, plus forty-one Egyptians, Saudis, and Kuwaitis, sixteen British, and two French. Of those killed, twenty-eight of the Americans were victims of one of the few Scuds not intercepted (they died in Dhahran, Saudi Arabia). Many of the others fell victim to friendly fire, and at least seven were killed by mines they were defusing as part of the French division. Overall, the enormous Iraqi Army achieved remarkably little.

It would be easy to attribute the result to the crushing air offensive. However, along with many Iraqis only too glad to surrender, the advancing coalition ground force did encounter many quite willing to fight, even after the coalition suspended its own attack. They stood, fought, and died. The coalition could thank both its superior weapons and the sheer inventiveness of the attack plan (which worked only because the force was so flexible and so mobile).

From Instant Thunder to Desert Storm: Developing the Gulf War Air Campaign's Phases

Diane T. Putney

During the weeks between the Iraqi invasion of Kuwait on August 2, 1990, and the commencement of Operation Desert Storm on January 17, 1991, American planners developed a comprehensive plan for the successful Gulf War air campaign. As Diane T. Putney of the Center for Air Force History explains, it was an evolutionary process involving both military and civilian personnel and eventually included four interrelated phases. These phases involved air, land, and sea operations despite the opinion of some Air Force personnel that the fourth phase, a ground war, would not be necessary because air power alone would drive the Iraqis out of Kuwait. This essay illustrating the complexity of modern warmaking planning was originally published in Air Power History *(41/3 [Fall 1994], 38–50) and is reprinted with permission.*

A study of the development of the plan for the Gulf War air campaign reveals a process that was both evolutionary and complex. The process was evolutionary because no war plan was ready to be implemented when Iraq invaded Kuwait on August 2, 1990. The 1002–90 plan of the United States Central Command (CENTCOM), still under development, was primarily for force deployment, not force employment. The air campaign plan developed during the entire five-month period of DESERT SHIELD and continued to evolve throughout the war. The process was complex because it involved more than one key player and staff. Gen. H. Norman Schwarzkopf, the commander in chief (CINC) of CENTCOM, and his CENTCOM staff and Lt. Gen. Charles A. Horner and his staff at United States Central Command Air Forces (CENTAF), who coordinated closely with representatives of the CENTCOM component commands, were involved, as were the Chairman of the Joint Chiefs of Staff and the Air Staff. Each key player recognized the advantage air power gave the United States, but each had his own view of how to employ air power. A study of the evolution of the air campaign plan reveals how the ideas of the commanders and planners emerged, took parallel or divergent courses, and then melded and produced distinct phases of the Gulf War air campaign—phases that would merge by the eve of the air war.

On Tuesday morning, August 7, 1990, five days after Iraq invaded Kuwait, Generals Schwarzkopf and Horner were at the airport in Jeddah, Saudi Arabia. They were part of a delegation President George Bush had sent to Saudi Arabia to offer U.S. military assistance to defend the Saudi kingdom; with King Fahd's acceptance of the U.S. offer, DESERT SHIELD deployment had commenced. Schwarzkopf then asked Horner to remain in theater to be the CENTCOM Forward commander and receive and bed down deploying forces.

As the CINC boarded the aircraft in Jeddah to return to MacDill AFB in Florida, he said to Horner, "Chuck, you are going to be tied up over here, and your staff is coming over here, so in the interim I'm going to have the Joint Chiefs of Staff look at a strategic targeting plan." General Horner assumed that the CINC was referring to the targeting plan that Horner had suggested to Schwarzkopf in April 1990 in preparation for the exercise INTERNAL LOOK; Horner's targets were part of a strategy to deter the use of chemical weapons.

The next morning, August 8, shortly after returning to MacDill AFB, Schwarzkopf telephoned the Joint Staff and the Air Staff. He wanted the Air Staff to develop a targeting plan for use if Saddam Hussein committed some "heinous" act, such as taking and harming hostages or using chemical weapons. The CINC knew that if such an act were committed, Gen. Colin Powell, Chairman of the Joint Chiefs, would immediately ask him about military options; so he had to be ready to brief options, especially ones which included broad sets of targets.

The Air Force vice chief of staff, Gen. John M. Loh, took the telephone call from the CINC, because Gen. Michael J. Dugan, the Air Force chief of staff, was out of town. Loh told Schwarzkopf that the Air Staff could develop such a plan and that a small Air Staff planning cell had already begun to look at a "strategic" set of targets, i.e., leadership capabilities and industrial targets. General Loh was referring to the Air Staff planning effort under the direction of Col. John A. Warden III, the deputy director for warfighting concepts. After the CINC's telephone call, General Loh directed Colonel Warden and his staff to go into "high gear" to prepare an air campaign—a "strategic" air campaign—for the CINC. The plan was to be "executable" in a short period of time. The staff, augmented very early on by officers from the Strategic Air Command, the Air Force Intelligence Agency, other Air Staff agencies, and CENTAF, worked intently on the plan in the Pentagon basement in the office space of the old CHECKMATE Division; hence, CHECKMATE became the shorthand name for the Air Staff organization deeply involved in air war planning. Weapon systems experts from Tactical Air Command (TAC) field units also assisted the planners. TAC headquarters eventually sent three colonels to assist the CHECKMATE effort and sent its own air campaign plan, which included ideas about "demonstrative attacks" and "escalating offensive operations." The CHECKMATE planners, with the consent of General Dugan, reviewed and simply set aside the TAC plan.

On Friday, August 10, Maj. Gen. Robert M. Alexander, director of plans, Colonel Warden, and a few other officers flew to MacDill AFB and briefed General Schwarzkopf on the concepts of the strategic air campaign. Their secret plan was titled "INSTANT THUNDER: A Strategic Air Campaign Proposal for CINCCENT."

INSTANT THUNDER signified a sudden, massive strategic air campaign, stunning in its intensity, in sharp contrast to ROLLING THUNDER, the graduated, failed air campaign of the Vietnam War. The strategic air campaign was to last from six to nine days, "minimize civilian casualties and collateral damage," and emphasize precision guided weapons.

The plan identified five strategic target categories and nine target sets. Under the first category, leadership, the two target sets were the Hussein regime, which was to be isolated and incapacitated, and communications, including both civil telecommunications and military command, control, and communications. The second target category, key production, had four targets sets: electricity; oil distribution and storage facilities; one nuclear, biological, and chemical (NBC) research facility in Baghdad; and military production and storage facilities, including SCUD-related targets.

The third target category, infrastructure, included railroads as a target set with one railway and highway bridge as a subset. The fourth target category, population, had three population target sets (Iraqis, foreign workers, and soldiers in Kuwait) that were to be struck with only nonlethal, psychological weapons—that is, leaflets and radio and television broadcasts—not explosive, destructive weapons. The fifth target category was the Iraqi fielded military force with two targets sets: the Iraqi strategic air defense system and the Iraqi strategic offensive system, with two components, bombers and missiles. The Iraqi army was not a target set under fielded force.

The five target categories originated with Colonel Warden many months before the Iraqis invaded Kuwait. He expressed them as five concentric strategic rings and described them as a modern nation state's "centers of gravity," borrowing that term from Carl von Clausewitz, the nineteenth-century military strategist, and using it to describe high-value, highly leveraged target categories. The Air Staff INSTANT THUNDER planners used the five strategic rings, written on a board in the Pentagon basement, as a model to identify Iraqi target sets.

Warden believed the most important strategic ring, and thus, the most important category, was leadership and that the least important of the five rings was the fielded military force. He wrote, "Although we tend to think of military forces as being the most vital in war, in fact they are means to an end. That is, their only function is to protect their own inner rings or to threaten those of an enemy." Air forces could overfly the fielded military force to hit the leadership element, thus destroying a nation's ability to command and control its fielded force. Emphasizing the primacy of the command ring, the leadership category, Warden stated, "The essence of war is applying pressure against the enemy's innermost strategic ring—its command structure. Military forces are a means to an end. It is pointless to deal with enemy forces if they can be bypassed, by strategy or technology, either in the defense or offense."

General Schwarzkopf expressed his "100 percent" approval of the INSTANT THUNDER plan at this early stage. During the briefing, most of the

CINC's questions and much discussion focused on when the plan would be executable and the changes required in the deployment flow to support its execution. In an important revelation, Schwarzkopf explained why he wanted and needed the Air Staff plan. He stated that Saddam Hussein was a "crazy man," who could "lash out" and attack Saudi Arabia, do something "nasty" to the hostages, or drop chemicals on Israel. The general needed a plan to "fall back on" in response to such "crazy" acts.

From Schwarzkopf's viewpoint, the strategic air campaign plan was a retaliation plan. At the August 10 briefing, the CINC approved of INSTANT THUNDER even though the strategic air campaign did not use air power directly against the Iraqi army in Kuwait. The general thought that if INSTANT THUNDER had to be executed soon, then only psychological operations should be used against the Iraqi troops in Kuwait. "This is where America has the edge," he stated. "After you do this, we'll drop leaflets on his front line forces and tell them they're out of business. If they don't believe it, let them try to call home." He continued by observing that using only psychological operations against the troops in Kuwait might save the nation from devastation. "If we invade Kuwait, they'll destroy it. This might leave Kuwait intact." The CINC instructed the planners to continue developing the INSTANT THUNDER plan, study the deployment flow, and assess if INSTANT THUNDER could be ready to execute on August 22. He told the planners to brief Chairman Powell on the plan by Monday, August 13.

In fact, Colonel Warden and a number of Air Force officers briefed Powell on Saturday, August 11. The chairman was less receptive of INSTANT THUNDER than General Schwarzkopf had been, but still thought it was a "good plan, very fine piece of work." Powell asked many practical questions about the logistics necessary to support an air campaign executable in eleven days. He wanted to know what assets would have to be put on hold in the deployment flow to allow space for INSTANT THUNDER assets—the "tradeoffs." He did not want to change the deployment flow and wanted to know when INSTANT THUNDER would be ready to execute without deployment changes.

After the briefing presentation and discussion about the strategic air campaign excluding targets in Kuwait, Chairman Powell dropped his bombshell question. "OK, it's day six," he asked, and the strategic air campaign is finished. "Now what?" Colonel Warden expressed confidence that INSTANT THUNDER would "induce" the Iraqis to withdraw from Kuwait. In the ensuing discussion, Powell remarked that he would not be happy until he saw tanks destroyed. He stated that if massive air attacks were launched against Iraq, the U.S. might as well finish the job and destroy the Iraqi army. Powell insisted, "I don't want them to go home—I want to leave smoking tanks as kilometer fence posts all the way to Baghdad." General Alexander observed that they needed to ensure that "operations to achieve tactical level objectives don't compromise success of the strategic air campaign." Powell replied, "Right—but I can't recommend only the strategic air campaign to the President."

As a result of Chairman Powell's direction to use air power to kill tanks, Colonel Warden directed his staff to develop an INSTANT THUNDER Phase II plan. Originally titled "An Operational Air Campaign Against Iraqi Forces in Kuwait" and subsequently, "Battlefield Air Operations against Iraqi Forces in Kuwait," the plan had four aims: achieve air superiority over Kuwait; attack Iraqi chemical weapons delivery systems; attack Iraqi command, control, and communications and military support structure in Kuwait, and attack Iraqi armored forces in Kuwait.

Chairman Powell also directed that INSTANT THUNDER be made a Joint plan. Consequently, throughout the week of August 11–17, four types of activity took place that gave the plan a Joint character and represented it as being sanctioned by the Joint Chiefs of Staff: first, personnel from the other military services joined the Air Staff planning teams; second, Air Staff personnel reported to CENTCOM and Joint Staff offices as liaison officers; third, officers from the Joint Staff and other services received INSTANT THUNDER briefings; and fourth, directors of the planning effort were appointed whose positions were on the Joint Staff. Although the planning effort became Joint in character, the CHECKMATE planning group remained dominant.

On Friday, August 17, the Air Staff planners returned to MacDill AFB to present the second and final INSTANT THUNDER briefing to General Schwarzkopf. They prepared for the CINC two top secret documents, a 180-page operations order and a 30-page briefing slide package.

By now they identified ten target sets, having added two, airfields and naval ports, and having merged two, the NBC facility and the military production and storage set. There were eighty-four targets; no targets were in Kuwait. The most important center of gravity was the Hussein regime. Significantly, the planners did not brief General Schwarzkopf on the INSTANT THUNDER Phase II plan, which described the employment of air power against the Iraqi army in Kuwait. Instead, they used one briefing slide near the end of the presentation to list the aircraft available in case the initiation of INSTANT THUNDER caused the Iraqi army to invade Saudi Arabia. The Air Staff planners held fixed and rotary wing aircraft in reserve to attack and stop an Iraqi invasion of Saudi Arabia. This reserve force consisted of four A–10 squadrons, two AV–8B squadrons, three F/A–18 squadrons, two AH–1W helicopter squadrons, and four AH–64 helicopter squadrons.

Again, the CINC reacted favorably to the INSTANT THUNDER strategic air campaign and observed that air power gave the United States an "overwhelming advantage" over Iraq. He ordered Colonel Warden to go to Saudi Arabia to brief General Horner on the plan. Colonel Warden flew to Riyadh on August 18/19, accompanied by three key planners, Lt. Col. David A. Deptula, Lt. Col. Bernard E. Harvey, and Lt. Col. Ronnie A. Stanfill.

Meanwhile, in Riyadh, General Horner was exercising CENTCOM command responsibilities for the DESERT SHIELD deployment, working with Saudi officials, other CENTCOM component commanders, and representatives of the international coalition. Horner directed Maj. Gen. Thomas R. Olsen, acting CENTAF commander, and the CENTAF staff to accomplish tasks associated with the responsibilities of the Joint Force Air Component Commander. These included generating a daily defensive and training air tasking order; establishing command, control, and communication links; building air defense and airspace control systems; producing a fully developed D–Day defensive plan and air tasking order; writing rules of engagement; developing search and rescue capabilities; and doing scores of other vital tasks. On August 17, when the U.S. Navy began to implement the naval embargo of Iraq, General Schwarzkopf telephoned General Horner, warned him that "an Iraqi attack might be imminent," and ordered him to put "naval and air forces on high alert." Horner was responsible for defending Saudi Arabia, and the threat from twenty-seven Iraqi divisions weighed heavily on his mind.

By August 20 General Horner's staff—particularly the staff under deputy director for operations Col. James C. Crigger, Jr.—had drafted an air plan, titled the "D–Day Game Plan," to defend Saudi Arabia against an Iraqi invasion. Colonel Crigger explained, "The objective of the 'D–Day' plan was defensive in nature. . . . Iraqi forces were less than 150 [nautical] miles from key oil fields, military installations, and port cities with no significant ground forces to oppose their advance into Saudi Arabia." The plan's first priority was for all alert aircraft to make a "hard initial thrust" against the Iraqi ground forces during the first seven hours of the Iraqi invasion. For the next thirty-six hours, aircraft, primarily from the USS *Eisenhower* and USS *Independence* carrier groups, would apply "continuous pressure" against Iraqi forces. Aerial tanker requirements would be heavy in this phase. The targeting strategy would depend on the number of electronic combat aircraft available. Sorties not involving F–4Gs and EF–111s would fly at low altitude against enemy concentrations and choke points and also on "road recce" missions. The F–4Gs and EF–111s would allow flexibility to attack point targets and second echelon assets, and air attacks would prevent follow-on forces from affecting the outcome of battle. The CENTAF staff would also study the probable routes of attack by Iraqi forces and develop air zones based on a map grid system, in which aircraft would hit enemy targets of opportunity.

Lt. Col. Samuel J. Baptiste, directing the combat operations planning staff, turned the D–Day plan into an executable air tasking order (ATO). The ATO was the "frag order" or detailed tasking order sent to multiservice and allied flying units providing them with specific information about missions, aircraft, call signs, targets, target coordinates, time over targets, tanker and refueling requirements, airspace control, and other special topics.

The CENTAF staff also initiated action, although low-key and small-scale, to develop an offensive air plan. This effort included the identification of high-value targets in Iraq, which was a continuation of the CENTAF targeting enterprise begun early in 1990. In Riyadh, General Horner prepared his defensive plan first, before developing his offensive plan. He explained that if a nation's army were being overrun, it did not matter much what targets were struck deep in the enemy's territory; what mattered was hitting the targets to immediately save the army. In his blunt manner, the general explained, "If your army is getting overrun, who gives a shit what you take out deep?"

On Monday, August 20, Colonel Warden briefed General Horner on the Air Staff INSTANT THUNDER plan. Both its place of origin and the plan itself displeased Horner immensely. He disliked that the plan originated in Washington, D.C., far removed from the theater of operations and the armed forces who might have to execute it. The involvement of the Air Staff in Washington reminded him of the Vietnam War, when targets had been selected half a world away from the battlefield, to the detriment of the effectiveness and morale of the forces in theater.

The plan itself irritated him, because INSTANT THUNDER implied that its air campaign alone would liberate Kuwait. The general rejected Colonel Warden's assertion that INSTANT THUNDER would induce the Iraqi army to leave Kuwait. Horner later recalled, "I sat there and listened to it, and I said, 'There are some really good thoughts here, *but* it is incomplete.' It developed the idea that air power was going to smash Iraq, and they were all going to give up and go home. Well, that is pure bull. I mean, anybody could see that."

Horner viewed INSTANT THUNDER as "incomplete," "embryonic," and a "partial answer." He knew, too, however, that the CINC wanted a retaliation plan. Horner selected Brig. Gen. Buster C. Glosson, who was already in theater as the deputy commander of the Joint Task Force Middle East, to head a Special Planning Group to continue the development of the strategic targeting plan and produce an "executable ATO" for it. Glosson's group later became known as the "Black Hole."

Meanwhile, back at CENTCOM in Florida after attending Colonel Warden's second INSTANT THUNDER briefing on August 17, General Schwarzkopf mulled over the plan and directed that it be incorporated into the offensive war planning that his J–5 planning staff had been doing in great secrecy. After the CINC had received the INSTANT THUNDER briefing the second time, the proverbial "light bulb" had gone on in his head when he realized that he now had a retaliation plan, INSTANT THUNDER, that could double as Phase I of his DESERT STORM offensive war plan. On Saturday morning, August 25, shortly before he departed the U.S. for Riyadh, General Schwarzkopf came to the Pentagon and briefed Chairman Powell on CENTCOM's four-phase DESERT STORM plan.

Phase I was the strategic air campaign, based on INSTANT THUNDER. Phase II was the Kuwait air campaign to gain air superiority over Kuwait to allow "unchallenged use of the skies for fixed wing and [helicopter] operations." Phase III was ground combat power attrition to "reduce Iraqi ground force capability, soften ground forces to assure successful penetration and exploitation, reduce ability to lay down chemicals, and destroy Republican Guard capability to reinforce into Kuwait." Phase IV was the ground attack to "eject Iraqi forces from Kuwait." These phases essentially formed a shell, a framework of general concepts of operation for the DESERT STORM war plan.

When General Horner learned of the four-phase DESERT STORM concepts, he directed that the name INSTANT THUNDER be dropped from the air campaign that General Glosson was working on; instead, the plan was titled "Offensive Campaign Phase I."

In Horner's view, Phase II originated directly from Schwarzkopf. In preparation for the INTERNAL LOOK exercise, Horner and Schwarzkopf had discussed at great length the importance of air superiority. The CINC's acknowledgement of its importance was crucial, but his placement of it in Phase II did not make much sense to Horner. "We have to get control of the air first," he stated. The air forces would achieve air superiority in Phase I, so that Phase I and the rest of the campaign could proceed successfully. Horner would give the CINC air "supremacy" in Phase II.

As the head of the Special Planning Group, General Glosson involved the wing commanders and operators in the planning effort to infuse the strategic plan with operational "sanity checks" and weapon system expertise. He immediately sought out the officers who knew how to produce an ATO, Maj. David L. Waterstreet and Maj. John D. Sweeney, and to coordinate tanker and mission refueling requirements, Lt. Col. James Pritchett and Maj. Scott Hente. Glosson's group grew quickly as he added representatives from the other services and specialists in such vital functions as intelligence, logistics, special operations, and the airborne warning and control system (AWACS). Brig. Gen. Larry L. Henry, director of the CENTAF electronic combat cell, and his staff assisted the Special Planning Group in designing the strategic attacks which took down the Iraqi integrated air defense system, a crucially important step towards gaining air superiority. Generals Horner and Glosson added the Republican Guard and SCUDs as distinct, separate Phase I target sets, increasing the strategic sets to twelve: ten from INSTANT THUNDER and two added in theater. The number of targets increased significantly as more intelligence disclosed valuable Iraqi assets.

Until mid-September, General Horner had relied on Col. Crigger to plan Phases II and III, because Crigger and his staff had already been focusing on attacking the Iraqi army in defense of Saudi Arabia via the D–Day ATO and its follow-on, ATO BRAVO. For Phase III, they planned according to the CINC's requirement for fifty percent attrition of armor and artillery prior to the start of Phase IV, the ground war. Colonel Crigger soon saw, however, that Phases II and III were "becoming more and more entwined" with Phase I, and he noted, "There were not clear break points when one phase would end and another would begin." The colonel suggested to General Horner that all offensive planning be consolidated in Glosson's Special Planning Group, which General Horner did in mid-September. By the middle of

October, Phases II and III of the air campaign had begun to receive a great deal of attention.

On October 10, General Glosson briefed the Joint Chiefs of Staff in the Pentagon on the air campaign Phases I, II, and III; on October 11, he gave the same briefing to the President and others at the White House. The objective of Phase II was to "conduct offensive strikes into Kuwait to roll back air defenses," and the objective of Phase III was to "attrit enemy ground forces." Maj. Gen. Robert B. Johnston, USMC, the CINC's chief of staff, and Lt. Col. Joseph H. Purvis, USA, a key CENTCOM augmentee planner, briefed Phase IV in the Pentagon and at the White House. While the President and his advisors viewed CENTAF's Phases I, II, and III as "sound," they had serious reservations about Phase IV and its attack into enemy strength.

Afterward, in theater, as ground force commanders and planners continued to struggle with Phase IV development, General Glosson continued to work on the development of Phase III and discussed its air objectives with planners of the ground offensive. In the Pentagon, General Loh asked Colonel Warden to provide answers to questions about the use of air power directly against the Iraqi army. When Colonel Warden studied the modeling results prepared by his staff, led by Maj. Roy Y. Sikes, and thought anew about the strength and lethality of air power, he became convinced that air power in Phase III would be so effective in destroying the Iraqi army that U.S. casualties from a ground war—predicted at from 17,000 to 30,000—would be negated and that, indeed, U.S. involvement in a land war would be unnecessary. Colonel Warden, however, initially advocated in Phase III striking only the Iraqi army in Kuwait, those front line troops facing the coalition ground forces, and not striking the Republican Guard, which had withdrawn to southern Iraq.

On October 22, Warden "faxed" a copy of CHECKMATE Phase III planning analysis to General Glosson, who welcomed the detailed analysis, but noted that he could not get through General Schwarzkopf's door with it unless Phase III prominently targeted the Republican Guard. After considerable discussion, the CHECKMATE staff, following the direction from General Glosson and the new Air Force chief of staff, General Merrill A. McPeak, prepared analyses to show numbers of aircraft, munitions, and timing for Phase III, split into two parts. Part One targeted the Republican Guard, and Part Two targeted the regular Iraqi army in Kuwait. The Republican Guard, therefore, became a target in both Phases I and III.

General Glosson used the analytical and modeling expertise of the Air Staff, including that of the Center for Studies and Analysis, to do computer runs based on his assumptions, which he purposely made conservative, such as target acquisition rates of only 75 percent. Glosson explained Phases II and III to General Horner on November 7. Horner questioned Glosson closely about strikes against artillery and discussed the phases with Lt. Gen. John Yeosock, the Army component commander.

Glosson then briefed the key members of the CENTCOM staff, without General Schwarzkopf, on November 8. On November 14, General Horner and other CENTCOM component, corps, and division commanders attended a meeting in Dhahran, where Schwarzkopf, who retained for himself the job of land component commander, delivered a rousing briefing of his four-phase DESERT STORM war plan. The phases were essentially the same as those the CINC had briefed Powell on August 25: Phase I, strategic air campaign; Phase II, air superiority in the Kuwait theater of operations; Phase III, battlefield preparation; and Phase IV, ground attack. The CINC's war plan now included the U.S. Army VII Corps moving into position to thrust into Iraq to seek and annihilate the Republican Guard. Even though the air plan had targeted the Republican Guard in Phases I and III, the CINC believed that the VII Corps would still have to battle and destroy the Guard, which he viewed as the primary center of gravity in Iraq.

A few days after the Dhahran meeting, General Glosson briefed the CINC on details of Phase III of the air campaign, which helped General Schwarzkopf to realize clearly that the time the air forces required for Phases I–III would enable the ground forces to move to their jumping off points for G–Day, the start of the land campaign and Phase IV. It showed the CINC, too, that air power was going to significantly "attrit" the Iraqi army prior to G–Day.

The main CENTAF staff in Riyadh prepared the Phase IV air campaign planning, which called for the use of air power in close, direct support of the ground attack. The staff worked closely with the representatives of the other services, the coalition partners, and the Joint Targeting Board on the procedures for identifying targets and executing Phase IV. They did not advertise what they were doing as DESERT STORM planning, but as the CENTAF "Concept of Operations for Command and Control of TACAIR in Support of Land Forces." Their planning products were at the secret level and received greater dissemination in theater than the Black Hole's top secret, special category, limited distribution planning for Phases I, II, and III. The staff developed a tactical air control system, which linked the "tactical air control center, control and reporting center, airborne elements, air support operations center, and tactical air control parties." In December General Horner reorganized his headquarters, integrating the Black Hole with the rest of the CENTAF staff. General Glosson was dual-hatted as the director of campaign plans and commander of the 14th Air Division, Provisional; Maj. Gen. John A. Corder was appointed the deputy chief of staff, operations.

On December 20 General Horner briefed Secretary of Defense Dick Cheney and Chairman Powell on the air campaign plan. With Phase IV, he explained his concept of close air support, "Push CAS." Push CAS sent sorties over the battlefield twenty-four hours a day for either preplanned CAS strikes or preplanned interdiction strikes. If unplanned CAS were needed, some of the preplanned strikes would be diverted to the new CAS mission;

otherwise strikes went as planned. In this way, Horner later said, "I always had my air employed. I didn't have the planes holding; I didn't have the planes waiting . . . or sitting on the ground idle."

In December 1990 and early January 1991, the arrival of additional aircraft in theater significantly influenced the air campaign plan. The increased air assets, part of the second stage of the DESERT SHIELD deployment announced by President Bush in November after the election, enabled the air campaign planners to schedule strikes on more targets simultaneously. General Glosson began to deliberately merge Phases I, II, and III, so that some targets from Phases II and III would be struck earlier than originally planned and at the time originally set aside for striking Phase I targets. For example, a target set from Phase II, surface-to-air missiles in Kuwait, became the thirteenth target set of Phase I.

When General Horner briefed Secretary Cheney and Chairman Powell on December 20, he used the concept "level of effort" to illustrate the progress of the air campaign. The phases merged throughout the campaign, as the level of effort shifted from Iraqi strategic and air defense targets to targets in the Kuwait theater of operations. Horner later said that the phases had "no meaning" other than to indicate an "emphasis on where we were going to put our efforts." Colonel Baptiste explained, "All those phases kind of blended into each other. . . . We didn't concentrate on the strategic campaign and then come down and say, 'OK, now we're going to get air superiority and knock out the radar threats in the KTO so we can execute at will down there and prepare the battlefield.' We did it all at once."

By the eve of the air war, the idea of separate, distinct air campaign phases was crumbling. The four phases were the CINC's idea, and the air campaign planners were never as comfortable with them as was General Schwarzkopf. Referring to the phases, General Glosson declared, "*In all candidness, it was unfortunate the air campaign was initially portrayed in that context, because it proved to be very cumbersome later on when we attempted to streamline the campaign to gain a more synergistic impact. So if we had initially laid it out as a strategic air campaign with a gradual shifting of the focus . . . to the tactical arena in the KTO it would have been easier to keep everyone oriented. It is certainly more accurate to portray the air campaign in that fashion than it is to try to segment it into four distinct phases.*"

Even as the air war commenced on January 17, 1991, planning continued for identifying targets for Phases I through III and for developing and coordinating procedures for the execution of Phase IV. Colonel Crigger noted, "All the targets that were selected for the 'D–Day' ATO that were in Kuwait or southern Iraq, as well as the grid square system for kill boxes that was developed for the 'D–Day' ATO, were integrated into Phase II and III planning and execution." The SCUD hunt was the major new wartime planning initiative.

In conclusion, the air war planning process was both complex and evolutionary. Various individuals and staffs were involved in developing the air campaign during the DESERT SHIELD period, and planners continued to refine air campaign plans throughout the war. All the participants in the planning process recognized the great advantage air power gave to the United States, leading some to question the necessity for Phase IV, the ground campaign. Colonel Warden believed fervently that Phase IV was unnecessary. Lt. Col. Deptula, Glosson's key deputy and masterful planner, describing the air campaign in November 1990, said, "The way I see it, our task is to ensure that no one is at home when the ground forces arrive to knock on the door." Secretary of the Air Force Donald B. Rice believed that if Phases I through III failed to force the Iraqis from Kuwait, Phase III should be repeated over and over. Not only Air Force personnel questioned the necessity for Phase IV. At the White House on October 11, President Bush, after hearing General Glosson's briefing, asked, "Why not do Phases I, II, and III, then stop?"

However, Chairman Powell and General Schwarzkopf were convinced that Phase IV was necessary. At the White House meeting, Powell answered President Bush's query about Phase IV; he did not defer to General Glosson, because Glosson made air power look too advantageous. Earlier, Powell had even told Glosson, "Tone it down, Buster." The Chairman explained to the President, "Phase I will devastate him, it will be massive, and I don't know how he will deal with it. Phase II will make it more difficult for him, and Phase III will be additive, but you will have no assurance or guarantee we would get him out of Kuwait. Because we can't guarantee he'll leave Kuwait, we must be prepared to do Phase IV."

After the war, General Horner was asked about the advantage of air power and the necessity for the ground war. He said he had not known at the time whether there would be a land war. "But," he added, "you are foolish not to plan for it."

In the end, the advantage air power gave the United States during the Gulf War and the liberation of Kuwait was overwhelming. Today, international adversaries have to reckon with the air power advantage—as do Army, Navy, Marine, and Air Force planners in the era of component command warfare.

XIV

❦

New Threats for the Twenty-First Century, 1992–

Somebody Else's Civil War

Michael Scott Doran

In the aftermath of the September 11, 2001 attacks on the World Trade Center and the Pentagon, most Americans at all levels attempted to analyze not only the nature of the Islamic terrorist attacks on the United States—"why us?"—but also how the nation should react to assure domestic security for its citizens both now and in the future. One of the most insightful analyses of the situation the nation faces in the twenty-first century was penned by Michael Scott Doran, Professor of Near Eastern Studies at Princeton University. In this essay Professor Doran dissects the Middle Eastern terrorists' goals in attacking the United States, examining them both from an ideological-religious and a historical perspective. Reprinted by permission of FOREIGN AFFAIRS, 8/1 *(Jan.–Feb. 2002). Copyright © 2002 by the Council on Foreign Relations, Inc.*

Call it a city on four legs
heading for murder. . . .
New York is a woman
holding, according to history,
a rag called liberty with one hand
and strangling the earth with the other.
   —Adonis [Ali Ahmed Said],
   "The Funeral of New York," 1971

In the weeks after the attacks of September 11, Americans repeatedly asked, "Why do they hate us?" To understand what happened, however, another question may be even more pertinent: "Why do they want to provoke us?"

David Fromkin suggested the answer in *Foreign Affairs* back in 1975. "Terrorism," he noted, "is violence used in order to create fear; but it is aimed at creating fear in order that the fear, in turn, will lead somebody else—not the terrorist—to embark on some quite different program of action that will accomplish whatever it is that the terrorist really desires." When a terrorist kills, the goal is not murder itself but something else—for example, a police crackdown that will create a rift between government and society that the terrorist can then exploit for revolutionary purposes. Osama bin Laden sought—and has received—an international military crackdown, one he wants to exploit for his particular brand of revolution.

Bin Laden produced a piece of high political theater he hoped would reach the audience that concerned him the most: the *umma*, or universal Islamic community. The script was obvious: America, cast as the villain, was supposed to use its military might like a cartoon character trying to kill a fly with a shotgun. The media would see to it that any use of force against the civilian population of Afghanistan was broadcast around the world, and the *umma* would find it shocking how Americans nonchalantly caused Muslims to suffer and die. The ensuing outrage would open a chasm between state and society in the Middle East, and the governments allied with the West—many of which are repressive, corrupt, and illegitimate—would find themselves adrift. It was to provoke such an outcome that bin Laden broadcast his statement following the start of the military campaign on October 7, in which he said, among other things, that the Americans and the British "have divided the entire world into two regions—one of faith, where there is no hypocrisy, and another of infidelity, from which we hope God will protect us."

Polarizing the Islamic world between the *umma* and the regimes allied with the United States would help achieve bin Laden's primary goal: furthering the cause of Islamic revolution within the Muslim world itself, in the Arab lands especially and in Saudi Arabia above all. He had no intention of defeating America. War with the United States was not a goal in and of itself but rather an instrument designed to help his brand of extremist Islam survive and flourish among the believers. Americans, in short, have been drawn into somebody else's civil war.

Washington had no choice but to take up the gauntlet, but it is not altogether clear that Americans understand fully this war's true dimensions. The response to bin Laden cannot be left to soldiers and police alone. He has embroiled the United States in an intra-Muslim ideological battle, a struggle for hearts and minds in which al Qaeda had already scored a number of victories—as the reluctance of America's Middle Eastern allies to offer public support for the campaign against it demonstrated. The first step toward weakening the hold of bin Laden's ideology, therefore, must be to comprehend the symbolic universe into which he has dragged us.

America, the Hubal of the Age

Bin Laden's October 7 statement offers a crucial window onto his conceptual world and repays careful attention. In it he states, "Hypocrisy stood behind the leader of global idolatry, behind the Hubal of the age—namely, America and its supporters." Because the symbolism is obscure to most Americans, this sentence was widely mistranslated in the press, but bin Laden's Muslim audience understood it immediately.

In the early seventh century, when the Prophet Muhammad began to preach Islam to the pagan Arab tribes in Mecca, Hubal was a stone idol that stood in the Kaaba—a structure that Abraham, according to Islamic tradition, originally built on orders from God as a sanctuary of Islam. In the years between Abraham and Muhammad, the tradition runs, the Arabs fell away from true belief and began to worship idols, with Hubal the most powerful of many. When bin Laden calls America "the Hubal of the age," he suggests that it is the primary focus of idol worship and that it is polluting the Kaaba, a symbol of Islamic purity. His imagery has a double resonance: it portrays American culture as a font of idolatry while rejecting the American military presence on the Arabian peninsula (which is, by his definition, the holy land of Islam, a place barred to infidels).

Muhammad's prophecy called the Arabs of Mecca back to their monotheistic birthright. The return to true belief, however, was not an easy one, because the reigning Meccan oligarchy persecuted the early Muslims. By calling for the destruction of Hubal, the Prophet's message threatened to undermine the special position that Mecca enjoyed in Arabia as a pagan shrine city. With much of their livelihood at stake, the oligarchs punished Muhammad's followers and conspired to kill him. The Muslims therefore fled from Mecca to Medina, where they established the *umma* as a political and religious community. They went on to fight and win a war against Mecca that ended with the destruction of Hubal and the spread of true Islam around the world.

Before the Prophet could achieve this success, however, he encountered the *Munafiqun*, the Hypocrites of Medina. Muhammad's acceptance of leadership over the Medinese reduced the power of a number of local tribal leaders. These men outwardly accepted Islam in order to protect their worldly status, but in their hearts they bore malice toward both the Prophet and his message. Among other misdeeds, the treacherous *Munafiqun* abandoned Muhammad on the battlefield at a moment when he was already woefully outnumbered. The Hypocrites were apostates who accepted true belief but then rejected it, and as such they were regarded as worse than the infidels who had never embraced Islam to begin with. Islam can understand just how difficult it is for a pagan to leave behind all the beliefs and personal connections that he or she once held dear; it is less forgiving of those who accept the truth and then subvert it.

In bin Laden's imagery, the leaders of the Arab and Islamic worlds today are Hypocrites, idol worshippers cowering behind America, the Hubal of the age. His sword jabs simultaneously at the United States and the governments allied with it. His attack was designed to force those governments to choose: You are either with the idol-worshiping enemies of God or you are with the true believers.

The al Qaeda organization grew out of an Islamic religious movement called the Salafiyya—a name derived from *al-Salaf al-Salih*, "the venerable forefathers," which refers to the generation of the Prophet Muhammad and his companions. Salafis regard the Islam that most Muslims practice today as polluted by idolatry; they seek to reform the religion by emulating the first generation of Muslims, whose pristine society they consider to have best reflected God's wishes for humans. The Salafiyya is not a unified movement, and it expresses itself in many forms, most of which do not approach the extremism of Osama bin Laden or the Taliban. The Wahhabi ideology of the Saudi state, for example, and the religious doctrines of the Muslim Brotherhood in Egypt and a host of voluntary religious organizations around the Islamic world are all Salafi. These diverse movements share the belief that Muslims have deviated from God's plan and that matters can be returned to their proper state by emulating the Prophet.

Like any other major religious figure, Muhammad left behind a legacy that his followers have channeled in different directions. An extremist current in the Salafiyya places great emphasis on jihad, or holy war. Among other things, the Prophet Muhammad fought in mortal combat against idolatry, and some of his followers today choose to accord this aspect of his career primary importance. The devoted members of al Qaeda display an unsettling willingness to martyr themselves because they feel that, like the Prophet, they are locked in a life-or-death struggle with the forces of unbelief that threaten from all sides. They consider themselves an island of true believers surrounded by a sea of iniquity and think the future of religion itself, and therefore the world, depends on them and their battle against idol worship.

In almost every Sunni Muslim country the Salafiyya has spawned Islamist political movements working to compel the state to apply the *shari`a*— that is, Islamic law. Extremist Salafis believe that strict application of the *shari`a* is necessary to ensure that Muslims walk on the path of the Prophet. The more extremist the party, the more insistent and violent the demand that the state must apply the *shari`a* exclusively. In the view of extremist Salafis, the *shari`a* is God's thunderous commandment to Muslims, and failure to adopt it constitutes idolatry. By removing God from the realm of law, a domain that He has clearly claimed for Himself alone, human legislation amounts to worshiping a pagan deity. Thus it was on the basis of failure to apply the *shari`a* that extremists branded Egyptian President Anwar al-Sadat an apostate and then killed him. His assassins came from a group often known as Egyptian Islamic Jihad, the remnants of which have in recent years merged with al Qaeda. In fact, investigators believe that Egyptian Islamic

Jihad's leaders, Ayman al-Zawahiri and Muhammad Atef (who was killed in the U.S. air campaign), masterminded the attacks of September 11. In his 1996 "Declaration of War against the Americans," bin Laden showed that he and his Egyptian associates are cut from the same cloth. Just as Zawahiri and Atef considered the current regime of Hosni Mubarak in Egypt to be a nest of apostates, so bin Laden considered the Saudi monarchy (its Wahhabi doctrines notwithstanding) to have renounced Islam. According to bin Laden, his king adopted "polytheism," which bin Laden defined as the acceptance of "laws fabricated by men . . . permitting that which God has forbidden." It is the height of human arrogance and irreligion to "share with God in His sole right of sovereignty and making the law."

Extremist Salafis, therefore, regard modern Western civilization as a font of evil, spreading idolatry around the globe in the form of secularism. Since the United States is the strongest Western nation, the main purveyor of pop culture, and the power most involved in the political and economic affairs of the Islamic world, it receives particularly harsh criticism. Only the apostate Middle Eastern regimes themselves fall under harsher condemnation.

It is worth remembering, in this regard, that the rise of Islam represents a miraculous case of the triumph of human will. With little more than their beliefs to gird them, the Prophet Muhammad and a small number of devoted followers started a movement that brought the most powerful empires of their day crashing to the ground. On September 11, the attackers undoubtedly imagined themselves to be retracing the Prophet's steps. As they boarded the planes with the intention of destroying the Pentagon and the World Trade Center, they recited battle prayers that contained the line "All of their equipment, and gates, and technology will not prevent [you from achieving your aim], nor harm [you] except by God's will." The hijackers' imaginations certainly needed nothing more than this sparse line to remind them that, as they attacked America, they rode right behind Muhammad, who in his day had unleashed forces that, shortly after his death, destroyed the Persian Empire and crippled Byzantium—the two superpowers of the age.

America, Land of the Crusaders

When thinking about the world today and their place in it, the extremist Salafis do not reflect only on the story of the foundation of Islam. They also scour more than a millennium of Islamic history in search of parallels to the present predicament. In his "Declaration of War," for instance, bin Laden states that the stationing of American forces on the soil of the Arabian peninsula constitutes the greatest aggression committed against the Muslims since the death of the Prophet in AD 632.

To put this claim in perspective, it is worth remembering that in the last 1,300 years Muslims have suffered a number of significant defeats, including but not limited to the destruction of the Abbasid caliphate by the

Mongols, an episode of which bin Laden is well aware. In 1258 the ruthless Mongol leader Hulegu sacked Baghdad, killed the caliph, and massacred hundreds of thousands of inhabitants, stacking their skulls, as legend has it, in a pyramid outside the city walls. Whatever one thinks about U.S. policy toward Iraq, few in America would argue that the use of Saudi bases to enforce the sanctions against Saddam Hussein's regime constitutes a world-historical event on a par with the Mongol invasion of the Middle East. Before September 11, one might have been tempted to pass off as nationalist hyperbole bin Laden's assumption that U.S. policy represents the pinnacle of human evil. Now we know he is deadly serious.

The magnitude of the attacks on New York and Washington make it clear that al Qaeda does indeed believe itself to be fighting a war to save the *umma* from Satan, represented by secular Western culture. Extreme though they may be, these views extend far beyond al Qaeda's immediate followers in Afghanistan. Even a quick glance at the Islamist press in Arabic demonstrates that many Muslims who do not belong to bin Laden's terrorist network consider the United States to be on a moral par with Genghis Khan. Take, for instance, Muhammad Abbas, an Egyptian Islamist who wrote the following in the newspaper *Al Shaab* on September 21:

> Look! There is the master of democracy whom they have so often sanctified but who causes criminal, barbaric, bloody oppression that abandons the moral standards of even the most savage empires in history. In my last column I listed for readers the five million killed (may God receive them as martyrs) because of the crimes committed by this American civilization that America leads. These five million were killed in the last few decades alone.

Similar feelings led another *Al Shaab* columnist that day, Khalid al-Sharif, to describe the shock and delight that he felt while watching the World Trade Center crumbling:

> Look at that! America, master of the world, is crashing down. Look at that! The Satan who rules the world, east and west, is burning. Look at that! The sponsor of terrorism is itself seared by its fire.

The fanatics of al Qaeda see the world in black and white and advance a particularly narrow view of Islam. This makes them a tiny minority among Muslims. But the basic categories of their thought flow directly from the mainstream of the Salafiyya, a perspective that has enjoyed a wide hearing over the last 50 years. Familiarity thus ensures bin Laden's ideas a sympathetic reception in many quarters.

In Salafi writings, the United States emerges as the senior member of a "Zionist-Crusader alliance" dedicated to subjugating Muslims, killing them, and, most important, destroying Islam. A careful reading reveals that this alliance represents more than just close relations between the United States and Israel today. The international cooperation between Washington and

Jerusalem is but one nefarious manifestation of a greater evil of almost cosmic proportions. Thus in his "Declaration of War" bin Laden lists 10 or 12 world hot spots where Muslims have recently died (including Bosnia, Chechnya, and Lebanon) and attributes all of these deaths to a conspiracy led by the United States, even though Americans actually played no role in pulling the trigger. And thus, in another document, "Jihad Against Jews and Crusaders," bin Laden describes U.S. policies toward the Middle East as "a clear declaration of war on God, His messenger, and Muslims."

As strange as it may sound to an American audience, the idea that the United States has taken an oath of enmity toward God has deep roots in the Salafi tradition. It has been around for more than 50 years and has reached a wide public through the works of, among others, Sayyid Qutb, the most important Salafi thinker of the last half-century and a popular author in the Muslim world even today, nearly 40 years after his death. A sample passage taken from his writings in the early 1950s illustrates the point. Addressing the reasons why the Western powers had failed to support Muslims against their enemies in Pakistan, Palestine, and elsewhere, Qutb canvassed a number of common explanations such as Jewish financial influence and British imperial trickery but concluded,

> All of these opinions overlook one vital element in the question . . . the Crusader spirit that runs in the blood of all Occidentals. It is this that colors all their thinking, which is responsible for their imperialistic fear of the spirit of Islam and for their efforts to crush the strength of Islam. For the instincts and the interests of all Occidentals are bound up together in the crushing of that strength. This is the common factor that links together communist Russia and capitalist America. We do not forget the role of international Zionism in plotting against Islam and in pooling the forces of the Crusader imperialists and communist materialists alike. This is nothing other than a continuation of the role played by the Jews since the migration of the Prophet to Medina and the rise of the Islamic state.

Sayyid Qutb, Osama bin Laden, and the entire extremist Salafiyya see Western civilization, in all periods and in all guises, as innately hostile to Muslims and to Islam itself. The West and Islam are locked in a prolonged conflict. Islam will eventually triumph, of course, but only after enduring great hardship. Contemporary history, defined as it is by Western domination, constitutes the darkest era in the entire history of Islam.

America and the Mongol Threat

When attempting to come to grips with the nature of the threat the modern West poses, extremist Salafis fall back on the writings of Ibn Taymiyya for guidance. A towering figure in the history of Islamic thought, he was born in Damascus in the thirteenth century, when Syria stood under the threat of invasion from the Mongols. Modern radicals find him attractive because he too faced the threat of a rival civilization. Ibn Taymiyya the firebrand exhorted his fellow Muslims to fight the Mongol foe, while Ibn Taymiyya the intellectual guided his community through the problems Muslims face when their social order falls under the shadow of non-Muslim power. It is only natural that bin Laden himself looks to such a master in order to legitimate his policies. Using Ibn Taymiyya to target America, however, marks an interesting turning point in the history of the radical Salafiyya.

Bin Laden's "Declaration of War" uses the logic of Ibn Taymiyya to persuade others in the Salafiyya to abandon old tactics for new ones. The first reference to him arises in connection with a discussion of the "Zionist-Crusader alliance," which according to bin Laden has been jailing and killing radical preachers—men such as Sheikh Omar Abdel Rahman, in prison for plotting a series of bombings in New York City following the 1993 bombing of the World Trade Center. Bin Laden argues that the "iniquitous Crusader movement under the leadership of the U.S.A." fears these preachers because they will successfully rally the Islamic community against the West, just as Ibn Taymiyya did against the Mongols in his day. Having identified the United States as a threat to Islam equivalent to the Mongols, bin Laden then discusses what to do about it. Ibn Taymiyya provides the answer: "To fight in the defense of religion and belief is a collective duty; there is no other duty after belief than fighting the enemy who is corrupting the life and the religion." The next most important thing after accepting the word of God, in other words, is fighting for it.

By calling on the *umma* to fight the Americans as if they were the Mongols, bin Laden and his Egyptian lieutenants have taken the extremist Salafiyya down a radically new path. Militants have long identified the West as a pernicious evil on a par with the Mongols, but they have traditionally targeted the internal enemy, the Hypocrites and apostates, rather than Hubal itself. Aware that he is shifting the focus considerably, bin Laden quotes Ibn Taymiyya at length to establish the basic point that "people of Islam should join forces and support each other to get rid of the main infidel," even if that means that the true believers will be forced to fight alongside Muslims of dubious piety. In the grand scheme of things, he argues, God often uses the base motives of impious Muslims as a means of advancing the cause of religion. In effect, bin Laden calls upon his fellow Islamist radicals to postpone the Islamic revolution, to stop fighting Hypocrites and apostates: "An internal war is a great mistake, no matter what reasons there are for it," because discord among Muslims will only serve the United States and its goal of destroying Islam.

The shift of focus from the domestic enemy to the foreign power is all the more striking given the merger of al Qaeda and Egyptian Islamic Jihad. The latter's decision to kill Sadat in 1981 arose directly from the principle that the cause of Islam would be served by targeting lax Muslim leaders rather than by fighting foreigners, and here, too, Ibn Taymiyya provided the key doctrine. In his day Muslims often found themselves living under Mongol rulers who had absorbed Islam in one form or another. Ibn Taymiyya argued that such rulers—who outwardly pretended to be Muslims but who secretly followed non-Islamic, Mongol practices—must be considered infidels. Moreover, he claimed, by having accepted Islam but having also failed to observe key precepts of the religion, they had in effect committed apostasy and thereby written their own death sentences. In general, Islam prohibits fighting fellow Muslims and strongly restricts the right to rebel against the ruler; Ibn Taymiyya's doctrines, therefore, were crucial in the development of a modern Sunni Islamic revolutionary theory.

Egyptian Islamic Jihad views leaders such as Sadat as apostates. Although they may outwardly display signs of piety, they do not actually have Islam in their hearts, as their failure to enforce the *shari`a* proves. This non-Islamic behavior demonstrates that such leaders actually serve the secular West, precisely as an earlier generation of outwardly Muslim rulers had served the Mongols, and as the Hypocrites had served idolatry. Islamic Jihad explained itself back in the mid-1980s in a long, lucid statement titled "The Neglected Duty." Not a political manifesto like bin Laden's tracts, it is a sustained and learned argument that targets the serious believer rather than the angry, malleable crowd. Unlike bin Laden's holy war, moreover, Islamic Jihad's doctrine, though violent, fits clearly in the mainstream of Salafi consciousness, which historically has been concerned much more with the state of the Muslims themselves than with relations between Islam and the outside world. The decision to target America, therefore, raises the question of whether, during the 1990s, Egyptian Islamic Jihad changed its ideology entirely. Did its leaders decide that the foreign enemy was in fact the real enemy? Or was the 1993 bombing in New York tactical rather than strategic?

The answer would seem to be the latter. Bin Laden's "Declaration of War" itself testifies to the tactical nature of his campaign against America. Unlike "The Neglected Duty," which presents a focused argument, the "Declaration of War" meanders from topic to topic, contradicting itself along the way. On the one hand, it calls for unity in the face of external aggression and demands an end to internecine warfare; on the other, it calls in essence for revolution in Saudi Arabia. By presenting a litany of claims against the Saudi ruling family and by discussing the politics of Saudi Arabia at length and in minute detail, bin Laden protests too much: he reveals that he has not, in fact, set aside the internal war among the believers. Moreover, he also reveals that the ideological basis for that internal war has not changed. The members of the Saudi elite, like Sadat, have committed apostasy. Like the Hypocrites of Medina, they serve the forces of irreligion in order to harm the devotees of the Prophet and his message:

> You know more than anybody else about the size, intention, and the danger of the presence of the U.S. military bases in the area. The [Saudi] regime betrayed the *umma* and joined the infidels, assisting them . . . against the Muslims. It is well known that this is one of the ten "voiders" of Islam, deeds of de-Islamization. By

opening the Arabian Peninsula to the crusaders, the regime disobeyed and acted against what has been enjoined by the messenger of God.

Osama bin Laden undoubtedly believes that Americans are Crusader-Zionists, that they threaten his people even more than did the Mongols—in short, that they are the enemies of God Himself. But he also sees them as obstacles to his plans for his native land. The "Declaration of War" provides yet more testimony to the old saw that ultimately all politics is local.

The Failure of Political Islam

If the attacks on the United States represented a change in radical Salafi tactics, then one must wonder what prompted bin Laden and Zawahiri to make that change. The answer is that the attacks were a response to the failure of extremist movements in the Muslim world in recent years, which have generally proved incapable of taking power (Sudan and Afghanistan being the major exceptions). In the last two decades, several violent groups have challenged regimes such as those in Egypt, Syria, and Algeria, but in every case the government has managed to crush, co-opt, or marginalize the radicals. In the words of the "Declaration of War,"

> the Zionist-Crusader alliance moves quickly to contain and abort any "corrective movement" appearing in Islamic countries. Different means and methods are used to achieve their target. Sometimes officials from the Ministry of the Interior, who are also graduates of the colleges of the shari`a, are [unleashed] to mislead and confuse the nation and the umma . . . and to circulate false information about the movement, wasting the energy of the nation in discussing minor issues and ignoring the main one that is the unification of people under the divine law of Allah.

Given that in Egypt, Algeria, and elsewhere regimes have resorted to extreme violence to protect themselves, it is striking that bin Laden emphasizes here not the brutality but rather the counterpropaganda designed to divide and rule. Consciously or not, he has put his finger on a serious problem for the extremist Salafis: the limitations of their political and economic theories.

Apart from insisting on the implementation of the shari`a, demanding social justice, and turning the umma into the only legitimate political community, radical Salafis have precious little to offer in response to the mundane problems that people and governments face in the modern world. Extremist Islam is profoundly effective in mounting a protest movement: it can produce a cadre of activists whose devotion to the cause knows no bounds, it can galvanize people to fight against oppression. But it has serious difficulties when it comes to producing institutions and programs that can command the attention of diverse groups in society over the long haul. Its success relies mainly on the support of true believers, but they tend to fragment in disputes over doctrine, leadership, and agenda.

The limitations of extremist Salafi political theory and its divisive tendencies come to light clearly if one compares the goals of al Qaeda with those of the Palestinian terrorist group Hamas, whose suicide bombers have also been in the headlines recently. The ideology of Hamas also evolved out of the Egyptian extremist Salafiyya milieu, and it shares with al Qaeda a paranoid view of the world: the *umma* and true Islam are threatened with extinction by the spread of Western secularism, the policies of the Crusading West, and oppression by the Zionists. Both Hamas and al Qaeda believe that the faithful must obliterate Israel. But looking more closely at Hamas and its agenda, one can see that it parts company with al Qaeda in many significant ways. This is because Hamas operates in the midst of nationalistic Palestinians, a majority of whom fervently desire, among other things, an end to the Israeli occupation and the establishment of a Palestinian state in part of historic Palestine.

The nationalist outlook of Hamas' public presents the organization with a number of thorny problems. Nationalism, according to the extremist Salafiyya, constitutes *shirk*—that is, polytheism or idolatry. If politics and religion are not distinct categories, as extremist Salafis argue, then political life must be centered around God and God's law. Sovereignty belongs not to the nation but to God alone, and the only legitimate political community is the *umma*. Pride in one's ethnic group is tolerable only so long as it does not divide the community of believers, who form an indivisible unit thanks to the sovereignty of the *shari`a*. One day, extremist Salafis believe, political boundaries will be erased and all Muslims will live in one polity devoted to God's will. At the moment, however, the priority is not to erase boundaries but to raise up the *shari`a* and abolish secular law. Nationalism is idolatry because it divides the *umma* and replaces a *shari`a*–centered consciousness with ethnic pride.

If Hamas were actually to denounce secular Palestinian nationalists as apostates, however, it would immediately consign itself to political irrelevance. To skirt this problem, the organization has developed an elaborate view of Islamic history that in effect elevates the Palestinian national struggle to a position of paramount importance for the *umma* as a whole. This allows Hamas activists to function in the day-to-day political world as fellow travelers with the nationalists. Thus one of the fascinating aspects of Palestinian extremist Salafiyya is a dog that hasn't barked: in contrast to its sibling movements in neighboring countries, Hamas has refrained from labeling the secular leaders in the Palestinian Authority as apostates. Even at the height of Yasir Arafat's crackdown against Hamas, the movement never openly branded him as an idolater.

Like al Qaeda, Hamas argues that a conspiracy between Zionism and the West has dedicated itself to destroying Islam, but for obvious reasons it magnifies the role of Zionism in the alliance. The Hamas Covenant, for example, sees Zionism as, among other things, a force determining many of the greatest historical developments of the modern period:

[Zionists] were behind the French Revolution, the communist revolution. . . . They were behind World War I, when they were able to destroy the Islamic caliphate [i.e., the Ottoman Empire]. . . . They obtained the Balfour Declaration [favoring establishment of a Jewish homeland in Palestine], [and] formed the League of Nations, through which they could rule the world. They were behind World War II, through which they made huge financial gains by trading in armaments, and paved the way for the establishment of their state. It was they who instigated the replacement of the League of Nations with the United Nations and the Security Council. . . . There is no war going on anywhere, without [them] having their finger in it.

Do a number of intelligent and educated people actually believe this? Yes, because they must; their self-understanding hinges on it. Since their political struggle must be for the greater good of the *umma* and of Islam as a whole, their enemy must be much more than just one part of the Jewish people with designs on one sliver of Muslim territory. The enemy must be the embodiment of an evil that transcends time and place.

Although the sanctity of Jerusalem works in Hamas' favor, in Islam Jerusalem does not enjoy the status of Mecca and Medina and is only a city, not an entire country. To reconcile its political and religious concerns, therefore, Hamas must inflate the significance of Palestine in Islamic history: "The present Zionist onslaught," the covenant says, "has also been preceded by Crusading raids from the West and other Tatar [Mongol] raids from the East." The references here are to Saladin, the Muslim leader who defeated the Crusaders in Palestine at the battle of Hattin in 1187, and to the Muslim armies that defeated the Mongols at another Palestinian site called Ayn Jalut in 1260. On this basis Hamas argues that Palestine has always been the bulwark against the enemies of Islam; the *umma*, therefore, must rally behind the Palestinians to destroy Israel, which represents the third massive onslaught against the true religion since the death of the Prophet.

Despite the similarities in their perspectives, therefore, al Qaeda and Hamas have quite different agendas. Al Qaeda justifies its political goals on the basis of the holiness of Mecca and Medina and on the claim that the presence of U.S. forces in Arabia constitutes the greatest aggression that the Muslims have ever endured. Hamas sees its own struggle against Israel as the first duty of the *umma*. The two organizations undoubtedly share enough in common to facilitate political cooperation on many issues, but at some point their agendas diverge radically, a divergence that stems from the different priorities inherent in their respective Saudi and Palestinian backgrounds.

The differences between al Qaeda and Hamas demonstrate how local conditions can mold the universal components of Salafi consciousness into distinct world views. They display the creativity of radical Islamists in addressing a practical problem similar to that faced by communists in the early twentieth century: how to build a universal political movement that can nevertheless function effectively at the local level. This explains why, when one looks at the political map of the extremist Salafiyya, one finds a large number of organizations all of which insist that they stand for the same principles. They do, in fact, all insist on the implementation of the shari`a, but the specific social and political forces fueling that insistence differ greatly from place to place. They all march to the beat of God's drummer, but the marchers tend to wander off in different directions.

The new tactic of targeting America is designed to overcome precisely this weakness of political Islam. Bin Laden succeeded in attacking Hubal, the universal enemy: he identified the only target that all of the Salafiyya submovements around the world can claim equally as their own, thereby reflecting and reinforcing the collective belief that the *umma* actually is the political community. He and his colleagues adopted this strategy not from choice but from desperation, a desperation born of the fact that in recent years the extremist Salafis had been defeated politically almost everywhere in the Arab and Muslim world. The new tactic, by tapping into the deepest emotions of the political community, smacks of brilliance, and—much to America's chagrin—will undoubtedly give political Islam a renewed burst of energy.

Explaining the Echo

The decision to target the United States allows al Qaeda to play the role of a radical "Salafi International." It resonates beyond the small community of committed extremists, however, reaching not just moderate Salafis but, in addition, a broad range of disaffected citizens experiencing poverty, oppression, and powerlessness across the Muslim world. This broader resonance of what appears to us as such a wild and hateful message is the dimension of the problem that Americans find most difficult to understand.

One reason for the welcoming echo is the extent to which Salafi political movements, while failing to capture state power, have nevertheless succeeded in capturing much cultural ground in Muslim countries. Many authoritarian regimes (such as Mubarak's Egypt) have cut a deal with the extremists: in return for an end to assassinations, the regime acquiesces in some of the demands regarding implementation of the shari`a. In addition, it permits the extremist groups to run networks of social welfare organizations that often deliver services more efficiently than does a state sector riddled with corruption and marred by decay. This powerful cultural presence of the Salafis across the Islamic world means not only that their direct ranks have grown but also that their symbolism is more familiar than ever among a wider public.

But the attack on America also resonates deeply among secular groups in many countries. The immediate response in the secular Arab press, for example, fell broadly into three categories. A minority denounced the attacks forcefully and unconditionally, another minority attributed them to the Israelis or to American extremists like Timothy McVeigh, and a significant majority responded with a version of "Yes, but"—yes, the terrorist attacks against you were wrong, but you must understand that your own policies in the Middle East have for years sown the seeds of this kind of violence.

This rationalization amounts to a political protest against the perceived role of the United States in the Middle East. Arab and Islamic commentators, and a number of prominent analysts of the Middle East in this country, point in particular to U.S. enforcement of the sanctions on Iraq and U.S. support for Israel in its struggle against Palestinian nationalism. Both of these issues certainly cause outrage, and if the United States were to effect the removal of Israeli settlements from the West Bank and alleviate the suffering of the Iraqi people, some of that outrage would certainly subside. But although a change in those policies would dampen some of bin Laden's appeal, it would not solve the problem of the broader anger and despair that he taps, because the sources of those feelings lie beyond the realm of day-to-day diplomacy.

Indeed, secular political discourse in the Islamic world in general and the Arab world in particular bears a striking resemblance to the Salafi interpretation of international affairs, especially insofar as both speak in terms of Western conspiracies. The secular press does not make reference to Crusaders and Mongols but rather to a string of "broken promises" dating back to World War I, when the European powers divided up the Ottoman Empire to suit their own interests. They planted Israel in the midst of the Middle East, so the analysis goes, in order to drive a wedge between Arab states, and the United States continues to support Israel for the same purpose. Bin Laden played to this sentiment in his October 7 statement when he said,

> What the United States tastes today is a very small thing compared to what we have tasted for tens of years. Our nation has been tasting this humiliation and contempt for more than eighty years. Its sons are being killed, its blood is being shed, its holy places are being attacked, and it is not being ruled according to what God has decreed.

For 80 years—that is, since the destruction of the Ottoman Empire—the Arabs and the Muslims have been humiliated. Although they do not share bin Laden's millenarian agenda, when secular commentators point to Palestine and Iraq today they do not see just two difficult political problems; they see what they consider the true intentions of the West unmasked.

Arab commentators often explain, for instance, that Saddam Hussein and Washington are actually allies. They ridicule the notion that the United States tried to depose the dictator. After all, it is said, the first Bush administration had the forces in place to remove the Baath Party and had called on the Iraqi populace to rise up against the tyrant. When the people actually rose, however, the Americans watched from the sidelines as the regime brutally suppressed them. Clearly, therefore, what the United States really wanted was to divide and rule the Arabs in order to secure easy access to Persian Gulf oil—a task that also involves propping up corrupt monarchies in Kuwait and Saudi Arabia. Keeping Saddam on a leash was the easiest way to ensure that Iran could not block the project.

Needless to say, this world view is problematic. Since World War I, Arab societies have been deeply divided among themselves along ethnic, social, religious, and political lines. Regardless of what the dominant Arab discourse regarding broken promises has to say, most of these divisions were not created by the West. The European powers and the United States have sometimes worked to divide the Arabs, sometimes to unify them. Mostly they have pursued their own interests, as have all the other actors involved. Bin Laden is a participant in a profoundly serious civil war over Arab and Muslim identity in the modern world. The United States is also a participant in that war, because whether it realizes it or not, its policies affect the fortunes of the various belligerents. But Washington is not a primary actor, because it is an outsider in cultural affairs and has only a limited ability to define for believers the role of Islam in public life.

The war between extremist Salafis and the broader populations around them is only the tip of the iceberg. The fight over religion among Muslims is but one of a number of deep and enduring regional struggles that originally had nothing to do with the United States and even today involve it only indirectly. Nonetheless, U.S. policies can influence the balance of power among the protagonists in these struggles, sometimes to a considerable degree.

Until the Arab and Muslim worlds create political orders that do not disenfranchise huge segments of their own populations, the civil war will continue and will continue to touch the United States. Washington can play an important role in fostering authentic and inclusive polities, but ultimately Arabs and Muslims more generally must learn to live in peace with one another so as to live comfortably with outsiders. Whether they will do so is anybody's guess.

It is a stark political fact that in the Arab and Muslim worlds today economic globalization and the international balance of power both come with an American face, and neither gives much reason for optimism. Osama bin Laden's rhetoric, dividing the world into two camps—the *umma* versus the United States and puppet regimes—has a deep resonance because on some levels it conforms, if not to reality, then at least to its appearances. This is why, for the first time in modern history, the extremist Salafis have managed to mobilize mass popular opinion.

This development is troubling, but the United States still has some cards to play. Its policies, for instance, on both West Bank settlements and

Iraq, are sorely in need of review—but only after bin Laden has been vanquished. These policy changes might help, but the root problem lies deeper. Once al Qaeda has been annihilated without sparking anti-American revolutions in the Islamic world, the United States should adopt a set of policies that ensure that significant numbers of Muslims—not Muslim regimes but Muslims—identify their own interests with those of the United States, so that demagogues like bin Laden cannot aspire to speak in the name of the entire *umma*. In 1991, millions of Iraqis constituted just such a reservoir of potential supporters, yet America turned its back on them. Washington had its reasons, but they were not the kind that can be justified in terms of the American values that we trumpet to the world. Today we are paying a price for that hypocrisy. This is not to say that we caused or deserved the attacks of September 11 in any way. It is to say, however, that we are to some extent responsible for the fact that so few in the Arab and Muslim worlds express vocal and unequivocal support for our cause, even when that cause is often their cause as well.

Since the events of September 11, innumerable articles have appeared in the press discussing America's loss of innocence. To foreigners, this view of Americans as naive bumpkins, a band of Forrest Gumps who just arrived in town, is difficult to fathom. Whether the MTV generation knows it or not, the United States has been deeply involved in other peoples' civil wars for a long time. A generation ago, for example, we supposedly lost our innocence in Vietnam. Back then, Adonis, the poet laureate of the Arab world, meditated on the ambivalence Arabs feel toward America. In the aftermath of the September 11 attacks, his poem seems prophetic:

> New York, you will find in my land
> . . . the stone of Mecca and the waters of the Tigris.
> In spite of all this,
> you pant in Palestine and Hanoi.
> East and west you contend with people
> whose only history is fire.

These tormented people knew us before we were virgins.

Are We Really at War?
Gary D. Solis

One of the major questions that arose in the wake of the September 11, 2001 attacks on the United States and President George W. Bush's subsequent call for a "war on terrorism" was how the nation could react in legally bringing the perpetrators to justice while carrying out an undeclared war. A second question was whether those terrorists taken into custody or captured in combat could or should be tried in civilian courts as criminals or as combatants under the Uniform Code of Military Justice. In this essay Lieutenant Colonel Gary D. Solis, U.S. Marine Corps (Retired), Marine Corps' Chief of Oral History with a doctorate in the law of war, examines these vital questions. This essay was first published in Naval Institute Proceedings, *December 2001. Reprinted from* Proceedings *with permission. Copyright © 2001 by U.S. Naval Institute/ www.navalinstitute.org.*

Is the war on terrorism actually a war? If not, what is it, and how will the actions of our armed forces be viewed in terms of international law? Are terrorists ordinary criminals to be tried in domestic courts, or are they enemy combatants? If captured, are al Qaeda fighters prisoners of war? May we try terrorists for war crimes in federal courts or by military commissions? As timely as these questions are, they are questions our country has faced before. We can look to history and to legal precedent for the answers.

What Constitutes a War?

In the context of the war on terrorism, the term *war* is "a metaphor to signify struggle, commitment, endurance," according to a *New York Times* op-ed piece by Michael Walzer, author of the classic book *Just and Unjust Wars*. But this is no metaphorical war. This is war, plain and simple. Even before our counterattacks on Afghanistan's Taliban and the al Qaeda terrorists, the United States was engaged in a war. We were at war at 0845 on 11 September 2001, a war "declared" by the Commander-in-Chief in his 20 September address before a joint session of Congress. Congress swiftly followed his declaration with a joint resolution supporting the use of force against terrorists. Our armed forces are now fighting that war, Professor Walzer's assessment notwithstanding.

But what legally constitutes a war? There is no court case, no text, no treaty that conclusively answers the question or defines the word. Only Congress can declare war—which it has not done—but can a state of war exist without a congressional declaration? On the basis of history alone, the answer is yes. The United States, which has employed military force more than 220 times in its history, has declared war only five times, most recently more than half a century ago. Korea, Vietnam, and the Gulf War all were undeclared combat actions.

Some say that war exists if there are armed hostilities between nations, or between citizens of the same nation. In 1846 President James Polk expressed this view in words pertinent to our situation today: "After reiterated menaces, Mexico has passed the boundary of the United States, has invaded our territory and shed American blood upon the American soil. She has proclaimed that hostilities have commenced, and that the two nations are now at war. . . . We are called upon by every consideration of duty and patriotism to vindicate with decision and honor, the rights and the interests of our country."

So it is with the 11 September terrorists. Behind the cry of "Jihad!" agents of Osama bin Laden and al Qaeda crossed our border and killed more American citizens in a single day than on any day since the Civil War. If estimates are correct, al Qaeda murdered more than 30 times the 148 U.S. battle deaths suffered in the Gulf War. We are at war, and no formal declaration is necessary.

Even if war can exist in the absence of a congressional declaration, can war be made on an individual, or a non-state group, such as "terrorists"? Indeed it can. In 1801, President Thomas Jefferson made undeclared war on the Barbary pirates, sending Marine Lieutenant Presley O'Bannon to the shores of Tripoli. It is true that in customary international law, war is a hostile contention by means of armed forces between states. The 1907 Hague Regulation III speaks of war being a circumstance between "states." But al Qaeda, Hamas, Hizballah, and other terrorist armed forces of international reach have taken the world community beyond what is customary. Nor is this a case of one man's terrorist, another man's freedom fighter. These fanatical groups are not resisting colonial governments, or fighting an alien occupation, or defying a racist regime. They breach borders to kill and destroy, intentionally targeting noncombatants and civilian locations, for reasons most Westerners find difficult even to articulate.

There is a well-reasoned argument that in international law, a declaration of war is passé, a policy relic of a not-so-distant past. That is because the U.N. Charter, ratified by the United States and thus the law of our land, requires that U.N. members "refrain in their international relations from the threat or use of force" unless directed by the United Nations. That provision prohibits force against "any state." Other charter provisions require that members "settle their international disputes by peaceful means." Those provisions, taken together, indicate little room today for a state's unilateral declaration of war.

The U.N. Charter does allow for force to be used in self-defense, however. In years past, self-defense has been described as requiring "a necessity of self-defense, instant, overwhelming, leaving no choice of means, and no moment for deliberation." That description does not closely fit our counterstrikes on the Taliban and al Qaeda. But international law, like all institutions, evolves and continues to mature. There is heated debate as to whether a state may, under the U.N. Charter or under customary international law, exercise anticipatory self-defense—that is, whether a threatened state may strike first. Twenty years ago, when Israel destroyed an Iraqi nuclear reactor shortly before it went critical, it cited anticipatory self-defense as justification and was condemned roundly by the United States and other governments. Fifteen years ago, however, our view was moderated when we bombed Libya after a Libyan-sponsored attack murdered two U.S. soldiers in a German discotheque. Although we were censored in international forums, anticipatory self-defense was the basis of our bombing.

If a nation's enemy masses on its border, that nation should not be required to await attack, providing a static target; to do so only invites a greater danger. It would border on the suicidal for the United States to stand docile and simply await the next armed terrorist assault. Reflecting evolving international law, there has been virtually no criticism of our war on terrorism, whether it be called self-defense or anticipatory self-defense. Even the United Nations, in rare support of the use of force, seconds the war and has voted to require U.N. members to act against terrorism.

Moreover, just as the get-away driver in a bank robbery is guilty of the robbery, so are the states that sponsor and succor terrorists guilty of the terrorists' crimes. Materially aiding and abetting terrorism in itself constitutes terrorism. Our extension of the war to such governments is no legal novelty, no breaking of new international ground.

So, yes, we are engaged in a war as surely as any formally declared war in our nation's history. An armed force that repeatedly has declared its intent to make war on us has breached our borders. It has murdered American civilians and killed our combatants. The initial battles of what promises to be a long conflict have been joined.

Are Terrorists Combatants or Criminals?

The United States traditionally has viewed terrorists merely as common-law criminals. Terrorism goes unmentioned in the 1949 Geneva Conventions and in Army Field Manual 27-10, *The Law of Land Warfare*. Even after elements of the Lebanese Party of God killed 220 Marines in the 1983 bombing of a Beirut barracks, and five years later kidnapped and murdered Marine Colonel William R. Higgins, the United States took no decisive military action. Since then, the United States has continued to view terrorism as a political issue, beyond the ambit of military solution. Six fundamentalists behind the 1993 bombing of the World Trade Center were tried and convicted in U.S. federal court. There are many other examples. U.S. armed forces sometimes delivered retaliation, usually little more than punitive slaps at the periphery rather than significant blows to the terrorists leadership or infrastructure. But on 11 September, terrorism graduated from criminality to clear-cut military attack.

If we accept that we are at war, the 1949 Geneva Conventions—the most widely observed treaties in the world, counting even Afghanistan among their signatories—lay out four requirements for fighters to be considered combatants, entitled to the protections of the law of armed conflict and prisoner-of-war status if captured: they must (1) be commanded by one responsible for their conduct, (2) have a fixed and distinctive sign that is recognizable at a distance, (3) bear arms openly, and (4) follow the law of war.

Terrorists ignore these requirements—even as they are diluted by the 1977 Protocols to the Conventions. In the law of armed conflict, that means terrorists are illegal combatants, not meriting prisoner-of-war status if captured and liable to trial for their acts. Of course, as illegal combatants, terrorists remain legitimate targets. To kill Osama bin Laden, for example, whether in an Afghan terrorist training camp or in his bed in Kabul, would be the lawful killing of an illegal enemy combatant.

The targeting of bin Laden should not be confused with assassination (simplistically, a murder for political reasons). U.S. military law first prohibited assassination in the 1863 Lieber Code, promulgated as Army General Orders 100. Although the Geneva Conventions are silent on the subject, today's *Law of Land Warfare* field manual continues the prohibition, as do the Defense Intelligence Agency and the Department of the Army's policy on special operations. Most notably, however, Executive Order 12333, reissued by every president since Gerald Ford, details a series of prohibitions against assassination in both peacetime and war. But, again accepting that we are at war, no order or manual precludes attack on individual soldiers or officers of the enemy, whether in the zone of hostilities, in occupied territory, or elsewhere. Thus it was within the law of war when, in 1943, U.S. Army pilots shot down and killed Japanese Admiral Isoruku Yamamoto, an officer of the enemy in a zone of hostilities. The 1942 killing of SS Obergruppenführer Reinhard Heydrich by British-trained Czech agents was a lawful killing of an enemy officer in an occupied country. The specific targeting of Osama bin Laden—a combatant, albeit an illegal one, who leads an enemy armed force—is not assassination.

President Bush's statement that Osama bin Laden is wanted, dead or alive, is more problematic. Field Manual 27-10, *The Law of Land Warfare*, explains that Article 23(b) of the Annex to 1907 Hague Convention IV "is construed as prohibiting assassination . . . or putting a price upon an enemy's head, as well as offering a reward for an enemy 'dead or alive.' " But the provision cited by the field manual is hardly a clear prohibition of any of those acts: "It is especially forbidden (b) To kill or wound treacherously individuals belonging to the hostile nation or army." There is no reference in the Hague Convention, even oblique, to either a bounty or a dead-or-alive policy. There is little law on the subject, although it generally is accepted that bounties and dead-or-alive pronouncements are not in conformance with customary international law. In any event, bin Laden's illegal combatant status makes him a legitimate target who may lawfully be killed. Should he one day offer to surrender, we are, of course, obligated to accept that surrender.

Where May Terrorists Be Tried?

When captured, terrorists may be tried for crimes they have committed. If being an unlawful combatant is itself a crime under the law of armed conflict, who may try the violator, and where, and in what forum?

Besides engaging in combat operations unlawfully, the crimes of the 11 September terrorists include multiple murder and hijacking, to name only the most obvious. A charge of genocide also appears appropriate. Terrorism, murder, and hijacking are domestic crimes within the jurisdiction of United States district courts—federal offenses. As many terrorists have found in past trials, federal sentences can be harsh. There is no federal crime of genocide per se. Murder, hijacking, and genocide, when committed by illegal combatants, also are violations of the law of armed conflict that can be tried under Article 18 of the Uniform Code of Military Justice (UCMJ), which is federal law.

There is no international tribunal now in existence that might try law-of-war violations. The jurisdiction of the International Criminal Tribunal for the Former Yugoslavia, established by the United Nations, is limited to crimes committed in Yugoslavia. The U.N.-established Rwandan Tribunal also is limited by geography. The World Court exercises jurisdiction over consenting nations, but not individuals. Although opposed by the United States, the International Criminal Court, once it comes into existence, will be a standing court with jurisdiction over war crimes, but its jurisdiction would not extend to acts alleged before it was established. The United Nations could establish another ad hoc international tribunal to try 11 September terrorists and their sponsors, but that possibility is not on the legal horizon. Any U.N. tribunal would exclude the possibility of the death penalty.

Although there is no suitable international tribunal, there is another method of putting terrorists on trial. In customary international law, violations of the law of armed conflict are universal crimes, that is, every nation considers them crimes, and any nation that has implementing legislation and has custody of accused war criminals may either try them or hand them over to another state willing to prosecute them. In other words, 11 September terrorists may be tried in the domestic courts of any nation holding them.

Captured enemy terrorists, then, face a broad variety of potential accusers. There is every possibility that some leaders of al Qaeda eventually will be captured, either following the fall of the Afghan Taliban government or through a military snatch operation. If captured by the forces of a country allied with the U.S. war on terrorism, the suspect quite likely would be turned over to the United States, with its greater interest in prosecution.

Presuming a U.S. prosecution, would trial be by a federal court or by a military tribunal? There will be no conclusive answer until the day of decision arrives, but there are compelling factors that suggest trial by military commission. The 1949 Geneva Conventions provide for trial of illegal combatants, allowing for trial by commission. In addition, Congress has provided for trial by military commission for offenses committed by illegal combatants, precluding any terrorist claim that military trial is not permitted because there were no ongoing hostilities between his group and the United States.

The military commission, a wartime court, first arose in 1847, when General Winfield Scott sought a means to try enemy civilians for criminal offenses against U.S. soldiers in the war with Mexico. In that day, as today, civilians, including civilians of the enemy state, were not subject to the Articles of War, the predecessors to the UCMJ, so General Scott established and employed military commissions. Essentially general courts-martial by another name, they are provided for in the *Manual for Courts-Martial*. Commissions are rare today, but were not always so. They were used frequently following the Civil War and after World War II. In 1865 a military commission convicted and sentenced to death Confederate Major Henry Wirz, the commandant of the Andersonville, Georgia, prisoner-of-war camp, where an estimated 12,000 Union soldiers died. In the same year another commission sentenced Dr. Samuel Mudd to life imprisonment for aiding and abetting the assassination of President Lincoln. General Tomoyuki Yamashita was the first major war criminal to be tried following World War II, sentenced to death by a military commission, as was Japanese Lieutenant General Masaharu Homma.

The United States' most notable military commission was held in 1942, after eight Nazi saboteurs—uniformed terrorists in many respects—were landed by submarine on U.S. shores: four on Long Island, New York, and four at Ponte Vedra, Florida. They were captured within days, before they could execute their missions, and President Franklin Roosevelt ordered a military commission convened. The three-week trial was conducted in secret and was prosecuted personally by the Army's Judge Advocate General. After the Supreme Court denied an accelerated jurisdictional appeal, all eight were convicted and the President approved the proceedings. Six were executed, and the other two received sentences of 30 years and life imprisonment.

The trial procedures employed by World War II commissions would in some specifics not be permitted today. There were troubling prosecution tactics and evidentiary rulings in all of the World War II commissions mentioned. The 1949 Geneva Conventions cure this problem by requiring that the legal procedure employed in trying prisoners of war be the same as that for trials of the prosecuting nation's own troops. A commission's procedure and evidentiary rules may vary, however.

What makes a military commission preferable to a domestic court for the trial of an al Qaeda terrorist accused of multiple murder as an illegal combatant is that commissions may be conducted in secret. In contrast, in federal court the prosecution's proof, including the disclosure of our most secret intelligence-gathering means and techniques, would have to be revealed. Further, courtroom security is simpler in trials conducted on military bases, and military jurors would be less susceptible than civilian jurors to possible terrorist retribution.

As illegal combatants in a technically undeclared war that is no less a war for that fact, terrorists are subject to trial in federal court as criminals, and for their law of war violations in a variety of forums, including U.S. military commissions. They may not claim prisoner-of-war status. Terrorists who invade our nation to kill and destroy, and who survive our self-defense efforts and are captured, will face the full weight of justice.